KU-225-223

• Polokwane

GAUTENG AND MPUMALANGA

PRETORIA   Nelspruit •

Johannesburg •

MBABANE

SWAZILAND

THE EAST COAST AND INTERIOR

• Kimberley

Bloemfontein •

MASERU

LESOTHO

• Durban

• Graaff-Reinet

E Port Elizabeth

EYEWITNESS TRAVEL GUIDES

SOUTH AFRICA

EYEWITNESS TRAVEL GUIDES

SOUTH AFRICA

Main contributors:
MICHAEL BRETT, BRIAN JOHNSON-BARKER
AND MARIËLLE RENSSEN

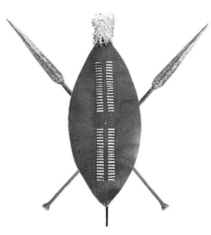

DK

LONDON, NEW YORK,
MELBOURNE, MUNICH AND DELHI
www.dk.com

Produced by Struik New Holland Publishing (Pty) Ltd,
Cape Town, South Africa

MANAGING EDITOR Claudia Dos Santos
MANAGING ART EDITORS Peter Bosman, Trinity Loubser-Fry
EDITORS Gill Gordon, Gail Jennings
DESIGNERS Simon Lewis, Mark Seabrook
MAP CO-ORDINATOR John Loubser
PRODUCTION Myrna Collins
PICTURE RESEARCHER Carmen Watts
RESEARCHER Jocelyn Convery

Dorling Kindersley Limited
EDITORIAL DIRECTOR Vivien Crump
ART DIRECTOR Gillian Allan
MAP CO-ORDINATOR David Pugh

MAIN CONTRIBUTORS
Michael Brett, Brian Johnson-Barker, Mariëlle Renssen

PHOTOGRAPHERS
Shaen Adey, Roger de la Harpe, Walter Knirr

ILLUSTRATORS
Bruce Beyer, Annette Busse, Bruno de Robillard,
Steven Felmore, Noel McCully, Dave Snook

Reproduced by Hirt & Carter (Pty) Ltd, Cape Town
Printed and bound by South China Printing Co. Ltd., China

First published in Great Britain in 1999
by Dorling Kindersley Limited
80 Strand, London WC2R 0RL

Reprinted with revisions 2001, 2002, 2003, 2005
Copyright © 1999, 2005 Dorling Kindersley Limited, London
A Penguin Company

**The information in this
Eyewitness Travel Guide is checked regularly.**
Every effort has been made to ensure that this book is as up-to-date as
possible at the time of going to press. Some details, however, such as
telephone numbers, opening hours, prices, gallery hanging
arrangements and travel information are liable to change. The
publishers cannot accept responsibility for any consequences arising
from the use of this book, nor for any material on third party websites,
and cannot guarantee that any website address in this book will be a
suitable source of travel information. We value the views and
suggestions of our readers very highly. Please write to: Publisher,
DK Eyewitness Travel Guides, Dorling Kindersley, 80 Strand,
London WC2R 0RL, Great Britain.

◁ **Stampeding eland in the Pilanesberg National Park near Sun City**

CONTENTS

Vasco Da Gama

INTRODUCING SOUTH AFRICA

CAPE TOWN

Camps Bay Beach, Cape Town

Red Disas on Table Mountain

A male leopard patrols his territory at Londolozi Game Reserve

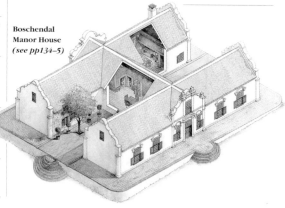

Boschendal
Manor House
(see pp134–5)

How to Use this Guide

THIS GUIDE helps you to get the most from a visit to South Africa, providing expert recommendations and detailed practical information. *Introducing South Africa* maps the country and sets it in its historical and cultural context. The four regional sections, plus *Cape Town*, describe important sights, using photographs, maps and illustrations. Throughout, features cover topics from food and wine to wildlife and culture. Restaurant and hotel recommendations can be found in *Travellers' Needs*. The *Survival Guide* contains practical tips on everything from transport to personal safety.

CAPE TOWN

The "mother city" has been divided into three sightseeing areas. Each has its own chapter opening with a list of the sights described. The *Further Afield* section covers many peripheral places of interest. All sights are numbered and plotted on an *Area Map*. Information on the sights is easy to locate as it follows the numerical order used on the map.

Sights at a Glance lists the chapter's sights by category: Museums and Galleries, Churches, Parks and Gardens, Historic Buildings etc.

All pages relating to Cape Town have red thumb tabs.

A locator map shows clearly where the area is in relation to other areas of the city.

1 Area Map
For easy reference, sights are numbered and located on a map. City centre sights are also marked on the Cape Town Street Finder maps (see pp108–15).

2 Street-by-Street Map
This gives a bird's-eye view of the key areas in each sightseeing area.

Stars indicate the sights that no visitor should miss.

A suggested route for a walk covers the more interesting streets in the area.

3 Detailed Information
All the sights in Cape Town are described individually. Addresses, telephone numbers and other practical information are also provided for each entry. The key to the symbols used in the information block is shown on the back flap.

GAUTENG AND SUN CITY

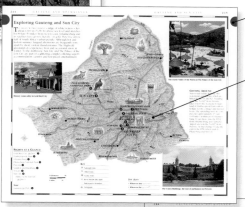

Exploring Gauteng and Sun City

The Union Buildings, the seat of parliament in Pretoria

1 Introduction

A general account of the landscape, history and character of each region is given here, explaining both how the area has developed over the centuries and what attractions it has to offer visitors today.

SOUTH AFRICA AREA BY AREA

Apart from Cape Town, the rest of the country has been divided into ten regions, each of which has a separate chapter. The most interesting towns and sights to visit are numbered on a *Pictorial Map* at the beginning of each chapter.

Each area of South Africa can be easily identified by its colour coding, shown on the inside front cover.

2 Pictorial Map

This shows the main road network and gives an illustrated overview of the whole region. All interesting places to visit are numbered and there are also useful tips on getting to, and around, the region.

Story boxes explore specific subjects further.

3 Detailed Information

All the important towns and other places to visit are described individually. They are listed in order, following the numbering on the Pictorial Map. *Within each entry, there is further detailed information on important buildings and other sights.*

The Palace of the Lost City

For all the top sights, a Visitors' Checklist provides the practical information you will need to plan your visit.

4 South Africa's Top Sights

The historic buildings are dissected to reveal their interiors; national parks have maps showing facilities and trails. The most interesting towns or city centres have maps, with sights picked out and described.

INTRODUCING
SOUTH AFRICA

Putting South Africa on the Map

THE SOUTHERNMOST COUNTRY on the African continent, South Africa is roughly five times the size of Britain. It covers an area of 1,223,201 sq km (472,156 sq miles), and has a population of around 41 million. The sovereign kingdoms of Swaziland and Lesotho lie within its borders. The Atlantic, which washes its western shores, and the Indian Ocean, which laps the East Coast, meet at Cape Agulhas, Africa's most southerly tip. To the north of South Africa lie the independent neighbouring states of Namibia, Botswana, Zimbabwe and Mozambique.

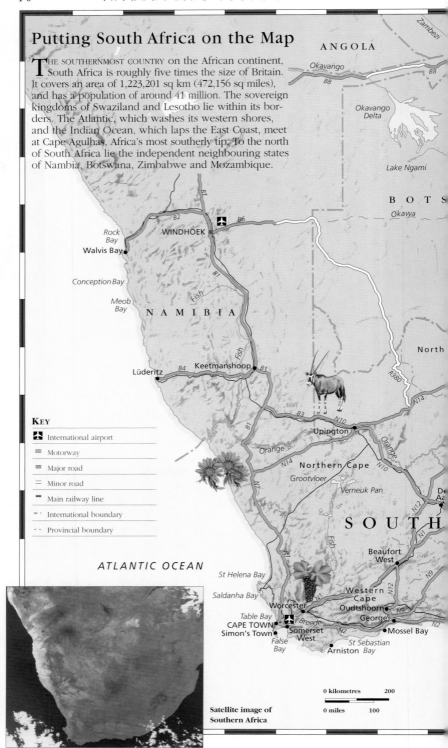

ANGOLA

Zambezi

Okavango

B8

B8

Okavango Delta

Lake Ngami

B O T S

Okawa

B1

B2

B6

✈

WINDHOEK

Rock Bay

Walvis Bay

Conception Bay

Meob Bay

B1

Fish

N A M I B I A

Fish

North

Lüderitz

B4

Keetmanshoop

B1

R380

N14

B1

B3

N10

Upington

Orange

Orange

N14

N10

Northern Cape

Grootvloer

Verneuk Pan

D
A

N12

N1

S O U T H

Fish

Beaufort West

N9

KEY

✈	International airport
▬	Motorway
▬	Major road
═	Minor road
▬	Main railway line
▪▪	International boundary
▪▪	Provincial boundary

ATLANTIC OCEAN

St Helena Bay

Saldanha Bay

Western Cape

N12

N9

Worcester

Oudtshoorn

George

Table Bay

N1

Breede

✈

CAPE TOWN

Somerset

Simon's Town

West

N2

Mossel Bay

N2

False Bay

St Sebastian Bay

Arniston

0 kilometres   200

0 miles   100

Satellite image of Southern Africa

◁ **The Eastern Buttress, Devil's Tooth and Inner Tower formations of the Drakensberg mountain range**

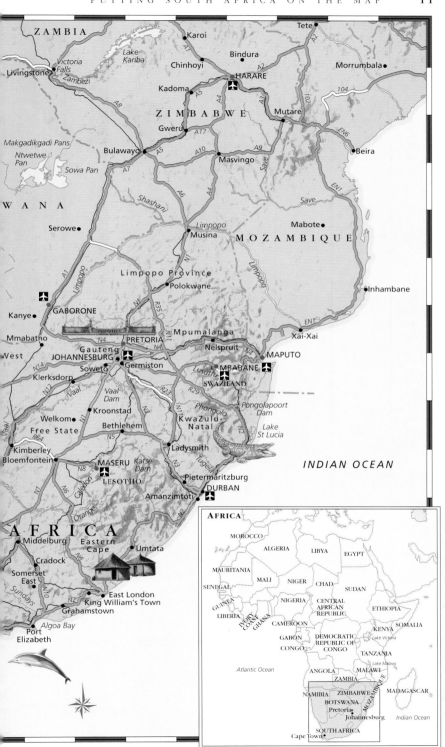

Road Map of South Africa

INTERNATIONAL AIRPORTS at Johannesburg, Cape Town and Durban link South Africa with the rest of the world, while domestic airports serve many of the smaller centres. International ocean liners dock at the ports of Cape Town, Durban and Port Elizabeth. An efficient road network spans the vast interior, linking cities and towns. This book divides the country into ten regions, with a separate chapter for Cape Town. Officially South Africa has nine provinces.

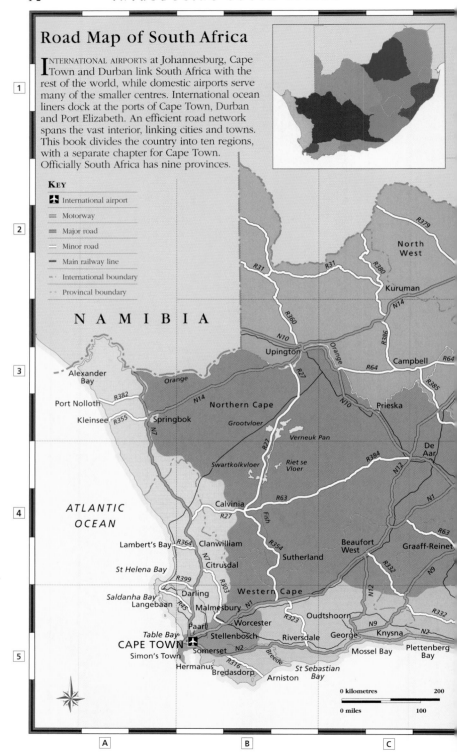

KEY

✈ International airport

═ Motorway

▬ Major road

— Minor road

▬ Main railway line

–·– International boundary

··· Provincial boundary

NAMIBIA

ATLANTIC OCEAN

North West

Kuruman

N14

R379

R380

Upington

R31

R31

R360

N10

R27

Orange

Campbell

R64

R386

R64

R385

Alexander Bay

Orange

Port Nolloth

R382

N14

Northern Cape

Prieska

N10

R384

Kleinsee

R355

Springbok

Grootvloer

Verneuk Pan

De Aar

N12

N7

Swartkolkvloer

Riet se Vloer

N1

Calvinia

R63

Lambert's Bay

R27

Fish

R364

Clanwilliam

R354

Beaufort West

R63

Graaff-Reinet

St Helena Bay

N7

Citrusdal

Sutherland

R332

N9

R399

Darling

R303

Western Cape

N12

Saldanha Bay

R45

Malmesbury

N1

Oudtshoorn

R332

Langebaan

Worcester

R323

N9

Paarl

Stellenbosch

Riversdale

George

Knysna

N2

Table Bay

CAPE TOWN ✈

Somerset

N2

Mossel Bay

Plettenberg Bay

Simon's Town

Breede

Hermanus

R316

St Sebastian Bay

Bredasdorp

Arniston

| 0 kilometres | 200 |
| 0 miles | 100 |

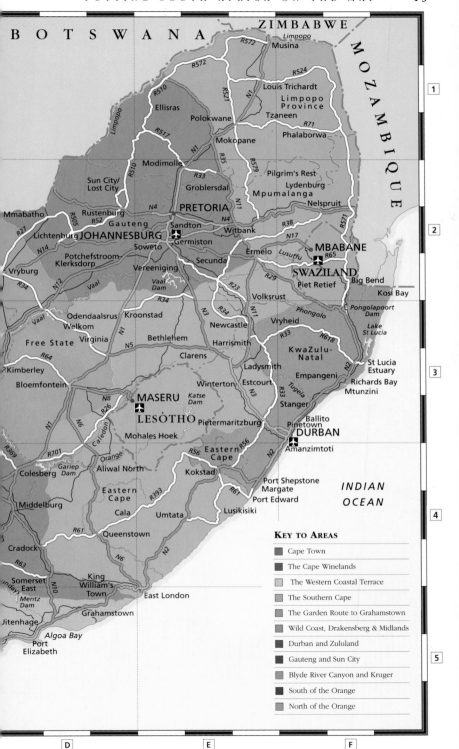

KEY TO AREAS

- Cape Town
- The Cape Winelands
- The Western Coastal Terrace
- The Southern Cape
- The Garden Route to Grahamstown
- Wild Coast, Drakensberg & Midlands
- Durban and Zululand
- Gauteng and Sun City
- Blyde River Canyon and Kruger
- South of the Orange
- North of the Orange

A PORTRAIT OF
SOUTH AFRICA

B LUE SKIES, GAME PARKS, *wilderness areas, and the promise of a sun-drenched holiday are what draws most visitors to South Africa. While the country continues to be troubled by deep-rooted racial divisions, the determination of her people to begin anew makes it an inspiring and beautiful place to explore.*

South Africa, roughly the size of Spain and France combined, encompasses an astonishing diversity of environments: from the dramatic arid moonscapes of the northwest to the forest-fringed coastline of the Garden Route; from the flat, dry Karoo interior to the craggy Drakensberg in the east; the manicured vineyards of the Cape to the spring flower fields of Namaqualand. South Africa is the only country in the world that can lay claim to an entire floral kingdom within its borders. Centred on a small area in the Western Cape, *fynbos* (literally "fine-leaved bush") comprises a unique variety of proteas, ericas and grasses.

King protea

The many wildlife parks further north are home to the Big Five: buffalo, elephant, leopard, lion and rhino, while the wetlands and marine reserves along the east coast teem with sea creatures and colourful birds, great and small, that are often overlooked.

And then there are the beaches, favourite holiday destination of the locals, for boardsailing, swimming, surfing, angling, and suntanning.

The "rainbow people of God" is how former Anglican Archbishop Desmond Tutu described the newly liberated South African nation – this conglomeration of beliefs, traditions, and heritages living within a country of breathtaking natural wonders.

Acacia trees survive along the parched fringes of the Kalahari desert

◁ **A young Zulu dancer in traditional costume**

Groote Schuur Hospital, where the world's first successful heart transplant was carried out in 1967

Yet, these stark contrasts do not exist in scenery alone. Many observers speak of two worlds within one country: a first and a third. Although 60 per cent of the continent's electricity is generated in South Africa, more than half of the nation's households still have to rely on paraffin, wood and gas for light, cooking, and heating their homes.

The modern South African state began as a halfway station. Dutch traders of the 17th century, on long sea voyages to their colonies in the East, replenished their stores at the Cape. A fertile land, South Africa is still largely self-reliant today, compelled

Pouring gold bars

to become so as a result of the long period of international political isolation that resulted from its former policy of racial discrimination known as *apartheid* (apartness).

South Africa became a world producer of gold and petroleum. Impressive advances were made in communication, weapons technology and mining, but apartheid stood in the way of harmony and economic growth. In the late 1960s, while the world's first human heart transplant was performed at Groote Schuur Hospital in Cape Town, the majority of South Africans struggled to fulfill their most basic needs of food, shelter and education.

Farm labourers relaxing on a hay wagon, West Coast

PEOPLE AND SOCIETY

Living in a land of such differences, it is hardly surprising that South Africans lack a collective identity. In 1994, English, Afrikaans, and nine Bantu tongues were recognized as official languages. Afrikaans, derived from Dutch and altered through contact with other tongues, is spoken by 18 per cent of the population.

South Africa's cultural mix has its roots in a colonial past. The original hunter-gatherer inhabitants of the Cape were joined, about 1,000 years ago, by migrating Bantu-speakers from the north. In the 17th century, European settlers appeared – first the Dutch, then the British and French – with their slaves from Indonesia, Madagascar, and India. Later followed indentured labourers from India. Settlers and slaves alike brought with them their culinary traditions, and if there is a national cuisine it is Cape Malay: mild lamb and fish curries sweetened with spiced fruit. Although seafood is relished, South Africans are really a meat-loving nation. The outdoor *braai* (barbecue) is popular all around the globe, but no one does it quite like South Africans, with fiercely guarded secret recipes, and competitions for the best *boerewors* (spicy sausage) and *potjiekos* (a tasty stew prepared in a three-legged cast iron pot).

Feast day preparations in a Cape Town mosque

Religion crosses many of the cultural and social divides. The African independent churches have a large following, as their approach includes aspects of tribal mysticism, and a firm belief in the influence of

ancestral spirits. The Dutch Reformed, Roman Catholic, Presbyterian, and Anglican churches draw worshippers from all population groups. Islam is strongly represented in the Western Cape, while Buddhists and Hindus are mainly found in Durban.

Penny whistler

CULTURE AND SPORT

A new awareness of African identity is increasingly apparent. Music, which has always played a central part in traditional ceremony and celebration, clearly leads the way. Regular church choir-festivals attest to the popularity of, especially, gospel and choral harmony. The distinctive sound of Zulu *mbube* (unaccompanied choral singing) has become one of South Africa's best known exports.

African choir performing an energetic song-and-dance routine

Sindiwe Magona is the author of several books about her life as a Black South African woman

be rather nostalgic, often evoking gentler times. By contrast, the music of the coloured people is lively, distinguished by bouncy melodies and cheerful, racy lyrics that belie the sadness and indignities of the past.

During the long, dark years of apartheid, oppression and suffering offered much ready-made source material for the arts. Although older South African literature undoubtedly has its luminaries *(see pp26–7)*, modern writers are moving away from racial introspection towards more universal themes.

The natural African gift for rhythm and harmony easily made the transition from rural area to city. Although the tunes are much influenced by popular North American music, jazz, soul, *kwela* (the inimitable piercing sound of the penny whistle), *kwaito* (transient pop), rock and reggae all have a determined local flavour.

The white Afrikaner's cultural heritage, accumulated over centuries of isolation from the European motherland, today embraces a powerful body of prose and poetry, and a very distinctive musical tradition. Afrikaans songs tend to

Cape minstrel

Most South Africans are passionate about sport – whether they are participating or merely watching. This ardour has shown a steep increase since the end of the sports boycott. The Rugby World Cup, which was held in Cape Town and other cities in 1995 and won by a jubilant South Africa, probably did more to unite the nation than anything else. South Africans countrywide celebrated their national team's victory. Soccer, cricket, boxing, horse racing and athletics also draw the expectant crowds.

Faces blazing with pride, a jubilant nation celebrates its Rugby World Cup victory in 1995

South Africans enjoy the outdoors, as here, on popular Clifton beach in Cape Town

SOUTH AFRICA TODAY

Perhaps the best starting point from which to chart the end of apartheid is the announcement of then President FW de Klerk regarding the unbanning of the African National Congress (ANC), and the Communist Party and Pan-Africanist Congress (PAC). On 11 February 1990, Nelson Mandela was released from the Victor Verster Prison near Paarl.

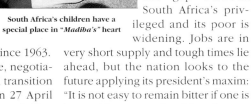

South Africa's children have a special place in *"Madiba's"* heart

He had been imprisoned since 1963.

Amid escalating violence, negotiations began for a peaceful transition to democracy. Finally, on 27 April 1994, all South Africans voted. Five days later the results were announced: the ANC had secured 63 per cent of the votes, and Nelson Mandela became the first Black president of the "New South Africa".

The new constitution was approved in May 1996 and has, arguably, the most enlightened Bill of Rights in the world. It outlaws discrimination on the grounds of ethnic or social origin, religion, gender, sexual orientation, and language.

Yet, many citizens still live very close to poverty. Despite the country's many natural resources, advanced technology and sophisticated infrastructure, the gap between South Africa's privileged and its poor is widening. Jobs are in very short supply and tough times lie ahead, but the nation looks to the future applying its president's maxim: "It is not easy to remain bitter if one is busy with constructive things."

A bold mural in Johannesburg portrays the multicultural nation

The Contrasting Coasts

TWO OCEAN CURRENTS influence the coastal climate of
South Africa: the tropical Agulhas Current, which
flows south down the East Coast, and the cold, north-
flowing Benguela Current along the western shores.
The two merge somewhere off lonely Cape Agulhas,
Africa's most southerly cape. Together with the winds
and mountains, these ocean movements determine
the region's coastal variance: the aridity of the west
versus the luxuriant forest in the east. The coastal
fauna and flora, both terrestrial and aquatic, display
interesting variations. Here, too, the west differs
substantially from the east, as plants
and animals have adapted to their
specific environments.

Blue whales, at 33 m (108 ft)
the largest mammals on earth,
are one of the whale species that
frequent South African coastal
waters during the Arctic winter.

Drosanthemums are
low-growing plants, well
adapted to arid West
Coast conditions. They
store precious water in
their small, thick leaves
and flower between
August and October.

Alexander Bay

0 kilometres 100

0 miles 50

ATLANTIC OCEAN

Cape Basin

The black korhaan
inhabits dry coastal
scrubland. The males
are strikingly coloured
and protect their terri-
tory with raucous calls.
Females are an incon-
spicuous mottled brown
and avoid detection by
standing perfectly still.

St Helena
Bay

Saldanha
Bay

Table Bay

CAPE TOWN

False Bay

Cape Point

Cape Agulhas

West Coast rock lobster,
important to the region's
economy, are harvested
under special licence.
They are not reared
on a commercial basis.

**The Benguela
Current** flows
north, carrying
cold water from
the Antarctic.

At Cape Agulhas, the waters
of the two currents converge.

Agulhas Bank

THE WEST COAST

Even in summer, water
temperatures average
only 14°C (57°F). This
precludes the formation
of rain-bearing clouds, and
annual precipitation is
below 250 mm (10 in). The
lack of fresh water means

Sea anemone

that only tough succulents survive on dew
from sea mists. The sea water, full of nutrients, sustains a rich and varied marine life.

CAPE AGULHAS

Memorial plaque at Cape Agulhas

The southernmost point of the African continent is not Cape Point, but unassuming Cape Agulhas on the rocky east side of the windswept, shallow Danger Point headland. The Portuguese word *agulhas*, from which it gets its name, means "needles". It was here, early navigators discovered, that the compass needle was not affected by magnetic deviation, but pointed true north. A plaque is set into the rock and markers give the distances to international cities.

Various dolphin species *can be seen frolicking in the warm currents off towns like Durban and Margate. They usually occur in groups of 10 to 15 individuals.*

Kosi Bay●

St Lucia Marine ● Reserve

***The genus* Crinum** *(amaryllis family) is commonly seen in swampy grassland along the East Coast. It flowers in summer.*

Umgeni River Estuary
DURBAN ●

Aliwal Shoal

The Grass owl *(Tyto capensis) occurs in swampy grassland along the east coast of South Africa.*

Natal Basin

INDIAN OCEAN

Algoa Bay

A g u l h a s   B a s i n

The warm Agulhas Current causes humid conditions along the East Coast.

Port Elizabeth crayfish *(or shoveller), one of many species of rock lobster found around the South African coast, has little commercial value.*

THE EAST COAST

The warm Agulhas Current that flows south through the Mozambique Channel creates hot, humid conditions along the East Coast. Vegetation is subtropical and mangrove forests flourish in the Umgeni River Estuary near Durban. The annual migration of big pilchard shoals is eagerly awaited by fish, bird and man. Coral reefs, rare in South African waters, are found in the St Lucia Marine Reserve.

Nudibranch

The Landscapes and Flora of South Africa

SOUTH AFRICA'S FLORA has charmed visitors and intrigued botanists for years. Many species are widely distributed within the country, but each region has produced distinct characteristics, the result of varying geographic, climatic and soil conditions. In the more arid western reaches of the country, plants tend to be small and low-growing, flowering briefly after the winter rains, while further east open grassland and bushveld dominate. Along the East Coast grow lush subtropical coastal forests.

Aloe flower

THE CAPE FLORAL KINGDOM

Pelargonium

The Southwestern Cape, one of the world's six floral kingdoms, boasts around 8,500 different plants in an area less than four per cent of the Southern African land surface. This so-called *fynbos* (fine-leaved bush) includes some 350 species of protea, as well as pelargoniums, ericas, reeds and irises. Most are endemic to the area, and is well represented in the Kirstenbosch National Botanical Garden *(see pp100–1)*.

SEMI-DESERT

In Southern Africa, true desert is confined to the Namib. The semi-desert Great Karoo region covers about one-third of South Africa. Its flora has evolved to withstand aridity and extreme temperatures. Many succulents, including the aloes, mesembryanthemums, euphorbias and stapelias, store water in their thick leaves or roots. The seeds of daisy-like ephemeral plants may lie dormant for years, only to germinate and flower briefly when the conditions are favourable *(see pp154–5)*. Trees tend to grow along seasonal river courses.

Succulent

NAMAQUALAND *(see pp154–5)*

Many succulent plants in this region survive only through the condensation of nightly mists that roll in from the Atlantic Ocean. Adaptation has led to many bizarre species, such as the *kokerboom* (quiver tree), *half-mens* (half-human), and the insectivorous plants of the Stapelia family. Dwarf shrubs and scraggy bushes are widely spaced over dusty land that is bare for most of the year, until even modest winter rains raise dense, multi-hued crops of daisy-like *vygie* blossoms.

Vygies

TEMPERATE FOREST

Dense evergreen forests thrive in the high-rainfall area around Knysna *(see pp176–7)*. They produce lovely rare hardwoods such as stinkwood and yellowwood, two types that also occur along the subtropical coastal belt of KwaZulu-Natal. Knysna's temperate forests have a characteristic under-growth of shrubs, ferns, fungi, and creepers, such as the wispy "old man's beard". Mature trees may reach a height of 60 m (195 ft), with a girth of seven metres (23 ft).

Forest fungus

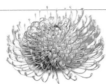

Erica patersonia
is one of over 625 erica species that occur in the Southwestern Cape. It is mainly found along streams.

Protea grandiceps
is one of the most widely distributed of its species. It grows at the higher altitudes of coastal mountains.

Pincushion proteas
bloom from June to December in colours ranging from yellow to deep red. Flower heads last for up to three weeks and attract sunbirds and insects.

Ericas *are found on Table Mountain, where Erica dichrus provides dense red splashes of colour.*

Yellow pincushion proteas *grow on a tall, shrub that is found near the coast.*

BUSHVELD

Large tracts of the interior are covered with tall grasses and low trees, most of them deciduous, fine-leaved and thorny. The Kruger National Park *(see pp272–5)* is an excellent example of several transitional types occurring between sparse shrub and savanna; here shrubs grow densely and larger tree types include marula, mopane and baobab. The large acacia family is characterized by pod-bearing trees and shrubs with clusters of small, golden-yellow flowers.

"Weeping boerbean" pod

HIGH MOUNTAIN

Mountain flora, zoned according to altitude and increasing severity of the environment, rises from dense heath to mixed scrub and grasses. A relatively small subalpine belt, 2,800 m (9,000 ft) above sea level, is confined to the Drakensberg region *(see pp206–7)*. Characteristic floral species are Helichrysum ("everlastings"), sedges and ericas. In many areas, annuals make brief, colourful spring appearances. Among the proteas growing in this region is the rare snow protea on the high peaks of the Cedarberg *(see pp152–3)*.

Watsonia

SUBTROPICAL COASTAL BELT

Brackish swamps, saline estuaries and lush plant growth are characteristic of the KwaZulu-Natal coast. Mangroves anchor themselves to their unstable habitat with stilt-like roots, while higher up on the banks grow palms and the broad-leaved wild banana of the Strelitzia family. A good example of typical East Coast vegetation can be seen at Kosi Bay *(see p233)*, where swamps surround lakes that are overgrown with water lilies and reeds. Dune forests and grasslands are dotted with wild palms.

Water lily

South Africa's Wildlife Heritage

BEFORE THE ARRIVAL OF THE WHITE COLONISTS, nomadic Khoina hunted wild animals for food, while to the east Zulu and Venda traded in ivory and organized ceremonial hunts – but their spears and pitfall traps had little impact. In comparison to 17th-century Europe, South Africa's wildlife seemed inexhaustible, and by the mid-19th century, the settlers' weapons had seen to it that the vast herds had disappeared – many species were in danger of extinction. Conservation measures over the past century have brought about a spectacular recovery, and South Africa's wildlife reserves are now among the finest in the world.

Giraffe

The klipspringer, agile and sure-footed, occurs in mountainous areas throughout the country.

Blue wildebeest

Bee-eaters, *one of around 840 bird species recorded in the country, gather in flocks along rivers in the Kruger National Park. They catch flying insects and return to their perch to consume their prey.*

Zebra

Nyala bulls can be distinguished from the similar-looking kudu by the orange colour of their lower legs.

Warthog

Princeps demodocus demodocus, *the attractive Christmas butterfly, is also known as the citrus swallowtail, and can be seen throughout South Africa from September to April. As its name suggests, the species often occurs in citrus groves.*

AT THE WATERHOLE

In the dry winter months (May to September), an ever-changing wildlife pageant unfolds as animals gather at waterholes to drink. Wooden hides have been erected at waterholes in KwaZulu-Natal's Hluhluwe-Umfolozi (*see p230*) and Mkuzi game reserves, while the rivers in the Kruger National Park offer the best vantage points.

AFRICA'S BIG FIVE

This term originated from hunting jargon for the most dangerous and sought-after trophy animals. Today, they are still an attraction, with Kruger National Park (*see pp272–5*) the prime Big-Five viewing destination. Hluhluwe-Umfolozi, and the Pilanesberg and Madikwe reserves, too, are well-known sanctuaries.

Lions, *the largest of the African cats, live in prides of varying size controlled by one or more dominant males.*

The black rhinoceros *is in serious danger of extinction. It is distinguished from the white rhino by its longer upper lip.*

THE FIRST WILDLIFE RESERVES

By the mid-19th century, hunters had decimated the big game. Subspecies like the quagga (relative of the zebra) and Cape lion had become extinct. As towns expanded people began to view wildlife as an asset and, in 1889, the Natal *Volksraad* (people's council) agreed to establish a wildlife reserve. In 1894, a strip of land between KwaZulu-Natal and Swaziland became the Pongola Game Reserve, Africa's first conservation area. Four years later, President Paul Kruger signed a proclamation that established the forerunner of a sanctuary that was later named Kruger National Park in his honour.

Early 19th-century hunting party

Quagga

Female impala

Nyala cows, usually accompanied by dominant bulls, are often spotted in the woodlands of northern KwaZulu-Natal.

Waterholes dry out rapidly in the summer heat and the animals suffer much hardship.

Vervet monkeys usually avoid the arid habitats.

The hunt is a brutal, yet timeless African sequence. Cheetah mainly prey on smaller gazelles, like springbok and impala.

Oxpeckers and kudu *are an example of the symbiosis that has evolved between different animals under the harsh African conditions. The birds free the antelope of parasites and are also an alarm system at waterholes.*

Spotted hyena are one of the most interesting of African predators. Loose family groups are led by females who, due to high levels of male hormones, also have male genitalia. Powerful pack hunters, they can bring down animals as large as buffalo.

Buffalo are the most abundant of the Big Five and occur in large herds. Old bulls become loners and may be extremely dangerous.

Leopards are shy cats that are largely nocturnal and often rest on tree branches.

Elephants live in tight-knit family groups led by a matriarch. The bulls remain solitary or may band together to form bachelor herds.

Literary South Africa

Afrikaans Bible

A RICH LITERARY TRADITION exists in all 11 national languages, which include nine Bantu tongues, mostly from the Nguni and Sotho branches. Most books were published in Afrikaans or English, while much of the African heritage was handed down orally. Books in African tongues are now beginning to enjoy a wider circulation, both locally and abroad, and are also appearing in foreign translation. Over the years, South Africa has inspired a number of outstanding authors and poets, among them Sir Percy FitzPatrick, Olive Schreiner, Sir Laurens van der Post, Nadine Gordimer and Mzwakhe Mbuli.

CJ Langenhoven wrote *Die Stem*, one of the two national anthems

Painting by Credo Mutwa, taken from the book *African Proverbs*

TRADITIONAL AFRICAN STORIES

M ANY AFRICAN communities have an oral tradition of entertaining, informative stories, genealogies, proverbs and riddles that have been passed on from generation to generation.

Izibongo, simplistically translated as praise songs, are very complex oral presentations delivered by a skilled performer known as *mbongi*. This rhythmic form of poetry uses exalted language, rich in metaphor and parallelisms. At the inauguration of Nelson Mandela, two *izibongo* were performed in Xhosa.

Among the best written works are SEK Mqhayi's historic *Ityala Lamawele* (Lawsuit of the Twins) and A Jordan's *Ingqumbo Yeminyanya* (The Wrath of the Ancestors), both in Xhosa, and Thomas Mofolo's *Chaka* in Sotho, BW Vilakazi's *Noma nini* in Zulu, and Sol Plaatjie's *Mhudi* in Tswana.

English publications of traditional African tales, novels and poetry include *Indaba my Children* and *African Proverbs* by Credo Mutwa.

Actor Patrick Mynhardt dramatizes Herman Charles Bosman's *A Sip of Jerepigo*

AFRIKAANS LITERATURE

T HE DUTCH spoken by the colonial authorities formed the basis of a local tongue that became known as Afrikaans, or simply *die taal* (the language). Efforts to translate the Bible into Afrikaans led to a vigorous campaign to have the language formally recognized. A direct result of these tireless efforts was the publication of almost 100 books before 1900.

The descriptive prose and lyrical poetry of literary greats like Gustav Preller, CJ Langenhoven, DF Malherbe and Totius (Jacob Daniël du Toit), who delighted in the use of their new language, helped to establish Afrikaans as the lingua franca.

Later writers, like PG du Plessis and Etienne Le Roux, placed Afrikaans literature in a wider context, while Adam Small and Breyten Breytenbach used it as a form of political and social protest against the white Afrikaner establishment.

"Afrikanerisms", deliberate use of Afrikaans words and sentence construction when writing in English, is a literary device used in Pauline Smith's *The Beadle*, and in Herman Charles Bosman's humorous short story *A Cask of Jerepigo*. Both works describe the life, joys and hardships of a rural Afrikaner community.

Afrikaans became a hated symbol of oppression during the apartheid years yet, today, it is more widely spoken than any other local tongue.

Jock of the Bushveld statue in the Kruger National Park

The 1924 publication of *The Flaming Terrapin* established Roy Campbell as a leading poet. Although the hardships of black South Africans had been highlighted in Herbert

Dhlomo's short stories and Peter Abrahams's *Mine Boy*, it was the subject matter of race relations in *Cry the Beloved Country* (1948) by Alan Paton that attracted the world's attention.

Among several superb female writers, Nadine Gordimer (*A Sport of Nature* and *July's People*, among others) became the recipient of a Nobel Prize for Literature in 1991. The author contributed greatly to the standard of writing in South Africa, and her struggle against another of the apartheid era's crippling laws – censorship – paved the way for many others. Rose Zwi's

Local edition of
A Sport of Nature

Another Year in Africa is an insight into the life of South Africa's Jewish immigrants, while the autobiographical *To my Children's Children* is Sindiwe Magona's account of a youth spent in the former homeland of Transkei, and of the daily struggle in Cape Town's townships.

CONTEMPORARY LITERATURE

AUTOBIOGRAPHIES and travelogues, popular genres for modern local writers, offer insights into the lives of South Africans. Nelson Mandela's *Long Walk to Freedom* was a national bestseller. *Country of my Skull* is Antjie Krog's narrative of her two years spent reporting on the Truth and Reconciliation Commission, while *Beckett's Trek* and *Madibaland* by Denis Beckett, and Sarah Penny's *The Whiteness of Bones* are entertaining jaunts through South Africa and its neighbours. Zakes Mda's award-winning *Ways of Dying* gives the reader a glimpse of the professional mourner, while Ashraf Jamal's *Love Themes for the Wilderness* takes a life-affirming trip into contemporary urbanity.

ENGLISH POETRY AND PROSE

OLIVE SCHREINER'S *Story of an African Farm* (1883), first published under a male pseudonym, presented the rural Afrikaner to an international audience for the first time. The book was startling, also, for its advanced views on feminism – sentiments that the author expanded on in *Woman and Labour* (1911).

Percy FitzPatrick's *Jock of the Bushveld* (1907) became one of the best-known of all South African titles. A blend of romantic adventure and realism, it tells the story of a transport rider and his dog on the early gold fields.

Later popular authors who achieved international sales include Geoffrey Jenkins, and Wilbur Smith whose novels, such as *Where the Lion Feeds*, have made him one of the world's best-selling writers. A more thought-provoking genre is that of Stuart Cloete's *The Abductors*, once banned in South Africa, and Sir Laurens van der Post's touching description of a dying culture in *Testament to the Bushmen*.

The works of André P Brink and JM Coetzee dealt mainly with social and political matters that were often viewed by the apartheid regime as attacks on the establishment. Brink's critical *Looking on Darkness* (1963) became the first Afrikaans novel to be banned in South Africa.

STRUGGLE POETRY

During the apartheid years, conflict and the repression of Africans provided recurring themes. Produced orally in various Bantu tongues and in written form in English, the new means of expression was termed "Struggle Poetry". Oswald Mtshali's *Sounds of a Cowhide Drum* (1971) signalled the shift in black poetry from lyrical themes to indirect political messages in free verse. Other creators of this form of protest were Mzwakhe Mbuli, known as "the people's poet", Mafika Gwala, James Matthews, Sipho Sepamla, Njabulo Ndebele and Mongane Wally Serote. Their verse expressed disapproval of the socio-political conditions in the country and was, at the same time, a conscious attempt to raise the level of awareness among their people.

Mongane Wally Serote, poet and politician

South African Architecture

D IVERSE FACTORS have influenced building styles in South Africa: climate, social structure, and the state of the economy have all shaped the country's homes. In earlier days, when suitable raw materials were often unavailable, ingenious adaptations resulted. Variations include the *hartbeeshuisie* (hard-reed house), a pitched-roof shelter built directly on the ground, and the beehive-shaped "corbelled" huts, built of stone in areas where structural timber was unobtainable, as in the Northern Cape. Modern South African building and engineering skills have kept abreast with international trends, and many different styles can be seen throughout the country.

Weaving the reed fence surrounding a traditional Swazi village

INDIGENOUS ARCHITECTURAL STYLES

Most traditional rural dwellings, often called "rondavels", are circular in shape. The conical roofs are traditionally constructed of a tightly woven reed or grass thatch, while the walls may be made of mud blocks mixed with cow dung, or consist of a framework of woven branches and covered with animal hide. Most of these homes, except the *matjieshuise* of the arid Namaqualand nomads for whom rain was no threat, are well insulated and waterproof. In recent times, materials like corrugated iron, plastic sheeting and cardboard have become popular, especially in informal settlements on the outskirts of cities.

Zulu "beehives" are a community effort. The stick framework is erected by the men, and the women thatch it.

*The **matjieshuise** (houses made of mats) of Khoina nomads consisted of portable hide- or reed-mats on a stick frame.*

Xhosa huts are built of mud. The circular type shown here has largely been replaced by rectangular patterns.

A capping of clay covers the ridge of the roof to keep the thatch in place.

The thatch is made of sheaves of grass, or reed.

Windows and decorations are symmetrically placed around the door.

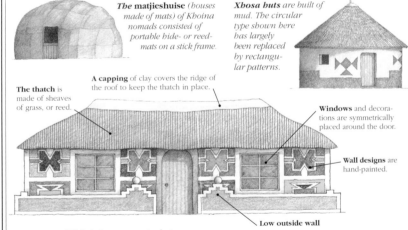

Wall designs are hand-painted.

Low outside wall

Ndebele homes are, perhaps, the most eye-catching local style. The walls of the rectangular structures are traditionally painted by women, using bright primary colours. No stencils are used for the bold geometric motifs.

Ndebele wall detail

Basotho huts, originally circular, are built of blocks of turf, mud, or stone, and plastered with mud. In rural areas, walls are still decorated with pebbles, but the use of paint is spreading.

CAPE DUTCH ARCHITECTURE

The vernacular of the Western Cape, recognized by its symmetrical design and prominent gables, evolved around the mid-18th century from a simple row of thatched rooms whose sizes depended on the length of the available beams. The forms of the gables were derived from the Baroque architecture of Holland. End gables prevented the roof from being torn off by high winds, while the centre gable let light into the attic.

Gable of Franschhoek Town Hall

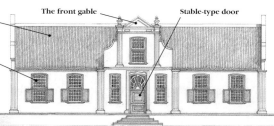

Thatching reed was widely available in the *vleis* (swamps).

Sash windows had many small panes, and only the lower half could be opened.

Rhone, near Franschhoek, is a good example of an 18th-century homestead. The front gable dates back to 1795.

The front gable

Stable-type door

GEORGIAN ARCHITECTURE

Modest examples of 18th-century Georgian-style architecture, with plain front pediments and flat roofs, survive along the narrow, cobbled streets of Cape Town's Bo-Kaap, or "Malay Quarter".

The neighbourhood of Artificers' Square in Grahamstown also has fine examples. Here, the houses display typical many-paned, sliding sash windows, plain parapets and a fanlight above the entrance.

Geometric brick detail

The chimney was designed to complement the house.

Bertram House, completed in 1839, is Cape Town's only surviving brick Georgian house.

The roof is protected by slate tiles.

Louvre shutters reduce the harsh glare of the sun.

Precise brick-laying adds attractive detail.

The wind lobby excludes draughts.

VICTORIAN ARCHITECTURE

The romantic Victorian style with its decorative cast-iron detail, brass fittings, and stained-glass windows became extremely popular, especially in Cape Town, around the turn of the century. Here, too, terrace housing, pioneered in 18th-century England by the Adam Brothers, provided affordable housing for a burgeoning middle-class. Fine examples may be seen in suburbs like Woodstock, Observatory, Mowbray and Wynberg.

Broekie lace detail, Prince Albert

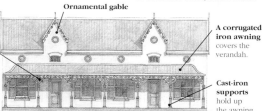

Cast-iron decorations were called *broekie* lace, because they resembled the lacy edging of ladies' drawers.

Oom Samie se Winkel (see p128), in Stellenbosch, displays a marked Cape Dutch influence. The porch encouraged patrons to linger.

Ornamental gable

A corrugated iron awning covers the verandah.

Cast-iron supports hold up the awning.

Multicultural South Africa

San Bushman rock painting

THE SOUTH AFRICAN NATION is composed of a medley of different beliefs and cultures. Early influences, such as the languages and religions of slaves from India, Madagascar, Indonesia, West and East Africa and Malaysia, are preserved by their descendants. South Africa's mineral wealth drew settlers from other parts of Africa, as well as Asia, America and Europe – heritages still reflected in today's faces. Most coloured people live in the former slave-owning Western Cape area, while many Indians live around Durban, where their ancestors worked on sugar plantations.

Very few San Bushmen still hunt and live in the traditional way

THE KHOINA

THEIR ROCK PAINTINGS, often found in caves overlooking the plains below, offer tantalizing evidence of the practical skills and the spiritual nature of the people who are almost certainly South Africa's original human inhabitants. *(See Drakensberg pp206–7 and Kagga Kamma p152.)* Many were hunter-gatherers, living lightly on the natural bounty of the land.

Under pressure from more material cultures, some Khoina withdrew inland, where their descendants (the San Bushmen) are still today found in parts of Namaqualand and in the Northern Cape.

Other Khoina eventually threw in their lot with the Dutch settlers. Many of today's Cape Coloured people are descended from them.

THE BANTU-SPEAKERS

THE BANTU LANGUAGES are indigenous to Africa, although not related to those of the Khoina. Each group has its own complex system of cultures and relationships, although Westernized culture is replacing many of the older, traditional ways. Cattle and cattle pens *(kraals)* have an important place in Zulu, Xhosa and Ndebele cultures, and Zulu handicrafts include works in earthenware, iron and wood. Basket-making and weaving are other skills. The Xhosa, most of whom live in the Eastern Cape, are known for their beautifully designed and executed beadwork. The Ndebele of the Limpopo Province and Gauteng are renowned for their remarkably colourful and intricate beadwork, and their decorative painting applied to buildings is particularly eye-catching.

Weaving is an important skill, and many Sotho, Xhosa and Tswana wear patterned or sombre ochre blankets as over-garments. In the northerly parts of Northern Province live the Venda, with a tradition, unusual in South Africa, of building in stone. The Venda are one of the few groups that traditionally used a drum as a musical instrument. Wood sculptures by leading Venda artists are treasured pieces.

The Wartburger Hof in KwaZulu-Natal looks like an alpine lodge

THE EUROPEAN COLONISTS

THE FIRST EUROPEAN settlers, in 1652, were Dutch and German. European politics further affected the composition of the Cape population, when French Huguenots were settled here from 1688, and French and German regiments were periodically brought in to boost the local defences against Britain. The British, however, took permanent possession of the Cape in 1806 and, during the

Many Xhosa women smoke long-stemmed pipes

depression that followed the Napoleonic Wars, dispatched several thousand settlers to farm in the Eastern Cape. More (pro-British) German settlers arrived after the Crimean War, and many British ex-soldiers elected to stay in South Africa, or returned to it, after the South African War of 1899–1902 and the World Wars. The British custom of hot Christmas dinner, for example, prevails in many quarters, despite its unsuitability in the stifling local climate.

Franschhoek, near Cape Town, retains some of the atmosphere of a French wine-growing region, while Eastern Cape villages settled by Germans still carry the names of German cities, such as Berlin and Hamburg.

ASIAN ORIGINS

EAST INDIAN islanders who opposed Dutch colonization of their territory in the 17th and 18th centuries were banished to the Cape of Good Hope. Slaves imported from Indonesia and the Indian subcontinent swelled the size of the oppressed minority. Nearly all of them belonged to the Islamic faith, while many others converted.

During the 19th century, thousands of indentured Indians worked in the sugar cane fields of KwaZulu-Natal, and elected to stay on at the end of their contract. In Kwa-Zulu-Natal, Cape Town and Gauteng, the striking Eastern mosques and temples are a noteworthy architectural feature. Religious festivals are regularly observed, and the bustling oriental markets yield a treasure trove of spices, jewellery and handicrafts.

AFRIKANERS

THE TERM "AFRIKANER" was first recorded in 1706, as referring to a South African-born, Afrikaans- (or Dutch-) speaking white person. In more recent times, however,

During Afrikaner festivals, traditional costumes are worn

just the first-language use of Afrikaans has become the identifying factor. Afrikaner men are often associated with a love for outdoor sport (especially rugby) and a passion for the *braai* (barbecue).

The tunes delivered by a *Boere-orkes* (literally "farmers' band") consist of concertina, banjo, piano accordion, and fiddles, and bear great similarity to North American "country" music.

THE COLOURED PEOPLE

THE TERM "Cape Coloured" has now been in use for almost two centuries to define members of what is sometimes called "the only truly indigenous population".

Many of these people are descended from relationships between settlers, slaves and local tribes, and many slave names survive in the form of surnames such as Januarie,

Temple dancing is still being taught in Durban

November, Titus, Appollis, Cupido and Adonis.

The most skilled fishermen, livery men as well as artisans were traditionally found in the Asian and Coloured communities, and many of the Cape's beautiful historic buildings were their creations.

A young Muslim girl prepares flower decorations for a festival

FROM ALL QUARTERS

COMPARED WITH other countries such as the United States and Australia, South Africa offered little scope for unskilled or semi-skilled white labour from Europe. However, small but steady numbers of immigrants did arrive, especially from Eastern European countries like Yugoslavia, Poland and Bulgaria.

South Africa has many citizens from Italy, Greece, Portugal and the Netherlands, as well as Jewish communities. These and other groups have formed common-interest societies seen at their most picturesque during colourful community carnivals.

Sport in South Africa

Given the country's favourable climate, sport plays a major role in the lives of many South Africans. In recent years, generous government funding and corporate sponsorship have resulted in the development of sporting facilities in the previously disadvantaged communities, encouraging much as yet unexplored talent. Sports events that are held in the major centres take place in world-class stadiums with superb facilities. Seats for the important matches are best bought through Computicket (see p361), while those for lesser events are obtainable directly at the respective venues.

Test matches are played by the national team, known as the Springboks, against the national sides of other rugby playing nations.

In 1995, South Africa was winner of the Rugby World Cup (contested every four years). The local rugby season begins in early February, continuing through the winter months and ending, in late October, with the Currie Cup Finals (see p34).

Soccer attracts spectators from all sectors of South African society

SOCCER

Without question the country's most popular sport, soccer is played all over South Africa, in dusty township streets and in the elite professional clubs. The most popular clubs attract huge spectator and fan followings, and can easily fill 80,000-seat stadiums for top matches. The soccer leagues are contested by clubs, and, unlike other major sports such as rugby and cricket, there is little emphasis on representation at provincial level.

The national soccer team, known as Bafana Bafana, has had success in the biennial African Cup of Nations, winning the contest in 1995 (when South Africa hosted the tournament) and reaching the finals in 1998. The team, ranked among the world's top 40, qualified for the World Cup Finals for the first time in 1998. Except for the hottest summer months (Dec–Feb), soccer is played year round.

RUGBY UNION

Rugby, the wealthiest sport in South Africa, is played at all levels, from school to regional club, provincial and national stage.

Teams from the 14 provincial unions contest the Currie Cup every season. These 14 unions supply players to the four regional teams that fight for victory in the Super 12, an international and regional tournament involving South Africa as well as Australia, and New Zealand.

CRICKET

South Africa has long been a major force in the world of cricket. Played during the summer months, cricket is a sport enjoyed by thousands of players and spectators at various levels, from club and provincial competitions to international test matches.

Development programmes have discovered great talent among the youth of once-disadvantaged communities.

Four-day provincial games and the more popular one-day matches are held, while five-day tests are contested between South Africa and visiting national teams.

One-day and day/night limited-overs international and provincial matches are particularly popular, usually played to packed stands.

The demand for tickets to these games is high, and advance booking is available through Computicket outlets countrywide or the cricket union hosting the match.

Rugby games draw crowds of up to 50,000 to the provincial stadiums

Two Oceans Marathon runners pass the crowds at Constantia Nek

MARATHONS AND ULTRA-MARATHONS

LONG-DISTANCE running is both a popular pastime and a serious national sport. South Africa boasts a number of the world's fastest marathon runners, such as Josiah Thugwane who won a gold medal in the 1996 Olympics.

The strenuous 56-km (35-mile) Two Oceans Marathon, which takes place around the Cape Peninsula on Easter Saturday, and the energy-sapping 85-km (53-mile) long Comrades Marathon, run between the KwaZulu-Natal cities of Durban and Pietermaritzburg in June, are two of the most difficult, yet popular, ultra-marathons in the country. Both events attract thousands of international and local entrants.

With its excellent training facilities and fine summer weather, South Africa is a popular place for European athletes to train during the winter months in Europe. During this season, the international Engen Grand Prix Athletics Series is held in various South African cities.

GOLF

SOUTH AFRICA boasts some of the finest golf courses in the world, and has also produced some of the world's finest golfers. The golfing prowess of Gary Player is legendary, while youthful Ernie Els ranks among the top three golfers in the world. Every December, Sun City hosts the Nedbank 2 Million Dollar Challenge *(see p35)*, where 12 contestants compete for the largest prize in the world – 2 million dollars. The South African Golf Tour also attracts professional golfers from around the globe.

Two local events, the South African Open and the Alfred Dunhill PGA, are both held in mid- to late January.

CYCLING

APART FROM VARIOUS local professional events, the Cape Peninsula hosts the largest timed cycle race in the world, the annual Cape Argus Pick 'n Pay Cycle Tour. Over 35,000 sweaty cycling enthusiasts, some dressed in flamboyant costumes, race or trundle 105 km (65 miles) around the Peninsula on the second Sunday in March. About one third of the contestants is from overseas.

EQUESTRIAN SPORTS

HORSE RACING, until recently the only legal form of gambling in the country, has been an enormous industry for many years. The "Met" (Metropolitan Stakes) held in Cape Town in January, and the Durban July are major social events, with fashion and high stakes the order of the day. Show jumping and horse trials attract crowds every spring to venues such as Inanda near Johannesburg.

The Cape to Rio race leaves Table Bay with huge fanfare

WATERSPORTS

SOUTH AFRICA's coastline offers superb opportunities for sports enthusiasts. The Gunston 500 surfing event, held in Durban each July, is a major attraction. Cape Town is a popular port of call for round-the-world yacht races, and is also the starting point for the Cape to Rio event that takes place early in January every three years.

Sun City's Golf Course hosts the Nedbank 2 Million Dollar Challenge

SOUTH AFRICA
THROUGH THE YEAR

THOUGH ORGANIZED festivals are a relatively new feature in South Africa, long, sunny days have given rise to a number of festivities, many of them outdoors. Cities, towns and villages host festivals to celebrate a variety of occasions: the start of the oyster and the wildflower season; the citrus, apple or grape harvest; even the

Dancers, FNB Vita Dance Umbrella

arrival of the southern right whale from its arctic breeding grounds – all are reason for celebration. The arts, music, religion, language and sport also take their places on the calendar of events. The diversity of festivals emphasizes the disparate origins of South Africa's many peoples and their gradual coming together as a single nation.

SPRING

ALL ACROSS the country, but especially noticeable in the semi-arid Western and Northern Cape regions, the onset of warmer weather raises colourful fields of wildflowers. In wildlife reserves throughout South Africa, the newborn of various species will soon be seen.

SEPTEMBER

Guinness Jazz Festival *(Sep–Oct)*, Johannesburg *(see pp246–7)*. Local and international musicians provide a jazz extravaganza.
Karoo Festival *(mid-Sep)*, Graaff-Reinet *(see pp292–3)*. Join guided walks through this historic country town.
Wildflower Festival *(late Sep)*. The country town of Caledon *(see p158)* celebrates its varied indigenous flora.

Wildflower Show *(late Sep)*, Darling *(see p149)*. Displays the unique West Coast flora and cultivated orchids.
Whale Festival *(last week in Sep)*, Hermanus *(see p160)*. From early spring onwards, the southern right whales and their calves can be seen close to shore in and around Walker Bay.
International Eisteddfod of South Africa *(Sep–Oct)*, Roodepoort. In what has become the country's premier cultural event, musicians, dancers and choirs and from around the world compete for top honours.
Magoebaskloof Spring Festival *(Sep–Oct)*, Magoebaskloof. A bustling arts, crafts and entertainment fair, which is held in a splendid forest setting.

Orchids from Darling

OCTOBER

Currie Cup Finals *(late Oct)*. Match between the two best provincial teams (the location varies from year to year.
Tulbagh Festival *(last weekend in Oct)*, Tulbagh *(see p149)*. Local produce and crafts are displayed in this country town.
The Johannesburg Biennale *(Oct of alternate years only)*, Johannesburg *(see pp246–7)*. Activities throughout the city.
Raisin Festival *(second Sat in Oct)*, Upington *(see p302)*. Music, choir contests and fun on the Orange River near the Augrabies Falls.
Model Aircraft Show *(Oct)*, Oudtshoorn *(see pp166–7)*. Model aircraft enthusiasts participate in this annual event at the local airport.

NOVEMBER

Cherry Festival *(third week in Nov)*, Ficksburg. Celebrate South Africa's only source of commercially grown cherries and asparagus.
National Choir Festival *(Nov–Dec)*, Standard Bank Arena, Johannesburg *(see pp246–7)*. The culmination of a national competition.
Nedbank Summer Concert Season *(Nov–Feb)*, Josephine Mill, Cape Town *(see p98)*. Outdoor concerts of choral,

The Oude Libertas open-air amphitheatre

SUMMER

MOST TOURISTS visit South Africa during the long summer months. The local long school-holidays extend from December well into January. With many South African families traditionally heading for the seaside and wildlife reserves, this is when the roads are at their busiest. Summer is a season spent outdoors. Christmas lunch is more likely to be celebrated around an informal *braai* (barbecue) than at a dining table. Over much of the country, summer rain arrives in the form of short, noisy thundershowers.

Carols by candlelight

DECEMBER

Carols by Candlelight *(pre-Christmas)*. These Advent celebrations take place in all major towns and cities.
Helderberg Festival of Lights *(Dec–Jan)*, Somerset West *(see p126)*. Main Street display of festive lights in rural Somerset West.
The Spier Summer Festival *(Dec–Mar)*, Spier, Stellen-bosch *(see p133)*. Local and international opera, music, dance, comedy and drama.
Miss South Africa, Sun City *(see p256)*. A glittering beauty pageant for the nine provin-cial beauty queens.
Nedbank 2 Million Dollar Challenge, Sun City *(see p256)*. An internationally renowned golfing event with 12 of the world's best golfers.

Shooting the Camps Drift rapids on the Duzi River

JANUARY

Summer Sunset Concerts *(every Sun evening, Jan–Mar)*, Kirstenbosch National Botanical Gardens, Cape Town *(see pp100–1)*. Musical performances on the Gardens' verdant lawns.
Duzi Canoe Marathon *(second week in Jan)*, Pietermaritzburg *(see pp212–3)*. A three-day canoe marathon to the Umgeni River mouth.
Maynardville Open-air Theatre *(Jan–Feb)*, Wynberg, Cape Town *(see p105)*. Shakespearean plays are performed in a well-known city park at night.
Oude Libertas Arts Programme *(Jan–Mar)*, Stellenbosch *(see pp130–1)*. Performances in an amphi-theatre among the vines.
Minstrel Carnival *(New Year)*, Cape Town *(see p18)*. A colourful musical proces-sion culminates in concerts at Green Point Stadium.

Cherries

FEBRUARY

FNB Vita Dance Umbrella *(Feb–Mar)*, Braamfontein, Johannesburg *(see pp246–7)*. One of the most important dance events in South Africa.
Bieliemieliefees *(Feb)*, Agricultural Showgrounds, Reitz, Free State. Concerts, traditional foods and sports to celebrate the Free State's main crop: the mealie (corn).
Paarl Show *(mid-Feb)*, Paarl *(see pp138–9)*. Craft stalls and local entertainment in a friendly wineland town.
Prickly Pear Festival *(early Feb)*, Willem Prinsloo Agricultural Museum, Pretoria *(see pp254–5)*. A showcase of 19th-century lifestyles and farming practices.
Kavady Festival *(Feb–Jul)*, Durban *(see pp218–21)*. A Hindu festival during which many penitents pierce their flesh with hooks and draw beautifully decorated carts through the streets.

Cape Town's minstrels are a colourful sight in early January

AUTUMN

WHEN DECIDUOUS TREES and grapevines begin to shed their leaves, a new round of country fairs is ushered in. The harvest festivals of many small towns celebrate crops like potatoes and olives; even sheep and gems are cause for cheerful get-togethers. A number of wine festivals are held from Paarl in the fertile Western Cape to Kuruman in the arid Northern Cape.

Over a million followers of the Zionist Church gather at Easter

MARCH

Beer and Bread Festival
(early Mar), Caledon *(see p158)*. Celebrating the wheat and barley harvests.
Harvest Festival of the Sea
(late Mar), Saldanha Bay, West Coast. Seafood such as *smoorsnoek (see p342)*, and a variety of watersports.
Klein Karoo Arts Festival
(Mar–Apr), Oudtshoorn *(see p166)*. A mainly Afrikaans cultural festival.
Rand Show *(Mar–Apr)*, Johannesburg *(see pp246–7)*. What began as an agricultural show has become a blend of entertainment and consumerism.
LifeCyle Week *(early Mar)*, Victoria & Alfred Waterfront *(see pp78–81)*. Cycling expo, a week before the annual 105-km (65-mile) Cape Argus Pick 'n Pay Cycle Tour.

APRIL

Zionist Church gathering
(Easter), near Polokwane (formerly Pietersburg, *see p262)* in the Northern Province. More than a million followers of this African Christian church gather at Moria (also known as Zion City) over the Easter weekend.
Festival of Light *(Good Friday)*, Pieter-maritzburg *(see pp212–3)*. At the Sri Siva, Soobramon-iar and Marria-men temples, visitors witness the grand and costly fireworks display.
Fire-walking *(Easter)*, Umbilo Hindu Temple, Durban *(see pp218–21)*. Devout Hindus,

Devotee, Festival of Light

after careful spiritual prepara-tion, walk uninjured across a bed of red-hot coals.
Two Oceans Marathon
(Easter), Cape Town. This 56-km (35-mile) marathon *(see p33)* around the Cape Peninsula is a qualifying race for the Comrades' Marathon.
Ladysmith Show *(Apr)*, Ladysmith, KwaZulu-Natal. An agricultural show with many craft stalls and entertainment.
Potato Festival *(Apr–May)*, Bethal, Mpuma-langa. A vibrant harvest festival with colourful street processions, arts and crafts stalls and entertainment.
Splashy Fen Music Festival
(last weekend in Apr), Splashy Fen Farm, Under-berg, KwaZulu-Natal. Main-stream, alternative, folk and traditional music styles.

MAY

Picnic concerts *(on alter-nate Sun, May–Sep)*, National Botanical Garden, Roode-poort. Choral singing and music in a garden setting.
Royal Show *(May–Jun)*, Pietermaritzburg *(see pp212–3)*. One of South Africa's leading agricultural shows.
Sabie Forest Fair *(May)* Sabie. This fair offers arts-and-craft stalls and local entertainment around a unique Forestry Museum.

Amusement park at the Rand Show in Johannesburg

WINTER

DRY SEASON for most of the country, only the winter-rainfall area along the South-western and Southern Cape coast is lush and green at this time. Inland, days are typically warm, although nightly frosts are common in high-lying areas. Snowfalls occur on the mountains of the Western and Eastern Cape and in the KwaZulu-Natal and Lesotho highlands. Late winter is particularly good for game-watching, as the thirsty wildlife gathers around waterholes.

Safari wildlife-viewing drive at Sabi Sabi, Mpumalanga

JUNE

Comrades' Marathon *(mid-Jun)*, between Durban and Pieter-maritzburg. This ultra long-distance running event attracts top-class runners from all over the world *(see p33)*.

JULY

Standard Bank National Arts Festival *(early to mid-Jul)*, Grahamstown *(see pp188–9)*. An extremely popular two weeks of local and international drama, film, dance, visual arts and music.
Hibiscus Festival *(Jul)*, South Coast of KwaZulu-Natal *(see pp224–5)*. Colourful craft stalls and plenty of entertainment.

High fashion, July Handicap

July Handicap *(first Sat in Jul)*, Greyville Race Course, Durban *(see pp218–9)*. This is the glamour event of the South African horse-racing fraternity.
Knysna Oyster Festival *(early Jul)*, Knysna *(see p176)*. The festival, centred on the commercial oyster beds in Knysna Lagoon, coincides with a forest marathon.
Berg River Canoe Marathon *(Jul)*, Paarl *(see pp138–9)*. A strenuous four-day canoe race that provides some high excitement and is staged annually when the river is in full flood.
Calitzdorp Port Festival *(late Jul)*, Karoo *(see p164)*. A celebration of the region's famous port-style wine.
Gunston 500 *(see pp196–7) (mid Jul)*, Durban *(see pp218–21)*. This popular week-long surfing championship attracts the world's best surfers and hordes of spectators.

Knysna oyster

AUGUST

Agricultural and Wildflower Show *(late Aug)*, Pietberg. The quality of this flower show, as well as the vividness of the colours and the range of species on display depends entirely on the rainfall during the preceding winter.
Food and Wine Festival, *(first weekend in Aug)*, Malmesbury *(see p149)*. This country fair features a variety of locally grown cereals and wines from nearby estates.
Cars-in-the-Park *(early Aug)*, Pretoria *(see pp254–5)*. Gleaming vintage vehicles are displayed by proud owners.
Arts Alive *(late Aug–early Sep)*, Johannesburg *(see pp246–7)*. An exciting urban arts festival, with performers ranging from world-class musicians to children eager to show off the skills they have acquired at workshops.

PUBLIC HOLIDAYS

New Year's Day (1 Jan)
Human Rights Day (22 Mar)
Good Friday (Apr)
Family Day (Apr)
Freedom Day (27 Apr)
Workers' Day (1 May)
Youth Day (16 Jun)
National Women's Day (9 Aug)
Heritage Day (24 Sep)
Day of Reconciliation (16 Dec)
Christmas Day (25 Dec)
Day of Goodwill (26 Dec)

Standard Bank National Arts Festival, Grahamstown

The Climate of South Africa

SITUATED HALFWAY between the Equator and the
Antarctic, South Africa has a temperate climate
with short-term exceptions in certain locations.
Day temperatures can soar to 50°C (122°F) over
low-lying coastal plains in summer and drop to
-16°C (3°F) during a winter's night over the higher
plateau areas. Rainfall increases from west to east.
The most popular time of year to visit South Africa
is during the summer months, from December to
February, but winter days are sunny and cool and
best for game viewing.

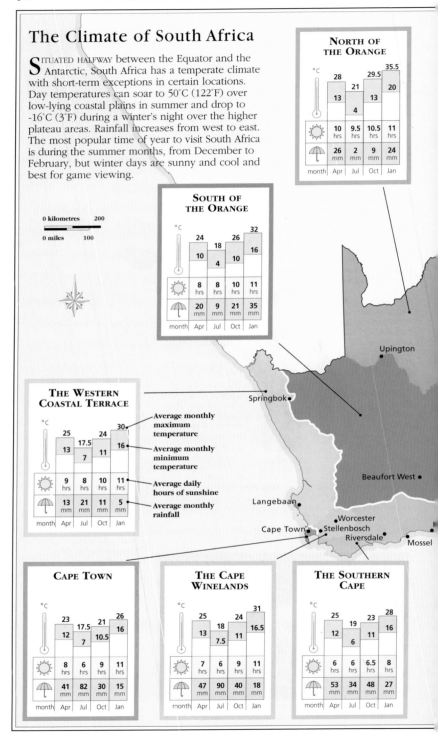

NORTH OF THE ORANGE

°C				35.5
	28		29.5	
		21		20
	13		13	
		4		
☀	10 hrs	9.5 hrs	10.5 hrs	11 hrs
☂	26 mm	2 mm	9 mm	24 mm
month	Apr	Jul	Oct	Jan

SOUTH OF THE ORANGE

°C				32
	24		26	
		18		16
	10		10	
		4		
☀	8 hrs	8 hrs	10 hrs	11 hrs
☂	20 mm	9 mm	21 mm	35 mm
month	Apr	Jul	Oct	Jan

0 kilometres   200
0 miles   100

THE WESTERN COASTAL TERRACE

°C				30
	25		24	
		17.5		16
	13		11	
		7		
☀	9 hrs	8 hrs	10 hrs	11 hrs
☂	13 mm	21 mm	11 mm	5 mm
month	Apr	Jul	Oct	Jan

Average monthly maximum temperature

Average monthly minimum temperature

Average daily hours of sunshine

Average monthly rainfall

Upington

Springbok

Beaufort West

Langebaan

Cape Town · Stellenbosch
Worcester
Riversdale
Mossel

CAPE TOWN

°C				26
	23		21	
		17.5		16
	12		10.5	
		7		
☀	8 hrs	6 hrs	9 hrs	11 hrs
☂	41 mm	82 mm	30 mm	15 mm
month	Apr	Jul	Oct	Jan

THE CAPE WINELANDS

°C				31
	25		24	
		18		16.5
	13		11	
		7.5		
☀	7 hrs	6 hrs	9 hrs	11 hrs
☂	47 mm	90 mm	40 mm	18 mm
month	Apr	Jul	Oct	Jan

THE SOUTHERN CAPE

°C				28
	25		23	
		19		16
	12		11	
		6		
☀	6 hrs	6 hrs	6.5 hrs	8 hrs
☂	53 mm	34 mm	48 mm	27 mm
month	Apr	Jul	Oct	Jan

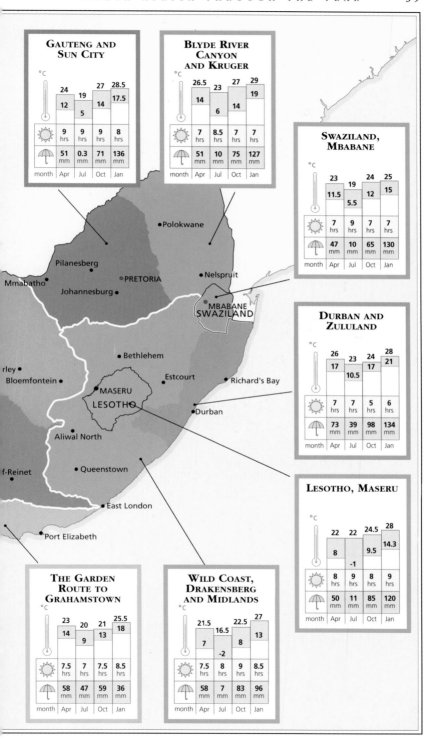

GAUTENG AND SUN CITY

°C

		27	28.5
24	19	14	17.5
12	5		

☀	9 hrs	9 hrs	9 hrs	8 hrs
☂	51 mm	0.3 mm	71 mm	136 mm
month	Apr	Jul	Oct	Jan

BLYDE RIVER CANYON AND KRUGER

°C

26.5	23	27	29
14	6	14	19

☀	7 hrs	8.5 hrs	7 hrs	7 hrs
☂	51 mm	10 mm	75 mm	127 mm
month	Apr	Jul	Oct	Jan

SWAZILAND, MBABANE

°C

23	19	24	25
11.5	5.5	12	15

☀	7 hrs	9 hrs	7 hrs	7 hrs
☂	47 mm	10 mm	65 mm	130 mm
month	Apr	Jul	Oct	Jan

DURBAN AND ZULULAND

°C

26	23	24	28
17	10.5	17	21

☀	7 hrs	7 hrs	5 hrs	6 hrs
☂	73 mm	39 mm	98 mm	134 mm
month	Apr	Jul	Oct	Jan

LESOTHO, MASERU

°C

22	22	24.5	28
8	-1	9.5	14.3

☀	8 hrs	9 hrs	8 hrs	9 hrs
☂	50 mm	11 mm	85 mm	120 mm
month	Apr	Jul	Oct	Jan

THE GARDEN ROUTE TO GRAHAMSTOWN

°C

23	20	21	25.5
14	9	13	18

☀	7.5 hrs	7 hrs	7.5 hrs	8.5 hrs
☂	58 mm	47 mm	59 mm	36 mm
month	Apr	Jul	Oct	Jan

WILD COAST, DRAKENSBERG AND MIDLANDS

°C

21.5	16.5	22.5	27
7	-2	8	13

☀	7.5 hrs	8 hrs	9 hrs	8.5 hrs
☂	58 mm	7 mm	83 mm	96 mm
month	Apr	Jul	Oct	Jan

Polokwane

Pilanesberg

Mmabatho

PRETORIA

Johannesburg

Nelspruit

MBABANE
SWAZILAND

Bethlehem

rley

Bloemfontein

Estcourt

MASERU
LESOTHO

Richard's Bay

Durban

Aliwal North

f-Reinet

Queenstown

East London

Port Elizabeth

THE HISTORY
OF SOUTH AFRICA

THE ANCIENT FOOTPRINTS discovered at Langebaan, a cast of which is now in the South African Museum in Cape Town, were made 117,000 years ago. They are the world's oldest traces of anatomically modern man, *Homo sapiens sapiens*. Other early hominid remains found at the Sterkfontein caves in Gauteng and at Taung near Bloemfontein belong to the group known as *Australopithecus africanus*.

Jan van Riebeeck, the founder of Cape Town

The African and European civilization drifted towards a cultural collision when the Dutch East India Company set up a refreshment station in Table Bay. The year was 1652, and the colonizers had come not just to visit, but to stay. On the whole, the Dutch sought to establish amicable relationships with the local Khoina, but a natural wariness and the inability to understand one another doomed many attempts and the pattern of relations over the subsequent centuries was set. Rivalry over water and grazing soon turned into open hostility, first around the bay and then further afield as Dutch "burghers" sought new land. Their trails initiated a wave of migration inland. Isolated clashes with indigenous groups escalated into the bitter frontier wars of the 18th and 19th centuries, a situation further aggravated by the arrival of the 1820 British settlers. Although outnumbered, the settlers' muskets, cannons and horses were an advantage that led to a prevailing sense of white supremacy, with both colonial and republican governments denying people of colour their rights.

Ironically, it was the exploitation of black labour in the mines of Kimberley and Johannesburg that ignited the spark of African nationalism, while the apartheid laws of the mid-1900s focused world attention and pressure on South Africa. The release of Nelson Mandela in 1990 was the beginning of a transformation that set the country on a new course: the road to democracy.

This surprisingly accurate map was produced in 1570 by Abraham Ortelius from Antwerp

◁ **Ancient San Bushman paintings adorn many rock walls like this one in the Cedarberg, Western Cape**

Prehistoric South Africa

Stone Age grinding tool

SOME 2–3 MILLION YEARS AGO, long after the dinosaurs, *Australopithecus africanus* inhabited South Africa's plains. *Australopithecines* were the ancestors of anatomically modern people whose remains in South Africa date at least as far back as 110,000 years. Rock art created by Bushman hunter-gatherers over the past 10,000 years, is widely distributed. Some 2,000 years ago, pastoral Khoina migrated southwestward, while black farming communities settled the eastern side of the country. Their descendants were encountered by the 15th-century Portuguese explorers.

EARLY MAN

◻ *Distribution in South Africa*

Australopithecus africanus
In 1925, Professor Raymond Dart, then dean of the University of the Witwatersrand's medical faculty, first identified man's ancestor based on the evidence of a skull found near Taung, North West Province.

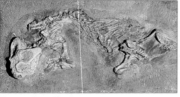

Langebaan Footprints
Homo sapiens *tracks at Langebaan Lagoon are around 117,000 years old. They are the world's oldest fossilized trail of anatomically modern human beings.*

Karoo Fossils
Diictodon *skeletons found in the Karoo (see p290) belonged to mammal-like reptiles that tunnelled into the mud along river banks some 255 million years ago.*

CRADLE OF MANKIND
Based on the evidence of fossilized remains from the Sterkfontein caves *(see p252)* and other sites in South and East Africa, palaeontologists believe that people evolved in Africa. Stone tools and bone fragments indicate that modern humans lived and hunted in South Africa some 110,000 years ago.

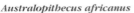

TIMELINE

c. 3,000,000 BC *Australopithecus africanus* lives in central South Africa		**c. 117,000 BC** Early modern man settlement at Langebaan	**c. 35,000 BC** Start of Late Stone Age, man uses refined tools and weapons	*Spear head*	
3,000,000 BC	**2,000,000 BC**	**1,000,000 BC**	**40,000 BC**	**30,000 BC**	**20,000 BC**
Hand axe	**c. 1,000,000 BC** *Homo erectus* displaces earlier apelike hominid species	**c. 200,000 BC** Middle Stone Age	**c. 38,000 BC** Iron ore is mined for its pigment at Ngwenya in Swaziland	**c. 26,000 BC** Earliest known example of rock art (Namibia)	

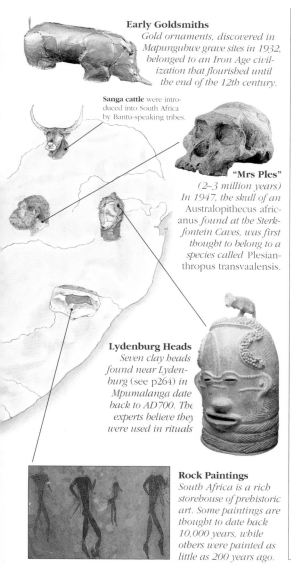

Early Goldsmiths
Gold ornaments, discovered in Mapungubwe grave sites in 1932, belonged to an Iron Age civilization that flourished until the end of the 12th century.

Sanga cattle were introduced into South Africa by Bantu-speaking tribes.

"Mrs Ples"
(2–3 million years)
In 1947, the skull of an Australopithecus africanus *found at the Sterkfontein Caves, was first thought to belong to a species called* Plesianthropus transvaalensis.

Lydenburg Heads
Seven clay heads found near Lydenburg (see p264) in Mpumalanga date back to AD 700. The experts believe they were used in rituals

Rock Paintings
South Africa is a rich storehouse of prehistoric art. Some paintings are thought to date back 10,000 years, while others were painted as little as 200 years ago.

WHERE TO SEE PREHISTORIC SOUTH AFRICA

The Natal Museum in Pietermaritzburg *(p213)*, McGregor Museum in Kimberley *(p304)* and Transvaal Museum in Pretoria *(p255)* hold important collections of rock art, archaeological and palaeontological artifacts. Rock paintings can be seen in the Cedarberg of the Western Cape *(p153)* and in the Drakensberg in Lesotho *(pp204–5)* and KwaZulu-Natal *(pp206–7)*. The South African Museum in Cape Town *(p72)* has dioramas of early people. Bloemfontein's National Museum *(p306)* and the museum in Lydenburg *(p264)* exhibit fossil finds. The Sterkfontein Caves *(p252)*, where Mrs Ples was found, are near Krugersdorp. Many of these museums can assist visitors with information on outings to individual sites.

Bushman Cave Museum *is an open-air site in the Giant's Castle Reserve (see pp206–7).*

The Sudwala Caves *(see p264) feature an interesting timeline display on the evolution of man.*

c. 8,000 BC Microlithic stone toolkit of the Bushman culture		c. AD 200 Black farmers and iron-workers settle south of the Limpopo River and plant sorghum crops		*San Bushman bow and arrows*	
10,000 BC	**AD 1**	**AD 350**	**AD 700**	**AD 1050**	**AD 1400**
	c. AD 1 Nomadic Khoina herders, originally from Botswana, move southwest into Cape coastal territory	*Sorghum*		**c. 1400** Stone settlements of Sotho people expand from the Highveld into present-day Free State	

Explorers and Colonizers

Bartolomeu Dias
(1450–1500)

PORTUGUESE NAVIGATORS pioneered the sea route to India, but it was the Dutch who set up a fortified settlement at the Cape in 1652. The indigenous Khoina who initially welcomed the trade opportunities were quickly marginalized. Some took service with the settlers, while others fled from the Dutch *trekboers* (migrant graziers). In 1688, the arrival of French Huguenot families swelled the numbers of the white settlers, driving even more Khoina away from their ancestral land.

EXPLORERS' ROUTES

➤ *Dias 1488*   ➤ *Da Gama 1498*

▢ *Cape colony 1795*

The Caravels of Dias
In 1988, a replica of the ship commanded by Bartolomeu Dias 500 years before retraced his voyage from Lisbon to Mossel Bay. The ship is now housed in Mossel Bay's Bartolomeu Dias Museum complex (see pp172–3).

Unique Early Postal Systems
In the 15th and 16th centuries, Portuguese captains anchored in Mossel Bay and left messages for each other engraved on flat rocks. One of these can be seen in the Old Slave Lodge in Cape Town (see p66).

Dutch flag

Jan van Riebeeck

Matchlock

JAN VAN RIEBEECK'S ARRIVAL

On 6 April 1652, Jan van Riebeeck landed at the Cape to establish a permanent settlement for the Dutch East India Company. The first commander of the new outpost and his wife, Maria de la Quellerie, are commemorated by statues erected near the site of their historic landing.

TIMELINE

1400	1450	1500	1550
	1486 Portuguese sail as far as today's Namibia.	**c. 1500** Shipwrecked Portuguese sailors encounter Iron Age farmers along South Africa's south coast.	
Vasco da Gama	**1498** Vasco da Gama discovers the route to India around the Cape of Good Hope	**1510** Dom Francisco d'Almeida, viceroy of Portuguese India, and 57 of his men are killed by Khoina in Table Bay	

The Vereenigde Oost-Indische Compagnie (VOC)

Several small trading companies joined in 1602 to form the Dutch East India Company (VOC). It was granted a charter to trade, draw up treaties and maintain an army and a fleet. The VOC was dissolved in 1798.

Beads and trinkets were offered as gifts to the Khoina.

Autshumao, leader of the local *Strandlopers* (a people living near the sea who ate mainly fish and mussels) had been taken to Java by the British in 1631. He had a basic knowledge of English and was able to negotiate with the Dutch.

Animal skins were worn by the native peoples of the Cape.

Superior Weaponry
Matchlocks secured the settlers' advantage over the clubs and throwing-spears of the Hottentots, and the bows and poisoned arrows used by the San Bushmen.

Almond Hedge
A remnant of the hedge that was planted to discourage unauthorized trading with the Khoina can be seen at Kirstenbosch National Botanical Gardens (see pp100–1).

WHERE TO SEE EXPLORERS AND COLONIZERS

Mossel Bay's museum complex houses a replica of Dias's caravel *(pp172–3)*, as well as the old milkwood tree in which passing sailors left messages for their fellow mariners. Castle Good Hope in Cape Town *(pp68–9)* is South Africa's oldest surviving structure.
The Huguenot Memorial Museum in Franschhoek *(p136)* honours the French heritage of the town and contains antique furniture and paintings. Early colonial artifacts are on display at the Old Slave Lodge in Cape Town *(p66)*.

The Kat Balcony, Castle Good Hope in Cape Town, leads to the rooms that house the William Fehr art collection.

The French Huguenots
Fleeing from religious persecution in France, about 200 Huguenots arrived at the Cape of Good Hope in 1688. They were assigned farms around Franschhoek (see pp136–7), where they planted vineyards.

1594 Portuguese barter with Khoina in Table Bay

Maria de la Quellerie

1652 Jan van Riebeeck and his wife, Maria de la Quellerie, arrive in Table Bay.

1693 Sheik Yusuf is exiled to the Cape after instigating a rebellion in Java. His *kramat* (shrine) near Faure (Western Cape) is revered by Muslims

| 1600 | 1650 | 1700 | 1750 |

1608 The Dutch barter with Khoina clans for food

1658 War against Khoina follows cattle raids and killing of settlers

1688 Huguenot refugees settle at the Cape

1713 Smallpox epidemic kills unknown hundreds of Khoina, as well as many white settlers

British Colonization

B Y 1778, SETTLER EXPANSION had reached the Eastern Cape and the Great Fish River was proclaimed the eastern boundary of the Cape Colony. As this was Xhosa territory, local herdsmen were deprived of their pastures and a century of bitter "frontier wars" ensued. In 1795, following the French Revolution, British forces were able to occupy the Cape. Having re-turned it to the Netherlands in 1802, they re-claimed it in 1806 and instituted a govern-ment-sponsored programme that assigned farms in the Zuurveld area to British settlers. To the east, Shaka Zulu was just beginning to build a powerful empire.

Hitching post, Graaff-Reinet

SETTLER EXPANSION

☐ 1814   — Cape today

Blockhouse ruins

Battle of Muizenberg (1795)

In this battle for possession of the Cape, British warships bombarded Dutch out-posts at Muizenberg (see p95). Britain was victorious and thus acquired a halfway station en route to India.

FORT FREDERICK

In the 19th century, many private homes were fortified, and a suc-cession of outposts and frontier forts were built in the Eastern Cape. Few were attacked; almost all are now in ruin. Fort Frederick in Port Elizabeth *(see pp182–3)* has been restored and is a superb example of what these frontier fortifications looked like.

Grave of Captain Francis Evatt, who oversaw the landing of the 1820 settlers.

Rustenburg House

After the battle of Muizenberg, the Dutch surrendered the Cape to Britain. The treaty was signed in this house in Rondebosch, Cape Town. Its present Neo-Classical façade probably dates from around 1803.

TIMELINE

1750s	1760s	1770s	1780s	
1750 Worldwide, Dutch influence begins to wane		**1770** Gamtoos River made boundary of Cape Colony	**1778** Fish River made boundary of Cape Colony	**1789** Merino sheep are imported from Holland and thrive in South Africa
1750	**1760**	**1770**	**1780**	**17**
1751 Rijk Tulbagh appointed Dutch Governor of the Cape (1751–71)		**1779** A year after it is made boundary of the Cape Colony, settlers and Xhosa clash at the Fish River – the first of nine frontier wars		

Merino sheep

Battle of Blaauwberg (1806)
This battle between the Dutch and the British was fought at the foot of the Blouberg, out of range of British warships. Outnumbered and poorly disciplined, the Dutch defenders soon broke rank and fled.

The 1820 Settlers
About 4,000 Britons, mostly artisans with little or no farming experience, settled around Grahamstown (see pp188–9).

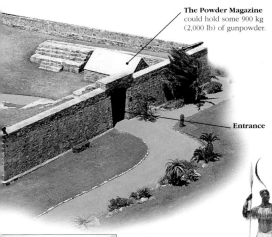

The Powder Magazine
could hold some 900 kg
(2,000 lb) of gunpowder.

Entrance

WHERE TO SEE BRITISH COLONIZATION

The museums in Umtata (the capital of the former Transkei) and the University of Fort Hare in Alice (in the former Çiskei) have interesting collections of colonial artefacts. Old weapons and ammunition, uniforms, maps, and even letters and medical supplies are displayed in the Military Museum at Castle Good Hope in Cape Town (*pp68–9*). The museums in King William's Town, Queenstown and Grahamstown all (*pp188–9*) exhibit collections of frontier-war memorabilia. The excellent MuseuMAfricA in Johannesburg (*p246*) has a superb collection of old prints and paintings.

MuseuMAfricA has three permanent exhibitions and various temporary displays.

Shaka Zulu
This gifted military strategist became Zulu chief after the death of Senzangakona in 1815. Shaka introduced the assegaai (short spear) and united lesser clans into a Zulu empire.

The Xhosa
The Xhosa had farmed in the Zuurveld (present Eastern Cape) for centuries. The arrival of the 1820 Settlers caused friction and dispute.

1795 Battle of Muizenberg and first British occupation	1800 The *Cape Town Gazette* and *African Advertiser* are first published	1806 Battle of Blaauwberg. Second British occupation of the Cape	1818 Shaka's military conquests in Zululand begin	*Typical settler house*	1820 4,000 British settlers arrive in Grahamstown	1829 The Khoina are released from having to carry passes. The University of Cape Town is founded
	1800		**1810**		**1820**	**1830**
•3 Lombard ak, the first ak in the ¡ntry, opens Cape Town	1802 Lady Anne Barnard, whose letters and diaries give an insight into colonial life, leaves the Cape	1814 British occupation of the Cape is ratified by the Congress of Vienna	1815 The Slagter's Nek rebellion, led by anti-British frontiersmen, ends with judicial executions near Cookhouse (Eastern Cape)		1828 Shaka is murdered by his half-brother, Dingane	

Colonial Expansion

A Voortrekker woman's bonnet

THE BRITISH COLONIAL administration met with hostility from the Cape's Dutch-speaking community. Dissatisfied Voortrekkers (Boer pioneers) headed east and north in an exodus that became known as the Great Trek. In 1838, Zulu chief Dingane had one group of Voortrekkers killed, but in the subsequent Battle of Blood River his own warriors were beaten. A short-lived Boer republic, Natalia, was annexed by Britain in 1843. By 1857, two new Boer states, Transvaal and Orange Free State, landlocked and impoverished but independent, had been consolidated north of the Orange and Vaal rivers.

VOORTREKKER MOVEMENT

☐ *1836 Great Trek*

☐ *British territory by 1848*

Emancipated Slaves

The freeing of 39,000 Cape Colony slaves in 1834 angered Boer farmers who relied on slave labour. The British decision was not due entirely to philanthropism, it was simply cheaper to employ free labour.

THE GREAT TREK

Dissatisfied with the British administration, convoys of Boer ox wagons trekked inland to seek new territory. The pioneers, armed with cannons and muskets, were accompanied by their families, black and coloured retainers and livestock. Each wagon was "home" for the duration of the journey and contained all that the family owned. At night, or under attack, the convoy would form a laager – a circle of wagons lashed together with chains.

The Battle of Vegkop

In 1836 the Ndebele found themselves in the path of trekker expansion northwards. Traditional weapons were no match for blazing rifles: the 40 Voortrekkers beat off an attack by 6,000 Ndebele warriors at Vegkop, killing 430, but losing most of their own sheep, cattle and trek oxen.

Barrels were used to store food, water and gunpowder.

Wagon chest

The drive shaft was attached to the yoke which was placed around the neck of the oxen.

TIMELINE

1838 Battle of Blood River follows the murder of Voortrekker leader, Piet Retief, and his men

Dingane

1830	1835	1840

1834 Slaves freed subject to a four-year "apprenticeship". Sixth Frontier War erupts; Voortrekkers travel to present-day Free State, KwaZulu-Natal, Northern Province and Namibia

1836 The Great Trek begins

1839 Boer Republic of Natalia is proclaimed

The Battle of Blood River
On 16 December 1838, the river ran red with blood as a 468-strong burgher commando defeated 12,500 Zulu warriors in retribution for the killing of Piet Retief.

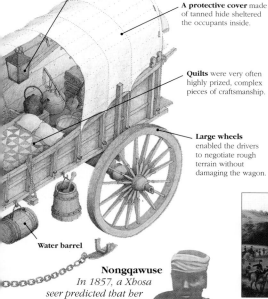

Tallow candles provided light.

A protective cover made of tanned hide sheltered the occupants inside.

Quilts were very often highly prized, complex pieces of craftsmanship.

Large wheels enabled the drivers to negotiate rough terrain without damaging the wagon.

Water barrel

Nongqawuse
In 1857, a Xhosa seer predicted that her people would regain their former power if they destroyed all their herds and crops, but the resulting famine further weakened their position.

WHERE TO SEE THE COLONIAL EXPANSION

British colonial history is well covered in cultural history and battle site museums nationwide. Museums at Grahamstown (pp188–9), Port Elizabeth (pp182–3), King William's Town and East London have displays of old weapons, maps and pioneer artifacts. MuseuMAfricA (p246) in Johannesburg exhibits historic documents, war memorabilia and maps. Kleinplasie Open-air Museum (pp142–3) is a living showcase of the lifestyles and farming processes of the Voortrekkers.

The Battle of Blood River Memorial, Dundee, shows a recreated, life-size laager.

The Kat River Rebellion
Khoina settlers on the Kat River in the Cape had fought for the government without compensation, but rebelled in the war of 1850. With their defeat, their land passed to white ownership.

1846 Seventh Frontier War (War of the Axe)	**1850** Eighth Frontier War, in which the Kat River Khoina join the Xhosa	**1854** Britain withdraws from the Orange River Sovereignty	**1856** British and German settlers placed on Eastern Cape border; the Colony of Natal is granted a representative government	
1845	**1850**	**1855**		**1860**
1852 The Cape is granted representative government by Britain. Zuid-Afrikaansche Republiek (Transvaal) is formed	**1853** Stamps available in the Cape Colony for the first time *First postage stamp*	**1857** Thousands of Xhosa living between the Keiskamma and Great Kei rivers (Eastern Cape) perish in a famine resulting from an ill-advised prophecy		

Clash for Gold and Diamonds

The crown of England

THE DISCOVERY OF DIAMONDS in the Northern Cape laid the foundation for South Africa's economy and created a massive migrant labour system. Subsequent strikes of gold in the east of the country promised an untold source of wealth best exploited under a single British authority. African kingdoms and two Boer republics were coerced to join a British confederation. Resistance to the British masterplan led to a series of skirmishes that culminated in the South African (Boer) War of 1899–1902.

AREAS OF CONFLICT

☐ *Boer strongholds, war zones*

Gold Fever
Finds of alluvial gold at Pilgrim's Rest (see p266) and Barberton preceded the 1886 discovery of Johannesburg's Main Reef.

Leander Jameson (1853–1917)
After the discovery of the Transvaal gold reefs, Jameson masterminded a revolt intended to topple President Paul Kruger of the Transvaal Republic.

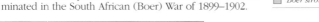

Cecil John Rhodes (1853–1902)
This ruthless financier became involved in organizing the Jameson Raid in 1896, while he was prime minister of the Cape. The interference in the affairs of another state effectively ended his political career.

TIMELINE

1867 A 21-carat diamond is found near Hopetown in the Northern Cape

1878 Walvis Bay (in today's Namibia) is proclaimed British territory

1860	1865	1870	1875

Cut diamond

1871 Diamonds found at Colesberg Kopje (Kimberley). Gold found in Pilgrim's Rest

1877 Britain annexes South African Republic

1879 Britain invades the Zulu kingdom of Cetshwayo, adjoining their colony of Natal

Jan Christiaan Smuts

General Smuts (1870–1950) played prominent roles in the South African War and in both World Wars. He also helped to draft the United Nations Charter, and was twice elected as prime minister of South Africa (1919–24 and 1939–48).

Isandlhwana Hill

Bayonets had to be used when the British ran out of ammunition.

Shields covered with cow hide were used to ward off the bayonets.

The *assegaai* (short stabbing spear) was useful in close combat.

British casualties were high; only a handful of men escaped alive.

WHERE TO SEE THE CLASH FOR GOLD AND DIAMONDS

Coach tours include the major sites on the Battlefields Route *(p210)* in KwaZulu-Natal. Audio cassettes for self-guided tours are available at Talana Museum *(p210)*. Gold Reef City *(pp248–9)* is an evocative recreation of the mining town from which Johannesburg developed. The Kimberley Mine Museum *(p305)* is one of several excellent historic sites in Kimberley.

Kimberley Mine Big Hole in Kimberley, Northern Cape.

BATTLE OF ISANDHLWANA

In an effort to subjugate the fiercely independent Zulu, British officials provoked several incidents. In 1879, a 1,200-strong British and colonial force was annihilated by 20,000 Zulu warriors at Isandhlwana Hill.

Modern Warfare

The South African War (1899–1902) was the first fought with high-velocity rifles and mechanical transport. Although the Boers were good shots and horsemen and could live off the land, limited manpower as well as the loose and informal structure of their armies counted against them.

1884 Lesotho becomes British protectorate	**1886** Discovery of the Main Reef on Witwatersrand (Gauteng)	**1894** Kingdom of Swaziland becomes British protectorate	**1896** Jameson Raid into Transvaal fails. Rinderpest kills countless head of cattle as well as wild animals	**1902** South African War ends
1880	**1885**	**1890**	**1895**	**1900**
1881 Boers defeat British army at Majuba	**1883** Olive Schreiner publishes *Story of an African Farm* **1885** Britain annexes part of Bechuanaland (Botswana)	**1893** Mohandas Karamchand Gandhi arrives in Durban to practise law	*Winston Churchill as war correspondent in South Africa*	**1899** Start of South African War. Sabie Game Reserve declared (forerunner of today's Kruger National Park)

Mahatma Gandhi

The Apartheid Years

"Free Mandela"

I N 1910, THE UNION of South Africa became a self-governing colony within the British Commonwealth. The future of black South Africans was largely left undecided, leading to the founding of the South African Native National Congress (later known as the ANC) in 1912. The Great Trek centenary of 1938 renewed the white Afrikaner's hope for self-determination. In 1948, the Afrikaner-based National Party (NP) came to power and, by manipulating the composition of parliament, managed to enforce a series of harsh laws that stripped black South Africans of most of their basic human rights. In 1961 Prime Minister Verwoerd led the country out of the Commonwealth and into increasing political isolation.

APARTHEID SOUTH AFRICA

— *Provincial boundaries (1994)*

▨ *Homelands up to 1984*

Delville Wood
One of the most vicious battles of World War I was fought at Delville Wood, in France. For five days, 3,000 South African soldiers held out against the German line.

The Great Trek Centenary
The ox wagons rolled again in 1938, headed for a solemn celebration in Pretoria, where the first stone of the Voortrekker Monument (see p255) was laid. This re-enactment of the Great Trek was an impressive display of Afrikaner solidarity, patriotism and political strength.

BURNING PASS BOOKS
The 1952 Natives Act required all black people over 16 to carry a pass book (permit to work in a "white" area) at all times, and present it to the police on demand. In 1960, thousands assembled at township police stations countrywide to burn their pass books. The law was repealed in 1986.

TIMELINE

1905 Cullinan Diamond found at Premier Diamond Mine	**1907** Sir James Percy FitzPatrick writes *Jock of the Bushveld*	**1912** South African Native National Congress founded (later becomes ANC)		**1928** Kirstenbosch Botanical Gardens and University of South Africa founded	**1936** Firs printing c the Bible i Afrikaan
1900		**1910**		**1920**	**1930**
1904 President Paul Kruger dies. *President Paul Kruger*		**1910** Formation of the Union of South Africa	**1914** South Africa declares war on Germany. Boer rebellion put down by Union government. The first National Party formed in Bloemfontein	**1922** Miners' rebellion breaks out at coal mines in Witbank	**1927** Compulsory racial segregation declared in many urban areas

APARTHEID

Afrikaans for "segregation", this word describes the government policy in force after 1948. In keeping with racial classification laws, skin colour dictated where people were allowed to live, work and even be buried. It determined where children were taught and influenced the quality of their education. Sex "across the colour bar" was punishable by imprisonment. Loss of land was among the system's most terrible inflictions.

Security police "house calls" enforced apartheid laws

African Nationalism

Drum, *first published in the 1950s, was important for black journalists. Not afraid to criticize the white regime, they rekindled African Nationalism.*

Apartheid's Architects

Dutch-born Hendrik Verwoerd (1901–66), prime minister from 1958 until his assassination, and Charles Robberts Swart (1894–1982), the minister of justice, implemented many apartheid measures.

WHERE TO SEE THE APARTHEID YEARS

District Six Museum, located on the edge of this former Cape Town precinct near the city centre, shows what life was like in this largely Muslim community before it was cleared under the Group Areas Act, starting in 1966. Exhibits at the Mayibuye Centre, University of the Western Cape, depict the oppression and struggle for democracy. The Old Slave Lodge *(p66)* in Cape Town and MuseuMAfricA *(p246)* in Johannesburg also have interesting displays. In Pretoria, the Voortrekker Museum and Monument *(p255)* offer an insight into the driving force behind Afrikaner Nationalism.

MuseuMAfricA in Johannesburg shows the living conditions in a township like Sophiatown.

District Six, "the life and soul of Cape Town", was declared a white area in 1966.

First edition of Afrikaans Bible

1939 South Africa declares war on Germany	**1948** National Party elected as the country's government	**1950** Communism is outlawed	**1955** Petrol is made from coal for the first time in South Africa
			1958 Hendrik Verwoerd becomes prime minister of South Africa
1940		**1950**	**1960**
	1949 Prohibition of Mixed Marriages Act, the first of many apartheid laws, is passed by Parliament		**1960** Police shoot 69 demonstrators at Sharpeville. Whites-only referendum opts for a republic

Age of Democracy

**Buttonhole,
1992 Referendum**

THE LAWS IMPOSED by the white Nationalist government outraged black African societies, and the decree that Afrikaans be the language of instruction at black schools sparked off the revolt of 1976. States of emergency came and went, and violence increased. It became clear that the old system of administration was doomed. In 1990, State President Frederik Willem de Klerk undertook the first step towards reconciliation by unbanning the ANC, Communist Party and 34 other organizations, and announcing the release of Nelson Mandela.

THE NEW SOUTH AFRICA

— *Provincial boundaries*

A World First
Christiaan Barnard (right) made medical history in 1967 when he transplanted a human heart.

Desmond Tutu won a Nobel Peace Prize (1984) and Martin Luther King Peace Prize (1986) for his dedicated anti-apartheid campaign.

The Soweto Riots
On 16 June 1976, police fired on Black students protesting against the use of Afrikaans in their schools. The picture of a fatally wounded boy became a world-famous symbol of this tragic struggle.

Arts Against Apartheid
The Black Christ (by Ronald Harrison) was inspired by the Sharpeville Massacre and banning of the then ANC president Chief Albert Luthuli (depicted as Christ). Banned for years, it now hangs in the South African National Gallery *(see p73).*

DEMOCRATIC ELECTION
On 27 April 1994, South Africans went to the polls – many for the first time. Five days later the result was announced: with 63 per cent of votes in its favour, the African National Congress (ANC) had achieved victory in all but two provinces and Nelson Mandela was the new State President.

TIMELINE

Old flag

1961 South Africa becomes a republic outside the British Commonwealth

1967 Professor Christiaan Barnard carries out first heart transplant

1971 International Court and UN Security Council recognize Namibia and revoke South Africa's mandate on the country

1976 Soweto riots erupt. Flight of foreign capital from South Africa

1960	1965	1970	1975	1980

1962 Nelson Mandela arrested. UN sanctions isolate South Africa politically and economically

1963 Guerrilla war begins in South West Africa (Namibia)

1968 Swaziland gains independence

1966 Prime Minister Verwoerd assassinated. Lesotho gains its independence

1974 United Nations demands that South Africa withdraw from Namibia

1980 ANC bombs Sasolburg Oil Refinery in the Free State

Kwaito – Sound of a New Generation
Boomshaka sings kwaito, *a uniquely South African sound that was born in the townships of Gauteng. The lyrics, influenced by* toyi-toyi *(protest) chants, have a similar repetitive quality.*

Free At Last
On 11 February 1990, after almost three decades in custody, Nelson Mandela emerged from the Victor Verster prison near Paarl. The high-profile event was watched by millions around the world.

Independent Electoral Commission monitor

Ballot paper

Sealed ballot box

Cricket World Cup 1992
Political change in South Africa saw the national cricket team included in a world event for the first time in over 20 years.

Freedom of Speech
The early 1980s saw flamboyant Evita Bezuiden-hout (see p149) on stage for the first time. Her outspoken, satirical views on internal politics made her famous in South Africa and abroad.

Sanctions Lifted ®
In 1993, trade sanctions (introduced in 1986) were lifted and brands became available again.

The Truth and Reconciliation Commission (TRC)
Established in 1994 under the chairmanship of former Archbishop of Cape Town Desmond Tutu, the aim of this commission was to establish the motives behind political crimes committed during the apartheid years.

1985	1990	1995	2000
	1990 South African involvement in SWA/Namibia ceases with Namibian independence. ANC, PAC and SACP unbanned. Nelson Mandela released	**1994** ANC wins SA's first democratic election. State President Nelson Mandela inaugurated	**1995** South Africa hosts and wins the Rugby World Cup **1999** Second democratic election
1984 New constitution for tricameral parliament	**1992** National referendum held regarding FW de Klerk's policy of change. South Africa participates in the Olympic Games, the first time since 1960		**1998** Truth and Reconciliation Commission hearings begin

The new flag

CAPE TOWN

Cape Town at a Glance

CAPE TOWN LIES ON A small peninsula at the southern tip of Africa which juts into the Atlantic Ocean. It is South Africa's premier tourist destination and its fourth largest urban centre. Enriched by Dutch, British and Cape Malay influences, the cosmopolitan atmosphere is a unique blend of cultures. Lying at the foot of its most famous landmark, Table Mountain, Cape Town has a host of well-preserved historical buildings. Many, such as the Old Townhouse on Greenmarket Square, now house museums. Outside the city, attractions include Chapman's Peak Drive along a winding coastline, where sheer cliffs drop to the swirling sea below, and a tour of the vineyards around Franschhoek and Stellenbosch.

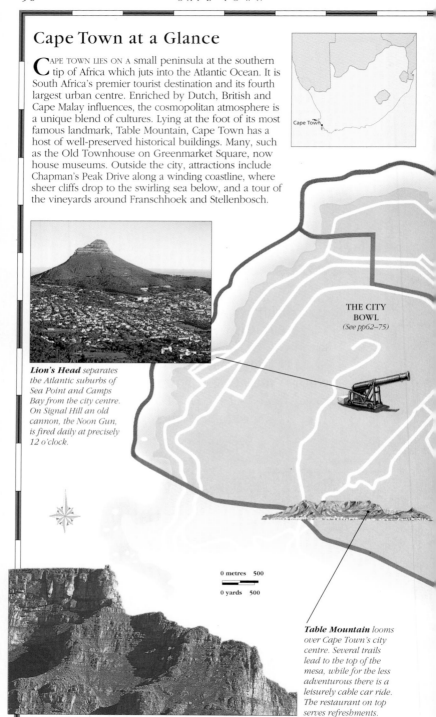

Cape Town

THE CITY BOWL
(See pp62–75)

Lion's Head *separates the Atlantic suburbs of Sea Point and Camps Bay from the city centre. On Signal Hill an old cannon, the Noon Gun, is fired daily at precisely 12 o'clock.*

0 metres 500

0 yards 500

Table Mountain *looms over Cape Town's city centre. Several trails lead to the top of the mesa, while for the less adventurous there is a leisurely cable car ride. The restaurant on top serves refreshments.*

◁ **Camps Bay beach, on the Atlantic seaboard, is a popular spot for sunbathing and people-watching**

Victoria Wharf Shopping Centre, an upmarket complex at the Waterfront (see pp78–9), is a veritable shopper's delight. The modern structures have been designed to fit in with renovated older buildings.

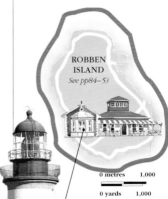

ROBBEN ISLAND
See pp84–5)

0 metres   1,000

0 yards   1,000

VICTORIA & ALFRED WATERFRONT
(See pp76–83)

The lighthouse on Robben Island (see pp84–5) *is 18 m (59 ft) high* and was *built in 1863. It stands near the "village", whose shoupiece, the Governor's House, now offers accommodation for visiting dignitaries.*

The Grand Parade is a lively market venue on Wednesdays and Saturday mornings. Wares range from fabrics, flowers and spices to cheap watches and toys. Beware of pickpockets, and don't carry expensive jewellery and cameras.

GREATER CAPE TOWN AREA

Robben Island

Table Bay

Hout Bay

False Bay

0 kilometres   20

Cape Point   0 miles   10

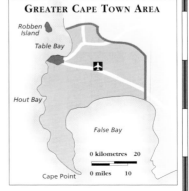

Castle Good Hope recreates the days of Jan van Riebeeck and the early settlers.

Street-by-street: City Centre

LOCATOR MAP
See Street Finder, map 5

THE COMPACT CITY CENTRE lends itself to walking, because most of its major sights are easily accessible. Cape Town is dissected by a number of thoroughfares, one of which is Adderley Street. The parallel St George's Mall is a lively pedestrian zone where street musicians and dancers entertain the crowds. Greenmarket Square, the focal point of the city, is lined with many historically significant buildings. One block west of here, towards Signal Hill, is Long Street. Some of the beautiful examples of the elaborate Victorian façades seen along this street are Bristol Antiques at No. 177, and the Traveller's Inn at No. 206.

Frieze on Koopmans de Wet House

★ Greenmarket Square
A produce market since 1806, and now a national monument, the cobbled square supports a colourful, daily open-air craft market. Among the historical buildings surrounding it is the Old Townhouse.

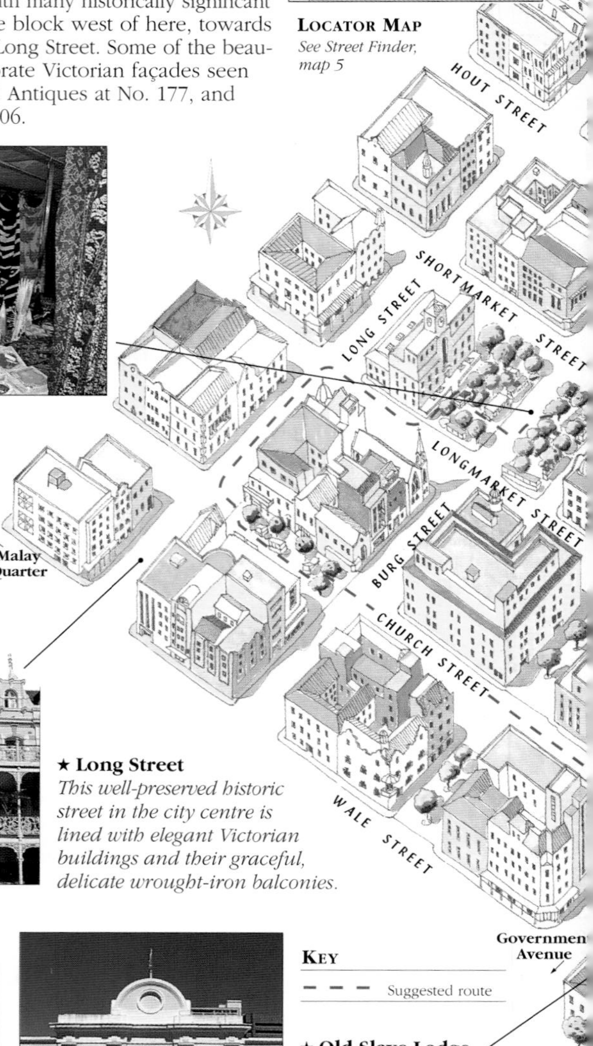

Malay Quarter

★ Long Street
This well-preserved historic street in the city centre is lined with elegant Victorian buildings and their graceful, delicate wrought-iron balconies.

Government Avenue

KEY
--- Suggested route

STAR SIGHTS
★ Old Slave Lodge
★ Greenmarket Square
★ Long Street

★ Old Slave Lodge
Now the Cultural History Museum, the exhibits illustrate the history and development of the city of Cape Town. It also served as brothel for a while ❷

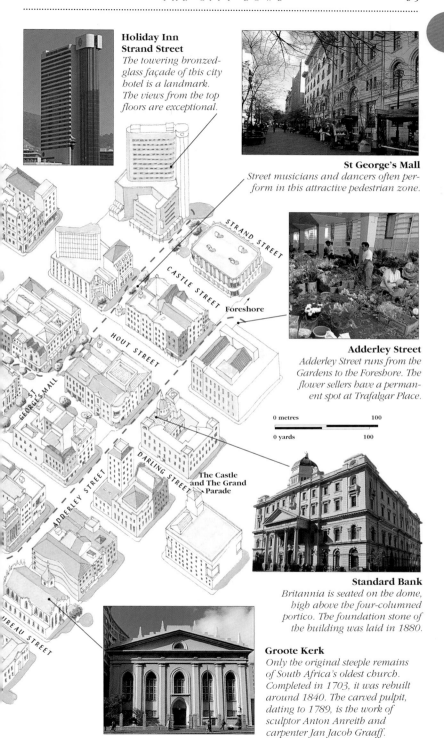

Holiday Inn
Strand Street
The towering bronzed-glass façade of this city hotel is a landmark. The views from the top floors are exceptional.

St George's Mall
Street musicians and dancers often perform in this attractive pedestrian zone.

STRAND STREET

CASTLE STREET

Foreshore

HOUT STREET

ST GEORGE'S MALL

Adderley Street
Adderley Street runs from the Gardens to the Foreshore. The flower sellers have a permanent spot at Trafalgar Place.

DARLING STREET

ADDERLEY STREET

The Castle and The Grand Parade

| 0 metres | 100 |
| 0 yards | 100 |

BUREAU STREET

Standard Bank
Britannia is seated on the dome, high above the four-columned portico. The foundation stone of the building was laid in 1880.

Groote Kerk
Only the original steeple remains of South Africa's oldest church. Completed in 1703, it was rebuilt around 1840. The carved pulpit, dating to 1789, is the work of sculptor Anton Anreith and carpenter Jan Jacob Graaff.

The Old Town House on Greenmarket Square

Old Town House ❶

Greenmarket Square. **Map** 5 B1.
[C] (021) 481-3933. ⏰ 10am–5pm
Mon–Fri, 10am–4pm Sat. ● Sun. 🖼

THIS NATIONAL MONUMENT on
Greenmarket Square was
first completed in 1761 and
initially served as the "Burgh-
erwacht Huys" (house of the
night patrol). The magistrate's
court and police station were
housed here until 1839, when
it was claimed as a town hall
by the newly formed municipality. After renovations in
1915, the building was handed
over to the Union Government
for use as a gallery.

The original art collection,
which was presented to the
city by the wealthy financier
and benefactor of the arts, Sir
Max Michaelis, was added to
by Lady Michaelis after the
death of her husband in 1932.

Today, many priceless works
by mainly Dutch and Flemish
artists of the 17th-century can
be viewed here, but there are
also important pieces from

the 16th and 18th centuries.
The portraits, in particular,
are significant aspects of
the gallery as they offer an
interesting insight into Dutch
society at the time.

Cape Town's coat of arms,
presented to the city in 1804
by Batavian Commissioner-
General Jacob Abra-
ham de Mist can
be seen above
the main portal.

In the garden is
a bronze bust of
Sir Max Michaelis
by the South
African sculptor
Moses Kottler.

**Postal stone,
Old Slave Lodge**

Old Slave Lodge ❷

Cnr Wale & Adderley sts. **Map** 5 B2.
[C] (021) 460-8200. ⏰ 9:30am–
4:30pm daily. 🖼 🚫

THE FIRST BUILDING on this site
was a lodge that housed
the slaves who worked in the
Company's Garden (see pp72–
3). It was built around 1679

on land that originally formed
part of the garden. Between
1809 and 1814, the slaves
were restricted to one section
of the building, to allow for
the construction of judges'
chambers and the addition of
an upper storey, designed by
Louis Michel Thibault. After
the Cape Colony's slaves had
officially been liberated in
1834, the lodge became the
seat of the Supreme Court,
which it remained until 1914.
At this time, the Old Supreme
Court, as it was then known,
also housed the post office
and public library, as well
as other government offices.

The present building once
extended into Adderley Street,
but this portion had to be
demolished when the road
was widened. However, the
original façade, designed by
Thibault, has been restored
to its former splendour.

Nowadays, the former slave
lodge contains the cultural
and historical col-
lections of the
South African
Museum (see
p72). Also on
view are various
interesting dis-
plays of Egyptian,
Greek and early
Roman artifacts,
and a presentation of the rich
Cape Malay culture, featuring
original items from Sri Lanka
and Indonesian islands.

Another interesting exhibit
is a collection of postal stones.
Left by early seafarers, these
constitute the earliest form of
postal communication. At first,
messages were carved into
the stone; later, letters were
stored underneath them.

THE MICHAELIS COLLECTION

This important art collection was established in 1914, when
Sir Max Michaelis donated 68 paintings collected by Lady
Phillips and Sir Hugh Lane. The gallery formally opened three
years later, and today comprises some 104 paintings and 312
etchings. It includes works by Frans Hals, Rembrandt, van
Dijck, David Teniers the Younger, Jan Steen and Willem van
Aelst. Although the collection is rather small in comparison
to international galleries, it presents a valuable source of
reference of the evolution of Dutch and Flemish art over two
centuries. One of the most famous paintings in the collection
is the Portrait of a Lady by Frans Hals.

Portrait of a Lady, Frans Hals (1640)

Many Cape Muslims have green-grocer stalls on the Grand Parade

Across the road from the Old Slave Lodge is the **Groote Kerk** (big church).

Soon after their arrival at the Cape, the Dutch held religious services on board of Jan van Riebeeck's ship, *Drommedaris*.

Later, they used a small side room at Castle Good Hope. However, when need arose for a decent burial place, a permanent site had to be chosen. The first, temporary structure at the northeast end of the Company's Gardens was replaced by a thatched church on the same site in 1700, at the order of Governor Willem Adriaan van der Stel.

The church was completely rebuilt in the 19th century, and the new building dedicated in 1841. All that remains of the original church today is the Baroque belfry, which, unfortunately, is now almost obscured by tall modern buildings.

Of interest in the church is the splendid original pulpit supported by carved lions. The story goes that sculptor Anton Anreith's original concept including the symbolic images of Hope, Faith and Charity was rejected as being too papist.

The façade of the church has high Gothic windows divided by bold pilasters. In front of the building is a statue of Andrew Murray, minister of the Dutch Reformed Church in Cape Town from 1864–71.

Andrew Murray (1828–1917)

🛈 **Groote Kerk**
Adderley St. **Map** 5 B2. ☎ *(021) 461-7044.* ⬚ *10am–2pm Mon–Fri .*

Grand Parade and City Hall ❸

Darling St. **Map** 5 C2. ☎ City Hall: *(021) 400-2230.* ⬚ *7:30am–5:30pm Mon–Sat.* ♿

THE GRAND PARADE was the site van Riebeeck selected for his first fort in 1652. The structure was levelled in 1674 when Castle Good Hope (*see pp68–9*) was completed; until 1821 the area was used as parade and exercise ground for the troops. As buildings went up around the perimeter, greengrocers established fruit stalls, precursors of today's fleamarket. Every Wednesday and Saturday morning the area bustles with market activity, while for the rest of the week the Grand Parade serves as a pay-and-display car park.

Overlooking the Grand Parade is Cape Town's large City Hall. Built in 1905 in the elaborate Italian Renaissance style, it presents its elegant façades on four different streets. A 39-bell carillon tower was added in 1923. The walls of the City Hall regularly resound to the soaring orchestral strains of the Cape Town Philharmonic, formerly known as the Cape Town Symphony Orchestra. It is well worth getting tickets for the popular lunchtime and evening concerts, which can be booked through any branch of Computicket (*see p104*).

Castle Good Hope ❹

See pp68–9.

Cape Town's City Hall opposite the Grand Parade

Castle Good Hope ❹

Dutch East India (VOC) monogram, 17th century

CASTLE GOOD HOPE in Cape Town is South Africa's oldest structure. Built between 1666–79, it replaced an earlier clay-and-timber fort erected by Commander Jan van Riebeeck *(see p44)* in 1652. The Castle overlooks the Grand Parade and is now a museum that also houses traditional Cape regiments and units of the National Defence Force.

Dolphin Pool
Descriptions and sketches made by Lady Anne Barnard (see p98) in the 1790s enabled the reconstruction of the dolphin pool over two hundred years later.

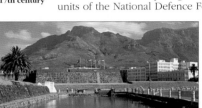

The Castle Moat
The restoration of the moat, which is a relatively recent addition to the Castle, was completed in 1999.

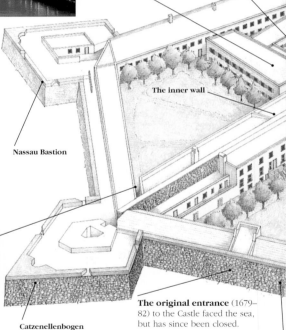

Het Bakhuys

The inner wall

Nassau Bastion

The Archway
Slate, taken from a quarry on Robben Island (see pp84–5) in the 17th century, was used for the paving stones inside the Castle.

Catzenellenbogen Bastion

The original entrance (1679–82) to the Castle faced the sea, but has since been closed.

STAR FEATURES

★ **The Castle Military Museum**

★ **William Fehr Collection**

★ **De Kat Balcony**

★ **The Castle Military Museum**
On display is an array of military artifacts, as well as weapons and uniforms from the VOC and British periods of occupation of the Cape.

★ **William Fehr Collection**
Exhibits include paintings by old masters such as Thomas Baines, as well as period furniture, glass ceramics and metalware.

VISITORS' CHECKLIST

Cnr Darling & Buitenkant sts. **Map** 5 C2. (021) 787-1249. Cape Town station. 9am–4pm daily; **Key Ceremony** 10am, noon. 25 Dec, 1 Jan. 11am, noon, 2pm Mon–Sat. W www.cape-town.org

Oranje
Bastion

Entrance Gable
A teak copy of the original VOC gable reflects martial symbols: a banner, flags, drums and cannon balls.

Leerdam Bastion
Leerdam, Oranje, Nassau, Catzenellenbogen and Buuren were titles held by Prince William of Orange.

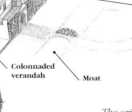

Colonnaded
verandah

Moat

The Castle Entrance
The original bell, cast in Amsterdam in 1697, still hangs in the belfry. The coat of arms of the United Netherlands can be seen on the pediment above the gate.

Buuren Bastion

★ **De Kat Balcony**
The original staircase, built in 1695 as part of a defensive crosswall, divided the square into an inner and outer court, and was remodelled between 1786 and 1790.

Lutheran Church and Martin Melck House ❺

Strand St. **Map** 5 B1. *(021) 421-5854.* 10am–2pm Mon–Fri.

SINCE THE RULING authority was intolerant of any religion other than that of the Dutch Reformed Church, the Lutheran Church began as a "storeroom". Wealthy Lutheran businessman, Martin Melck, built it with the intention of modifying it into a place of worship once the religious laws were relaxed, and the first service was held in 1776. A few years later, the sexton's house was added.

From 1787–92, the German-born sculptor Anton Anreith embellished the church and added a tower. Today, both the church and the sexton's house are national monuments. The Martin Melck House, next door, was built in 1781 and declared a national monument in 1936. The building is a rare example of an 18th-century Cape town-house that features an attic.

In April 2001, the Gold of Africa Museum opened on the premises, featuring a collection of over 350 19th- and 20th-century gold objects from Mali, Senegal, Ghana and the Ivory Coast. Plans for expansion include the acquisition of further treasures from the entire African continent, a training studio and boutique.

The dining room in Koopmans-De Wet House

Koopmans-De Wet House ❻

35 Strand St. **Map** 5 B1. *(021) 481-3935.* 9:30am–4pm Tue–Thu.

THIS NEO-CLASSICAL HOME WAS built in 1701 when Strand Street, then close to the shore, was the most fashionable part of Cape Town. The building was enlarged in subsequent centuries; a second storey was added and renowned French architect, Louis Michel Thibault, remodelled the façade around 1795 in Louis XVI-style.

The De Wet family was the last to own the house. After the death of her husband, Johan Koopmans, Maria de Wet lived here with her sister, from 1880 until her death in 1906. Over the years, the De Wet sisters assembled the many fine antiques that can still be seen in the museum today.

Maria de Wet, apart from being a renowned society hostess who entertained famous guests like President Paul Kruger *(see p241)* and the mining magnate Cecil John Rhodes *(see p50)*, was also responsible for taking the first steps to protect Cape Town's many historic buildings. It was thanks to her intervention that the destruction of part of the Castle was prevented when the new railway lines were being planned.

Bo-Kaap Museum ❼

71 Wale St. **Map** 5 A1. *(021) 481-3939.* 9:30am–4pm Mon–Sat. Eid (variable), Good Fri, 25 Dec. of Bo-Kaap area 10am, 2pm Mon–Sat.

THE BO-KAAP MUSEUM, which dates back to the 1760s, is the oldest house in the area still in its original form. The characteristic feature is a *voorstoep* (front terrace) with a bench at either end, emphasizing the social aspect of the Cape Muslim culture: the front of the house was an important gathering place.

The museum highlights the cultural contribution made by early Muslims, many of whom were skilled tailors, carpenters, shoemakers and builders. It contains 19th-century furnishings which include a fine Cape drop-leaf dining table, Cape Regency-style chairs and a bridal chamber decorated to match the bride's dress.

Table Mountain ❽

See pp 74–5.

The Lutheran Church in Strand Street

Malay Culture in Cape Town

THE ORIGINAL MALAYS were brought to the Cape from 1658 onwards by the Dutch East India Company. Most of them were Muslims from Sri Lanka, Indonesian islands and India. A large proportion of them were slaves, while others were political exiles of considerable stature. After the abolition of slavery in the early 1830s, the Cape Malays (or Cape Muslims as they now prefer to be called) settled on the slope of Signal Hill in an area called Bo-Kaap ("above Cape Town") to be near the mosques that had been built there (Auwal Mosque dates from 1794). The Malays had a significant influence on the Afrikaans tongue, and many of their culinary traditions *(see p342)* were absorbed by other cultures. Today, the Muslim community is very much a part of Cape Town: the muezzins' haunting calls, ringing out from minarets to summon the faithful, are an integral part of the city.

Mango atchar

STREETS OF THE BO-KAAP

Just above modern Cape Town, within easy walking distance of the city centre, lies the traditional home of the Cape Muslims. Here, narrow-fronted houses in pastel colours open onto cobbled streets.

Ornate parapets and plasterwork adorn the houses, most of which date from around 1810.

Cobbled streets still exist, but many of them have now been tarred.

Muslim tradition dictates that formal attire be worn on festive occasions. This includes the traditional fez for men, while women don the characteristic chador *(full-length veil or shawl).*

The fez, of Turkish origin, is still worn occasionally, but knitted, or cloth, caps are more common nowadays.

The Mosque in Longmarket Street, like many of the Bo-Kaap's mosques, stands wedged in-between the homes of residents. Religion is a fundamental part of every devout Muslim's life.

Signal Hill is the traditional home of the Cape Muslim community. Many of the quaint, Bo-Kaap cottages have been replaced by modern apartment blocks higher up.

Table Mountain

Cable car

T HE CAPE PENINSULA mountain chain is a mass of sedimentary sandstone lying above ancient shales that were deposited some 700 million years ago, as well as large areas of granite. The sandstone sediment, which forms the main block of the mountain, was deposited about 450 million years ago when the Peninsula, then a part of Gondwana, lay below sea level. After the subsidence of the primeval ocean, the effects of wind, rain, ice and extreme temperatures caused erosion of the softer layers, leaving behind the characteristic mesa of Table Mountain.

Royal Visitors
In 1947, King George VI and the future Queen Mother accompanied Prime Minister Smuts on a hike.

Kirstenbosch National Botanical Garden
The garden (see pp 100–01) nestles at the foot of the Peninsula range. Three major trails and numerous paths lead up the mountain slopes.

King's Blockhouse
This is the best preserved of the three 18th-century stone forts that were built during the first British occupation of the Cape (see pp46–7).

SOUTHERN SUBURBS

Kirstenbosch National Botanical Garden

Contour Path

Forest Station

Newlands Reservoir

Newlands

Maclear's Beacon 1,087 m (3,566

University of Cape Town

Rhodes Memorial

King's Blockhouse

Woodstock Cave

Devil's Peak 1,000 m (3,280 ft)

Plumpudding Hill 291 m (955 ft)

Queen's Blockhouse

Prince of Wales Blockhouse

CITY CENTRE AND FORESHORE

CITY CEN

TABLE MOUNTAIN FAUNA AND FLORA

Disa orchid

Over 1,400 plant species of the 2,285 that make up the Cape Floral Kingdom of the Peninsula can be found in the protected natural habitat of Table Mountain. They include *Disa uniflora* (also called Pride of Table Mountain), which mostly grows near streams and waterfalls, and several members of the regal protea family. Wildlife, consisting mostly of small mammals, reptiles and birds, includes the rare and secretive ghost frog that is found in a few perennial streams on the plateau.

Ghost frog

KEY

▬	Major road
═	Road
- -	Hiking trail
☆	Viewpoint
🏃	Hiking trail starting point
🚲	Mountain bike access
🌸	Wildflowers
P	Parking

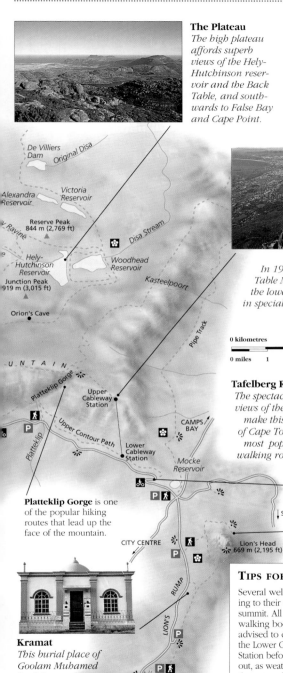

The Plateau

The high plateau affords superb views of the Hely-Hutchinson reservoir and the Back Table, and southwards to False Bay and Cape Point.

Viewing Platform

In 1998, extensive upgrading of the Table Mountain Cableway as well as the lower and upper stations resulted in special reinforced viewing platforms at strategic vantage points.

Tafelberg Road

The spectacular views of the city make this one of Cape Town's most popular walking routes.

Platteklip Gorge is one of the popular hiking routes that lead up the face of the mountain.

A circular route leads up Lion's Head

Kramat

This burial place of Goolam Muhamed Soofi is one of six Muslim shrines that form a holy circle around the Cape Peninsula.

TIPS FOR WALKERS

Several well-marked trails, graded according to their degree of difficulty, lead to the summit. All hikers must wear proper walking boots and are advised to check with the Lower Cableway Station before setting out, as weather conditions may deteriorate without warning. Hiking on windy or misty days is not recommended.

Hikers on the plateau

The Victoria & Alfred Waterfront ❶

THE VICTORIA AND ALFRED WATERFRONT is a shopper's
haven, offering designer boutiques and others
selling quirky hand-painted clothing, health and beauty
shops, homeware and gift speciality stores, and over 40
ethnically diverse food outlets. Most eating places have
harbour views, and alfresco dining on the wharfs and
waterside platforms is extremely popular. Many bars
and bistros offer live music, with excellent jazz at the
Green Dolphin, while regular outdoor concerts are
staged at the Waterfront Amphitheatre. Excursions of all
kinds start at the Waterfront, from boat tours around the
harbour and to Robben Island, helicopter flips over the
peninsula to sunset champagne cruises off Clifton Beach.
The Waterfront also boasts luxurious hotel accommodation.

LOCATOR MAP

☐ Illustrated Area

☐ Extent of V&A Waterfront

★ BMW Pavilion
*This modern BMW
showroom displays
the company's latest
models and is open
late into the evening.*

The Scratch Patch
affords visitors the opportunity to choose their own
selection of polished semi-
precious stones, such as
amethyst and tiger's-eye.

★ Two Oceans Aquarium
*Shatterproof glass tanks
and tunnels are filled
with shoaling fish such
as yellowtail, steenbras,
and musselcracker, as
well as turtles, and even
a short-tailed stingray.*

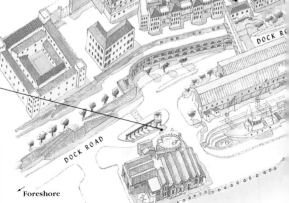

STAR FEATURES

★ BMW Pavilion

★ Victoria Wharf
  Shopping Centre

★ Two Oceans
  Aquarium

---

0 metres   50

0 yards   50

Table Bay Hotel
One of the latest and best appointed hotels built at the Victoria & Alfred Waterfront, the glamorous Table Bay offers the ultimate in comfort and luxury. Each room has wonderful views of Table Mountain and the busy harbour.

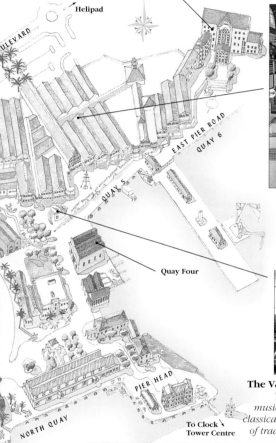

Helipad

ULEVARD

EAST PIER ROAD

QUAY 6

QUAY 5

Quay Four

PIER HEAD

NORTH QUAY

To Clock
Tower Centre

★ Victoria Wharf Centre
Exclusive shops, boutiques, cosy eateries and informal "barrow" stalls give this shopping centre a festive, market-day feel.

The V&A Waterfront Amphitheatre
This venue offers a vast array of musical and other events. Jazz, rock, classical concerts and even the rhythms of traditional drumming appear here.

The Cape Grace Hotel
Another of the Victoria & Alfred Waterfront's fine accommodation offerings, The Cape Grace on West Quay has wonderful views.

VISITORS' CHECKLIST

Cape Town harbour. **Map** 2 D–E 3–4. 🚶 *Visitor's Centre (021) 408-7600.* 🚌 *Shuttle bus between city centre, Table Mountain, International Airport and Waterfront.* 🚢 *to Robben Island; Jetty 1 (see p85).* ⏰ *9am–midnight. Dragon Boat Races (Nov); Cape To Rio (Jan, every three years); Wine Festival (May).* 🍴 ♿ 🚻 📷
🌐 www.waterfront.co.za

Exploring the Waterfront

THE VICTORIA & ALFRED WATERFRONT is one of Cape Town's most visited attractions. The multibillion-rand redevelopment scheme incorporates ideas from other ventures, like San Francisco's harbour project. Easily accessible, it has its own bus service running to and from the railway station in Adderley Street, and provides ample covered and open-air parking for vehicles. Major stores are open from 9am to 9pm, and most restaurants close well after midnight. Some of the city's newest hotels are here.

Whitbread Round-the-World racers moor at the Waterfront

➤ Two Oceans Aquarium

Dock Rd. **Map** 2 D4. ☎ (021) 418-3823. ◐ 9:30am–6pm daily. 🏪 ♿
🍴 🎁 🖥 www.aquarium.co.za
The aim of this complex is to introduce visitors to the incredible diversity of sealife which occurs in the ocean around the Cape coast. A world first is the interesting exhibit of a complete river ecosystem that traces the course of a stream from its mountain source down to the open sea. One of the most fascinating features is a ceiling-high glass tank that holds various shoals of line fish, like Red Roman, swimming placidly among the waving tangles of a kelp forest. Apart from other waterbirds like wagtails, there is also a resident colony of jackass penguins, a tank full of mischievous seals and the popular touch pool that has wide-eyed children exploring delicate underwater creatures like crabs, starfish and sea urchins.

Alfred Basin (West Quay)

Off Dock Rd. **Map** 2 E4. ♿
Overlooked by the elegant Cape Grace Hotel *(see p315)*, Alfred Basin forms a crucial part of the working harbour as fishing boats chug to the Robinson Graving Dock for repair and maintenance. Alongside the dry dock is the Waterfront Craft Market, which is one of South Africa's largest indoor markets. Available are handcrafted gifts ranging from toys and furniture to candles and art. Adjoining the blue craft shed is the **South African Maritime Museum**, which contains South Africa's largest model ship collection. The SAS *Somerset*, a former naval defence vessel, is part of the museum. Visits to explore the ship are included in the entrance fee.

🏛 South African Maritime Museum

Shop 17, Dock Rd. ☎ (021) 405-2880. ◐ 9:30am–5pm daily. 🔴 Good Fri, 25 Dec. 🏪 ♿ 🚫

Victorian clocktower

Victoria Basin

Map 2 E3.
The Waterfront's most popular venue, Quay Four *(see p346)*, is located at the edge of the basin, with superb views of the harbour and its constant boat traffic. The large Agfa Amphitheatre regularly stages free recitals and concerts, from the Cape Town Philharmonic Orchestra to African musicians and their energetic dance routines. In the **Red Shed**, visitors can observe glass-blowers at work, buy handmade pottery and ceramics, leathercraft, hand-painted fabrics, jewellery and gifts. Nearby, in the **King's Warehouse**, the catch of the day is stacked side by side with crisp vegetables and fragrant herbs. Equally tempting is the aroma of exotic crushed spices and the many deli luxuries, such as hand-rolled pasta and freshly made Italian biscotti.

🎁 Red Shed

Opposite Imax. ☎ (021) 408-7846.
◐ 9am–9pm daily. ♿

🍴 King's Warehouse

Breakwater Blvd. ◐ 9am–9pm daily.
♿

Inside the BMW Pavilion

BMW Pavilion

Cnr. Portswood & Dock rds.
Map 2 D3. ☎ (021) 419-7365.
◐ until 11pm. ♿ 🍴
The BMW Pavilion is a modern building that serves as a showroom for the company's latest cars. BMW's ritziest new models are immaculately presented here and, with the centre open late into the evening, visitors are free to roam and admire the collection at their leisure.

The pavilion provides a well-equipped conference centre and is also used to host temporary exhibitions from time to time.

Exhibits at the Two Oceans Aquarium

An INNOVATIVE APPROACH to education has assured the popularity and success of this venture. The complex is constantly upgraded to accommodate new exhibits, such as the recently installed jellyfish tank. Future displays will include an unusual quarantine section. All the exhibits introduce the public to unfamiliar aspects of the fragile marine environment and the need for its preservation.

Starfish

Young visitors, in particular, enjoy the hands-on experience. Alpha Activities Centre offers an interesting daily programme in the vicinity of the entertaining seal tank. Novel "sleep-overs" in front of the Predator Tank are a hit with children between the ages of six and 12. Adventurous visitors in possession of a valid scuba licence may book dives during the day, although not during feeding sessions in the Predator and Kelp tanks.

THE DISPLAYS

The aquarium's displays are well planned and create an interesting, stimulating environment. Quite a few of them are interactive, offering visitors the opportunity to experience sealife at first hand. The latest technology is used to reveal the secrets of even the tiniest of sea creatures.

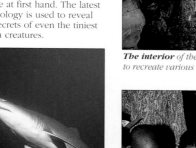

The interior of the aquarium has been carefully designed to recreate various ocean and riverine habitats.

The Touch Pool invites children to handle and examine sea creatures like crabs and starfish.

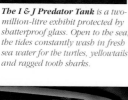

The I & J Predator Tank is a two-million-litre exhibit protected by shatterproof glass. Open to the sea, the tides constantly wash in fresh sea water for the turtles, yellowtails and ragged tooth sharks.

Jackass penguins, rescued from oil spills, have a small colony in the aquarium complex.

The Intertidal Pool contains mussels, barnacles, starfish, sea anemones and various sponges.

A short-tailed stingray, like this one, can be seen in the Predator Tank.

The Victoria & Alfred Waterfront is a hive of activity until late at night ▷

Robben Island ❷

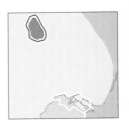

N AMED "ROBBE EILAND" (seal island) by the Dutch in the mid-17th century due to its abundant seal population, Robben Island has seen much human suffering. As early as 1636 it served as a penal settlement, and was taken over by the South African Prisons Service in 1960. When the last political prisoners were released in 1991, the South African Natural Heritage Programme nominated the island for its significance as a seabird breeding colony – rare species include the migrant Caspian tern and the jackass penguin. Today, the island is an important ecological and historical heritage site.

World War II battery

★ Governor's House
This splendid Victorian building dates from 1895 and was originally the home of the Island Commissioner. Today it serves as a conference centre and provides upmarket accommodation for visiting dignitaries and VIPs.

0 metres   500

0 yards   150

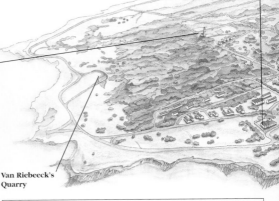

Van Riebeeck's Quarry

The Lighthouse
This lighthouse was built in 1863 to replace the fire beacons in use until then. It is 18 m (59 ft) high and its beam can be seen from a distance of 25 km (15 miles).

STAR FEATURES

★ Governor's House

★ Lime Quarry

★ The Prison

POLITICAL PRISONERS

In the 18th century, high-ranking princes and sheikhs from India, Malaysia and Indonesia were sent to Robben Island by the Dutch East India Company for inciting resistance against their European overlords. The British banished rebellious Xhosa rulers to the island in the early 1800s. And in 1963, Nelson Mandela and seven other political activists were condemned to life imprisonment here by the South African government.

Exiled Xhosa chiefs, Robben Island, 1862

Offshore Island

This flat, rocky island lies 11 km (7 miles) north of Cape Town in the icy Atlantic Ocean. Composed mainly of blue slate, it is only 30 m (98 ft) above sea level at its highest point. None of the trees on the island are indigenous.

VISITORS' CHECKLIST

Road map B5. **(** (021) 409-5100. *Jetty 1, Victoria & Alfred Waterfront 9am, 10am, 11am, noon, 1pm, 2pm, 3pm.* high wind/ rough seas. obligatory. inform ticket office beforehand. @ info@robben-island.co.za

Caspian Tern

This endangered migrant bird species breeds on the northern part of the island.

★ The Prison

Robben Island served as a place of banishment from 1658, when Jan van Riebeeck sent his interpreter here. The maximum security prison was completed in 1964.

Murray's Bay Harbour

The kramat was constructed in 1969 over the grave of an Indonesian prince. It is a place of pilgrimage for devout Muslims.

The Church of the Good Shepherd

Designed by Sir Herbert Baker, this stone church was built by lepers in 1895, for use by men only. Worshippers had to stand or lie because there were no pews.

Faure Jetty

★ Lime Quarry

Political prisoners, required to work in this quarry for at least six hours a day, suffered damage to their eyesight due to the constant dust and the glare of the sunlight on the stark white lime cliffs.

An aerial view of Sea Point on Cape Town's Atlantic seaboard

Green Point and Sea Point ❶

Main or Beach rds. **Map** 1 B4, 3 C1.

SINCE THE DEVELOPMENT of the Victoria & Alfred Waterfront began in 1995, the real estate value in neighbouring seaside suburbs like Green Point and Mouille Point has soared. Beach Road, only a stone's throw from the sea, is today lined with a row of expensive high-rise apartments, as well as trendy restaurants and modern, upmarket office blocks.

Green Point Common backs

the residential strip. It started in 1657 as a farm granted to Jan van Riebeeck, but the soil proved unfit for cultivation. The sports complex that was built on the common comprises hockey, soccer, rugby and cricket fields, bowling greens, tennis and squash courts, a sports stadium and an 18-hole golf course.

Green Point's red and white candy-striped lighthouse, built in 1824, is still functional. Its resonant foghorn is notorious for keeping Mouille Point's residents awake when mist rolls in from the sea. Further on along

Mouille Point lighthouse has a foghorn to warn ships at sea

Beach Road lies the suburb of Sea Point. It, too, has undergone intensive development over the years and sports towering apartment blocks, hotels and offices. Sea Point used to be Cape Town's most popular entertainment strip. However, the opening of the Victoria & Alfred Waterfront provided a new and more convenient attraction, with its upmarket eateries, pubs and amphitheatre, so Sea Point's glamour has faded somewhat, although the suburb still teems with restaurants, bars, and night spots.

All day long, the 3-km (2-mile) Sea Point promenade is abuzz with joggers, rollerbladers, children, tanned people-watchers and older residents strolling along with their lap dogs.

The promenade ends with a pavilion which adjoins a large parking area and the open-air **Sea Point Swimming Pool**, which is filled with seawater.

Small sandy coves (packed with sunbathers in summer) dot the rocky shoreline. The tidal pools among the rocks are always a source of amazement, particularly for children, who enjoy scrambling around looking for sea anemones, tiny starfish, shells and the occasional octopus. Graaff's Pool is a secluded bathing spot. It is open to the sea and, by tradition, for men only.

Sea Point Swimming Pool
Beach Rd. ▐ *(021) 434-3341.*
◗ *Dec–Jan: 7am–6:30pm daily;
Feb–Nov: 7am–4:30pm daily.*
● *only in bad weather.* 🌊 🏊

LION'S HEAD AND SIGNAL HILL

A relatively easy climb to the top of Lion's Head, 670 m (2,198 ft) high, affords breathtaking views of the City Bowl and Atlantic coastline. Climbers can leave their cars at a parking area along Signal Hill Road (take the right-hand fork at the top of Kloof Nek Road), which opens to the contour path that encircles Lion's Head. At the end of Signal Hill Road is a viewpoint and another parking area. This spot is popular for its night vistas of the city. Signal Hill is the site of Cape Town's noon gun, a battery originally built by the British in 1890 to defend the harbour. Every day the cannon is loaded with 1.5 kg (3 lb) of gunpowder and fired off at precisely noon.

The view from Lion's Head is spectacular

Mariner's Wharf has an excellent fresh fish market

Hout Bay Museum

4 Andrews Rd. 📞 (021) 790-3270.
🕐 8:30am–4:30pm Tue–Fri, 10am–
4:30pm Sat. ● public hols. 🎫 🚻

This museum has interesting displays on the history of the Hout Bay valley and its people, focusing on forestry, mining and the fishing industry up to modern times. The museum also organizes weekly guided nature walks into the surrounding mountains.

ENVIRONS: Just north of Hout Bay, the remarkable **World of Birds Wildlife Sanctuary** is presently the largest bird sanctuary in Africa and the second largest in the world.

The high, landscaped, walk-through aviaries feature 450 bird species. Around 3,000 individual birds are kept in the sanctuary for rehabilitation purposes, many of them brought in injured. Others are endangered species which are introduced for a captive breeding programme. Wherever possible, birds are released into their natural habitat again once they are fit to survive.

Visitors can watch them feed, build nests and incubate their eggs. The World of Birds also plays an important secondary role in educating the public on conservation and other environmental matters.

Among the endangered bird species that have benefited from special breeding projects are the Egyptian vulture, which is extinct in South Africa, the blue crane and the citron-crested cockatoo.

Rare primates can also be seen at the sanctuary, among these the endangered pygmy marmoset and Geoffrey's tufted-ear marmoset.

🦅 World of Birds Wildlife Sanctuary

Valley Rd. 📞 (021) 790-2730. 🕐
9am–5pm daily. 🎫 ♿ 🚻 🛍
🌐 www.worldofbirds.co.za

Black-shouldered kite

LINEFISH OF THE WESTERN CAPE

The cold, nutrient-bearing water along the West Coast results in a greater number of fish than off the East Coast, but not as great a variety. The biggest catches are of red roman, kabeljou and white stumpnose. The uniquely South African national fish, the galjoen, has now become very rare. The deep gulleys along the rocky shores of the Western Cape, with their characteristic kelp beds, are perfect fishing spots for anglers.

***Red Roman** Particularly tasty when stuffed and baked, this fish is found in great numbers off the Cape reefs.*

***Snoek** Winter and early spring see the "snoek run", when this predatory fish migrates south in search of its prey – pilchards. Its rich, rather oily flesh is either canned, smoked or dried.*

***Kabeljou (kob)** One of the most common food fishes, this is invariably served as the "linefish catch of the day".*

***White stumpnose** A delicious sport fish, it is eagerly sought by ski-boat anglers.*

***Yellowtail** This is one of the finest seasonal gamefish available in South African waters. The flesh is very firm and tasty, but can be coarse, especially in older and larger fish.*

***Cape salmon** Its flesh is similar to that of its cousin, the kob, but more flavourful .*

Touring the Cape Peninsula ❹

TOURS OF THE PENINSULA should start on the Atlantic coast and include Chapman's Peak Drive, a scenic route that took seven years to build. The drive, cut into the cliff face, has splendid lookout points with picnic sites. A highlight of the tour is the panorama at Cape Point, where the peninsula juts into the sea. The views encompass False Bay, the Hottentots Holland mountains and Cape Hangklip, 80 km (50 miles) away. The return journey passes the penguin colony at Boulders and goes through charming Simon's Town.

Chapman's Peak ①
The highest point rises to 592 m (1,942 ft). An observation platform is on sheer cliffs which drop 160 m (525 ft) to the swirling seas below.

0 kilometres 5

0 miles 2

Kommetjie ②
Flashes from the powerful beams of Slangkop Lighthouse can be seen from Hout Bay at night.

KEY

- Tour route
- Other roads
- Park or reserve boundary
- Viewpoint
- Shore-based whale watching

TIPS FOR DRIVERS

Length: *160 km (99 miles). From De Waal Drive via Camps Bay and Chapman's Peak Drive to Cape Point, returning through Simon's Town and Muizenberg, then back to the city via the M3.*
Duration of journey: *To fully appreciate the beauty of both coastlines, Cape Point and the peninsula, it is advisable to do the route in two stages.*

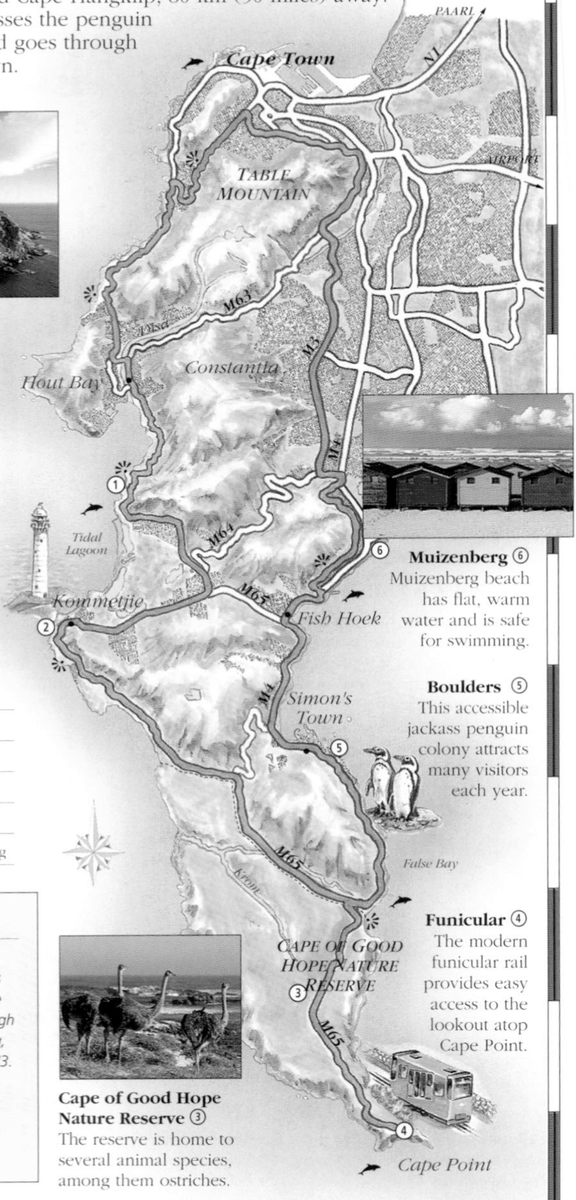

Muizenberg ⑥
Muizenberg beach has flat, warm water and is safe for swimming.

Boulders ⑤
This accessible jackass penguin colony attracts many visitors each year.

Funicular ④
The modern funicular rail provides easy access to the lookout atop Cape Point.

Cape of Good Hope Nature Reserve ③
The reserve is home to several animal species, among them ostriches.

Horse riding on Noordhoek Beach is a popular pastime

Noordhoek **❺**

Road map B5. Via Chapman's Peak Drive or Ou Kaapse Weg.

THE BEST FEATURE of this little coastal settlement is its 6-km (4-mile) stretch of pristine white beach. Strong currents make the water unsafe for swimming but is popular with surfers and paddleskiers. The shore is good for horse riding and long walks (tourists are advised to walk in groups) while along its length lies the wreck of the *Kakapo*, a steamer that was beached here during a storm in 1900. Part of the Hollywood movie *Ryan's Daughter* was filmed here.

ENVIRONS: Another coastal hamlet, **Kommetjie**, adjoins a tidal lagoon situated inland from Noordhoek Beach. Long Beach, which stretches north as far as Klein Slangkop Point, is a venue for surfing championships and is very popular among boardsailors.

Scarborough, at the mouth of the Schuster's River, is a sought-after residential area. In summer, the seasonal lagoon is very popular.

Cape of Good Hope Nature Reserve **❻**

Road map B5. M4 via Simon's Town. **☎** *(021) 780-9100 (from 9am–5pm).* **☐** Main gate: *Oct–Mar: 6am–6pm (spring/summer) daily; Apr–Sep: 7am–5pm (autumn/winter) daily. The gate closes at 6pm in winter & sunset in summer.* 🖼 🍴 🏧 🚻 🛍 ♿

NAMED *Cabo Tormentoso* (Cape of Storms) by Bartolomeu Dias in 1488, the peninsula was later renamed *Cabo de Boa Esperança* (Cape of Good Hope) by King John of Portugal, who saw it as a positive omen for a new route to India.

The reserve that now exists on the tip of the peninsula is exposed to gale-force winds. As a result, the vegetation is limited to hardy milkwood trees and *fynbos*. Small antelope such as eland, bontebok, grey rhebok and grysbok occur here, as do Cape mountain zebra. Visitors will also encounter troops of chacma baboons, which can be aggressive as a result of unlawful feeding by humans.

To view the point from the upper station, the visitor can either climb aboard the funicular or walk the steep, paved pathway to the top. From here, the views are marvellous and the sea pounds relentlessly against the rocks some 300 m (98 ft) below.

The original lighthouse, whose base still stands at the viewpoint, always used to be swathed in fog. The *Lusitania*, a Portuguese liner, was wrecked on Bellows Rock, directly below this lighthouse, in April 1911. As a result, the present lighthouse was constructed lower down on the Cape Point promontory in 1911.

Along the reserve's east coast, the tidal pools at Venus Pool, Bordjiesrif and Buffels Bay and the numerous picnic spots attract hordes of holidaymakers. Buffels Bay has public facilities and a boat-launching ramp. A number of easy and scenic walking trails along the west coast include the Thomas T Tucker shipwreck trail and the path to Sirkelsvlei; maps are available at the reserve's entrance gate.

Bontebok, Cape of Good Hope

The Flying Dutchman

THE FLYING DUTCHMAN

This legend originated in 1641, when the Dutch captain Hendrick van der Decken was battling wild seas off Cape Point while sailing home. No match against the storm, his battered ship started sinking, but Van der Decken swore that he would round the Cape, whether it took him until Judgement Day. Since then many sightings of a phantom ship, its masts smashed and sails in shreds, have been reported in bad weather. The most significant was recorded in July 1881 in the diary of a certain midshipman sailing on HMS *Bacchante*. He was crowned King George V of England in 1910.

Classic architecture along the main road in Simon's Town

Simon's Town ❼

Road map B5. 🏊 *4,000*. 🚉 from Cape Town station, Adderley St. 🛈 *111 St George's St, Simon's Town, (021) 786-2436.* 🖥 *www.simonstown.com*

Picturesque simon's town in False Bay has been the base of the South African navy since 1957. It was named after Simon van der Stel (*see p96*) who visited this sheltered little spot around 1687.

Since the Cape's winter storms caused extensive damage to the ships that were anchored in Table Bay, the Dutch East India Company decided, in 1743, to make Simon's Bay their anchorage point in winter.

From 1814, until handover to South Africa, it served as the British Royal Navy's base in the South Atlantic. The town's characterful hotels and bars have been frequented by generations of seamen.

Simon's Town's naval history is best absorbed by joining one of the interesting **Historical Walks** that take place every Tuesday and Saturday morning. The walks begin near the railway station and end at the Martello Tower on the East Dockyard, taking in the **Simon's Town Museum**, the South African Naval Museum, and the Warrior Toy Museum. The Simon's Town

Jackass penguin

Museum is housed in The Residency, believed to be the town's oldest building. It was built in 1777 as weekend retreat for Governor Joachim van Plettenberg. Later, it also served as a naval hospital. Among the exhibits is a replica of a World War II royal naval pub and the cramped quarters of the original slave lodge. Martello Tower, the walk's endpoint, was built in 1796 as a defence against the French.

🏴 Historical Walk
🔵 *Simon's Town station, (021) 786-1805.* 🔵 *10am Tue and Sat.* 📷

🏛 Simon's Town Museum
Court Rd. 🔵 *(021) 786-3046.* 🔵 *9am–4pm Mon–Fri, 10am–4pm Sat, 11am–4pm Sun and public hols.* 🔴 *25 Dec, 1 Jan, Good Fri. Donations.*

Environs: Between Simon's Town and the Cape of Good Hope Nature Reserve, the M4 passes through charming settlements that offer safe swimming and snorkelling in a number of protected bays such as Froggy Pond, Boulders and Seaforth. The big granite rocks after which Boulders is named provide excellent shelter when the southeaster blows. A walk along the beach between Boulders and Seaforth leads to secluded little coves. A major attraction at Boulders is the protected, land-based colony of over 2,300 jackass penguins.

Further south, Miller's Point has grassed picnic areas, a slipway, and tidal rock pools. The Black Marlin Restaurant here is loved for its views and fresh seafood. At Smitswinkel Bay, a lovely cove lies at the foot of a very steep path.

ABLE SEAMAN JUST NUISANCE

In Jubilee Square, overlooking Simon's Bay's naval harbour, stands the statue of a Great Dane. During World War II this dog was the much-loved mascot of British sailors based in Simon's Town. Just Nuisance, formally enrolled in the Royal Navy, was given the title Able Seaman. When he died in a Simon's Town naval hospital, he was honoured with a full military funeral, which was attended by 200 members of the British Royal Navy. One room at the Simon's Town Museum is filled with memorabilia of the unusual cadet.

Just Nuisance and friend

Fish Hoek ❽

Road map B5. M4, False Bay. 👥 9,000. 🚉 from Cape Town station, Adderley St. ℹ️ 11 First Avenue. 📞 (021) 782-3991.

ONLY RECENTLY was liquor allowed to be sold in Fish Hoek; until then it was a "dry" municipality. This condition had been written into a property grant made by Governor Lord Charles Somerset in 1818, and was only repealed in the 1990s.

The broad stretch of Fish Hoek beach is lined with changing rooms, cafés and a yacht club, and is popular with families and the sailing fraternity. Regattas are held regularly, and catamarans and Hobie Cats often line the beach. Jager's Walk, a pleasant pathway overlooking sea and beach, runs along the edge of the bay.

ENVIRONS: The M4 continues northwards, staying close to the shore. It passes through the seaside suburb of St James which has a small, safe family beach and is characterized by a row of wooden bathing huts that have all been painted in bright primary colours.

At the picturesque little fishing harbour of Kalk Bay, the daily catches of fresh fish, particularly snoek, are sold directly from the boats. The height of the snoek season varies, but usually extends from June to July. The Brass Bell restaurant, sandwiched between the railway station and the rocky shore, has a popular pub, good seafood,

Muizenberg's beachfront seen from Boyes Drive

and at high tide, waves crash against the breakwater between the restaurant and the sea. Kalk Bay is also popular for its many antique and art shops that line Main Road.

Muizenberg ❾

Road map B5. M4, False Bay. 👥 5,800. 🚉 from Cape Town station, Adderley St. ℹ️ Beach Rd. 📞 (021) 788-6193. 🕐 9am–5:30pm Mon–Fri, 9am–1pm Sat.

THE NAME Muizenberg comes from the Dutch phrase *Muijs zijn berg*, meaning "Muijs's mountain". Wynand Willem Muijs was a sergeant who, from 1743, commanded a military post on the mountain overlooking the beach.

Muizenberg's white sands, which curve for 40 km (25 miles) around False Bay as far as the town of Strand, rightly earned the town its status as the country's premier holiday retreat in the 19th century. Traces of this early popularity are still visible in the now-shabby façades of

once-grand beach mansions. Today a fast-food pavilion, seawater pool and wide lawns attract young and old alike.

The railway station perches on a rocky section of shoreline, where the curve of the bay is known as Surfer's Corner, due to its popularity among novice surfers.

Rhodes Cottage

ENVIRONS: Cecil John Rhodes, prime minister of the Cape Colony from 1890–5, started a fashion trend when he bought Barkly Cottage in Muizenberg in 1899. Soon, holiday mansions began to mushroom at the seaside resort, although most were in stark contrast to his simple, stone-walled, thatch cottage. The cottage is today a museum in Main Road and has been renamed **Rhodes Cottage**.

It contains photographs and personal memorabilia of the powerful empire builder and statesman, including his diamond-weighing scale and the chest in which he carried his personal belongings.

🏛️ **Rhodes Cottage**
Main Rd. 📞 (021) 788-1816. 🕐 9:30 am–4:30pm daily. ⚫ 25 Dec. 📷

Fish Hoek beach offers safe bathing

Groot Constantia ⑩

Newly appointed commander of the cape, Simon van der Stel named this farm Constantia; it was the first piece of land granted to him in 1685. The most likely of several theories regarding the origin of the name is that it honours the daughter of Rijckloff van Goens, who supported the governor's land application. After Van der Stel's death in 1712, the farm was subdivided into three. The portion with the manor house, built around 1685, was renamed Groot Constantia. Hendrik Cloete bought the estate in 1778. His family owned it for three generations thereafter, and was responsible for the present appearance of the buildings.

Carriage Museum
A collection of simple carts and other implements tells the story of transport in the Cape's early colonial days.

★ Cloete Wine Cellar
This façade, commissioned by Hendrik Cloete and built in 1791, is attributed to Louis Thibault. The Rococo pediment was sculpted by Anton Anreith.

Cape Gable
The very tall gable of the manor house was added between 1799 and 1803. The sculpted figure of Abundance that decorates its lofty niche is the work of respected sculptor, Anton Anreith.

★ Manor House
This museum contains an authentic representation of a wealthy, 19th-century farming household. Most of the antiques were donated by Alfred A de Pass, member of a Dutch family.

STAR FEATURES

★ **Manor House**

★ **Cloete Wine Cellar**

★ **Jonkershuis**

Groot Constantia

The Mediterranean climate of temperate summers and cool, rainy winters has ensured the success of the vines planted on this estate.

VISITOR'S CHECKLIST

Road map B5. Groot Constantia off-ramp from M3 (Van der Stel Freeway) onto Ladies Mile. ☎ *(021) 794-5128.* ☐ *Dec–Apr: 9am–6pm daily (to 5pm May–Nov).* ● *Good Fri, 25 Dec, 1 Jan.* ✔ *cellar: (021) 794-5128. 10am–4pm daily.* 🖼 ♿ 🚻 🖩 🛍

Vin de Constance

This naturally sweet Muscat de Frontignan by Klein Constantia (until 1712 part of the Groot Constantia estate) is made in the style of the early 18th-century wines.

★ Jonkershuis

Once the abode of the estate owner's bachelor sons, the quaint Jonkershuis is now a restaurant that serves traditional Cape dishes (see p342).

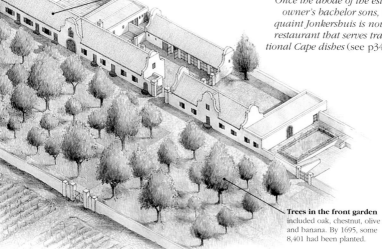

Trees in the front garden
included oak, chestnut, olive and banana. By 1695, some 8,401 had been planted.

THE DEVELOPMENT OF GABLE DESIGN

Government House (1756) is an example of the concave, or lobed, gable style.

Libertas (1771) has a convex-concave gable style, also called the Cape Baroque.

Klein Constantia (1799) has a classical gable, inspired by the Italian Renaissance.

Nederburg (1800) has a convex-concave outline, broken pediment and low pilasters.

Newlands Forest, a popular destination for weekend excursions

Kirstenbosch National Botanical Garden ⓫

See pp100–101.

Newlands ⓬

Road map B5. 🚆 *fm Cape Town station, Adderley St.* 🚌 *Terminus in Strand St to Mowbray station.*

AN EXCLUSIVE SUBURB nestled at the foot of Table Mountain's southern slopes, Newlands is the headquarters for the Western Province rugby and cricket unions. The big Newlands sports grounds, which were renamed Newlands-Norwich in 1996, have served as the venue for many international matches. The rugby stadium can hold up to 50,000 spectators, and hosted the opening game of the 1995 Rugby World Cup *(see p32)*.

Newlands Forest runs along the edge of the M3, a major route that links Muizenberg with the southern suburbs and the city centre. Local residents love to take long walks and exercise their dogs through the forest's tall blue gums, pines and silver trees, which are watered by the Newlands stream.

Exhibits at the small **Rugby Museum**, situated close to the Newlands-Norwich sports grounds, include boots, jerseys, blazers, ties and caps worn by South Africa's rugby greats, past and present.

Some 1,500 photos depict various national teams, as well as individual players of note. A vast collection of related mementos includes items that date back to 1891, when South Africa played their first international match against Britain.

A little further on stands a beautifully restored national monument, **Josephine Mill**. This mill with its cast-iron

Josephine Mill

wheel was built in 1840 by the Swede, Jacob Letterstedt, on the bank of the Liesbeeck River, to grind wheat. It was named after the Swedish Crown Princess, Josephine.

Today, the mill is managed by Cape Town's Historical Society. Demonstrations take place on request and fresh biscuits and flour are for sale.

The society also arranges guided walks along the Liesbeeck River, and during the summer months (Nov–Feb) Sunday evening concerts are held on the river banks.

🏛 **Rugby Museum**
Boundary Rd. 🔲 *(021) 686-2151.*
◯ *8:30am–5pm Mon–Fri.* 🗓 🔲 🔲

🏭 **Josephine Mill**
Boundary Rd. 🔲 *(021) 686-4939.*
◯ *9am–4pm Mon–Fri.* ◯ *weekends and public hols.* 🗓 🔲

Mostert's Mill ⓭

Road map B5. Rhodes Drive. 🚌 *Golden Acre terminus in Strand St to Mowbray station.* 🔲 *(021) 762-5127.*
◯ *phone to book.* 🗓

THIS OLD-FASHIONED windmill dates to 1796 and stands on part of the Groote Schuur estate bequeathed to the country's people by financier Cecil John Rhodes *(see p50)*. Rhodes bought the estate in 1891, donating a portion to the University of Cape Town, which today sprawls across the lower slopes of the mountain, its red-tiled roofs and ivy-covered walls an unmistakable landmark above Rhodes Drive (M3). The mill was restored in 1936 with aid from the Netherlands. There is no guide on the site.

ENVIRONS: Directly east of Mostert's Mill, in the suburb of Rosebank, is the **Irma Stern Museum**, dedicated to one of South Africa's most talented and prolific modern

---

LADY ANNE BARNARD (1750–1825)

A gracious Cape Georgian homestead in Newlands, now the Vineyard Hotel, was once the country home of 19th-century hostess, Lady Anne Barnard, who lived at the Cape from 1797 to 1802 with her husband Andrew, the colonial secretary. A gifted writer, she is remembered for her witty and astute accounts of life in the new colony. She was also a talented artist: dainty sketches often accompanied her letters and the entries in her personal journal.

Lady Anne Barnard

Mostert's Mill dates back to 1796

painters, who died in 1966. Her magnificent home, The Firs, is filled with 200 paintings and her valuable personal collection of antiques.

Travelling northwest from Mostert's Mill along the busy M3 that leads into town, the road curves around Devil's Peak to become De Waal Drive, which heads into the city centre. On the right-hand side is the famous **Groote Schuur Hospital** where, in 1967, the world's first heart transplant was performed by Professor Christiaan Barnard.

🏛 Irma Stern Museum
Cecil Rd, Rosebank. **[** (021) 685-5686. **○** 10am–5pm Tue–Sat. **●** public hols. **▨**

Rhodes Memorial ⓮

Road map B5. Groote Schuur Estate. Exit off M3. **ⓘ** (021) 689-9151. **▯**

D IRECTLY OPPOSITE Groote Schuur homestead – the state president's official Cape Town residence – the Rhodes Memorial overlooks the busy M3, and affords sweeping views of the southern suburbs.

The white granite, Doric-style temple on the slopes of Devil's Peak was designed by Sir Herbert Baker as a tribute to Cecil John Rhodes, and unveiled in 1912. It contains a bust of Rhodes by JM Swan, who also sculpted the eight bronze lions which guard the stairs. Beneath the bust is an inscription from "The Burial"

written by one of Rhodes' good friends, Rudyard Kipling. The focus of the memorial, however, is the bronze equestrian statue, titled "Physical Energy", which was executed by George Frederic Watts.

The sweeping views from the monument across the southern suburbs and out to the distant Hottentots Holland mountains are superb. Mixed oak and pine woodlands cover the mountain slopes around the memorial. They still harbour a small, free-living population of fallow deer, as well as a few Himalayan tahrs, first introduced on Groote Schuur estate in the 1890s by Cecil John Rhodes.

Ratanga Junction theme park logo

South African Astronomical Observatory ⓯

Road map B5. Off Liesbeeck Pkway, Observatory Rd. **[** (021) 447-0025. **○** 8pm on 2nd Sat of every month. **▨** groups of 10 or more must book.

T HE SITE FOR THE Royal Observatory was selected in 1821 by the first Astronomer Royal stationed at the Cape, Reverend Fearon Fellows. Today, as the national headquarters for astronomy in South Africa, it controls the Sutherland laboratory in the Great Karoo and is responsible for transmitting

the electronic impulse that triggers off the daily Noon Day Gun on Signal Hill *(see p75)*, thus setting standard time for the entire country.

Ratanga Junction ⓰

Road map B5. Off N1, 10 km (6 miles) N of Cape Town. **[** 086 120 0300. **○** 10am–5pm Wed–Sun. **●** 25 Dec. **▨** **W** www.ratanga.co.za

R ATANGA JUNCTION is the country's first full-scale theme park. The highly imaginative venue is situated some 12 km (7 miles) from the city centre on the N1, at the Century City shopping, hotel and office complex.

Ratanga Junction provides entertainment for the entire family. Chief among its many attractions are the thrilling tube ride through Crocodile Gorge, the spine-chilling Cobra rollercoaster, and a breath-taking 18.5-m (60-ft) log-flume drop on Monkey Falls.

Also on offer are various shows, "jungle cruises", fun rides specifically designed for younger children, and the usual host of fast-food outlets. There is also plenty for adult visitors, with over 20 themed restaurants, a cinema complex, laser shows, cabaret and comedy performances, a 3-D theatre, and an array of bars, pubs and games venues.

The Rhodes Memorial, designed by Sir Herbert Baker

Kirstenbosch National Botanical Garden ⓫

Daisy

IN JULY 1913, THE SOUTH AFRICAN government handed over the running of Kirstenbosch estate (which had been bequeathed to the state by Cecil John Rhodes in 1902) to a board of trustees. The board established a botanical garden that preserves and propagates rare indigenous plant species. Today, the world-renowned garden covers an area of 5.3 sq km (2 sq miles), of which 7 per cent is cultivated and 90 per cent is covered by natural *fynbos* and forest. Kirstenbosch is spectacular from August to October when the garden is ablaze with spring daisies and gazanias.

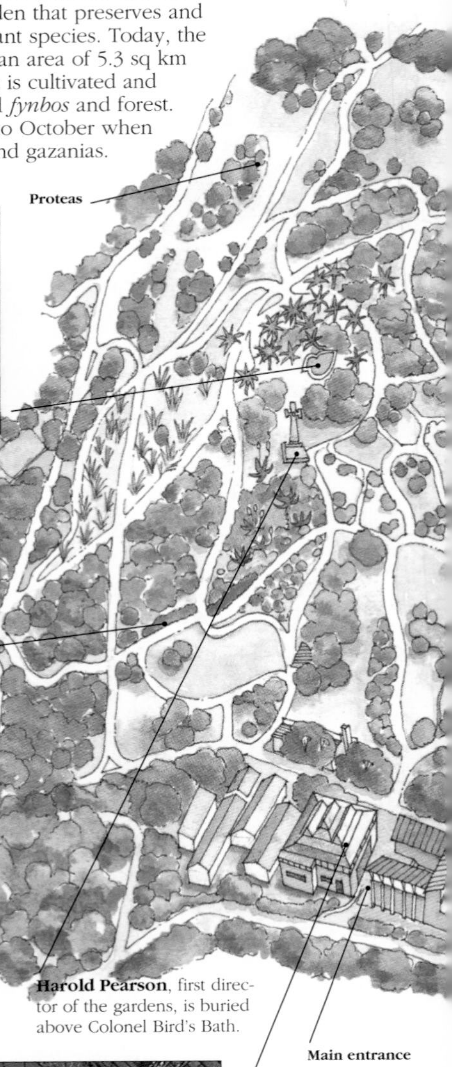

Proteas

★ Colonel Bird's Bath
Tree ferns and Cape Holly trees surround this pool, named after Colonel Bird, deputy colonial secretary in the early 1800s.

Van Riebeeck's Almond hedge
In the 1650s a hedge was planted to keep the Khoina out of the settlement and discourage illegal trading.

Birds
Proteas attract the indigenous sugarbirds.

Harold Pearson, first director of the gardens, is buried above Colonel Bird's Bath.

Main entrance

STAR FEATURES
★ Conservatory
★ Colonel Bird's Bath
★ Camphor Avenue

★ Conservatory
This glasshouse, with a baobab at its centre, displays all the floral regions of the country, from lush coastal forest to arid and alpine.

Braille Trail
A guide rope leads visually impaired visitors along this interesting 470-m (1,542-ft) long walk through a wooded area. Signs in large print and braille describe the plant species that grow along the trail.

VISITORS' CHECKLIST

Road map B5. Rhodes Ave turn-off on M3. 🚈 *Mowbray Station.*
🚌 *Fm Golden Acre in Adderley St and Mowbray Station.*
📞 *Mon–Fri: (021) 799-8899, Sat–Sun: (021) 761-4916.*
◯ *Apr–Aug: 8am–6pm daily; Sep–Mar: 8am–7pm, daily.* 🎫 *10am Tue & Sat.* 📷 🏠 🍴 🛍️ 🚻
♿ 🌐 *www.nbi.ac.za*

0 metres 100
0 yards 100

Floral Splendour
After the winter rains, carpets of indigenous Namaqualand daisies and gazanias echo the flower display found along the West Coast (see p154).

Two Gift Shops
The shop located at the upper entrance to the Gardens sells indigenous plants and seeds, while the lower shop offers a variety of natural history books, gifts and novelty items.

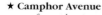
Parking

★ Camphor Avenue
This avenue of camphor trees was planted by Cecil John Rhodes around the end of the 19th century to link his cottage in Muizenberg with his Groote Schuur estate.

SHOPPING IN CAPE TOWN

CAPE TOWN has a variety of attractive shopping options that are sure to appeal to the most discerning tastes. The bustling Victoria & Alfred Waterfront *(see pp 78–81),* in convenient proximity to the city centre, is just one of a host of large, sophisticated shopping complexes that offer everything under one roof – from groceries and fresh produce to international fashion outlets and fine, gourmet dining. The lively Long and Kloof streets and the pedestrianized St George's Mall,

Art gallery logo

on the other hand, present shops with more local colour and appeal, with their streetside art displays, talented buskers and stalls crammed with African masks, beadwork, carvings and other curios. Cape Town is also the textile centre of South Africa, and brightly coloured, handmade clothing is sold at many informal markets in and around the city, such as Greenmarket Square. The surrounding suburbs like Hout Bay regularly host outdoor craft stalls and noisy fish markets.

Inside the Tygervalley Centre

OPENING HOURS

MOST SHOPS are open from 8:30am–5pm during the week, and from 9am–5pm on Saturdays. Fridays are usually the busiest time of the week and many stores stay open until 9pm. Supermarkets and delis are open on Sundays, as, of course, are most of the craft and flea markets.

SHOPPING MALLS

CAPE TOWN'S malls offer one-stop dining, entertainment, banking and shopping with convenient parking. **Canal Walk**, the largest, has over 400 upmarket shops and is a ten minute drive from the city centre. The 185 shops in elegant **Cavendish Square** offer high fashion, homeware and gourmet fare, while the **Victoria & Alfred Waterfront**, a unique centre in the heart of the old harbour, is an attractive modern shopping venue.

ARTS AND CRAFTS MARKETS

IN THE CENTRE of Cape Town, **Greenmarket Square** is the city's oldest open-air market. Mondays to Saturdays, weather permitting, one can buy everything from handmade clothing to leather goods, sandals and fashion jewellery. The **Hout Bay Arts and Crafts Market**

offers a variety of wares each Sunday, from African curios to baskets, ceramics and shell art. The **Red Shed Craft Workshop** in the Victoria Wharf and **Constantia Craft Market** (first and last Sunday of the month) sell quality handwork ranging from furniture to items made from wire and pottery.

Exterior of African Image curios

AFRICAN CRAFTS

MUCH OF THE African art available in Cape Town comes from West Africa, Zimbabwe and Zambia. **African Image**, **Out of Africa** and the **Pan African Market** stock choice fabrics and ethnic furniture, beads, utensils and sculptures. **Africa Nova** offers locally produced wire art, as well as ceramics, pewter ware, basketry and quality textiles. **The African Craft Market** also offers mainly local works like masks and decorated gourds. Freight to foreign destinations can be arranged at most of the stores.

Cobbled Greenmarket Square is one of the city's most popular markets

DELIS AND FOOD MARKETS

Cape Town's main supermarket chains, **Woolworths** and **Pick 'n Pay** sell groceries, fresh produce and South African specialities like *rooibos* tea *(see p152)* and biltong *(see p343)*. **New York Bagel** in Sea Point has a superb deli, while the **Mariner's Wharf Fish Market** further out in Hout Bay has plentiful supplies of fresh fish.

WINE

While many supermarkets stock wine, the specialist shops also offer advice and freight facilities, and are able to suggest wine route itineraries. **Vaughan Johnson's Wine Shop** at the Waterfront, which is open daily, stocks a number of unusual Cape wines like the high-quality Meerlust, Cordoba and Welgemeend.

Caroline's Fine Wine Cellar stocks over a thousand wines including classic imported wines from France, Italy, Spain and Australia. The shop holds regular wine tasting evenings on an informal basis.

Vaughan Johnson's Wine Shop at the Waterfront

BOOKS

The most comprehensive bookstore chain, **Exclusive Books**, sells CDs, newspapers, coffee table publications, maps, guides, novels and a wide range of magazines. The Cavendish Square branch even has an in-store coffee shop.

The shop at the Kirstenbosch Botanical Gardens also carries an excellent range of travel, plant and wildlife guides to South Africa.

For general stationery needs, shop at branches of the main newsagents, **CNA** and **PNA**.

PLANTS

Gardeners wanting to buy indigenous South African plants and seeds from any climatic zone in the country can do so in the gardening section of the **Kirstenbosch National Botanical Garden** shop. A horticulturalist is on duty every day to give advice.

DIRECTORY

MALLS

Canal Walk
Century City.
(*(021) 555-4444.*

Cavendish Square
Dreyer St, Claremont.
(*(021) 671-8042.*

Victoria & Alfred Waterfront
Map 2 D3–4, E3–4.
(*(021) 408-7600.*

ARTS AND CRAFT MARKETS

Constantia Craft Market
Alphen Common.
(*(021) 531-2653.*

Greenmarket Square
Cnr Shortmarket and Burg sts, Cape Town.
Map 5 B1.

Hout Bay Arts and Crafts Market
Village Green, Main Rd.
(*(021) 790-3474.*

Red Shed Craft Workshop
Victoria Wharf, Victoria & Alfred Waterfront.
Map 2 D3.
(*(021) 408-7846.*

AFRICAN ARTS

The African Craft Market
Harare Rd, Khayelitsha.
(*(021) 975-1840.*

African Image
Cnr Church and Burg sts, Cape Town.
Map 5 B1.
(*(021) 423-8385.*
Victoria Wharf, Waterfront
(*(021) 419-0382.*

Africa Nova
35 Main Rd, Hout Bay.
(*(021) 425-5123.*

Out of Africa
Victoria Wharf, Victoria & Alfred Waterfront.
Map 2 E3.
(*(021) 418-5505.*

Pan African Market
76 Long St, Cape Town.
Map 5 A2.
(*(021) 426-4478.*

DELIS AND FOOD MARKETS

Mariner's Wharf Fish Market
Harbour Rd, Hout Bay.
(*(021) 790-1100.*

New York Bagel
51 Regent Rd, Sea Point.
Map 3 C1.
(*(021) 439-7523.*

Pick 'n Pay
28 branches in Cape Town.
(*080011 2288 (Customer service)*

Woolworths
30 branches in Cape Town.
Map 2 B5
(*(021) 407-9111.*

WINE

Caroline's Fine Wine Cellar
8 King's Warehouse, Victoria Wharf, Victoria & Alfred Waterfront **Map** 1 B1.
(*(021) 425-5701.*

Vaughan Johnson's Wine Shop
Pierhead, Dock Rd, Victoria & Alfred Waterfront. **Map** 2 E3.
(*(021) 419-2121.*

BOOKS

CNA (Central News Agency)
Victoria Wharf, Victoria & Alfred Waterfront
(*(021) 418-3510.*
Branches all over town.

Exclusive Books
Cavendish Sq, Claremont.
(*(021) 674-3030.*
Branches all over town.

PNA
Garden's Centre, Gardens.
(*(021) 465-7654.*
Branches all over town.

PLANTS

Kirstenbosch National Botanical Garden
Rhodes Drive, Newlands.
Natural World Merchants
(*(021) 799-8782.*

ENTERTAINMENT IN CAPE TOWN

MUCH of Cape Town's leisure activity centres on the beaches and mountains, and the city does not have quite the reputation for its nightlife and cultural events that Johannesburg has. Many happenings take place al fresco, and in spring and summer various music productions are staged in amphitheatres and parks. Unusual venues, such as the top floor of a trendy shop or the parade ground at Castle of Good Hope, draw audiences to music, cabaret and comedy and military tattoos. Jazz bands play at clubs, restaurants and bars, as well as in the open air. Many Capetonians enjoy dinner followed by a visit to the cinema, but the city also caters for serious clubbers. The action is focused on the fashionable clubs and bars in the city centre and at the Victoria & Alfred Waterfront.

Ster Kinekor company logo

Computicket booking office, Victoria & Alfred Waterfront

INFORMATION

FOR DETAILS of entertainment in the city, check the daily and weekend newspapers. They review and list events in the cinema, arts and theatre industries. Reviews and listings also appear in a number of magazines that are sold in the newsagents as well as some clubs and bars. Good choices are *SA City Life*, *Cape Review* and *The Big Issue* (sold by homeless or vulnerably accommodated street vendors).

BOOKING TICKETS

RESERVE THEATRE SEATS by calling **Computicket**, which has branches in all the major centres countrywide.

To make telephone bookings for Ster-Kinekor cinemas, call **Ticketline**. Most theatres and cinemas do not accept telephone bookings without credit card payment.

CINEMA

THE COUNTRY'S fledgling film industry is only beginning to make a name for itself, both locally and abroad. Mainstream Hollywood productions are extremely popular and the main fare in Cape Town's **Ster-Kinekor** and **Nu Metro** cinema complexes.

There are three art-house cinemas in Cape Town offering stimulating and challenging independent and cult movies, as well as international art releases. **Cinema Nouveau**, at Cavendish Square, and also the Cinema Nouveau on the Victoria and Alfred Waterfront, and the **Labia Theatre** in Cape Town all offer good alternatives to the run-of-the-mill Hollywood movie.

THEATRE, OPERA AND DANCE

ALTHOUGH CAPETONIANS, in general, prefer the cinema to drama, the standard of local theatre is excellent. The city's flagship venue for cultural events is the **Nico Theatre Centre**. The Nico, as it is called, hosts world-class performances of classic opera and ballet, drama and satire. A calendar of events is available from the box office.

A stage production at the Nico Theatre Centre

The Baxter Theatre in Rondebosch

Another cultural venue is the **Baxter Theatre Centre**, which hosts cabaret, classical and contemporary music and dance performances and art exhibitions. Its children's theatre is well attended, too.

It is worth checking in the local press for details of performances hosted by the University of Cape Town's **Little Theatre** and the **Maynardville Open-Air Theatre**, where Shakespearean plays are performed under the stars in January and February. These open-air events are very special and many theatre-goers extend the outing by taking along a pre-performance picnic to eat in the park.

COMEDY

Comedy performances always draw large crowds. At the **Theatre on the Bay**, farce is the standard fare, while at **Evita Se Perron** in the town of Darling *(see p149)*, a short drive from Cape Town, the razor-sharp wit of Pieter-Dirk Uys launches hilarious attacks on current political issues. Both venues, along with the popular **On Broadway**, in Somerset Road, also showcase cabaret and drag troupes.

CLASSICAL MUSIC

Music in a superb outdoor setting is what summers in Cape Town are all about. Popular occasions are the sunset concerts held at

Kirstenbosch National Botanical Garden *(see pp100–1)* and in the leafy and sheltered gardens of the **Josephine Mill** *(see p98)*.

The Nico Theatre Centre is the home of the **Cape Town Philharmonic Orchestra**, which usually gives performances here on Thursday evenings. Occasionally, rather unusual concert venues are chosen, such as the Two Oceans Aquarium or the South African Museum (watch the press for details). The Nico Theatre Centre also stages musicals, as well as popular lunchtime and Sunday afternoon concerts.

The **Baxter Theatre Centre**, where the **South African College of Music** performs its repertoire of chamber music, string ensembles, organ recital and superb orchestral productions, also offers occasional lunchtime concerts.

Cellist, Cape Town Philharmonic

AFRICAN JAZZ AND FUSION

Cape town is well known for its unique, indigenous style of jazz, which is heavily influenced by traditional African rhythms and melodies. After years in self-imposed exile, renowned jazz musician Abdullah Ibrahim, once again resides in the city of his birth.

There are many other talented musicians performing at fashionable venues such as **Dizzy Jazz Café** and **Winchester Mansions Hotel**, which is especially good for lazy Saturday afternoons.

Heritage Square, a complex of shops, restaurants and art galleries in a restored 18th-century building, offers al fresco dining to live jazz and classical music over weekends.

The Victoria & Alfred Waterfront is where you will find the popular **Green Dolphin**, an excellent restaurant and cocktail bar that offers live jazz performances every night. Also in the vicinity is the trendy venue and restaurant **West End**, which hosts resident jazz bands on Friday and Saturday nights.

During the long summer season when darkness falls at around 9pm, **St George's Mall** bustles with gifted street musicians. The AGFA Amphitheatre at the Victoria & Alfred Waterfront often hosts free performances. On Heritage Day (24 Sep), look out for the many free music festivals; they're advertised by the local press and radio.

A jazz band at the Green Dolphin restaurant, V&A Waterfront

BARS AND CLUBS

IT IS NOT ALWAYS VERY easy to distinguish between clubs and bars in Cape Town, as drinking and dancing usually take place at the same venue.

British-style pubs are becoming more popular, however, and there are many lively late-night eateries, particularly in the student-filled Observatory.

Cape Town's young and trendy set is, of course, as fickle as it is elsewhere, so it is best to read the listings and the local press to learn what is in and what is not. The City Bowl is a nightlife hotspot and the bars in Loop and Long streets and at the Victoria & Alfred Waterfront are good bets.

City pub logo

For live music, the local radio stations like Good Hope FM, newspapers and magazines are good sources of information. International live acts usually perform at the **3 Arts Theatre** ice rink or Green Point Stadium, while local rock bands favour **The Purple Turtle** in town, as well as **The River Club**, a big centre with a number of venues that also has good eateries.

In December the River Club hosts an enormously popular drag party organized by Mother City Queer Projects. The River Club is also the venue for the Barleycorn Music Club, featuring original compositions by local folk- and fusion-inspired musicians. Contemporary and African music can be heard at **The Space** in Kalk Bay, jazz and blues at **The Brass Bell**.

The Sports Café, Victoria & Alfred Waterfront

CAPE TOWN STREET FINDER

THE MAP REFERENCES appearing with the sights, shops and entertainment venues that are mentioned in the Cape Town chapter refer to the maps in this section. The key map below shows the areas covered including: the City Bowl, the Central Business District, the historical Gardens area and the Victoria & Alfred Waterfront. All the principal sights

mentioned in the text are marked, as well as useful information like tourist information offices, police stations, post offices and public parking areas, always at a premium in the inner city. A full list of symbols appears in the key. Map references for Cape Town's hotels *(see pp-314–19)* and restaurants *(see pp344–47)* have been included in the Travellers' Needs section.

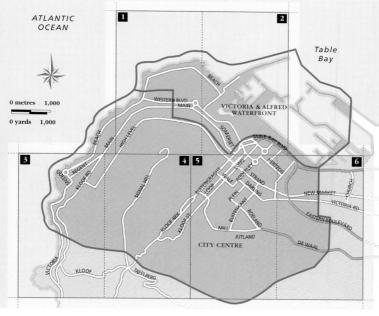

KEY

▢ Major sight	ℹ Tourist information	⚡ Viewpoint
▢ Place of interest	✚ Hospital with casualty unit	═ Railway line
▢ Other building	🚓 Police station	One-way street
🚆 Transnet station	🚴 Mountain biking access	Pedestrianized street
🚌 Bus terminus	🏊 Bathing beach	Road (no public access)
Minibus terminus	✝ Church	
⛴ Ferry boarding point	☾ Mosque	**SCALE FOR STREET FINDER PAGES**
🚕 Taxi rank	✡ Synagogue	0 metres 500
P Parking	⊠ Post office	0 yards 500

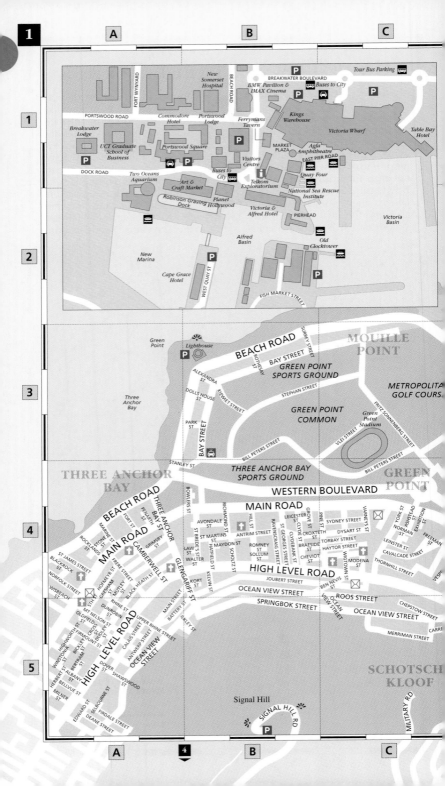

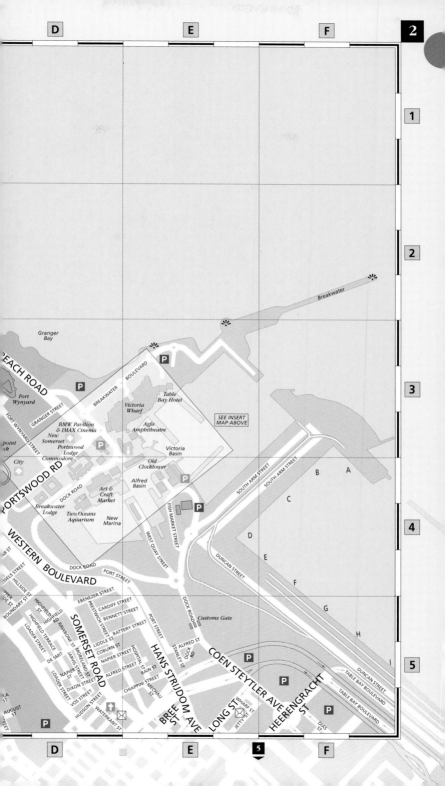

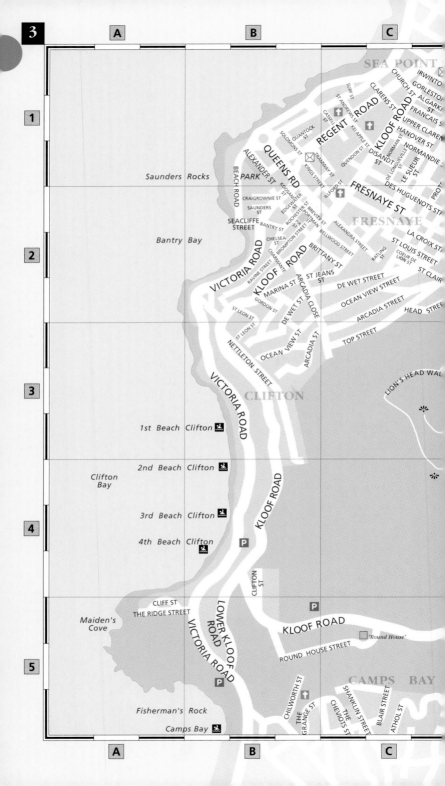

3

A   B   C

1

SEA POINT

IRWINTO

GORLESTON

CHURCH ST ALGARK!

FRANCAIS S

SURE ST

ST ANDREWS ST

CLARENS ST

REGENT

KLOOF ROAD

HANOVER ST

UPPER CLAREN

CASSEL

ROAD

NORMANDIE

SOLOMONS ST

QUANTOCK ST

TRAMWAY ST

KEL APPLE ST

QUENDON ST

DISANDT

DE LONGUEVILLE

LE SUEUR ST

NORMAN ST

Saunders Rocks

ALEXANDER ST

QUEENS RD

KINGS STREET

ILFORD ST

DES HUGUENOTS ST

PROT

BEACH ROAD

PARK

FRESNAYE ST

ALEXANDER ST

CRAIGROWNIE ST

FRESNAYE

SAUNDERS ST

EDGEWATER

LA CROIX ST

SEACLIFFE STREET

BANTRY ST

ROCHESTER ST

BREVITY ST

PORTMAN

ST LOUIS STREET

2

Bantry Bay

CHELSEA ST

BROMPTON STREET

BELLWOOD STREET

ALEXANDRA STREET

RATING ST

COEUR DE LION ST

ST CLAIR

CHARMANTE

BRITTANY ST

VICTORIA ROAD

RAVINE STREET

KLOOF ROAD

ST JEANS ST

DE WET STREET

MARINA ST

ARCADIA CLOSE

OCEAN VIEW STREET

GORDON ST

DE WET ST

ST LEON ST

ARCADIA STREET

HEAD STREE

ST LEON ST

OCEAN VIEW ST

ARCADIA ST

TOP STREET

NETTLETON STREET

3

CLIFTON

LION'S HEAD WAL

VICTORIA ROAD

1st Beach Clifton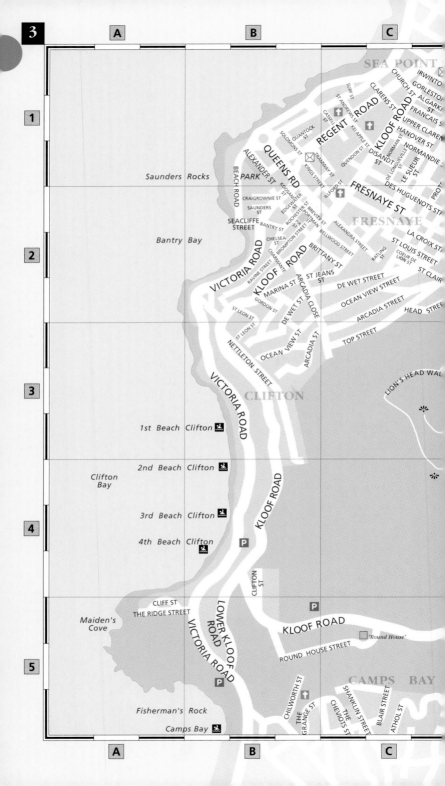

4

2nd Beach Clifton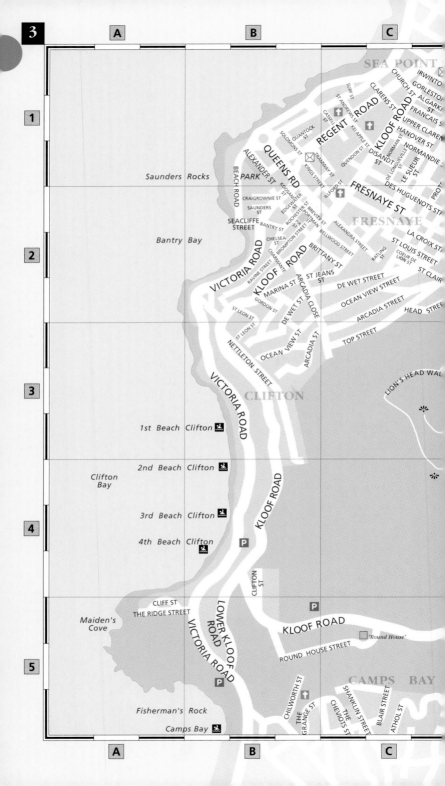

Clifton Bay

KLOOF ROAD

3rd Beach Clifton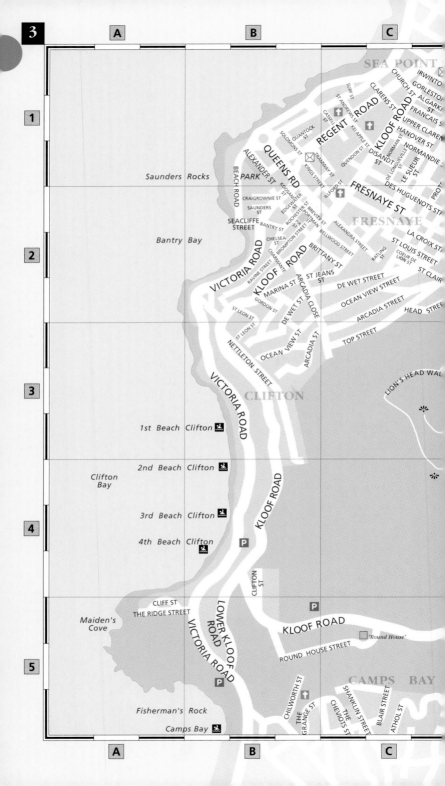

4th Beach Clifton

🅿

CLIFTON ST

CLIFF ST

THE RIDGE STREET

🅿

Maiden's Cove

LOWER KLOOF ROAD

KLOOF ROAD

"Round House"

ROUND HOUSE STREET

VICTORIA ROAD

5

🅿

CAMPS BAY

Fisherman's Rock

CHILWORTH ST

THE GRANGE ST

THE CHEVIOTS ST

SHANKLIN STREET

BLAIR STREET

ATHOL ST

Camps Bay

A   B   C

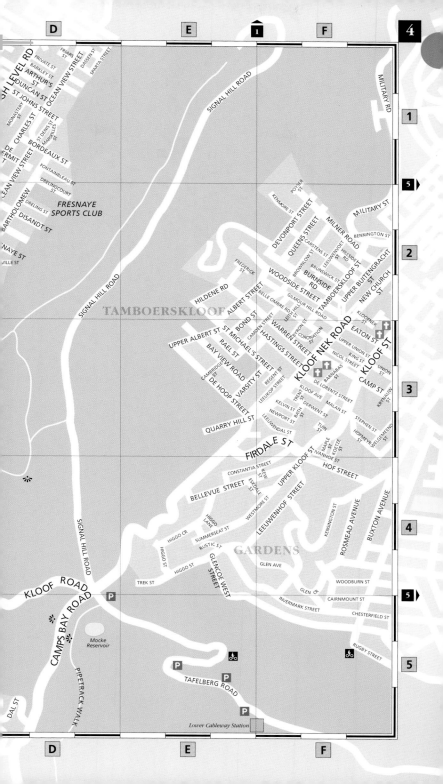

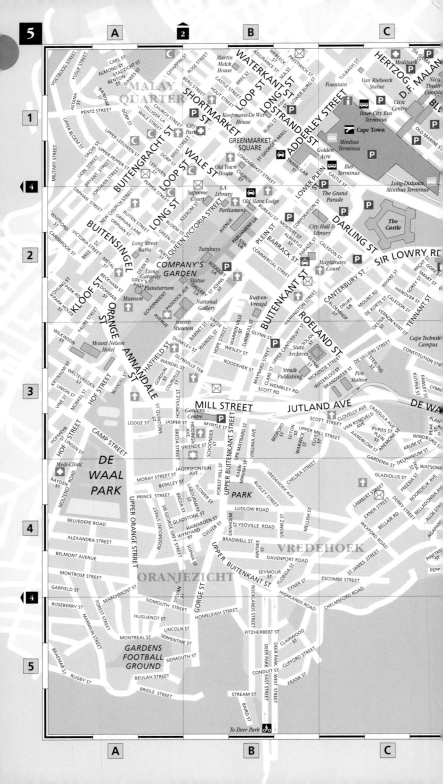

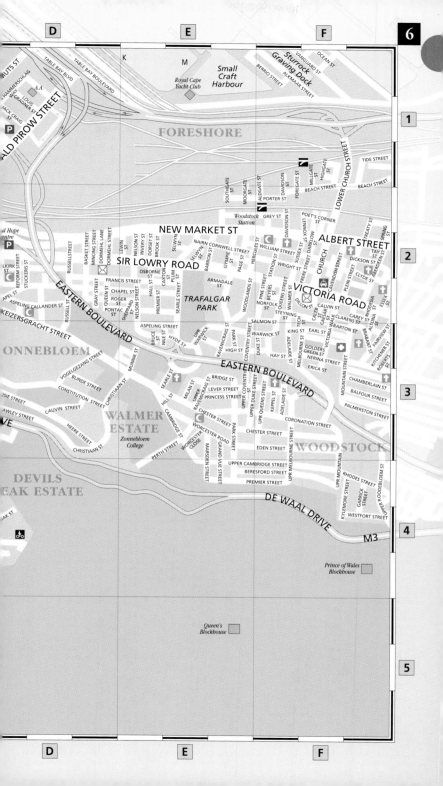

Cape Town Street Finder Index

Introducing the Western and Southern Cape

THIS REGION IS DOMINATED by a rugged mountain chain, comprising what is geologically known as the Cape folded mountains. The landscapes found in this territory are diverse. The arid and rather barren West Coast gives way to fertile winelands, cradled by jagged mountains. Beyond the terraced valleys, dramatic passes that traverse the massive mountain ranges of the Southern Cape are a testament to the efforts of early road builders. The spectacular Cango Caves lie here and, on the other side of the mountains, the spectacular Garden Route. All along the rocky coastline, which is one of the most dangerous in the world and where swells can reach up to 30 m (98 ft) in height, fishermen reap the harvest of the sea.

Namaqualand

0 kilometres 50

0 miles 25

THE WESTERN
COASTAL TERRACE
(See pp144–55)

***The Manor House at
Boschendal*** *near Franschhoek forms a stately backdrop
for the vineyards of the estate.
Wine tasting here is one of the
highlights of the wine route.*

A myriad wildflowers
*occurs in this region
after good spring rains,
when the dry West Coast
comes alive with colour.*

*Cape
Columbine*

***Cape Columbine light-
house*** *on the West Coast
warns ships of the dangerous rocks along the shore.
It is the last manned lighthouse in South Africa.*

*Boschendal
Estate*

THE CAPE WINELANDS
(See pp124–43)

THE SOUTHERN CAPE
(See pp156–67)

Hermanus *is best known for the southern
right whales that come here to give birth to
their calves. The best time of the year for
whale watching is around September.*

◁ **In spring, double Namaqualand daisies provide carpets of colour**

Knysna Forest is known for its tall stinkwood trees and ancient yellowwoods, some of which are 650 years old. The dense canopy is alive with birds, such as the elusive, emerald-green lourie.

Addo Elephant National Park in the Eastern Cape is a major tourist attraction. The park is home to around 300 elephants.

Port Elizabeth's attractions include an aquarium on the beachfront, where dolphin shows are the most popular event. In the city, a host of historic buildings and statues date back to British colonial times.

THE GARDEN ROUTE
TO GRAHAMSTOWN
(See pp168–89)

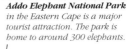

ngo Caves

Knysna

Port
Elizabeth

The Cango Caves near Oudtshoorn contain many fascinating dripstone formations, caused by the constant percolation of water through limestone.

Pinotage Wine-Making

P INOTAGE IS A UNIQUE South African cultivar that was developed in 1925 by Stellenbosch University professor, Abraham Perold, from a cross of pinot noir and cinsaut (then called hermitage). The world's first commercially bottled pinotage was released in 1961 under the Lanzerac label. The distinctly fruity, purple-red wine has, since then, achieved international acclaim. Pinotage comprises only a small percentage of South African total grape plantings, with most of the crop grown around Stellenbosch. In recent years, cuttings have been exported to Zimbabwe, California and New Zealand.

Old grape press in the Stellenryck Museum, Stellenbosch

Pinot noir

Cinsaut

Pinotage

THE PINOTAGE CULTIVARS

Pinot noir, the noble cultivar from France's famous Burgundy district, contributed complexity, flavour, and colour, while cinsaut improved the yield. Today, pinotage is an early ripening cultivar that results in a light- to medium-bodied wine with unique flavour characteristics.

*The large **oak barrels** used for maturation and storage of red wines are often decorated with hand-carved designs, like this beautiful example from the Delheim cellar in Stellenbosch.*

Stellenbosch *(see pp128–33)* is surrounded by gentle hills that are ideal for growing pinotage.

PINOTAGE INTERNATIONAL AWARDS

1987: Kanonkop (1985) – Beyers Truter voted Diners' Club "Winemaker of the Year"

1991: Kanonkop (1989 Reserve) – Robert Mondavi Trophy (USA)

1996: Kanonkop (1992) – Perold Trophy (International Wine and Spirit Competition)

1997: L'Avenir (1994) – Perold Trophy

1997: Jacobsdal (1994) – gold medal at Vin Expo Competition (France)

Two of South Africa's well-known pinotage labels

Lanzerac, in Stellenbosch, combines a luxury country hotel with a working winery. Pinotage is one of a range of wines made by the estate.

THE RED WINE-MAKING PROCESS

Wine is a natural product and winemakers take great care during harvesting, production and maturation to ensure that their wines are of a high quality and meet the requirements of the consumer. Modern trends call for minimal interference in the vineyard and cellar in order to allow the wines to "speak" for themselves.

Harvesting *is carefully timed to achieve the best flavours and characters from the grape. Red wines are traditionally harvested later than white wines, to allow the development of riper and more concentrated fruit.*

Grapes are cut off the vine with sharp shears to minimize damage to the mature berries

Destalking *removes the stems, whose high tannin content influences the wine's flavour. The grapes are then lightly crushed before being put into a vat for fermentation to begin.*

Destalker and crusher

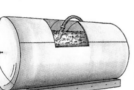

Fermentation tank

Fermentation *occurs over three to five days. The juice is periodically pumped over the "cap" formed by the skins to extract the desired amount of colour and tannin. After fermentation, the juice is separated from the skins, and matured before blending and bottling.*

Storage tanks and barrels

Racking *is the transfer of fermented wine from one tank or cask to another to remove the "lees", sediments that would cause the end product to appear cloudy. Filtration and fining, often using egg whites, removes impurities.*

Maturation *of pinotage takes 12–15 months. Traditionally, big vats were used, but the modern trend is to use small barrels made of French or American oak. The size of the barrel, type of wood and maturation time combine to shape the character of the wine. Once matured, the red wines are ready for bottling.*

Wooden maturation barrels

The South African Pinotage Producers, Association, *formed in November 1995, strives to maintain a consistently high standard for South African pinotage. It holds an annual competition to judge the year's ten best wines.*

Over 130 pinotages are made in South Africa

Whale-Watching

Shop sign in Hermanus

SOME 37 WHALE AND DOLPHIN species and around 100 different types of shark occur in Southern African waters. Only a small number come in close to the coast however. Of the dolphins, bottlenose, common and Heaviside's are the most prolific, while common predatory sharks include the great white, tiger, ragged-tooth, oceanic white tip, bull (Zambezi), and mako. A large portion of the world's 4,000–6,000 southern right whales migrates north annually, with numbers increasing by seven per cent every year. They leave their subantarctic feeding grounds from June onwards to mate and calve in the warmer waters of the protected rocky bays and inlets that occur along the South African coastline.

WHALE-WATCHING

☐ *Best vantage points*

An albino calf was born in Hermanus in 1997.

Callosities *are tough, wart-like growths on the whale's skin, not barnacles as is often thought. Scientists use these unique markings to distinguish between individuals.*

THE SOUTHERN RIGHT WHALE

Early whalers named this species "southern right" *(Eubalaena australis)* because it occurred south of the Equator and was the perfect quarry. Its blubber was rich in oil, the baleen plates supplied whalebone for corsets, shoe horns and brushes, and when dead it floated, unlike other whales which sank. A protected species, they can migrate by up to 2,600 km (1,615 miles) annually.

A characteristic V-shaped "blow" *can be seen when the southern right exhales. The vapour is produced by condensation, as warm breath comes into contact with cooler air.*

The "Whale Crier" *patrols the streets of Hermanus, blowing a kelp horn to inform passers-by of the best sightings of the day.*

WHALE ANTICS

The reasons for some types of whale behaviour are, as yet, unclear. Breaching, for example, may either indicate aggression, or joyfulness; it may also simply help the animal get rid of lice.

Breaching: *the whale lifts its upper body out of the water and falls back into the sea with a massive splash.*

...uthern right whales
...rse their calves for at ...st six months.

Blowhole   **Callosities**

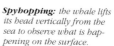
Lobtailing: *the flukes slap on the surface to produce a loud clap.*

Spyhopping: *the whale lifts its head vertically from the sea to observe what is happening on the surface.*

Shore-based whale watching
is superb at Hermanus.

Humpback whales *are well known for their spectacular breaching behaviour, lifting their bodies well above the water. A striking feature of this species is its extremely long flippers.*

WHALE EXPLOITATION

In the years from 1785 to around 1805, some 12,000 southern right whales were killed off the Southern African coast, but the northern right whale was the most ruthlessly hunted and is virtually extinct today. After the introduction of cannon-fired harpoons, humpbacks were the first large whale to be exploited. Some 25,000 were killed between 1908 and 1925. By 1935, when the League of Nations' Convention for the Regulation of Whaling came into effect, fewer than 200 southern right whales remained in Southern African waters. Although numbers are increasing steadily, today's total population is only a fraction of what it once was.

Early whalers in False Bay

THE CAPE WINELANDS

THE CAPE'S WINELANDS *are a scenically enchanting region of lofty mountains and fertile valleys and slopes planted with orchards and vines. Nestled in the valleys are graceful Cape Dutch manor houses, of which stately Nederburg in Paarl (which hosts a famous wine auction), elegant Boschendal near Franschhoek and the charming Lanzerac Hotel in Stellenbosch are the best known.*

Stellenbosch was the first of the wineland towns to be established by Simon van der Stel, who had succeeded Jan van Riebeeck as governor in 1679. After Van der Stel visited the area in November of that year and proclaimed it to be well watered and fertile, the first free burghers (early Dutch settlers who were granted tracts of land together with implements and oxen to help them establish farms) were sent to this valley to start a new life. Settlement in the Franschhoek valley followed with the arrival of the French Huguenots (Protestant refugees from Europe), and later Dutch as well as French pioneers established themselves in the Paarl area. The temperate Mediterranean climate of the Cape has ensured the survival of the early wine-making traditions.

The cool mountain and sea breezes create diverse conditions, and variable soil types – from the acidic and sandy alluvial soils of Stellenbosch (good for red wines) to the lime-rich soils of Robertson (excellent for white wines) – ensure a wide range of superb wines, making South Africa the world's seventh-largest producer. The 91 estates, 66 co-operatives and more than 100 private cellars in the Western Cape support about 300,000 farm workers and their dependents.

Most of the estates and co-ops offer tastings, and the architectural legacy of the settlers is evident on a drive through any of the Wineland towns.

Klein Constantia in Cape Town is a particularly picturesque wine estate

◁ **The Gazebo at Boschendal estate on the Franschhoek wine route**

Exploring the Cape Winelands

A FTER TABLE MOUNTAIN, the Victoria & Alfred Waterfront and Cape Point, the winelands are the Western Cape's most popular attraction. The towns of Stellenbosch and Paarl are special for their elegant, gabled architecture, while Franschhoek enjoys an exquisite valley setting. Viewed from majestic mountain passes, the vineyards of Worcester and Robertson fit together like puzzle pieces, and the drawcard of Tulbagh *(see p149)* is its row of quaint, historical houses, meticulously restored after a devastating earthquake in 1969.

Spier wine estate serves meals on the terrace in warm weather

SIGHTS AT A GLANCE

SEE ALSO

Delheim's vineyards, Stellenbosch

GETTING AROUND
The winelands are served by two major national routes, the N1 and N2. All of the connecting principal roads are clearly signposted. Franschhoek, Paarl and Worcester are accessed from the N1, Stellenbosch from either the N1 or N2 national route. Robertson is reached from Worcester via the R60.

The scenic mountain passes are well worth an excursion and own transport is essential if you wish to tour these areas. Alternatively, visitors can join one of the coach tours organized by major tour operators like Intercape (see p385) and Mainline Passenger Services (see p383). Cape Town International is the closest airport.

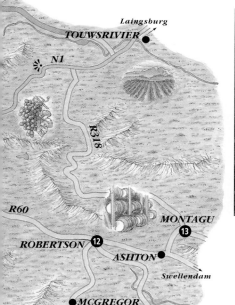

Montagu is renowned for its hot springs

Laingsburg

TOUWSRIVIER

N1

R318

R60

MONTAGU

ROBERTSON ⑫

ASHTON

Swellendam

MCGREGOR

BOESMANSKLOOF
⑭ TRAVERSE

GREYTON

⑬

0 kilometres   50

0 miles   25

Rhebokskloof has converted a cellar into a cosy wine-tasting venue

KEY
☰ Motorway
▭ National route
▬ Main road
▬ Scenic route
▬ River, lake or dam
☼ Viewpoint

Street-by-Street: Stellenbosch ❶

Stained glass, Moederkerk

A CENTRE OF VITICULTURE and learning, the historical university town of Stellenbosch is shaded by avenues of ancient oaks planted in 1685 when Governor Simon van der Stel established the town. The streets are lined with homes in the Cape Dutch, Cape Georgian, Regency and Victorian styles. Through the centuries, Stellenbosch has been ravaged by three fires and several homes have had to be restored. The town is best explored on foot; pamphlets of a walk are available from the tourist information bureau on Market Street.

The Burgher House was built in 1797. Its gable is an early example of the Neo-Classical style. The house is the headquarters of the Historical Homes of South Africa foundation.

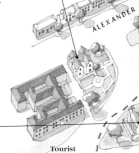

VOC Kruithuis
The powder magazine of the VOC (Dutch East India Company) was built in 1777 to defend the early settlement. It now houses a small military museum.

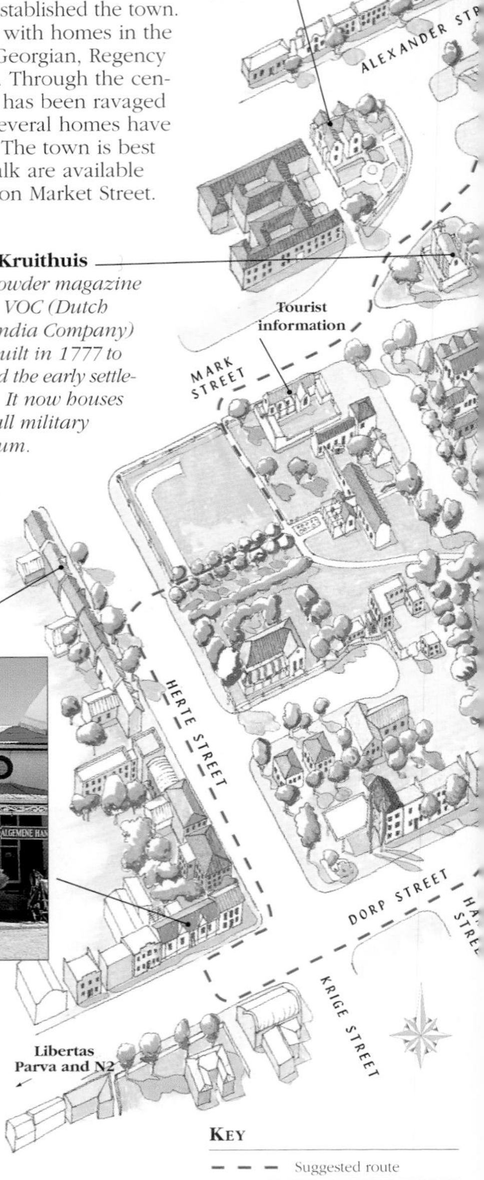

Slave Houses, built around 1834 for the settlers' servants, are no longer thatched but still retain their original character.

★ **Oom Samie se Winkel**
In this "olde-worlde" village store (see p130) shoppers can step back in time and buy antiques, collectables, sticky toffee and biltong (see p343).

Libertas Parva and N2

STAR SIGHTS

★ **Dorp Street**

★ **Oom Samie se Winkel**

KEY

– – – Suggested route

| 0 metres | 250 |
| 0 yards | 250 |

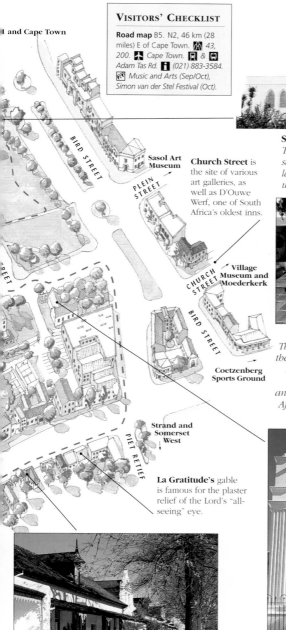

VISITORS' CHECKLIST

Road map B5. N2, 46 km (28 miles) E of Cape Town. 🚌 43, 200. 🚂 Cape Town. 🚍 & 🏢 Adam Tas Rd. 🛈 (021) 883-3584. 🎭 Music and Arts (Sep/Oct), Simon van der Stel Festival (Oct).

and Cape Town

BIRD STREET

Sasol Art Museum

PLEIN STREET

Church Street is the site of various art galleries, as well as D'Ouwe Werf, one of South Africa's oldest inns.

CHURCH STREET

Village Museum and Moederkerk

BIRD STREET

Coetzenberg Sports Ground

Strand and Somerset West

PIET RETIEF

La Gratitude's gable is famous for the plaster relief of the Lord's "all-seeing" eye.

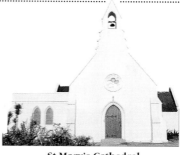

St Mary's Cathedral
This church adjoins the town square, Die Braak (fallow land). Laid out in 1703, it was used as a parade ground.

The Village Museum
The historic houses that comprise the Village Museum on Ryneveld Street (see pp130–1) are decorated in different period styles and are regarded as one of South Africa's best restoration projects.

The Rhenish Church
The church was built in 1823 as a school for slaves' children and "coloured" people.

★ **Dorp Street**
Some of the best-preserved historical façades in Stellenbosch are found on this oak-lined street.

Exploring Stellenbosch

THE HEART OF THE WINELANDS, this beautiful university town is also the historical cradle of Afrikaans culture. Founded in 1679, the town's proud educational heritage began in 1863 with the establishment of the Dutch Reformed Theological Seminary. The Stellenbosch College was completed in 1886, the forerunner of the university, which was established in 1918. Today, the university buildings are beautifully integrated with the surrounding historical monuments, reinforcing the town's dignified atmosphere of culture and learning.

🏛 Rhenish Complex

Herte St. *Opening times of buildings vary and are subject to change.* **C** *(021) 883-3584 for information.*
This lovely group of old buildings, which is flanked by two modern educational centres – the Rhenish Primary School and the Rhenish Institute – is representative of most of all the architectural styles that have appeared in Stellenbosch over the centuries.

Parts of the Cape Dutch-style Rhenish parsonage are much older than the date of 1815 noted on the building's gable. The parsonage houses a museum of miniature rooms fitted with period furniture and a 50-sq-m (538-sq-ft) model railway set in a diminutive reconstruction of the landscape around Stellenbosch.

Leipoldt House, which was built around 1832, is an interesting combination of Cape Dutch and English Georgian architectural styles, while the Rhenish Church, facing Bloem Street, was erected in 1823 by the Missionary Society of Stellenbosch as a training centre and school for slaves and "coloured" people.

Oom Samie se Winkel

🏛 Oom Samie se Winkel

84 Dorp St. **C** *(021) 887-0797.* ◯ *8:30am–5:30pm (6pm summer) Mon–Fri, 9am–5:30pm (5:30pm summer) Sat, Sun.* ● *Good Fri, 25 Dec, 1 Jan.*
This charming, restored Victorian shop, whose name means "Uncle Samie's Store", has been operating as a general store since 1904. Its original proprietor, bachelor Samie Volsteedt, used to live in the house next door. The store, a Stellenbosch institution and a national monument, has bric-a-brac ranging from bottled preserves, basketry, candles and curios to 19th-century butter churns, plates and kitchen utensils. Visitors may also browse in Samie's Victorian Wine Shop for a special vintage or take tea under the leafy pergolas of the Koffiehuis restaurant.

🏛 Toy and Miniature Museum

Market St (next to tourist information office). **C** *(021) 887-2948.* ◯ *9:30am–5pm Mon–Sat, 2–5pm Sun.* ● *Sun (May–Aug).* 🖼 🚻 **W** *www.museums.org.za/stellmus*
The Toy and Miniature Museum offers a world of enchantment for both young and old and is well worth a visit. Housed in the old Rhenish Parsonage of 1815, the museum is the first of its kind in Africa. On display is an amazing collection of historical toys, including antique dolls and Dinky Toy motor cars, as well as a model railway-layout and miniature houses. The museum also boasts a number of finely detailed and exquisite 1:12 scale miniature rooms, each with delicate filigree work.

On sale in the small museum shop are furniture and accessories for dolls' houses, as well as momentos of the museum's unique treasures.

🏛 The Village Museum

18 Ryneveld St. **C** *(021) 887-2902.* ◯ *9am–5pm Mon–Sat, 2–5pm Sun.* ● *Good Fri, 25 Dec.* 🖼 ♿ 🖳
The Village Museum complex features houses from Stellenbosch's early settlement years to the 1920s, although the Edwardian and other early 20th-century houses are not open to the public. The museum presently comprises four buildings. Schreuder House was built in 1709 by Sebastian Schreuder. It is the oldest of the houses and shows the spartan, simple lifestyle of the early settlers. Bletterman House, erected in 1789, belonged to Hendrik Bletterman, a wealthy *landdrost* (magistrate). Parts of

The Rhenish Complex, a splendid example of Cape Dutch architecture

ARTS AND CRAFTS IN STELLENBOSCH

Nurtured by Stellenbosch's environment of culture and learning, a community of artists, graphic designers, ceramists and screen-printers has settled in the town. Multiple galleries and studios such as the Dorp Street Gallery at 176 Dorp Street and the Stellenbosch Art Gallery at 34 Ryneveld Street show the works of respected contemporary South African and local artists. Outside Stellenbosch, off Devon Valley Road, the Jean Craig Pottery Studio showcases all stages of its pottery production, and on Annandale Road, off the R310, visitors can watch spinners and weavers at work at Dombeya Farm. A detailed arts and crafts brochure is available from the Stellenbosch tourist information centre.

Work by Hannetjie de Clerq

The 18th-century middle-class Schreuder House at the Village Museum

Grosvenor House, the most elegant of the four, date back to 1782, but later additions to the house represent the Classicism of the 1800s. The house has period furnishings of the 1800s.

Constructed in 19th-century Victorian style, the interiors of Bergh House, occupied by Olof Marthinus Bergh from 1837 to 1866, accurately reflect the comfortable life-style of a wealthy burgher of the 1850s.

🏛 Sasol Art Museum
Eben Donges Centre, 52 Ryneveld St. 📞 *(021) 808-3695.* ⏰ *Tue–Fri 9am–4pm, Sat 9am–5pm.* ⬤ *Mon, Sun, Good Fri, 25 Dec.* 📷♿📷

The interesting exhibition at the Sasol Art Museum focuses on anthropology, cultural history and art. Of particular interest to many visitors are the prehistoric artifacts, reproductions of San rock art and crafted utensils and ritual objects from South, West and Central Africa.

🖼 Van Ryn Brandy Cellar
R310 from Stellenbosch, exit 33. 📞 *(021) 881-3875.* ⏰ *9am–4:30pm Mon–Fri, 9am–2:30pm Sat.* ⬤ *Sun, public hols.* 📷♿📷📷

At this cellar just southwest of Stellenbosch, where the well-known local brands Van Ryn and Viceroy are made, guided tours introduce the visitor to the intricate art of brandy production. Brandy courses are offered and include a lecture, an audio-visual presentation, as well as a brandy tasting and dinner.

ENVIRONS: The **Jonkershoek Nature Reserve** lies in a valley 10 km (6 miles) southeast of Stellenbosch that is flanked by the scenic Jonkershoek and Stellenbosch mountain ranges. The scenery is characterized by wooded ravines, pine plantations and montane *fynbos*, which in spring and summer includes tiny pink and white ericas, blushing bride *(Serruria florida)* and the king protea. The waterfalls and streams of the Eerste River provide abundant water for hikers, mountain bikers and horse riders. For the less energetic, there is a 12-km (7.5-mile) scenic drive into the mountains. Baboons and dassies may be sighted, and sometimes the elusive klip-springer. Of the many bird species in the reserve, the Cape sugarbird and malachite and orange-breasted sunbirds are most likely to be seen.

🦌 Jonkershoek Nature Reserve
Jonkershoek Rd. 📞 *(021) 866-1560.* ⏰ *8am–6pm daily.* ⬤ *heavy rains (Jun–Aug).* 📷📷
Ⓦ www.capenature.org.za

The sandstone mountains of the Jonkershoek Nature Reserve

Stellenbosch Winelands ➋

THE STELLENBOSCH WINE ROUTE was launched in April 1971 by the vintners of three prominent estates: Spier, Simonsig and Delheim. Today, the route comprises a great number of estates and co-operatives. Tasting, generally for a small fee, and cellar tours are offered throughout the week at most of the vineyards. A few of them can be visited by appointment only and many are closed on Sundays, so phoning ahead is advisable.

Zevenwacht ①
This is one of the most beautiful estates. The manor house, a national monument has views of both oceans. Backed by terraced vineyards, it lies at the edge of a tranquil lake.
𝄆 (021) 903-5123.

Morgenhof ⑥
Established in 1692, this historic farm is owned by the Huchon-Cointreau family of Cognac, in France.
𝄆 (021) 889-5510.

Delheim ⑦
Particularly atmospheric is Delheim's wine cellar with its brick arches, wooden benches and mellow light.
𝄆 (021) 888-4600.

Delaire ⑤
"Vineyard in the sky" on the Helshoogte Pass.
𝄆 (021) 885-1756.

Neethlingshof ②
The Lord Neethling restaurant in the old manor house serves Thai, Indonesian and Vietnamese cuisine.
𝄆 (021) 883-8988.

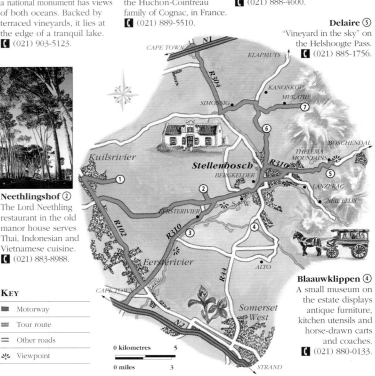

CAPE TOWN · N1 · KLAPMUTS · R304 · SIMONSIG · KANONKOP · MURATIE · ⑦ · ⑥ · Kuilsrivier · Stellenbosch · BERGKELDER · R310 · THELEMA MOUNTAINS · BOSCHENDAL · ⑤ · LANZERAC · NEIL ELLIS · ① · ② · EERSTERIVIER · S.F.W. · ③ · R102 · R310 · ④ · ALTO · R44 · Eersterivier · CAPE TOWN · Somerset West · STRAND · N2

KEY
▬ Motorway
▭ Tour route
═ Other roads
🍃 Viewpoint

0 kilometres 5
0 miles 3

Blaauwklippen ④
A small museum on the estate displays antique furniture, kitchen utensils and horse-drawn carts and coaches.
𝄆 (021) 880-0133.

Spier Estate ③
This complex consists of the manor house, a riverside pub, farm stall, three restaurants, wine centre, a dam and an open-air amphitheatre.

TIPS FOR DRIVERS
Tour length: *Due to the great number of wine estates, most visitors tour three or four cellars, stopping for lunch at one of the superb estate restaurants.*
Getting there: *Visitors need a car, unless they join one of the coach tours (see p 385).*

Spier Wine Estate ❸

Road map B5. Stellenbosch. N2, then R310. ☎ *(021) 809-1100.* 🚃 *Spier Vintage Train from Cape Town. Phone estate for schedules.* ☐ *tastings: 10am–4pm daily.* 🅿 ♿ 🍴 🛏 🛍 🚻 🅦 www.spier.co.za

BOUNDED BY the Eerste River, this extensive complex is the result of major renovations undertaken since 1993 after businessman Dick Enthoven purchased the estate from the Joubert family.

The Spier development also includes an experimental farm that was previously owned by the University of Stellenbosch. Future plans are to extend the present vineyards with mainly red grape varietals – merlot, cabernet, shiraz and pinotage – to be planted by 2002. Spier has three excellent restaurants; the Jonkershuis (*see p349*), offers a superb Indonesian and Cape Malay buffet.

Very popular with visitors are picnics on the rolling lawns surrounding the lake, after having stocked up on the mouthwatering delicacies available at Spier's farm stall.

In summer, the 1,075-seat open-air amphitheatre stages live entertainment ranging from opera, jazz and classical music to ballet and stand-up comedy.

Spier operates a luxury train, the Spier Vintage Train, which departs from its own private station close to the main Cape Town Station and delivers guests directly to the estate.

The beautiful formal gardens at Morgenhof

Morgenhof ❹

Road map B5. Stellenbosch. Off R44. ☎ *(021) 889-5510.* ☐ *9am–5:30pm Mon–Fri, 9am–5pm Sat & Sun.* ⬤ *Good Fri, 25 Dec, 1 Jan.* 🅿 🍴

FIRST ESTABLISHED IN 1692, the farm is now owned by the Huchon-Cointreau family, and produces 300,000 bottles of wine per year.

The sand-coloured, red-tiled estate buildings have been extensively renovated and are arranged around formal, French-style gardens. The airy tasting room features floor-to-ceiling feature windows that overlook a brick-vaulted cellar used for the barrel-ageing of white wines. Morgenhof's superb red wines, mainly from pinotage, merlot and cabernet sauvignon grapes, mature in a magni-

Choice white wine of the area

ficent cellar. In summer, lunch is served in the garden and, in winter, a fire is lit in the glass gazebo.

Vergelegen ❺

Road map B5. Somerset West. Lourensford Rd from R44. ☎ *(021) 847-1334.* ☐ *9:30am–4:30pm daily.* ⬤ *Good Fri, 25 Dec, 1 May.* 🅿 *10:30am, 11:30am, 3pm.* 🅿 🍴 🛍

THE VINES and the five old camphor trees in front of the manor house were planted in 1700, when the farm belonged to Willem Adriaan van der Stel. Today, Vergelegen is the joint property of Anglo-American Farms Limited and the mining giant De Beers, who contributed to the construction of a unique cellar, built into the slopes of Helderberg Mountain. The ripe grapes are fed into underground destalking, crushing and steel maturation tanks from above the ground, thus maximizing the effect of gravity and minimizing bruising. This results in a special brand of velvet-smooth wines.

The estate also has a wine museum and serves light lunches in the charming Lady Phillips Tea Garden (Lady Florence Phillips lived here from 1917 to 1940). The extensive renovations undertaken by the Phillips couple revealed the foundations of an octagonal garden, built by Willem van der Stel, which has now been restored.

Visitors enjoying an outdoor meal at the Spier estate

Boschendal Manor House ❻

Boschendal picnic basket

I N 1685, SIMON VAN DER STEL granted the land on which the manor house stands to the French Huguenot Jean le Long. Originally named "Bossendaal" (which literally means "forest and valley"), the property was transferred in 1715, together with adjacent fertile farmland, to another Huguenot settler, Abraham de Villiers. It remained in the wine-farming De Villiers family for 100 years. Jan de Villiers built the wine cellar and coach house in 1796. His youngest son, Paul, was responsible for Boschendal Manor House in its present H-shaped form, which he built in 1812. Rhodes Fruit Farms, a company that was established by Cecil John Rhodes in 1898, owns the historic estate today.

The Back Entrance
Visitors to Boschendal enter the elegant Manor House via the gabled back door.

Crafted Room Dividers
Screens divided the front and back rooms in elegant Cape Dutch homes. Boschendal's original teak-and-yellowwood screen is decorated with geometric designs in dark ebony.

Rounded pilasters
supported the end gables. The front and back pilasters have a more classic design.

STAR FEATURES

★ **Master Bedroom**

★ **Kitchen**

★ **Sitting Room**

Brick-paved courtyard

★ **Master Bedroom**
This antique stinkwood four-poster bed was crafted in 1810 by local artisans. It is decorated with a hand-crocheted lace hanging and a light, embroidered cotton bedspread, both of which date from around 1820.

VISITORS' CHECKLIST

Road map B5. On R45 from Stellenbosch. *(021) 870-4252.*
8:30am–4:30pm daily.
W www.boschendal.com

★ Kitchen
The original clay floor was washed with a mixture of water and cow dung to keep it cool and vermin-free. Walls were painted dark brown or red to hide the dirt.

Long-Case Clock
This Dutch clock, made in 1748, shows the date, day of the week, month, zodiac sign, moon phases and the tide in Amsterdam.

The sash windows are all mounted by similarly curved mouldings that reflect the shape of the gables.

★ Sitting-Room
A gabled armoire, crafted in oak with a walnut veneer, contains a collection of Ming Dynasty porcelain (1573–1620) created for the Chinese export market.

The reception room has an original section of the 1812 wall frieze.

The drop-fanlight had to be raised to allow visitors to enter.

FRIEZES

Painted wall decoration using oil-based pigments is a craft believed to derive from Europe. Pilasters and swags would feature in reception and dining rooms, entwined roses in drawing rooms and, in less important rooms, a dado of a single colour on a plain background would suffice. The original 1812 wall frieze (in the reception rooms) of black acorns and green leaves was discovered during restoration in 1975.

The Gift and Wine Shop
Boschendal wines, as well as preserves, souvenirs and gifts are sold at this shop.

Franschhoek ➐

ARMS IN THIS BEAUTIFUL VALLEY encircled by the Franschhoek and Groot Drakenstein mountains were granted to several French Huguenot families *(see p45)* by the Dutch East India Company (VOC) in 1694. The new settlers brought with them considerable skill as farmers, crafters and viticulturalists, leaving a marked influence on the area, which the Dutch named *De Fransche Hoek* (French Corner).

Victory statue

VISITORS' CHECKLIST

Road map B5. N1, exit 47, R45.
🏠 6,800. ✈ Cape Town 79 km
(49 miles) E. 🏢 Huguenot St,
(021) 876-3603. ⏰ 9am–5pm
daily. 🎨 Bastille Day (14 Jul).

A collection of period furniture in the Franschhoek Huguenot Museum

Exploring Franschhoek

Upon arrival, the town's French heritage is immediately evident in lilting names like Haute Cabrière, La Provence and L'Ormarins. The main attraction, besides an exquisite setting, is its gourmet cuisine, accompanied by the area's excellent wines. Around 30 restaurants *(see p348)* offer superb Malay, country and Provençale dishes.

Franschhoek's wine route was established in 1980 by Michael Trull, a former Johannesburg advertising executive. He formed the Vignerons de Franschhoek, with five founder cellars; today there are 20 estates.

A unique experience is a visit to **Cabrière Estate**. After an interesting cellar tour, host Achim von Arnim cleanly shears the neck off a bottle of his Pierre Jourdan sparkling wine with a sabre, an old technique known as *sabrage*, before serving the wine.

Visible at the top end of the main street is the **Huguenot Monument**, unveiled in 1948 to commemorate the arrival of the French settlers. Among the lawns and fragrant rose beds, a wide semi-circular colonnade forms an amphitheatre for three tall arches. They are representative of the Holy Trinity and rise behind the figure of a woman who stands on a globe with her feet on France. On a tall spire that surmounts the central arch is the "Sun of Righteousness".

🍷 Cabrière Estate
☎ (021) 876-2630. ⏰ 9am–5pm Mon–Fri, 11am–1pm Sat. Wine tasting: 11am, 3pm Mon–Fri & 11am Sat. 📷 for groups (by advance booking only). ♿

🏛 Huguenot Memorial Museum
Lambrecht St. ☎ (021) 876-2532. ⏰ 9am–5pm Mon–Sat, 2–5pm Sun. ⬤ Good Fri, 25 Dec. 🎨♿⬜📷
This museum was inaugurated in 1967 and functions primarily as a research facility covering the history and genealogy of the Cape's Huguenot families and their descendants. Among the exhibits are 18th-century furniture, Huguenot graphics, title deeds, and other early documents and letters. Of special note is a copy of the Edict of Nantes (1598), which permitted freedom of worship to Protestants in France.

There is also a fine collection of old Bibles, one of which was printed in 1636.

The Huguenot Monument in Franschhoek was built in 1943

Franschhoek's French Heritage

The emblem of Cabrière Estate

Franschhoek is a charming little country town with a distinctly French character. Wine-making traditions introduced by the early French Huguenot settlers are still pursued by viticulturalists with surnames like Malherbe, Joubert and du Toit. Restaurants called Le Quartier Français and La Petite Ferme offer Provençale cuisine in light-filled, airy interiors, while Chez Michel flies the French flag and serves delicacies like escargots, and Camembert marinated in Calvados brandy. Architecturally, the influence of French Classicism is evident in the graceful lines of the historic buildings. A good example is the Huguenot Memorial Museum, which was based on a design by the 18th-century French architect, Louis Michel Thibault.

Freedom of religion is symbolized by the dramatic central figure at the Huguenot Monument, which depicts a woman holding a Bible in her right hand and a broken chain in the left.

Refined classic gables like that of the Huguenot Museum replaced the Baroque exuberance of earlier gables.

Powdered wig

The tricorn was worn by gentlemen.

Mother-of-pearl buttons on garments were very fashionable.

THE FRENCH HUGUENOTS

After King Louis XIV of France revoked the Edict of Nantes in 1685, countless French Huguenots were forced to flee to Protestant countries. The Dutch East India Company's offer of a new life at the Cape of Good Hope was eagerly accepted by some 270 individuals.

Many Khoina were employed as slaves.

Hoop skirts were reinforced by stiff petticoats made from whalebone.

Grape presses like this one, which stands outside the Huguenot Museum, were used by the French settlers to produce the first wines of the region.

Restaurants in Franschhoek exude typical French joie de vivre and ambience.

Rocco Catoggio (1790–1858), depicted here with his grandson Rocco Cartozia de Villiers, married into a prominent Huguenot family.

Paarl ●

I̲N̲ 1687 FARMS WERE ALLOCATED to early Dutch colonists in the pretty Berg River Valley, which is flanked to the north by Paarl Mountain. The name Paarl comes from the Dutch *peerlbergh* (pearl mountain), given to the outcrops by early Dutch explorer Abraham Gabbema when he spotted the three smooth domes after a rain shower. Mica chips embedded in the granite glistened in the sun, giving it the appearance of a shiny pearl. The town of Paarl was established in 1690.

VISITORS' CHECKLIST

Road map B5. On the N1. 🏠 73,500. ✈ *Cape Town 56 km (35 miles) SW.* 🚌 *Huguenot Station, Lady Grey St.* 🚌 *International Hotel, Lady Grey St.* ℹ *216 Main Rd, (021) 872-3829.* ◻ *9am–5pm Mon–Fri, 9am–1pm Sat, 10am–1pm Sun.* 🎨 *Nederburg Wine Auction (Apr).*

The three granite domes on the outskirts of Paarl

Exploring Paarl

Large agricultural, financial and manufacturing companies are based in Paarl, making it a major player in the industry of the Western Cape. Its many tree-lined streets and graceful gabled homes, however, lend it a certain country charm. Paarl's 11-km (7-mile) Main Street, which runs along the Berg River, is shaded by oak trees and makes a very good starting point for exploring the town. A number of well-preserved 18th- and 19th-century Cape Dutch and Georgian houses are found along both sides of Main Street, some of the later ones displaying marked Victorian architectural influences.

La Concorde, a stately old structure in the Neo-Classical style built in 1956, is the headquarters of the *Kooperatiewe Wijnbouwers Vereeniging* (KWV), the Cooperative Wine Farmers Association. The KWV was a controlling body which aimed to administer wine production, check the quality and develop export markets. It has since been privatized.

Antique cupboard, Paarl Museum

Further along Main Street, the **Paarl Museum** presents historical aspects of the town. Exhibits include a collection of stinkwood chairs, a Dutch linen press and yellowwood armoires. An excellent porcelain collection features Imari, Kang Hsi, VOC and Canton pieces, and the kitchen is crammed with authentic utensils and furniture. Temporary displays covering a wide field of related themes, such as the Khoina (*see pp44–5*), are also arranged regularly.

Just off Paarl's Main Road lies **Laborie Estate**, first granted to a Huguenot settler in 1688. In 1774 it was acquired by Hendrick Louw, who subsequently built the Cape Dutch homestead on it. It was carefully restored after KWV purchased the estate in 1972.

🏛 Paarl Museum
303 Main St. ☎ (021) 872-2651. ◻ *9am–5pm Mon–Fri, 9am–noon Sat.* ● *Good Fri, 25 Dec.* 🎨 ▢ ✉

🍷 Laborie Estate
Off Main Rd, Paarl. ☎ (021) 807-3390. ◻ *wine tastings: 9am– 5pm Mon–Fri, also Sat in summer.* ● *25 Dec, 1 Jan.* ✉ *booked in advance.* 🎨 ♿ 🏠

ENVIRONS: Just off Main Street, opposite La Concorde, is Jan Phillips Drive, an 11-km (7-mile) route to Paarl Mountain. The 500 million-year-old massif is the world's second-largest granite outcrop, after Uluru in Australia, and can be climbed with the aid of handholds.

The entrance to the Paarl Mountain Nature Reserve also lies on Jan Phillips Drive. From here, visitors can gain access to the **Language Monument** *(Taalmonument)*. Designed by the architect Jan van Wyk, it was constructed around 1975, and is a tribute to the official recognition of the Afrikaans language 100 years earlier. The imposing monument is composed of three domes and three small pillars, all of varying height and size, as well as a tall obelisk and a soaring column. Each of the elements acknowledges the linguistic influence and contribution of a different culture.

Language Monument
Signposted from Main St. ☎ (021) 863-2800. ◻ *9am–10pm Tue–Sat, 9am–5pm Sun–Mon.* ♿

The Language Monument, Paarl

Paarl Winelands Tour ➒

PICTURESQUE WINE FARMS spread out to either side of the imposing Paarl Mountain with its three rounded domes. Estates dotted along its eastern slopes face the Klein Drakenstein and the Du Toitskloof mountains, while those on the west face look towards Table Mountain and False Bay.

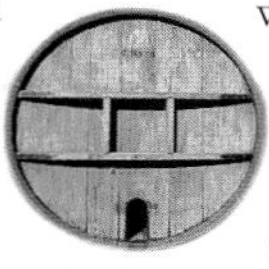

Wine barrel

The vineyards around Paarl produce about one-fifth of South Africa's total wine crop. All of the estates on this route, which include well-known names like Nederburg and Laborie, offer wine tasting and sales daily, except on Sundays. Certain farms arrange cellar tours by appointment only.

Nederburg ➄
Nederburg is famous for its annual Wine Auction, for many years presided over by British wine auctioneer Patrick Grubb.

Rhebokskloof Estate ➀
This estate is named after the small antelope (rhebok) that once lived in its valleys.

Fairview ➁
The estate's Saanen goats can climb and enter this tower via the spiralling wooden ramp that encircles it. Delicious goat's milk cheeses are sold.

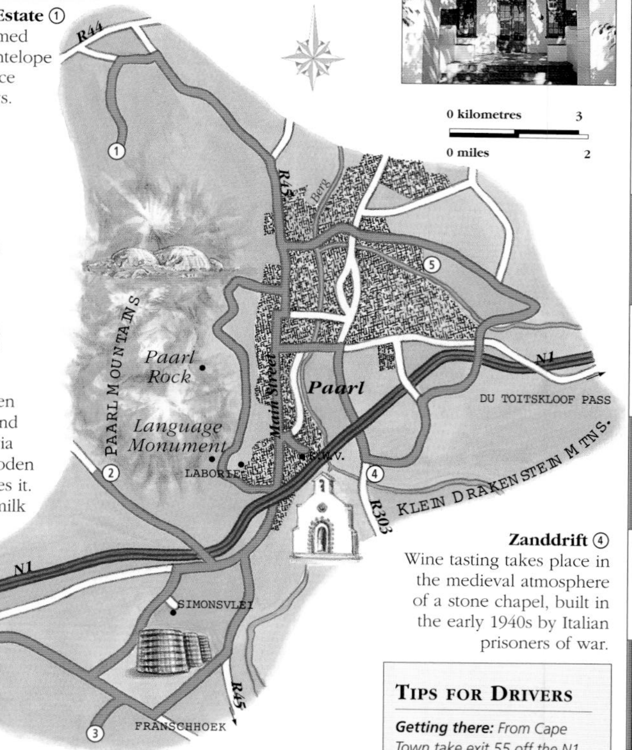

0 kilometres 3

0 miles 2

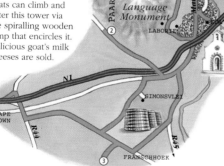

R44

Paarl Rock

PAARL MOUNTAINS

Language Monument

LABORIE

Main Street

Paarl

R45

DU TOITSKLOOF PASS

N1

KLEIN DRAKENSTEIN MTNS.

R303

Zanddrift ➃
Wine tasting takes place in the medieval atmosphere of a stone chapel, built in the early 1940s by Italian prisoners of war.

N1

CAPE TOWN

R44

SIMONSVLEI

FRANSCHHOEK

R45

KEY

▰ Motorway

▰ Tour route

═ Other roads

✻ Viewpoint

Backsberg ➂
In 1977 the late Sydney Back, a Paarl wine farmer, pioneered the formation of Paarl Vintners to address issues like the social upliftment of wine workers. Skills programmes include wine tasting.

TIPS FOR DRIVERS

Getting there: From Cape Town take exit 55 off the N1. This joins the R45, which then becomes Paarl's Main Street.
Stopping-off points: Simonsvlei and Laborie have formal restaurants.
Tour length: Depends on how many of the estates are visited (best limited to three or four).

The road to Worcester leads through the scenic Du Toit's Kloof Pass

Worcester ⑩

Road map B5. N1 from Cape Town via Du Toit's Kloof Pass. 🚶 91,000. 🚉 Worcester Station. 🛈 Worcester Information Center, (023) 348-2795.

WORCESTER, named after the Marquis of Worcester, the brother of one-time Cape governor Lord Charles Somerset lies some 110 km (68 miles) east of Cape Town. It is the biggest centre in the Breede River Valley and the largest producer of table grapes in South Africa. Its wineries produce about one quarter of the country's wine. Several of the estates, such as Nuy and Graham Beck, are open to the public for tastings and sales.

The attraction of a trip to Worcester is the drive through the Du Toit's Kloof Pass, which climbs to a height of 823 m (2,700 ft). Construction of the Huguenot Tunnel in 1988 shortened the pass by 11 km (7 miles), but the route still affords scenic views of Paarl and the Berg River Valley.

At Church Square in the town, there is a Garden of Remembrance designed by landscape artist Hugo Naude. The World War I Memorial is also here, together with a stone cairn erected at the time of the symbolic *Ossewa* (ox wagon) Trek of 1938 *(see p52)* that was undertaken to commemorate the historic Great Trek *(see pp48–9)*.

Hugo Naude House, located two blocks further south of Church Square, was the artist's home until his death in 1941. Today, it is an art gallery that hosts various revolving exhibitions featuring works by various contemporary South African artists. The exhibitions are changed monthly.

Northeast of Church Square, in a building known as Beck House, is the **Worcester Museum**, furnished like a late-19th-century home.

🏛 **Worcester Museum**
Cnr Church and Baring sts. 📞 (023) 342-2225. 🕐 9am–4:30pm Mon–Fri, 10:30am–4:30pm Sat. 🌑 public hols.
🏛 **Hugo Naude House**
Russell St. 📞 (023) 342-5802. 🕐 8:30am–4:30pm Mon–Fri, 9:30am–noon Sat. 🌑 public hols. ♿

ENVIRONS: The **Karoo National Botanic Garden**, located some 3 km (2 miles) north of Worcester, covers 1.44 sq km (0.556 sq miles) and contains plants that thrive in a semi-desert environment.

Jewel-bright mesembryanthemums are lovely in spring, while the unusual year-round species include the prehistoric welwitschias, and the *halfmens* (half-human) and quiver trees.

One section features plants grouped together according to regional and climatic zones. The succulent plant collection, the largest in Africa, is ranked by the International Succulent Organization as one of the most authentic of its kind in the world. There is also a Braille Trail.

Old water pump in Worcester

🌺 **Karoo Desert Botanic Garden**
Roux Rd, Worcester.
📞 (0233) 347-0785. 🕐 8am–7pm daily. 🎫 📷 (Aug–Oct only) ♿ 📷

Kleinplasie Open-Air Museum ⑪

See pp142–3.

The Dutch Reformed Church in Worcester

Robertson's Dutch Reformed Church

Robertson ⑫

Road map B5. R60 from Worcester or Swellendam. 15,950. Cnr Reitz and Voortrekker sts, (023) 626-4437. www.robertsonr62.com

R OBERTSON LIES IN THE Breede River Valley where sunny slopes create perfect conditions for vineyards and orchards. In addition to wine and table grapes, dried fruit is a major industry. The Robertson Wine Route comprises 24 private and co-operative

Swan, Montagu Inn

cellars, many of which, like van Loveren, are acclaimed for their choice Chardonnays.

Montagu ⑬

Road map B5. N15 fm Robertson. 11,000. Bath St, (023) 614-2471.

T HE CHARM OF Montagu lies in its many houses dating back to the early 1850s. In Long Street alone are 14 national monuments. The best known feature is the thermal springs (at a constant

43°C, 109°F), situated 2 km (1 mile) from town. The hotel and timeshare resort nearby offer a comfortable stay.

The scenery of the northern edge of the Langeberg range has led to the establishment of trails for hikers, mountain bikers and 4WD enthusiasts.

The route to Montagu from Robertson passes through a 16-m (52-ft) long tunnel, above which stands the ruined Sidney Fort built by the British during the South African War.

Avalon hot springs in Montagu

BOESMANSKLOOF TRAVERSE ⑭

This popular five-hour walking trail follows a gap through the Riviersonderend mountains. It runs between the rustic hamlets of Greyton and McGregor and can be tackled from either village. Hikers will need to be reasonably fit as the trail ascends and descends the mountainside. The views here are impressive, and the stream running along the scenic McGregor section of the trail ensures an abundant water supply. The Oakes Falls, 9 km (6 miles) from Greyton, a series of waterfalls and pools, are ideal for swimming. There are no overnight huts.

The start of the hiking trail from Greyton

ROBERTSON

McGregor

BONNIEVALE

Takkap

Hoeks

Nooienskop
1,391 m (4,562 ft)

P Die Galg
Interpretation Trail Start

Interpretation Trail End

Gobos

Oakes Falls

Genadendal

Perdekop
1,346 m (4,414 ft)

Skilpadkop
1,510 m (4,952 ft)

Greyton

P

Riviersonderend

R406

R406

CALEDON AND SWELLENDAM

TIPS FOR WALKERS

Starting point: Die Galg, 14 km (9 miles) SW of McGregor; or from Main Street in Greyton.
Getting there: R21 from Robertson; or N2 to Caledon, take the McGregor turn-off.
Best time: Avoid winter (Jun–Aug). Book permits three months ahead from Vrolijkheid Nature Reserve. (023) 625-1671.

KEY

══ Tarred road

- - Trail

⚶ Viewpoint

0 kilometres 4

0 miles 2

Kleinplasie Open-Air Museum ⓫

Candle holder

THE RECREATED BUILDINGS of this living "little farm" museum, which opened in 1981, portray the lifestyle of the early Cape pioneer farmer. Each one houses a particular home industry activity that was practised between 1690 and 1900. Here, visitors can watch cows being milked, wholewheat bread and traditional *melktert* (milk tart) being baked in an outdoor oven and the making of tallow candles and soap. At times the museum hosts seasonal activities such as wheat threshing and winnowing, grape treading and the distilling of *witblits* (a potent homemade brandy).

Tobacco Shed
Dried tobacco leaves are twisted together in this 19th-century, windowless farm shed.

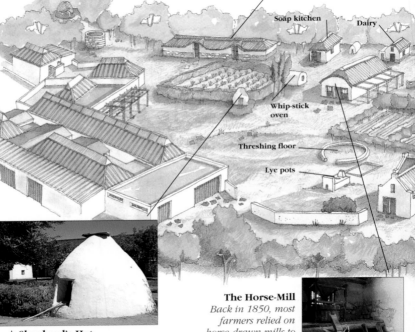

Soap kitchen

Dairy

Whip-stick oven

Threshing floor

Lye pots

The Horse-Mill
Back in 1850, most farmers relied on horse-drawn mills to grind flour, a slow, laborious process.

★ Shepherd's Hut
Shepherds who tended distant flocks lived in temporary shelters like this one. In the treeless Karoo, domed stone roofs were used instead of wooden beams and trusses.

STAR FEATURES

★ Shepherd's Hut

★ Labourer's Cottage

★ The Blacksmith

Canisters
This collection of 19th-century storage tins is displayed in the museum restaurant. Occasionally, these tins are found in "junk" stores today.

★ **The Blacksmith**
The smithy door, as well as the bellows used by the black-smith, date from 1820. The rest of the building has walls cast in clay and gables built in raw brick. The blacksmith can be seen daily, forging nails, hinges, forks and tripods.

VISITORS' CHECKLIST

Road map B5. N1, signposted fm Worcester. *(023) 342-2225.* check website for times www.worcester.org.za/kleinplasie.

★ **Labourer's Cottage**
Simply furnished and thatched with rye straw, one-roomed dwellings like this one date from the mid-19th century. They housed farm labourers and their families.

Farmhouse

Water mill

Wine cellar

Dipping kraal

Graveyard

Harness Room
This is a replica of an 1816 coach house, stable and harness room. The tanning of skins took place here, too.

BRANDY DISTILLING

Homemade brandies, first distilled in 1672 from peaches and apricots, became known as *witblits* (white lightning). To create this potent liquor, crushed fruit is fermented in large vats for ten days. The pulp is then poured into a brandy still and heated so that the alcohol evaporates. The resulting vapour is conducted from the dome of the still into a water-cooled condensation spiral, which causes the alcohol to become liquid again. The first extraction, called the "heads", is discarded. Only the second, "the heart", is bottled; the rest is used as liniment.

Furnace   Still

Coil

Brandy

Donkey Power
To draw water, a donkey rotated the bucket pump. Small buckets on a looped chain scooped water from the well and emptied it into irrigation furrows.

THE WESTERN COASTAL TERRACE

THE DRY, SUNBAKED LANDSCAPE OF SOUTH AFRICA'S *western coastal terrace is bounded to the east by the rugged Cedarberg mountain range and to the west by the rocky, wind-blown Atlantic coastline. An unexpected surprise in this forbidding terrain is the appearance every spring of colourful fields of exquisite wildflowers in Namaqualand, the West Coast's most famous tourist attraction.*

The West Coast extends north of Cape Town to the Namibian border, where the fringes of the Namib desert epitomize the extremes of this vast, rain-deprived area. The arid, bleak and infertile vegetation zones support only hardy, drought-resistant succulents and geophytes (plants whose bulbs, corms or tubers store water and nutrients). The *fynbos* area south of Nieuwoudtville possesses a stark beauty, embodied in the weird forms of the Cedarberg's outcrops that were eroded over millennia by wind and rain.

Further inland the country's wheatbelt centres on Malmesbury, and is an area of undulating golden corn whose texture changes constantly with the play of light on the rippling fields.

The upwelling of the Atlantic Ocean's cold Benguela Current along the coast brings rich phytoplanktonic nutrients to the surface, attracting vast shoals of pelagic fish (especially anchovies). This harvest from the sea supports an important fishing industry in the Western Cape. Saldanha Bay, a rather unappealing industrial town, is the fishing and seafood processing hub. It is also a major centre for the export of iron ore, which is mined at Sishen further inland in the Northern Cape Province. Sishen is the site of the largest iron ore deposits in the world.

The Namaqualand is an arid belt stretching north of the Cedarberg almost to the Namibian border, which is marked by the mighty Orange River. This belt only receives about 140 mm (6 inches) of rainfall during March and April, but the brief downpours provide sufficient moisture to clothe the landscape with colourful blooms from August to October every year.

Fishing nets with bright yellow floats on the beach at St Helena Bay

◁ A carpet of yellow *Pentzia suffruticosa* frames this fisherman's cottage at Paternoster

Exploring the Western Coastal Terrace

ALTHOUGH FIRST APPEARANCES seem to indicate that the West Coast is a hot, barren wilderness, it is a magnet to visitors during the spring months when flowering daisies and gazanias paint the landscape with bold colour splashes. The region is also known for its spectacular walking and hiking trails in the Cedarberg mountains, which are famous for their contorted rock formations and breathtaking views. Along the coastline, the cold waters of the Atlantic yield a vast array of delicious seafood, from rock lobster and black mussels to fresh linefish, which can be sampled at a number of *skerms* (open-air restaurants) that have been established on the beaches.

Fishing trawlers at anchor in Lambert's Bay harbour

The Wolfberg Arch in the Cedarberg

SIGHTS AT A GLANCE

Cedarberg **9**
Citrusdal **7**
Clanwilliam **8**
Darling **4**
Lambert's Bay **3**
Malmesbury **5**
Tulbagh **6**

West Coast **1**
West Coast National Park pp150–1 **2**

Driving Tour
Namaqualand Tour **10**

KEY

▭	National route
▭	Other route
▭	Scenic route
~	River, lake or dam
···	Park or reserve boundary
☆	Viewpoint

0 kilometres 50

0 miles 25

White Namaqualand daisies *(Dimorphotheca pluvialis)*, tall yellow bulbinellas *(Bulbinella floribunda)* and magenta *Senecio* open their petals to the sun

GETTING AROUND

A car is essential for touring this region as no regular public transport service exists. Private coach companies do operate along this section of coast however. During the flower season, a large number of organized coach tours are available from operators based in Cape Town. The N7, a major national route, runs straight up the West Coast from Cape Town to the Namibian border, with main roads leading off to the coast and interior. Between Cape Town and St Helena Bay, the R27 offers a more scenic route with intermittent views of the coastline. The closest international airport is in Cape Town.

SEE ALSO

Upington

SPRINGBOK

NAMAQUALAND
oen

N7

Olifants

R27

R27

Calvinia

R27

VANRHYNSDORP

R364

LAMBERT'S BAY
3
R364

9 CEDARBERG

8 CLANWILLIAM
Clanwilliam Dam

Doring

7 CITRUSDAL

KAGGA KAMMA

EST COAST
R27

1

PATERNOSTER
Berg

PIKETBERG

GEBAAN

R44

**EST
OAST
TIONAL
ARK**

2
R27

4

DARLING 5

6 TULBAGH

MALMESBURY

N7

*Cape
Town*

Lookout, West Coast National Park

Fishermen drag their boat to the water at Paternoster

The West Coast ❶

Road map A4, A5.

FROM CAPE TOWN, the R27 leads up the West Coast to the Olifants River, linking the coastal towns. Between Milnerton, Bloubergstrand and Melkbosstrand, Marine Drive (M14), which becomes Otto Du Plessis Drive, is a scenic road with wonderful views of the dunes and sea. Travelling north, the village of Bloubergstrand, today a sought-after residential area, is famous for its unsurpassed views of Table Mountain seen across the 16-km (10-mile) wide expanse of Table Bay, and lies at the foot of the Blouberg (blue mountain). The broad beaches and bays of Bloubergstrand are popular with watersports enthusiasts and families, although south-easterly summer gales can create windy conditions.

Heading north along the R27, silver domes come into view. They belong to **Koeberg Nuclear Power Station**, the only nuclear facility in Africa, which offers guided tours.

A left turn from the R27 onto the R315 leads to Yzerfontein, whose claim to fame is its prolific crayfish (rock lobster) reserves. The sweet-tasting flesh of this shellfish is a sought-after local delicacy and during the crayfishing season (Dec–Apr), the local campsite attracts countless divers and their families. Permits, allowing daily catches of four crayfish per person, are obtainable at any post office.

Continuing north on the R27, past the industrial fishing hub and harbour of Saldanha, is Vredenburg. From here, a 16-km (10-mile) drive leads to Paternoster, a typical little wind-blown fishing village with whitewashed cottages. Legend recounts that the Portuguese sailors shipwrecked here recited the Paternoster (Our Father) to give thanks for their survival.

Around a rocky headland, the village of **St Helena** perches at the edge of a sheltered bay. Just before the village a sign-posted turnoff leads to the monument commemorating Portuguese navigator Vasco da Gama's landing on these shores on St Helena's Day, 7 November, in 1497.

The fishing industry here benefits from the cold, north-flowing Benguela Current. It ensures a ready supply of rich nutrients that sustain the vast populations of anchovies and other shoals of pelagic fish.

Koeberg Nuclear Power Station
📞 *(021) 550-4089.* ⏰ *7:30am–4:30pm Mon–Fri.* ● *public hols.* 📷 *ring to book.*

West Coast National Park ❷

See pp150–1.

A seal pup relaxes on the rocks of Bird Island, Lambert's Bay

Lambert's Bay ❸

Road map A4. 🏘 *5,000.* 🏢 *Church St, Lambert's Bay (027) 432-1000. Lambert's Bay Charter Office (083) 726-2207.* ⏰ *8am daily (groups only).*

THIS LITTLE FISHING town, a two-hour drive north of St Helena on a gravel road, was named after Rear-Admiral Sir Robert Lambert. This senior Royal Navy officer who was stationed in Durban, monitored the marine survey of this section of coastline.

For visitors, the main attraction is **Bird Island**, which lies

---

OPEN-AIR SEAFOOD FEASTS

Along the West Coast, restaurateurs have established open-air eating places known as *skerms* (Afrikaans for "shelters") with names like Die Strandloper *(see p349)*, in Langebaan,

and Die Muisbosskerm *(see p349)*, in Lambert's Bay. Reed roofs provide shade and mussel shells are used as utensils, but the major appeal is the fresh seafood on offer: smoked angelfish, *snoek* (a large gamefish that tastes best when barbecued), spicy mussel stews, thin slices of *perlemoen* (abalone), and calamari.

Lunch at Die Strandloper

about 100 m (328 ft) offshore and is accessible via a break-water-cum-harbour wall.

The island is a breeding ground for thousands of jackass penguins, Cape cormorants and the striking Cape gannet with its painted face. A viewing tower allows visitors to remain unobtrusive while observing the birds' behaviour.

The Lambert's Bay Charter Office offers one-hour trips on a boat called *Wolf-T,* which leaves at 8am every day. From August to October, groups of visitors are taken out to spot southern right whales, while penguins, Cape fur seals and Heaviside's dolphins, endemic to the West Coast, can be seen throughout the year. Guided excursions through the striated dunes in the southernmost reaches of the Namib desert are unfortunately no longer available.

Darling ❹

Road map B5. R307. 👥 *4,750.* ℹ️
Cnr Pastorie & Hill sts, (022) 492-3361.

DARLING IS SURROUNDED by a farming region of wheat-fields, vineyards, sheep and dairy cattle, but the small town is best known for its annual springflower show *(see p.34).* The first show was held in 1917, and the tradition has been maintained ever since.

Darling also lays claim to satirist Pieter-Dirk Uys *(see p55),*

A National Monument on historical Church Street in Tulbach

who gained fame for the portrayal of his female alter ego, Evita Bezuidenhout, fictitious ambassadress of the equally fictitious homeland called Baphetikosweti. **Evita se Perron** (Evita's platform) is situated on a defunct railway platform and draws crowds to hear the hilarious, razor-sharp analyses of local politics.

🎭 Evita se Perron

📞 *(022) 492-2831.* 🅿️ 🍴 ♿ 🛍️

Malmesbury ❺

Road map B5. 👥 *15,900.* 🚌 *Boko-mo Rd.* ℹ️ *De Bron Centre, (022) 487-1133.*

MALMESBURY, THE HEART of South Africa's wheatland, lies in the *Swartland* (black country), a term that has, at

times, been attributed to the region's soil, at others to its renosterbush, a local shrub that turns a dark hue in winter. This town is South Africa's major wheat distributor and site of one of its largest flour mills. The surrounding wheat-fields undergo constant meta-morphosis, and the velvety shoots rippling in the breeze or cropped furrows with bales piled high are a lovely sight.

Tulbagh ❻

Road map B5. R44. 👥 *3,353.* 🚉
Station Rd. 🚌 *along Church St.*
ℹ️ *4 Church St, (023) 230-1348.*

IN 1700, GOVERNOR Willem Adriaan van der Stel initiated a new settlement in the Breede River Valley, naming it Tulbagh after his predecessor.

Encircled by the Witzenberg and Winterhoek mountains, the town made headlines in 1969 when it was hit by an earthquake measuring 6.3 on the Richter scale. Eight people died and many historic buildings were badly damaged. The disaster resulted in a five-year restoration project undertaken along Church Street, lined with no less than 32 18th- and 19th-century Victorian and Cape Dutch homes. The oldest building, Oude Kerk (old church) Volksmuseum, dates back to 1743 and contains the original pulpit, pews and Bible. De Oude Herberg, Tulbagh's first boarding house (1885), is now a guest house and art gallery.

Cape gannets populate Bird Island in their thousands

West Coast National Park ➋

Watch out – tortoises on the road

THE WEST COAST NATIONAL PARK encompasses Langebaan Lagoon, the islands Schaapen, Jutten, Marcus and Malgas, and the Postberg Nature Reserve, which is opened to the public each spring (Aug–Sep) when it is carpeted with colourful wildflowers like daisies and gazanias.

The park is one of South Africa's most important wetlands, harbouring some 250 000 waterbirds including plovers, herons, ibis, and black oystercatchers. Antelope species such as eland, kudu and zebra can also be seen. Accommodation in the park consists of a guesthouse, cottages and a houseboat on the lagoon.

Cape cormorants
Abundant on the coast, they feed on pelagic shoaling fish, but have been affected by overfishing.

SEABIRDS

Langebaan Lagoon, 15 km (9 miles) long, at an average depth of 1 m (3 ft), offers a sheltered haven for a great number of seabirds, including waders, gulls, flamingos, and pelicans. Resident and migrant species take advantage of the Atlantic's nutrient-rich water to rear their chicks.

The curlew sandpiper's curved bill enables it to probe for small crustaceans.

Hartlaub's gulls are endemic to the West Coast and forage for food along the shore in the early morning hours.

Lesser flamingos, distinguished from greater flamingos by their smaller size and red bill, often congregate in large flocks.

White Pelicans
Langebaan Lagoon is home to one of only a handful of white pelican breeding colonies in Southern Africa. The species feeds on fish, which it scoops up in the large pouch under its beak. Pelicans fly and feed in formation.

★ **Geelbek Goldfields Environmental Centre**
This educational centre in the park is a mine of fascinating information on the fauna, flora and ecology of the region. Birdwatchers can observe many different species from the nearby hide.

STAR FEATURE

★ **Geelbek Goldfields Environmental Centre**

Plankie
Stoney Head
Kreeftebaai
Vondeling Island
Pree
Sixteen Mile Beach
Churchhaven
Geelb Goldfie Environn Cen
Bird hide
Strandveld Educational Trail
Entrance

Yzerfontein

| 0 kilometres | 5 |
| 0 miles | 2.5 |

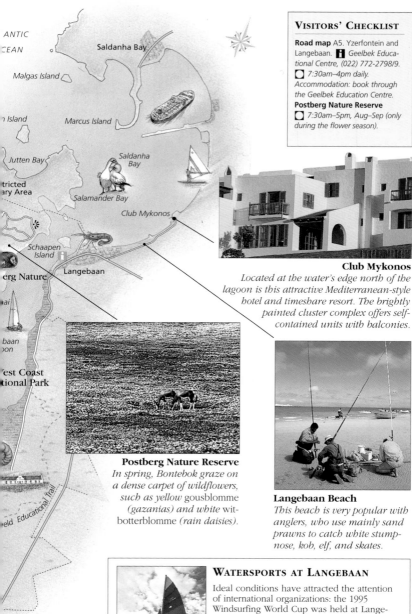

ANTIC
CEAN

Saldanha Bay

Malgas Island

n Island   Marcus Island

Saldanha
Bay

Jutten Bay

tricted
ary Area

Salamander Bay

Club Mykonos

Schaapen
Island

rg Nature   Langebaan

ai

baan
on

est Coast
tional Park

eld Educational Trail

Club Mykonos
Located at the water's edge north of the lagoon is this attractive Mediterranean-style hotel and timeshare resort. The brightly painted cluster complex offers self-contained units with balconies.

Postberg Nature Reserve
In spring, Bontebok graze on a dense carpet of wildflowers, such as yellow gousblomme *(gazanias) and white wit-botterblomme (rain daisies).*

Langebaan Beach
This beach is very popular with anglers, who use mainly sand prawns to catch white stump-nose, kob, elf, and skates.

KEY

══ Tarred road

══ Untarred road

-- Trail

▌ Information

※ Viewpoint

WATERSPORTS AT LANGEBAAN

Ideal conditions have attracted the attention of international organizations: the 1995 Windsurfing World Cup was held at Langebaan Lagoon, and in 1998 it was nominated to host the prestigious Production-Board World Championships. In order to protect the natural environment without curtailing the activities of other interest groups, the lagoon has been zoned into three recreational areas, with the northern tip demarcated for all watersports enthusiasts and the central part of the lagoon out of bounds for motorboats.

Catamaran on the beach

Zinc-roofed houses along Church Street in Clanwilliam

Citrusdal ❼

Road map B4. 🏚 *2,900*. 🚉 *fm Cape Town station to Church St.* 🛈 *Voortrekker St, (022) 921-3210.*

Frost-free winters and the Olifants River Irrigation Scheme have made Citrusdal South Africa's third-largest citrus district. The first orchard was planted with seedlings from Van Riebeeck's garden at the foot of Table Mountain *(see pp74–5)*. One tree, after bearing fruit for some 250 years, is now a national monument.

The Goede Hoop Citrus Co-operative has initiated scenic mountain bike trails around Citrusdal, like the old Ceres and Piekenierskloof passes.

Clanwilliam ❽

Road map B4. 🏚 *4,000*. 🚉 *fm Cape Town station.* 🛈 *Main Rd, (027) 482-2024.*

Clanwilliam is the head-quarters of the *rooibos* (red bush) tea industry. The shoots of the wild shrub are used to make a caffeine-free tea that is low in tannins and also considered to have medicinal properties.

Clanwilliam Dam, encircled by the Cedarberg Mountains, stretches for 18 km (11 miles) and is popular with water-skiers. Wooden holiday cabins line the banks, and an attractive camp-site has been established right at the water's edge.

Cedarberg ❾

Road map B4. Ceres. Algeria Cape Nature Conservation turnoff fm N7. 🛈 *(027) 482-2812. Anyone wishing to hike or stay in the Cedarberg area will require a permit.* 🅰 🚶 🎣 🚗

From the north, the Cedarberg is reached via Pakhuis Pass and the Biedouw Valley, 50 km (31 miles) from Clanwilliam. Coming from the south, take the N7 from Citrusdal. The Cedarberg range is a surreal wilderness of sandstone peaks that have been eroded into jagged formations. It is part of the Cedarberg Wilderness Area which was proclaimed in 1973 and covers 710 sq km (274 sq miles). The attraction of the range is its recreational appeal – walks, hikes, camping and wonderful views. The southern part, in particular, is popular for its dramatic rock formations: the Maltese Cross, a 20-m (66-ft) high pillar, and the Wolfberg Arch with its sweeping views of the area. At the Wolfberg Cracks, the main fissure measures over 30 m (98 ft). The snow protea *(Protea cryophila)*, endemic to the upper reaches of the range, occurs on the Sneeuberg which, at 2,028 m (6,654 ft), is the highest peak. The Clanwilliam cedar, after which the area was named, is a species that is protected in the Cedarberg Wilderness Area. At the southern end of the Cedarberg lies the **Kagga Kamma** reserve where some of the last Bushman families live. Tours allow you to interact with members of the clan and observe fire-making and beadcraft skills. Artifacts are for sale (a portion of the proceeds goes back to the community). Game drives are arranged and cottages and huts offer accommodation.

Road marker at Kagga Kamma

🐾 Kagga Kamma
Southern Cedarberg. 🛈 *Tour reservations (021) 872-4343 (to be prebooked).* 🌙 *daily.* 🛏 🍴 *(meals included).* 🛎

Scenic view over Clanwilliam Dam to the Cedarberg mountains

Rock Formations of the Cedarberg

During the palaeozoic pre-Karoo Era several hundred million years ago, the formations that over time became the Cape Folded Mountains were under water. Of the sandstones, shales and quartzites of these Cape formations, Table Mountain sandstone was the most resilient. In the Karoo Period, tectonic forces produced the crumpled folds of the Cape mountains. Subsequent erosion wore away the soft rock, leaving the harder layer. The resulting formations can be seen today in the Cedarberg's twisted landscape. The original grey-coloured sandstone of the bizarre terrain has frequently been stained a rich red by iron oxides.

Hiking
Paths made by woodcutters some 100 years ago now provide access for hikers.

Softer layers erode faster, causing a thinner base.

THE MALTESE CROSS
This unusual 20-m (66-ft) high rock formation, a day hike from Dwarsrivier Farm (Sanddrif), consists partly of Table Mountain sandstone. More resistant to erosion, it forms the upper portion of the cross.

Cedarberg Cedar
Some 8,000 trees are planted annually to ensure the survival of this endemic species. The cedars were once popularly used as telephone poles.

The scree slope, composed of fallen debris from above.

Wolfberg Cracks
Lovely views greet hikers at the Wolfberg Cracks, a 75-minute walk from the Wolfberg Arch.

Wolfberg Arch
The majestic Wolfberg Arch is the Cedarberg's most unique formation. A favourite with photographers, it provides a natural frame for memorable images.

Bizarre rock sculptures supported on brittle pillars.

Cracks are caused by the expansion and contraction of the rock.

The Arch, 30 m (98 ft) high, overlooks a region known as the Tankwa Karoo.

Erosion
Over aeons, wind and water have carved the Cedarberg into a fairytale landscape. Pinnacles, arches and fissures resemble the strange castles of another world, while the rock outcrops seem alive with gargoyles and goblins.

Namaqualand Tour ⑩

NAMAQUALAND, an area of about 48,000 sq km (18,500 sq miles), from the Orange River in the north to the mouth of the Olifants River in the south, is a region of sharp contrasts. In spring, this scrub-covered, arid land blazes with colour – from fuchsia pinks to neon yellows and oranges – as a myriad daisies and flowering succulents open their petals to the sun. The seeds of the drought-resistant plants lie dormant in the soil during the dry months, but if the first rains (usually around March and April) are good, they burst into bloom from August to October.

Gazania krebsiana

KEETMANSHOO

Orange

Alexander Bay

Noordoewer

Steinkopf

R382

R355

Springbo

Kamieskr

Hondeklipbaai

0 kilometres   50
0 miles   25

Skilpad Wild Flower Reserve ⑥
Lying 17 km (11 miles) west of Kamieskroon, the reserve was purchased by WWF-SA (World Wide Fund for Nature in South Africa) in 1993 to protect the area's plant life. The higher rainfall resulting from the reserve's proximity to the West Coast guarantees excellent displays. Bright orange daisies (*Ursinia* sp) and gazanias are at their most spectacular here.

Tienie Versveld Reserve ①
After attending the Darling wildflower and orchid shows, visitors can drive to this nearby reserve and view expanses of wildflowers in their natural habitat. Namaqualand's best displays vary from season to season, depending on the rainfall patterns.

Postberg Nature Reserve ②
This is the most popular flower-viewing spot among locals, as it is an easy day-trip from Cape Town, and visitors are not often disappointed at its multicoloured bands of annuals stretching as far as the eye can see.

KEY

▬ Tour route

= Other roads

--- Park boundary

🌼 Viewpoint

🔲 Wildflower viewing

Goegap Nature Reserve ⑦
Situated 15 km (9 miles) east of Springbok, the "capital" of Namaqualand, the Goegap Nature Reserve's flat plains and granite koppies support hundreds of succulents. Over the years, the reserve has recorded 580 plant species within its boundaries.

Nieuwoudtville Wildflower Reserve ⑤
This reserve contains the world's largest concentration of geophytes (plants with bulbs, corms or tubers). Of the 300 plant species, the more prominent ones are the irises and lily family.

Vanrhynsdorp ④
This town is situated in the stony *Knersvlakte* (a name that literally translates as "gnashing plains"). Spring ushers in dramatic displays of succulents such as *vygies*, and annuals like *botterblom* and *gousblom* (*Ursinia* sp).

Biedouw Valley ③
This valley is famous for its mesembryanthemums, a succulent species more commonly known by its Afrikaans name, *vygie*. Daisies and mesembryanthemums form the major group of Namaqualand's 4,000 floral species.

TIPS FOR DRIVERS

Tour length: *Due to the extent of the area, trips can vary from one to three days. For details of coach tours, call Captour.*
☎ *(021) 426-4260.*
When to go: *Flowers bloom Aug–Oct – call Namaqualand Information Bureau for the best viewing areas. Flowers only open on sunny days, and are best between 11am and 4pm; drive with the sun behind you and flowers facing you.*
Where to stay and eat: *Each town has its own hotel, as well as guesthouses and a campsite. Private homes may also offer accommodation.*
ℹ *Namaqualand Information Bureau, (0277) 12-8000.*

Exploring the Southern Cape

A<small>N ALTERNATIVE ROUTE</small> to the N2 over Sir Lowry's Pass, which drops down into wheatfields and farmland dotted with cattle and woolly merino sheep, is the R44, a scenic road that hugs the coastline from Gordon's Bay to Hermanus. Coastal hamlets like Cape Agulhas – official meeting point of two oceans – offer a calm contrast to the majestic passes that lead through the mountains. Oudtshoorn is where the mansions of former "ostrich barons" can be seen, and nearby lies the underground splendour of the Cango Caves.

MATJIESFONT

N1
Worcester and
Cape Town

Touws

BARRYD
SWELLENDAM

Wind-blown sand dunes at De Hoop Nature Reserve

N2

Breede

Cape Town

R317

R318

CALEDON

BETTY'S
BAY
KLEINMOND
HERMANUS
R326
Walker Bay
R43

BREDASDORP
R316

DE HO
NATU
RESE

GANSBAAI

ARNISTON

CAPE AGULHAS

Rocky beach near Arniston's cave

GETTING AROUND

The N2 over Sir Lowry's Pass cuts right across the Southe Cape to Riversdale, where the R323 heads north to Oud hoorn, the Cango Caves and the country's most dramat passes, which are linked by the R328. All of the coastal towns are accessed via main routes feeding off the N2. The De Hoop Nature Reserve can be reached via an untarred road from both Bredasdorp and the N2. Coach tours offer day trips, otherwise public transport service are severely limited, so a car is essential for touring this region. The closest international airport is in Cape Tow

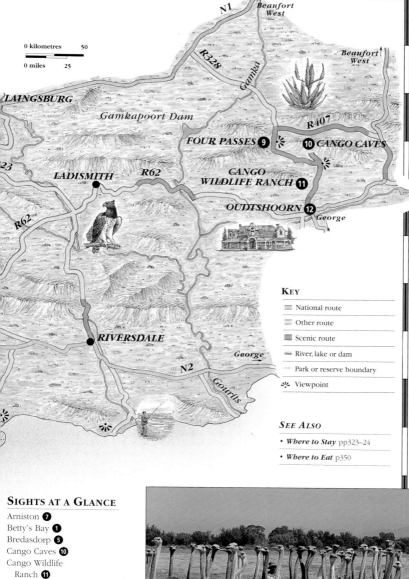

FOUR PASSES 9

10 **CANGO CAVES**

CANGO WILDLIFE RANCH 11

OUDTSHOORN 12

George

LAINGSBURG

Gamkapoort Dam

LADISMITH

R62

R62

23

RIVERSDALE

George

N2

Beaufort West

N1

R328

Gamka

Beaufort West

R407

KEY

National route

Other route

Scenic route

River, lake or dam

Park or reserve boundary

Viewpoint

SEE ALSO

- **Where to Stay** pp323–24

- **Where to Eat** p350

SIGHTS AT A GLANCE

Arniston 7

Betty's Bay 1

Bredasdorp 5

Cango Caves 10

Cango Wildlife
  Ranch 11

Cape Agulhas 6

De Hoop Nature
  Reserve 8

Gansbaai 4

Hermanus 3

Kleinmond 2

Oudtshoorn 12

Driving Tour

Four Passes Tour pp164–5 9

A group of residents at High Gate Ostrich Farm, near Oudtshoorn

Betty's Bay ❶

Road map B5. R44 SE of Gordon's Bay.
🏠 *170.* ✈ *Cape Town International.*
ℹ *Kleinmond, (028) 271-5657.*

T HIS SEASIDE VILLAGE, named
after Betty Youlden, the
daughter of a property deve-
loper who lived here in the
1900s, is a popular weekend
retreat. People cherish its
remote solitude, a testament
to which is the fact that
electrification of some local
homes occurred only in 1993.

Of significance is the **Harold
Porter National Botanical
Garden** on the slopes of the
Kogelberg which rises behind
Betty's Bay. Harold Porter, a
partner in a property agents'
business in the town, bought
this tract of land in 1938 to
preserve the rich mountain
and coastal *fynbos* vegetation.
Over 1,600 species of ericas,
proteas and watsonias – one
of the densest
concentrations in
the Western Cape
– attract sugar-
birds and sunbirds. A
permit is required
for the Leopard
Kloof Trail that
runs through
dense riverine forest
to a picturesque
waterfall. The penguin
reserve at Stoney Point
protects a small breed-
ing colony of African
jackass penguins.

**Erica, Harold
Porter Gardens**

🌿 **Harold Porter National
Botanical Garden**
☎ *(028) 272-9311.* 🕐 *8am–
4:30pm (7pm summer) daily.*
♿ 🖥 🚶 🚻

The tranquil Harold Porter Botanical Gardens at Betty's Bay

Wide lagoon mouth and beach at Kleinmond

Kleinmond ❷

Road map B5. R44 E of Betty's Bay. 🏠
2,900. ℹ *Spar Centre (028) 271-5657.*

S URROUNDING KLEINMOND, the
stony hills with their thin
green veneer of *fynbos* scrub
once harboured small bands
of Khoina and runaway slaves.

In the 1920s Klein-
mond, at the foot
of the Palmietberg,
was a fishing settle-
ment; today it is a
holiday spot where
rock angling for
kabeljou (kob), and
fishing for yellowtail
and tunny are popular
pastimes. Kleinmond
Lagoon, where the Pal-
miet River reaches the
sea, offers safe swim-
ming and canoeing.

Visitors can appreciate
the beautiful sea and mountain vistas from a well-planned
network of hiking trails in the
Kogelberg Nature Reserve
and maybe even
glimpse some
of the dainty, shy gazelle
species like klipspringer, as
well as grysbok and steenbok
that occur in the coastal
fynbos and on the lower
slopes of the mountain.

🌿 **Kogelberg Nature
Reserve**
Betty's Bay. ☎ *(028) 271-5138.*
🕐 *8am–5pm daily.* ♿ 🚶

Hermanus ❸

Road map B5. 🏠 *6,600.* 🚉 *Bot River
30 km (18 miles) N on N2.* ℹ *Hermanus Stn, Mitchell St, (028) 312-2629.*

O NCE A FASHIONABLE seaside
and retirement resort with
august establishments like the
Marine, Windsor and Astoria
hotels, Hermanus's grandeur
is, today, a little faded.

The focal point of the town
is the **Old Harbour Museum**,
which traces the history of
the town's whaling days, and
contains a whale skull and
old weapons. Fishermen's
boats dating from 1850 to the
mid-1900s lie restored and
hull-up on the old ramp. On
the higher rocks are *bokkom*
stands, racks on which fish
are hung to dry in the sun.

Today, Hermanus is famous
for its superb whale-watching
sites. Every year, southern
right whales *(see p122–3)* migrate
from the subantarctic to calve
in the shelter of Walker Bay.
They arrive in June and leave
again by December, but the
peak whale-watching season
is from September to October
when visitors are guaranteed
daily sightings of the large
mammals frolicking offshore.

The town's official whale crier blows his kelp horn as he walks along Main Street, bearing a signboard that shows the best daily sighting places.

Despite having lost some of its charm to development and the annual influx of tourists, Hermanus has a beautiful coastline. Unspoilt beaches such as Die Plaat, a 12-km (7-mile) stretch from Klein River Lagoon to De Kelders, are perfect for walks and horse-riding. A clifftop route extends from New Harbour to Grotto Beach; the regularly placed benches allow walkers to rest and enjoy the superb views.

Approximately 20 km (12.5 miles) east of Hermanus lies **Stanford**, a rustic crafts centre. The heart of this little village contains many historical homes built in the late 1800s and early 1900s, and has been proclaimed a national conservation area. The early school building and Anglican Church both date back to 1880, while the reputedly haunted Spookhuis (ghost house) is dated about 1885.

Old Harbour Museum

Market Place. *(028) 312-1475.* 9am–4:30pm Mon–Sat, noon–4pm Sun. public hols.

The popular Marine Hotel in Hermanus

Gansbaai ❹

Road map B5. R43 SE of Hermanus. 2,800. *Cnr Main Rd and Berg St, (028) 384-1439.*

THE NAME GANSBAAI (Bay of Geese) originates from the flocks of Egyptian geese that used to breed here.

Gansbaai is renowned for the tragedy of HMS *Birkenhead*, which, in February 1852, hit a rock off Danger Point, 9 km (6 miles) away, and sank with 445 men – all the women and children were saved. To this day, the phrase "Birkenhead Drill" describes the custom of favouring women and children in crisis situations.

From Gansbaai there are boat trips to Dyer Island to watch great white sharks feeding on the seals that breed on nearby Geyser Island.

WHALE WATCHING IN HERMANUS

The World Wide Fund for Nature (WWF) has recognized Hermanus as one of the best land-based whale-watching spots on earth. October sees a peak in whale numbers (from 40 to 70 have been recorded). The mammals can be seen as close as 10 m (11 yd) away. Particularly special is the Old Harbour Museum's sonar link-up. A hydrophone buried in the seabed transmits the whale calls to an audio room on shore.

Whale Route logo

The rocky coastline around Hermanus offers good vantage points for whale watchers

Bredasdorp **5**

Road map B5. 9,800. Lang St, (028) 424-2584.

BREDASDORP LIES in a region of undulating barley fields and sheep pasture. The town is a centre for the wool industry, but serves mainly as an access route to Cape Agulhas (via the R319) and Arniston (via the R316).

The town's most interesting feature is the **Shipwreck Museum**, which pays tribute to the southern coast's tragic history. This treacherous length of coastline has been labelled the "graveyard of ships" as its rocky reefs, gale-force winds and powerful currents make it one of the most dangerous in the world. Since 1552, more than 130 ships have foundered here, an average of one wreck per kilometre of coast.

🏛 Shipwreck Museum

Independent St. (028) 424-1240. 9am–4:45pm Mon–Fri, 11am–3:45pm Sat & Sun.
This museum was officially opened in April 1975 and is housed in an old rectory and church hall, both of which are national monuments.

The rectory, built in 1845, is furnished like a 19th-century townhouse typical of South Africa's southern coast. The interiors and furnishings were influenced by the many shipwrecks that occurred along this capricious stretch of coastline. The salvaged wood, as well as ships'

A 19th-century kitchen in the Shipwreck Museum at Bredasdorp

decor, frequently reappeared in door and window frames and in the ceiling rafters.

Many of the maritime artifacts that were donated by the town locals have been incorporated into the refurbished home. The beautiful marble-topped wash-stand in the bedroom was salvaged from the *Queen of the Thames*, which sank in 1871, while the medicine chest came from the *Clan Mac-Gregor*, which was shipwrecked in 1902.

The church hall, dating back to 1864, is now called the Shipwreck Hall. Its rather gloomy interior is a suitable environment for the interesting and diverse relics displayed in glass-cases, all of which were recovered from major shipwrecks in the area.

Figurehead, Shipwreck Museum

Cape Agulhas **6**

Road map B5. R319, 45 km (28 miles) S of Bredasdorp. Lang St, (028) 424-2584.

CAPE AGULHAS was named by early Portuguese naviga-tors, the first to round Africa in the 15th century. At the southernmost point of their journey, the sailors noticed that their compass needles were unaffected by mag-netic deviation, pointing true north instead. They called this point the "Cape of Needles".

At this promontory, where the tip of the African continental shelf disappears undramatically into the sea to form what is known as the Agulhas Bank (*see p20*), the Atlantic and Indian oceans merge. The only phys-ical evidence of this conver-gence is a simple stone cairn. The wreck of Japanese trawler, *Meisho Maru 38*, can be seen 2 km (1 mile) west of the Agulhas lighthouse.

🏛 Lighthouse and Museum

(028) 435-6078. 9am–4:30pm daily.
Agulhas Lighthouse, whose design is based on the Pharos lighthouse of Alexandria in Egypt, was built in 1848. After the Green Point lighthouse, it is the oldest working light-house in Southern Africa. It fell into disuse, but was restored and reopened in

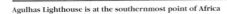

Agulhas Lighthouse is at the southernmost point of Africa

March 1988. Today, its 7.5 million-candlepower lamp is visible for 30 nautical miles.

The museum attached to the lighthouse was opened in 1994. There are 71 steps to the top of the tower, which affords superb views of the coast and seascape.

Arniston ➐

Road map B5. 🏠 *800.* ℹ️ *Lang St, Bredasdorp, (028) 424-2584.*

ARNISTON'S NAME originates from the British vessel, *Arniston*, which was wrecked east of the settlement in May 1815. Tragically, of the 378 soldiers, homebound from Ceylon (Sri Lanka), only six passengers survived.

The little fishing settlement is located some 24 km (15 miles) southeast of Bredasdorp off the R316 and is characterized by its turquoise waters. The locals call the village Waenhuiskrans (wagonhouse cliff), after a cave that is large enough to accommodate several fully spanned ox-wagons and is situated 2 km (1 mile) south of the modern Arniston Hotel *(see p323)*. The cave is accessible only at low tide, however, and visitors should beware of freak waves washing over the slippery rocks.

Kassiesbaai is a cluster of rough-plastered and thatched fishermen's cottages with traditional tiny windows to keep out the midday heat. This little village lies to the north of Arniston, very close to undulating white sand dunes. Further to the south lies Roman Beach; continuing further from here is a windy, wild rocky point that attracts many hopeful anglers.

Dramatic cliffs at the De Hoop Nature Reserve

De Hoop Nature Reserve ➑

Road map B5. R319, 56 km (35 miles) W of Bredasdorp. 📞 *(028) 425-5020.* 🕐 *7am–6pm. Permits required.* ♿

THIS RESERVE, located some 15 km (9 miles) north of Arniston, encompasses a 50-km (30-mile) stretch of coastline, weathered limestone cliffs and spectacular sand dunes, some of which tower as high as 90 m (295 ft). De Hoop's main attraction is a 14-km (8-mile) wetland that is home to 12 of South Africa's 16 waterfowl species.

Thousands of red-knobbed coot, yellow-billed duck and Cape shoveller, as well as Egyptian geese can be seen here, although populations do fluctuate with the water level of the marshland. The birdwatching is best between the months of September and April, when migrant flocks of Palaearctic waders arrive.

Eland at De Hoop Nature Reserve

Of the 13 species that have been recorded, visitors may expect to see ringed plover, wood and curlew sandpiper, greenshank, and little stint.

The rich variety of *fynbos* species includes the endemic Bredasdorp sugarbush *(Protea obtusfolia)*, stinkleaf sugarbush *(Protea susannae)* and pincushion protea *(Leucospermum oliefolium)*.

Wildlife can also be seen in the reserve and there is a short circular drive from the rest camp to Tierhoek. Species to look out for are Cape mountain zebra and small gazelle, like bontebok, grey rhebok and the rather shy and elusive mountain reedbuck.

For visitors who enjoy cycling, a mountain bike trail traverses the Potberg section of the reserve which contains a breeding colony of the rare Cape vultures. The sites, however, are not accessible, to avoid disturbing the birds.

Comfortable campsites and self-catering cottages are available for visitors who wish to stay overnight.

Arniston's fishermen live in Kassiesbaai

Elevated walkways bring the visitor into close contact with lion

Cango Wildlife Ranch ⓫

Road map C5. R328 to Cango Caves. ☎ (044) 272-5593. ⏷ 8am–4:30pm daily. 🖾 🍴 🅆 www.cango.co.za

THE RANCH LIES 3 km (2 miles) north of Oudtshoorn. Since the establishment here in 1993 of the Cheetah Conservation Foundation, the ranch ranks among the leading cheetah breeders in Africa and is one of the world's top five protection institutions. The breeding enclosure is not accessible, but visitors may enter a fenced area to interact with tame cheetah.

Walkways elevated over a natural bushveld environment allow the visitor close-up views of some other powerful hunters: lion, jaguar and puma. Crocodiles and alligators, of which there are over 400, are also bred at the ranch, and exotic snakes on show include a South American albino python, a 4-m (13-ft) boa constrictor and a copperhead viper. A breeding programme is underway for the endangered Cape wild dog.

The ranch restaurant, which overlooks a watering hole with flamingos and black swans, is a pleasant place to eat.

Nile crocodiles at the Cango Wildlife Ranch are a top attraction

Oudtshoorn ⓬

Road map C5. N12 from George. 🏛 42,500. ☎ Baron van Reede St, (044) 279-2532. 🅆 www.oudtshoorn.co.za

AT THE FOOT of the Swartberg mountains, the town of Oudtshoorn was established in 1847 to cater to the needs of the Little Karoo's growing farming population. It gained prosperity when the demand for ostrich feathers, to support Victorian, and later Edwardian, fashion trends, created a sharp rise in the industry in 1870–80.

The Karoo's hot, dry climate proved suitable for big-scale ostrich farming – the loamy soils yielded extensive crops of lucerne, which forms a major part of the birds' diet, and the ground was strewn with the small pebbles that are a vital aid in its somewhat unusual digestive processes.

Oudtshoorn's importance as ostrich-farming centre continued for over 40 years, and the town became renowned for its sandstone mansions, built by wealthy ostrich barons. But World War I and changes in fashion resulted in the industry's decline – many farmers went bankrupt. Ostrich farming recovered in the 1940s with the establishment of the tanning industry. Today, ostrich products include eggs and leather, meat and bonemeal. The town also produces crops of tobacco, wheat and grapes.

A sandstone "feather palace" on the outskirts of Oudtshoorn

The early 20th-century sandstone façade of the CP Nel Museum

🏛 CP Nel Museum

3 Baron van Rheede St. 🛈 (044) 272-7306. ⏱ 9am–5pm, Mon–Fri, 9am–4pm Sat. ⬤ public hols. 🌐

This building, formerly the Boys' High School of Oudtshoorn, was designed in 1906 by the local architect Charles Bullock. Its green-domed sandstone façade is considered to be one of the best examples of stone masonry found anywhere in South Africa. The school hall was designed in 1913 by JE Vixseboxse.

The museum was named in honour of its founder, Colonel CP Nel. A series of dioramas traces the history of ostriches and the impact of ostrich farming on the town and its community. Displays also depict the cultural history and lifestyle of the people of the Klein Karoo region, and the museum prides itself on its excellent replica of an early 20th-century pharmacy. There is a section devoted to the vital role played by the Jewish community in the development of Oudtshoorn's feather industry.

A carved ostrich egg lamp

🏛 Le Roux Townhouse

146 High St. 🛈 (044) 272-3676. ⏱ 8am–1pm and 2–5pm, Mon–Fri, Sat & Sun by app. ⬤ public hols. 🌐

Built around 1895, this is an outstanding example of the feather palaces of the time. An annex of the CP Nel Museum, its exhibits include authentic European furniture from the period 1900–20 and a collection of porcelain, glassware and pieces made from Cape silver.

THE OSTRICH'S UNUSUAL EATING HABITS

Ostriches have neither teeth nor a crop, so have developed the habit of eating stones, which help to grind and digest their food. Perhaps by extension of this habit, or perhaps because they are naturally curious, there is little that an ostrich won't eat. A few years ago, an Oudtshoorn farmer was mystified by the theft of his washing – shirts, socks, trousers vanished every washday, until the death of one of his ostriches revealed the culprit! The birds have also been seen to eat babies' shoes, combs, sunglasses, buttons and earrings (ripped from the shirts and ears of tourists).

Spark plugs and bullet cases – ostriches eat almost anything

🦤 Highgate Ostrich Show Farm

Off R328 to Mossel Bay. 🛈 (044) 272-7115. ⏱ 7:30am–5pm daily. 🌐 multilingual. 🅿 🍴

Located 10 km (6 miles) south of Oudtshoorn, this large farm offers a tour of its ostrich breeding facilities where visitors can learn more about the various stages of the bird's development, and have an opportunity to cuddle the chicks, handle the eggs and visit an ostrich pen. The adventurous may even ride an ostrich. Those who don't have the nerve, can watch jockeys take part in an ostrich derby. The tour length is 1.5 to 2 hours and the fee includes refreshments.

The curio shop offers ostrich feather products, handbags, wallets, belts and shoes.

Coloured ostrich plumes are available in stores in Oudtshoorn

🦤 Safari Show Farm

Off R328 to Mossel Bay. 🛈 (044) 272-7311/2. ⏱ 8am–4:30pm daily. 🌐 🍴 🅿 🍴

Situated 5 km (3 miles) from Oudtshoorn, this show farm has over 2,500 ostriches. The conducted tours leave every half-hour and include an ostrich race and visits to the breeding camp and museum.

Place your bet on the race winner at one of the ostrich farms

Exploring the Garden Route to Grahamstown

THE GARDEN ROUTE, from Wilderness to the end of the Tsitsikamma National Park, where the N2 heads inland for the last stretch to Port Elizabeth, is a scenic treat. On leaving the town of Wilderness, vehicles can park at Dolphin's Point for an uninterrupted view of the coastline with its long white rollers. After Wilderness, the N2 hugs the coast almost all the way to Knysna. From here it passes through indigenous forest as far as Storms River. Between Nature's Valley and Storms River, detours can be made off the N2 to cross the spectacular old pass routes of Grootrivier and Bloukrans. Lush vegetation, mountains, lagoons, rivers and the sea combine to make this route a visual feast.

The Edward Hotel, Port Elizabeth

The Outeniqua Choo-Tjoe en route between Knysna and George

KEY

▬	National route
▭	Other route
▬	Scenic route
≈	River, lake or dam
···	Park or reserve boundary
☀	Viewpoint

SEE ALSO

- *Where to Stay* pp324–27
- *Where to Eat* pp350–51

GETTING AROUND

The N2 traverses the entire length of the Garden Route, from Mossel Bay to Port Elizabeth and beyond, on its way up the east coast. Although coach tours to the area are available, travel by car is ideal as it allows the visitor to explore the pretty coastal towns along the way at leisure. The seven- and five-day hiking trails of the Tsitsikamma, as well as shorter forest walks, may also entice visitors to linger. There are domestic airports at Port Elizabeth and George.

At a waterhole in the Addo Elephant National Park

0 kilometres 50

0 miles 25

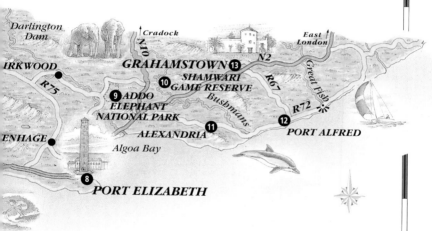

A view of Knysna Lagoon as seen from the Heads

SIGHTS AT A GLANCE

Bartolomeu Dias Museum Complex (Mossel Bay) ❶

THE BARTOLOMEU DIAS Museum Complex, established in 1988, celebrates the 500th anniversary of Dias's historic landfall. A full-sized replica of his ship was built in Portugal in 1987 and set sail for Mossel Bay, arriving on 3 February 1988. Here, the 25-ton vessel was lifted from the water and lowered into the specially altered museum with its high, angled roof, clerestory windows and sunken floor for the keel.

★ The Caravel
The intrepid Spanish and Portuguese seafarers of the 15th and 16th centuries sailed into the unknown in small two- or three-masted ships like this.

Portuguese flag

Lateen sails are characteristic of Mediterranean ships.

Letter Box
Mail posted in this unusual post box in the museum complex is marked with a special postmark.

Post Office Tree
The 16th-century seafarers left messages for each other in a shoe suspended from a milkwood tree like this one, next to the museum building.

Rudder

Barrels filled with fresh water were stored in the hold.

Crew Cabin
Cramped confines in the crew's quarters left little room for privacy on sea voyages that often lasted many months.

STAR FEATURES

★ The Caravel

★ Stained-Glass Windows

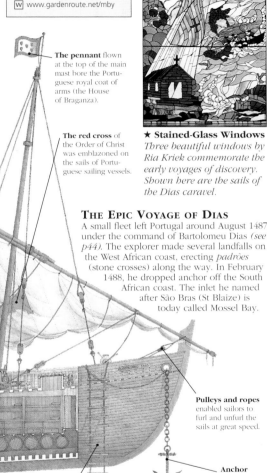

The pennant flown at the top of the main mast bore the Portuguese royal coat of arms (the House of Braganza).

The red cross of the Order of Christ was emblazoned on the sails of Portuguese sailing vessels.

★ **Stained-Glass Windows**
Three beautiful windows by Ria Kriek commemorate the early voyages of discovery. Shown here are the sails of the Dias caravel.

THE EPIC VOYAGE OF DIAS

A small fleet left Portugal around August 1487 under the command of Bartolomeu Dias *(see p44).* The explorer made several landfalls on the West African coast, erecting *padrões* (stone crosses) along the way. In February 1488, he dropped anchor off the South African coast. The inlet he named after São Bras (St Blaize) is today called Mossel Bay.

Pulleys and ropes enabled sailors to furl and unfurl the sails at great speed.

Anchor

Rope ladder

Exploring Mossel Bay and the Bartolomeu Dias Museum Complex

One of the main attractions in the seaside town of Mossel Bay, situated 397 km (246 miles) east of Cape Town, is the interesting museum complex and the historic centre, both overlooking the harbour.

Seafaring history is the subject at the Bartolomeu Dias Museum Complex. Apart from the outstanding reconstruction of Dias's caravel, there are old maps, photographs and documents detailing the first explorations around the tip of Africa. The complex also includes the **Old Post Office Tree Manor**, which commemorates the custom of early navigators who left messages for each other in a shoe.

The town is probably best known for its controversial and costly Mossgas development, initiated by the discovery of natural offshore gas fields.

But the real charm of the settlement lies in its natural beauty – fine beaches and walks. The 15-km (9-mile) St Blaize Hiking Trail winds along an unspoilt stretch of coastline from Bat's Cave to Dana Bay. Santos Beach, the only north-facing beach in South Africa, guarantees sunny afternoons and safe swimming.

Regular cruises take visitors out to **Seal Island**, while **Shark Africa** offers the excitement of a shark cage dive or snorkelling and certification diving courses.

🚢 **Romonza–Seal Isle Trips**
(044) 690-3101.
Shark Africa
Cnr Upper Cross & Kloof sts.
(044) 691-3796, (082) 455 2438.

The Old Post Office Tree Manor

BARTOLOMEU DIAS MUSEUM COMPLEX

Maritime Museum

MARKET ST

CHURCH ST

Tourist Information

GRAVE ST

SANTOS RD

Post Office Tree

FOOTPATH

Malay Graves

Fountain

Munrohoek Cottages

FOOTPATH

Shell Museum

0 metres 100

0 yards 100

George ❷

Road map C5. 🏠 *48,300.* ✈ *10 km (6 miles) NW of town.* 🚉 *George Station, Market St.* 🚌 *St Mark's Sq.* ℹ *124 York St, (044) 801-9295.*

THE WIDE STREETS of George were laid out in 1811 during the British occupation of the Cape. Named after King George III, the town was officially known as George's Drostdy. Today the Garden Route's largest centre, it primarily serves the farming community, with a focus on wheat, hops, vegetables, sheep and dairy cattle. George's best-known attraction is the Outeniqua Choo-Tjoe, a narrow-gauge steam train that takes visitors on a scenic ride from George to Knysna *(see p176)*, a pretty little town further up the Garden Route.

On the outskirts of George lies the prestigious Fancourt Hotel and Country Club, with its immaculate and challenging 27-hole golf course designed by the internationally famous South African golfer, Gary Player. The hotel also boasts an excellent health spa.

The **Outeniqua Nature Reserve** is the starting point for 12 separate day walks in the indigenous forest of the Outeniqua Mountains. At least 125 tree species grow here and over 30 forest birds have been recorded. The scenic Tierkop Trail is a circular overnight route that covers 30 km (18 miles) in two days. The

Beach houses at Victoria Bay

more difficult Outeniqua Trail covers 108 km (67 miles) in seven days.

🥾 Outeniqua Nature Reserve
Witfontein. On R28 NW of George. 📞 *(044) 870-8323.* ⏰ *8am–4pm Mon–Fri.* 🎫 *Permits at office.*

Wilderness ❸

Road map C5. *N2 12 km (7 miles) SE of George.* 🏠 *1,250.* 🚉 *Fairy Knowe.* ℹ *Leila's Lane, (044) 877-0045.*

LOCATED 10 km (6 miles) east of George is South Africa's lake district. This chain of salt- and freshwater lakes at the foot of luxuriant, forested mountain slopes forms part of the **Wilderness National Park**. Protecting some 30 km (19 miles) of unspoilt coastline, the park incorporates two long white beaches called Wilderness and Leentjiesklip; swimming is not safe here due to strong undercurrents.

Of the five lakes, the three westernmost ones, Island

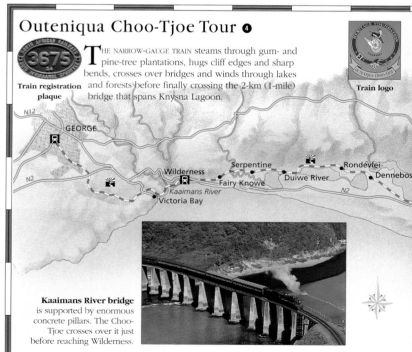

Outeniqua Choo-Tjoe Tour ❹

THE NARROW-GAUGE TRAIN steams through gum- and pine-tree plantations, hugs cliff edges and sharp bends, crosses over bridges and winds through lakes and forests before finally crossing the 2-km (1-mile) bridge that spans Knysna Lagoon.

Train registration plaque

Train logo

N12

GEORGE

N2

Wilderness
Kaaimans River
Victoria Bay

Fairy Knowe

Serpentine

Duiwe River

Rondevlei

Dennebos

N2

Kaaimans River bridge is supported by enormous concrete pillars. The Choo-Tjoe crosses over it just before reaching Wilderness.

Lake, Langvlei and Rondevlei, are all linked and fed by the Touws River via a natural water channel called the Serpentine. Swartvlei is the largest and deepest lake, and is connected to the sea by an estuary, although its mouth silts up for six months of the year. Groenvlei, which is the only lake not located within the Wilderness National Park, is not fed by any river and has no link to the sea. Instead, it receives its water through springs and rainfall, so is the least brackish. Birdlife in the park is excellent, with 79 of the country's waterbird species having been recorded. Five species of kingfisher can be spotted here – pied, giant, half-collared, brown-hooded and malachite. The area is also popular for angling and a variety of watersports, but these activities are restricted in order to protect the sensitive ecology of the area. Horse riding is permitted along Swartvlei's shores. A scenic drive starting at

Fairy Knowe, a popular hotel near Wilderness

Wilderness runs along Lakes Road, which skirts the lake chain and meets up with the N2 at Swartvlei.

The **Goukamma Nature Reserve** borders on the Wilderness National Park and offers similar activities. The reserve supports grysbok and blue duiker. Resident Cape clawless otters are present, but are seldom seen. Buffels Bay, a seaside resort at the

easternmost extent of the reserve, has a magnificent beach for walking, swimming and sunbathing.

⚐ Wilderness National Park
Wilderness. **📞** (044) 877-1197. **ℹ**
(012) 428-9111 for reservations.
◯ 8am–5pm daily. 📶 🏃
⚐ Goukamma Nature Reserve
Wilderness. **📞** (044) 343-1855. **◯**
8am–5pm Mon–Fri. 📶 🏃 ⚓ 🏊

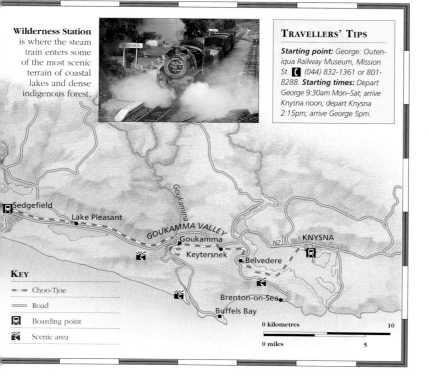

Wilderness Station is where the steam train enters some of the most scenic terrain of coastal lakes and dense indigenous forest.

TRAVELLERS' TIPS

Starting point: George: Outeniqua Railway Museum, Mission St. **📞** (044) 832-1361 or 801-8288. **Starting times:** Depart George 9:30am Mon–Sat; arrive Knysna noon; depart Knysna 2:15pm; arrive George 5pm.

KEY

- – – Choo-Tjoe
- ═══ Road
- 🚉 Boarding point
- ⚒ Scenic area

Sedgefield
Lake Pleasant
GOUKAMMA VALLEY
Goukamma
Keytersnek
Belvedere
KNYSNA
Brenton-on-Sea
Buffels Bay

0 kilometres   10
0 miles   5

Paddle cruiser on the Knysna Lagoon

Knysna ❺

Road map C5. 🏘 25,000. 🚉 Outeniqua Choo-Tjoe. 🚌 Main St. 🛈 40
Main St, (044) 382-5510. 🖵 www.
visitknysna.com

A MAN FEATURING significantly
in Knysna's history was
George Rex, who, according
to local legend, was the son
of King George III and his first
wife, a Quaker named Hannah
Lightfoot (she never gained
royal approval and was
exiled after the birth of
her son). The claim,
made as a result of
Rex's opulent life-
style, was never
proved. He
played a
leading
role in devel-
oping the lagoon harbour and
his ship, the *Knysna*, regularly
traded along the coast. At the
time of his death, in 1839, he
was the most prominent land-
owner in the area.

Furniture, boat building and
oysters cultivated in the lagoon
are Knysna's major industries.

Knysna lourie

ENVIRONS: One of Knysna's
most attractive features is the
17-km-long (11-mile) Knysna
Lagoon, protected from the
sea by two sandstone cliffs,
the Knysna Heads.

George Rex Drive provides
access to Leisure Island on the
eastern Head, from where
there are superb views.

On the western Head, which
is accessible via a free
ferry service, is the
**Featherbed Nature
Reserve**, a World
Heritage Site. Here,
visitors can join a 2.5-
km long (1.5-mile)
guided nature walk,
the Bushbuck Trail.

The lagoon itself is an
ideal venue for a great
variety of watersports.
Cabin cruisers may be
hired from **Lightleys**, while
daily sightseeing cruises and
sunset trips to the Heads are
offered by **Knysna Ferries**
and the *John Benn*, a large
luxury pleasure cruiser.

Angling, too, is a popular
pastime. Fish are abundant in
the area and catches include

white steenbras, stumpnose
and blacktail. From December
to April, fishermen can charter
deep-sea skiboats to try and
net tuna, bonito and marlin.

South Africa's largest commercial oyster-farming centre
is based at Knysna Lagoon.
The delicious Pacific oysters
(*Crassostrea gigas*) can be
sampled at the **Knysna
Oyster Company** on Thesen's
Island (accessible via a causeway) or at Jetty Tapas.

Another spot favoured by
the locals is the mock-Tudor-
style Crab's Creek, which has
wooden benches under tall
shade trees. Crab's Creek lies
right at the edge of the
lagoon as one enters Knysna
from the west.

About 6 km (4 miles) east
of Knysna, a turnoff to Noetzie
ends at a clifftop parking area.
From here visitors can descend
a path to a secluded bay that
is guarded by five castles, all
of which are private homes.

🏊 **Featherbed Nature
Reserve**
📞 (044) 381-0590. 🚢 8:45am, 10am,
11:45am, 3pm daily. Ferry leaves from
Municipal Jetty. 🅿

🚤 **Lightleys**
Knysna Lagoon. 📞 (044) 386-0007. 🅿

🚤 **Knysna Ferries**
Knysna Lagoon. 📞 (044) 382-5520. 🅿

🚤 **John Benn Cruises**
Waterfront. 📞 (044) 382-1693. 🕐
Apr–Sep: 12:30pm, 5pm; Nov–
Apr and school hols: 10:15am,
12:30pm, 2pm, 6pm.

Knysna Oyster Company
Thesen's Island. 📞 (044) 382-6942.
🕐 8am–5pm Mon–Fri; 9am–4pm
Sat & Sun. 🍴

The Knysna Heads promontories guard the lagoon entrance

❀ Knysna Forest

The magnificent indigenous forest that surrounds Knysna offers walking trails, scenic drives, cycling routes and picnic sites. Most notable of the hikes is the seven-day **Outeniqua Hiking Trail**, which traverses 105 km (65 miles).

Goldfields Drive leads to a picnic site at Jubilee Creek, which is lined with gold-panning relics, and then goes on to the old mineshafts and machinery of Millwood, a former gold-mining settlement.

From the **Diepwalle Forest Station** a 13-km (8-mile) scenic drive, a cycling route and the Elephant Walk lead through tall Outeniqua yellowwood, ironwood and stinkwood trees. The yellowwoods are often draped with lichen known as "old man's beard" *(Usnea barbarta)*. Together with the lush ferns and twisted lianas they create a fairy-tale atmosphere, where the lucky may spot a brilliant green Knysna lourie. In the Diepwalle State Forest is the King Edward Tree, a gigantic, old Outeniqua yellowwood. It is 39 m (128 ft) tall with a circumference of 7 m (20 ft), and is believed to be 600 years old.

Kranshoek scenic drive, some 10 km (6 miles) east of Knysna, ends at a rocky coastline that falls sheer to the sea below. Back on the N2, the route traverses the "Garden of Eden", where many trees are labelled.

🚶 Outeniqua Hiking Trail
Knysna. **☎** *(044) 382-5466.*
🌲 Diepwalle Forest Station
☎ *(044) 382-9762.* **◷** *7:30am–5pm daily.* 🚶 🏕 ♿

One of the five private castles along Noetzie Beach

Plettenberg Bay ❻

Road map C5. 👥 *7,947.* ✈ *S of town.* 🚌 *Shell Ultra City, Marine Way.* ℹ *Main St.* **☎** *(0445) 33-4065.*

UPMARKET PLETTENBERG BAY, 30 km (19 miles) east of Knysna, is the holiday playground of the wealthy. A coast of lagoons, rivers and 12 km (7 miles) of white beaches, "Plett", as it is called by the locals, earned the name *Bahia Formosa* ("beautiful bay") from early Portuguese sailors.

The village is perched on red sandstone cliffs that rise above the coastline and the lagoon formed by the Keurbooms and Bietou rivers.

Plett's most recognized feature is a large luxury hotel and timeshare complex on Beacon Isle.

South of the village, the **Robberg Nature and Marine Reserve** juts out into the sea, its cliffs rising to 148 m (486 ft) in places. A series of walking trails affords contrasting views of the dramatically churning seas and pristine secluded bays where anglers try their hand at catching elf, musselcracker, galjoen and red roman in the deep, natural gulleys. Seals and dolphins are often seen, while whales occur in spring (Sep onwards).

Further along the coast, east of Plettenberg Bay, a winding scenic route off the N2 leads to Nature's Valley, a coastal resort that forms part of the Tsitsikamma National Park *(see pp178–9)* and is studded with holiday homes.

🦌 Robberg Nature and Marine Reserve

☎ *(0445) 33-3424.* **◷** *6am–6pm Feb–Nov; 6am–8pm Dec–Jan. Permits required (avail. at gate)* 🚗 🐟 🚶

The pansy shell is Plettenberg Bay's emblem

The Beacon Isle Hotel seen from Signal Hill, Plettenberg Bay

THE KNYSNA FOREST ELEPHANTS

The last true forest elephant

During the 19th century, 400–500 elephants lived around Knysna and were perfectly adapted to the forest habitat. Ruthless hunting reduced their numbers drastically, and by the early 1900s only 50 of the gentle giants remained. Today, only a single one exists from the original herd. Two young elephants were introduced from the Kruger National Park, but the relocation venture failed. The last elephant is elusive and very shy, and is seldom seen. It belongs to the African elephant species *Loxodonta africana*, and is the only completely free-ranging elephant that remains in South Africa.

The promontory known as the Knysna Heads marks the gateway between lagoon and sea ▷

Tsitsikamma National Park **❼**

THE TSITSIKAMMA NATIONAL PARK, designated in 1964, extends for 68 km (42 miles) from Nature's Valley to Oubosstrand and stretches seawards for some 5.5 km (3 miles), offering licensed snorkellers and divers a unique "underwater trail". Within the park's boundaries lie two of South Africa's most popular hikes, the Tsitsikamma and Otter trails. Primeval forest, rugged mountain scenery, an abundance of water from rivers and streams, and panoramic views contribute to their popularity with hikers.

Cape clawless otter

★ Yellowwood trees
Once considered inferior and used for building, today yellowwood is highly valued.

Bloukrans River
gorge is the site of an overnight trail hut.

Fynbos
The typical vegetation of this area is coastal fynbos which consists of low-growing species of ericas and proteas.

Tsitsikamma Trail

Keurbos

Bloukrans River

Bloukrans

N2

R102

Groot River

Bloukrans River

Bloukrans Forest Station

Vark River

Cold Stream

Coldstrea

R102

N2

Covie

Tsitsikamma National Park

Nature's Valley

Kalander

Groot River Lagoon

André

Otter Trail

Oakhu

Tsitsikamma Marine Reserve

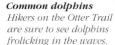

Common dolphins
Hikers on the Otter Trail are sure to see dolphins frolicking in the waves.

STAR FEATURES

★ **Otter Trail**

★ **Tsitsikamma Trail**

★ **Yellowwood trees**

★ Otter Trail
This five-day coastal hike was the country's first official trail and stretches from the mouth of the Storm's River to the superb beach at Nature's Valley. Hikers may spot whales, dolphins, seals and Cape clawless otters along the way.

★ *Tsitsikamma Trail*
The relatively easy inland walking route leads 60 km (37 miles) through fynbos and indigenous forest in the Tsitsikamma mountains and takes five days to complete.

VISITORS' CHECKLIST

Road map C5. Keurboomstrand 14 km (8 miles) E of Plettenberg Bay on N2. ✖ *Plettenberg Bay.* 🚌 *Hopper and Baz buses to De Vasselot camp.* ℹ *National Parks Board Reservations national numbers: (011) 678-8870, (012) 428-9111.* ⏰ *7am–7pm.* **Otter Trail:** *41 km (25 miles).* **Tsitsikamma Trail:** *60 km (37 miles).* 🏕 🍴 ⛺ 🚶 *(permit required for trails).* 🖥 www.saparks.co.za

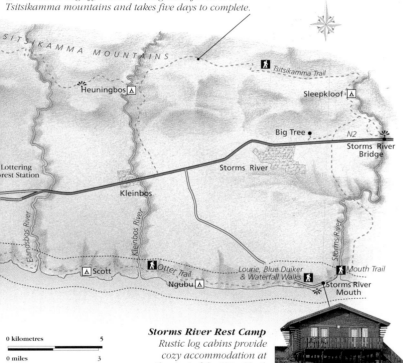

Storms River Rest Camp
Rustic log cabins provide cozy accommodation at the start of the Otter Trail.

KEY

▬▬	Motorway
▬▬	Major road
▬▬	Tarred road
- - -	Trail
☀	Viewpoint
🚶	Hiking
⛺	Overnight trail huts

En route to Storms River Mouth

TIPS FOR WALKERS

Visitors should be fit, and sturdy walking shoes are essential. For the longer hikes, all provisions as well as cooking gear and sleeping bags must be carried, as the overnight huts are only equipped with mattresses. The Bloukrans River along the Otter Trail can only be forded by swimming or wading, so waterproof backpacks are advised.

Street-by-Street: Port Elizabeth ❽

Statue of Queen Victoria

THE THIRD LARGEST port and fifth largest city in the country, Port Elizabeth faces east across the 60-km (38-mile) wide sweep of Algoa Bay. Many of its attractions are concentrated along the seafront. Modern Port Elizabeth has spread inland and northward along the coast from the original settlement. It is often referred to as the "Friendly City" and its wide open beaches are popular with visitors. Among the many attractions in this major tourist centre are a host of well-preserved historic buildings, splendid architecture, Bayworld, Snake Park, Donkin Reserve and Happy Valley.

Donkin Lighthouse
Built in 1861, the lighthouse is in the Donkin Reserve.

CHAPEL STREET

DONKIN STREET

Horse Memorial

HAVELOCK STREET

BELMONT TERRACE

PEARSON STREET

Art Gallery, Pearson Conservatory and War Memorial

Donkin Reserve is situated on a hillside overlooking the city.

★ Donkin Street
The row of quaint, double-storey Victorian houses lining this street was built between 1860–80. The entire street was declared a national monument in 1967.

Protea Hotel Edward
This well-preserved Edwardian building is a city landmark, located in the heart of Port Elizabeth's historical district. The hotel is renowned for its sumptuous breakfasts and has a vintage lift that is still fully operational.

STAR SIGHTS
★ **Donkin Street**
★ **City Hall**
★ **Fort Frederick**

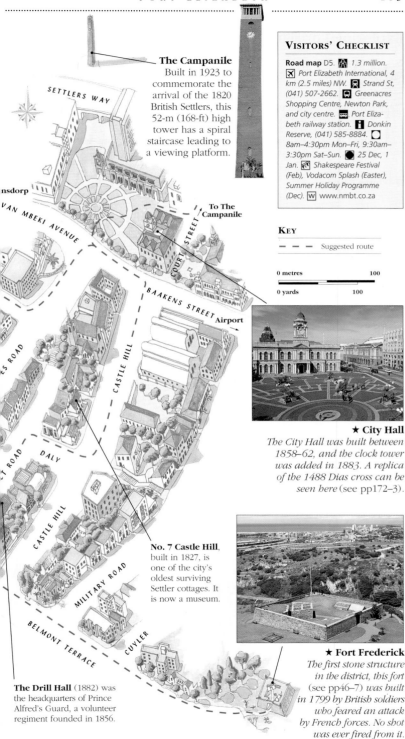

The Campanile
Built in 1923 to commemorate the arrival of the 1820 British Settlers, this 52-m (168-ft) high tower has a spiral staircase leading to a viewing platform.

VISITORS' CHECKLIST

Road map D5. 🏠 1.3 million.
✈ Port Elizabeth International, 4 km (2.5 miles) NW. 🚌 Strand St, (041) 507-2662. 🚌 Greenacres Shopping Centre, Newton Park, and city centre. 🚉 Port Elizabeth railway station. 🛈 Donkin Reserve, (041) 585-8884. ◯ 8am–4:30pm Mon–Fri, 9:30am–3:30pm Sat–Sun. ● 25 Dec, 1 Jan. 🎭 Shakespeare Festival (Feb), Vodacom Splash (Easter), Summer Holiday Programme (Dec). 🌐 www.nmbt.co.za

KEY

– – – Suggested route

0 metres 100
0 yards 100

★ **City Hall**
The City Hall was built between 1858–62, and the clock tower was added in 1883. A replica of the 1488 Dias cross can be seen here (see pp172–3).

No. 7 Castle Hill, built in 1827, is one of the city's oldest surviving Settler cottages. It is now a museum.

★ **Fort Frederick**
The first stone structure in the district, this fort (see pp46–7) was built in 1799 by British soldiers who feared an attack by French forces. No shot was ever fired from it.

The Drill Hall (1882) was the headquarters of Prince Alfred's Guard, a volunteer regiment founded in 1856.

Exploring Port Elizabeth

MODERN PORT ELIZABETH sprawls inland and northward on the windy shores of Algoa Bay. Many of the city's most popular attractions, such as Bayworld with its dolphin and seal shows, can be found along Humewood Beach. Port Elizabeth is very proud of its settler heritage and a wealth of historic buildings and museums, as well as memorials and statues, await exploration further inland.

Signpost

🜨 Donkin Reserve
Belmont Terrace. 🈂 (041) 585-8884. ◐ 8am–4:30pm Mon–Fri; 9:30am–3:30pm Sat–Sun. ● 25 Dec, 1 Jan. 🈁

In this attractive park-like reserve is the pyramid-shaped memorial that then acting governor of the Cape, Sir Rufane Donkin, dedicated to his late wife in 1820. A few days earlier he had named the settlement Port Elizabeth in her honour.

Donkin Memorial

The adjacent lighthouse was completed in 1861. The entire site was declared a national monument in 1938.

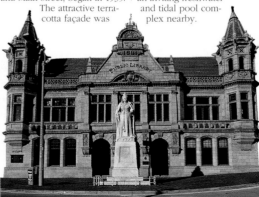

The Horse Memorial

🜨 Horse Memorial
Cape Road.
During the South African War, Port Elizabeth was the port of entry for the horses of British soldiers. After the war, local resident Harriet Meyer raised money to honour the estimated 347,000 horses that had died. The statue by sculptor Joseph Whitehead, unveiled in 1905, was relocated to its present site in 1957. The inscription reads: "The greatness of a nation consists not so much in the number of its

people or the extent of its territory as in the extent and justice of its compassion."

🌿 St George's Park
Park Drive.
The setting of the well-known play, *Master Harold and the Boys*, by Athol Fugard, this lovely park is home to the oldest cricket ground and bowling green in South Africa. It also contains tennis courts, a swimming pool, a botanic garden and several historic monuments, like the War Memorial in the northeast corner of the park.

The Pearson Conservatory, named after Henry Pearson who served as mayor of the city for 16 terms, was completed in 1882 and houses a collection of exotic plants.

🜨 Main Public Library
Market Square. 🈲 (041) 585-8133.
Work on the building, located on the corner of Whites Road and Main Street, began in 1935. The attractive terracotta façade was

made in England, shipped out, and the numbered segments assembled on site. The lovely stained-glass dome on the second floor is a masterpiece. A statue of Queen Victoria, one of at least three in South Africa, stands right in front of the entrance to the building.

♠ Fort Frederick
Belmont Terrace.
In 1799, a British garrison was sent to Algoa Bay to prevent an invasion by French troops supporting the rebel republic of Graaff-Reinet *(see pp292–3).* Small, square Fort Frederick *(see pp46– 7)* was built on a low hill overlooking the mouth of the Baakens River, and named after the Duke of York, who was commander-in-chief of the British army at the time. Although it was defended by eight cannons, no salvoes were ever fired from them in an act of war. The arrival of the English settlers in 1820 was supervised by the commander of the garrison, Captain Francis Evatt, whose grave can be seen at the fort.

🜨 Humewood Beach
2 km (1 mile) S of the city centre.
The recreation hub of Port Elizabeth, Humewood Beach is bordered by Marine Drive, which provides quick access to all the attractions that line the shore. An attractive covered promenade provides welcome shelter from the wind and hosts a fleamarket over weekends. There is also an inviting freshwater and tidal pool complex nearby.

The Queen Victoria statue in front of the Main Public Library

The all-important "19th hole" at Humewood Golf Course

Lifeguards are stationed at all the main beaches. Sailing and scuba diving are popular here, and the windy expanse of Algoa Bay is often punctuated by the white sails of yachts.

Many hotels and holiday apartments line Marine Drive and there are numerous little restaurants and eateries, especially at Brookes Pavilion near the Museum Complex.

Bayworld's dolphin and seal shows always attract the crowds. The "stars" were all born in captivity, and are not replaced when they die.

➤ The Museum Complex and Bayworld

Marine Drive. **☎** (041) 584-0650. **◗** 9am–4:30pm daily. Shows at 11am and 3pm. 🗒 🍴 🛒 **W** www.bayworld.co.za

The jetty at Humewood Beach

The Museum Complex and Bayworld is the flagship of the beachfront, and also includes a snake park and Tropical House. The entrance to the museum itself is lined with several open enclosures containing water birds. The interesting exhibits inside include a marine gallery containing salvaged items, fully rigged models of early sailing ships, and a fascinating display of the Xhosa people.

Tropical House is well worth a visit. Numerous forest bird species scurry through the dense undergrowth or roost in tree tops in this spacious exhibit. A path circles the rocky 7-m (23-ft) high man-made hill at the centre of the building, offering a bird's-eye view of, among others, crocodiles and flamingos.

On view at the Snake House are snakes from around the world, including South African species like the puffadder.

🦋 Happy Valley

3 km (2 miles) S of the city centre. A sandy underpass connects Humewood Beach and Happy Valley, an attractive, tranquil park in a shallow valley. Several walking paths meander across the well-kept lawns, past a little stream, lily ponds and small waterfalls.

ENVIRONS: The championship **Humewood Golf Course**, some 3 km (2 miles) south along the coast from Humewood is considered to be one of the best in South Africa. At the clubhouse, golfers can enjoy a well-earned drink and marvel at the splendid views across the bay.

A lovingly restored little narrow-gauge steam train that has been named the Apple Express occasionally departs from Humewood Station on weekends. It puffs to the village of Thornhill, 48 km (30 miles) east of Port Elizabeth, and completes the return journey to the city after lunch.

About 3 km (2 miles) south of Humewood lies the cape that marks the entrance to Algoa Bay. **Cape Recife** and its surrounding nature reserve are an ideal destination for bird spotting and exploring the unspoilt rocky shore.

A 9-km-long (6-mile) hiking trail explores the reserve and traverses several different coastal habitats that include redbuds and dune vegetation. The route passes the Cape Recife lighthouse, a spot that is a favourite with divers. A rocky outcrop near the lighthouse shelters a small colony of Jackass penguins.

Of the number of ships that have been wrecked at Cape Recife, the Greek vessel *Kapodistrias* was the most recent casualty. The bulk carrier struck Thunderbolt Reef in July 1985.

⚡ Humewood Golf Course

☎ (041) 583-2137.

One of the performing bottlenose dolphins at Bayworld

Addo Elephant National Park ❾

Road map D5. 50 km (31 miles) NE of Port Elizabeth. [(012) 428-9111. ◯ 7am–7pm daily. ⧉ ✔ ⦿ �
W www.addoelephantpark.com

IN THE PAST, elephants occurred throughout the Cape Colony, but as the land was settled they were hunted to extinction. In 1919 Major Philip Pretorius was appointed to exterminate the last survivors and succeeded in shooting 120 over 11 months. Only 15 terrified elephants survived in the densest thickets.

When public opinion turned in their favour, a 68 sq km (26 sq mile) tract of surplus land was declared national park territory in 1931. However, the animals raided nearby farms at night and a suitable fence was needed to prevent escapes.

After numerous experiments, warden Graham Armstrong constructed a guard from railway tracks and elevator cables. By 1954, some 23 sq km (9 sq miles) had been fenced in this way and the elephants were safely contained.

For many years, Addo resembled a large zoo. Oranges were placed below the rest camps at night to lure the shy beasts out of the bush, while the stout fences separated visitors and animals. The herd responded well to protection – increasing to 265 by 1998 – making it necessary to enlarge their territory. Today, the Addo

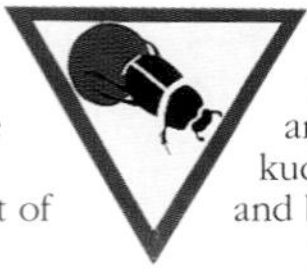

Dung beetles are protected in the park

Elephant Park includes the Zuurberg mountains to the north and its size has increased to 600 sq km (232 sq miles). South African National Parks plans to quadruple it in size.

Addo's main focus is the rest camp that offers a restaurant, shop, swimming pool, caravan park and 24 comfortable Cape Dutch chalets. A network of game-viewing roads allows visitors to explore the southern region of the park. Kadouw Lookout is one of several from which to view the elephants.

Among the many other animals inhabiting the dense thicket, are buffalo, black rhino, kudu, eland, hartebeest and bushbuck. But visitors tend to overlook one of the park's smallest and most fascinating creatures. The flightless dung beetle is an insect that is virtually restricted to Addo. Signs warn motorists not to drive over them.

Addo's dense *spekboom* (*Portulacaria afra*) bushland sustains the highest concentration of large mammals in the country. To assist in monitoring the effects that the elephant, buffalo and black rhino populations have on the vegetation a botanical reserve has been established. A 6-km (4-mile) walking trail explores this interesting reserve in which many of the indigenous trees have been labelled.

A herd of elephants at a waterhole in the Addo Elephant National Park

Shamwari Game Reserve ❿

Road map D5. 72 km (44 miles) N of Port Elizabeth. [(042) 203-1111. ⧉ ✔ 11am–6pm daily (booking essential; lunch included). ✻ � W www.shamwari.com

AT 140 SQ KM (54 sq miles), Shamwari is the largest private reserve in the Eastern Cape and the only one in the province where the Big Five (*see pp24–5*) can be seen. It consists of undulating bushveld country in the catchment area of the Bushmans River. The recipient of four international awards, Shamwari is the brainchild of entrepreneur Adrian Gardiner, who originally bought the ranch in the hills near Paterson as a retreat for his family. Over the years, several neighbouring farms were incorporated and wildlife re-introduced. The reserve is now home to 33 elephant, 12 white rhino, buffalo, zebra, giraffe and 16 antelope species including eland, kudu, impala, gemsbok, hartebeest, springbok and black wildebeest.

Shamwari is the only private reserve in the Eastern Cape where the endangered black rhino is found. Five were translocated from

A rustic chalet in the Addo Elephant National Park

KwaZulu-Natal and, as the reserve's vegetation provides an ideal habitat, four calves have thus far been born. The lion pride, once kept in a separate camp, now roams the entire reserve.

The reserve offers luxury accommodation *(see p327)* and an African wildlife experience that has attracted many famous visitors, including the late Princess Diana. Rangers conduct game-viewing drives in open vehicles twice daily.

White Rhino, Shamwari Game Reserve

Alexandria ⓫

Road map D5. R72, E of Port Elizabeth.

ALEXANDRIA was founded in 1856 around a Dutch Reformed Church. A dirt road, just west of town, crosses chicory fields before entering the enchanting Alexandria forest. Superb specimens of yellowwood, one of the 170 tree species found here, tower above the road. The forest and the largest active dune system in South Africa are protected by the 240 sq km (93 sq miles) **Alexandria State Forest**. The two-day, 35-km (22-mile) Alexandria Hiking Trail, one of the finest coastal walks in South Africa, passes through gloomy, dense indigenous forest to reach sand dunes rising to 150 m (488 ft) above the sea, before returning via a circular route.

Overnight huts are located at the start and at Woody Cape.

🏕 Alexandria State Forest
8 km (5 miles) off R72. 📞 (046) 653-0601, (042) 233 0556. ⏰ 7am–7pm daily. 🅿 🚶

Port Alfred ⓬

Road map D5. R72, 150 km (93 miles) E of Port Elizabeth. 🚶 5,000. 🅿 Halyards Hotel. ℹ Causeway Rd, (046) 624-1235.

PORT ALFRED, a charming seaside resort in the Eastern Cape, is well known for its superb beaches. Those west of the river mouth are more developed, while those to the east are unspoilt and excellent for long walks. Kelly's Beach offers safe bathing. The entire stretch of coast is perfect for

surfing and also popular with rock and surf fishermen.

Outside the **Kowie Museum**, which preserves the town's history is, a figurehead from an old sailing ship.

ENVIRONS: The Kowie River is navigable for 25 km (16 miles) upriver in small vessels. The two-day Kowie Canoe Trail allows canoeists to savour the beauty of the river and the forested hills that surround it. At the overnight stop, 21 km (13 miles) upstream in the Waters Meeting Nature Reserve, a footpath explores the dense bush and forest, and a variety of birds and small animals can be seen.

🏛 Kowie Museum
Pascoe Crescent. 📞 (046) 624-4713. ⏰ 10am–1pm Mon–Fri. ⬤ public hols. 🅿

Many luxury yachts, catamarans and fishing vessels are moored at Port Alfred's marina

Grahamstown ⓮

A FTER THE FOURTH FRONTIER WAR OF 1812, Colonel John Graham established a military post on an abandoned farm near the southeast coast. In an attempt to stabilize the region, the Cape government enticed 4,500 British families to the farmlands. Many of these "1820 Settlers" prefered an urban life, and Grahamstown became a thriving trading centre, home to the largest concentration of artisans outside Cape Town.

Arts Festival logo

Exploring Grahamstown

Grahamstown is known for its over 50 churches, university and superb schools. Its major attractions lie within a 500-m (1,625-ft) walk from the City Hall in High Street. Some 60 buildings have been declared national monuments, and a host of beautifully restored Georgian and Victorian residences line the streets.

🔒 Cathedral of St Michael and St George

High St. 📞 (046) 622-3976.
🕐 8am–4:30pm daily. ♿
The cathedral is the town's most prominent landmark – its spire towers 51 m (166 ft) above the town centre. The original St George's Church, built in 1824, is the oldest Anglican Church in South Africa, and the massive organ is one of the finest in the country.

🔒 Methodist Church

Bathurst St. 📞 (046) 622-7210. 🕐 daily. ♿
The Commemoration Church is noted for its Gothic Revival façade and lovely stained-glass windows. It was completed in 1850.

🏛 Albany Museum Complex

📞 (046) 622-2312.
The complex incorporates five separate venues. Two of them, the **History and Natural Sciences museums** display fossils, settler artifacts and Xhosa dress. Another, the **Old Provost**, opposite Rhodes University, was built in 1838 as a military prison. **Drostdy Gateway**, which frames the university entrance, is all that remains of the 1842 magistrate's offices. **Fort Selwyn** (see pp46–7), adjacent to the 1820 Settlers Monument, was built in 1836 and offers scenic views of the town.

🏛 History and Natural Sciences museums

Somerset St. 📞 (046) 622-2312. 🕐 9am–1pm, 2–5pm Mon–Fri, 9am–1pm Sat. ● Good Fri, 25 Dec. 🎫 ♿

🏛 Old Provost

Lucas Ave. 📞 (046) 622-2312. 🕐 Fri 9am–1pm. ● Sat–Thu, Good Fri, 25 Dec. 🎫 ♿

🏛 Fort Selwyn

Fort Selwyn Dr. 📞 (046) 622-2312. 🕐 by appointment only. 🎫 ♿

Drostdy Gateway, the entrance to Rhodes University

🏛 Observatory Museum

Bathurst St. 📞 (046) 622-2312. 🕐 9am–1pm, 2–5pm Mon–Fri, 9am–1pm Sat. ●, Good Fri, 25 Dec. 🎫 ♿ (except turret).
The attraction at this historic home and workshop of a mid-19th-century Grahamstown jeweller is the Victorian camera obscura in the turret, which projects images of the town onto a wall.

🏛 Rhodes University

Artillery Rd. 📞 (046) 603-8111. 🎫 multi-entry ticket. 🌐 www.ru.ac.za
This beautiful old university complex also houses the world-famous **JLB Smith Institute of Ichthyology**, where the most interesting displays are two rare coelacanth specimens. This prehistoric species of deep-water fish was presumed extinct until its "discovery" in 1939. There is also a collection of other marine and freshwater fish. Visitors interested in traditional African music should visit the **International Library of African Music**, also on the campus.

Statue at the 1820 Settlers Monument

🏛 JLB Smith Institute of Ichthyology

Rhodes University. 📞 (046) 603-8425. 🕐 8am–1pm, 2–5pm Mon–Fri. ● Sat–Sun, Good Fri, 25 Dec. ♿

🏛 International Library of African Music

Rhodes University. 📞 (046) 603-8557. 🕐 by appointment. ♿

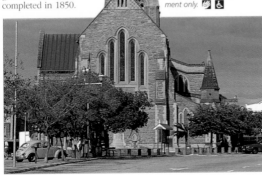

The Cathedral of St Michael and St George in High Street

🏛 National English Literary Museum

Beaufort St. 📞 (046) 622-7042. ⭕
8am–1pm, 2–5pm, Mon–Fri. ● Good
Fri, 25 Dec. ♿ W www.ru.ac.za/nelm
Preserved here are documents,
early manuscripts and personal
letters relating to South Africa's
most important writers.

🏛 1820 Settlers Monument

Gunfire Hill. 📞 (046) 622-7115. ⭕
8am–4:30pm Mon–Fri. ♿ 🖥
Reminiscent of an old fort, this
monument on Gunfire Hill was
built in 1974 in the shape of a
ship and commemorates the
British families who arrived in
the area in 1820. The modern
Monument Theatre complex
nearby is the main venue for
the popular 11-day Standard
Bank National Arts
Festival (see p37)
held here annually.
Many paintings
decorate the
impressive
foyer.

The Old Provost was once a military prison

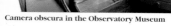

ENVIRONS: 34 km (21 miles)
north of Grahamstown lies
the 445-sq-km (172-sq-mile)
Great Fish River Reserve.
After the Fifth Frontier War
of 1819, the land between
the Keiskamma and Great
Fish rivers was declared neu-
tral territory, and British
settlers were brought in to
act as a buffer against the
Xhosa incursions. Today, the
area is the largest wildlife
reserve in the Eastern Cape
province, home to kudu,

eland, hartebeest, hippo, black
rhino, buffalo and leopard.
    Accommodation is provided
in comfortable lodges. A two-
day guided trail follows the
river; hikers stay overnight in
a tented camp.

🐾 Great Fish River Reserve

Fort Beaufort Rd. 📞 (040) 635-2115.

VISITORS' CHECKLIST

Road map D5. 🏘 100,000. ✈
Port Elizabeth, 127 km (79 miles)
to NE. 🚉 High St. 🚌 Cathcart
Arms Hotel, Market Square. 🛈
63 High St, (046) 622-3241. ⭕
8:30am–5pm Mon–Fri, 8:30am–
noon Sat. ● Good Fri, 25 Dec,
public hols. 🎭 Standard Bank
National Arts Festival (Jul).
W www.grahamstown.co.za

Camera obscura in the Observatory Museum

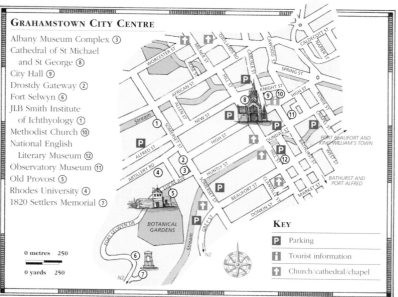

GRAHAMSTOWN CITY CENTRE

Albany Museum Complex ③
Cathedral of St Michael
    and St George ⑧
City Hall ⑨
Drostdy Gateway ②
Fort Selwyn ⑥
JLB Smith Institute
    of Ichthyology ①
Methodist Church ⑩
National English
    Literary Museum ⑫
Observatory Museum ⑪
Old Provost ⑤
Rhodes University ④
1820 Settlers Memorial ⑦

0 metres   250

0 yards   250

KEY

🅿 Parking

🛈 Tourist information

✝ Church/cathedral/chapel

THE EAST COAST
AND INTERIOR

Introducing the East Coast and Interior

CROWNED BY SOUTHERN AFRICA'S highest mountains, a serrated spine that runs the length of this region, the Eastern Cape, Lesotho and KwaZulu-Natal offer rugged mountain scenery, undulating hills, and superb beaches. The powerful currents of the warm Indian Ocean carve the wave-battered cliffs of the Wild Coast. Although an almost continuous chain of coastal resorts extends 160 km (100 miles) south of Durban, Africa's largest port, much of the coastline remains unspoilt and accessible only along winding dirt roads. In the far north, subtropical forests and savannah provide a haven for an abundance of big game and birds, while coastal lakes and the ocean lure fishermen and holiday-makers.

Golden Gate National Park

Golden Gate Highlands National Park *in the northeastern Free State lies in the foothills of the Maluti mountains. Magnificent scenery, impressive sandstone formations like Sentinel Rock, abundant wildlife and pleasant walks are the attractions in this park* (see p207).

```
0 kilometres        300

0 miles        150
```

WILD COAST,
DRAKENSBERG
AND MIDLANDS
(See pp198–213)

Wild Coast

The Hole in the Wall *is situated just off the coast at the mouth of the Mpako River. It is one of the best known sites on the romantic Wild Coast* (see p203).

◁ **Loggerhead turtle hatchlings on Sodwana Bay beach, along the Maputaland Coast**

Cape Vidal *separates the Indian Ocean and Lake St Lucia. It forms part of the Greater St Lucia Wetland Park* (see p232), *which borders on the unspoilt Maputaland coast, the breeding ground of leatherback and loggerhead turtles.*

Sodwana Bay

DURBAN AND
ZULULAND
(See pp214–33)

Pietermaritzburg

Church Street Mall *in Pietermaritzburg is surrounded by a number of historic buildings like the beautiful City Hall, which was built in 1893* (see p212).

Durban's Beachfront*, a 6-km (4-mile) long stretch of hotels, restaurants and entertainment venues along the Indian Ocean shoreline, is also known as the Golden Mile* (see p218).

Zulu Culture

Clay pot

KEY

KwaZulu-Natal

THE REPUTATION of being a fierce warrior nation, fuelled by written accounts of the 1879 Anglo-Zulu War, has been enhanced by dramatic films like *Zulu* and, more recently, the internationally acclaimed television series *Shaka Zulu*. Many sites associated with Zulu history can be visited in the Ulundi, Eshowe and Melmoth districts of KwaZulu-Natal. It is true that the Zulu fought determinedly to defend their land, but their culture also reflects other, gentler, aspects in beadwork, pottery and basketry. In the remote Tugela River Valley and the northern parts of the province, rural people uphold many old customs and dances.

Oxhide was stretched on the ground and cured to make clothing and shields.

Fence made of poles and woven reeds.

Zulu Beehive Hut
A framework of saplings is covered with plaited grass or rushes. A hide screen affords additional privacy.

ZULU CRAFTS

The Zulu people are renowned as weavers and for their colourful beadwork. Baskets and mats made from *ilala* palm fronds and *imizi* grass are very decorative and especially popular. Most baskets display the traditional triangle or diamond shape, a symbol representing the male and female elements. Shiny glass beads introduced by the early 19th-century traders created a new custom. Today, artistic beadwork forms an important part of Zulu culture. Every pattern and colour has symbolic significance, as in the *incwadi*, or love-letters, that are made by young women and presented to eligible men.

Zulu beadwork and spoon

Maize, the staple diet, is ground and boiled to form a stiff, lumpy porridge.

Basket weaver

Utshwala *(beer) is prepared by the women, using sorghum. The fermented liquid is then strained through long grass sieves to separate the husks.*

Zulu dances require stamina and agility

TRADITIONAL DANCING

In Zulu society, social gatherings almost always involve dancing. Most Zulu dances require a high level of fitness – and a lack of inhibition. While ceremonial dances can involve large crowds of gyrating, clapping and stamping performers, small groups of performers need only the encouragement of an accompanying drum and singing, whistling or ululating onlookers. Lore and clan traditions may be related through the dance; alternatively, the movements may serve as a means of social commentary.

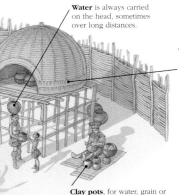

Water is always carried on the head, sometimes over long distances.

Clay pots, for water, grain or sorghum beer, are smoothed and decorated before firing.

Grain Storage
To protect their grain from birds and rodents, the Zulu stored maize and sorghum in a hut on long stilts.

***Cattle** are a symbol of wealth and play an important part in Zulu society. They are kept in a kraal (securely fenced enclosure) at night.*

THE ZULU KRAAL

Historically the *imizi* (Zulu kraal) was a circular settlement that enclosed several *uhlongwa* (beehive-shaped grass huts) grouped around an enclosure in which the cattle were corralled at night. Although the principle of the kraal continues, traditional architectural styles are seldom seen nowadays. Cement, bricks, concrete blocks and corrugated iron sheeting are the modern choices.

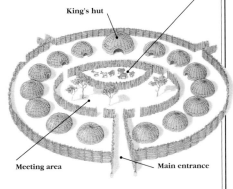

King's hut

Meeting area

Main entrance

***Traditional weapons** are still an integral part of Zulu culture, even today, and men often carry wooden staffs and clubs. At political meetings and rallies, tempers tend to flare, and as a result the carrying of traditional weapons has been outlawed.*

Durban's Surfing Scene

Glen D'Arcy surfing logo

IN THE 1960s, fibreglass boards replaced the earlier canvas-covered wooden versions, causing a surge in devotees to the sport. Durban, with its warm ocean currents, perfect waves and wide beaches, quickly became the surfing capital of the country. Some of the international greats the city produced were Max Wetland and Shaun Thomson, while current champions include Paul Canning and David Weare. Although surfing venues vary with weather conditions, ocean currents and the deposition or erosion of sand, favourite Durban hotspots are North Beach, New Pier, Snake Park Beach and Cave Rock at the Bluff, south of the harbour.

Paul Canning, a current hero, was the first South African to qualify for the World Championship Tour. The competition is restricted to the world's top 44 surfers.

"Cranking" is a term that is used to describe the manoeuvres at the base of a wave, in order to execute a "floater" (when the surfer rides back over the crest of an approaching wave).

The perfect wave provides an exhilarating ride. Durban is famous for its superb waves.

Modern boards *are smaller, lighter and more manoeuvrable than the clumsy early models.*

Competition long boards must exceed 2.8 m (9 ft) in length and weigh between 5.2–7 kg (11–15 lbs).

Short boards are lighter, more manoeuvrable, and are not allowed to exceed 3.2 kg (7 lbs) to qualify for contests.

Dr Zogs Sex Wax is rubbed on boards to improve the surfer's foothold.

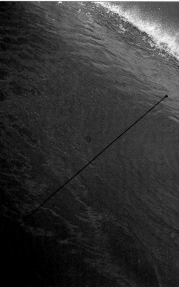

CAVE ROCK

Cave Rock is Durban's premier surfing spot. The presence of a deep ocean channel *(see p21)* and a reef near the shore produces powerful waves that compare with those which made Hawai'i world-famous.

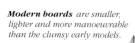

Shaun Thomson (middle) became a local hero and surfing icon when he won the World Championship title in 1977.

SURFING CULTURE

Surfing has produced a unique life-orientation and philosophy followed by dedicated devotees around the globe. Laid-back and easy-going, it strives for simplicity and centres on the enjoyment of one of nature's most powerful forces: water. Graffiti and murals in Durban integrate the thrills and ills of surfing with the cityscape, transforming the bland walls into roaring tubes of salt and spray.

The lip forms as the base of the wave encounters the reef.

Fashion is a lucrative spin-off industry. The Gunston 500 attracts imaginative creations that reflect laissez faire, *and popular brand labels like Gotcha and Hang Ten now command designer-wear prices.*

The tube of the wave curls up and around behind the surfer.

Surfing heroes attain cult status. The big events draw devoted "groupies" and autograph hunters.

The Gunston 500, South Africa's premier surfing event, takes place over six days every July. First staged in 1969 with prize money of R500 (which gave rise to the contest's name), it was the first professional surfing event to be held outside Hawai'i.

SURFING LINGO

Tube – ride through the concave curve formed by the body of the wave.
Lip – the tip of the wave (its most powerful part).
Barrel – ride through the curve of a wave that ends in the wave breaking on the surfer.
Bomb – enormous wave.
Filthy – excellent surf.
Grommet – a beginner.
Shundies – thank you.
Tassie – a young woman.
Cactus – any person that surfers do not like.

WILD COAST, DRAKENSBERG AND MIDLANDS

T HE ZULUS CALL THE JAGGED PEAKS *of Southern Africa's highest mountains* Ukhahlamba, *"a barrier of spears". Where the lofty summits of the Drakensberg slope down toward the coastline, the unspoiled Wild Coast promises excellent fishing and hiking.*

Some 1,000 years ago the lush, well-watered valleys of the Drakensberg were home to hunter-gatherer San Bushmen who stalked antelope with their bows and arrows. The colonizing vanguards of Zulu, Xhosa, Afrikaner and British soon drove them from the region, but, apart from the delicate paintings that survive under overhangs and in caves, the diminutive hunters left no evidence of their presence.

At the beginning of the 19th century, the Xhosa's heartland was part of the expanding Cape colony, while the centre of the Zulu kingdom stretched north of the Tugela River. Facing attacks on several fronts, the Basotho tribe sought refuge in the high mountains that would eventually become the kingdom of Lesotho. By 1848 the Kei River had become the frontier line between the British and Xhosa, while to the north, the territory between the Mzimkhulu and Tugela rivers was declared the Colony of Natal. Over the centuries, countless territorial wars raged in this fertile region now known as the Midlands, and many of the old battle sites can still be visited today.

In 1976 the Xhosa territory of Transkei was officially declared "independent", but reincorporated into South Africa in 1994. This is an area of immense natural beauty and splendour. The enchanted coastline, too remote for modern development, has remained virtually unspoilt and offers secluded bays and beaches, rocky headlands and some of the best fishing to be found anywhere along the coast.

The sandstone buildings at the Rorke's Drift battle site

◁ **Bushman's River and Giant's Castle in the Drakensberg range, seen from the Giant's Castle Game Reserve**

Exploring the Wild Coast, Drakensberg and Midlands

THE REMOTE LESOTHO HIGHLANDS and the Drakensberg, Southern Africa's highest mountain range, form the backbone of this region. Breathtaking views, and streams flowing through secluded valleys attract nature lovers, hikers, birdwatchers and trout fishermen. A plateau dotted with traditional Xhosa huts lies between the mountains and the Wild Coast's sheltered coves and forested cliffs. North of here, in the Natal Midlands, a pastoral landscape of green hills and forest patches serves as the perfect backdrop for charming country hotels, a myriad arts and crafts enterprises and dairy farms.

The distant Champagne Castle, Monk's Cowl and Cathkin Peak in the Drakensberg mountains

KEY

≣	Motorway
≣	National route
≣	Other route
≣	Scenic route
⇌	River, lake or dam
···	Park or reserve boundary
- -	International boundary
✲	Viewpoint

The memorial *laager* (encampment) on the site of the Battle of Blood River (1838), near Dundee

Johannesburg

KROONSTAD

N1

WELKOM

Bloemfontein

Bloemfontein

MASERU

Caledon

LESOTI

A2

Bloemfontein

N6

Orange

ALIWAL NORTH

R58

R56

R56

White Kei

R61

R61

QUEENSTOWN

Black Kei

Great Kei

N6

Port Elizabeth

EAST LONDON

San Bushman rock art in the Giant's Castle Game Reserve, Drakensberg

GETTING AROUND

The N2 links East London with KwaZulu-Natal. Roads leading to the Wild Coast are mostly untarred and private transport is necessary to reach the remote beaches. Many Lesotho roads require a 4WD vehicle, although the network is being extended. There is no easy road access to Lesotho from the east. The N3 highway in KwaZulu-Natal, which carries one-tenth of South Africa's traffic, provides access to the Drakensberg resorts. Roads leading to the hotels and resorts are mostly tarred. Large bus companies offer regular services between regional centres. There are domestic airports in East London, Umtata and Pietermaritzburg and an international airport at Maseru.

SIGHTS AT A GLANCE

Cathedral Peak **7**
Champagne Castle **5**
Giant's Castle **4**
Golden Gate Highlands
   National Park **9**
Kamberg **3**
Lesotho pp204–5 **2**
Midlands Meander **12**
   Natal Drakensberg
National Park **6**
Pietermaritzburg **13**
Royal Natal National Park **8**
Spioenkop Nature Reserve **11**
Wild Coast **1**

Tour
Battlefields Tour p210 **10**

SEE ALSO

• *Where to Stay* pp327–29

• *Where to Eat* pp351–52

0 kilometres 50

0 miles 25

The City Hall of Pietermaritzburg

The Wild Coast ❶

THE SECOND LARGEST CITY in the Eastern Cape and the country's only river port, East London is a good starting point for exploring the shores of the former Transkei *(see p189)*. Appropriately named "Wild Coast", this area is one of South Africa's most under-developed, where rural communities adhere to age-old traditions, and spectacular beaches front a section of the Indian Ocean that is notorious for its shipwrecks. Much of the land here is communally owned by the Xhosa-speaking inhabitants.

East London's Orient Beach is popular with bathers and surfers

Exploring the Wild Coast

The Wild Coast is an outdoor paradise with rugged cliffs, an unspoilt coastline, sheltered bays, pounding breakers and dense coastal forests. Most resorts, reserves and villages are accessible from the N2, but many roads are untarred and in poor condition. There is no public transport to speak of, the best option is the Baz Bus, which covers the N2.

East London

Road map E5. 🏢 101,300. ✈ R72, 12 km (7 miles) W of East London. 🚉 Station Rd. 🚌 Oxford St. 🛈 Shop 1 & 2, King's Tourism Centre Esplanade *(043) 722-6015.*

East London is a pleasant seaside town on the Buffalo River. Several good swimming beaches are washed by the warm waters of the Indian Ocean.

Among several interesting sites is the statue in front of the City Hall of Black Consciousness leader, Steve Biko. Born in the Eastern Cape, he died under dubious circumstances while in police custody.

Latimer's Landing, the city's waterfront, offers good river and harbour views.

Rock angling is a popular sport

🏛 East London Museum

319 Oxford St. ☎ *(043) 743-0686.* ⏰ 9:30am–5pm Mon–Fri, 2–5pm Sat; 11am–4pm Sun & pub hols. ⬤ Good Fri, 25 Dec. 🗓 🎫 🅿

Kwelera

Road map E4. 26 km (17 miles) E of East London. 🛈 Yellow Sands Resort, *(043) 734-3043.*
Kwelera is one of the most attractive estuaries in the region. There is a resort on the north bank and canoeists can paddle upriver, past hills dotted with huts and cycads, and which echo with the cries of fish eagles. An extensive coastal forest reserve, south of the river mouth, is an ideal habitat for bushbuck.

Morgan's Bay and Kei Mouth

Road map E4. Off the N2, 85 km (53 miles) E of East London. 🛈 Morgan's Bay Hotel, *(043) 841-1062.*
These coastal villages lie on a stretch of coast renowned for its scenery. At Kei Mouth, a pont transports vehicles across the Great Kei River to the former Xhosa "homeland" known as Transkei. A family hotel at Morgan's Bay *(see p328)* adjoins the beach and the Ntshala Lagoon offers safe swimming. Walks along the cliffs afford superb views of the sea.

Further south, at Double Mouth, a spur overlooking the ocean and estuary provides one of the finest views in the whole country.

Kei Mouth to Mbashe River

Road map E4. 95 km (59 miles) E of East London. 🛈 *(043) 841-1004.*
The Kei River marks the start of the Wild Coast. Twenty rivers enter this 80-km (50-mile) long stretch, along which is strung a succession of old-fashioned family hotels. Kei Mouth is only an hour's drive from East London, making it a popular weekend destination.

Further north, Dwesa Nature Reserve extends along the coast from the Nqabara River. The reserve is home to rare tree dassies and samango monkeys. The grassland,

---

COELACANTH

In 1938 a boat fishing off the Chalumna River mouth near East London netted an unusual fish. The captain sent it to the East London Museum, whose curator, Marjorie Courtenay-Latimer, contacted Professor JLB Smith, ichthyologist at Rhodes University. The fish belonged to a species believed to have become extinct with the dinosaurs. The reward offered for another *Latimeria chalumnae* was claimed only in 1952, when one was netted off the Comoros Islands. The coelacanth is steel-blue and covered in heavy scales; it is distinguished by its six primitive, limb-like fins.

The coelacanth

Traditional Xhosa huts dot the hillsides of the former Transkei

coastline and forest are all pristine. The Haven is on the banks of the Mbashe River within the Cwebe Nature Reserve. Adjoining reserves conserve 60 sq km (23 sq miles) of dense forest, home to bushbuck and blue duiker, as well as coastal grasslands inhabited by eland, harte-beest, wildebeest and zebra. A hiking trail follows the entire Wild Coast, but the section from Mbashe to Coffee Bay is the most spectacular.

Coffee Bay

Road map E4. Off the N2. *Ocean View Hotel, (047) 575-2005/6.*
Allegedly named after a ship carrying coffee which was wrecked at the site in 1863, Coffee Bay is popular for fishing, swimming and beach

walks. There are a number of superbly sited hotels set above the sandy beaches. A prominent detached cliff, separated from the mainland by erosion, has been named Hole in the Wall; it is a conspicuous landmark located 6 km (4 miles) south along the coast. Many centuries of swirling wave action have carved an arch through the centre of the cliff.

Umngazi Mouth

Road map E4. 25 km (16 miles) S of Port St Johns. *Umngazi River Bungalows, (047) 564-1115/6/8/9.*
An idyllic estuary framed by forested hills, the Umngazi offers superb snorkelling, canoeing and board-sailing. Umngazi River Bungalows *(see p329),* on the northern

bank, and renowned for its food and service, is one of the leading resorts on the Wild Coast. There is a lovely, sandy beach and the rugged coastline extends south to the cliffs that are known in Xhosa as *Ndluzulu,* after the crashing sound of the surf.

Mkambati Game Reserve

Road map E4. Off R61 N of Port St Johns. *Eastern Cape Tourism Board, (040) 635-2115.*
Wedged between the Mzikaba and Mtentu rivers, Mkambati is the Wild Coast's largest nature reserve. Apart from conserving a 13-km (8-mile) long strip of grassland and unspoilt, rocky coastline, the reserve is known for its endemic plants such as the Mkambati palm, which is found only on the north banks of the rivers. Cape vultures breed in the Mzikaba Gorge. The Mkambati River flows through the reserve in a series of waterfalls of which Horseshoe Falls, near the sea, is the most striking.

Accommodation ranges from a stone lodge to cottages. Outdoor activities include swimming, fishing and horseriding. Animals include eland, springbok, blesbok, impala, blue wildebeest and zebra. An added attraction is that the reserve is near the Wild Coast Sun Hotel and Casino *(see p224).*

The Xhosa word for Hole in the Wall, *esiKhaleni,* means "the place of sound"

Lesotho ❷

SURROUNDED BY SOUTH AFRICA, this mountain kingdom, or "Kingdom in the Sky" as it is sometimes referred to, achieved independence from Britain on 4 October 1966. The rugged highlands of Lesotho, which encompass the Drakensberg, Maluti and Thaba-Putsoa mountains, are a popular destination for visitors who enjoy camping, hiking and climbing. Lesotho also boasts fertile river valleys, a rich variety of flora and fauna, and a strong cultural heritage that is very much kept alive by the Basotho people.

Basotho hat

The Cave Houses at Mateka, sculpted from mud, are good examples of indigenous architecture.

★ **Teyateyaneng**
This town, easily accessible from Maseru, is the "craft capital" of Lesotho. The colourful woven jerseys, carpets and wall-hangings are a local speciality.

Maseru
Founded by the British in 1869, Maseru lies on the Caledon River. Buildings and roads destroyed in political turmoil toward the end of 1998 are being restored and rebuilt.

STAR FEATURES

★ **Katse Dam**

★ **Sani Pass**

★ **Teyateyaneng**

Snowfalls
In May and June the high country becomes a winter wonderland, but no commercial skiing ventures exist.

Map labels: Johannesburg, LESOTHO, Cape Town, Ficksburg, Hlot, Din, Tr, Peka, Phuth, Moletsar, Ladybrand, Teyateyaneng, Cave H, N8, A1, Mateka, Sefikeng, MASERU, Thaba Bosiu, Mazenod, Roma, Bl, Mou, Pa, Makhaleng, Likalane, Caledon, Kolo, Morija, Ramabanta, A2, Mafeteng, Rock Paintings, Bird Park, Thabana Morena, Semonko, Cannibal Caves, Dinosaur Tracks, Mohale's Hoek, Mount Moorosi, Mou, For, A2, Telle-Bridge, Dinosaur Tracks, Pa, Moyeni (Quthing), Ral

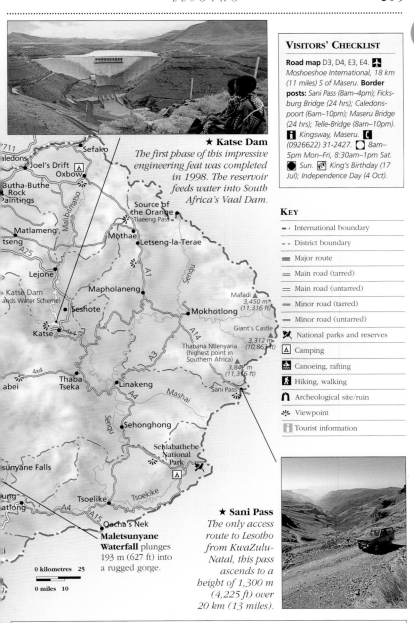

★ **Katse Dam**
The first phase of this impressive engineering feat was completed in 1998. The reservoir feeds water into South Africa's Vaal Dam.

VISITORS' CHECKLIST

Road map D3, D4, E3, E4. ✈
Moshoeshoe International, 18 km (11 miles) S of Maseru. **Border posts:** *Sani Pass (8am–4pm); Ficksburg Bridge (24 hrs); Caledonspoort (6am–10pm); Maseru Bridge (24 hrs); Telle-Bridge (8am–10pm).*
ℹ *Kingsway, Maseru.* 📞 *(0926622) 31-2427.* 🕐 *8am–5pm Mon–Fri, 8:30am–1pm Sat.* 🌑 *Sun.* 🎉 *King's Birthday (17 Jul); Independence Day (4 Oct).*

KEY

▬ ·	International boundary
▬ ▬	District boundary
▬▬	Major route
▬▬	Main road (tarred)
▬▬	Main road (untarred)
▬▬	Minor road (tarred)
▬▬	Minor road (untarred)
🏞	National parks and reserves
⛺	Camping
🚣	Canoeing, rafting
🚶	Hiking, walking
🏛	Archeological site/ruin
🔆	Viewpoint
ℹ	Tourist information

★ **Sani Pass**
The only access route to Lesotho from KwaZulu-Natal, this pass ascends to a height of 1,300 m (4,225 ft) over 20 km (13 miles).

Maletsunyane Waterfall plunges 193 m (627 ft) into a rugged gorge.

0 kilometres   25

0 miles   10

ROCK PAINTINGS AND DINOSAUR TRACKS

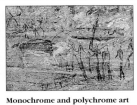

Monochrome and polychrome art

Due to its remoteness, Lesotho has remained relatively uncommercialized. The high mountains, where stout Basotho ponies are often the only form of transport, contain some of the finest examples of rock art in Southern Africa. Thaba Bosiu near Maseru and the Sekubu Caves at Butha-Buthe in the north are just two of the more than 400 worthwhile sites. Fossilized dinosaur tracks are found at places like Moyeni (Quthing), and the Tsikoane Mission at Hlotse.

Kamberg ❸

Road map E3. Estcourt. 🛈 *KwaZulu-Natal Nature Conservation, (033) 845-1000.* ⏰ *8am–6pm Mon–Thu, 8am–4:30pm Fri, 8am–noon Sat, Sun.* 🖾
🚶 ⚔ ⬇

Sᴛᴜᴀᴛᴇᴅ ɪɴ ᴛʜᴇ Mooi River valley, Kamberg is known for its trout fishing locations. There are several small dams near the trout hatchery, which is open to the public and offers guided tours. Walking trails explore the valley or meander along the river.

Shelter Cave has superb San Bushman rock paintings and can be visited with a guide; the return walk takes about four hours. A small chalet camp overlooks the valley.

Kamberg offers good trout fishing in a beautiful setting

Giant's Castle ❹

Road map E3. Estcourt. 🛈 *KwaZulu-Natal Nature Conservation, (033) 845-1000.* ⏰ *as Kamberg.* 🖾 🚶 ⚔

Iɴ 1903 ᴀ sᴀɴᴄᴛᴜᴀʀʏ was established in this area to protect some of the last surviving

The high-lying Giant's Castle is covered with snow in winter

eland in South Africa. They now number around 1,500 – one of the largest populations in the country.

A camouflaged hide allows visitors to view endangered bearded vultures (lammergeier), an estimated 200 pairs of which are found here.

Accommodation is in comfortable bungalows and small cottages. The main camp overlooks the Bushman's River, with Giant's Castle (3,314 m; 10,770 ft) dominating the skyline. A number of trails leads off from the camp and a short walk brings visitors to a cave where 500 San Bushman rock paintings, some of which are 800 years old, can be seen.

Champagne Castle ❺

Road map E3. Winterton.

Cʜᴀᴍᴘᴀɢɴᴇ Cᴀsᴛʟᴇ, at 3,377 m (10,975 ft), is the second highest peak in South Africa. It juts out from the surrounding escarpment and dominates the horizon in a delightful valley. A 31-km (19-mile)

connecting road from the N3 provides convenient access to a cluster of luxury hotels and timeshare resorts, such as the The Nest and the luxurious Drakensberg Sun. Famous institutions like the internationally acclaimed Drakensberg Boys' Choir School, as well as the Dragon Peaks and Monk's Cowl caravan parks are found in this region.

Natal Drakensberg Park ❻

Road map E3. Winterton. 🛈 *KwaZulu-Natal Nature Conservation, (033) 845-1000.* ⏰ *as Kamberg.* 🖾 🚶 ⚔ 🅰

Tʜᴇ ᴅʀᴀᴋᴇɴsʙᴇʀɢ's dramatic and rugged escarpment provides an awesome backdrop to much of the pastoral KwaZulu-Natal Midlands.

The Natal Drakensberg Park covers an area of 2,350 sq km (907 sq miles) and preserves some of South Africa's finest wilderness and conservation area, as well as its highest mountain peaks. Secluded valleys and mist-shrouded,

THE DRAKENSBERG RANGE

The Drakensberg, "dragon mountains", is South Africa's greatest mountain wilderness. It follows the border of Lesotho for 250 km (155 miles) – an escarpment that separates the high, interior plateau from the subtropical coast of KwaZulu-Natal. The Drakensberg is divided into the rocky High Berg and the pastoral Little Berg. Both are superb hiking venues.

Giant's Castle

Giant's Castle Pass

Die Hoek

Hodgson's Peaks

dense forests are home to an abundance of wildlife, while many rock overhangs shelter some of the finest remaining examples of San Bushman rock art in South Africa today. Since these ancient paintings and etches represent a priceless cultural heritage they must never be touched, or, even worse, be splashed with water to enhance their colours.

KwaZulu-Natal Nature Conservation has established five rest camps within the park which can accommodate 370 visitors, and there are many pleasant campsites, mountain huts and caves that cater for hikers and mountaineers. On the boundaries of the park, particularly in the Cathkin Peak valley, many hotels and resorts offer comfortable accommodation and outdoor sports.

Cathedral Peak ❼

Road map E3. Winterton.

SOME OF THE Drakensberg's finest scenery is found in this region, and the area around Cathedral Peak offers some of the best hiking in the entire range.

The road from Winterton winds for 42 km (26 miles) through Zulu villages that are scattered across the gentle folds of the Mlambonja Valley. The Drakensberg's towering peaks form a dramatic backdrop. From the conservation office near the Cathedral Peak hotel, Mike's Pass gains 500 m (1,625 ft) in 5 km (3 miles). Ndedema Gorge, where many San Bushman paintings adorn rocky overhangs, protects the largest forest in the range.

Royal Natal National Park ❽

Road map E3. Winterton. 🛈 *Tendele camp, (036) 438-6411.* 🎫 *National Parks Board Reservations: (012) 343-1991, (031) 304-4934, or (0338) 45-1000.* ⭕ *daily.* 🏕 🚶 🎣 ⛺ 🅦 *www.saparks.co.za*

THE ROYAL NATAL National Park has some of Africa's most spectacular scenery. The awe-inspiring Amphitheatre, a crescent-shaped basalt wall 6 km (4 miles) wide, soars to a height of 1,500 m (4,875 ft). Here, the Tugela River plunges 948 m (3,080 ft) into the valley below, making it the second highest waterfall in the world.

Bearded vulture

Tendele rest camp, above the Tugela River, provides unrivalled views of the countryside below.

In the valleys, the Royal Natal Hotel and Mahai campsite provide easy access to an extensive network of trails that explore the 88-sq-km (34-sq-mile) reserve.

Golden Gate Highlands National Park ❾

Road map E3. Clarens. 🎫 *National Parks Board Reservations: (012) 428-9111, (058) 255-0012.* ⭕ *daily.* 🏕 🚶 🎣 ⛺ 🅦 *www.saparks.co.za*

SITUATED IN THE foothills of the Maloti Mountains in the eastern Free State, Golden Gate Highlands National Park encompasses 48 sq km (18 sq miles) of grassland and spectacular sandstone formations. The park was proclaimed in 1963 to protect the sandstone cliffs above the Little Caledon valley. Black wildebeest, grey rhebok, oribi, blesbok and mountain reedbuck can be seen, as well as the endangered bearded vulture (lammergeier), black eagle and steppe buzzard.

Accommodation in Glen Reenen Camp consists of chalets and a caravan park, while Brandwag Lodge offers more sophisticated cottages.

The Royal Natal National Park, an unspoilt wilderness

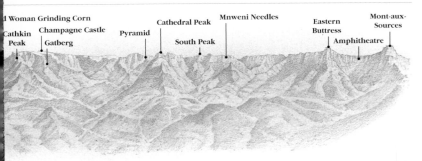

Woman Grinding Corn · Cathkin Peak · Champagne Castle · Gatberg · Pyramid · Cathedral Peak · South Peak · Mnweni Needles · Eastern Buttress · Amphitheatre · Mont-aux-Sources

Cattle grazing in the Giant's Castle reserve at the foot of the mighty Drakensberg Mountains ▷

Battlefields Tour ⑩

THE PEACEFUL, rolling grasslands and treed hills of northwestern KwaZulu-Natal retain few reminders of the bloody battles that were waged in this corner of South Africa during the 19th century. In the 1820s, Zulu king Shaka's campaign to seize control over the scattered tribes plunged the entire region into turmoil. Over

Monument at Rorke's Drift

the following 80 years many wars were fought, pitting Zulu against Ndwandwe, Afrikaner against Zulu and English against Afrikaner and Zulu. A detailed guide to the battle-fields lists over 50 sites of interest and is available from the local publicity associations and the Talana Museum, where expert guides can be hired as well.

Elandslaagte ②
The Boer and British forces clashed here on 22 October 1899, during a severe storm. The British were forced to retreat to nearby Ladysmith.

Talana Museum ③
This museum commemorates the first battle of the South African War (20 October 1899) when 4,500 British soldiers arrived in Dundee to defend the town and its coal mines.

Rorke's Drift ⑤
This museum depicts the battle during which some 100 British soldiers repelled 4,000 Zulus for 12 hours, earning them a total of 11 Victoria crosses.

Ladysmith ①
On 2 November 1899, Boer general Piet Joubert laid siege to Ladysmith and its 12,000 British troops for 118 days.

KEY

▬	Motorway
▭	Tour route
⁼	Other roads
☀	Viewpoint
☒	Battle site

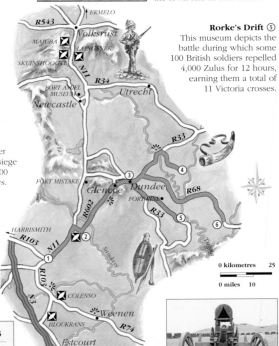

0 kilometres   25

0 miles   10

TIPS FOR DRIVERS

Length: 380 km (236 miles).
Stopping-off points: The towns of Ladysmith and Dundee have restaurants and accommodation. Audio tapes can be bought from the Talana Museum in Dundee and at Fugitives Drift, which also offers guided tours and accommodation.

Isandlhwana ⑥
Zulu *impis*, angered by an invasion of their territory, attacked a British force on 22 January 1879.

Blood River ④
For years regarded as a symbol of the Afrikaners' political and religious victory over the Zulus, this battle gave rise to a public holiday in South Africa – 16 December.

Midmar Dam is surrounded by a tranquil nature reserve

Spioenkop Public Resort Nature Reserve ⓫

Road map E3. 35 km (22 miles) SW of Ladysmith on Winterton Rd. 🚘 (036) 488-1578. ⏰ 6am–6pm daily.
🏊 🅰 🦌 💦 🎣 🚤

THE PICTURESQUE dam nestles at the foot of the 1,466-m high (4,764 ft) Spioenkop which was scene of a decisive battle between British and Boer forces in 1891 during the South African War *(see p51)*. Countless graves and memorials are scattered across the mountain's summit as a grim reminder.

Today, Spioenkop is popular with outdoor enthusiasts. The dam offers fishing and boating, while eland, hartebeest, zebra, giraffe, kudu, buffalo and white rhino can be seen in the surrounding nature reserve. Here, there is also a

pleasant campsite, as well as a swimming pool, battlefields museum, tennis courts, children's playground and a slipway on the southern shore. Picnic sites are situated along the southern shoreline, and two short trails encourage visitors to view game on foot.

Two bush camps offer luxury accommodation. Ntenjwa overlooks the peaceful upper reaches of the large dam and is only accessible by private boat or the ferry service provided by Nature Conservation.

Iphika, at the foot of Spioenkop on the northern shore, is a secluded tented safari camp, reached by a private track. As other vehicles are not permitted in this sector, visitors are offered a unique wilderness experience.

Midlands Meander ⓬

Road map E3 Mooi River ℹ️ (0332) 66-6308.

THE UNDULATING hills of the Natal Midlands, with their green patches of forest and their dairy farms, have long been a retreat favoured by artists and craftspeople. In 1985 six studios established an arts and crafts route: the Midlands Meander. The route quickly gained popularity and now consists of around 140 participating members and studios.

Tapestry detail, Rorke's Drift

There are four routes that meander between the small towns of Hilton, Nottingham Road and Mooi River. Goods on offer include herbs, cheese, wine, pottery, woven cloth, leather itms, furniture, stained glass and antiques.

Of interest is a monument on the R103, just past Midmar Dam, that marks the spot where Nelson Mandela *(see p55)* was arrested by security police on 5 August 1962.

Accommodation along the way ranges from idyllic country hotels, tranquil guest farms and picturesque lodges to comfortable bed and breakfast establishments. There is also a well-known health spa and many quaint country pubs and eateries.

The monument to the Battle of Spioenkop overlooks the dam

Street-by-Street: Pietermaritzburg ⑬

FROM ITS HUMBLE BEGINNINGS as an irrigation settlement established by Afrikaner farmers in 1836, Pietermaritzburg has developed into the commercial, industrial and administrative centre of the KwaZulu-Natal Midlands. An intriguing blend of Victorian, Indian, African and modern architecture and culture combine to produce a distinctly South African city. Many historic buildings and monuments, as well as galleries and museums, are located around the city centre and in the western suburbs, which nestle at the foot of a range of densely wooded hills. Visitors can ramble through the surrounding forests and botanic gardens, and visit several nature reserves and recreation resorts located within the city or a few minutes' drive away.

Gandhi statue
In Pietermaritzburg, in 1893, Gandhi had to leave a first-class train, because he wasn't white.

★ Tatham Art Gallery
Housed in the old Supreme Court, displays at this gallery include works by South African artists, as well as European masters like Edgar Degas, Henri Matisse and Pablo Picasso.

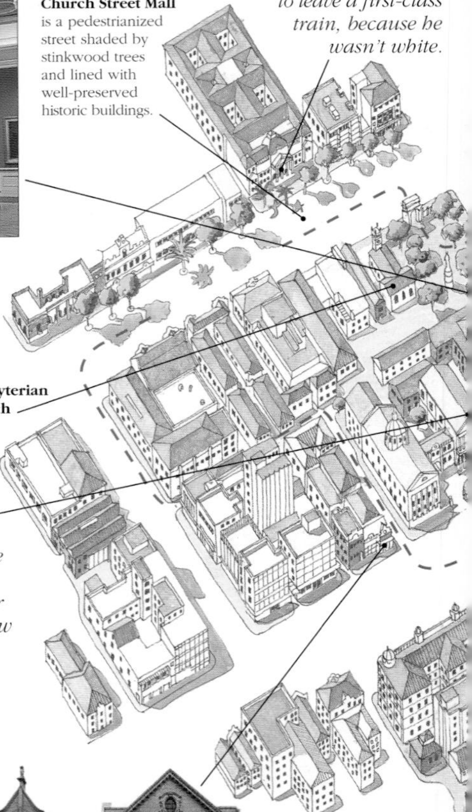

Church Street Mall
is a pedestrianized street shaded by stinkwood trees and lined with well-preserved historic buildings.

Presbyterian Church

Parliament Building
The seat of the colonial government prior to 1910, it now houses KwaZulu-Natal's provincial legislature.

KEY

– – – Suggested route

STAR SIGHTS
★ Natal Museum
★ Tatham Art Gallery
★ City Hall

Colonial Houses
The Renaissance Revival JH Isaacs building and the Edwardian First National Bank are two examples of colonial architecture in Longmarket Street.

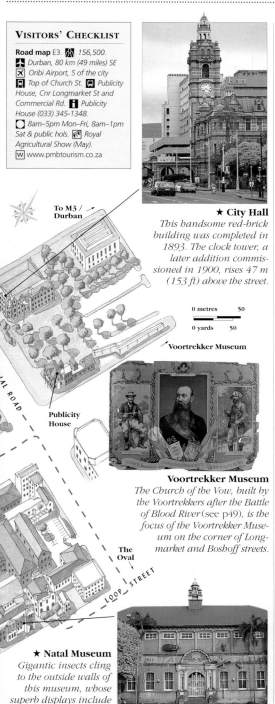

**To M3 /
Durban**

★ **City Hall**
This handsome red-brick building was completed in 1893. The clock tower, a later addition commissioned in 1900, rises 47 m (153 ft) above the street.

```
0 metres        50
0 yards         50
```

Voortrekker Museum

Publicity House

Voortrekker Museum
The Church of the Vow, built by the Voortrekkers after the Battle of Blood River (see p49), is the focus of the Voortrekker Museum on the corner of Longmarket and Boshoff streets.

The Oval

LOOP STREET

★ **Natal Museum**
Gigantic insects cling to the outside walls of this museum, whose superb displays include African mammals, birds and dinosaurs.

Exploring Pietermaritzburg

The town is a treasure trove of architecture and lends itself well to walking excursions. One of the oldest quarters, the Lanes – a labyrinth of narrow alleys between Church and Longmarket streets – gives an idea of what Pietermaritzburg was like in days gone by.

ENVIRONS: Midmar Dam, a weekend and holiday venue for watersports enthusiasts and fishermen, lies 27 km (17 miles) north of Pietermaritzburg in the **Midmar Dam Resort**. A small wildlife reserve on the southern shore is home to several antelope species, among them black wildebeest, eland, hartebeest, springbok, blesbok and zebra.

The origins of Howick, some 18 km (11 miles) north of Pietermaritzburg, date back to 1850. In the town, a viewing platform and restaurant overlook the beautiful Howick Falls, equal in height to the Victoria Falls in Zimbabwe.

On the Karkloof Road, just outside Howick, the **Umgeni Valley Nature Reserve** offers hiking trails through the steep-sided, boulder-strewn valley carved by the Umgeni River. The track leading from the entrance gate provides scenic views of the gorge.

🏊 **Midmar Dam Resort**
Howick. **(** *(033) 330-2067.* 🕐 *24 hours daily.* 🎭 🚻 🚕 🅿
🏊 **Umgeni Valley Nature Reserve**
Howick. **(** *(033) 330-3931.*
🕐 *8am–4:30pm daily.* ● *25 Dec.*
🎭 🚶

The Howick Falls

DURBAN AND ZULULAND

Caressed by the warm currents *of the Indian Ocean, this picturesque region is one of the country's leading tourist destinations. Abundant rainfall and year-round sunshine sustain a prosperous sugar industry and a profusion of coastal holiday resorts. North of the Tugela River, an untamed tapestry of wildlife, wilderness and wetland evokes the essence of Africa.*

Near the end of the 15th century a sailing ship captained by the Portuguese mariner, Vasco Da Gama, passed the east coast of Africa on Christmas Day. The intrepid seafarer sighted a large bay, flanked by forested dunes, and named it "Rio de Natal", the Christmas River. Subsequently, on sailors' maps, the name "Natal" was given to the uncharted land that lay beyond the wide beaches and forested dunes along the coast.

In the 1820s, rumours of the Zulu chief and military genius, Shaka, *(see p47)* began to reach the Cape Colony. Shaka forged the scattered clans of the Natal region into a near-irrepressible force, and 60 years would pass before the British Empire succeeded in subduing the mighty Zulu army. The passage of time has brought many changes. "Rio de Natal" has developed into Durban, today the largest port in Africa and third largest city in the country. Where the coastal grasslands and forests once tumbled down to the sea, a wide band of sugar cane plantations now separates luxury hotels overlooking sandy beaches and the warm currents of the Indian Ocean from the rolling hills of the interior. Many major rivers meander through the undulating hills of the interior, and the coastline is enhanced by tranquil estuaries and lagoons rich in birdlife.

In the northern corner of the region, some of the country's finest game reserves, with melodious Zulu names like Hluhluwe-Umfolozi, Mkuzi, Ndumo and Tembe, preserve a timeless landscape that has remained unchanged since the reign of Shaka.

Traditional reed fishtrap, Kosi Bay

◁ **The marvellous interior of the Hindu Temple of Understanding near Durban**

Exploring Durban and Zululand

THIS REGION IS RENOWNED for its subtropical climate, sandy beaches, tepid ocean currents and unspoilt game reserves. Durban, with its superb hotels, beach-front and shopping centres, is perfectly situated for exploring a scenic and varied coastline, and the N2 coastal motorway allows holiday-makers easy access to many attractions. Apart from tourism, this coastal belt also sustains the vast plantations that produce most of South Africa's sugar. North of Richards Bay, three hours from Durban on excellent roads, beckons a wilderness of swamps, forests and savannah. The Greater St Lucia Wetland Park is a paradise for bird-watchers and nature lovers. The wooded hills of the nearby Hluhluwe-Umfolozi Park are home to rhino, zebra, elephant, buffalo and lion.

Grazing Burchell's zebra in the Hluhluwe-Umfolozi Park

Aerial view of Durban's attractive beachfront development, with Sea World in the foreground

SIGHTS AT A GLANCE

Durban ❶
Greater St Lucia Wetland Park ❽
Hluhluwe-Umfolozi Park ❻
Itala Nature Reserve ❼
Kosi Bay ❿
Tembe Elephant Park ⓫
North Coast ❸
Phinda Resource
    Reserve ❾
Shakaland ❺
Simunye Lodge ❹
South Coast ❷

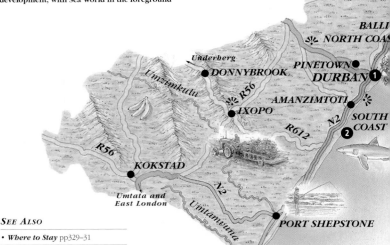

Tugela

R614

BALLI
❄ NORTH COAS

Underberg
●DONNYBROOK   PINETOWN●
Umzimkulu   DURBAN❶

R56

AMANZIMTOTI❄

●IXOPO   N2   SOUTH
        COAST
R612   ❷

R56

KOKSTAD

Umtata and
East London   N2

Umtamvuna   PORT SHEPSTONE

❄PORT EDWARD

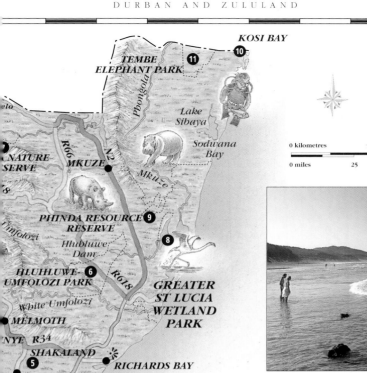

KOSI BAY

TEMBE ELEPHANT PARK

Phongola

Lake Sibaya

Sodwana Bay

NATURE SERVE

R66

N2

MKUZE

Mkuze

Imfolozi

PHINDA RESOURCE RESERVE

Hluhluwe Dam

HLUHLUWE-UMFOLOZI PARK

R618

White Umfolozi

GREATER ST LUCIA WETLAND PARK

MELMOTH

NYE R34

SHAKALAND

RICHARDS BAY

HOWE

N2

TUGELA MOUTH

ANGER

| 0 kilometres | 50 |
| 0 miles | 25 |

The unspoilt beach at Cape Vidal, near St Lucia, on the North Coast

GETTING AROUND

The N2 national route that leads from the Eastern Cape Province and Wild Coast runs parallel to the coast from Port Shepstone onwards. It provides quick and safe access to the region's attractions. Durban has an international airport, with domestic airports at Margate and Richards Bay. Several Durban-based touring companies offer package tours to the splendid northern game reserves.

Sugar cane is a major crop in subtropical Zululand

KEY

≡ Motorway

▬ National route

▭ Other route

▬ Scenic route

— River, lake or dam

--- Park or reserve boundary

- - International boundary

☆ Viewpoint

Durban ❶

Life ring

Vasco da Gama's port Natal was renamed Durban in honour of Cape Governor Benjamin D'Urban after Zulu chief, Shaka had given the land to the British in 1824. The former trading post is, today, the holiday capital of KwaZulu-Natal. Sunny days and the warm Indian Ocean draw visitors to a beachfront flanked by high-rise hotels and holiday apartments. Attractions such as Water World and the Umgeni River Bird Park lie north of South Africa's principal harbour.

An aerial view of the Paddling Pools on Durban's Golden Mile

Exploring Durban

Most of the city's modern holiday attractions are strung out along the beachfront, conveniently close together and within comfortable walking distance from the hotels. But Durban is not only about seaside fun; the city centre has many historic buildings, as well as museums, theatres and exciting markets.

The Golden Mile

Marine Parade.

The land side of this 6-km (4-mile) long holiday precinct is lined with a continuous row of hotels, while the seaward edge consists of amusement parks, an aerial cableway, craft sellers, pubs, restaurants, ice-cream parlours, piers, sandy beaches and a promenade.

Along the Golden Mile is where visitors will find the brightly decorated rickshaws that have become a unique local form of entertainment. The colourful rickshaw drivers, festooned in beads and tall, elaborate headdresses, are a curious amalgamation of traditional African practices and Indian influences.

uShaka Marine World offers an excellent aquarium and dolphinarium. The aquarium's main tank is home to many species of tropical fish, turtles and sting rays. Scuba divers enter the tank twice a day to feed the fish. Shows at the dolphinarium feature dolphins, seals and penguins. The **FitzSimons Snake Park** exhibits indigenous snakes, as well as crocodiles, lizards and tortoises. It also plays the vital role of being South Africa's major producer of snake-bite serum.

uShaka Marine World
1 Bell St, Point Rd. (031) 328-8000.
 10am–5pm daily.
 www.ushakamarineworld.co.za

FitzSimons Snake Park
248 Lower Marine Parade, Golden Mile. (073) 156-9606.
 9am–4:30pm daily.

Durban Waterfront
Victoria Embankment.

The bright murals and pink staircase that lead to the **BAT Centre** (Bartel Arts Trust) are an appropriate introduction to Durban's innovative dockside art-and-music scene.

The centre has a 300-seat theatre and music venue, a dance studio, art galleries and shops. Next door, are a pub and a fine restaurant, both of which overlook the harbour.

Photographs and memorabilia of Durban's seafaring past are displayed in the **Natal Maritime Museum**. The tugboats *Ulundi* and *JR More* and the minesweeper SAS *Durban* form part of the exhibits.

BAT Centre
Victoria Embankment. (031) 332-0451. 8:30am–4pm Mon–Fri, 10am–2:30pm Sat. public hols.

Natal Maritime Museum
Victoria Embankment. (031) 311-2230. 8:30am–4pm Mon–Sat, 11am–4pm Sun.

The Wheel
55 Gillespie St. (031) 332-4324.
 9am–5pm daily. 1 Jan.

The top floor of this shopping centre, which comprises 140 shops and restaurants and 12 cinemas, is modelled after a Moroccan village, but the main focus is a gigantic ferris wheel.

Modern art exhibit at the BAT Centre

The mock-Tudor façade of The Playhouse

Central Durban

Beautifully restored buildings and interesting museums can be found in the city centre. All are situated within walking distance of one another. The cafés and restaurants that line the streets offer respite from the heat and humidity.

Completed in 1910, Durban's City Hall was modelled after that of Belfast, in Northern Ireland. The central dome is 48 m (156 ft) high while statues symbolizing art, literature, music and commerce flank the four smaller domes.

The **Natural Science Museum** is situated on the ground floor of the City Hall. Exhibits vary from a display of South African wildlife to a geological collection, a bird hall, a dinosaur exhibit and an Egyptian mummy. Fascinating,

if disturbing, are the oversized insects featured in the *Kwa-Nunu* section of the museum.

Upstairs, the **Durban Art Gallery** began collecting black South African art in the 1970s, the first in the country to do so.

What was once Durban's Court now houses the **Local History Museum**. It contains relics of early colonial life in what was then Natal.

The Playhouse, opposite the City Hall, offers top-class entertainment, ranging from opera to experimental theatre.

🏛 **Natural Science Museum**
City Hall, Smith St. [(031) 311-2242.
◯ 8:30am–5pm Mon–Sat, 11am–5pm
Sun & public hols. ● Good Fri, 25 Dec.
🏛 **Durban Art Gallery**
City Hall, Smith St. [(031) 311-2264. ◯ 8:30am–4pm Mon–Sat, 11am–4pm Sun. ● Good Fri, 25 Dec.

VISITORS' CHECKLIST

Road map F3. KwaZulu-Natal Province. 🏙 352,200. ✈ 14 km (9 miles) SW of city centre. 🚉 New Durban Station, Umgeni Rd. 🚉 New Durban Station. 🛈 Old Station Bldg, 160 Pine St. (031) 304-4934. 🎭 Comrades Marathon (Jun); Rothmans July Handicap (Jul); Gunston 500 (Jul). Ⓦ www.durban.kzn.org.za

🏛 **Local History Museum**
Cnr Smith & Aliwal sts. [(031) 311-2225. ◯ 8:30am–4pm Mon–Sat, 11am–4pm Sun. ● Good Fri, 25 Dec.
🎭 **The Playhouse**
231 Smith St. [(031) 369-9555.

In the Natural Science Museum

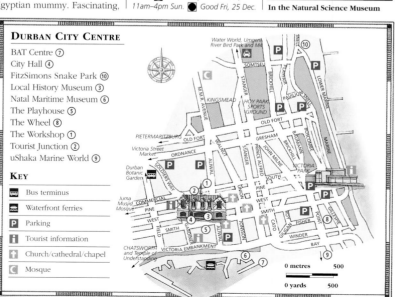

DURBAN CITY CENTRE

BAT Centre ⑦
City Hall ④
FitzSimons Snake Park ⑩
Local History Museum ③
Natal Maritime Museum ⑥
The Playhouse ⑤
The Wheel ⑧
The Workshop ①
Tourist Junction ②
uShaka Marine World ⑨

KEY

🚍	Bus terminus
⛴	Waterfront ferries
🅿	Parking
🛈	Tourist information
✝	Church/cathedral/chapel
C	Mosque

0 metres 500
0 yards 500

Exploring Durban

A WAY FROM THE CITY CENTRE, beautiful mosques, richly decorated temples and vibrant street markets await the visitor. Nature reserves and sanctuaries are situated on the outskirts of Durban, among them the Umgeni River Bird Park, north of the city, which houses exotic birds in walk-through aviaries. Water World is a perfect destination on a hot day, while the Hindu Temple of Understanding, in the suburb of Chatsworth, never fails to impress with its grandiose opulence. Tour operators offer tailor-made coach trips to all of these sights.

Exotic curry and masala spice

Tourist Junction

Station Building, 160 Pine St. (031) 304-4934. 8am–5pm Mon–Fri, 9am–2pm Sat–Sun.

Tucked between Commercial and Pine streets stands the former railway station. The four-storey, red-brick building was completed in 1894 and now houses the tourist centre. In the entrance of the building stands a statue in memory of Mahatma Gandhi, who bought a train ticket to Johannesburg here in June 1893.

The building's most curious feature is the roof, designed to carry the weight of 5 m (16 ft) of snow. The London firm of architects accidentally switched plans – and the roof of Toronto station caved in during the first heavy snowfalls.

The Tourist Junction has a comprehensive range of maps and brochures, and the staff can advise on several walking tours of the city centre. There is also a useful booking office for accommodation at the national parks (the only other offices are in Cape Town and Pretoria) and a booking office for long-distance bus tours.

The Workshop

99 Aliwal St. (031) 304-9894. 8:30am–5pm Mon–Fri, 10am–4pm Sat & Sun.

Durban's premier shopping experience, The Workshop is housed in a vast, steel-girded Victorian building that was once the railway workshop.

Extensive renovations have transformed it into a postmodern complex, with "old-world" touches like fanlights, brass- and wrought-iron trimmings.

The Workshop houses over 120 shops, boutiques, jewellers, a supermarket and several cinemas, as well as a large fast food and restaurant area.

Opposite The Workshop, on the opposite side of Aliwal Street, in the direction of the beach, are the big grounds of the Durban Exhibition Centre. A bustling outdoor market is held here on every Sunday morning. It is very popular and draws many shoppers to its craft, fruit and vegetable stalls and the colourful curio displays.

Victoria Street Market

Cnr Queen & Victoria sts. (031) 306-4021. 6am–6pm Mon–Fri, 6am–2pm Sat, 10am–2pm Sun.

At the end of the N3 flyover, where the highway meets the streets of central Durban, is the Victoria Street Market. The building is a striking city feature – each one of its 11 domes was modelled on a notable building in India.

In this crowded and noisy bazaar, visitors can sample the tastes and aromas of the Orient as they browse through 116 stalls offering spices and incense. Upstairs, 56 shops sell silk, linen and other fabrics, as well as brassware, leather goods and ceramics.

Bananas

Juma Musjid Mosque

Cnr Queen & Grey sts. (031) 306-0026. 10am–noon, 2–3pm Mon–Sat. to be booked in advance.

The impressive Juma Musjid Mosque, also known as Grey Street Mosque, lies across the road from the Victorian Street Market. Completed in 1927, it is the largest mosque on the African continent.

Visitors are allowed inside at certain times. A strict dress code is enforced and shoes must be removed before entering the building.

Durban Botanic Gardens

Sydenham Rd. (031) 201-1303. 7:30am–5.15pm Apr–Sep; 7:30am–5:45pm Sep–Apr.

Heading north on Grey Street, the Durban Botanic Gardens is located near the Greyville

The Workshop houses a wide variety of shops

racecourse. It was established in 1849 as an experimental station for tropical crops.

The Ernest Thorp Orchid House, named after an early curator, gained renown as the first naturalistic botanical display in South Africa.

The spectacular cycad and palm collection on the 15-ha (38-acre) property is one of the largest of its kind in the world. It includes several rare species, like a male *Encephalartos woodii* from the Ngoye forest, which was successfully transplanted in 1916.

Among the garden's 480 tree species are the oldest jacarandas in South Africa, originally imported from Argentina.

Other attractions include a Braille trail, a sunken garden, a herbarium, an ornamental lake and a tea garden.

The Temple of Understanding in Chatsworth

Durban's Botanic Gardens is the perfect setting for a picnic

Waterworld

Battery Beach Rd. **(** (031) 337-6336. ☐ 9am–5pm Mon–Fri, 8am–5pm Sat & Sun. ☒

This theme park is based on having fun in the water and is easily accessible from the northern beaches which are situated along the Golden Mile.

Given Durban's hot, at times even sultry, climate throughout most of the year, Water World is an extremely popular destination. It offers thrilling water slides, cool wave pools and water chutes in a tropical setting framed by palm trees.

Umgeni River Bird Park

490 Riverside Rd, Northway. **(** (031) 579-4600. ☐ 9am–4pm daily. ● 25 Dec. ☒ ☐ ☒

Bordered on three sides by steep cliffs, and overlooking the north bank of the Umgeni River, 1.5 km (1 mile) from its mouth, the Umgeni River Bird Park enjoys a superb location. Four waterfalls cascade down

the cliffs into ponds fringed by palms and lush vegetation. The four large walk-through aviaries allow visitors a face-to-face encounter with some of the 3,000 birds. Among the 400 resident species are rare exotic parrots, toucans, cranes macaws, and hornbills.

Entertaining bird shows are held daily at 11am and 2pm, except Mondays.

Temple of Understanding

Chatsworth. **(** (031) 403-3328. ☐ 4:30am–8pm daily. ☒

This large, ornate temple of the International Society for Krishna Consciousness was designed by the Austrian architect, Hannes Raudner. It is encircled by a moat and a beautiful garden laid out in the shape of a lotus flower.

The daily guided tours take in the awe-inspiring marble temple room and the inner sanctuary, as well as an interesting audio-visual show.

THE HINDU POPULATION OF DURBAN

When the first sugar was produced from sugar cane in 1851, the Natal Colony experienced a major economic boom. Cheap labour was required to work in the plantations, and the colony entered into negotiations with the colonial government in India. Between 1860 and 1911, a total of 152,000 indentured labourers was shipped to Durban from Madras and Calcutta. Tamil and Hindi were the main languages spoken. At the end of their five-year contracts, the workers were offered a free passage back to India. Over half of them opted to remain in South Africa, and became active as retailers and vegetable farmers; in later years many entered commerce, industry and politics. Of the current population of over one million (the largest Indian community outside of Asia), an estimated 68 per cent are Hindu. Deepavali is their most important festival, and begins with the lighting of a lamp for the Goddess of Light, symbolizing the conquest of good over evil.

Statue of Bhaktivedanta Swami, a respected religious teacher

Durban's North and South Coasts

DURBAN IS THE CENTRAL FOCUS of South Africa's most popular holiday coastline. Blessed with a subtropical climate, this picturesque area is a delightful blend of sun, sand, surf and nature reserves. Extending 162 km (100 miles) south of Durban is a string of coastal towns and holiday resorts, like Scottburgh and Port Edward. Uncrowded beaches at holiday villages such as Ballito are hallmarks of the 154-km (96-mile) stretch of coast that lies north of Durban.

Traditional Zulu basket

Oribi Gorge

The Oribi Gorge, 21 km (13 miles) inland from Port Shepstone, is a scenic, thickly forested area where cliffs rise from the deep chasms and open out to reveal the spectacular Samango Falls.

Croc World

In a 60-ha (148-acre) indigenous botanic garden near Scottburgh, Croc World has 12,000 Nile crocodiles and the largest eagle cage on the African continent.

Vernon Crookes Nature Reserve

Umkomaas

Umk

Itafa

R612

uMzinto

Scottburg

N2

Park Rynie

Oribi Gorge Nature Reserve

Umzimkulu

Umzimkulwana

Mzumbe

R102

Sezela

0 kilometres 5

0 miles 3

Ndongeni's Grave

Hibberdene

N2

Port Shepstone

Umtamvuna Nature Reserve

Margate

San Lameer

R61

Port Edward

Port Edward

This village near the Umtamvuna Nature Reserve is the location of Caribbean Estates, a popular timeshare resort.

San Lameer

Two good golf courses, a private beach and a nature reserve make San Lameer a sought-after holiday resort.

Johannesburg

Durban

Cape Town

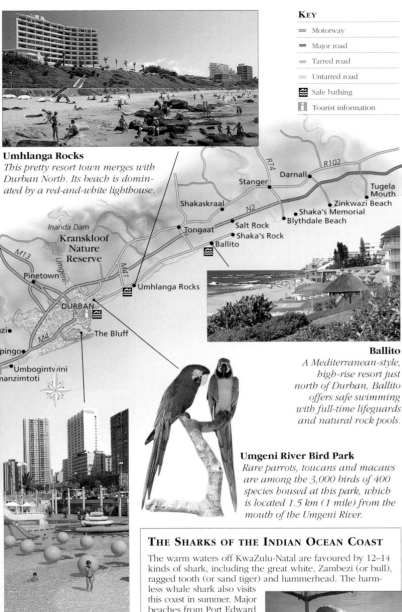

KEY

═══ Motorway

▬▬▬ Major road

═══ Tarred road

═══ Untarred road

🏖 Safe bathing

ℹ Tourist information

Umhlanga Rocks
This pretty resort town merges with Durban North. Its beach is dominated by a red-and-white lighthouse.

Ballito
A Mediterranean-style, high-rise resort just north of Durban, Ballito offers safe swimming with full-time lifeguards and natural rock pools.

Umgeni River Bird Park
Rare parrots, toucans and macaws are among the 3,000 birds of 400 species housed at this park, which is located 1.5 km (1 mile) from the mouth of the Umgeni River.

Durban
This large city has the most developed beachfront in the country, with amusement parks, paddling pools, fun rides, a water park and a salt water pool.

THE SHARKS OF THE INDIAN OCEAN COAST

The warm waters off KwaZulu-Natal are favoured by 12–14 kinds of shark, including the great white, Zambezi (or bull), ragged tooth (or sand tiger) and hammerhead. The harmless whale shark also visits this coast in summer. Major beaches from Port Edward to Richards Bay are protected by shark nets beyond the surf, 500 m (545 yds) from the shore. These are maintained by the KwaZulu-Natal Sharks Board, which finds about 1,200 sharks caught in the nets each year.

A "great white" encounter

The South Coast ❷

Furry-ridged triton

A YEAR-ROUND COMBINATION of sunshine, sand, sea and surf has created an irresistible drawcard for visitors coming from the cooler inland climates or the Northern Hemisphere. Some 30 inviting resort towns form a coastal playground that stretches for 162 km (100 miles) from the Eastern Cape border to Durban. The attractions entail much more than the obvious seaside fun. From nature reserves and bird sanctuaries to glittering casinos – this coast has it all.

Port Edward

Road map E4. N2, 20 km (12 miles) S of Margate. ✈ 🏠 Margate. 🛈 Panorama Parade, Margate, (039) 312-2322.

The village of Port Edward on the Umtamvuna River is the southernmost beachside resort in KwaZulu-Natal. Port Edward is popular for swimming, fishing and boating, and the estuary is navigable far upstream, making it ideal for ski-boats.

The lush Caribbean Estates on the north bank is rated as one of the country's top time-share resorts.

Between 1976 and 1994 the land south of the Umtamvuna River bridge fell within the homeland known as Transkei. At that time, gambling was illegal under South African law and a casino resort, the Wild Coast Sun, was built here to lure visitors from Durban and the South Coast. Today, it overlooks an unspoilt coastline covered in dense forest and grassland. A challenging 18-hole golf course stretches from the banks of the river to the shores of the lagoon.

The Mzamba Village Market opposite the resort's main entrance offers a range of

locally crafted curios, such as woven grass baskets, stone and wood carvings and beadwork. The **Umtamvuna Nature Reserve**, some 8 km (5 miles) north of Port Edward protects a 30-km (19-mile) section of the Umtamvuna River gorge. The trails that explore the dense, subtropical forest are excellent for bird-watching.

🦌 Umtamvuna Nature Reserve

Port Edward. Road to Izingolweni. 📞 (039) 311-2383. 🛈 Ezemvelo Kzn Wildlife Service, (033) 845-1000. 🔘 daily.

Margate

Road map E4. N2. 🏘 12,000. ✈ 4 km (2.5 miles) inland. 🏠 Beachfront. 🛈 Panorama Parade, (039) 312-2322. Ⓦ www.sunnymargate.com

Margate is the tourist capital of the South Coast. Daily flights from Johannesburg land at the town's small airport.

Margate's focal point is a broad expanse of golden sand lined by the tall, white towers of dozens of hotels and apartments. Marine Drive, which runs parallel to the coast one block inland, is the

town's main business centre, and banks, restaurants, pubs, fast-food outlets, shops, estate agencies and cinemas all compete for the available street frontage.

The approach to the sandy beach leads across well-tended palm-shaded lawns that attract many sunbathers. Along the main beachfront a variety of attractions compete for the holiday-maker's attention. Among these are the paddling pools, a fresh-water swimming pool, water slides, a mini-golf (putt-putt) course, paddle boats and many ice-cream parlours.

Margate's fishing area is one of the drawcards of the town

Uvongo

Road map E4. N2, 12 km (7 miles) N of Margate. 🏘 6,000. 🛈 Panorama Parade, Margate, (039) 312-2322.

Just before it empties into the sea, the Vungu River plunges down a 23-m (75-ft) waterfall into a lagoon. High cliffs, overgrown with wild bananas, protect the sheltered lagoon. With its spit of sandy beach separating the river from the ocean, Uvongo is one of the most attractive features along the South Coast.

Boating is popular in the lagoon and the beach, a safe playground for children, is also the site of a daily craft, fruit and basketry market. A restaurant, timeshare resort, tidal pool and paddling pool are a short walk inland.

On the main road, less than 2 km (1.2 miles) south of the beach, the small Uvongo Bird Park is home to many species of exotic birds.

The swimming pool of the Wild Coast Sun

BANANA EXPRESS

The Banana Express provides visitors to the South Coast with the rare opportunity of a steam train journey on a narrow-gauge railway. The Express departs from Port Shepstone on Thursdays and steams along the coastline before turning inland. It winds its way through sugar and banana plantations before reaching Izotsha village and returning to the coast. On Wednesdays the train climbs 550m (1,788ft) to Paddock, 39 km (24 miles) from Port Shepstone. After a guided walk in the Oribi Gorge Nature Reserve, which includes lunch, guests board the train for the return journey. Telephone (039) 682-2455 for reservations.

The Banana Express

Oribi Gorge Nature Reserve

Road map E4. 21 km (13 miles) inland of Port Shepstone. *(033) 845-1000.* daily.

In a region where population densities are high and where sugar cane plantations and coastal resort developments have replaced most of the natural vegetation, the ravine carved by the Umzimkulwana River is a delight for nature lovers. The impressive gorge is 24 km (15 miles) long, up to 5 km (3 miles) wide and 300 m (975 ft) deep.

The reserve has a small rest camp with eight huts perched on the southern rim of the chasm. There is a scenic circular drive, three walking trails and many beautiful picnic spots along the river.

Small, forest-dwelling animals like bushbuck, duiker, samango monkey and leopard occur in the dense forest, which comprises some 500 different tree species.

Oribi Gorge was formed by the Umzimkulwana River

Scottburgh's beaches and lawns are popular with sunbathers

Scottburgh

Road map E4. N2, roughly 30 km (19 miles) S of Amanzimtoti. 4,300. Scott St, (039) 976-1364.

An almost continuous carpet of sugar cane plantations lines this stretch of South Coast, and the town of Scottburgh was once used as a harbour for exporting the crop. Today, the neat and compact little town has a distinct holiday atmosphere, and is a popular beach resort. It occupies the prominent headland overlooking the mouth of the Mpambanyoni River, and most of the hotels and holiday apartments offer superb sea views.

In the previous century, a spring used to cascade from the bank above the river, but today a large water slide occupies the site. A restaurant, small shops, a miniature railway and tidal pool are added attractions. Further south, a caravan park adjoins the beach and the town's popular golf course has a prime site overlooking the Indian Ocean surf.

Frangipani

Amanzimtoti

Road map F4. N2, 27 km (17 miles) S of Durban. 16,300. Durban. 95 Beach Rd, (031) 903-7498.

It is claimed that Amanzimtoti derives its name from a remark made by Shaka Zulu *(see p47)*. In the 1820s, returning home from a campaign further down the South Coast, Shaka drank from a refreshing stream and is said to have exclaimed, "*amanzi umtoti*" (the water is sweet). Today, Amanzimtoti is a lively coastal resort. Its beaches are lined with hotels, holiday apartments, take-away outlets, restaurants and beachwear shops.

The most popular beach extends for 3 km (2 miles) north of the Manzimtoti River and offers safe bathing, picnic sites and a fine salt-water pool.

The N2 passes within 400 m (1,300 ft) of the coast, providing easy access to the town's attractions, such as the small bird sanctuary, a nature reserve and two fine golf courses in the vicinity of the beach.

North Coast ❸

THIS SUBTROPICAL REGION is renowned for its attractive towns, sheltered bays and estuaries, uncrowded beaches and forested dunes that give way to a green carpet of sugar cane and timber plantations. Northern KwaZulu-Natal has escaped the rampant development that characterizes the South Coast and offers unspoilt nature at its best.

One of the guest rooms at the cross-cultural bush lodge of Simunye

Umhlanga Rocks

Road map F3. 20 km (12 miles) NE of Durban. 👥 *12,600.* 🚌 *Umhlanga Express.* ℹ️ *Chartwell Drive, (031) 561-4257.*

The premier holiday resort on the North Coast, Umhlanga Rocks has excellent beaches, timeshare resorts, hotels and restaurants. This is a fast-growing, upper-income town, but the stylish outdoor cafés and bistros, make it seem more like a peaceful coastal centre than a fast-paced resort. The promenade, which extends along the coastline for 3 km (2 miles), provides stunning views of the golden sands that have made Umhlanga famous.

Further north, at the mouth of the Ohlanga River, forested dunes fringing the beach form part of a nature reserve. Here a boardwalk crosses the river and the forest teems with blue duiker, birds, monkeys.

Hibiscus flower

Ballito

Road map F3. N2, 30 km (19 miles) N of Umhlanga Rocks. 👥 *2,700.* 🚌 *Baz Bus.* ℹ️ *Dolphin Coast Publicity, Cnr Ballito Dr/Link Rd, (032) 946-1997.*

Ballito and the neighbouring Salt Rock, extend for 6 km (4 miles) along a coast known for its beaches, rocky headlands and sheltered tidal pools alive with a menagerie of sea creatures. Lining the main coastal road are many good restaurants. Accommodation ranges from luxury holiday apartments and timeshare resorts to family hotels and attractive caravan parks.

Mtunzini

Road map F3. N2, 29 km (19 miles) SW of Richards Bay. 🚌 *Baz Bus.* ℹ️ *Hely-Hutchinson St, (035) 340-1421.*

The pretty village, whose name means "in the shade", is set on a hillside overlooking the sea. Its streets are lined with coral trees and in winter their red flowers add splashes of colour to the townscape. A golf course adjoins the main shopping street, and near the railway station there is a grove of raffia palms. The nearest known group of these plants is on the Mozambique border, 260 km (163 miles) north. The rare palm-nut vulture is a fruit-eating raptor that may be spotted here, and the swamp forest and raffia palms can be seen from a raised boardwalk.

Mtunzini lies in a belt of unspoiled coastal forest that falls within the Umlalazi Nature Reserve. Comfortable log cabins, tucked into the forest, border a broad marsh, and along the banks of the Mlazi River there is a circular walk through a mangrove swamp that is alive with crabs and mud-skimmers.

From the picnic site on the bank of the Mlazi River, a boat trip to the river mouth will reveal glimpses of fish eagles and kingfishers, and walking trails lead through the forest to a wide, sandy beach. Along the many trails, shy forest animals such as vervet monkey, red duiker and bushbuck are often seen.

Simunye Lodge ❹

Road map F3. Melmoth. D256. 📞 *(035) 45-03111.* ⏰ *7am–5pm daily.* 🍴 🛏️ Ⓦ *www.proteahotels.com*

A UNIQUE LODGE tucked into the Mfule Valley 6 km (4 miles) from Melmoth allows visitors to experience both traditional and contemporary Zulu culture. The creation of linguist Barry Leitch, Simunye overlooks the Mfule River in a

Holiday apartments and hotels line the beach at Ballito

◁ **Shaka's Rock, near Ballito, is a subtropical holiday resort, typical of the North Coast**

typical Zululand scenery of
thorn trees and grassy hills.
To reach the lodge, visitors
have to ride on horseback for
6 km (4 miles), then continue
by ox- or donkey-cart.

Overnight guests have the
option of staying in a stone
lodge or traditional Zulu *kraal*
(see pp194–5). Guides tell the
fascinating history of the Zulu
nation, and there are demonstrations of traditional dances,
sparring and spear-throwing.
Guests also visit working Zulu
homesteads for a first-hand
experience of rural Zulu life.

The entrance to the cultural village of Shakaland

Shakaland ❺

Road map F3. Eshowe. R68, Norman
Hurst Farm, Nkwalini. 📞 *(035) 460-
0912.* ⬭ *6am–9pm daily.* 📷 *11am,
2pm daily* 🍴 🏠
ⓦ www.shakaland.com

FOR THE PRODUCTION of the TV
series *Shaka Zulu*, several
authentic 19th-century Zulu
kraals were constructed
in 1984. The series was
sold to many overseas
networks and princi-
pal actor, Henry
Cele, became a
star. For the series'
grand finale, the
villages were set
alight; only that of
Shaka's father was
spared and opened
to the public as Shakaland.

**Zulu "love-letter"
pouch, Shakaland**

The unique Zulu village is
open for day visits, while those
wishing to stay overnight are
accommodated in one of the
Protea Hotel chain's most
unusual destinations. A video
explaining the origin of the

Zulu people is shown, and
guests sleep in beehive huts
and enjoy traditional Zulu fare,
followed by a dancing display.

On a tour of the 40-hut
village, visitors are introduced
to a variety of traditional skills
such as hut building, spear-
making, beer brewing, artistic
beadwork and pottery.

Framed by thorn trees and
aloes, Goedertrou Dam
in the valley below
is an attractive
body of water.
The sunset river
boat cruises are
an added attraction.
In the hills east
of Shakaland, and
commanding a
superb view over
the wide Mhlatuze
Valley, is the site of Shaka's
famed military stronghold,
KwaBulawayo. Construction
of this historic facility began
in 1823, but today, almost
nothing remains of the citadel
that once held so much of
Southern Africa in its grasp.

TRADITIONAL HEALING

In traditional Zulu society,
the *inyanga* (herbalist) was
male and concentrated on
medicinal cures, while the
isangoma (diviner) was a
woman who possessed
psychic powers and the
ability to communicate
with the ancestral spirits.
Today, this strict division
is no longer accurate.
Muthi is an assortment of
medicine and remedies
made from indigenous
bulbs, shrubs, leaves, tree
bark and roots. Animal
products like fat, claws,
teeth and skin are also
often used. Despite the
advances of Western cul-
ture, the faith in traditional
healing methods is still
wide-spread in rural and
urban settlements. In order
to meet the demand for the
plants and to ensure a regular supply, special "*muthi*
gardens" have been estab-
lished in a number of
nature reserves.

Zulu *inyanga* (herbalist)

Shakaland offers unusual hotel accommodation

Hluhluwe-Umfolozi Park ⑥

Road map F3. *30 km (18 miles) W of Ulundi, or from N2.* ☎ *(035) 562-0255 or (033) 845 1000.* ⏰ *Apr–Sep: 6am–6pm daily; Nov–Feb: 5am–7pm; Oct & Mar: 8am–7pm.* 🦎 ❚❚ 🅿 ⓦ www.kznwildlife.com

AN UNSPOILT WILDERNESS of rolling hills, subtropical forest, acacia woodland and palm-fringed rivers, the 964-sq-km (372-sq-miles) park is world-renowned for its rhino conservation programme.

In 1895 two wildlife reserves, Hluhluwe and Umfolozi, were established to protect the last rhinos in South Africa. In the early 1950s a corridor of land between the two was added. The park was consolidated in 1989, and is now the fourth largest in the country. One of Africa's leading wildlife sanctuaries, it is home to an astonishing diversity of wildlife. The varied vegetation supports large herds of nyala, impala, wildebeest, kudu, zebra and buffalo, as well as elephant, rhino, giraffe, lion, leopard, hyena and cheetah.

Over the years, animals that had become extinct in this region were re-introduced.

In 1958 a single male lion suddenly appeared – possibly from the Kruger National Park some 350 km (220 miles) to the north. Two lionesses were relocated from the Kruger park some time later, and their offspring have re-established prides throughout the park.

Southern bald ibis roosting site in the Hluhluwe-Umfolozi Park

Elephants, first transported from Kruger in 1981, have adapted extremely well to their new environment and now number around 200.

Nyalazi Gate, the park's main entrance, is reached from the N2 at Mtubatuba. It is a perfect starting point for exploring the park's 220-km (138-mile) road network. Heading south, the route traverses open woodland before fording the Black Umfolozi River. Then it ascends to Mpila Camp, which has magnificent views over the reserve.

A trio of exclusive reed-and-thatch rest camps on the banks of the Black Umfolozi, Sontuli, Gqoyeni and Nselweni rivers allow visitors to savour the most secluded corners of this wilderness. Game rangers conduct game-viewing walks.

From Nyalazi Gate north, the route follows a tarred road that curves across rolling hills teeming with wildlife. The journey to Hluhluwe climbs a range of hills, 400 m (1,300 ft) above the Hluhluwe River.

These hills trap moisture-laden clouds resulting in an average rainfall of 985 mm (38 inches) per year. In the dense woodland and forests live red duiker, bushbuck, nyala and samango monkey. Buffalo, zebra, white rhino and elephant can be seen roaming the northeastern grasslands near Memorial Gate.

Hilltop Camp, at an altitude of 450 m (1,460 ft), offers panoramic views over the surrounding countryside and can accommodate up to 210 guests in its chalets. Facilities at the central complex include a restaurant, bar, shop, petrol station and swimming pool.

A short trail through the adjoining forest is excellent for bird-watching.

A female waterbuck at Hluhluwe-Umfolozi Park

Itala Game Reserve ⑦

Road map F3. Vryheid. R69 via Louwsburg, 50 km (31miles) NE of Vryheid. ☎ *(033) 845-1000.* ⏰ *Nov–Feb: 5am–7pm daily; Mar–Oct: 6am–6pm daily.* 🦎 ❚❚ ⓦ www.kznwildlife.com

FROM THE UNHURRIED village of Louwsburg on the R69, a tarred road descends a steep escarpment to the wilderness of Itala, a 296-sq-km (114-sq-mile) tract of grassland with dramatic mountain scenery and densely wooded valleys.

The reserve was established in 1972, and over the years 13 farms have become one of South Africa's top sanctuaries. The Phongolo River flows along the northern boundary

Hilltop Camp at Hluhluwe-Umfolozi Park

Mhlangeni Bush Camp, Itala Game Reserve

for some 37 km (23 miles). Seven tributaries have carved the deep valleys that dissect this park and enhance its scenic splendour. The Ngoje escarpment rises dramatically to 1,446 m (4,700 ft), providing a striking backdrop to Itala's game-viewing roads.

A 7-km (4-mile) tarred road leads from the entrance to the prestigious Ntshondwe Camp, which nestles at the foot of an imposing escarpment. Its 40 self-catering chalets have been carefully tucked away between boulders and wild fig trees. The central complex contains a reception area, restaurant, store and coffee shop, and offers panoramic views over the entire reserve. In front of the building, an extensive wooden platform overlooks a reed-fringed water hole and is perfect for bird-watching. As no fences surround the camp, animals such as warthog often wander

between the chalets. A path leads to a swimming pool tucked into a clearing at the base of the mountain.

An additional three exclusive bush camps offer guided walks led by resident rangers. Ntshondwe Lodge is a lavish, three-bedroomed cabin perched on a hill top. The far-reaching vista from its wooden deck and sunken swimming pool is arguably Itala's finest.

Game-viewing at Itala is excellent. Visitors will see white rhino, giraffe, hartebeest, kudu, eland, impala, wildebeest, warthog and zebra, as well as the only population in KwaZulu-Natal of the rare tsessebe antelope. Elephant, buffalo, leopard and black rhino are also present, but are generally more difficult to locate.

Ngubhu Loop, a 31-km (19-mile) circuit, which crosses a broad basin backed by the escarpment and then hugs the cliff face on the return journey, is the best drive in the park. Another route winds down the thickly wooded Dakaneni Valley to the Phongolo River. Although game is not as plentiful here as on the higher grasslands, the scenery is spectacular.

Game-viewing in the Itala Game Reserve

THE WHITE AND THE BLACK RHINO

A white (square-lipped) rhino

At first glance, it may seem impossible to classify the grey hulks, yet there are a number of clear distinguishing factors between the white *(Ceratotherium simum)* and black *(Diceros bicornis)* rhino. The term "white" does not describe colour, but is a bastardization of the Dutch *wijd* (wide), referring to the lips of the animal. The white rhino is a grazer that carries its large, heavy head close to the ground as it rips off grass with its wide, square lips. The black rhino, on the other hand, is a browser and holds its small head up to feed off leaves with its elongated, prehensile upper lip. Black rhinos are smaller and occur singly or in very small groups, while white rhinos may weigh up to 2,300 kg (5,000 lb) and gather in larger social groups. Today the Hluhluwe-Umfolozi Park protects a total of 1,200 white and 400 black rhino.

African fish eagle

Greater St Lucia Wetland Park ❽

Road map F3. St Lucia. Approx. 53 km (33 miles) NE of Empangeni. ℹ️ (035) 550-4059. ⏰ daily, some areas are restricted. 🅿️ 🚗 🏪 🍴 ⚓ 🏕️ 🅰️ 🆆 www.leisure.satel.co.za

L AKE ST LUCIA, 368 sq km (142 sq miles) in size, is the focal point of the third largest wildlife sanctuary in South Africa. Stretching from the game-filled Mkuzi plains in the north to the St Lucia Estuary in the south, the 1,700-sq-km (656-sq-mile) Greater St Lucia Wetland Park encompasses a diversity of habitats: mountain, bushveld, palm groves, sand forest, grassland, wetland, coastal forest, coral reef and ocean.

The coastal village of St Lucia is a popular holiday destination, with a range of facilities and accommodation. Regular cruises offer close-up views of hippos, crocodiles, pelicans, fish eagles and rare waterbirds. The Crocodile Centre, north of the village, is the finest in the country.

Cape Vidal, 32 km (20 miles) north of St Lucia Estuary,

GREATER ST LUCIA WETLAND PARK

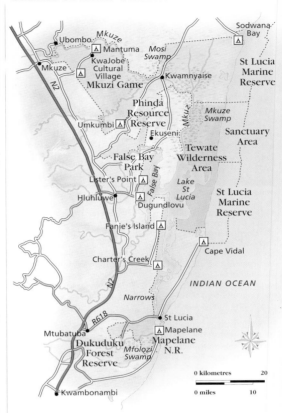

KEY

▬	Major route
═	Road (tarred)
─	Road (untarred)
🅰️	Camping

St Lucia Estuary offers excellent shore-based fishing

boasts a reef-shielded beach, tropical waters, deep-sea fishing and a freshwater lake.

The coastline from Cape Vidal to Ponta Do Ouro is a protected marine reserve; the sandy beaches provide vital nesting sites for loggerhead and leatherback turtles. Fishing is allowed in certain areas.

Located 65 km (41 miles) north of St Lucia Estuary, along an unspoilt and uninhabited coastline, **Sodwana Bay** is a popular destination for deep-sea fishing and scuba diving expeditions.

The road from Sodwana to the N2 passes the southern boundary of the **Mkuzi Game Reserve**; its four game-viewing hides are renowned for their close-ups. **KwaJobe Cultural Village** near Mantuma camp gives visitors an insight into traditional Zulu culture.

One of the beaches at Kosi Bay, the northernmost part of KwaZulu-Natal

Ndumo Game Reserve, renowned for the richness of its riverine life, particularly its water-related birds – an amazing 420 species have been recorded. Hides on the Nyamithi and Banzi pans afford excellent views. The pans also sustain large hippo and crocodile populations, and animals such as nyala, red duiker, and white and black rhino can be seen. To appreciate the beauty of the pans, book one of the guided Land Rover tours. A small rest camp and a tented safari camp overlook Banzi Pan.

Ndumo Game Reserve
(033) 845-1000. ◯ daily.

Sodwana Bay
(035) 571-0051.
Mkuzi Game Reserve
(035) 573-9004.
KwaJobe Cultural Village
(035) 573-9004.

Phinda Resource Reserve ❾

Road map F3. 80 km (50 miles) NE of Empangeni. (011) 809-4300. ◯ restricted access. ⓦ www.ccafrica.com

EXTENDING OVER 170 sq km (65 sq miles) of bushveld, wetland, savannah and sand forest, luxurious privately-owned Phinda adjoins the Greater St Lucia Wetland Park. Activities on offer include sunset cruises on the beautiful Mzinene River, outdoor meals under a spreading acacia tree, game-viewing drives led by experienced rangers as well as bush walks and fishing or diving expeditions to the nearby coast. Wildlife is abundant and includes nyala, kudu, wildebeest, giraffe, zebra, elephant, white rhino, lion and cheetah. Visitors can stay in Nyala Lodge, which offers panoramic views over the surrounding bushveld, or in the exclusive, glass-walled Forest Lodge, which is so much a part of the sand forest that its rooms are framed by trees and enclosed by dense foliage. The reserve has its own air strip and arranges regular air transfers from Johannesburg, or road transfers from Richards Bay.

Kosi Bay ❿

Road map F2. Approx. 155 km (96 miles) NE of Mkuze. (033) 845-1000. ◯ restricted access.

KOSI BAY NATURE RESERVE is an 80-sq-km (31-sq-mile) aquatic system that incorporates an estuary, mangrove swamps and four interconnecting lakes. It can be reached from Mkuze, just south of Pongolapoort Dam. The system hosts many fresh- and salt-water fish species, and angling and boating are popular. Tonga fish traps (fences built from sticks and reeds) have been a feature of the Kosi system for over 500 years. There is a campsite and a few thatched chalets, and guided walks and boat trips can be arranged. A 4-day circular trail allows hikers to explore the lakes on foot.

ENVIRONS: About 50 km (31 miles) west of Kosi Bay is the

Tembe Elephant Park ⓫

Road map F3. Approx. 110 km (68 miles) N of Mkuze. (031) 202-9090. ◯ restricted access. ⓦ www.tembe.co.za

THIS EXCLUSIVE 290-sq-km (112-sq-mile) wilderness reserve protects the flood plain of the Phongolo River along the northern boundary of KwaZulu-Natal. The park was established in 1983 to protect the KwaZulu-Natal elephants. As the terrain is sandy, access is limited to 4WD vehicles. Visitor numbers are strictly controlled; only ten visitors are allowed in per day. There is a small, tented camp near the entrance and two hides overlook areas where elephants come to drink. The park also conserves South Africa's largest population of suni antelope.

Loggerhead turtles lay their eggs on sandy beaches

Introducing Gauteng and Mpumalanga

FROM NATURAL WONDERS AND WILDLIFE to the "City of Gold", this region offers something for everyone. Johannesburg is the throbbing life of the streets and the sophistication of exclusive suburbs, while Soweto, Johannesburg's "other half", provides an insight into the daily lives of the country's urban black people. To the east, the land drops over 1,000 m (3,281 ft) to the hot Lowveld plains and the Kruger National Park. West lies the arid heartland of the subcontinent, and beyond, the Magaliesberg range seems to rise from the waters of the Hartbeespoort Dam. The most fascinating destination of all, perhaps, is glittering Sun City and the near-mythical grandeur of the Lost City.

The Palace of the Lost City, a part of the opulent Sun City resort and casino complex, is a spectacular architectural indulgence of age-stressed concrete, beautifully crafted pillars and ornate domes set in a man-made tropical garden and surrounded by a variety of water features such as Roaring Lagoon.

Sun City

GAUTENG AND SUN CITY
(See pp242–59)

Johannesburg

Johannesburg is the largest city in South Africa and the one in which extremes are most evident. Poverty and wealth, historic buildings and modern office blocks, create stark contrasts.

◁ **The lion is one of the "Big Five" African animals, seen here in the Kruger National Park**

Lions (Panthera leo) *can live in almost any habitat except desert and thick forest. They are both nocturnal and diurnal and occur in prides of 3 to 40 individuals (although 6 to 12 is more usual). In the Kruger, which is accessible through several gates, they are often seen resting in the shade of a tree.*

Kruger National Park

BLYDE RIVER CANYON AND KRUGER
(See pp260–77)

Bourke's Luck Potholes

Pilgrim's Rest

Bourke's Luck *is a series of intriguing potholes, scoured into the yellow dolomite rock by the Treur and Blyde rivers. The potholes were named after gold miner, Tom Bourke, who owned the land adjacent to the main gold-bearing reef.*

| 0 kilometres | 50 |
| 0 miles | 25 |

Pilgrim's Rest *is a beautifully restored old mining town, which owes its existence to South Africa's first gold rush in 1873. By the end of that year, more than 1,500 diggers had converged on the area and Pilgrim's Rest had grown into a large mining camp.*

Conservation in the Kruger National Park

National Parks Board logo

THE KRUGER NATIONAL PARK stretches for 352 km (220 miles) along South Africa's northeastern border. The 19,633-sq-km (7,580-sq-mile) conservation area supports an astounding array of fauna and flora. Although the park sustains the animals in their natural habitat, a fence along much of its boundary does restrict their free movement. Wildlife is concentrated in the lusher southern parts, which calls for careful management. Periodically, rangers have to limit the numbers this contained ecosystem can safely support by translocating young and healthy animals to other reserves.

EXTENT OF THE KRUGER NATIONAL PARK

☐ *Park boundaries*

Dry hills provide a habitat for kudu and eland, animals that do not need to drink water regularly.

Zebra flourish when artificial water points are provided. Large zebra herds have a negative impact on animals who require tall grass, like roan, sable and reedbuck.

Zebra

The Olifants River *is the largest of the park's seven major watercourses. Since water is scarce, artificial water points have allowed elephants to move into areas that were previously only accessible in wet summer months.*

Giraffe

Tall trees along the riverbed shelter animals such as baboon, grey duiker, bushbuck and giraffe.

MANAGING FOR DIVERSITY

Scientists are only now beginning to understand the complicated African savannah. In an effort to manage the ecosystem in a way that maintains its diversity, artificial water points, which caused habitat-modifiers like elephant to flourish (to the detriment of other species), are now being closed.

Giraffe *are the tallest of the browsers and favour areas where acacias are abundant.*

Kudu *are large antelope that do not need to drink frequently and occur in dense woodland.*

Sable *antelope require tall grass of a high quality that grows on well-drained soils.*

Radio tracking *enables scientists to monitor the endangered predators. Only 180 cheetah and 400 wild dog inhabit the park's vast expanse. Research has shown that competition from the more aggressive lion is a major limiting factor.*

DROUGHT STATISTICS

Although park managers endeavour to limit the impact of drought, animal populations in the park are never static. Some species like wildebeest and giraffe are hardly affected, while buffalo, sable and roan antelope exhibit sharp declines.

SPECIES	1989	1992	1995
Elephant	7,468	7,600	8,371
White rhino	1,284	1,803	2,800
Wildebeest	13,709	13,960	12,723
Giraffe	4,877	4,600	4,902
Impala	123,433	101,416	97,297
Buffalo	29,575	21,900	19,477
Sable	1,651	1,232	880
Roan	200	60	44

Severe destruction takes place around waterholes.

Artificial water point

Elephant are termed habitat-modifiers, because they destroy trees, which brings about significant changes in vegetation.

Roan

Impala

Destructive feeders, *elephants strip bark off umbrella thorn acacias and fever trees. Kruger's 8,700 elephant each consume up to 250 kg (550 lb) of vegetation daily and comprise one-quarter of the park's total biomass.*

Endangered roan antelope require open woodland, with tall grass to hide their young, and are unable to adapt to the short-grass conditions caused by an increase in zebra herds around artificial water points.

Bush encroachment, resulting from elephants damaging tall trees and from concentrations of grazing animals near water, benefits browsers like impala, kudu and giraffe.

TOURIST GUIDELINES

To ensure the safety of visitors and maintain the park's essential attributes, a few regulations are necessary. It is important to observe speed limits, as the animals, too, use the roads as thoroughfares. Since camp closing times are strictly enforced, a good rule of thumb is to calculate an average travelling speed, including stops, at 20 kph (12 mph). Visitors are not permitted to leave their cars except at the 22 designated picnic sites and facilities at 13 of the larger camps – all of the animals are wild and unpredictable, and the predators are superbly camouflaged. Although baboons and vervet monkeys may beg for food, particularly on the road between Skukuza and Lower Sabie, feeding is a punishable offence. It disrupts natural behaviour, and often produces aggression, particularly in male baboons.

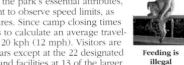

Feeding is illegal

Visitors blatantly ignoring the rules

Gold Mining

Kruger rands

Vast natural resources make South Africa one of the richest countries on earth. Ancient sediments in this geological treasure chest yield silver, platinum, chromite, uranium, diamonds – and gold. Over the years, small-scale miners have left behind evidence of their labour all around the country. The most poignant of these historic sites is Pilgrim's Rest (see p266), a well-preserved mining town in Mpumalanga. Today, controlled by giant corporations, South Africa produces about one-quarter of the world's gold.

EXTENT OF GOLD FIELDS

☐ *Main mining operations*

The processing plant produces gold bars of 90 per cent purity, ready for transport to the refinery.

Johannesburg in 1889 was a sprawling tent settlement. Three years earlier, a prospector named George Harrison had discovered the greatest gold reef in history on a farm named Langlaagte, just west of today's Johannesburg.

Office blocks house the administration and human resources staff, as well as engineers, geologists, surveyors, mechanics and planners.

SHAFT 9 – VAAL REEFS
This vast gold mine near Klerksdorp straddles the North West and Free State provinces. It is the world's largest gold-mining complex, and is now in the process of selling some of its 11 shafts to black empowerment groups such as Rainbow Mining.

The main shaft, sunk to a depth of 60 m (197 ft), is encased in a concrete "collar" to support the headgear. South African gold-mine shafts are the deepest in the world, because the reefs are located several miles underground.

Miners work underground on eight-hour shifts. Rock temperatures in the confined working place (stope) may reach up to 55°C (131°F).

Canteen staff *have to cater for the different traditional diets of miners, as well as their exceptionally high calorie intake.*

headgear, set up after the initial has been sunk, carries the ropes, els and other mining equipment.

The ore *is crushed and pumped into a leach tank where cyanide is added to dissolve it. The product is then heated to remove impurities and smelted into gold bars of about 90 per cent purity. A yield of one troy ounce (31.1 grams) of gold from a ton of ore is considered very rich indeed.*

Mine dumps*, yellow heaps on the outskirts of Johannesburg, contain the waste solids of the extraction process. 'Greening' the dumps has seen the return of smaller animals and birds.*

Miners' accommodation also includes sporting facilities, libraries and parks.

The gold price *is determined twice daily (except on weekends and British bank holidays) by a group of London bullion dealers. It is quoted in US dollars per troy ounce.*

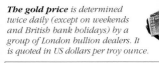

A carat *denotes the purity of gold (measured per part of gold in 24 parts other metal).*

THE KRUGER MILLIONS

Legend has it that when Paul Kruger, last president of the Zuid-Afrikaansche Republiek (1883–1900), left to go into exile in Europe in 1900, all the gold in the State Mint at Pretoria travelled with him to keep it out of the hands of the advancing British army. At the town of Nelspruit (Mpumalanga), the presidential train was delayed while mysterious wooden crates were unloaded and carried away into the bush. Kruger had little money (or any assets at all) in Europe, and it is surmised that the missing gold – in Kruger pounds, coin blanks and bars – still awaits discovery somewhere between Nelspruit and Barberton. The search continues to this day.

President Paul Kruger

GAUTENG AND SUN CITY

SOWETO AND JOHANNESBURG *are part of the urban conglomerate that developed around the rich gold mines of the Witwatersrand in Gauteng. To the north of these cities lies sedate and elegant Pretoria, founded before the discovery of gold and today South Africa's administrative capital. In the northwest, the glittering Sun City resort and casino complex offers fast-paced entertainment.*

After the discovery of the main reef in 1886, gold fast became the basis of the national economy and dictated the development of the then mostly rural Transvaal Boer republic. Gold prospectors uncovered many other minerals, such as the coal fields of the eastern Highveld, which now provide the power for further development.

Those who wish to escape the cities do not have far to go. Northwest of Johannesburg and Pretoria is the large Hartbeespoort Dam, where watersports enthusiasts flock on weekends, and the shores are lined with resorts and holiday homes. The Magaliesberg mountain range is a nature retreat nearby whose lower slopes are all but immersed in the water. To the south, the Vaal Dam is another source of water, and recreation, for the province.

The ambitious Sun City development turned the most unpromising terrain in the former homeland of Bophuthatswana, now part of the North West Province, into an opulent leisure resort. Subsequent expansion on a tide of success produced the exotic fantasy called The Palace of the Lost City, where the visitor wants for nothing. Tropical jungle now covers what once was overgrazed farmland in the crater of an extinct volcano, and computer-generated waves wash onto pristine, man-made beaches. Even those who do not find the complex to their taste have to admire the effort and planning that went into its creation.

Visitors in search of an authentic Africa experience should head for the tranquil beauty of the Pilanesberg National Park a little further north.

In October, the streets of Pretoria are ablaze with lilac jacaranda blossoms

◁ The impressive Elephant Walk leads to the Palace of the Lost City at Sun City

Exploring Gauteng and Sun City

THE ROCKY WITWATERSRAND – ridge of white waters – lies about 1,600 m (5,250 ft) above sea level and stretches for 80 km (50 miles) from west to east. Johannesburg and its satellites have grown, literally, on gold. Here live almost half of South Africa's urban people. Although hot and lush in summer, languid afternoons are frequently torn apart by short, violent thunderstorms. The Highveld grasslands do experience frost and occasional snow in winter. To the northwest, Sun City and The Palace of the Lost City are part of a glittering complex offering superb accommodation, casinos and fast-paced entertainment.

History comes alive in Gold Reef City

THABAZIMBI

PILANESBERG
NATIONAL PARK
9

Vaalko
Dam

SUN CITY **8**

R565

R

N4

Motopo

MMABATHO

LICHTENBURG

R30

N14

SC
N

Kuruman

R53

POTCHEFSTROOM

SASOLI
N

Kimberley

Vaal

Bloemfo

SIGHTS AT A GLANCE

Gold Reef City pp248–9 **2**
Hartbeespoort Dam **6**
Johannesburg **1**
Pilanesberg National Park **9**
Pretoria **7**
Sandton and Randburg **4**
Soweto **3**
Sun City **8**
   *Palace of the Lost City ·
   pp258–9*

Tour
Touring Gauteng pp252–3 **5**

| 0 kilometres | 50 |
| 0 miles | 25 |

KEY

▬	National route
▭	Other route
▬	Scenic route
━	River, lake or dam
···	Park or reserve boundary
✺	Viewpoint

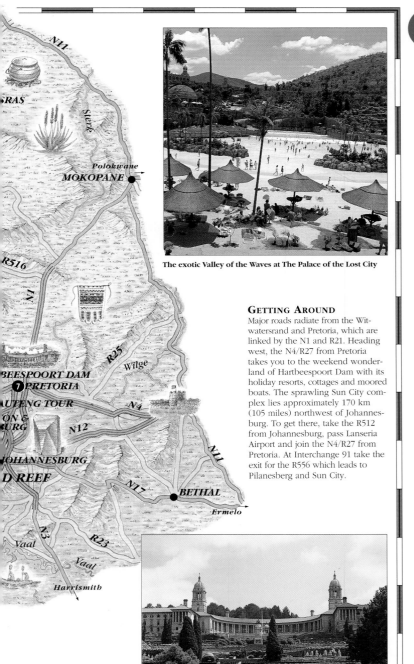

The exotic Valley of the Waves at The Palace of the Lost City

GETTING AROUND

Major roads radiate from the Witwatersrand and Pretoria, which are linked by the N1 and R21. Heading west, the N4/R27 from Pretoria takes you to the weekend wonderland of Hartbeespoort Dam with its holiday resorts, cottages and moored boats. The sprawling Sun City complex lies approximately 170 km (105 miles) northwest of Johannesburg. To get there, take the R512 from Johannesburg, pass Lanseria Airport and join the N4/R27 from Pretoria. At Interchange 91 take the exit for the R556 which leads to Pilanesberg and Sun City.

The Union Buildings, the seat of parliament in Pretoria

Johannesburg ❶

A taste of Africa

THE COUNTRY's financial and commercial heartland, densely populated Johannesburg has many names. Most of them, like Egoli and Gauteng itself, mean "place of gold", for gold and glamour are close companions in this city which has grown from primitive mine camp to metropolis in little over a century. The city pulsates with entrepreneurial energy while, at the same time, having retained the spirit of a frontier town. It lies at an altitude of 1,763 m (5,784 ft) above sea level, but at Western Deep gold mine, the shafts reach 3,777 m (12,388 ft) below ground.

Traditional arts and crafts are sold at many markets

Exploring Johannesburg

Johannesburg is undergoing considerable change, with the once quiet neighbourhoods of Sandton and Randburg, north of the city, fast becoming fashionable places to live. The city centre, however, still has a host of interesting sights.

Johannesburg is not a safe city to explore on foot and with its poor public transport system, visitors are advised to embark on an organized tour.

CITY CENTRE
🏛 University of the Witwatersrand
Cnr Jorissen & Bertha sts. 📞 (011) 717-1000. ☐ 8:30am–4:30pm Mon–Fri, Sat (bookings only). ⬤ Sun, public hols. ♿

Splendid African carvings and ceremonial and ritual objects can be seen at the Gertrude Posel Gallery on the campus.

The James Kitching Gallery of the Bernard Price Institute has the largest collection of prehistoric fossils in the country.

🎭 Market Theatre Complex
Bree Street. 📞 (011) 832-1641. ☐ 9am–5pm daily. 🍴 🛒 ♿

The Market Theatre Complex is the centre of the Newtown Cultural Precinct that includes the South African Breweries Museum, the Workers' Museum and Library, and MuseuMAfricA.

Originally an Indian fruit market, it now houses three theatres, two art galleries, restaurants, cafes and shops.

Each Saturday morning, flea-market traders gather on the square outside to sell everything from curios to clothing.

Opposite the Market Theatre, but part of the complex, the Africana Museum (1935) was relaunched in 1994 as **MuseuMAfricA**. The theme is Johannesburg and its people at various stages of socio-political transformation.

🏛 MuseuMAfricA
Newtown. 📞 (011) 833-5624. ☐ 9am–5pm Tue–Sun. ⬤ Mon. ♿ 🛒

🏢 Johannesburg Stock Exchange Building
Diagonal St. 📞 (011) 298-2800. ⬤ to the public.

This rather impressive glass-walled building is set somewhat incongruously in a truly African downtown area of street vendors and tiny shops selling everything from plastic buckets to blankets and traditional herbal medicines. The building formerly housed the Johannesburg Stock Exchange (JSE) on one of its floors, but the exchange has now moved to new premises in Sandton.

🏬 Kwa Zulu Muti
14 Diagonal St. 📞 (011) 836-4470. ☐ 8am–5pm Mon–Fri, 8am–1pm Sat. ⬤ Sun, public hols.

This herbalist shop represents a traditional side of Africa that is very much a part of daily life for many South Africans.

Not all the remedies, potions and medicines are herbal. Stock includes animal skins, bones, horns and claws, as well as dried bats, frogs and insects, and a variety of herbs and plants, dried and fresh.

🏛 Johannesburg Art Gallery and Sculpture Park
Klein St, Joubert Park. 📞 (011) 725-3130. ☐ 10am–5pm Tue–Sun. ⬤ Good Fri & 25 Dec. 🛒

This gallery in Joubert Park displays traditional, historical and modern South African art, as well as paintings from European schools, collections of ceramics, sculptures, furniture and textiles.

Unfortunately, the small park has now become a haven for vagrants and hustlers and visitors must be on guard.

Traditional African herbalist

MuseuMAfrica is part of the Market Theatre Complex in Newtown

VISITORS' CHECKLIST

Road map E2. Gauteng Province.
🏛 712,500. ✈ 20 km (12 miles)
E of the city. 🚌 Rotunda terminal, cnr Rissik and Wolmarans
sts, Braamfontein. 🚌 Rotunda
terminal. ℹ Sandton Mall, Level
4, Entrance 6, Sandton, (011) 784–
9596/7/8 ◯ daily. 🎭 FNB Vita
Dance Umbrella (Feb–Mar); Windy-
brow Festival (Mar); Arts Alive
(Sep); Johannesburg Biennale
(Oct, only in odd-numbered
years). 🌐 www.gauteng.net

🏛 Constitution Hill

San Hancock St. 📞 (011) 274-5300.
◯ 9am–5pm daily. ● Good Fri, 25
Dec. 🎫 except Tue.

This remarkable development is a living museum documenting South Africa's turbulent past and its transition to democracy. The site incorporates the Old Fort Prison Complex, a notorious jail for over a century where many, including Nelson Mandela, were imprisoned. South Africa's Constitutional Court, established in 1994 after the country's first democratic elections, now occupies the eastern side of the complex.

HILLBROW

One of Johannesburg's oldest suburbs, Hillbrow has a very high population density. Noisy, active, and exuberant, it offers many restaurants, entertainment venues and bars. Due to the high crime rate, visitors should join an organized tour.

🏟 Ellis Park Sports Stadium

Cnr Cerrey and Staib sts, Doornfontein.
📞 (011) 402-8644. 🚌 fm Rotunda
terminal. 🚉 Ellis Park station.

Homeground of the Gauteng Lions rugby team, this 60,000-seat stadium was built in 1982. It hosts regular matches and fixtures, and also features an Olympic-sized swimming pool.

ENVIRONS

West of the Market Theatre, along Jeppe Street, the **Oriental Plaza** bazaar is permeated by the exotic aroma of Eastern spices. Here, some 300 shops and stalls sell everything from carpets to clothing. Many of the traders are the descendants of Indians who came to the Witwatersrand in the 19th century, after their contracts on the sugar plantations of Natal had expired.

South of the city, **Santarama Miniland** houses landmark buildings from around the country, accurately reconstructed on a miniature scale.

🏬 Oriental Plaza

Main & Bree sts, Fordsburg. 📞 (011)
838-6752. ◯ 8:30am–5pm Mon–Fri,
8:30am–2pm Sat. ● Fri 12–2pm,
Sun, public hols. 🍴 🏬 🎫

🏯 Santarama Miniland

Rosettenville Rd, Wemmerpan.
📞 (011) 435-0543. ◯ 9am–
5pm daily. 🚻 🎫 🍴

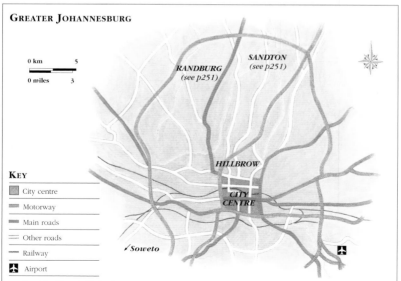

GREATER JOHANNESBURG

0 km 5
0 miles 3

RANDBURG
(see p251)

SANDTON
(see p251)

HILLBROW

CITY CENTRE

Soweto

KEY

▨	City centre
▬	Motorway
▬	Main roads
═	Other roads
─	Railway
✈	Airport

Gold Reef City ❷

THIS LIVELY AND IMAGINATIVE reconstruction of Johannesburg of the 1890s is situated some 8 km (5 miles) south of the city. It was built around Shaft 14, a gold mine that was in use from 1887–1971. The Gold Reef City theme and fun park aims to recapture that transient time during which Johannesburg slipped, quite unobtrusively, from mining camp to city. There are interesting museums to visit and an informative underground tour of the now disused mine. Daily displays of tribal, gumboot and cancan dancing complement the festive atmosphere.

Cancan dancer

Golden Loop
The daring loop is one of 26 rides that can be enjoyed free of charge.

Main Gate
People short enough to pass under the miner's hands without touching (1.2 m; 4 ft) enter free of charge.

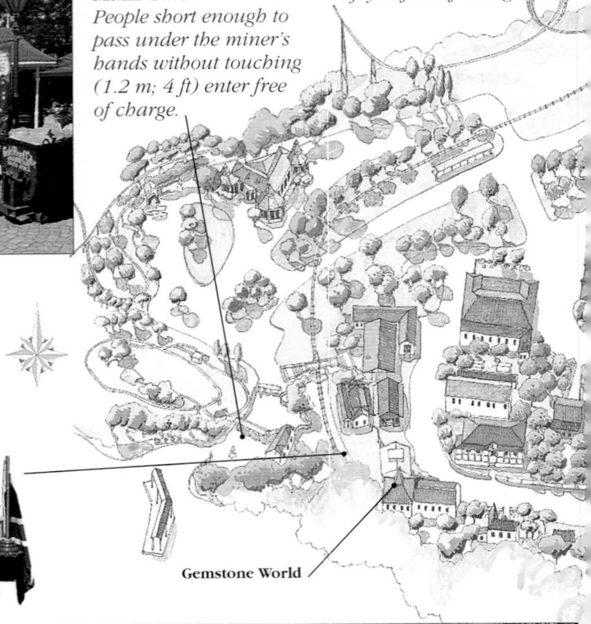

Gemstone World

Gold Reef City Train
For visitors wishing to gain an overview of the theme park, the Gold Reef City Train offers a leisurely mode of transport and stops at three different stations.

★ Gumboot Dancing
The gumboot dance is said to be based on an Austrian folk dance that was taught by missionaries who were scandalized by "pagan" African dances. The deliberately heavy-footed response is a gentle rebuke to those who saw merit only in their own customs.

STAR FEATURES
★ Gold Pouring
★ Gumboot Dancing
★ Main Street

★ **Main Street**
Restaurants, pubs, shops, banking facilities, and the Gold Reef City Hotel line this wide street, which also acts as a stage for impromptu dance displays.

VISITORS' CHECKLIST

Road map E2. Shaft 14, Northern Parkway, Ormonde, Johannesburg.
(011) 248-6800. 55 from city centre; major hotels offer shuttle buses. 9:30am–5pm Tue–Sun. 25 Dec. incl. all rides & shows. multilingual.
www.goldreefcity.co.za

The Digger Joe's Prospector Camp
Here visitors can experience the thrill of panning for gold in a swift-running stream. An experienced gold digger is on hand to explain the process and give expert advice.

Victorian
merry-go-round

Town
square

Scale model of
the gold mine

Vintage car
display

0 metres   50
0 yards   50

Victorian Funfair
This fair is suitable for visitors of all ages and available to use at no additional cost. The fair affords a unique opportunity to experience authentic, Victorian-era rides.

★ **Gold Pouring**
Gold Reef City is the only venue in the entire country where the public can attend a gold pouring demonstration.

The Spirit of Sophiatown

Sophiatown – 10 km (6 miles) from Johannesburg's city centre in the 1950s – was a rather seedy shanty town, yet it was also the cradle of a developing urban black culture, and became part of South Africa's mythology. Much of the creative black African talent of Johannesburg lived in this overcrowded slum. Artists and journalists from *Drum* (the first "black" magazine

Township shuffle

in the country), stylish dressers and musicians would meet in the vibrant dance halls and debate politics in the shebeens (illegal bars). But the magic ended abruptly in the 1950s when the government ordered the forcible removal of the community to Meadowlands, a characterless settlement on the far edge of the city – and the white suburb of Triomf replaced Sophiatown.

Sophiatown Gangs
Gangsters looked to the USA for role models. The most admired gang in Sophiatown was a snappily dressed, limousine-driving group known as "The Americans".

ESSENCE OF SOPHIATOWN
Despite the poverty, squalor, petty crime and violence, Sophiatown's stimulating vibe differed from that of other townships in the country. People of all races could (and did) buy and own properties here.

Shebeens
The Casbah Gang Den was the most notorious shebeen. At these illegal drinking spots, workers and teachers, both white and black, would meet.

Tap water was unavailable in most homes.

The Sounds of Music
The sounds of the penny whistle, saxophone, harmonica, piano, trumpet and clarinet filled the streets and halls.

Skokiaan was a potent, back-yard-brewed cocktail.

Building materials were bits of wood, cardboard boxes, tin and old sacks.

Leaving Sophiatown
It took four years to remove all of the inhabitants to Meadowlands (now Soweto). By 1959 Sophiatown had been demolished.

Graffiti on a wall in Soweto

Soweto ❸

Road map E2. 👥 *5.5 million.*
ℹ️ *118469 Senokonyana St, Orlando West, (011) 982-1050.* ⏰ *8:30am–5pm Mon–Fri.*

F EW WHITE SOUTH AFRICANS have visited Soweto or any of the other townships built beyond the limits of the once "whites-only" suburbs. Soweto has few parks or reserves, museums or malls, but it is home to at least five or six million people.

It was in Soweto, in 1976, that the final phase of resistance to apartheid began. The anniversary of this uprising, 16 June, is commemorated as Youth Day. There is a modest monument in the suburb.

Numerous reliable tour companies *(see p365)* organize day trips to Soweto, usually including a visit to a traditional shebeen, as well as a backyard, or spaza, shop. It is not advisable for visitors to enter Soweto alone.

Sandton and Randburg ❹

Road map E2. 👥 *191,800.* ✈️ *Johannesburg International.* 🚌 *Magic Bus, (011) 394-6902.* ℹ️ *Village Walk, cnr Rivonia Rd & Maud St, (011) 783-4620.* ⏰ *9am–4:30pm Mon–Sat, 9am–1pm Sun.*

N ORTH OF JOHANNESBURG, the metropolitan sprawl blends into expensively laid-out residential areas with high walls, spacious gardens, swimming pools and tennis courts.

Affluent Sandton is a fashionable shoppers' paradise, with Sandton City reputedly the most sophisticated retail centre in the Southern Hemisphere. It is especially noted for its speciality shops, trendy boutiques, jewellers and dealers in African art, curios and leatherwork. The centre also has 16 cinemas and 20 superb restaurants and bistros. A number of five-star graded hotels adjoin the Sandton City complex and Sandton Square,

where an Italianate fountain is the focal point in a little piazza that is lined with coffee shops and restaurants. The Village Walk, close to Sandton City, has restaurants, cinemas and up-market boutiques selling clothing and accessories that have been imported from fashion centres in Europe.

Situated about 10 km (6 miles) northwest of Sandton City is another of Johannesburg's more vibrant suburbs – Randburg – which is a sought-after residential area.

Sandton's Village Walk mall

Randburg's pedestrian mall was among the first in the country. The Randburg Waterfront is a lakeside centre with a variety of shops, pubs, restaurants, craft markets, cinemas, live musical shows, an entertainment area for children and a floodlit musical fountain in the evenings.

On the Witkoppen Road, north of Randburg and Sandton, the Klein Jukskei Vintage Car Museum features a collection of early vehicles.

The Randburg Waterfront is a popular entertainment venue in Johannesburg's northern suburbs

Touring Gauteng ⑤

Although much of Gauteng consists of the industrial areas that have helped to shape the national wealth, the vibrant metropolitan centres of Johannesburg and Pretoria are surrounded by a green belt that offers various facilities for outdoor recreation. Popular destinations like the De Wildt cheetah station, Hartbeespoort Dam and the hiking trails of the Magaliesberg mountain range are accessible via an excellent network of highways.

Mask, Heia Safari Ranch

De Wildt ⑦
This sanctuary near Brits initiated a breeding programme for captive king cheetahs in 1971. Although experts predicted failure, the project is a success.

0 kilometres   10

0 miles   5

The Magaliesberg Range ⑥
This chain of low hills between Pretoria and Rustenburg is very popular with hikers. The area has many hotels, guest farms, caravan parks and camp sites.

KEY

- ▬ Motorway
- ▬ Tour route
- ▬ Other roads
- ☀ Viewpoint

(Map labels: THABAZIMBI, R511, Cablew..., Hartbeespoort, Kosmos, Hartbe... Da..., RUSTENBURG, Mooinooi, Buffelspoort Dam, MAGALIESBERG, Nooitgedacht Battlesite, Blockhouse, R560, WITWATERSBERG, R563, Rhino Park, UPINGTON, Krugersdorp, Roodepoort)

Kromdraai Conservancy ⑤
Caves, old gold mines, fossil sites, a trout farm and a game reserve are visited on guided walks and overnight trails.

TIPS FOR DRIVERS

Length: 200 km (124 miles) Hartbeespoort Dam is an hour's drive from Pretoria and Johannesburg on good roads.
Stopping-off points: There are good restaurants at Heia Safari, the Aloe Ridge Game Reserve and around the Hartbeespoort Dam area.

Sterkfontein Caves ④
The sheer number of fossils found in these extensive dolomite caverns makes this one of the world's most important archeological sites. Conducted tours leave every 30 minutes.

Aloe Ridge Game Reserve ②
At this reserve near Muldersdrift visitors can see white rhino, buffalo, hippo and many antelope and bird species. There is also a Zulu craft centre.

Hartbeesport Dam ⑧
A 17-sq-km (6.6-sq-mile) water surface makes this dam a prime weekend destination for the citizens of Johannesburg and Pretoria.

Crocodile River Arts and Crafts Ramble ⑨
On the first weekend of every month, visitors driving along this route can stop off at the workshops to watch the craftspeople and buy fine art, furniture and metalwork.

Lion Park ⑩
A one-way road passes through a 200-ha (493-acre) lion enclosure and a separate park stocked with blesbok, black *wildebeest* (gnu), impala, gemsbok and zebra, to reach a picnic site.

Witwatersrand National Botanical Gardens ①
The Witpoortjie Falls form the focus of the gardens, where indigenous highveld flora like aloes and proteas attract many bird species.

Heia Safari Ranch ③
Impala, blesbok and zebra wander freely through the grounds, which also incorporate a conference centre, restaurant, and bungalows on the banks of the Crocodile River.

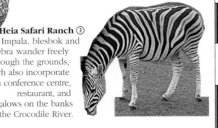

Power-boating is popular on Hartbeespoort Dam

Hartbeespoort Dam ❻

Road map E2. On R514 take cableway turnoff. ℹ *(012) 251-0992*.

THIS DAM FORMS part of the **Hartbeespoort Nature Reserve**. Boating is permitted and the dam is popular with water-skiers, boardsailors and yachtsmen, while anglers cast for *kurper* (a species of bream), carp, and yellowfish.

The circular drive includes a short tunnel leading to the dam wall, on which you emerge to experience wide views over the captive waters of the Crocodile and Magalies rivers. The route is studded with holiday cottages, retirement homes and holiday resorts, as well as farm stalls, kiosks, and curio shops.

Other attractions include an aquarium, claimed to be the largest freshwater aquarium in Africa. It houses most species of South African freshwater fish, crocodiles, penguins and seals.

ENVIRONS: In Schoemansville village is the entrance to the **Hartbeespoort Dam Snake and Animal Park**, a private zoo that houses snakes and other reptiles, lions, panthers, tigers, cheetahs and leopards. A passenger launch offers cruises from the zoo area.

🗡 **Hartbeespoort Dam Snake and Animal Park**
Schoemansville. 🄲 *(012) 253-1162.* ◑ *8am–5pm daily.* 🖼 🚻 ♿ 🚢

Map labels: R566, 3, R514, N4, R513, R511, esburg

Pretoria ❼

Delville Wood Memorial

THE MONUMENTS AND grandiose official buildings, some dating back to the 19th century, are softened by Pretoria's many parks and gardens. Each spring, the flowers of the jacaranda trees add splashes of deep lilac to the streets. First imported from Rio de Janeiro in 1888, some 70,000 jacarandas now line the avenues of South Africa's administrative capital, which is also one of the country's foremost academic centres.

Paul Kruger Monument, Church Square, Pretoria

Exploring Pretoria

Historical buildings, gracious parks, theatres, and restaurants can be found throughout this elegant, compact city, which centers on the attractive, pedestrianized Church Square.

🦓 National Zoological Gardens

Cnr Paul Kruger & Boom sts. ((012) 328-3265. ○ 8am–5:30pm daily (summer), 8am–5pm (winter).

Better known as Pretoria Zoo, this parkland lies in the heart of the city on the bank of the Apies River. One of the top ten in the world, Pretoria Zoo is very conservation conscious. Much time and effort is spent on breeding programmes of rare or endangered species like the African bateleur eagle and the stately Arabian oryx.

🏛 Church Square

Cnr Church and Paul Kruger sts. Among the buildings on the square are the **Raadsaal** (1890), onetime parliament of the former Boer Republic, and the Palace of Justice (1899), used as a military hospital until 1902 by the British.

Anton van Wouw's statue of Paul Kruger was cast in Italy in 1899, the year the Transvaal Republic went to war against the British Empire.

🎭 State Theatre

Cnr Prinsloo & Church sts.
((012) 392-4000. ○ daily
This complex, in Japanese style, houses five theatres where ballets, dramas, operas, musicals and classical concerts are performed regularly.

🏛 City Hall

Paul Kruger St.
Opposite the Transvaal Museum, this imposing building is a mixture of Neo-Greek and Roman architecture.

Two statues depict Marthinus Pretorius, founder of the city, and his father, Andries, after whom Pretoria was named.

🏛 Transvaal Museum

Paul Kruger St. ((012) 322-7632. ○ 8am–4pm Mon–Sun.
This natural history museum has a remarkable collection of stuffed animals, as well as permanent archaeological and geological exhibitions.

Many of South Africa's indigenous birds are displayed in the Austin Roberts Bird Hall.

🏛 Melrose House

275 Jacob Maré St. ((012) 322-2805. ○ 10am–5pm Tue–Sun.
● Mon, public hols.
In the 1880s, British architect William Vale designed this house for wealthy transport contractor, George Heys. He incorporated almost every form of precast embellishment available, and mixed the styles of an English country house with Indian pavilion and Cape Dutch. Today, the museum, set in a picturesque garden, is furnished with many of its original contents.

During the South African War, Melrose House was the residence of Lord Kitchener, British commander-in-chief. It was here that the Treaty of Vereeniging was signed on 31 May 1902, ending the war.

NDEBELE ARTS AND CRAFTS

The Ndebele are noted for their colourful dress and their art, which includes sculpted figurines, pottery, beadwork, woven mats, and their celebrated wall painting *(see p359)*. An outstanding example is the beaded *nguba*, a "marriage blanket" which the bride-to-be, inspired by her ancestors, makes under the supervision and instruction of the older women in her tribe. Traditionally, the women work the land and are the principal decorators and artists, while the men fashion metal ornaments such as the heavy bracelets, anklets and neck rings that are worn by women.

Typical Ndebele art

♨ Union Buildings

Church St, Meintjies Kop. ◯ *daily (grounds only).*

Designed by the renowned architect, Sir Herbert Baker, the Union Buildings were built to house the administrative offices of the Union of South Africa in 1910. Baker himself chose the imposing hill site from where the two large office wings, linked by a semicircular colonnade, overlook landscaped gardens and an impressive amphitheatre.

Although the building is not open to the public for reasons of security, the impressive Renaissance building with its Cape Dutch and Italian influences may be admired from the peaceful gardens.

ENVIRONS: Visible on the left as one approaches Pretoria on the N1 from Johannesburg, the **Voortrekker Monument** and museum commemorate the Afrikaner pioneers who trekked from the Cape in the 1830s to escape British domination.

Begun in 1938, the centenary of the Battle of Blood River *(see p49)*, it became a focus of Afrikaner unity. The structure features a cenotaph in the Hall of Heroes which is lit by a beam of sunlight at precisely noon on 16 December, the day of the Battle of Blood River.

The Voortrekker Monument

East of Pretoria on the R104, signposted from the Bronk-horstspruit Road, lies **Sammy Marks Museum**, once the elegant residence of industrial pioneer Sammy Marks (1843–1920), the founder of the South African Breweries. The house is furnished in period style.

VISITORS' CHECKLIST

Road map E2. Gauteng Province. 🏛 468,000. ✈ Johannesburg, 50 km (31 miles) SW of Pretoria. ☒ Cnr Shelding and Paul Kruger sts. ☐ Tourist Rendezvous Centre. 🅸 Church Square, (012) 337-4337. ◯ 8am–4pm Mon–Fri. 🎪 Pretoria Show (Aug). 🆆 www.tshwane.gov.za

♨ Sammy Marks Museum

Route 104, Bronkhorstspruit Rd. 📞 (012) 802-1150. 🕐 10am–4pm Tue–Sun (tours obligatory). ● 25 Dec, Good Fri. 🎫 🚻

♨ Voortrekker Monument

Eeufees Rd. 📞 (012) 326-6770. ◯ 8am–5pm daily. 🎫
Museum 📞 (012) 323-0682. 🎫

Historic Melrose House is set in a splendid garden

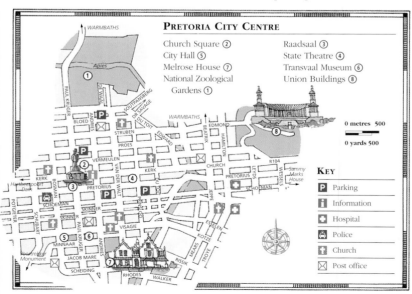

PRETORIA CITY CENTRE

Church Square ②
City Hall ⑤
Melrose House ⑦
National Zoological Gardens ①

Raadsaal ③
State Theatre ④
Transvaal Museum ⑥
Union Buildings ⑧

0 metres 500
0 yards 500

KEY

🅿	Parking
🅸	Information
✚	Hospital
⬛	Police
✝	Church
⊠	Post office

The Cascades Hotel at Sun City

Sun City ⑧

Road map D2. Rustenburg. N4, take R565 turnoff. ✈ 6 km (4 miles) from Sun City. 🚌 Johannesburg (011) 780-7800. 🕿 (014) 557-1000. ◯ daily. 🛂🛗🚻🍽🏧🛍

Set in a fairly bleak part of Southern Africa, two hours by road from the metropolitan centres of the Witwatersrand, "the city that never sleeps" is a glittering pleasure resort. Sun International (see p313) and Computicket (p361) offer regular coach tours from Gauteng and there are daily flights from Johannesburg International Airport.

Sun City is the inspiration of self-made multimillionaire hotelier Sol Kerzner. In the 1970s, when the complex was built, the land formed part of the quasi-independent "republic", Bophuthatswana, where gambling, officially banned in South Africa at the time, was legal. The casino was a key element in the resort's initial success, which then included only one luxury hotel, a man-made lake and a challenging 18-hole golf course designed by the former South African golfing champion, Gary Player.

Within a few years, it became apparent that the complex could not cope with the influx of visitors, and a further two hotels were added in 1980 and 1984 respectively,

Casino entrance

the Cabanas and the attractive Cascades. Accommodation at the 284-room Cabanas Hotel caters mainly for families and day visitors with outdoor interests, and costs slightly less than elsewhere in the resort.

Although recent changes in gambling legislation mean that casinos have sprung up around the country and punters no longer have to drive to Sun City, the resort continues to attract visitors due to its many other features, particularly the entertainment centre, still one of the principal attractions. Not only does it offer a chance of winning a fortune at the spin of a wheel, there are elaborate stage shows featuring lines of feathered and sequinned dancers, regular music concerts and beauty pageants and a variety of sports events. The complex also houses a vast array of restaurants, curio shops, boutiques and coffee shops. **The Palace of the Lost City** (see pp258–9) is the latest addition to the vast complex.

In the vicinity of Sun City are several worthwhile natural attractions that should not be missed. Located at the entrance to the resort is the fascinating

Sun City is a spectacular man-made oasis in the North West Province

Paths and bridges wind through the jungle gardens

Kwena Gardens, where Nile crocodiles can be viewed in their natural habitat, with special walkways leading to observation areas.

🐾 **Kwena Gardens**
Sun City. 📞 (014) 552-1262. 🕐 10am–6pm Mon–Sun. Feeding: 4:30pm daily. 🎫 🖥 🚻

Pilanesberg National Park ❾

Road map D2. Take Mogwase turnoff from R510. 📞 (014) 553-6135.
🕐 6am–6pm daily (times may vary).
🎈 🐾 🦌

THE CIRCULAR LAYOUT of the park can be traced to prehistoric times, when this area was the fiery crater of a volcano. Around the central Mankwe Dam lie three rings of little hills – mounds of cooled lava – and the whole area is raised above the plain.

The decision to establish a reserve here was economic: to benefit the local people, and to complement the nearby resort of Sun City.

Re-stocking the overgrazed farmland turned into one of the most ambitious game relocation ventures ever attempted in South Africa. Appropriately called Operation Genesis, it involved the release of 6,000 mammals of 19 species into the new reserve. To ensure the success of the ambitious venture, alien plants were removed and replaced with indigenous ones, telephone lines were diverted, farming structures demolished and the ravages of erosion repaired.

Elephant, black rhino and leopard head an impressive list of wildlife that can be seen at Pilanesberg today. Qualified rangers take guests on safaris in open vehicles. For visitors staying overnight, there is the excitement of night drives.

The Pilanesberg is also home to a number of birds, notably a variety of raptors. Cape vultures nest on the steep cliffs of the Magaliesberg mountains and a number of feeding stations have been established to encourage the survival of this endangered bird.

Pilanesberg National Park offers a choice of accommodation, from the luxurious Kwa Maritane Lodge, Tshukudu Bush Camp and Bakubung Lodge, which overlooks a hippo pool, to tented camps and thatched huts. In the vicinity is a private camp with bungalows and a pleasant caravan park.

Young elephants in the Pilanesberg National Park

The Palace of the Lost City

IN AN ANCIENT VOLCANIC CRATER, some 180 km (112 miles) northwest of Johannesburg, lies the mythical "lost city" of a vanished people, where time seems to have stood still. Here, innovative design and fanciful architecture in a lush, man-made jungle have created a complex that promises an unforgettable holiday experience: luxurious hotels, world-class golf courses, the glamorous Superbowl entertainment centre, glittering casinos, hanging bridges and blue waves lapping white, palm-fringed beaches.

Palace light

The King's Suite
Maple panelling, a private library, bar and panoramic views make this the hotel's most opulent suite.

King Tower

Buffalo Wing

Lost City Golf Course
This 18-hole championship course offers a choice of tees. A crocodile pool at the 13th hole is a unique water hazard.

Cheetah Fountain
This superb bronze sculpture shows impala, frozen in flight from the feared predator.

LOST CITY COMPLEX

① Grand Pool
② Temple of Courage
③ Adventure Mountain
④ Roaring Lagoon
⑤ Bridge of Time
⑥ Superbowl

KEY

═══ Road (tarred)

▢ Building

P Parking

PILANESBERG
Village Wall
Lost City Golf Course Clubhouse
Baobab Forest
The Palace Hotel
Sway Bridge
Hidden Cave Falls
Rainforest and Hippo Pool
Lake of
Old East Gate Bridge
Royal
Royal Amphitheatre
CASCADES
SUN CITY

0 metres　　20
0 yards　　25

★ Elephant Atrium and Shawu Statue

This sculpture honours an elephant bull that roamed the Kruger National Park, until his death in 1986, aged 80. It graces a large chamber at the end of the vaulted Elephant Atrium.

VISITORS' CHECKLIST

Road map D2. N4 from Rustenburg, then R565; or R556, 70 km (43 miles) past Brits. North West Province. ✈ Sun City: Airlink *(011) 978-1111.* 🚌 *from Johannesburg (014) 557-1684.*
ℹ *Sun International Central Reservations (011) 780-7800.*
🏨 *The Palace of the Lost City (014) 557-1000.* ◯ *daily.* 📷 🅿
♿ 🍴 🛍 💺 🌐 🏊 ⛱ ✂
🆆 www.suninternational.co.za

Royal Suites

Queen Tower

Elephant Atrium

Some **600,000** mature trees and shrubs were planted at the Lost City.

★ Central Fresco
The fresco that adorns the dome of the reception area measures 16 m (52 ft) in diameter and took 5,000 hours to complete.

The porte-cochère leads to the domed lobby.

Roaring Lagoon
Every 90 seconds a 2-m (6.56 ft) wave rolls onto the white sand beach.

STAR FEATURES

★ Central Fresco

★ Elephant Atrium and Shawu Statue

BLYDE RIVER CANYON AND KRUGER

THE ATTRACTIONS IN THE NORTHEASTERN PART *of the country include a deeply carved canyon and the nature reserves that surround it, panoramic views, trout-fishing dams, and the charming gold mining town of Pilgrim's Rest, preserved as a living museum.*

South Africa's topography is at its most dramatic where the Drakensberg's northern reaches drop sheer to the hot bushveld plains below. From here, visitors can look out over the Eastern Escarpment to where the savannah merges with the distant coastal plains of Mozambique, and hike through the ravines of the Blyde River Canyon.

High rainfall on the steep mountain slopes contributes to the growth of dense forests, as well as the country's greatest concentration of waterfalls. More timber is produced here than anywhere else in South Africa, and there are vast pine and eucalyptus tree plantations. Scenic drives include the Panorama Route with its unobstructed view sites, which is accessible from the busy little town of Graskop.

Much of the Lowveld plains is occupied by the Kruger National Park, one of the world's oldest and largest wildlife reserves. The southern part, south of the Letaba River and closer to the metropolitan area of Gauteng, is very popular and more frequently visited. Tourist numbers are considerably less in the east, and in the remote north, renowned for its long-tusked elephants. Strict management policies preserve the park from becoming a victim of its own success, while some of the tourist pressure is relieved by the privately run luxury reserves along the Kruger National Park's western border.

Lowveld farming produces a variety of citrus fruit from a number of large estates. Tobacco, nuts, mangoes and avocados are also sucessfully grown.

The graceful impala gazelle, a common sight in the Kruger National Park

◁ At the confluence of the Blyde and Treur rivers, pebbles have scoured gigantic potholes into the rock

Exploring the Blyde River Canyon and Kruger

EARLY PROSPECTORS flocked to the eastern part of the country in search of gold, and found it in the rivers and streams. Today, visitors are attracted by the natural beauty and the superb nature reserves. Here, the Blyde River has cut a mighty canyon, and close by, the edge of the Drakensberg range rises from the grassy plains a kilometre below. This is wildlife conservation country, home of the renowned Kruger National Park and a cluster of exclusive private reserves. There are airstrips and excellent accommodation – just a few hours' drive away from the Witwatersrand.

SIGHTS AT A GLANCE

Blyde River Canyon **5**
Dullstroom **1**
Kruger National Park **6**
Lydenburg **2**
Pilgrim's Rest
   Alanglade pp268–9 **4**
Private Reserves **8**
Swaziland pp276–7 **9**

Tour

Waterfalls Tour p265 **3**
Southern Kruger Tour p274 **7**

SEE ALSO

KEY

▭	National route
▭	Other route
▭	Scenic route
〜	River, lake or dam
⋯	Park or reserve boundary
–·	International boundary
☆	Viewpoint

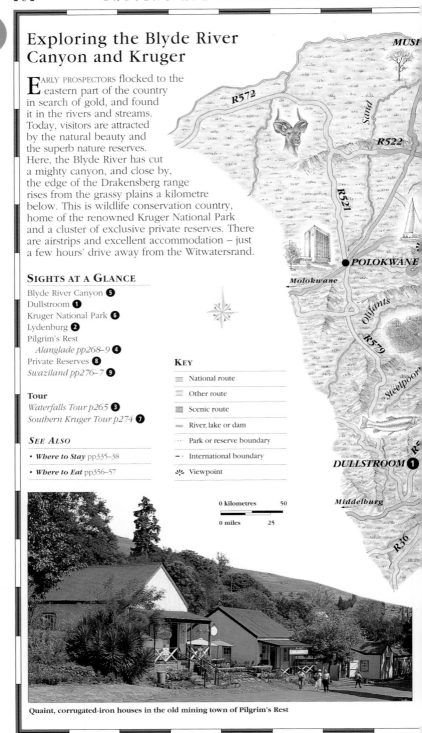

MUSI

R572

Sand

R522

R521

Molokwane

POLOKWANE

Olifants

R579

Steelpoor

DULLSTROOM **1**

Middelburg

R36

0 kilometres 50

0 miles 25

Quaint, corrugated-iron houses in the old mining town of Pilgrim's Rest

The mighty canyon carved by the Blyde River

GETTING AROUND

The N4 national road, running east from Pretoria, is the smoothest and most direct route to the border of Mozambique. Leave Johannesburg on the N12, which joins the N4 near Witbank. For destinations in the Kruger Park or at Blyde River, turn north onto other good, tarred roads – a few of the escarpment passes may seem narrow and steep. The Panorama Route, one of the highest and most scenic roads in South Africa, includes the picturesque old mining village of Pilgrim's Rest *(see pp266–7)*. Slow down and use the car's headlamps and fog lights in misty conditions (usually during late winter and early summer).

Wildlife gathers at a waterhole in the Kruger National Park

The serpentine curves of Long Tom Pass near Lydenburg

Dullstroom ❶

Road map E2. Middelburg. 🏠 *430.*
ℹ️ *Huguenote St, (013) 254-0254.*
🆆 *www.dullstroom.biz*

NAMED IN 1893 after a Dutch official called "Dull" and the *stroom* (stream) of the Crocodile River, Dullstroom is South Africa's fly-fishing centre. It has the highest railway station in South Africa, at 2,076 m (6,811 ft) above sea level. In winter, temperatures can drop to -13°C (9°F).

ENVIRONS: The **Dullstroom Dam Nature Reserve**, on the eastern outskirts of the town, is an area of attractive wooded gorges surrounding a tranquil dam known for its trout fishing. Sheltered camping and caravan sites lie close to the shores amid the unusual and luxuriant sub-alpine vegetation. Bird life is rich, and the countryside is traversed by scenic hiking trails like Misty Valley, Ratelspruit and Salpeterkrans.

The **Verloren Vlei Nature Reserve** lies 14 km (9 miles) by road north of Dullstroom, at the heart of a wetlands conservation area boasting a wealth of floral species. The endangered wattled crane is the subject of a conservation project, which aims to release the bird back into the wild.

Along the road to Nelspruit, the **Sudwala Caves** are filled with bizarre dripstone formations. There are regular guided tours. The network of caverns, is named after a Swazi leader who took refuge here during the mid-1800s.

A short walk from the caves is an interesting timeline of the developement of man, as well as a park with life-sized models that portrays prehistoric wildlife in a convincing setting of palms, shrubs and cycads.

🦌 **Dullstroom Dam Nature Reserve**
📞 *(013) 254-0151.* 🕐 *daily.* 📷
🦌 **Verloren Vlei Nature Reserve**
📞 *(013) 254-0799.* 🕐 *by appointment.* 📷
🛖 **Sudwala Caves**
📞 *(013) 733-4152.* 🕐 *daily.* 📷

Lydenburg ❷

Road map F2. 58 km (36 miles) N of Dullstroom. 🏠 *6,000.* ℹ️ *Jock's Country Stall, (013) 235-3076.*

LYDENBURG MEANS "town of suffering" and refers to the failed attempt to establish a town in the malaria-infested area to the north. Survivors headed south in 1850 to found a new settlement. Interesting historic buildings from that early period are the old church and the Voortrekker school.

The most interesting exhibits in the **Lydenburg Museum** are replicas of the Lydenburg Heads *(see p43)*, seven large, unique terracotta masks dating back to about AD 500 and believed to have been used in ceremonial rituals.

🏛 **Lydenburg Museum**
Long Tom Pass Rd. 📞 *(013) 235-2121.* 🕐 *8am–1pm, 2–4:30pm Mon–Fri, 8am–5pm Sat–Sun.* ● *25 Dec.* 📷

ENVIRONS: Sabie, some 53 km (33 miles) east of Lydenburg, is surrounded by vast forestry plantations and is reached via the scenic **Long Tom Pass**, originally part of a wagon road. In places the rocks still bear the marks of metal-rimmed wheel ruts. In the 19th century exotic, fast-growing trees were planted around Sabie to provide timber for use in the many local gold mines. Timber is still the area's mainstay. The **Safcol Forestry Industry Museum** is dedicated to wood and its many uses.

🏛 **Safcol Forestry Museum**
10th Ave, Sabie. 📞 *(013) 764-1058.*
🕐 *8:30am–4pm Mon–Fri, 10am–3pm Sat & Sun.* 📷

TROUT FISHING IN DULLSTROOM

In 1890, brown trout were successfully introduced to the inland waters of KwaZulu-Natal for the first time and were later distributed in cold streams throughout the country. The rainbow trout with its sparkling reddish-mauve side stripe was introduced in 1897. The trout-rich waters around Dullstroom allow for dam and river angling, mostly from private ground. Temporary membership of the Dullstroom Fly-Fishers' Club allows temporary access to sites, as well as sound advice from experienced local anglers. Details may be obtained on admission to Dullstroom Dam, or from the Town Clerk. Accommodation in the district ranges from wooden cabins to luxurious guesthouses.

Tranquil dam near Dullstroom

The Waterfalls Tour ❸

HIGH-LYING GROUND, generous rainfall and heavy run-off have created spectacular waterfalls in this old gold-mining area along the Drakensberg escarpment. There are, in fact, more waterfalls here than anywhere else in Southern Africa. Several of them can be seen on an easy round trip of under 100 km (60 miles) between the towns of Sabie and Graskop. Most are well signposted and easy to reach by car. Enchanting as they are, waterfalls can be slippery and dangerous and visitors are urged to heed the warning notices.

Berlin Falls ⑦
The water flows through a natural sluice before falling 80 m (263 ft) to the deep, dark-green pool below.

Lisbon Falls ⑥
The Lisbon Falls crash 90 m (295 ft) down a rocky cliff. The old miners named many local places after towns in their home countries.

MacMac Falls ④
The 70-m (230-ft) fall was named for the Scottish miners who panned for gold in this area. There is a picnic site at the nearby MacMac pools.

Maria Shires Falls ⑤
These falls in the forest are noted for their thundering sound, especially after heavy rainfall.

Bridal Veil Falls ③
Delicate wisps of spray that billow like a veil have given this water-fall its name.

KEY

▬	Tour route
═	Other roads
⋯	Trail
☼	Viewpoint

Lone Creek Falls ②
From almost 70 m (230 ft), the spray of the falls drifts down onto dense pockets of fern and mountain forest.

Horseshoe Falls ①
Cascading in an almost perfect horseshoe, these falls are on private land and reached after a short walk through a campsite.

0 kilometres   5
0 miles   3

TIPS FOR DRIVERS

Starting point: Sabie.
Length: 100 km (60 miles).
Getting there: From Sabie, turn left on to the R532 for the Horse-shoe, Lone Creek and Bridal Veil falls. For the MacMac, Maria Shires, Lisbon, Berlin and Forest falls, take the R532 from Sabie towards Graskop.

Pilgrim's Rest ❹

Gravestone

Prospectors struck it rich in 1874, ending their search for gold in a picturesque Low-veld valley. Their original village, today restored to its modest glory, is unique: the diggers built in "tin and timber" thinking that, once the gold was exhausted, they would move on. But the gold lasted almost 100 years, and Pilgrim's Rest, 15 km (10 miles) west of the Drakensberg escarpment, is a living part of history.

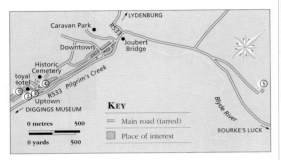

KEY
⎓ Main road (tarred)
▢ Place of interest

Dredzen's store with its colourful bargains from a bygone era

KEY TO TOWN PLAN

The Old Print House ①
Information Centre ②
The Miner's House ③
Dredzen & Company ④
Alanglade ⑤

Exploring Pilgrim's Rest

The entire village, situated 35 km (21 miles) north of Sabie, is a national monument. A single ticket, available from the Information Centre, affords access to the buildings.

A leisurely downhill stroll from St Mary's Church to the Post Office passes the old "uptown area", where one can visit the cemetery. Most interesting of all the tombstones is the enigmatic Robber's Grave.

At the Diggings Site, on the bank of Pilgrim's Creek, visitors may try their luck at panning for alluvial gold.

The Old Print House is typical of local buildings: corrugated iron sheets on a timber frame. Newspapers were the only news medium in days gone by, and printers were among the town's early residents.

The Miner's House puts the life of prospectors into perspective: they may have been surrounded by gold, but their way of life was simple.

Dredzen & Company, the general dealer, displays essential household requisites of a century ago.

Stately Alanglade, the mine manager's residence, was situated in a wooded glen, well away from the dust and noise of the village (*see pp268–9*).

ENVIRONS: Timber and tourism are the mainstays of this area on the dramatic escarpment of the Drakensberg mountains.

From the village, the tarred R533 winds across Bonnet Pass to Graskop, a convenient centre for exploring both the escarpment and the Kruger National Park, whose main camp, Skukuza, is just 70 km (44 miles) away.

View from God's Window

The R534, also known as the Panorama Route, starts 3 km (2 miles) north of Graskop and passes cliff-top sites and lovely waterfalls (*see p265*). The escarpment drops almost 1,000 m (3,281 ft) to the Low-veld plains below. In places, the view extends 100 km (60 miles) towards Mozambique. The scenery in this area has been called the most beautiful in South Africa, and the vistas are spectacular.

The bar of the Royal Hotel was once a chapel

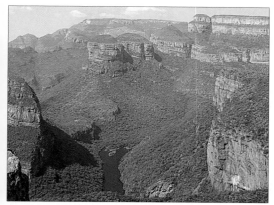
The Three Rondavels in the Blyde River Canyon

Blyde River Canyon ❺

Road map F2. On R534. **(013) 761-6019.** ○ 7am–5pm daily.

THE FAST-FLOWING Blyde River has, over the centuries, carved its way through 700 m (2,300 ft) of shale and quartzite to create a scenic jumble of cliffs, islands, plateaus and bush-covered slopes that form a 20-km (12-mile) canyon. At the heart of this canyon lies the Blydepoort Dam.

The forested slopes of the ravine are home to several large antelope species, as well as smaller mammals, birds, hippo and crocodile. Only in the Blyde River Canyon are all the Southern African primates found: chacma baboon, vervet and samango monkeys, and both species of bushbaby. The abundant flora ranges from lichens and mosses to montane forest, orchids and other flowering plants.

Exploring the Blyde River Canyon Nature Reserve

A 300-km (186-mile) circular drive from Graskop via Bosbokrand, Klaserie, Swadini and Bourke's Luck affords panoramic vistas of the escarpment rising above the plains, the Blydepoort Dam and the breathtaking view deep into the canyon itself. There are several overnight trails and short walks, and accommodation is available at the resorts of Swadini and Blydepoort.

Kowyn's Pass

The tarred R533 between Graskop and the Lowveld provides views of the escarpment and its soaring cliffs. It also passes the scenic Panorama Gorge with its feathery waterfall.

Swadini Aventura

(015) 795-5141. ○ daily. Ⓦ www.aventura.co.za

This resort, set deep in the canyon on the shores of Blydepoort, offers accommodation, a restaurant and a base for boating trips on the dam. The visitors centre and low-level view site have information on the dam and the Kadishi Falls, the world's largest active tufa (calcium carbonate) formation.

Three Rondavels

Resembling the traditional cylindrical huts of the Xhosa or Zulu, these three hills were shaped by the erosion of soft rock beneath a harder rock "cap" that eroded more slowly. The capping of Black Reef quartzite supports a growth of

Bourke's Luck potholes

evergreen bush. The Three Rondavels is one of three sites that can be viewed from the road which overlooks the canyon – the other two are World's End and Lowveld View.

Bourke's Luck

(013) 761-6019. ○ 7am–5pm daily.

Grit and stones carried by the swirling waters at the confluence of the Blyde ("joyful") and Treur ("sad") rivers have carved potholes, from which early prospectors extracted large quantities of gold. Off the R532, Bourke's Luck is the reserve's headquarters, with an information centre.

The Pinnacle, Panorama Route

Panorama Route

The 18-km (11-mile) stretch of the R534 that loops along the top of the cliff, right at the very edge of the escarpment, is a scenic marvel. Wonderview and God's Window may sound like purely fanciful names until one explores the sites and stands in silent awe at the breathtaking scenery.

The Pinnacle

This impressive column of rock, also on the Panorama Route, appears to rise sheer from a base of evergreen foliage. Optical illusions seem to place it almost within reach. Exposed layers of sandstone show the rock's sedimentary origins. It becomes clear that, even at this lofty height above present sea level, the top of the escarpment was once covered by a primordial sea.

Pilgrim's Rest: Alanglade

Palatial by Pilgrim's Rest standards, Alanglade was occupied by a succession of Transvaal Gold Mining Estate managers. It is, however, most strongly associated with its first occupants. Alan and Gladys Barry moved into the newly built house with their young family in 1916. Today, the mansion is a period museum furnished in the Edwardian style, and seems to await the return of its first owners.

Wooden rocking horse

★ The Kitchen
The kitchen staff had to cook for many people, so the kitchen includes two pantries, a larder, scullery and milk room.

Electric Bell
An ingenious bell system connected to a numbered, glazed box informed the staff in which room service was required.

Blocks of local stone line the base of the house.

Glazed double doors
separate the rooms and let in light

Arched windows offset the entrances from the rest of the house.

Enclosed Verandahs
Airy verandahs doubled as sleeping space for the Barry household, which included seven children and many servants.

Star Features

★ The Kitchen

★ Erica's Bedroom

Alanglade, built in 1915

VISITORS' CHECKLIST

Pilgrim's Rest. 3 km (2 miles) NE at R533 fork. ℹ *Information Centre, (013) 768-1060.* 📷 *11am, 2pm Mon–Sat. Booking essential.* ♿

Hunting trophies reflect the game of the lowveld area.

★ **Erica's Bedroom**
The eldest daughter, Erica, was the only child to have her own bedroom, even though she only visited during school holidays.

Antique Furniture
Museum Services furnished Alanglade with a number of exquisite antiques, such as this rosewood armoire.

Day nursery

Floor coverings consist of woven mats made of coir, grass or sisal fibre.

The Rose Garden
Only the small rose garden still displays the strict, original period layout of bold lines, geometric patterns and herbaceous borders.

ALAN BARRY'S LEGACY

On 15 August 1930, Richard Alan Barry, the General Manager of Transvaal Gold Mining Estates Ltd, wrote this diary entry: "Leave Pilgrim's Rest. A very sad parting from work and friends and associates." This, the third Alanglade (the other two were in Johannesburg), had been the family's home for 14 years and had seen a new generation of Barrys grow up. So strong was the association with these first owners that the house is called Alanglade to this day.

Three of the Barry children

The Kruger National Park ⑥

KRUGER IS SOUTH AFRICA'S largest national park, and unquestionably one of the best wildlife sanctuaries in the world. From the Limpopo River in the north to the Crocodile in the south, the park extends for 352 km (220 miles), and averages 60 km (38 miles) from east to west. This vast wilderness covers an area of 19,633 sq km (7,580 sq miles), equivalent in size to Israel. The park has 16 distinct sections, based on the type of vegetation found there.

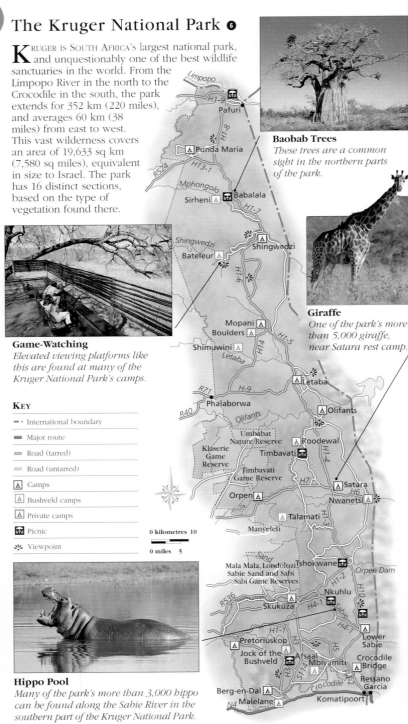

Baobab Trees
These trees are a common sight in the northern parts of the park.

Giraffe
One of the park's more than 5,000 giraffe, near Satara rest camp.

Game-Watching
Elevated viewing platforms like this are found at many of the Kruger National Park's camps.

KEY

- ‑·‑ International boundary
- ▬ Major route
- ═ Road (tarred)
- ═ Road (untarred)
- Ⓐ Camps
- Ⓐ Bushveld camps
- Ⓐ Private camps
- 🚻 Picnic
- ✹ Viewpoint

0 kilometres   10
0 miles   5

Hippo Pool
Many of the park's more than 3,000 hippo can be found along the Sabie River in the southern part of the Kruger National Park.

◁ **Zebra and impala share a drink at one of the Kruger National Park's many waterholes**

Mopane trees and red sand near Punda Maria in northern Kruger

NORTHERN KRUGER

Kruger's semi-arid northern region is an immense, arid wilderness of mopane trees. Several rivers, often little more than sandy courses, sustain some of the park's most intriguing habitats. Apart from providing sanctuary for large herds of elephant and buffalo, the north also hosts antelope species such as sable, roan, eland, Lichtenstein's hartebeest, tsessebe and grysbok.

Punda Maria

The remote northernmost corner of Kruger will appeal to visitors seeking solitude. Punda Maria's huts date back to 1933. The Pafuri picnic spot, at the northern extremity of the park, attracts birdwatchers in pursuit of the exquisite crimson-and-green Narina trogon. Longtailed starlings, crested guinea fowl and white-fronted bee-eaters are also found in this tranquil haven within the park. Wild fig, fever, mahogany, ebony and baobab trees border the Luvuvhu River, where nyala feed quietly in the shade.

Shingwedzi and Mopani

Shingwedzi, 47 km (29 miles) south, occupies a hill summit overlooking the Pioneer Dam. In this hot, dry region, the camp's swimming pool offers year-round relief. Mopani, 63 km (39 miles) further, is an ideal base from which to explore the area. A network of roads follows both banks of the beautiful Shingwedzi River, which sustains elephant, buffalo, nyala, waterbuck, lion and leopard.

Letaba

Enjoying a commanding position on the south bank of the Letaba River is one of Kruger's finest camps. Chalets are arranged in semi-circles overlooking the river. In the Elephant Hall is a display of tusks from the "Magnificent Seven", believed to be the largest tusks ever found in Southern Africa.

CENTRAL KRUGER

Although no major rivers flow across the flat plains of Kruger's central region, the open grassland supports large herds of antelope and other game. As prey animals are plentiful, half of the park's lions inhabit this region and are regularly sighted. During winter, large herds of impala, zebra, wildebeest, buffalo and giraffe gather to drink at the artificial waterholes and dams that have been constructed across sandy riverbeds.

Crested guinea fowl

There are some superb vantage points on the road north from Lower Sabie that overlook the Kruger's dams. Mlondozi Dam has good picnic facilities and a shady terrace overlooking the valley. The very popular Nkumbe lookout point offers unparalleled views over the plains below. The water of Orpen Dam, at the foot of the N'wamuriwa hills, attracts kudu, elephant and giraffe.

Olifants

This attractive camp overlooks the broad floodplain of the Olifants River. This area supports large herds of elephant. Lion, antelope and buffalo can often be found along the roads that follow the river.

Satara and Orpen

Satara, the second largest camp, is located in an area where lion are common. Gravel roads along the Sweni, Nuanetsi and Timbavati rivers offer superb game-viewing. To the west of Satara, Orpen camp is close to the private Timbavati Game Reserve.

Near Satara, zebra and giraffe enjoy fresh grazing after the summer rains

Southern Kruger Tour ❼

Although the southern region covers only about one-fifth of the Kruger National Park's total area, it attracts the most visitors, as it is easily accessible from Gauteng. Three of the five largest camps are found here, and the traffic volume can be high, but it is considered to be the best game-viewing area. It is also a very scenic region, where granite *koppies* (outcrops) punctuate the woodland, and the Sabie River carves a verdant corridor across the plains.

Skukuza ①
The largest camp, able to accommodate around 1,000 visitors, is at the centre of the Kruger's best wildlife-viewing area. Camp facilities include an airport, car-hire service, bank, post office, museum, library, restaurant, shop and bakery.

Tshokwane Picnic Site ②
A pleasant place for breakfast, lunch or a cup of tea, refreshments can be bought from the kiosk. Tshokwane is located on the old transport wagon trail, cut through the bush in the 1880s.

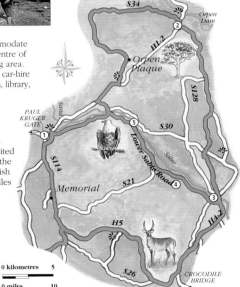

Nkuhlu Picnic Site ⑤
On the shady banks of the Sabie River, the picnic spot is often visited by monkeys who descend from the trees to snatch food off plates. Fish eagles may be seen, and crocodiles float in the river.

Lower Sabie Road (H4-1) ④
Connecting Skukuza to Lower Sabie, the road closely follows the Sabie River for 43 km (27 miles). It is the most popular road in the park, as there is much wildlife in the area.

0 kilometres   5

0 miles   10

Lower Sabie ③
At the modest-sized Lower Sabie camp, many of the chalets survey an expanse of the Sabie River where elephant, buffalo, hippo, ducks and herons are often seen.

KEY
— Tour route
= Other roads
☀ Viewpoint

TIPS FOR DRIVERS

Starting point: *From Paul Kruger Gate to Skukuza, Tshokwane and Lower Sabie, and onto the H4-1.*
Length: *100 km (62 miles).*
Getting there: *Take the N4 from Nelspruit, the R538 to Hazyview and R536 to Paul Kruger Gate.*

Private Reserves ❽

A LONG THE WESTERN BOUNDARY of the national park, and bordered by the Sabie and Olifants rivers, a mosaic of private reserves provides a vital buffer between the densely populated areas of Lebowa and Gazankulu, and the Kruger. A fence, erected along the park's boundary in the 1960s to prevent the spread of diseased animals, also blocked migration routes. An agreement between all parties made possible its removal, and by 1994 herds were free once again to trek along their ancient paths.

Hippo in the natural pool at Sabi Sabi Game Reserve

Exploring the Private Reserves

Luxury lodges, often recipients of international awards for service excellence, offer exclusive "bush experiences" to small groups of visitors. Emphasis is placed on personal attention, and experienced rangers guide visitors on night drives and interesting bush walks.

Sabie Sand Complex

Mpumalanga. *bookings: Selati (011) 483-3939; Bushlodge (011) 483-3939; Mala Mala (011) 809-4300; Londolozi (011) 809-4300. access restricted. fully incl.*
This famous complex includes the Mala Mala, Londolozi and Bushlodge reserves and shares a 33 km (21 mile) boundary with Kruger. Sightings of the Big Five are virtually guaranteed, and hyena, cheetah and wild dog may also be seen.

The choice of accommodation alternatives ranges from exclusive bush camps to luxury lodges. Popular camps like Selati, Sabie River, the Bushlodge, Mala Mala and Londolozi offer access to the southern Sabi-Sabi region with its abundant wildlife.

Manyeleti

Mpumalanga. *(013) 735-5753. access restricted. fully incl.*
Exclusive Manyeleti adjoins the Orpen area of the Kruger National Park, which is known for its variety of wildlife. Visitors can choose to stay either in the comfortable tented Honeyguide Camp, or at the beautiful and luxurious Khoka Moya chalets.

Tourists on a game drive

Timbavati

Mpumalanga. *bookings for the different lodges: (015) 793-1453. restricted access. fully incl.*
The 550-sq-km (210-sq-mile) Timbavati reserve, adjoining Kruger's central region, has some of the best game-viewing in South Africa. Five lodges each with access to a different part of the reserve offer drives and guided walks.

M'bali, a tented camp, and Umlani Bush Camp are situated in the north, while the luxurious Kambaku, Ngala and Tanda Tula lodges lie in the central region.

Klaserie

Mpumalanga. *bookings: Thornybush (011) 883-7918; King's Camp (015) 793-1123; Umhlali (012) 346-4028; Motswari (011) 463-1990. access restricted. fully incl.*
Klaserie is an area that encompasses many private reserves, making it the second largest private sanctuary in the country. It extends over 620 sq km (235 sq miles) and borders on the Kruger National Park, as well as on the Olifants River.

The Klaserie River meanders across the semi-arid bushveld and is the reserve's central focus as countless birds and animals gather on the river banks to drink. Until 1995, Klaserie reserve was not accessible to the general public, but since then, its many splendid bushcamps and lodges have become a firm favourite.

A luxurious lounge at Mala Mala Private Reserve

Swaziland ❾

Traditional Swazi hut at Mlilwane

THE KINGDOM OF SWAZILAND achieved its independence from Britain on 6 September 1968. King Mswati III has ruled the almost one million Swazis since 1986. In the west of the country, the highlands offer many opportunities for hikers. The middleveld has the perfect growing conditions for tropical fruit and is known for its arts and crafts. In the east, lush sugar cane plantations contrast with the dense brown bushveld of game reserves and ranches.

★ Mbabane

Swaziland's capital city developed around the site where Michael Wells opened a pub and trading post at a river crossing in 1888. Today, trade is brisk at the Swazi Market.

★ Mlilwane Wildlife Sanctuary

Mlilwane, which supports white rhino, giraffe, zebra and antelope, covers 45 sq km (17 sq miles). The rest camp's Hippo Haunt restaurant overlooks a hippo pool.

STAR SIGHTS

- ★ Hlane Royal National Park
- ★ Mbabane
- ★ Mlilwane Wildlife Sanctuary
- ★ Piggs Peak

Manzini

Swaziland's biggest town is situated close to the airport. An industrial centre, it also has colourful markets that sell fresh produce, crafts and fabric.

★ Piggs Peak
Local artists display their craft on the road that leads to the casino hotel north of this timber centre.

Phopanyane Nature Reserve is privately owned. The sub-tropical vegetation attracts a great many birds.

VISITORS' CHECKLIST

Road map F2. ✈ *Matsapha (Manzini) 34 km (21 miles) SE of Mbabane.* 🚌 *City Liner from Durban to Pretoria via Mbabane.*
Border posts: *Ngwenya (7am–10pm); Bulembu (8am–4pm); Matsamo (7am–8pm); Mananga (8am–6pm); Lavumisa (7am–10pm); Mahamba (7am–10pm).* 🛈 *Swazi Plaza, Mbabane.* 📞 *(09268) 404-9675.* ◯ *8am–5pm Mon–Fri, 9am–12pm Sat.* ⬤ *Sun, public hols.* 📷 *Umhlanga Reed Dance (Aug/Sep); Independence Day (6 Sep).* **Mlilwane Wildlife Sanctuary** 📞 *(09268) 528-3992.*
Hlane Royal National Park
📞 *(09268) 528-3992.*
@ *reservations@biggame.co.sz*

Malolotja Nature Reserve
Ngwenya, in the reserve, is the oldest mine in the world. Specularite and haematite, used for cosmetics, were excavated here 43,000 years ago. From here there are spectacular views over the countryside.

At Big Bend, near the Lubombo Mountains, sugar cane thrives along the Lusutfu River.

★ Hlane Royal National Park
Hlane and the adjacent Mlawula reserve protect 370 sq km (143 sq miles) of dense woodland and the Lubombo Mountains. Elephant, white rhino, antelope, hippo and giraffe can be seen. Lion and cheetah are kept in separate camps. Guided walking safaris can be arranged on request.

KEY

▬ ▪ International boundary	△ Camping
▪ ▪ Provincial boundary	⚓ Canoeing, rafting
▬ Major route	🚶 Hiking, walking
═ Road (tarred)	☀ Viewpoint
═ Road (untarred)	🛈 Tourist information

THE ARID
INTERIOR

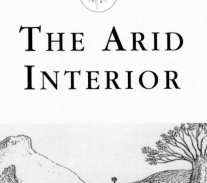

Introducing the Arid Interior

THE SEMI-ARID, sparsely populated Karoo extends across the Northern Cape and parts of the Free State, Eastern and Western Cape provinces. Sleepy country towns and villages, often treasure chests of Cape Dutch and Victorian architecture, serve as supply centres for surrounding farms. North of the Orange River lie the red dunes of the Kalahari desert, one of South Africa's finest wilderness areas. A rich assortment of wildlife inhabits this remote territory. In the Northern Cape, the most famous diamond mines in the world extract shining riches from the earth.

The Richtersveld *is a bleak moonscape with curious flora such as the* kokerboom *(quiver tree), from which Khoina hunters made arrows.*

Upington

Richtersveld

SOUTH OF THE ORANGE
(See pp286–97)

The Camel Rider Statue *in Upington honours the memory of the policemen and their tireless mounts who patrolled the Kalahari in the early 20th century.*

◁ **A *kokerboom* (quiver tree) in the barren semi-desert of the Augrabies Falls National Park**

Kimberley's diamond mines, *once owned by De Beers Mining Company, are nowadays controlled by the Anglo-American Corporation. Impressive headgear dominates the skyline on the outskirts, while in the town itself lie many beautiful historic buildings, like the City Hall.*

Bloemfontein's Civic Centre, *a tall modern structure of glass and concrete, represents a bold departure from the traditional, stately sandstone buildings in the town.*

NORTH OF THE ORANGE
(See pp298–307)

Kimberley

Bloemfontein

The Gariep Dam *is the largest water project on the Orange River and has become a popular weekend resort.*

Gariep Dam

u-Bethesda

Nieu-Bethesda's *quaint Dutch Reformed Church was completed in 1905. The main drawcard of this little Karoo town, however, is the bizarre Owl House.*

| 0 kilometres | 100 |
| 0 miles | 50 |

Life in the Desert

Velvet mite

THE KALAHARI DESERT forms part of a vast inland steppe that stretches from the Orange River to the equator. It extends across portions of the Northern Cape and Namibia, and also covers much of Botswana. Rainfall in this region varies from 150–400 mm (6–16 in) per year and is soon soaked up or simply evaporates. There is little surface water and the flora consists mainly of grass, shrubs and the hardy camelthorn acacias that line the dry beds of ancient rivers. Although the landscape may appear to be lifeless, it supports an astonishing variety of wildlife that is superbly adapted to survive in this harsh environment.

Seasonal river beds, such as that of the Auob, carry water only every few years, usually after exceptionally heavy downpours.

*The **Gemsbok** (oryx) feeds on grass, leaves and roots, and can do without water. The animal's temperature fluctuates in response to climatic changes: during the day it may soar to above 45°C (113°F).*

*The **quiver** contains arrows poisoned with the juice of beetle larvae.*

Bat-eared foxes' large ears allow them to detect underground prey, such as harvester termites and beetle larvae, in the barren areas.

***Kalahari lions** are unique to the Kgalagadi Transfrontier Park, and have learned to depend on smaller prey, taking porcupines and bat-eared foxes when antelope migrate.*

*The **brown hyena** is primarily a scavenger, but also eats wild fruit, beetles, termites, birds' eggs and small animals. Restricted to the drier desert regions of Southern Africa, it can survive without fresh water for extended periods of time.*

*The **Tsama melon's** bitter-tasting flesh is eaten by Bushmen and animals, as it is a vital source of vitamin C and moisture.*

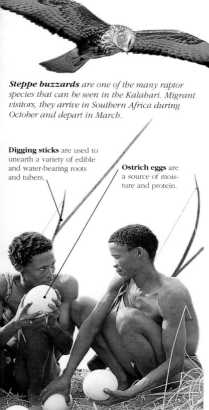

Steppe buzzards are one of the many raptor species that can be seen in the Kalahari. Migrant visitors, they arrive in Southern Africa during October and depart in March.

Namaqua sandgrouse males fly distances of up to 60 km (37 miles) every three to five days to drink and to soak their specially adapted chest feathers. The water retained in these feathers sustains the chicks.

Digging sticks are used to unearth a variety of edible and water-bearing roots and tubers.

Ostrich eggs are a source of moisture and protein.

The puff adder is highly poisonous and bites readily when threatened. The snake propels itself forward leaving deep, straight tracks which can sometimes be seen on the Kalahari sand dunes.

THE BUSHMEN

These nomads have all but vanished from the subcontinent. A small band lives on land south of the Kgalagadi Transfrontier Park allocated to them in 1997. The modern age has severely affected their culture. Even in the remote reaches of Botswana, clans now live in settlements around waterholes – the nomadic lifestyle replaced by a sedentary existence. Before these camps were established, water and food were obtained from the bush: the Bushmen knew of 20 edible insects and 180 plants, roots and tubers.

Barking geckos herald sunset in the desert by emitting a series of sharp clicking sounds. When threatened they tend to freeze, camouflaged against the red sand.

The **Sparrmannia flava** *scarab has a furry coat which enables it to remain active at night when temperatures can drop drastically.*

Wind mills pump precious water from below the surface into metal reservoirs. Agricultural activities in the Kalahari region include Karakul sheep, goat and wildlife farming, while hardy Afrikander cattle only survive where a water supply is assured.

The Orange River

Soutth africa is predominantly a dry country, with precipitation decreasing from east to west and only 8 per cent of rainfall reaching the few major rivers. The mighty Orange and its tributaries drain 47 per cent of the country. For much of the 2,450-km (1,530-mile) long journey from its source in northeast Lesotho to the Atlantic Ocean, the Orange meanders across the arid plains of the Northern Cape. Here, wooden wheels draw the precious water from canals to sustain a narrow, fertile corridor of vineyards, date palms, lucerne and cotton fields, tightly wedged between the river and the unrelenting desert.

Quiver tree

Richtersveld National Park *was established in 1991, and is located in a jagged, mountainous landscape. A network of scenic 4WD trails crisscrosses the park.*

Alexander Bay *is the site of large-scale diamond dredging operations. The nearby Orange River estuary is a wetland renowned for its splendid birdlife.*

The Fish River Canyon lies across the Namibian border.

Ai-Ais and Fish River Canyon Park
Rosh Pinah
Restricted Access
Richtersveld National Park
Khubus
Peace of Paradise
Vioolsdrif
Noordoewer
Goodhouse
Oranjemund
Alexander Bay
Wa
Hom
Haib
B1
N7
Brak
R382

0 kilometres   50
0 miles   25

Orange River canoe trips
(see p364) *have become increasingly popular over the last few years. Several Cape Town-based adventure companies offer exciting canoeing and rafting tours that include camping along the river banks.*

Augrabies Falls, *christened Aukoerebis ("place of great noise") by the early Khoina inhabitants of this region, is where the Orange River plunges 56 m (182 ft) into a constricted granite gorge. The falls and surrounding area were declared a national park in 1966.*

Onseepkans, a small settlement and border post, serves as a departure point for canoe trips down the Orange River.

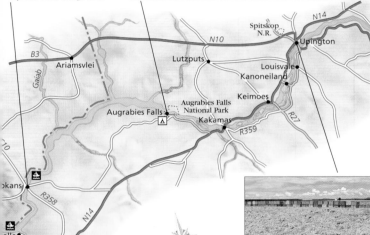

Pella Mission, *with its rows of date palms and the tall spire of its Catholic church, exudes a distinctly Mexican ambience. The church was built by two missionaries whose only building manual was an encyclopaedia.*

Upington, *on the north bank of the Orange River, is the largest town along its course. An important centre for the dried fruit industry, a common sight along the road are sultanas drying in the sun. The municipal resort, on an island in the river, is a popular stop-over.*

KEY

- -	International boundary
▬	Major route
═	Road (tarred)
═	Road (untarred)
🏕	Camping
🛶	Canoeing / rafting

SOUTH OF THE ORANGE

V AST AND UNRELENTING, THE GREAT KAROO *is a uniquely South African landscape of dolerite outcrops, buttes and endless plains. In restful towns and villages the harshness of the terrain is softened by the large, low, sandstone homesteads, typical of Karoo architecture. Since the 1970s, several nature reserves have been established to conserve the territory's fascinating wildlife.*

The indigenous Khoina called the region *Karoo* ("land of great thirst") and the Dutch colonists of the 17th century were hesitant to venture into this forbidding terrain. Ensign Schrijver was the first European to explore the eastern reaches of the Karoo in 1689, and by 1795 the Cape Colony had expanded to include the southern and eastern Karoo regions. The vast plains were partitioned into sheep ranches, and large migrating herds of springbuck, hartebeest, black wildebeest, eland and quagga were decimated through uncontrolled hunting. Some 80 years later, the quagga was extinct, and the large herds of Cape mountain zebra and black wildebeest had been reduced to tiny remnant populations.

With the expanding frontier, several new towns were established. Graaff-Reinet, founded in 1786, prospered quickly as it became an important centre for the surrounding community of sheep farmers. Today, it has the highest number of national monuments in South Africa and is renowned for its Cape Dutch architecture. Elsewhere, the typical Karoo vernacular includes steep-roofed sandstone farm houses surrounded by broad verandahs and delicate latticework.

The Karoo Nature Reserve surrounds Graaff-Reinet on three sides, while the Karoo National Park lies just north of Beaufort West. The Mountain Zebra National Park, near Cradock, is credited with saving the Cape mountain zebra from extinction. In the eastern Karoo, where South Africa's largest water project, the Gariep Dam on the Orange River, provides water to the drought-prone Eastern Cape, many water-based resorts have sprung up.

A fiery show of low-growing *vygies*, a drought-resistant plant that flowers only after it has rained

◁ The windpump silhouetted against a glowing sky is the unofficial emblem of this arid region

Exploring South of the Orange

THE KAROO IS A REGION of endless vistas and clear blue skies, where the road runs straight as an arrow to the distant horizon. Large sheep farms produce much of South Africa's mutton and wool. Steel windmills, standing in the blazing sun, supply the area's life-blood: water. Only 70 small towns and villages, of which Beaufort West is the largest, cling tenaciously to the drought-prone land. Many of them, for example Graaff-Reinet, are architectural treasure chests. At Beaufort West, Graaff-Reinet and Cradock, nature parks conserve the characteristic landscape, fauna and flora of the region.

SIGHTS AT A GLANCE

Cradock **6**
Gariep Dam **7**
Graaff-Reinet pp292–3 **2**
Karoo National Park **1**
Karoo Nature Reserve **3**
Mountain Zebra National Park **5**
Nieu Bethesda **4**

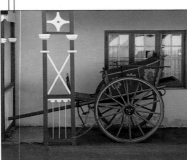

A painted horse cart on a verandah in Cradock

SEE ALSO

• *Where to Stay* p338
• *Where to Eat* p357

Ostrich in the Mountain Zebra National Park

GETTING AROUND

The N1 national route that links Cape Town and Johannesburg passes right through Beaufort West. The N9, which connects Graaff-Reinet to the Southern Cape coast, branches off the N1 at Colesberg. Cradock and the nearby Mountain Zebra National Park to the west of the town are located on the N10. Tarred provincial roads connect most of the smaller villages, allowing visitors to explore the more remote parts of the region. Although distances are great, traffic volumes are moderate and many of the Karoo towns have comfortable bed-and-breakfast establishments and restaurants. The long-distance bus companies stop in Beaufort West, Graaff-Reinet and Cradock.

The Drostdy in Graaff-Reinet, a typical example of a Cape Dutch-style magistrate's office

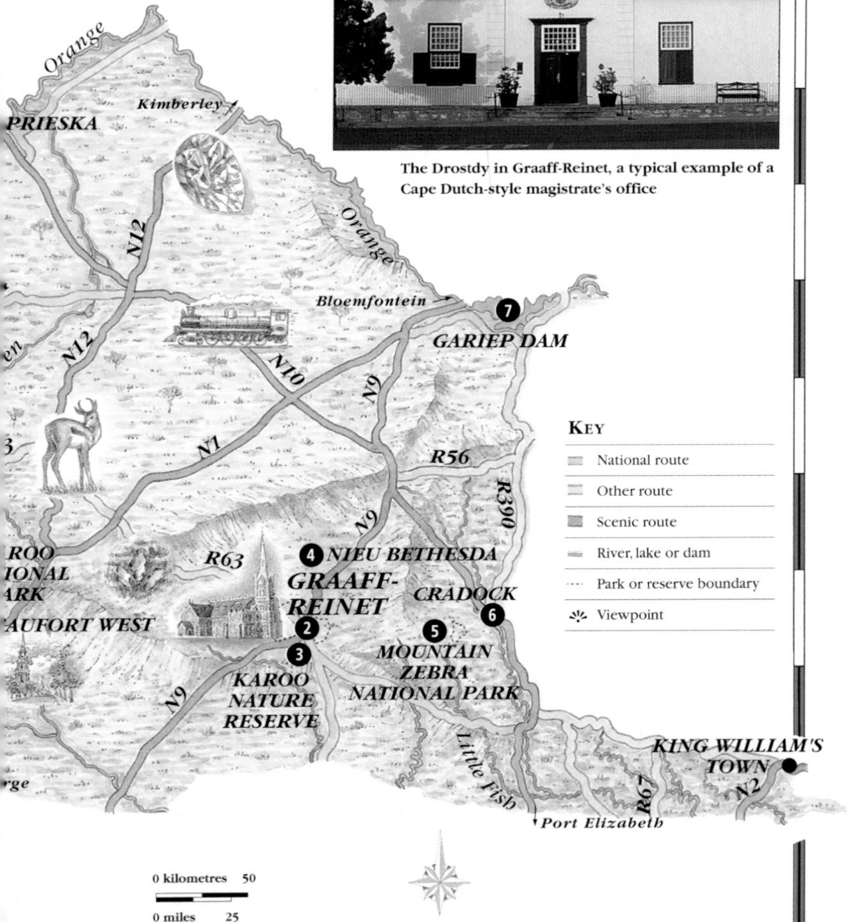

Orange
Kimberley
PRIESKA
N12
N12
Orange
Bloemfontein
GARIEP DAM 7
N10
N9
N7
R56
R390
R63
NIEU BETHESDA 4
GRAAFF-REINET 2
CRADOCK 6
3
5 **MOUNTAIN ZEBRA NATIONAL PARK**
KAROO NATURE RESERVE
ROO IONAL ARK
AUFORT WEST
N9
Little Fish
KING WILLIAM'S TOWN
R67
N2
Port Elizabeth

KEY

▬	National route
▬	Other route
▬	Scenic route
～	River, lake or dam
⋯	Park or reserve boundary
☀	Viewpoint

0 kilometres 50
0 miles 25

Karoo National Park ❶

Road map C4. N1, 2 km (1 mile) S of Beaufort West. ℹ️ *(023) 415-2828.*
ℂ *booking: (012) 428-9111.*
🕐 *5am–10pm daily.* 🖼️ 🎥 🏕️
ⓦ *www.saparks.co.za*

THE KAROO NATIONAL PARK was established on the outskirts of Beaufort West in 1979, to conserve a representative sample of the region's unique heritage. It has been enlarged over the years and now encompasses vast, flat plains as well as the rugged Nuweveld Mountains. Animals such as mountain reedbuck, grey rhebok, kudu, steenbok, jackal and aardwolf occur naturally, while reintroduced species include springbuck, hartebeest, gemsbok (oryx), black wildebeest (gnu), Cape mountain zebra and the endangered black rhino and riverine rabbit. Some 196 bird species have been recorded, and the park also sustains more than 20 black eagle pairs.

A comfortable rest camp is set at the base of the Nuweveld Mountains. Its spacious Cape Dutch chalets provide a convenient overnight stop that is easily accessible from the N1. The camp has a shop, swimming pool, restaurant and caravan park. Nearby, the historic Ou Skuur Farmhouse contains the park's infor-

Springbok once roamed the Karoo plains in their thousands

mation centre. A 4WD trail has been laid out in the rugged western region of the park, and night drives provide the very best chances of seeing many of the region's shy nocturnal animals, such as the aardwolf.

The short Fossil and Bossie trails are accessible from the rest camp and allow visitors to learn about the Karoo's fascinating 250-million-year-old geological history and its unique vegetation. The Fossil Trail accommodates wheelchairs and incorporates braille boards. An easy circular day hike of 11 km (7 miles) is also accessible from the rest camp.

Graaff-Reinet ❷

See pp292–3.

Karoo Nature Reserve ❸

Road map C4. Graaff-Reinet.
ℹ️ *(04989) 2-3453.* 🕐 *6am–6pm Apr–Sep; 6am–7pm Oct–Mar.*
ⓦ *www.graaffreinet.co.za*

IN A BID TO CONSERVE typical Karoo landforms and wildlife, an area of 145 sq km (56 sq miles) around Graaff-Reinet *(see pp292–3)* was set aside. West of the town is the Valley of Desolation, a popular landmark in the reserve. Here, spectacular columns of weathered dolerite tower 120 m (390 ft) over the valley floor.

A 14-km (9-mile) road leads to a view site and a short walk, while the circular day hike is reached from the Berg-en-dal gate on the western edge of town. A two- to three-day hike explores the scenic mountainous terrain in the southeast.

The eastern region of the nature reserve includes the Driekoppe peaks, which rise 600 m (1,950 ft) above the plains. This section sustains more than 220 species of bird. The population of Cape mountain zebra, buffalo, hartebeest, springbok, kudu and blesbok is expanding, and many of them may be seen.

There are game-viewing roads and picnic sites around the Van Ryneveld's Pass Dam in the centre of the reserve, and both boating and fishing are permitted.

The Valley of Desolation in the Karoo Nature Reserve

The back yard of the Owl House is populated with many strange figures

Nieu Bethesda ➍

Road map C4. 50km (31 miles) N of Graaff-Reinet. 🏠 950. ℹ️ *Church St, (049) 892-4248.*

THE TURN-OFF TO this village lies on the N9, 27 km (17 miles) north of Graaff-Reinet. From there, a good dirt road traverses the Voor Sneeuberg ("in front of snow mountain") and leads to Nieu-Bethesda.

The Kompasberg (Compass Peak), at 2,502 m (8,131 ft), is the highest point in the Sneeuberg range. It received its name in 1778 when Cape Governor Baron van Plettenberg, accompanied by Colonel Jacob Gordon, visited the mountain while on a tour of the interior and noted that the surrounding countryside could be surveyed from its summit.

Nieu-Bethesda was founded by Reverend Charles Murray, minister of the Dutch Reformed Church in Graaff-Reinet. The fertile valley in the arid terrain reminded him of the Pool of Bethesda *(John 5:2)*, and so he named the town after it.

In 1875 he acquired a farm in the valley and by 1905 the church (now in Parsonage Street) was completed. It cost £5,600 to build, but at the time of its consecration two-thirds of the amount was still outstanding. To raise funds, arable church land was divided into plots and sold at a public auction. The debt was finally settled in 1929.

Today, Martin Street, the quaint main road, is lined with pear trees, and many of the bordering properties are framed by quince hedges. Irrigated fields and golden poplar trees complement and soften the rugged Karoo mountains, which create a bold contrast.

Pienaar Street crosses over the Gat River to its western bank, and passes an old water mill that was built in 1860 by the owner of the original farm, Uitkyk. The first water wheel was made of wood, but was later replaced with the existing steel wheel.

In recent years, the peaceful village has attracted much artistic talent, including one of South Africa's leading playwrights, Athol Fugard, who achieved world acclaim for his thought-provoking plays such as *Master Harold and the Boys (see p184)*.

🏛 The Owl House

River St. 🕐 *9am–5pm daily.* ☎ *(049) 841-1603.* ♿

The Owl House is considered one of South Africa's top 50 heritage sites. Its garden is cluttered with an intriguing assembly of concrete statues: owls, sheep, camels, people, sphinxes and religious symbols, created over more than 30 years by Helen Martins and her assistant, Koos Malgas. The walls, doors and ceilings of the house are decorated with finely ground coloured glass. Mirrors reflect the light from candles and lamps. Her work, unusual in its quantity and range of subject, has been classified as "Outsider Art" (art that falls outside the artistic mainstream as a result of isolation or insanity) and "Naive" (an expression of innocence and fantasy).

Owl statue

HELEN MARTINS (1897–1976)

Born in Nieu-Bethesda on 23 December 1897, Helen left home to study at a teachers' training college in Graaff-Reinet, and later married a young diplomat. The relationship did not last. Neither did a second marriage, and Helen returned home to nurse her irascible, elderly father. After his death, the naturally retiring woman retreated increasingly into her own fantasy world, and began to populate her garden with bizarre figures, an expression of her personal, mythical universe. In later years her eyesight began to fail due to having worked with ground glass over a long period of time. In August 1976, aged 78, she committed suicide by drinking a lethal dose of caustic soda. As an artist she remains an enigma.

The bedroom with its "wallpaper" of ground glass

Street-by-Street: Graaff-Reinet ❷

Display in Urquhart House

I N 1786 A *LANDDROST* (MAGISTRATE) was appointed by the Dutch East India Company to enforce Dutch law and administration along the remote eastern Karoo frontier. The settlement that grew up around the magistrate's court was named after Governor Cornelis Jacob van de Graaff and his wife, Hester Cornelia Reinet. Nine years later, the citizens of Graaff-Reinet expelled the *landdrost* and declared the first Boer Republic in South Africa. Within a matter of a few months, however, colonial control was re-established.

The War Memorial
The memorial honours the fallen of both World Wars.

Spar
Ke

Dutch Reformed Church
The beautiful Groot Kerk (great church), completed in 1887, was constructed using two different types of local stone.

Huguenot Monument

PARK STREET

Town Hall

Valley of Desolation

NORTH STREET

CALEDON STREET

CHURCH STREET

Old Library Museum

SOMERSET STREET

PARLIAMENT STREET

STRETCH'S COURT

The South African War Memorial
This monument, unveiled in 1908, commemorates the efforts of Boer soldiers against the British troops.

0 metres   100
0 yards   100

KEY

– – – Suggested route

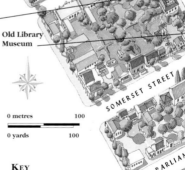

STAR SIGHTS

★ Stretch's Court

★ The Old Residency

★ Reinet House

★ Stretch's Court
These cottages were built in the 1850s to house labourers and freed slaves.

Spandau Kop looms over the town

VISITORS' CHECKLIST

Road map C4. 🏘 50,000. ✈ Port Elizabeth, 236 km (147 miles) SE. 🚌 Kudu Motors, Church St. ℹ Publicity Association (049) 892-4248. ⏰ 8am–5pm Mon–Fri, 9am–noon Sat, Sun. **Reinet House** 📞 (049) 892-3801. ⏰ 8am–12:30pm, 2–5pm Mon–Fri, 9am–3pm Sat, 9am–noon, 2–5pm Sun. 🌐 www.graffreinet.co.za

Exploring Graaff-Reinet

Graaff-Reinet lies in a valley eroded by the Sundays River. The gardens and tree-lined avenues form a striking contrast to the bleak expanse of the surrounding Karoo. Many of the town's historic buildings have been painstakingly restored, and over 200 houses have been declared national monuments. The main architectural attractions lie between Bourke and Murray streets.

🔒 Dutch Reformed Church

This beautiful church is considered to be the finest example of Gothic architecture in the country. Completed in 1886, it was modelled on Salisbury Cathedral.

♨ Stretch's Court

In 1855 Captain Charles Stretch bought land near the Drostdy for his labourers. Restored in 1977, the cottages are now an annex of the Drostdy Hotel.

🏛 Old Library Museum

Church St. 📞 (049) 892-3801. ⏰ 9am–12:30pm, 2–5pm Mon–Fri. Completed in 1847, this building now houses the information office and also displays historic photographs and Karoo fossils.

🏛 Hester Rupert Gallery

Church St. 📞 (049) 892-2121. ⏰ 10am–noon, 3pm–5pm Mon–Fri, 10am–noon Sat, Sun. On display in this former Dutch Reformed Mission Church are works by contemporary South African artists, among them the well known Cecil Skotnes (see p306) and Irma Stern.

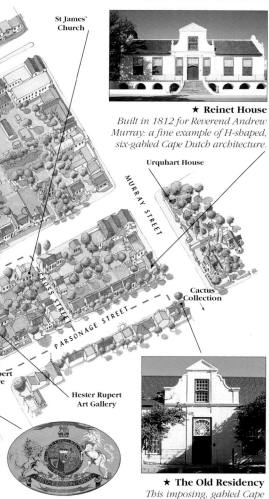

St James' Church

Urquhart House

MURRAY STREET

CROSS STREET

PARSONAGE STREET

Cactus Collection

Hester Rupert Art Gallery

★ **Reinet House**
Built in 1812 for Reverend Andrew Murray: a fine example of H-shaped, six-gabled Cape Dutch architecture.

The Drostdy
Heraldic detail on a plaque at the Drostdy (magistrate's court), a building designed by French architect Louis Michel Thibault in 1804.

★ **The Old Residency**
This imposing, gabled Cape Dutch manor was completed in the 1820s, and the original fanlight can still be seen above the front door. Today the manor is an annex of Reinet House.

The Dutch Reformed Church

A Cape mountain zebra in the Mountain Zebra National Park

Mountain Zebra National Park ❺

Road map D4. 26 km (16 miles) W of Cradock. ☎ (048) 881-2427. ◷ 7am–6pm May–Sep; 7am–7pm Oct–Apr. 🖼 🎫 🚶 Ⓐ ⓦ www.parks-sa.co.za

W HILE THE national park west of Cradock is the second smallest in the country, its modest acreage in no way detracts from the visitor's enjoyment. It was originally conceived as a sanctuary that was intendend to rescue the Cape mountain zebra from imminent extinction. When the park was proclaimed in 1937, there were six zebra; by 1949 only two remained. Conservation efforts were successful, however, and the park now protects about 270 zebra. Several breeding herds have been relocated to other parks, but the Cape mountain zebra still remains rare. Also to be seen are springbok,

hartebeest, eland, mountain reedbuck and black wilde-beest. When additional land is acquired, cheetah and black rhino will be reintroduced.

The rest camp, which over-looks a valley, consists of chalets, a caravan park, a restaurant, shop and infor-mation centre. A short walk leads past the chalets to the swimming pool set at the base of a granite ridge.

For convenience, the park can be divided into two sections. From the camp, a circular drive of 28 km (18 miles) explores the wooded Wilgeboom Valley, noted for its rugged granite land forms. The road passes the Doornhoek Cottage where *The Story of an African Farm* was filmed, and leads to a shady picnic site at the base of the mountains.

The northern loop, which starts just before Wilgeboom, climbs steeply to the Rooi-plaat Plateau, which offers splendid views across the vast Karoo and where most of the park's wildlife congregates. The early mornings and late afternoons are the best times to visit the area. Alternatively, a three-day circular hike, which begins at the camp, explores the southern part of the park, where the granite Bankberg mountains are at their most spectacular.

Cradock ❻

Road map D4. 🚻 11,500. 🚉 Church St. 🚌 Struwig Motors, Voortrekker St. ℹ Stockenstrom St, (048) 881-2383.

I N 1812, TOWARDS THE END of the Fourth Frontier War, Sir John Cradock established two military outposts to secure the eastern border. One was at Grahamstown, the other at Cradock.

Merino sheep flourished in this region, and Cradock soon developed into a sheep-farming centre.

The Dutch Reformed Church was inspired by London's St Martin's-in-the-Fields. Completed in 1867, it dominates the town's central square.

The **Great Fish River Museum** behind the town hall preserves the history of the early pioneers.

In Market Street, **Die Tuishuise** (*see p338*) is the result of an innovative project to restore a series of 14 mid-19th-century houses and create comfortable bed-and-breakfast establishments. Each portrays the architectural style of a particular era.

About 5 km (3 miles) north of town, the **Cradock Spa** is renowned for its indoor and outdoor swimming pools that are fed by hot sulphur springs.

The Dutch Reformed Church in Cradock

🏛 **The Great Fish River Museum**
87 High St. ☎ (048) 881-4361. ◷ 8am–1pm, 2–4pm Tue–Fri; 9am–noon Sat. ● Mon, Sun. 🖼

OLIVE EMILIE SCHREINER (1855–1920)

The Story of an African Farm is widely regarded as the first South African novel of note. Olive Schreiner began writing while she worked as a governess on farms in the Cradock district. The manuscript was released in 1883 under the male pseudonym Ralph Iron, and was an immediate success. Schreiner, an active campaigner for women's equality and a supporter of "Native" rights, wrote extensively on politics. She died in Wynberg (Cape Town) in 1920. Her husband, Samuel Cronwright-Schreiner, buried her on Buffelskop, 24 km (15 miles) south of Cradock, beside their daughter who had died 25 years earlier just 18 hours after her birth, and Olive's dog.

Olive Schreiner

Cottages with striped awnings and painted *stoeps* (verandahs) line the streets of Cradock

Cradock Spa
Marlow Rd. ((048) 881-2709.
7am–8pm daily.

Gariep Dam ❼

Road map D4. NE of Colesberg on R701. ((051) 754-0060 (Gariep Hotel).

THE ORANGE RIVER is South Africa's largest and longest river. Together with its tributaries (excluding the Vaal River) it drains a total of one-third of the country.

In 1779, when Colonel Robert Gordon reached the banks of a watercourse that was known to the Khoina as *Gariep*, he renamed it the Orange River, in honour of the Dutch Prince of Orange. Little did he know that a dam would be constructed at this point nearly 200 years later.

In 1928 Dr AD Lewis advanced the idea of building a tunnel linking the Orange River to the Eastern Cape. Although a report was presented to the government in 1948, it was only in 1962 that then prime minister Hendrik Verwoerd gave the ambitious project the go-ahead. Work began in 1966 and in September 1970 the last gap in the wall was closed. The Gariep is South Africa's largest body of water. The dam wall rises 90 m (297 ft) above its foundations and has a crest length of 948 m (3,110 ft). At full supply level it covers an area of 374 sq km (144 sq miles).

At Oviston, midway along the shoreline, the Orange-Fish Tunnel diverts water along a stretch of 83 km (52 miles) to the headwaters of the Great Fish River near Steynsburg. This tunnel, completed in 1975, is the second longest water conduit in the world. With a diameter of 5 m (17 ft) it can divert one-quarter of the Orange River's water flow.

A corridor of bushveld surrounds the Gariep Dam, and the land that lies between the Caledon and the Orange rivers has been developed into three beautiful nature reserves with a combined area of 452 sq km (174 sq miles). Springbok, blesbok and the rare Cape mountain zebra and black wildebeest have been successfully re-introduced here.

The **Aventura Midwaters** resort, at the dam wall, offers comfortable chalets, a camp-site and a range of outdoor activities including boating, fishing, golf, tennis, horse riding and swimming.

At the headwaters of the dam, an aptly-named game reserve, **Tussen-die-Riviere** ("between the rivers"), supports herds of springbok, black wildebeest, hartebeest, eland, gemsbok, zebra and white rhino. Chalets overlook the confluence of the rivers, and hiking trails explore the eastern half of the reserve.

Aventura Midwaters
Gariep Dam. ((051) 754-0045.
daily.
Tussen-die-Riviere Game Reserve
Gariep Dam. ((051) 763-1114.
daily.

Chalets built on the water's edge at the Gariep Dam

Ancient mountains provide a dramatic backdrop to the guest cottages in the Karoo National Park ▷

NORTH OF THE ORANGE

THE RED DUNES OF THE KALAHARI DESERT *stretch north of the Orange River like the waves of an inland sea. Three mountain ranges break the monotony until the dunes give way, at last, to the grasslands of the Highveld plateau. In this remote wilderness, oasis-like towns such as Upington welcome the traveller, and in a narrow band along the river, vineyards produce sultana grapes and fine wines.*

At the beginning of the 19th century, the uncharted Northern Cape was home to the last nomadic hunter-gatherers, the San Bushmen. In 1820, Robert and Mary Moffat built a mission and school in Kuruman, 263 km (163 miles) northeast of Upington, and devoted 50 years to translating and printing the Bible in the Setswana language. The journeys of exploration undertaken by their son-in-law, David Livingstone, focussed European attention on Africa.

In the Cape Colony Afrikaner farmers became increasingly discontented with the British administration and many trekked north in search of new land. In 1836, a group of Voortrekkers *(see pp48–9)* crossed the Orange River and settled near Thaba Nchu, east of the present-day Bloemfontein, where they established an independent republic, the Orange Free State, in 1854.

The discovery of diamonds in 1866 transformed South Africa's economy. At the town of Kimberley, countless fortune-seekers carved out the Big Hole, an enormous crater that had yielded a total of 2,722 kg (5,988 lb) of diamonds by the time work stopped in 1914.

Further west along the Orange River, a local Griqua leader invited early missionary, Reverend Christiaan Schröder, to establish a mission station on the banks of the river, and the town of Upington was founded. Irrigation canals soon transformed the desert into a fertile crescent of vineyards, orchards, wheat and lucerne fields.

Although mining is still the main contributor to the region's economy, today visitors are enticed by the area's history, desert scenery and diverse wildlife, such as various raptor species and the unique Kalahari lion.

Suricates, or slender-tailed meerkat, live in closely knit family groups

◁ A *halfmens*, or half-human, *(Pachypodium namaquanum)* stands out over misty Richtersveld plains

Exploring North of the Orange

UPINGTON IS THE PERFECT BASE for exploring South Africa's last frontier: the red-dune wilderness bordering the Kalahari Desert. Although no permanent rivers have flowed across this ancient landscape for thousands of years and grass-covered dunes seem to stretch to infinity, wildlife is abundant. Kimberley was once the scene of the world's greatest diamond rush and retains many reminders of its frenetic heyday. Driving eastward, annual rainfall increases. The grasslands of the Free State support cattle and sheep, as well as fields of sunflowers and maize. Historic Bloemfontein, once the capital of a Boer republic named Orange Free State, has many superb old buildings.

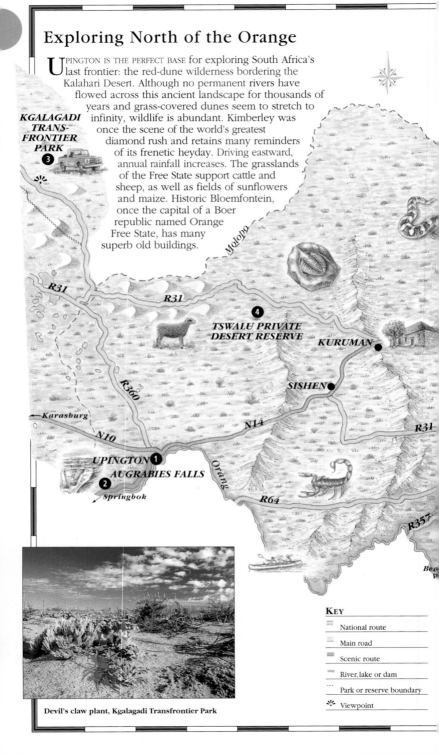

KGALAGADI TRANS-FRONTIER PARK ❸

Molopo

R31

R31

TSWALU PRIVATE DESERT RESERVE ❹

KURUMAN

R360

SISHEN

Karasburg

N10

N14

R31

UPINGTON ❶

AUGRABIES FALLS ❷

Springbok

Orange

R64

R357

Bee

Devil's claw plant, Kgalagadi Transfrontier Park

KEY

▬	National route
▬	Main road
▬	Scenic route
▬	River, lake or dam
⋯	Park or reserve boundary
☀	Viewpoint

SIGHTS AT A GLANCE

Augrabies Falls National Park ❷
Bloemfontein ❻
Kgalagadi Transfrontier Park ❸
Kimberley ❺
Tswalu Private Desert Reserve ❹
Upington ❶

0 kilometres   50

0 miles   25

The Big Hole in Kimberley, begun in the 1870s

GETTING AROUND

Most of the towns north of the Orange River lie more than
200 km (125 miles) apart, and there are few petrol stations or
refreshment stops along the way. But as traffic volumes are low
and all the main roads are tarred, travel in this region need
not be arduous. The R360 runs north from Upington to the
Kgalagadi Transfrontier Park. Although the roads in the park
are sandy, 4WD vehicles are not required. National roads
link the major regional centres to Johannesburg and to
the Western and Eastern Cape. The east–west R64
connects Upington, Kimberley and Bloemfontein.
There are regional airports in all three centres, and
long-distance coaches provide links to other towns.

SEE ALSO

• *Where to Stay* pp339

• *Where to Eat* p357

**Sunflowers constitute one of the Free
State's major crops**

The Reverend Christiaan Schröder's cottage in Upington

Upington ●

Road map B3. 🏔 36,300. 🚗
Schröder St, (054) 332-6064. ✗
7 km (4 miles) NE of town. 🚉 🚌
Upington station.

UPINGTON LIES IN a vast plain
dotted with low shrubs.
Only where the road reaches
the Orange River does the
landscape change abrupt-
ly, as the river paints a
green stripe across
the barren territory.
   The Northern
Cape's second
largest town after
Kimberley, Upington
serves a district of
lucerne, cotton, fruit
and wine farms lining
a fertile corridor on the river.
   In the late 19th century the
Northern Cape was a wild
frontier. The nomadic bands
of Khoina hunter-gatherers
resented the intrusion of the
white settlers into this region
and frequently stole
livestock from them.
In 1871, however, at
the request of Korana
chief Klaas Lukas, the
Reverend Christiaan
Schröder established
a mission station in
the wilderness and
the first irrigation
canals were dug. His
original church is part
of **The Kalahari–
Oranje Museum** in
Schröder Street. Here
too, is the statue of
a camel and rider,
which honours the
policemen and their

The "stone" plant

tireless mounts who once
patrolled this desert region.
   Occupying an island in the
Orange River, just outside
town, Die Eiland is one of the
finest municipal resorts in South
Africa. Sunset cruises down
the river depart from here.
   The five wine cellars in this
arid region all belong to the
OranjeRivier Wine Cellars,
which offers tours and
tastings. On the south-
ern bank of the river,
the South African
Dried Fruit Co-op on
Louisvale Road is
capable of proces-
sing up to 250 tonnes
of dried fruit daily.

🏛 **The Kalahari–
Oranje Museum**
Schröder St. 📞 (054) 332-6064. ◯
8am–12:30pm, 1:30–5pm Mon–Fri. ♿
🍷 **OranjeRivier Wine Cellars**
📞 (054) 337-8800. ◯ 8am–5pm
Mon–Fri, 9am–noon Sat. ● public
hols. 🎫

Augrabies Falls
National Park ❷

Road map B3. 100 km (62 miles) W
of Upington. 🏠 (054) 452-9200.
◯ daily. 📞 bookings: (012) 343-
1991. 🏕 🎣 🚶 🏊 ⛺
🌐 www.parks-sa.co.za

THE AUGRABIES FALLS National
Park was established in
1966 to protect the Augrabies
Fall, which rushes through
the largest granite gorge in
the world. During periods of
normal flow, the main waterfall plunges 56 m (182 ft) into
the gorge. The lesser Bridal
Veil Waterfall, located along
the northern wall of the
gorge, cascades 75 m (244 ft)
into the river below.
   At the main complex near
the entrance to the park is a
shop, restaurant and bar. Paths
lead from here down to the
falls. Despite safety fences to
prevent visitors from falling
into the chasm, you should
take care near the waterfall,
as the rocks are very slippery.
   Apart from the waterfall
itself and the attractive rest
camp which consists of 59
chalets, three swimming pools
and an extensive campsite,
Augrabies has much to offer.
The 39-km (24-mile) long Klip-
springer Trail explores the
southern section of the park
and affords superb views of
the gorge and surrounding
desert. The Black Rhino
Adventure Company offers
trips downriver in a rubber
dinghy, as well as tours of the
park's northern section where
black rhino may be seen.

The Augrabies Falls in the national park of the same name

Kgalagadi Transfrontier Park ❸

Road map B2. 280 km (174 miles) N of Upington. ☎ (054) 561-2000.
📞 bookings: (012) 428-9111.
🕐 daily. 📋 🎥 👤 🅰
Ⓦ www.saparks.co.za

Aᴺ ɪᴍᴍᴇɴsᴇ wilderness of grass-covered dunes traversed by two dry, ancient riverbeds, this national park (formerly the Kalahari Gemsbok National Park) is Africa's largest and extends over 34,390 sq km (13,278 sq miles) across territory almost twice the size of the Kruger National Park. Jointly managed by South Africa and Botswana, the border within the park is unfenced and the wildlife is free to migrate.

From Upington the new R360 cuts a course across a landscape that seems devoid of human habitation. The tar roads ends near Andriesvale and a sandy track hugs the border fence for 58 km (36 miles) before reaching the southern entrance. A dusty campsite is situated near the gate, while the nearby camp of Twee Rivieren offers chalets, a restaurant and a swimming pool. From Twee Rivieren, two roads follow the dry courses of the Auob and Nossob rivers on their way to the camps of Mata Mata and Nossob. There are four lovely picnic spots along the Nossob.

Although Twee Rivieren is situated in the most arid region of the park, wildlife is surprisingly plentiful. The Kgalagadi does not support the diversity of antelope found in savannah parks, but an astonishing 19 species of carnivore are present, including the black-maned Kalahari lion, cheetah, brown hyena, wild cat and honey badger. Raptors such as martial, tawny and bateleur eagles as well as the pale chanting goshawk are commonly sighted.

A total of 40 windmills have been erected in the riverbeds, providing water for wildlife.

Springbok *(Antidorcas marsupialis)*, Kgalagadi Transfrontier Park

Tswalu Private Desert Reserve ❹

Road map C2. 115 km (71 miles) NW of Kuruman. ☎ information and bookings: (053) 781-9211. 📋
Ⓦ www.tswalu.com

Aɴ ᴀᴍʙɪᴛɪᴏᴜs project without equal, Tswalu is South Africa's largest private reserve. It protects 750 sq km (285 sq miles) of red Kalahari dunes and the picturesque Korannaberg mountains. The reserve came into existence through the tireless efforts of British businessman Stephen Boler, who, after careful selection, bought and amalgamated 26 cattle farms. Work teams then began to remove some 800 km (500 miles) of fencing, as well

Buffalo bull

as 2,300 km (1,440 miles) of electric lines, 38 concrete dams and the farmsteads. Approximately 7,000 cattle were sold off and the reserve was fenced.

Boler has invested over R54 million to develop the reserve. A total of 4,700 animals, representing 22 species, have been reintroduced, including lion, leopard, cheetah, white rhino, buffalo, zebra, giraffe, sable, tsessebe, eland and gemsbok. But the jewels in Tswalu's crown are, without doubt, the eight black desert rhinos (subspecies *Diceros bicornis bicornis*) relocated with the permission of the Namibian government. The rhinos were later followed by seven desert elephants.

Tswalu's very expensive luxury lodge has its own tarred airstrip and is managed by the Conservation Corporation. Guests are accommodated in nine thatched units and there is an attractive swimming pool.

Sɪʀ Lᴀᴜʀᴇɴs ᴠᴀɴ ᴅᴇʀ Pᴏsᴛ (1906–96)

Soldier, writer, philosopher, dreamer and explorer, Laurens van der Post was the son of an Afrikaner mother and a Dutch father. During World War II he obtained the rank of colonel and was a prisoner of the Japanese in Java until 1945. Upon his return to South Africa, he began his journeys into the wilderness. A fascinating account of his expedition in search of the San Bushmen of the Kalahari was published in 1958. *The Lost World of the Kalahari* was one of the first books to detail this intriguing and highly spiritual culture. A personal friend of the British Royal Family, the late Van der Post is remembered for his insightful, philosophical writings, most of which deal with the moral and social issues of his time.

Sir Laurens van der Post

Kimberley ❺

THE FIRST DIAMOND RUSH in the Kimberley district took place in 1869 when diamonds were found in the walls of a house on the farm Bultfontein. In July 1871 prospectors camped at the base of a small hill, 4.5 km (3 miles) to the northwest. The party's cook was sent to the summit as punishment for a minor offence and returned with a diamond. Within two years, New Rush tent town, renamed Kimberley in 1873, had become home to 50,000 miners. By the time Cecil John Rhodes (*see p50*) arrived, 3,600 claims were being worked.

A re-created street scene at the Kimberley Mine Big Hole

Exploring Kimberley

The angular street pattern of Kimberley is in contrast to the neat, parallel, grid pattern characteristic of other South African cities, a legacy from its formative, tent-town years. Although reminders of the past are not always apparent, Kimberley has several interesting historic landmarks that are well worth visiting.

⛏ Kimberley Mine Big Hole

West Circular Rd. ((053) 833-1557.
🖼 🔓 📷
The quaint museum village, laid out around the rim of the Big Hole, consists of cobbled streets lined with diverse historic buildings. A small church, the pharmacy, an assortment of shops and an old bar are all decorated with authentic fittings.

♞ Kimberley Club

70–72 Du Toitspan Rd. ((053) 832-4224. 🔓 daily. 🔓 📷
Completed in 1896, this luxurious club was the meeting place of the mining magnates and saw much wheeling and dealing. In keeping with tradition, women are not permitted in the main bar.

♣ Oppenheimer Memorial Gardens

Jan Smuts Blvd.
In the gardens, five bronze miners surround the Digger's Fountain. A marble colonnade contains a bust of Sir Ernest Oppenheimer, the German-born diamond buyer who in 1917 founded the giant Anglo American Corporation.

VISITORS' CHECKLIST

Road map D3. 👥 72,200. ✈ 7 km (4 miles) S of town. 🚌 Old de Beers Rd. 🚌 Shell Ultra City. ℹ 121 Bultfontein Rd, *(053) 832-7298.*

🏛 William Humphreys Art Gallery

Cullinan Crescent. ((053) 831-1724. 🔓 10am–5pm Mon–Sat, 2–5pm Sun. 🖼 free on Wed and first weekend of month. 🔓
Across the road from the Memorial Gardens, the gallery houses a superb collection of paintings by European masters and South African artists.

🏛 McGregor Museum

Egerton Rd. ((053) 839-2700. 🔓 9am–5pm Mon–Sat, 2–5pm Sun. 🖼 🔓 🔓
Cecil John Rhodes stayed in this building, completed in 1897, during the South African War. It now houses a museum of natural and cultural history and has important ethnological and archeological displays, as well as rock paintings.

🏛 Duggan-Cronin Gallery

Egerton Rd. ((053) 839-2700. 🔓 9am–5pm Mon–Sat, 2–5pm Sun. The gallery contains 8,000 photographs of anthropological interest taken over a 20-year period by Alfred Duggan-Cronin, who, having arrived in Kimberley in 1897, became deeply interested in the indigenous people of the Northern Cape.

🏛 Honoured Dead Memorial

Dalham & Oliver rds.
The memorial, designed by Sir Herbert Baker, honours the memory of the British soldiers who died during the siege of Kimberley in 1899. It is flanked by Long Cecil, a cannon built in the De Beers workshops.

The McGregor Museum, Kimberley

The Kimberley Diamond Rush

KIMBERLEY MINE, or the Big Hole, as it is known, is the most famous of the four diamond mines in the Kimberley area. Within two years of the discovery of diamond-bearing kimberlite pipes in 1871, the claims were being worked by up to 30,000 miners at a time. Early photographs reveal a spider's web of cables radiating upward from the edge of the excavation. With little more than picks and shovels to aid them, the miners dug

Barney Barnato

deep into the earth, and by 1889 the hole had reached an astounding depth of 150 m (488 ft). The deeper the miners delved, the more difficult it became to extract the diamond-bearing soil, and the chaotic arrangement of cables, precipitous paths and claims lying at varying heights encouraged the diggers to form syndicates. These groupings were absorbed into various companies that were later acquired by Cecil John Rhodes.

The Cullinan Diamond is the largest diamond ever found. A replica is displayed at the Kimberley Mine Museum.

Cecil John Rhodes, depicted as victorious empire builder in this 19th-century Punch cartoon, was one of the most influential people in Kimberley.

THE BIG HOLE
Covering an area of 17 ha (43 acres), the hole has a perimeter of 1.6 km (1 mile). It eventually reached a depth of 800 m (2,600 ft), the first 240 m (780 ft) of which was laboriously dug by hand. An underground shaft increased the depth to 1,098 m (3,569 ft). By 1914, some 22.6 million tons of rock had been excavated, yielding a total of 14.5 million carats of diamonds.

Diamond miners' lives were exhausting during the 1870s: they worked six days a week, surrounded by heat, dust and flies.

Cocopans (wheelbarrows on narrow-gauge tracks) were used to transport diamond-bearing rock out of the hole.

De Beers Consolidated Mines, owned by Cecil John Rhodes, bought Barney Barnato's diamond mines for the sum of £5,338,650 in 1889.

The Big Hole was closed as a working mine in 1914. It is the largest man-made hole in the world, and the central focus of the Kimberley Open-Air Mine Museum.

Bloemfontein 6

SITUATED IN THE HEARTLAND of South Africa, Bloemfontein, capital of the Free State and seat of the province's parliament, is also the judicial capital of South Africa. It lies at the hub of six major routes that traverse the country. An altitude of 1,400 m (4,550 ft) means that summers are moderate and winters mild to cool. The city was named after a fountain, west of the present business district, where early travellers stopped on their treks through the interior. The city's history, and many of its stately old sandstone buildings, are firmly connected with the Afrikaners' struggle for independence. In 1854, when Major Henry Warden, the region's official British representative, was recalled to the Cape, the Afrikaners established a republic with Bloemfontein as their capital.

The Appeal Court building, Bloemfontein

Exploring Bloemfontein

Although Major Warden's fort has long disappeared, a portion of Queen's Fort, dating back to 1848, can still be seen south of the city centre.

President Brand Street is lined with many fine old sandstone buildings, such as the Appeal Court, built in 1929, opposite the Fourth Raadsaal, which now houses the Free State's provincial legislature. This brick-and-sandstone building was constructed around 1893, during the presidency of Frederick Reitz.

🏛 The National Museum

36 Aliwal St. 🄲 (051) 447-9609. ◯ 8am–5pm Mon–Fri, 10am–5pm, noon–5pm Sun. 🖼 ▣ 🅦 www.nasmus.co.za
This museum contains a good collection of dinosaur fossils, and a reconstruction of a typical 19th-century Bloemfontein street, complete with a cluttered general dealer's store and a pharmacy.

🏛 National Museum for Afrikaans Literature

Cnr President Brand & Maitland sts. 🄲 (051) 405-4711. ◯ 8am–5pm Mon–Fri, 9am–noon Sat.
Near the Appeal Court, this museum is devoted to leading Afrikaans writers, even those who, like André Brink *(see p27)*, opposed apartheid.

Detail of the Women's Memorial

⚰ Old Presidency

President Brand St. 🄲 (051) 448-0949. ◯ 10am–4pm Mon–Fri.
Three blocks south from the Literature Museum lies the Old Presidency, completed in 1861. The attractive building stands on the site once occupied by the homestead of Major Warden's farm.

⚰ First Raadsaal

St George's St. 🄲 (051) 447-9610. ◯ 10am–1pm Mon–Fri. 🖼 ♿
This, the oldest building in the city, is a white, unpretentious structure near the National Museum. Built by Warden in 1849, it was used as a school. After Warden had been withdrawn in 1854, it became the meeting place of the republic's *Volksraad* (people's council).

⛪ Tweetoringkerk

Charles St. 🄲 (051) 430-4274.
Dedicated in 1881, this twin-spired Dutch Reformed church is unique in the country. It was inspired by Europe's Gothic cathedrals and designed by Richard Wocke. The interior, too, is Gothic. Especially noteworthy is the woodwork around the pulpit and organ.

🍃 King's Park

King's Way. 🄲 (051) 405-8483.
On the western edge of the city, this park will appeal to lovers of the outdoors. Shade trees, flower beds and rolling lawns surround a lake, Loch Logan, and a small zoo.

🏛 National Women's Memorial and War Museum

Monument Rd. 🄲 (051) 447-3447. ◯ 8am–4:30pm Mon–Fri, 10am–4:30pm Sat, 2–4:30pm Sun. 🖼
South of the city, this site commemorates the countless Boer and Black African women and children who died in British concentration camps during the South African War.

Emily Hobhouse, a British woman who campaigned for better treatment of the prisoners, is buried at the foot of the monument.

ENVIRONS: North of the city centre, the **Franklin Nature Reserve** occupies Naval Hill. The name originated during the South African War when a cannon was mounted here by the British Naval Brigade. In 1928, the University of

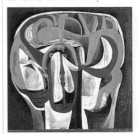

Abstract painting by Cecil Skotnes, Oliewenhuis Art Gallery

Exterior of the Oliewenhuis Art Gallery, Bloemfontein

Michigan (USA) built an observatory on the summit. Over 7,000 star systems were discovered before it closed in 1972. It now houses a theatre.

Further north of the city, on Harry Smith Street, **Oliewenhuis Art Gallery** is set in a spacious garden. This gallery is renowned for its superb collection of South African art.

Several excellent wildlife reserves can be found north of Bloemfontein. The **Soetdoring Nature Reserve** borders on the expansive Krugerdrif Dam whose wall, at 5 km (3 miles), is one of the longest in South Africa.

The river and shoreline of this reserve provide excellent picnic spots and attract many birds. Antelope species like black wildebeest and gemsbok roam free, while predators like lions and wild dogs are kept in a large separate camp.

The turn-off to the **Willem Pretorius Game Reserve** lies some 150 km (93 miles) north of Bloemfontein on the N1. The grassland around the Allemanskraal Dam supports large herds of gazelle. The hills on the northern shore are home to kudu, eland, buffalo, giraffe and white rhino. Birds like korhaan and double-banded courser are also commonly seen.

The chalets of the **Aventura Aldam Resort** perch on the northern shore of the dam.

🦌 Franklin Nature Reserve
Union Ave, Naval Hill. 🕐 daily.
🏛 Oliewenhuis Art Gallery
Harry Smith St. 📞 (051) 447-9609.
🕐 8am–5pm Mon–Fri, 10am–5pm
Sat, 1–5pm Sun. 📷
🦌 Soetdoring Nature Reserve
R64 (Kimberley Rd). 📞 (051) 433-9002. 🕐 7am–6pm daily. 🎫 🍴 🚶

🦌 Willem Pretorius Game Reserve
N1 to Kroonstad. 📞 (057) 651-4003.
🕐 daily. 🎫 🍴
🦌 Aventura Aldam Resort
N1 to Kroonstad. 📞 (057) 652-2200.
🕐 daily. 🎫 🍴 🚶

Giraffe, Franklin Nature Reserve on Naval Hill, Bloemfontein

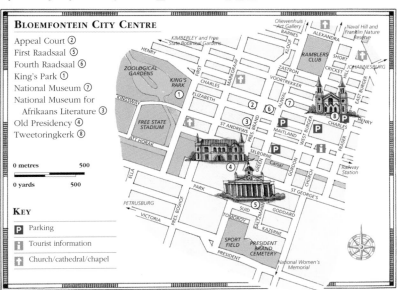

BLOEMFONTEIN CITY CENTRE

Appeal Court ②
First Raadsaal ⑤
Fourth Raadsaal ⑥
King's Park ①
National Museum ⑦
National Museum for
    Afrikaans Literature ③
Old Presidency ④
Tweetoringkerk ⑧

| 0 metres | 500 |
| 0 yards | 500 |

KEY

🅿 Parking

ℹ Tourist information

✝ Church/cathedral/chapel

TRAVELLERS' NEEDS

WHERE TO STAY

THE SLOW JOURNEYS of earlier centuries, when the vast distances between settlements had to be covered on horseback or by ox wagon, led to a proud local tradition. In South Africa "hospitality" is more than a catchword, and establishments, from the largest hotel chain to the smallest bed-and-breakfast, do their utmost to make the modern traveller feel welcome. The wide range of accommodation available is a reflection of the diversity of the country itself. A fantasy resort hotel like the Palace of the Lost City at Sun

Doorman at the Mount Nelson Hotel

City *(see pp258-9)* and Cape Town's elegant colonial hotel, the Mount Nelson *(see p315)*, offer every conceivable luxury and bear comparison with the best in the world. Charming alternatives are the guest cottages found in most *dorps* (country villages), where tranquillity and hearty, home-cooked fare is valued far more than modern convenience. Farmsteads and safari lodges provide a lavish and expensive Africa experience, while camp sites and backpacker's hostels offer basic amenities and cater for younger visitors on limited budgets.

WHERE TO LOOK

VISITORS TOURING South Africa by car may be worried by the distances that separate cities and towns. Fortunately, hotels, bed-and-breakfasts, motels and self-catering cottages are found in even the remotest villages. Farm accommodation is also plentiful.

South Africa's cities offer a great variety of places to stay, whether you want family, luxury or business accommodation. In well-visited country and resort areas, there is also accommodation to suit every taste and pocket: many game parks, for example, offer luxurious lodges as well as basic camp sites, while most coastal resorts offer hotels, camp sites, B&Bs and guesthouses. Enquire at the local tourist information office (usually well signposted) or contact one of the many umbrella associations such as the

AA Travel Information Centre, The National Accommodation Selection, Youth Hostel Association or the Guesthouse Association of Southern Africa (see p313). If you are travelling through the smaller towns without having made prior arrangements, ask at the post office, one of the local stores or police stations for accommodation advice.

If you are seeking quiet surroundings, try the smaller and more simple hostelries, inland or away from obvious attractions on the coast. Most private game reserves offer superb safari lodges.

HOTEL PRICES

PRICES TEND to be per room rather than per person, but may be advertised as "per person sharing". Taxes (and sometimes gratuities) are usually included in the rates, but tips are appreciated. Ten

Mala Mala safari lodge *(see p275)*

to 15 per cent of the cost or value of goods or service received is the norm.

Where rates are stated as "dinner, bed and breakfast" or "bed and breakfast", you are likely to be charged for these meals whether or not you take them. If you advise the host in time, it may be possible to avoid payment for advertised meals that are not taken. Also notify the hosts in advance if you are vegetarian, for example. "Special offers" are seldom further negotiable.

Rooms with a shower are usually cheaper than those with a bath, and those with views are more expensive.

Prices vary slightly, outside of high season (Nov–Feb, Easter weekend and the mid-year school holidays). But do ask your travel agent about possible special offers made by hotel groups, or contact them directly. Hotels do not close during winter (May–Aug).

Thatched rondavels at Olifants camp, Kruger National Park *(see p273)*

◁ **A herd of elephant makes its way across the Addo Elephant Park near Port Elizabeth**

The beautifully situated Fairy Knowe Motel on the Garden Route

HOTEL GRADING

SOUTH AFRICAN HOTELS are classified by a number of organizations, such as **Satour**, the national tourism authority, and **Portfolio of Places**. Satour divides hotels into five categories, indicated by a plaque carrying from one to five stars. A typical five-star hotel is luxurious, offering suites as well as rooms and a wide range of services, such as hair dressing, dry cleaning and room service. In a country town, a one-star hotel may prove to be comfortable and entirely satisfactory, while in a city it may be little more than a liquor outlet or a noisy local rendezvous spot.

Many charming hotels have lower ratings, and some hotels with higher ratings – although they boast more than the required minimum of facilities and service – turn out to be impersonal business warrens.

Some self-catering cottages and guesthouses are also accredited by Satour.

FACILITIES

FACILITIES VARY according to location and grading. Parking is usually available, but is not always under cover or supervised by a guard. Some hotels offer a daily car-wash, and may also have courtesy vehicles for hire, either with or without a driver.

Most hotels provide a telephone in the bedroom, but it is usually cheaper to use a public telephone. Television sets in rooms (without cable channels) are fairly common, and there is almost always a set in the guests' lounge.

Central heating in winter is not the norm, although most places of accommodation do provide portable heaters. Many self-catering cottages, particularly those on farms, have indoor fireplaces.

Some more upmarket small guesthouses and B&Bs offer an "honesty bar" with cold beers, wine, soft drinks and mineral water.

In country towns, the hotel frontage may be on the main street. If there is no bypass road, the noise level may be uncomfortable, especially at night. Before asking to be moved to a room at the back, however, check that there are no large cooling units tucked away, as those are likely to be even more disturbing.

Hotels usually have a locked and secure safe where guests can deposit valuables.

HOTEL GROUPS

MANY OF THE BETTER class hotels are controlled by one of the national hotel chains *(see p313)*, offering incentives or package deals that include lower family rates or out-of-season tariffs. Some, however, are graded lower than others, so have a different rates' structure.

CHILDREN

DON'T PRESUME THAT your venue of choice will cater for children. Many upmarket hotels, guesthouses and safari lodges do not accept children under the age of ten.

Where children are accepted, families may be able to share a room at little extra cost, as tariffs are "per room" rather than "per person".

BOOKING

IF POSSIBLE, confirm a telephone booking in writing or by fax. It is likely that a deposit will be required, which you will forfeit if you cancel your booking at short notice.

The hotel is legally obliged to inform you if there has been a tariff increase since you made your booking.

Even if you have reserved a specific room, ask to see it before you sign the register. And if you require special arrangements, first ensure that these are satisfactory.

Unless otherwise stated, the occupation period generally extends from noon to noon.

Reception area in the Palace of the Lost City at Sun City *(see pp258–9)*

SELF-CATERING

CHOICE IN STYLE and price of self-catering accommodation in South Africa is vast, with cottages sometimes also referred to as chalets, bungalows or *rondavels* (if they are round and grass-thatched).

Many of the game parks have luxurious, East African-style safari tents with private outdoor kitchens, while farm-style cottages in the vast Karoo *(see pp290–1)* feature large, indoor hearths to fend off the bitter cold on winter nights. Municipal chalets in caravan parks may offer only the mere basics, while cottages on the wine estates of the Cape *(see pp128–41)*, for example, may even be equipped with microwaves and satellite television.

Guest cottage at the Blyde River Canyon resort *(see p267)*

Club Mykonos units, Langebaan

The larger resorts and game reserves will usually have a selection of cottages. These may be self-contained units or have shared kitchen, laundry and bathroom facilities. Self-catering cottages usually have well-equipped kitchens, are comfortably furnished and may even include towels and bedding, although it is always advisable to ask beforehand.

Upon arrival, a member of staff may check to ensure that all the items on the inventory are supplied and intact. You could also be asked to pay a small deposit (refundable at the end of your stay) to cover potential loss or breakage.

It is advisable to approach individual tourist information offices of towns or regions for the addresses and contact numbers of self-catering cottages. Agencies like **Roger & Kay's Travel Selection** may also be able to assist.

COUNTRY COTTAGES

COTTAGES on farms and in peaceful villages. are to be found in Mpumalanga (**Jacana Country Homes and Trails**), the KwaZulu-Natal Midlands (**The Under-**

berg Hideaway), and in the wine- and fruit farming areas around Cape Town. A memorable aspect of a stay in the country is the hospitality and catering in true local style.

BED AND BREAKFAST

ACCOMMODATION IN private homes has become very popular, especially along the Garden Route and in bigger cities like Cape Town, Port Elizabeth and Johannesburg. The hosts, who concentrate on a small number of guests staying only a night or two, take pride in being able to provide personal attention.

GUEST FARMS

RELATIVELY INEXPENSIVE outdoor family holidays are provided by guest- or holiday farms all around the country. Visitors stay in the farmhouse or in a nearby cottage. Sometimes meals are eaten with the resident family, otherwise there are equipped kitchens. Guests can also take part in daily activities, such as collecting the eggs and milking the cows.

GAME LODGES

GAME LODGES in most private reserves *(see pp366–7)* cater for affluent visitors. They typically offer excellent cuisine, luxurious pseudo-rustic accommodation, highly skilled staff and game rangers who ensure that guests see as much of the African wildlife as possible. National parks are much more basic, yet very comfortable.

Victorian-style Koornhoop Guesthouse, Observatory, Cape Town

BUDGET ACCOMMODATION

Hosteling international provides accommodation in several hostels. The YMCA and YWCA offer similar basic facilities. No age limit is imposed on guests, although preference is usually given to the younger travellers.

Backpackers' lodges are more suited to young people, as facilities and meals are few and privacy is non-existent. Staying in a youth hostel may be fairly accurately described as "roughing it".

Camping in the Natal Drakensberg Park *(see p206)*

CARAVAN PARKS

You don't have to tow a caravan to qualify for residence, as many caravan parks have caravans to let, along with prefabricated or rustic cottages. Allocated sites are usually connected to water mains and electricity supplies.

Larger caravan parks have a shop, restaurant and swimming pool, and sometimes even tennis courts or a bowling green.

Most campers do their own cooking– the method of choice is the South African *braaivleis* or barbecue. Cooking-places or "braai sites" are provided – one per site – and good, dry firewood is usually available from the park office.

Camping sites can be noisy at night, so choose a spot well away from the entrance gate, which usually also serves as the exit point. The **AA Travel Services** will be able to supply contact details of caravan parks and camping sites.

REST CAMPS

Rest camps are the "standard" version of the luxurious game lodge and are found in national parks and provincial game reserves *(see pp366–7)*. Most of them offer a variety of facilities such as swimming pools, shops and communal dining areas, with accommodation options ranging from bungalows to bigger chalets.

UNDER CANVAS

Numerous camping grounds are situated along South Africa's major rivers or at the sea. Sites are separated from each other by calico screens or hedges. Communal ablution blocks are provided. Many of the camp sites are run as part of a local caravan park.

MINERAL SPRINGS

There are resorts at most South African hot springs, such as the one at Cradock *(see p294)*. The attraction is the water itself, in swimming pools or in the form of medicinal baths. Accommodation is in hotels or at camp sites.

DIRECTORY

MAIN HOTEL GROUPS CENTRAL BOOKING OFFICES

Southern Sun
((0861) 447-744.

Sun International
((011) 780-7800.

Protea Hotels
((0861) 119-000.

Conservation Corporation Africa
((011) 809-4300.

Holiday Inn Garden Court
((0861) 447-744.

Portfolio of Places
((011) 880-3414.

City Lodge
((011) 884-0660.

Formule 1 Hotel
((011) 392-1453.

Aventura Resorts
((011) 207-3600.

COUNTRY HOMES

Jacana Country Homes and Trails
Box 95212, Waterkloof, Pretoria, 0145.
((012) 346-3550.

The Underberg Hideaway
Box 1218, Hilton, KwaZulu-Natal, 3245.
((033) 343-1217.

CAMPING

National Parks Board Bookings
((012) 428-9111 or (011) 678-8870.
W www.saparks.co.za

KwaZulu-Natal Nature Conservation Services
((033) 845-1000.
W www.kznwildlife.com

Aventura Resorts
((011) 207-3600.

GUESTHOUSES AND BED-AND-BREAKFASTS

Roger & Kay's Travel Selection
Box 405, Bergvliet, Cape Town, 7864.
((021) 715-7130.

Bed 'n' Breakfast Bookings
Box 91309, Auckland Park, Gauteng, 2006.
(011) 482-2206 or (021) 683-3505.

Guest House Association of Southern Africa
Box 18416, Wynberg, Cape Town, 7824.
((021) 762-0880.
W www.gaza.co.za

GENERAL

AA Travel Services
Box 7118, Johannesburg, 2000.
((011) 799-1400.
W www.aatravel.co.za

South African Tourism (Satour)
Private Bag X164, Pretoria, 0001. ((011) 778-8000.
W www.satour.com

Hosteling International
((021) 421-7721.

Choosing a Hotel

THE HOTELS in this guide have been selected from a wide price range for their good value or exceptional location, comfort and style. The chart highlights some of the factors which may influence your choice and gives a brief description of each hotel. Entries are listed by price category within the towns, with colour-coded thumbtabs to indicate the regions covered on each page.

	NUMBER OF ROOMS	SWIMMING POOL	RESTAURANT	CHILDREN'S FACILITIES	GARDEN
CAPE TOWN					
CITY BOWL: *The Cape Colonial* w www.thecapecolonial.com ®® 13 Union Street Gardens. **Map 4 B3.** ((021) 423-7382. FAX (021) 423-7382. Housed in a beautifully restored Victorian townhouse and located in a quiet residential area at the foot of Table Mountain. Colonial-style rooms and attention to detail. Ten minutes walk from city centre. 🔳 TV 🗐 🗐 🗐 🔳	6				●
CITY BOWL: *Formule 1 Hotel* @ all@formule1.co.za ®® Jan Smuts Ave, Foreshore, 8001. **Map 5 D1.** ((021) 418-4664. FAX (021) 418-4661. Part of an affordable chain of budget establishments, this hotel offers no-frills accommodation a short drive from the Waterfront. 🔳 TV 🗐 🗐 🗐 🔳	64				
CITY BOWL: *Palm Tree Manor* ®® 11 Glynnville Terrace, Gardens, 8001. **Map 5 B3.** ((021) 461-3698. FAX (021) 462-3330. The African-Colonial decor adds an air of elegance to this restored Victorian townhouse. All the rooms have superb views. 🔳 TV 🗐 🔳	4				
CITY BOWL: *Acorn House* w www.acornhouse.co.za ®®®® 1 Montrose St, Oranjezicht, 8001. **Map 5 A4.** ((021) 461-1782. FAX (021) 461-1768. This accredited guesthouse offers accommodation in a colonial-style mansion designed by Sir Herbert Baker in 1904. 🔳 TV 🗐 🗐 🔳 🔳	7	▦			●
CITY BOWL: *Cape Gardens Lodge Hotel* ®®®® 88 Queen Victoria St, Gardens, 8001. **Map 5 B2.** ((021) 423-1260. FAX (021) 423-2088. @ info@capegardens.co.za Centrally situated directly opposite the former Company Gardens, this comfortable hotel in the heart of the city offers a country atmosphere and wonderful views. 🔳 TV 🗐 🗐 🗐 🔳	56	●	▦		
CITY BOWL: *Cape Heritage Hotel* w www.capeheritage.co.za ®®®® Heritage Square, 92 Bree St, 8001. **Map 5 A1.** ((021) 424-4646. FAX (021) 424-4949. This hotel borders on the historical BoKaap district. The rooms are decorated to reflect Cape Town's diverse cultural heritage. 🔳 TV 🗐 🗐 🗐 🔳 🔳 🔳	15	●			
CITY BOWL: *Cape Town Lodge* w www.capetownlodge.co.za ®®®® 101 Buitengracht St, Cape Town, 8001. **Map 5 A1.** ((021) 422-0030. FAX (021) 422-0090. A comfortable hotel situated within easy reach of the city centre. Facilities for physically disabled visitors. 🔳 TV 🗐 🗐 🗐 🔳 🔳 🔳	114	●	▦		
CITY BOWL: *Holiday Inn Garden Court De Waal* ®®®® Mill St, Gardens, 8001. **Map 5 B3.** ((021) 465-1311. FAX (021) 461-6648. Centrally situated, this member of the international chain lies within walking distance of the Company Gardens. 🔳 TV 🗐 🗐 🗐 🔳 🔳 🔳	136	▦	●		
CITY BOWL: *iKhaya Guest Lodge* w www.ikhayalodge.co.za ®®®® Dunkley Sq, Gardens, 8001. **Map 5 A3.** ((021) 461-8880. FAX (021) 461-8889. This guesthouse is decorated in ethnic style. Carved doors, wood ceilings and sandstone walls create a distinctive ambience. 🔳 TV 🗐 🗐 🗐 🔳 🔳	17		●		
CITY BOWL: *Leeuwenvoet House* w www.leeuwenvoet.co.za ®®®® 93 New Church St, Tamboerskloof, 8001. **Map 4 F2.** ((021) 424-1133. FAX (021) 424-0495 This beautiful historical monument, built in 1892, has individually decorated rooms and caters mainly for business travellers. There are many restaurants in walking distance. 🔳 TV 🗐 🗐 🗐 🔳 🔳	12	▦		▦	●
CITY BOWL: *Lion's Kloof Lodge* w www.lionskloof.co.za ®®®® 26 Higgo Crescent, Higgovale, 8001. **Map 4 E4.** ((021) 426-5515. FAX (021) 422-2047. This guesthouse on the slopes of Table Bay Mountain is set in a magnificent garden with a sparkling pool overlooking the city. 🔳 TV 🗐 🗐 🔳 🔳	7	▦			●

						Number of Rooms	Swimming Pool	Restaurant	Children's Facilities	Garden

Price categories for a standard double room per night including tax and service charges, but not including breakfast:
- ® under R150
- ®® R150–R300
- ®®® R300–R500
- ®®®® R500–R1000
- ®®®®® over R1000

SWIMMING POOL
These are usually quite small and outdoors.

RESTAURANT
Restaurant on the premises, usually open to non-residents.

CHILDREN'S FACILITIES
Baby-sitting services, cots for small children and play parks are available. Some hotels also provide half portions and high chairs in their restaurants.

GARDEN
Hotel with a garden or terrace.

Listing	Rooms	Pool	Restaurant	Children's	Garden
CITY BOWL: *Table Mountain Lodge* ®®®® 10A Tamboerskloof Rd, Tamboerskloof, 8001. **Map 4 F2.** (021) 423-0042. FAX (021) 423-4983. W www.tablemountainlodge.co.za Nestled at the foot of Signal Hill, this guesthouse offers splendid views of Table Mountain.	8	■			●
CITY BOWL: *Town House Hotel* W www.townhouse.co.za ®®® 60 Corporation St, Cape Town, 8001. **Map 5 B2.** (021) 465-7050. FAX (021) 465-3891. Centrally situated and close to Parliament, this hotel exudes the quiet elegance and comfort of a private club.	104	■	●		●
CITY BOWL: *Underberg Guesthouse* ®®® 6 Tamboerskloof St, Tamboerskloof, 8001. **Map 4 F2.** (021) 426-2262. FAX (021) 424-4059. W www.underbergguesthouse.co.za This Victorian manor house (1860) has been transformed into a comfortable guesthouse, with original designs and features.	11			■	●
CITY BOWL: *Villa Lutzi* W www.villalutzi.com ®®®® 6 Rosmead Ave, Oranjezicht, 8001. **Map 4 F4.** (021) 423-4614. FAX (021) 426-1472. Situated in a quiet residential area, this guesthouse lies within walking distance of the city, and is comfortably furnished.	11	■		■	
CITY BOWL: *Holiday Inn* W www.southernsun.com ®®®® Strand St, Cape Town, 8001. **Map 5 B1.** (021) 488-5100. FAX (021) 423-1861. An upmarket, modern 32-storey hotel located in the heart of the city, with views of Table Mountain and the Waterfront.	368	■	●	■	
CITY BOWL: *Mount Nelson Hotel* W www.mountnelson.co.za ®®®®® 76 Orange St, Gardens, 8001. **Map 5 A2.** (021) 483-1000. FAX (021) 423-1060. Cape Town's *grande dame* opened her doors in 1899 for passengers of the Union Castle Shipping Line. Opulent, luxurious, famed for impeccable service and set in beautiful gardens.	226	■	●		●
CITY BOWL: *No. 1 Chesterfield* W www.one-chesterfield.com ®®®® 1 Chesterfield Rd, Oranjezicht, 8001. **Map 4 F5.** (021) 461-7383. FAX (021) 461-4688. Another Herbert Baker-designed 1920s home in the elite neighbourhood of Oranjezicht that has been converted into a comfortable guesthouse. Children over 14 are welcome.	8	■	●		●
CITY BOWL: *Villa Belmonte* W www.villabelmontehotel.co.za ®®®®® 33 Belmont Ave, Oranjezicht, 8001. **Map 5 A4.** (021) 462-1576. FAX (021) 462-1579. This restored Victorian mansion at the foot of Table Mountain offers every luxury to the discerning traveller. Warm hospitality and excellent cuisine have earned this guesthouse many coveted awards.	14	■	●	■	
CITY BOWL: *Welgelegen Guesthouse* W www.welgelegen.co.za ®®®®® 6 Stephen St, Gardens, 8001. **Map 4 F3.** (021) 426-2373. FAX (021) 426-2375. A Victorian manor dating back to 1890, Welgelegen has elegant decor, a swimming pool and lies in a quiet cul de sac.	8	■		■	
V & A WATERFRONT: *Breakwater Lodge* @ info@proteahotels.com ®®® Portswood Rd, 8001. **Map 2 D4.** (021) 406-1911. FAX (021) 406-1070. Unusual budget accommodation in a complex that incorporates the former Breakwater Prison (1854).	291		●	■	
V & A WATERFRONT: *Victoria Junction* @ info@proteahotels.com ®®® Somerset Rd, Greenpoint, 8001. **Map 2 D5.** (021) 418-1234. FAX (021) 418-5678. Trendy, modern hotel blending Art Deco, techno and industrial chic. Short walk to the Waterfront.	172	■		■	
V & A WATERFRONT: *Cape Grace Hotel* ®®®®® West Quay, 8001. **Map 2 E4.** (021) 410-7100. FAX (021) 419-7622. W www.capegrace.com Surrounded by water on three sides, with views across the city. Cross the drawbridge to the Waterfront.	121	■	●	■	

Price categories for a standard double room per night including tax and service charges, but not including breakfast: Ⓡ under R150 ⓇⓇ R150–R300 ⓇⓇⓇ R300–R500 ⓇⓇⓇⓇ R500–R1000 ⓇⓇⓇⓇⓇ over R1000	**SWIMMING POOL** These are usually quite small and outdoors. **RESTAURANT** Restaurant on the premises, usually open to non-residents. **CHILDREN'S FACILITIES** Baby-sitting services, cots for small children and play parks are available. Some hotels also provide half portions and high chairs in their restaurants. **GARDEN** Hotel with a garden or terrace.	NUMBER OF ROOMS	SWIMMING POOL	RESTAURANT	CHILDREN'S FACILITIES	GARDEN

V & A WATERFRONT: *The Commodore* ⓇⓇⓇⓇ
Portswood Rd, 8001. **Map 2 D4.** 📞 *(021) 415-1000.* FAX *(021) 415-1100.*
@ hotels@legacyhotels.co.za Enjoy views of Table Mountain and across the bay from this hotel adjacent to the historical Waterfront. 🛏 📺 🅿️ 🍴 ♿ 🎠 Ⓟ 🔒

| 236 | ■ | ● | ■ | |

V & A WATERFRONT: *Portswood Hotel* ⓇⓇⓇⓇ
Portswood Sq, 8001. **Map 2 D4.** 📞 *(021) 418-3281.* FAX *(021) 419-7570.*
@ hotels@legacyhotels.co.za All rooms have wonderful views and there is a well in the lobby. Short walk to the Waterfront. 🛏 📺 🅿️ 🍴 ♿ 🎠 Ⓟ 🔒

| 103 | ■ | ● | ■ | |

V & A WATERFRONT: *Radisson* W www.radisson.com ⓇⓇⓇⓇ
Granger Bay, 8001. **Map 2 D5.** 📞 *(021) 418-5729.* FAX *(021) 418-5717.*
Adjacent to V & A Waterfront, with own private marina. Spectacular views across Table Bay to Robben Island. 🛏 📺 🅿️ 🍴 ♿ Ⓟ

| 182 | ■ | ● | ■ | |

V & A WATERFRONT: *The Table Bay Hotel* ⓇⓇⓇⓇ
Quay 6, 8001. **Map 2 E3.** 📞 *(021) 406-5000* FAX *(021) 406-5767.*
Luxury accommodation on a grand scale from this Sun International flagship. Sweeping views across Table Bay to Robben Island and over the city to Table Mountain. Enjoy resort ambience with the convenience of being close to the Waterfront, city centre and other attractions. 🛏 📺 🅿️ 🍴 ♿ 🎠 Ⓟ

| 329 | ■ | ● | ■ | |

V & A WATERFRONT: *Victoria & Alfred Hotel* ⓇⓇⓇⓇ
Pierhead, 8001. **Map 2 E4.** 📞 *(021) 419-6677.* FAX *(021) 419-8955.*
W www.vahotel.co.za Situated at the heart of the Waterfront. Superior accommodation in colonial-style bedrooms with magnificent views. Well situated for shopping and lively nightlife. 🛏 📺 🅿️ 🍴 ♿ 🎠 Ⓟ

| 68 | | ● | ■ | |

FURTHER AFIELD: *Lion's Head Lodge* W www.lions-head-lodge.co.za ⓇⓇ
319 Main Rd, Sea Point, 8001. **Map 1 A4.** 📞 *(021) 434-4163.* FAX *(021) 439-3813.*
Small hotel and self-catering accommodation, perfectly situated close to shops, restaurants, the Waterfront and beaches. 🛏 📺 🅿️ Ⓟ

| 49 | ■ | ● | | ● |

FURTHER AFIELD: *Afton Grove Country Guest House* ⓇⓇⓇ
Chapman's Peak Dr, Noordhoek, 7985. **Road map B5.** 📞 *(021) 785-2992.*
FAX *(021) 785-3456.* W www.afton.co.za Cape cottages in a country setting, offering luxury rooms, birdwatching and horse riding. 🛏 📺 🅿️ 🍴 Ⓟ 🔒

| 7 | ■ | | ■ | ● |

FURTHER AFIELD: *Boulders Beach Guesthouse* ⓇⓇⓇ
4 Boulders Place, Simon's Town, 7975. **Road map B5.** 📞 *(021) 786-1758.* FAX *(021) 786-1825.*
W www.bouldersbeach.co.za Cosy accommodation close to Boulders Beach. The adjacent coastal reserve has a small Jackass penguin colony. 🛏 🅿️ Ⓟ 🔒

| 12 | | ● | ■ | |

FURTHER AFIELD: *Brenwin* W www.brenwin.co.za ⓇⓇⓇ
1 Thornhill Rd, Green Point, 8001. **Map 1 C4.** 📞 *(021) 434-0220.* FAX *(021) 439-3465.*
Friendly staff and beautifully furnished rooms are the hallmarks of this cottage-style guesthouse. Children over 12 are welcome. 🛏 📺 🅿️

| 13 | ■ | | | ● |

FURTHER AFIELD: *Centurion Hotel* ⓇⓇⓇ
275 Main Rd, Sea Point, 8001. **Map 1 A4.** 📞 *(021) 434-0006.* FAX *(021) 434-0051.*
Affordable. Close to sea and restaurants, this hotel is upgraded every two years in order to maintain the highest standards. 🛏 📺 🅿️ ♿ Ⓟ

| 45 | ■ | | | |

FURTHER AFIELD: *Cotswold House* W www.cotswoldguesthouse.com ⓇⓇⓇ
6 Cotswold Dr, Milnerton, 7441. **Road map B5.** 📞 *(021) 551-3637.* FAX *(021) 552-4228.*
The Cape Dutch homestead, built by a former governor general of South Africa, has been converted into a cosy guesthouse, with landscaped gardens and stunning views of Table Bay and the mountain. 🛏 📺 🅿️ 🍴 Ⓟ 🔒

| 6 | ■ | | | ● |

FURTHER AFIELD: *La Splendida Luxury Suites* ⓇⓇⓇ
121 Beach Rd, Mouille Point, 8001. **Map 1 A4.** 📞 *(021) 439-5119.* FAX *(021) 439-5112.*
W www.lasplendida.co.za This Art Deco-inspired hotel is located between the Waterfront and Sea Point and also has a plunge pool. 🛏 📺 🅿️ Ⓟ 🔒

| 22 | ■ | ● | ■ | |

FURTHER AFIELD: *Leisure Bay Luxury Suites* ⓇⓇⓇ | 32
Lagoonbeach Rd, Milnerton, 7441. **Road map** B5. (*(021) 551-7440.* FAX *(021) 551-7441.*
W *www.leisurebay.co.za* Executive accommodation only 30 m (32 yd) from the
long, white beach and a 15-minute drive from Cape Town. 🔑 TV 🎷 ▤ P 🔧

FURTHER AFIELD: *Lord Nelson Inn* W *www.simonstown.com* ⓇⓇⓇ | 10
St George's St, Simon's Town, 7975. **Road map** B5. (*(021) 786-1386.* FAX *(021) 786-1009.*
Decorated with naval mementos, this hotel overlooks the bay and is close
to the Boulders penguin colony, shops and restaurants. 🔑 TV 🎷 🔧

FURTHER AFIELD: *Namaste* @ *namasteb@mweb.co.za* ⓇⓇⓇ | 3
62 Ixia St, Milnerton, 7435. **Road map** B5. (*(021) 438-5704.* FAX *(021) 794-0560.*
In the heart of the leafy Constantia Valley, this welcoming B&B is convenient
for trips to the vineyards, restaurants and shops nearby. 🔑 TV 🎷 P

FURTHER AFIELD: *Toad Hall* @ *vano@iafrica.com* ⓇⓇⓇ | 2
9 AB Bull Rd, Froggy Farm, Simonstown **Map** 3 B5. (& FAX *(021) 786-3878.*
Bed and Breakfast accommodation in a luxurious private apartment (one twin
and one double room) with glorious views over False Bay. 🔑 TV 🎷 P

FURTHER AFIELD: *Villa Rosa Guesthouse* W *www.villa-rosa.com* ⓇⓇⓇ | 9
277 High Level Rd, Sea Point, 8001. **Map** 1 A5. (*(021) 434-2768.*
FAX *(021) 434-3526.* Beautiful red Victorian-style mansion overlooking
the sea, conveniently situated close to all amenities. 🔑 TV 🎷 P

FURTHER AFIELD: *Whale View Manor* W *www.whaleviewmanor.co.za* ⓇⓇⓇ | 9
402 Main Rd, Simon's Town, 7975. **Road map** B5. (*(021) 786-3291.*
FAX *(021) 786-2455.* A light and airy guesthouse close to family beaches, and
perfect for whale-watching. Children over 12 are welcome. 🔑 🎷 🔧

FURTHER AFIELD: *Alphen Hotel* W *www.alphen.co.za* ⓇⓇⓇⓇ | 34
Alphen Dr, Constantia, 7800. **Road map** B5. (*(021) 794-5011.* FAX *(021) 794-5710.*
The main building, a national monument, was built in 1752 and forms part
of a regal old Cape estate in a country setting, only 20 minutes from the city
centre. Relax by the pool after a long day's sightseeing. 🔑 TV 🎷 ▤ 🍴 🔧

FURTHER AFIELD: *Ambassador Hotel & Suites* ⓇⓇⓇⓇ | 100
34 Victoria Rd, Bantry Bay, 8001. **Map** 3 B5. (*(021) 439-6170.* FAX *(021) 439-6336.*
W *www.ambassador.co.za* Perched on the rocks high above the Atlantic
Ocean, guests can enjoy spectacular sunsets and wonderful views
from the bar. 🔑 TV 🎷 ▤ P 🔧

FURTHER AFIELD: *Andros* W *www.andros.co.za* ⓇⓇⓇⓇ | 9
6 Paradise View Rd, Claremont, 7700. **Road map** B5. (*(021) 797-9777.*
FAX *(021) 797-0300.* Mansion with a sparkling pool set in extensive gardens.
A short walk from a major suburban shopping centre. 🔑 TV 🎷 ✂ P 🔧

FURTHER AFIELD: *Bantry Bay Luxury Suites* ⓇⓇⓇⓇ | 41
8 Alexander Rd, Bantry Bay, 8001. **Map** 3 B1. (*(021) 434-8448.* FAX *(021) 434-8212.*
@ *bantrybay@relais.co.za* Exclusive hotel with beautiful sea views, close to the
famous Clifton beaches, restaurants and shops. 🔑 TV 🎷 ▤ 🔧 P 🔧

FURTHER AFIELD: *Protea Cape Castle Hotel* ⓇⓇⓇ | 63
3 Main Rd, Green Point, 8001. **Map** 1 A4. (*(021) 439-1016.* FAX *(021) 439-1019.*
W *www.proteahotels.com* In close proximity to the Waterfront, the Cape Castle
offers self-catering accommodation, with fully equipped kitchens, lounges,
dining areas and a communal barbeque *(braai)* facility. 🔑 TV 🎷 ▤ ✂ 🔧 P 🔧

FURTHER AFIELD: *Constantia Lodge* W *www.constantialodge.com* ⓇⓇⓇ | 8
Duntaw Cl, Constantia, 7800. **Road map** B5. (*(021) 794-2410.* FAX *(021) 794-2418.*
Tastefully furnished accommodation set in large, tranquil grounds with
an all-weather tennis court, this estate is well-protected from the wind
and is near a number of golf courses. 🔑 TV 🎷 ✂ 🔧 P 🔧

FURTHER AFIELD: *Courtyard Hotel* @ *info@citylodge.co.za* ⓇⓇⓇ | 70
Liesbeeck Pkwy, Mowbray, 7700. **Road map** B5. (*(021) 448-3929.* FAX *(021) 448-5494.*
This Cape Dutch manor house, built around 1815, has been declared a
national monument. In the garden stands South Africa's second oldest
fig tree, reputedly planted in 1840. 🔑 TV 🎷 ▤ ✂ 🔧 P 🔧

FURTHER AFIELD: *Glen Hotel* W *www.glenhotel.co.za* ⓇⓇⓇ | 11
3 The Glen, Sea Point, 8001. **Map** 1 A5. (*(021) 439-0086.* FAX *(021) 439-3552.*
A Victorian-style manor house located in a quiet residential area,
yet close to a variety of shops and restaurants. 🔑 TV 🎷 ✂ 🔧 P 🔧

Price categories for a standard double room per night including tax and service charges, but not including breakfast: Ⓡ under R150 ⓇⓇ R150–R300 ⓇⓇⓇ R300–R500 ⓇⓇⓇⓇ R500–R1000 ⓇⓇⓇⓇⓇ over R1000	**SWIMMING POOL** These are usually quite small and outdoors. **RESTAURANT** Restaurant on the premises, usually open to non-residents. **CHILDREN'S FACILITIES** Baby-sitting services, cots for small children and play parks are available. Some hotels also provide half portions and high chairs in their restaurants. **GARDEN** Hotel with a garden or terrace.	**NUMBER OF ROOMS**	**SWIMMING POOL**	**RESTAURANT**	**CHILDREN'S FACILITIES**	**GARDEN**
FURTHER AFIELD: *Greenways Hotel* ⓦ www.greenways.co.za ⓇⓇⓇⓇ 1 Torquay Ave, Claremont, 7700. **Road map** B5. **(** *(021) 761-1792.* **FAX** *(021) 761-0878.* Charming accommodation in a gracious homestead built in the 1920s and set in large, tranquil gardens. 🛏 📺 ✉ 🗐 ♿ 🅿 🔧	14	■	●		●
FURTHER AFIELD: *Houtkappersspoort* ⓇⓇⓇⓇ Constantia Nek, Cape Town. **Map** 1 A5. **(** *(021) 794-5216.* **FAX** *(021) 794-2907.* ⓦ www.houtkappersspoort.co.za Accommodation in cottages constructed from local stone and timber, which sleep between 2 and 8 persons. 🛏 📺 ✉ 🅿	9	■		■	●
FURTHER AFIELD: *Olaf's Guesthouse* ⓦ www.olafs.co.za ⓇⓇⓇⓇ 24 Wisbeach Rd, Sea Point, 8001. **Map** 1 A4. **(** *(021) 439-8943.* **FAX** *(021) 439-5057.* Voted the B&B establishment of the year in 1996 by South Africa's tourist organization, SATOUR, this guesthouse offers the ultimate in comfort. Close to restaurants and shops. Children over 12 are welcome. 🛏 📺 ✉	11	■			●
FURTHER AFIELD: *Palm House* ⓦ www.palmhouse.co.za ⓇⓇⓇⓇ Oxford St, Wynberg, 7800. **Road map** B5. **(** *(021) 761-5009.* **FAX** *(021) 761-8776.* An elegant guesthouse in the southern suburbs, close to shopping centres and 20 minutes from Cape Town International Airport. 🛏 📺 ✉ 🗐 🅿 🔧	11	■		■	●
FURTHER AFIELD: *Romney Park Luxury Suites* ⓇⓇⓇⓇ Romney Rd, Green Point, 8001. **Map** 1 B4. **(** *(021) 439-4555.* **FAX** *(021) 439-4747.* ⓦ www.romneypark.co.za Elegant accommodation for the discerning traveller, this establishment is near the city, beaches and the Waterfront. 🛏 📺 ✉ 🗐 ♿ 🅿	34	■		■	
FURTHER AFIELD: *Southernwood Country House* ⓇⓇⓇⓇ 19 Ave, Constantia, 7800. **Road map** B5. **(** *(021) 794-3208.* **FAX** *(021) 794-7551.* @ souwood@mweb.co.za On a wooded estate in the suburb of Constantia, near the Kirstenbosch Botanical Gardens. Children over 12 are welcome. 🛏 📺 ✉ 🅿	5	■			●
FURTHER AFIELD: *Villa Sunshine* ⓦ www.villasunshine.co.za ⓇⓇⓇⓇ 1 Rochester Rd, Bantry Bay, 8001. **Map** 3 B2. **(** *(021) 439-8224.* **FAX** *(021) 439-8219.* Comfortable Mediterranean-style guesthouse overlooking the sea, close to beaches, many restaurants and public transport. 🛏 📺 ✉ ✂ 🅿 🔧	7	■			
FURTHER AFIELD: *Vineyard Hotel* @ enquiries@vineyard.co.za ⓇⓇⓇⓇ Colinton Rd, Newlands, 7700. **Road map** B5. **(** *(021) 657-4500.* **FAX** *(021) 657-4501.* Built for Lady Anne Barnard in 1799, this national monument has beautiful gardens, a heated pool and a fitness centre. The award-winning restaurant specializes in classic French cuisine. 🛏 📺 ✉ 🗐 ✂ ♿ 🅿 🔧	160	■	●	■	●
FURTHER AFIELD: *Welgeleë Guesthouse* @ welgelee@mweb.co.za ⓇⓇⓇⓇ Dressage Cl, Constantia, 7800. **Road map** B5. **(** *(021) 794-7397.* **FAX** *(021) 794-7397.* The silos of this old homestead have been professionally rebuilt and renovated to create unusual three-storey accommodation. 🛏 📺 ✉ 🗐 🅿	10	■			●
FURTHER AFIELD: *Winchester Mansions Hotel* ⓇⓇⓇⓇ 221 Beach Rd, Sea Point, 8001. **Map** 1 A4. **(** *(021) 434-2351.* **FAX** *(021) 434-0215.* ⓦ www.winchester.co.za A privately owned hotel with an Italian-style interior piazza, palms and water fountains. Children over 12 are welcome. 🛏 📺 ✉ 🔧	53	■	●		
FURTHER AFIELD: *Cellars-Hohenort Hotel* ⓇⓇⓇⓇⓇ 93 Brommersvlei Rd, Constantia, 7800. **(** *(021) 794-2137.* **FAX** *(021) 794-2149.* ⓦ www.cellars-hohenort.com A luxury country hotel, whose wonderful gardens adjoin Kirstenbosch Botanical Gardens. The restaurant is an epicure's delight, offering local and imported wines. Children over 14 welcome. 🛏 📺 ✉ 🗐 🅿 🔧	53	■	●		●
FURTHER AFIELD: *Clifton House* ⓦ www.cliftonhouse.co.za ⓇⓇⓇⓇⓇ 1 Clifton St, Clifton, 8001. **Map** 3 B4. **(** *(021) 438-2308.* **FAX** *(021) 438-3716.* Situated on the slopes of Lion's Head, with spectacular sea and mountain views, this establishment does not cater for children. 🛏 📺 ✉ 🗐 🅿 🔧	5	■			●

FURTHER AFIELD: *Constantia Uitsig Country Hotel* ⓇⓇⓇⓇ | 16
Spaanschemat River Rd, Constantia, 7800. **Road map** B5. 【 *(021) 794-6500.*
⒡⒳ *(021) 794-7605.* ⓦ www.constantiauitsig.co.za Superb accommodation on a historic
wine farm. The two restaurants are among Cape Town's finest. 🚪 📺 🅢 🅿 🛏

FURTHER AFIELD: *Peninsula All-suite Hotel* ⓇⓇⓇⓇ | 109
313 Beach Rd, Sea Point, 8001. **Map** 1 A4. 【 *(021) 439-8888.* ⒡⒳ *(021) 439-8886.*
@ hotel@peninsula.co.za Fully appointed self-catering suites and spectacular
views across the bay make this hotel a popular choice. 🚪 📺 🅢 🅔 🛁 🍴 🅿 🛏

FURTHER AFIELD: *Protea Hotel President* ⓇⓇⓇⓇ | 349
Alexander Rd, Bantry Bay, 8001. **Map** 3 B1. 【 *(021) 434-8111.* ⒡⒳ *(021) 434-9991.*
ⓦ www.proteahotels.com A friendly hotel, decorated in a breezy island style, which
affords single lady travellers special VIP treatment. Close to beachfront promenade,
with easy access to the Waterfront and the city. 🚪 📺 🅢 🅔 🛁 🅿

FURTHER AFIELD: *Sea Castle* ⓦ www.primi-seacastle.com ⓇⓇⓇⓇ | 9
15 Victoria Rd, Clifton, 8001. **Map** 3 B5. 【 *(021) 438-4010.* ⒡⒳ *(021) 438-4015.*
The spacious, airy apartments are exquisitely furnished with marble, granite
and maple wood fittings. Sea views from all balconies. 🚪 📺 🅢 🅿 🛏

FURTHER AFIELD: *Steenberg Hotel* ⓦ www.steenberghotel.com ⓇⓇⓇⓇ | 24
Steenberg Rd, Constantia, 7800. **Road map** B5. 【 *(021) 713-2222.* ⒡⒳ *(021) 713-2221.*
Cape Dutch manor house (1682) on a tranquil wine estate in the Constantia
Valley. Luxuriously appointed rooms with views of the vineyards or the
gardens. Newly developed 18-hole golf course. 🚪 📺 🅢 🅔 🅿 🛏

FURTHER AFIELD: *The Bay Hotel* ⓦ www.thebay.co.za ⓇⓇⓇⓇ | 78
Victoria Rd, Camps Bay, 8001. **Map** 3 B5. 【 *(021) 438-4444.* ⒡⒳ *(021) 438-4455.*
A member of the Small Luxury Hotels of the World. Sophisticated and modern,
in a superb setting opposite Camps Bay beach. Watch the sun set over the
Atlantic Ocean while you sip cocktails on the terrace. 🚪 📺 🅢 🅔 🛁 🅿 🛏

THE CAPE WINELANDS

FRANSCHHOEK: *Auberge Bligny* ⓦ www.bligny.co.za ⓇⓇⓇ | 8
28 Van Wijk St, 7690. **Road map** B5. 【 *(021) 876-3767.* ⒡⒳ *(021) 876-3483.*
Accredited guesthouse located in a beautifully restored homestead, surrounded
by green vineyards and wonderful mountain scenery. 🚪 📺 🅢 🛁 🅿

FRANSCHHOEK: *Franschhoek Country Guesthouse* ⓇⓇⓇ | 14
Main Rd, 7690. **Road map** B5. 【 *(021) 876-3386.* ⒡⒳ *(021) 876-2744.*
ⓦ www.fch.co.za A lovingly restored Victorian homestead built in 1890, on
the outskirts of the town, close to restaurants and shops. 🚪 📺 🅢 🅩 🅿 🛏

FRANSCHHOEK: *Rusthof Guesthouse* ⓦ www.rusthof.com ⓇⓇⓇ | 5
12 Huguenot Rd, 7960. **Road map** B5. 【 *(021) 876-3762.* ⒡⒳ *(021) 876-3682.*
Pleasant, affordable accommodation in individually furnished rooms with
underfloor heating and air conditioning. 🚪 📺 🅢 🅔 🅿 🛏

FRANSCHHOEK: *L'Auberge le Quartier Français* ⓇⓇⓇⓇ | 15
16 Huguenot Rd, 7960. **Road map** B5. 【 *(021) 876-2151.* ⒡⒳ *(021) 876-3105.*
ⓦ www.lequartier.co.za Stylish accommodation in the heart of this historic village. The
restaurant serves award-winning Cape-Provençale cuisine. 🚪 📺 🅢 🅔 🛁 🅿 🛏

HERMON: *Bartholomeus Klip Farmhouse* ⓇⓇⓇⓇ | 5
Off R44 from Tulbagh/Wellington. **Road map** B5. 【 *(022) 448-1820.* ⒡⒳ *(022) 448-1829.*
@ bartholomeus@icon.co.za This period farmhouse, dating to 1903, offers
charming country-style accommodation in a beautiful setting. 🚪 🅢 🅩 🅿

KUILS RIVER: *Zevenwacht Country Inn* ⓦ www.zevenwacht.co.za ⓇⓇⓇ | 20
Langverwacht Rd, 7580. **Road map** B5. 【 *(021) 903-5123.* ⒡⒳ *(021) 906-1570.*
This Cape Dutch-style manor house offers fine dining, cellar tours and
cheese-making demonstrations. 🚪 📺 🅔 🅩 🅿 🛏

MONTAGU: *Kingna Lodge* ⓦ www.kingnalodge.co.za ⓇⓇⓇ | 8
11 Bath St, 6720. **Road map** B5. 【 *(023) 614-1066.* ⒡⒳ *(023) 614-2405.*
In a Victorian manor dating from around 1885, this guesthouse also
offers guests fragrant health therapy. 🚪 📺 🅢 🅔

MONTAGU: *Mimosa Lodge* ⓦ www.mimosa.co.za ⓇⓇⓇ | 16
Church St, 6720. **Road map** B5. 【 *(023) 614-2351.* ⒡⒳ *(023) 614-2418.*
Built in 1861, this double-storey Victorian villa is run by a Swiss
couple and exudes warmth and hospitality. 🚪 🅢 🅩 🛁 🅿

<table>
<tr><td>

Price categories for a standard double room per night including tax and service charges, but not including breakfast:
ⓡ under R150
ⓡⓡ R150–R300
ⓡⓡⓡ R300–R500
ⓡⓡⓡⓡ R500–R1000
ⓡⓡⓡⓡⓡ over R1000

</td><td>

SWIMMING POOL
These are usually quite small and outdoors.
RESTAURANT
Restaurant on the premises, usually open to non-residents.
CHILDREN'S FACILITIES
Baby-sitting services, cots for small children and play parks are available. Some hotels also provide half portions and high chairs in their restaurants.
GARDEN
Hotel with a garden or terrace.

</td></tr>
</table>

	NUMBER OF ROOMS	SWIMMING POOL	RESTAURANT	CHILDREN'S FACILITIES	GARDEN
MONTAGU: *Montagu Country Hotel* ⓡⓡⓡⓡ 27 Bath St, 6720. **Road map** B5. (*(023) 614-3125.* FAX *(023) 614-1905.* W www.montagucountryhotel.co.za Well-preserved, original Art Deco building, surrounded by wonderful mountain views. Access to numerous hiking and walking trails. 🔲 TV 🖼 🍴 P 🛏	23	▦	●	▦	●
PAARL: *Goedemoed Country Inn* W www.goedemoed.com ⓡⓡⓡ Cecilia St, 7646. **Road map** B5. (*(021) 863-1102.* FAX *(021) 863-1104.* Country hospitality in this gracious guesthouse, set in pleasant gardens with a welcoming pool and views across the vineyards. 🔲 TV 🖼 🍴 P 🛏	8	▦		▦	●
PAARL: *Lemoenkloof Gastehuis* W www.lemoenkloof.co.za ⓡⓡⓡ 396A Main Rd, 7646. **Road map** B5. (*(021) 872-7520.* FAX *(021) 872-7532.* Comfortable guesthouse in national monument, located in the heart of town, within easy reach of the wine route. 🔲 TV 🖼 🍴 🔁 P 🛏	20	▦		▦	●
PAARL: *Mountain Shadows Guesthouse* ⓡⓡⓡ Klein Drakenstein Rd, 7620. **Road map** B5. (*(021) 862-3192.* FAX *(021) 862-6796.* W www.mountainshadow.co.za Comfortable Cape Dutch manor house nestling against a mountain backdrop. The manor enjoys a quiet country wineland setting. 🔲 TV 🖼 🍴 P 🛏	11	▦	●	▦	●
PAARL: *Pontac Manor Hotel & Restaurant* W www.pontac.com ⓡⓡⓡⓡ 16 Zion St, 7646. **Road map** B5. (*(021) 872-0445.* FAX *(021) 872-0460.* Beautiful 250-year-old farmhouse situated below Paarl Rock. Conveniently situated for touring the cellars of the KWV nearby. 🔲 TV 🖼 🍴 P	16	▦	●	▦	●
PAARL: *Grande Roche Hotel* W www.grandroche.com ⓡⓡⓡⓡⓡ Plantasie St, 7646. **Road map** B5. (*(021) 863-2727.* FAX *(021) 863-2220.* Built in 1707, this historical estate has been tastefully restored. The international award-winning hotel offers five-star accommodation in chalets set among the vineyards. Bosman's Restaurant is consistently rated as one of the country's best. Member of the Relais et Châteaux group. 🔲 TV 🖼 🍴 🔁 ♿ 📶 P 🛏	35	▦	●	▦	●
PAARL: *Roggeland Country House* W www.roggeland.co.za ⓡⓡⓡⓡ Roggeland Rd, 7623. **Road map** B5. (*(021) 868-2501.* FAX *(021) 868-2113.* Situated 15 km (9 miles) from Paarl, this historic farmstead is decorated with wonderful antiques and offers country-style living complete with duck pond. Quality regional cuisine. 🔲 TV 🖼 ♿ P	11	▦	●	▦	●
ROBERTSON: *The Grand Hotel & Guesthouse* ⓡⓡⓡ 68 Barry St, 6705. **Road map** B5. (*(023) 626-3272.* FAX *(023) 626- 1158.* W www.grandhotel.co.za A cosy and comfortable hotel situated some 800 m (870 yd) from the main road in a quiet residential area. 🔲 TV 🖼	10	▦	●	▦	
SOMERSET WEST: *Albourne Guesthouse* W www.albourne.co.za ⓡⓡⓡ 61 Lourensford Rd, 7130. **Road map** B5. (*(021) 852-2184.* FAX *(021) 852-7050.* Guests at this classic Cape Dutch residence enjoy membership of the exclusive Erinvale Golf Course 2 km (1.5 miles) away. The landlord here speaks Dutch, German, Spanish and French. 🔲 TV 🖼 P 🛏	16	▦			●
SOMERSET WEST: *Die Ou Pastorie Guesthouse* ⓡⓡⓡ 41 Lourens St, 7130. **Road map** B5. (*(021) 852-2120.* FAX *(021) 851-3710.* W www.dieoupastorie.co.za This elegant guesthouse is a national monument dating from 1819. Ideal location for golfing enthusiasts since it is situated close to three outstanding golf courses. 🔲 TV 🖼 P 🛏	16	▦	●		●
SOMERSET WEST: *Erinvale Estate Hotel* W www.erinvale.co.za ⓡⓡⓡⓡ 1 Erinvale Ave, 7130. **Road map** B5. (*(021) 847-1160.* FAX *(021) 847-1169.* Gracious manor house hotel nestled at the foot of the majestic Helderberg Mountains and surrounded by well-kept gardens. There is also the challenge of the renowned Erinvale Golf Course. 🔲 TV 🖼 🍴 ♿ P 🛏	57	▦	●	▦	●

SOMERSET WEST: *Somerton Manor* w www.somerton.co.za ⓇⓇⓇ
13 Somerset St, 7130. **Road map** B5. █ (021) 851-4682. **FAX** (021) 851-4672.
This grass-thatched Cape Dutch-style guesthouse has a sauna, gymnasium,
Jacuzzi, large swimming pool, snooker room, and a wine cellar stocked
with some 2000 bottles of wine. 🔒 TV 🖼 ▤ 💈 🍴 P 🔔
12

SOMERSET WEST: *Straightway Head Country House* ⓇⓇⓇ
Parel Catley Rd, 7130. **Road map** B5. █ (021) 851-7088. **FAX** (021) 851-7091.
w www.straightwayhead.com A comfortable guesthouse surrounded by
mountains, only 9 km (5.6 miles) from the False Bay beaches. 🔒 TV 🖼 & P
19

SOMERSET WEST: *Zandberg Farm Country Guesthouse* ⓇⓇⓇ
Winery Rd, 7130. **Road map** B5. █ & **FAX** (021) 842-2945.
w www.zandberg.co.za Country accommodation on a 300-year-old wine estate.
Enjoy Cape-Provençale cuisine in the adjacent award-winning restaurant. The
historic chapel, herb garden and dam are added attractions. 🔒 TV 🖼 & P
11

SOMERSET WEST: *Lord Charles Hotel* ⓇⓇⓇⓇ
Faure & Stellenbosch rds, 7130. **Road map** B5. █ (021) 855-1040. **FAX** (021) 855-1107.
w www.the-lord-charles.co.za Situated in the heart of the Cape Winelands, this
magnificent hotel is set on a nine-hectare private estate. There are several golf
courses close by and it is also close to the beaches. 🔒 TV 🖼 ▤ 💈 & P 🔔
197

SOMERSET WEST: *Willowbrook Lodge* ⓇⓇⓇⓇ
1 Morgenster Ave, 7130. **Road map** B5. █ (021) 851-3759. **FAX** (021) 851-4152.
w www.willowbrook.co.za Elegant riverside lodge, set in award-winning gardens.
The à la carte restaurant offers innovative modern cuisine. 🔒 TV 🖼 &
11

STELLENBOSCH: *Bonne Esperance Guest Lodge* ⓇⓇⓇ
17 Van Riebeeck St, 7600. **Road map** B5. █ (021) 887-0225. **FAX** (021) 887-8328.
@ stay@bonneesperance.com An accredited guesthouse in a comfortably refurbished
Victorian-style villa with turret and wrap-around verandah. 🔒 🖼 ▤ 💈 P 🔔
15

STELLENBOSCH: *De Goue Druif* @ gouedruif@new.co.za ⓇⓇ
110 Dorp St, 7599. **Road map** B5. █ (021) 883-3555. **FAX** (021) 883-3588.
This building, declared a national monument, dates back to 1792,
and is tastefully furnished with antiques. 🔒 TV 🖼 ▤ 🍴 P 🔔
4

STELLENBOSCH: *Ryneveld Lodge* @ ryneveld@iafrica.com ⓇⓇ
67 Ryneveld St, 7600. **Road map** B5. █ (021) 887-4469. **FAX** (021) 883-9549.
A comfortably refurbished slave house that also has several fully
self-contained family cottages available. 🔒 TV 🖼 ▤ & P
15

STELLENBOSCH: *Yellow Lodge Guesthouse* ⓇⓇ
32 Herold St, 7600. **Road map** B5. █ (021) 887-9660. **FAX** (021) 887-5686.
w www.yellow-lodge.com Spacious lodge in a garden planted with banana trees.
Local and German satellite television channels. 🔒 TV 🖼 💈 P 🔔
11

STELLENBOSCH: *Dorpshuis Boutique Hotel* ⓇⓇⓇ
22 Dorp St, 7600. **Road map** B5. █ (021) 883-9881. **FAX** (021) 883-9884.
w www.dorpshuis.co.za Decorated with genuine antiques, this guesthouse
is situated on charming, historic Dorp St. 🔒 TV 🖼 ▤ & 🍴 P
22

STELLENBOSCH: *D'Ouwe Werf* w www.ouwewerf.com ⓇⓇⓇ
30 Church St, 7600. **Road map** B5. █ (021) 887-4608. **FAX** (021) 887-4626.
South Africa's oldest inn, in the heart of Stellenbosch, was built on the
foundations of the very first church in the country, the original floors of
which can still be seen under the restaurant. 🔒 TV 🖼 ▤ P 🔔
25

STELLENBOSCH: *Eendracht Gastehuis* ⓇⓇⓇ
161 Dorp St, 7600. **Road map** B5. █ (021) 883-8843. **FAX** (021) 883-8842.
w www.eendracht-hotel.com A comfortable residence, rebuilt in the architectural
style of 1710, that offers accommodation in the heart of town. 🔒 TV 🖼 💈 & P 🔔
12

STELLENBOSCH: *Lanzerac Manor & Winery* ⓇⓇⓇⓇ
Lanzerac Rd, 7600. **Road map** B5. █ (021) 887-1132. **FAX** (021) 887-2310.
w www.lanzerac.co.za Luxury country estate hotel, set among the vineyards, and
surrounded by the magnificent Jonkershoek and Helderberg mountains. The
elegant splendour recalls Lanzerac's 300-year history. 🔒 TV 🖼 ▤ & P 🔔
48

TULBAGH: *De Oude Herberg* @ ingam@mweb.co.za ⓇⓇ
6 Church St, 6820. **Road map** B5. █ & **FAX** (023) 230-0260.
Accredited guesthouse in a national monument (1840) right in
the centre of the historic town of Tulbagh. 🔒 TV 🖼 💈 & P
5

Price categories for a standard double room per night including tax and service charges, but not including breakfast: ® under R150 ®® R150–R300 ®®® R300–R500 ®®®® R500–R1000 ®®®®® over R1000	**SWIMMING POOL** These are usually quite small and outdoors. **RESTAURANT** Restaurant on the premises, usually open to non-residents. **CHILDREN'S FACILITIES** Baby-sitting services, cots for small children and play parks are available. Some hotels also provide half portions and high chairs in their restaurants. **GARDEN** Hotel with a garden or terrace.	**NUMBER OF ROOMS**	**SWIMMING POOL**	**RESTAURANT**	**CHILDREN'S FACILITIES**	**GARDEN**
TULBAGH: *Rijk's Ridge* w www.rijks.co.za　　　®®®® Off Church St, 6820. **Road map** B5. (*(023) 230-1006.* FAX *(023) 230-1125.* This charming Cape Dutch farmhouse is set in the Tulbagh Valley and is surrounded by the spectacular scenery of the Winterhoek and Witzenberg mountains which are often snow-capped in winter. 🛏 TV 🍴 ♿ P	15	■	●		●
WELLINGTON: *Diemersfontein Gastehuis*　　　®®® On the R303 to Wellington. **Road map** B5. (*(021) 873-2671.* FAX *(021) 864-2095.* w www.diemersfontein.co.za Gracious, turn-of-the-century homestead offers vineyard horse trails and scenic mountain walks. 🛏 🍴 P 🚼	18	■	●		●
WORCESTER: *Church Street Lodge* w www.churchst.co.za　　　®®® 36 Church St, 6850. **Road map** B5. (*(023) 342-5194.* FAX *(023) 342-8859.* Comfortable rooms in a Cape Dutch house that is centrally located in the heart of historic Worcester. 🛏 TV 🍴 🛁 ♿ P 🚼	21	■			●

THE WESTERN COASTAL TERRACE

CEDARBERG: *Bushmanskloof Wilderness Reserve*　　　®®®®® R364. Box 53405, Kenilworth, 7945. **Road map** B4. (*(021) 797-0990.* FAX *(021) 685-5210.* w www.bushmanskloof.co.za Luxury thatched lodges in the Cedarberg Mountains, just three hours from Cape Town. View zebra, wildebeest, eland and a host of small game or visit the 125 Bushman rock art sites in the area. 🛏 🍴 📶 P 🚼	10	■	●		
CLANWILLIAM: *Saint du Barrys Country Lodge*　　　®®®® 13 Augsburg Dr, 8135. **Road map** B4. (*(027) 482-1537.* FAX *(027) 482-1537.* w www.saintdubarrys.co.za This thatched lodge, named after a 19th-century Swiss Saint, offers generous hospitality and comfort to its guests. Situated in the village of Clanwilliam, close to the Cedarberg mountains. 🛏 TV 🍴 ♿ P	5	■			●
DARLING: *Trinity Lodge* @ mclaughlin@worldonline.co.za　　　®®® 19 Long St, 7345. **Road map** B5. (& FAX *(022) 492-3430.* A tastefully renovated Victorian home in the old part of Darling, offering a peaceful retreat and exclusive guest accommodation. 🛏 TV P	5	■		■	●
KAMIESKROON: *Kamieskroon Hotel*　　　®®® Old National Rd, 8241. **Road map** A4. (*(027) 672-1614.* FAX *(027) 672-1675.* @ kamieshotel@kingsley.co.za This comfortable country hotel, in the heart of the Namaqualand wildflower region, has been offering eco-tours and photographic workshops since 1984. Booking essential in the spring wildflower season. 🛏 🍴	21	■	●	●	
LANGEBAAN: *Falcon's Rest Guesthouse* @ info@falconrest.co.za　　　®®® 21A Zeeland St, 7357. **Road map** A5. (& FAX *(022) 772-1112.* Uninterrupted views over the lagoon from this double-storey house near the golf course. Children are welcome and meals can be arranged. 🛏 TV 🍴 🚼	12	■	●	■	
LANGEBAAN: *The Farmhouse Hotel*　　　®®® 5 Egret St, 7357. **Road map** A5. (*(02277) 2-2062.* FAX *(022) 772-1980.* w www.thefarmhouselangebarn.co.za This traditional farmhouse was built in 1860. It sits adjacent to the West Coast National Marine Park and overlooks the tranquil lagoon. 🛏 TV 🍴 🚼	18	■	●		●
MOOREESBURG: *Karbonaatjieskraal Guest House*　　　®® N1 (near Mooreesburg). **Road map** B5. (*(023) 358-2134.* FAX *(023) 358-2133.* Convenient for travellers, this stylish house looks onto the Matroosberg Mountains, which are often snow-capped in winter. 🛏 🍴 🛁 P ⟳	12	■	●		●
PIKETBERG: *Noupoort Guest Farm & Conference Centre*　　　®® N7. PO Box 101, Piketberg, 7320. **Road map** B4. (*(022) 914-5502.* FAX *(022) 914-5834.* @ martintdh@absamail.co.za Tranquillity, clean air and great views, 90 minutes from Cape Town. Hiking trails, a sauna and spa bath. 🛏 🍴 📶 🛁 ♿ P 🚼	32	■	●	■	

RIEBEEK WEST: *Riebeek Valley Hotel* W www.riebeekvalley.co.za   ℝℝℝℝ | 16
4 Dennehof St, 7306. **Road map** B4. **(** *(022) 461-2672*. **FAX** *(022) 461-2692*.
This rambling Victorian-style house (1904) oozes charm and character, and
provides a romantic, luxury retreat in the country. 🛏 🍽 🍴 ⚡ **P** ☷

SPRINGBOK: *Masonic Hotel*   ℝℝℝ | 35
Van Riebeeck St. **Road map** A3. **(** *(027) 712-1505*. **FAX** *(027) 712-1730*.
Clean, modern hotel in the heart of the Namaqualand wildflower region, at its
best after the spring rains, from September to October. 🛏 📺 🍽 🍴 **P** ☷

VELDDRIF: *Doornfontein Bird & Game Lodge*   ℝℝ | 10
Doornfontein, PO Box 17, Velddrif, 7965. **Road map** A4. **(** *(022) 783-0853*.
FAX *(022) 783-0853*. **@** doornfontein@xsinet.co.za   Attentive owners and game
drives on a fully working farm. Victorian/Colonial decor. 🛏 🍴 ⚡ **P** ☷

VELDDRIF: *Kersefontein Farm* **@** info@kersefontein.co.za   ℝℝ | 2
Off R45. Box 15, Hopefield, 7355. **Road map** A4. **(** *& **FAX** (022) 783-0850*.
Thatched Cape cottage and restored outbuildings on a national monument
farm on the banks of the Berg River. Swimming, hiking, birdwatching,
boating and cycling are available. 🛏 📺 🍽 **P**

YZERFONTEIN: *Auberge* **@** yzerfonteinauberge@kingsley.co.za   ℝℝ | 33
16 Mile, Yzerfontein, 7351. **Road map** A5. **(** *& **FAX** (022) 451-2424*.
Prime Atlantic Ocean beach-front location, on the leeward side
of the dunes. Rustic barnyard style. 🛏 ⚡ **P**

THE SOUTHERN CAPE

ARNISTON: *The Arniston Hotel* W www.arnistonhotel.com   ℝℝℝℝ | 40
Beach Rd, 7280. **Road map** B5. **(** *(028) 445-9000*. **FAX** *(028) 445-9633*.
This modern sea-facing hotel, near a 200-year-old fishing village close to
the southernmost tip of Africa, offers panoramic views and is within reach
of the famous sea-cave and beaches. 🛏 📺 ⚡ **P** ☷

BETTY'S BAY: *Buçaco Sud Guesthouse* W www.bucacosud.co.za   ℝℝℝ | 5
2609 Clarence Dr, 7141. **Road map** B5. **(** *& **FAX** (028) 272-9750*.
This guesthouse is surrounded by *fynbos*. Centrally located along the
whale coast, close to beaches and a penguin colony. There are fireplaces
for cold winter days and spectacular sea views. 🛏 🍽 ⚡ **P**

BREEDE RIVER: *Breede River Lodge*   ℝℝℝ | 21
Breede River, Witsands, 6761. **Road map** B5. **(** *(028) 537-1631*. **FAX** *(028) 537-1650*.
@ brl@telkomsa.net   A very popular fishing lodge on the Breede River estuary,
it overlooks the bay where concentrations of southern right whales gather
from May to October. The establishment is relaxed and informal and the
restaurant serves fresh local oysters in season. 🛏 📺 🍽 **P**

GRABOUW: *Houw Hoek Inn* W www.houwhoekinn.co.za   ℝℝℝ | 47
Off the N2, 7160. **Road map** B5. **(** *(028) 284-9646*. **FAX** *(028) 284-9112*.
This inn, situated in a quiet valley an hour's drive from Cape Town, prides
itself on being the oldest in the country (1792). 🛏 📺 🍽 🍴 ♿ **P** ☷

GREYTON: *The Post House* W www.posthouse.co.za   ℝℝℝ | 12
Main St, 7233. **Road map** B5. **(** *(028) 254-9995*. **FAX** *(028) 254-9920*.
All the rooms of this guesthouse are decorated and named after Beatrix
Potter characters. Greyton is only 90 minutes' drive from Cape Town
and is a popular weekend getaway. 🛏 🍽 ⚡ ☷

GREYTON: *The Greyton Lodge* W www.greytonlodge.com   ℝℝℝ | 18
46 Main St, 7233. **Road map** B5. **(** *(028) 254-9876*. **FAX** *(028) 254-9672*.
Built in 1880, this comfortable lodge at the foot of the mountains is
perfect for walks and hikes. Relax on the terrace before enjoying the
country cuisine. Cosy pub and a good wine list. 🛏 🍽 ⚡ **P** ☷

HERMANUS: *Auberge Burgundy*   ℝℝℝℝ | 14
16 Harbour Rd, 7200. **Road map** B5. **(** *(028) 313-1201*. **FAX** *(028) 313-1204*.
@ auberge@hermanus.co.za   Luxury Provençal-style house with courtyards and
herb gardens in the centre of town, close to the Old Harbour, shops, restaurants
and beaches. The acclaimed Burgundy Restaurant is next door. 🛏 📺 🍽 ⚡ **P** ☷

HERMANUS: *Whale Rock Lodge* W www.whalerock.co.za   ℝℝℝ | 11
26 Springfield Ave, 7200. **Road map** B5. **(** *(028) 313-0014*. **FAX** *(028) 312-2932*.
This beautiful thatched lodge overlooking the sea is only a 10-minute walk
away from a top whale-watching spot on the famous cliff path. 🛏 📺 🍽 ⚡

Price categories for a standard double room per night including tax and service charges, but not including breakfast:
Ⓡ under R150
ⓇⓇ R150–R300
ⓇⓇⓇ R300–R500
ⓇⓇⓇⓇ R500–R1000
ⓇⓇⓇⓇⓇ over R1000

SWIMMING POOL
These are usually quite small and outdoors.

RESTAURANT
Restaurant on the premises, usually open to non-residents.

CHILDREN'S FACILITIES
Baby-sitting services, cots for small children and play parks are available. Some hotels also provide half portions and high chairs in their restaurants.

GARDEN
Hotel with a garden or terrace.

	NUMBER OF ROOMS	SWIMMING POOL	RESTAURANT	CHILDREN'S FACILITIES	GARDEN
HERMANUS: *The Marine Hotel* 🅦 www.marine-hermanus.co.za ⓇⓇⓇⓇ Marine Dr, 7200. **Road map** B5. 📞 *(028) 313-1000.* ☎ *(028) 313-0160.* This luxury hotel has recently been refurbished and its unique cliff-top position makes it a perfect base for whale watching. There are two restaurants, a helipad and access to sports facilities. 🛏 📺 🍽 ♨	47	■	●		●
KLEINMOND: *The Beach House* @ beachhouse@relais.co.za ⓇⓇⓇ 13 Beach Rd, 7195. **Road map** B5. 📞 *(028) 271-3130.* ☎ *(028) 271-4022.* In winter, whales can often be seen from the restaurant overlooking the beach, only 300 m (320 yd) away. All rooms have mountain or sea views. 🛏 📺 🍽 🔧	23	■	●		
MALGAS: *Malgas Hotel & Conference Centre* ⓇⓇⓇ Main Rd, 6666. **Road map** B5. 📞 *(028) 542-1049.* ☎ *(028) 542-1718.* 🅦 www.malgashotel.co.za Some 50 km (31 miles) from Swellendam, the inn offers canoe and boat trips on the Breede River, and is near the boarding point for South Africa's only remaining hand-pulled ferry, the *Pont.* 🛏 📺 🍽 ♨ 🔧 P 🔧	21	■	●	●	●
McGREGOR: *The Old Mill Lodge* @ mcgregor@lando.co.za ⓇⓇⓇ Meul St, 6708. **Road map** B5. 📞 *(023) 625-1841.* ☎ *(023) 625-1841.* This quiet retreat, built in 1860, is set in beautiful countryside and lies on the outskirts of picturesque McGregor village. 🛏 🍽 P	10	■	●		●
OUDTSHOORN: *De Oude Meul Country Lodge* ⓇⓇ Schoemanspoort, 6620. **Road map** C5. 📞 & ☎ *(044) 272-7190.* @ deoudemeul@mweb.co.za Family lodge on the Grobbelaars River, within reach of the Cango Caves, crocodile ranch and ostrich farms. 🛏 🍽 ♨ P 🔧	12	■	●		●
OUDTSHOORN: *Altes Landhaus Country Lodge* ⓇⓇⓇ Schoemanshoek, 6620. **Road map** C5. 📞 *(044) 272-6112.* ☎ *(044) 279-2652.* Situated on ostrich farm. Cape Dutch house dates from 1898. 🛏 📺 🍽 ▤ P	6	■			●
OUDTSHOORN: *Queen's Hotel* 🅦 www.queenshotel.co.za ⓇⓇⓇ 5 Baron Van Rheede St, 6620. **Road map** C5. 📞 *(044) 272-2101.* ☎ *(044) 272-2104.* Old fashioned Colonial-style hotel conveniently situated in the town centre, close to the ostrich museum. 🛏 📺 🍽 ▤ 🔧 P 🔧	40	■	●	■	
OUDTSHOORN: *Hlangana Lodge* 🅦 www.hlangana.co.za ⓇⓇⓇ 51 North St, 6620. **Road map** C5. 📞 *(044) 272-2299.* ☎ *(044) 279-1271.* A comfortable lodge, situated on the outskirts of town on the road to the Cango Caves. 🛏 📺 🍽 ▤ ♨ 🔧 P 📺	19	■	●	■	●
OUDTSHOORN: *Rosenhof Country Lodge* ⓇⓇⓇⓇ 264 Baron van Rheede St, 6620. **Road map** C5. 📞 *(044) 272-2232.* ☎ *(044) 272-3021.* 🅦 www.rosenhof.co.za Charming Victorian-style house set in a fragrant rose garden. Overlooking the Swartberg mountains and close to the Cango Caves. Traditional home-cooked country cuisine. 🛏 📺 🍽 ▤ ♨ 🔧 P	12	■	●		●
SWELLENDAM: *The Rose Garden B&B* ⓇⓇ 19 Andrew Whyte St, 6740. **Road map** B5. 📞 & ☎ *(028) 514-1471.* Accommodation and home-cooked meals in a private residence. The patio overlooks a rose garden with a view of the Langeberg mountains. 🛏 📺 🍽 P	3			■	●
SWELLENDAM: *Klippe Rivier* 🅦 www.klipperivier.co.za ⓇⓇⓇⓇ Voortrekker St, 6740. **Road map** B5. 📞 *(028) 514-3341.* ☎ *(028) 514-3337.* Transformed into a quaint guesthouse, this 1827 original Cape Dutch manor is surrounded by mountains, vineyards and wheatfields. 🛏 🍽 ♨ P	7	■	●		●

THE GARDEN ROUTE TO GRAHAMSTOWN

	NUMBER OF ROOMS	SWIMMING POOL	RESTAURANT	CHILDREN'S FACILITIES	GARDEN
ADDO: *Cosmos Cuisine Guesthouse* 🅦 www.cosmoscuisine.co.za ⓇⓇⓇ Main St, 6105. **Road map** D5. 📞 & ☎ *(042) 234-0323.* Comfortable accommodation near the Addo Elephant Park and the Fitz-Patrick Lookout over the Sundays River Valley. 🛏 📺 🍽 ▤ ♨ P 🔧	6	■	●		●

THE CRAGS: *Hog Hollow Country Lodge* ⓇⓇⓇⓇ | 12
Askop Rd, 6602. **Road map** C5. 📞 & FAX *(04453) 4-8879.*
ⓌⓌ www.hog-hollow.com Rustic retreat 16 km (9 miles) east of Plettenberg Bay.
The cottages have private decks, cosy fireplaces and splendid views. 🛏 🍴 P 🛗

GEORGE: *Hilltop Country Lodge* ⓇⓇⓇⓇ | 7
Victoria Bay t/off fm N2 between George & Wilderness. **Road map** C5. 📞 *(044) 889-0199.*
FAX *(044) 889-0151.* Ⓦ www.hilltopcountrylodge.co.za Located in a private fynbos
reserve, this B&B offers splendid sea views and whale watching. 🛏 📺 🍴 🍴 P

GEORGE: *Protea Hotel King George* Ⓦ www.proteahotels.com ⓇⓇⓇⓇ | 64
Box 9292, KingGeorge Drive 6529. **Road map** C5. 📞 *(044) 874-7659.*
FAX *(044) 874-7664.* Ideally located for both business and pleasure, this
hotel is renowned for old-fashioned service and attention to detail.
The superb, luxurious rooms overlook the famous George Golf course.
🛏 📺 🍴 🍴 ♿ P 🛗

GEORGE: *Fancourt Hotel and Country Club* ⓇⓇⓇⓇⓇ | 100
Montagu St, Blanco, 6529. **Road map** C5. 📞 *(044) 804-0000.* FAX *(044) 804-0700.*
Ⓦ www.fancourt.co.za Exclusive resort with a 27-hole championship course,
luxury accommodation in a historical 1845 colonial manor house or garden lodges.
There are four restaurants, and various sporting activities. 🛏 📺 🍴 ▤ 🍴 🍴 P 🛗

GRAHAMSTOWN: *The Cock House Guesthouse* ⓇⓇⓇ | 9
10 Market St, 6140. **Road map** D5. 📞 *(046) 636-1287.* FAX *(046) 636-1285.*
Ⓦ www.cockhouse.co.za An 1826 homestead with yellowwood floors.
Within walking distance of historic Church Square. 🛏 📺 🍴 🍴 P 🛗

GRAHAMSTOWN: *Evelyn House Country Lodge* ⓇⓇⓇ | 7
16 High St, 6140. **Road map** D5. 📞 *(046) 622-2366.* FAX *(046) 622-2424.*
@ grahotel@intekom.co.za Gracious accommodation in a double-storey Georgian
house, in a quiet part of town, close to the university. 🛏 📺 🍴 ▤ 🍴 ♿ 🍴 P 🛗

GRAHAMSTOWN: *7 Worcester Street* Ⓦ www.worcesterstreet.co.za ⓇⓇⓇⓇ | 10
7 Worcester St, 6140. **Road map** D5. 📞 *(046) 622-2843.* FAX *(046) 622-2846.*
An eclectic collection of artwork is found throughout this house including
indigenous African art. Accommodation is luxurious. 🛏 📺 🍴 ♿ P

JEFFREY'S BAY: *Stratos Guest House* @ stratos@agnet.co.za ⓇⓇⓇ | 8
11 Uys St, 6330. **Road map** D5. 📞 *(042) 293-1116.* FAX *(042) 293-3072.*
Modern, stylish house close to the famous surfing beach. 🛏 🍴 🍴 P

KNYSNA: *Point Lodge Luxury Guesthouse* ⓇⓇⓇ | 9
Point Cl, 6570. **Road map** C5. 📞 *(044) 382-1944.* FAX *(044) 382-3455.*
Ⓦ www.pointlodge.com Overlooking the lagoon, 3 km (1.8 miles) west of Knysna,
this small guesthouse is excellent for birdwatchers. 🛏 📺 🍴 🍴 P

KNYSNA: *Wayside Inn* @ waysideinn@pixie.co.za ⓇⓇⓇ | 15
48 Main Rd, 6570. **Road map** C5. 📞 & FAX *(044) 382-6011.*
Sisal carpets and wrought-iron bedsteads create an "Out of Africa" theme.
Breakfast is served through a panel in the door. 🛏 📺 🍴 P 🛗

KNYSNA: *Falcon's View Manor* Ⓦ www.falconsview.com ⓇⓇⓇ | 9
2 Thesen Hill, 6570. **Road map** C5. 📞 *(044) 382-6767.* FAX *(044) 382-6430.*
Victorian manor house c1898, with fine furnishings. Expansive views of
the lagoon and the Heads from the verandah. Short walk into town.
Table d'hôte dinners by candlelight. 🛏 📺 🍴 ▤ 🍴 P

KNYSNA: *Portland Manor* @ portlandmnr@mweb.co.za ⓇⓇⓇ | 24
Rheenendal Rd, off N2. **Road map** C5. 📞 & FAX *(044) 388-4604.*
Situated 20 minutes out of town on a historic citrus farm with its own
mini wildlife park, the restored stone manor house (1864) still displays
the original gleaming yellowwood floors and ceilings. 🛏 🍴 🍴 🛗

KNYSNA: *Belvidere Manor* Ⓦ www.belvedere.co.za ⓇⓇⓇⓇ | 30
Duthie Dr, 6570. **Road map** C5. 📞 *(044) 387-1055.* FAX *(044) 387-1059.*
On the shores of Knysna lagoon, the main house (1834) is surrounded by
quaint cottages, each with verandah and fireplace. 🛏 📺 🍴 🍴 ♿ P 🛗

KNYSNA: *St James of Knysna* Ⓦ www.stjames.co.za ⓇⓇⓇⓇ | 16
The Point, 6570. **Road map** C5. 📞 *(044) 382-6750.* FAX *(044) 382-6756.*
Stylish comfort on the edge of the tranquil lagoon, five minutes from the centre
of town. Suites all have superb bathroom with separate shower, lounge with
direct dial telephone and satellite television. 🛏 📺 🍴 ▤ 🍴 P 🛗

							NUMBER OF ROOMS	SWIMMING POOL	RESTAURANT	CHILDREN'S FACILITIES	GARDEN

Price categories for a standard double room per night including tax and service charges, but not including breakfast:
(R) under R150
(R)(R) R150–R300
(R)(R)(R) R300–R500
(R)(R)(R)(R) R500–R1000
(R)(R)(R)(R)(R) over R1000

SWIMMING POOL
These are usually quite small and outdoors.
RESTAURANT
Restaurant on the premises, usually open to non-residents.
CHILDREN'S FACILITIES
Baby-sitting services, cots for small children and play parks are available. Some hotels also provide half portions and high chairs in their restaurants.
GARDEN
Hotel with a garden or terrace.

Hotel	Price	Rooms	Pool	Rest.	Child.	Garden
MOSSEL BAY: *The Point Hotel* w www.pointhotel.co.za Point Rd, 6500. **Road map** C5. (*(044) 691-3512.* FAX *(044) 691-3513.* A superbly located hotel in the heart of the Garden Route. Built on the rocks and offering magnificent sea views from its balconies.	(R)(R)	48		●		
MOSSEL BAY: *Eight Bells Mountain Inn* Robinson Pass on the R328. **Road map** C5. (*(044) 631-0000.* FAX *(044) 631-0004.* w www.eightbells.co.za Tranquil 160-ha (400-acre) estate with magnificent mountain scenery, log cabins and thatched rondavels.	(R)(R)(R)	25	■	●	■	●
MOSSEL BAY: *Protea Hotel Mossel Bay* w www.oldposttree.co.za Cnr Church & Market sts, 6500. **Road map** C5. (*(044) 691-3738.* FAX *(044) 691-3104.* This hotel is housed in one of the oldest buildings in Mossel Bay and forms part of the Dias Museum complex. Good views over the harbour.	(R)(R)(R)(R)	30		■	■	●
PLETTENBERG BAY: *Mallard River Lodge* Rietvlei Rd, 6600. **Road map** C5. (*(044) 533-2982.* FAX *(044) 533-0687.* @ mallard@pixie.co.za Charming building on the bank of the Bitou River, with panoramic views from all rooms.	(R)(R)(R)(R)	5	■			
PLETTENBERG BAY: *Country Crescent Hotel* Piesang Valley Rd, 6600. **Road map** C5. (*(044) 533-3033.* FAX *(044) 533-2016.* w www.crescenthotels.com In the heart of the rural Piesang River valley, minutes from the sea and beaches. Gardens and pool deck.	(R)(R)(R)(R)(R)	39	■	●		
PLETTENBERG BAY: *Hunter's Country House* Off the N2. **Road map** C5. (*(044) 532-7818.* FAX *(044) 532-7878.* w www.hunterhotels.com Thatched manor house, 10 km (6 miles) from Plettenberg Bay. Individual garden suites surrounded by indigenous forest. Acclaimed as one of the country's top hotels. Facilities include wine cellar, conservatory and shop. Member of Relais et Châteaux.	(R)(R)(R)(R)(R)	23	■	●		●
PLETTENBERG BAY: *The Plettenberg* w www.plettenberg.com 40 Church St, 6600. **Road map** C5. (*(044) 533-2030.* FAX *(044) 533-2074.* Elegant, stylish hotel on a rocky headland overlooking two beaches, where whales are seen from July to October. Bedrooms are designed to take advantage of the stunning views. Every comfort has been catered for at this prestigious Relais et Châteaux hotel, including fine cuisine and wines.	(R)(R)(R)(R)(R)	40	■	●	■	
PORT ALFRED: *The Halyards* w www.riverhotels.co.za Royal Alfred Marina, 6170. **Road map** D5. (*(046) 624-2410.* FAX *(046) 624-2466.* A luxury waterfront resort with plentiful comforts such as ensuite rooms. It forms the centrepiece of the marina, just minutes from town.	(R)(R)(R)(R)	37	■	●	■	●
PORT ELIZABETH: *Brighton Lodge* w www.brightonlodge.co.za 21 Brighton Dr, Summerstrand, 6001. **Road map** D5. (*(041) 583-4576.* FAX *(041) 583-4104.* Magnificent views of Algoa Bay from this conveniently situated, comfortable lodge in a popular seaside residential suburb.	(R)(R)	11	■			●
PORT ELIZABETH: *Villa Hestia* w www.villahestia.co.za 14 10th Ave, 6001. **Road map** D5. (*(041) 583-3927.* FAX *(041) 503-8513.* Situated on Pollock Beach, Villa Hestia offers three self-catering units with private entrances, as well as rooms. Breakfast and dinner by request.	(R)(R)	10	■			●
PORT ELIZABETH: *Beach Hotel* w www.pehotels.co.za Marine Dr, 6001. **Road map** D5. (*(041) 583-2161.* FAX *(041) 583-6220.* Hobie Beach is just across the road from this modern holiday hotel with its magnificent views of Algoa Bay.	(R)(R)(R)(R)	58		●	■	
PORT ELIZABETH: *Hacklewood Hill Country House* 152 Prospect Rd, Walmer, 6070. **Road map** D5. (*(041) 581-1300.* FAX *(041) 581-4155.* w www.pehotels.co.za Stylish Victorian manor house (1898), in the garden suburb of Walmer, close to the airport.	(R)(R)(R)(R)	8	■	●		●

PORT ELIZABETH: *Protea Marine Hotel* ⓦ www.proteahotels.com Ⓡ Ⓡ Ⓡ Ⓡ
Marine Dr, 6001. **Road map** D5. Ⓒ *(041) 583-2101.* FAX *(041) 583-2076.*
Modern hotel on the beach, offering the traveller all modern conveniences
and beautiful views. 🚗 TV 📧 🍽 ⚡ & P 🏊

73	■	●	

PORT ELIZABETH: *Shamwari Game Reserve* Ⓡ Ⓡ Ⓡ Ⓡ Ⓡ
Box 32017, Summerstrand, 6019. **Road map** D5. Ⓒ *(042) 203-1111.* FAX *(042) 235-1224.*
ⓦ www.shamwari.com Private 12,000-ha (29,600-acre) reserve 72 km
(45 miles) from Port Elizabeth. Luxury accommodation in restored homesteads.
Day and night game drives in open vehicles. 🚗 TV 📧 🍽 ⚡ P

54	■	●	■

SEDGEFIELD: *Lake Pleasant Hotel* ⓦ www.lakepleasanthotel.com Ⓡ Ⓡ Ⓡ Ⓡ
N2. Box 2, Sedgefield, 6573. **Road map** C5. Ⓒ *(044) 349-2400.* FAX *(044) 349-2401.*
Small family hotel on the shores of Groenvlei, 6 km (3.5 miles) from Sedgefield
on the Garden Route. Offers birdwatching and water-sports in a nature
reserve that includes the lagoon and sea. 🚗 TV 📧 P 🏊

33	■	●	

WILDERNESS: *Protea Wilderness Hotel* ⓦ www.proteahotels.com Ⓡ Ⓡ Ⓡ Ⓡ
On the N2. **Road map** C5. Ⓒ *(044) 877-1110.* FAX *(044) 877-0600.*
A family hotel close to the beach, offering a children's programme, trampoline,
squash and tennis courts, mini golf (putt-putt), heated pool and sauna.
Conveniently situated for travellers. 🚗 TV 📧 🍽 ⚡ & 🍴 P 🏊

158	■	●	■

WILD COAST, DRAKENSBERG & MIDLANDS

BALGOWAN: *Granny Mouse Country House* Ⓡ Ⓡ Ⓡ
R103. Old Main Rd, 3275. **Road map** E3. Ⓒ *(033) 234-4071.* FAX *(033) 243-4429.*
ⓦ www.grannymouse.co.za Well-appointed thatched cottages in a country setting
on the banks of a river in the heart of the Natal Midlands. Renowned restaurant
specializes in country cooking; there is a comprehensive wine list. 🚗 TV 📧 P 🏊

16	■	●	●

BERGVILLE: *Karos Mont-Aux-Sources Hotel* Ⓡ Ⓡ Ⓡ
R74 (near Royal Natal National Park). **Road map** E3. Ⓒ & FAX *(036) 438-6230.*
ⓦ www.orion-hotels.co.za In the northern part of the Drakensberg,
this hotel has splendid views of the Amphitheatre. At 3,248 m (10,650 ft),
Mont-Aux-Sources is the highest peak in the country. 🚗 TV 📧 & 🍴 P 🏊

75	■	●	■	●

BERGVILLE: *Sandford Park Lodge* ⓦ www.sandford.co.za Ⓡ Ⓡ Ⓡ
Box 7, Bergville, 3350. **Road map** E3. Ⓒ *(036) 448-1001.* FAX *(036) 448-1047.*
This 150-year-old thatched coach house, on a garden property,
lies close to the Drakensberg mountains. 🚗 📧 🍴 P 🏊

26	■	●	●

EAST LONDON: *Hotel Osner* ⓦ www.catleasure.co.za Ⓡ Ⓡ
Court Crescent, 5201. **Road map** E5. Ⓒ & FAX *(043) 743-3433.*
A member of 'Osner Resorts', this hotel is situated near the beachfront
close to buzzing nightclubs. 🚗 TV 📧 🍽 ⚡ 🍴 P 🏊

113	■	●	●

EAST LONDON: *Kennaway Hotel* ⓦ www.catleasure.co.za Ⓡ Ⓡ
Esplanade, 5201. **Road map** E5. Ⓒ & FAX *(0437) 22-5531.*
An 'Osner Resorts' hotel, conveniently located close to the beachfront and the
centre of town. Affordable family accommodation. 🚗 TV 📧 ⚡ & P 🏊

106		●	■

EAST LONDON: *King David Hotel* @ kingdavidhotel@africa.com Ⓡ Ⓡ Ⓡ
Inverleith Terrace & Currie St, 5201. **Road map** E5. Ⓒ *(043) 722-3174.* FAX *(043) 743-8019.*
Decorated in a Middle Eastern theme, this hotel is 2 km (1 mile) from the city
and very close to the beach. 🚗 TV 📧 🍽 ⚡ & P 🏊

80		●	

FOURIESBURG: *Wyndford Holiday Farm* ⓦ www.wyndford.co.za Ⓡ Ⓡ
Caledonspoort, 9725. **Road map** E3. Ⓒ *(058) 223-0274.* FAX *(058) 223-0664.*
In the Free State Province. Family accommodation close to the Golden Gate
area of the Drakensberg. Swimming pool, hiking, tennis, horse riding, games
room. Children welcome. Low season discounts for senior citizens. 🚗 TV 📧

26	■	●	●

HIMEVILLE: *Sani Pass Hotel & Leisure Resort* Ⓡ Ⓡ Ⓡ
Sani Pass Rd, 3256. **Road map** E3. Ⓒ *(033) 702-1320.* FAX *(033) 702-0220.*
ⓦ www.sanipasshotel.co.za This friendly hotel has its own nine-hole golf course,
bowling greens, tennis courts and swimming pools. At an altitude of 1,566m
(5,138 ft) above sea level, at the foot of the Sani Pass across the Drakensberg
into Lesotho, only accessible to four-wheel-drive vehicles. 🚗 TV 📧 P 🏊

87	■	●	●

KEI MOUTH: *Kei Mouth Beach Hotel* ⓦ www.keimouthbeachhotel.co.za Ⓡ Ⓡ Ⓡ
R349. Box 8, Kei Mouth, 5260. **Road map** E4. Ⓒ *(043) 841-1017.* FAX *(043) 841-1175.*
A comfortable Wild Coast hotel, 60 minutes' drive from the nearest city, with
spectacular solitary beaches, wildlife, fauna and flora. 🚗 📧 🍴 P 🏊

29	■	●	●

Price categories for a standard double room per night including tax and service charges, but not including breakfast:
® under R150
®® R150–R300
®®® R300–R500
®®®® R500–R1000
®®®®® over R1000

SWIMMING POOL
These are usually quite small and outdoors.

RESTAURANT
Restaurant on the premises, usually open to non-residents.

CHILDREN'S FACILITIES
Baby-sitting services, cots for small children and play parks are available. Some hotels also provide half portions and high chairs in their restaurants.

GARDEN
Hotel with a garden or terrace.

	NUMBER OF ROOMS	SWIMMING POOL	RESTAURANT	CHILDREN'S FACILITIES	GARDEN
LESOTHO: *Katse Lodge* @ fedicsles@leo.co.za ®®® Katse Dam. **Road map** E3. ((0926622) 91-0202. FAX (0926622) 91-0004. Situated on the banks of scenic Katse Dam in the northeast of Lesotho, this small lodge offers superb views and a chance to observe the abundant birdlife around the water.	14		●	■	●
LESOTHO: *Lesotho Sun* @ lesoresw@sunint.co.za ®®®® Hilton Rd, Maseru. **Road map** D3. ((0926622) 31-3111. FAX (0926622) 31-0104. A shuttle service to and from Maseru's international airport is only one of the conveniences at this large, modern hotel. There is also a casino, a cinema and the renowned Lehaha Grill restaurant.	198	■	●	■	●
LESOTHO: *Maseru Sun* @ maserus@sunint.co.za ®®®® 12 Orpen Rd, Maseru. **Road map** D3. ((0926622) 31-2434. FAX (0926622) 31-0158. Conveniently located 5 km (3 miles) from the Maseru Bridge border post, this luxury hotel has all the modern conveniences, as well as a sauna, casino, photo studio and access to a nearby golf course.	115	■	●	■	●
LIDGETTON: *Penny Lane Guesthouse* ®®® Farm No 13, Old Main Rd. **Road map** E3. ((033) 234-4332. FAX (033) 234-4617. @ pennylane@pixie.co.za Country lodge which blends African elements with a traditional country feel. On the Midlands Meander, in a tranquil area renowned for trout fishing. Cosy pub with roaring fire on cold nights.	7	■	●	■	●
MIDMAR DAM: *FernHill Hotel* w www.fernhillhotel.co.za ®® On the Midlands Meander route. **Road map** E3. ((033) 330-5071. FAX (033) 330-5092. Built in 1851 as a trading post, this hotel is set in extensive grounds opposite the Midmar Dam and Nature Reserve. Facilities are excellent.	26	■	●	■	●
MOOI RIVER: *Hartford House* w www.hartford.co.za ®®® Giant's Castle Rd, Mooi River, 3300. **Road map** E3. ((033) 263-2713. FAX (033) 263-2818. Accommodation on a stud farm breeding Arab stallions for the sheiks of Dubai. Splendid manor house has underfloor heating and log fires in winter, gardens blooming with daffodils, roses and flowering cherries in summer. In easy reach of battlefields, scenic drives. Bass and trout fishing dams.	11	■	●		●
MORGAN'S BAY: *Morgan Bay Hotel* @ morganbay@telkom.sa ®®® R349. Morgan's Bay, 5292. **Road map** E4. ((043) 841-1062. FAX (043) 841-1130. Small family hotel catering especially for children. There is an old *Strandloper* trail and an extensive beach to explore.	33	■	●	■	●
NOTTINGHAM ROAD: *Rawdons Hotel* @ hotel@rawdons.co.za ®®®® R103. Old Main Rd, 3280. **Road map** E3. ((033) 266-6044. FAX (033) 266-6048. Gracious thatch-roofed building lies beside a tranquil lake that is perfect for trout fishing. There is an English-style pub, gym, sauna, bowling green, tennis court, swimming pool and brewery on the premises. The Sunday carvery lunch is a legend in the area.	29	■	●	■	●
PENNINGTON: *Selborne Hotel* w www.selborne.com ®®®®® Old Main Rd, 4184. **Road map** E3. ((039) 975-1133. FAX (039) 975-1811. Built in the early 1950s but recently refurbished, this golf resort complex on the south coast boasts a private beach and, naturally, good golfing facilities.	49	■	●	■	●
PIETERMARITZBURG: *Imperial Protea Hotel* ®®®® 224 Loop St, 3201. **Road map** E3. ((033) 342-6551. FAX (033) 342-9796. w www.proteahotels.com Comfortable chain hotel in the heart of this historic town. Secure parking, a laundry service and a cocktail bar.	70		●	■	
PIETERMARITZBURG: *Redlands Hotel and Lodge* ®®®® 1 George McFarlane Lane, 3201. **Road map** E3. ((033) 394-3333. FAX (033) 394-3338. @ redlands@mweb.co.za Small luxury hotel with a good restaurant, in an attractive parklike estate not far outside Pietermaritzburg.	20	■	●	■	●

PIETERMARITZBURG: *Wartburger Hof Country Hotel*   ⓇⓇⓇⓇ | 20
53 Noodsberg Rd, 3233. **Road map E3.** 【 & FAX *(033) 503-1482.*
Ⓦ www.wartburgerhof.co.za Cosy Alpine-style hotel 30 minutes from
Pietermaritzburg. A "Germany in Africa" atmosphere. 🖥 TV 🎫 ⚡ 🔌 P 🏊

PORT EDWARD: *The Estuary Guesthouse* Ⓦ www.estuary.co.za   ⓇⓇⓇⓇ | 31
Main Rd, 4295. **Road map E4.** 【 *(039) 311-2675.* FAX *(039) 311-2689.*
Restored Cape Dutch manor overlooking the estuary and a protected
bathing beach. Just 5 km (3 miles) from the Wild Coast Casino. Activities
include games room, hiking and fishing. 🖥 TV 🎫 ≡ ⚡ P 🏊

PORT ST JOHNS: *Umngazi River Bungalows* Ⓦ www.umngazi.co.za ⓇⓇⓇ | 66
R61. Box 391, Pinetown, 3600. **Road map E4.** 【 *(047) 564-1115.* FAX *(047) 564-1115.*
Thatched chalets, 10 km (6 miles) from Port St Johns, overlooking the lagoon
and the Indian Ocean. Fully inclusive. Convenient airstrip nearby. 🖥 🎫 ⚡ P 🏊

RICHMOND: *The Oaks Hotel at Byrne* Ⓦ www.oaksatbyrne.co.za   ⓇⓇⓇ | 43
Byrne Valley, 3780. **Road map E3.** 【 *(033) 212-2324.* FAX *(033) 212-2211.*
This Midlands country hotel caters for children, with a playground,
playroom, horses, trampolines and tennis. 🖥 TV 🎫 ≡ 🔌 P 🏊

RORKE'S DRIFT: *i'Sibindi Lodge* Ⓦ www.isibindiafrica.co.za   ⓇⓇⓇ | 6
Box 124, Dundee, 3000. **Road map E3.** 【 *(035) 474-1473.* FAX *(035) 474-1490.*
In the i'Sibindi Eco Reserve. Guests are accommodated in traditional Zulu-
style huts with wooden decks, overlooking the valley bushveld and riverine
forests. Close to Rorke's Drift and Isandhlwana battlefields. 🖥 🎫 ⚡ P

RORKE'S DRIFT: *Fugitives' Drift Lodge*   ⓇⓇⓇⓇⓇ | 8
R33. Rorke's Drift, 3016. **Road map E3.** 【 *(034) 642-1843.* FAX *(034) 271-8053.*
Ⓦ www.fugitives-drift-lodge.com Set in a 1,620-ha (4,000-acre) wildlife reserve on
the Buffalo River, the lodge overlooks several Anglo-Zulu battlefields. Guided tours
to nearby Isandhlwana and Rorke's Drift, as well as fishing, walking and
birdwatching. Rooms are decorated with artefacts from the area. 🖥 🎫 ⚡ P 🏊

VAN REENEN: *Oaklands Country Manor* Ⓦ www.oaklands.co.za   ⓇⓇⓇⓇ | 13
Skaapdrift Rd, 3372. **Road map E3.** 【 *(058) 671-0067.* FAX *(058) 671-0077.*
Comfortable manor house in superb mountain setting near Van Reenen's
Pass and close to the battlefields route. 🖥 🎫 ⚡ P 🏊

VRYHEID: *Villa Prince Imperial* ＠ princeimperial@intekom.co.za   ⓇⓇⓇ | 12
201 Deputasie St, 3100. **Road map F3.** 【 & FAX *(034) 983-2610.*
This accredited guesthouse is in the vicinity of the Itala Game Reserve
and at the heart of the battlefields route. 🖥 TV 🎫 ⚡ P 🏊

WINTERTON: *Cathedral Peak Hotel* Ⓦ www.cathedralpeak.co.za   ⓇⓇⓇⓇ | 42
R74. PO Winterton, 3340. **Road map E3.** 【 *(036) 488-1888.* FAX *(034) 983-2619.*
Choice holiday destination in the Drakensberg foothills. Walks lead to San
paintings and nearby waterfalls, or visitors can take a ride in the hotel's
helicopter to view the Drakensberg from the air. 🖥 TV 🎫 🔌 🎾 P 🏊

WINTERTON: *Cayley Lodge* ＠ cayley@global.co.za   ⓇⓇⓇⓇ | 24
R74. Box 241, Winterton, 3340. **Road map E3.** 【 & FAX *(036) 468-1020.*
Thatched lodge with splendid views of the Drakensberg, surrounded by 115 ha
(286 acres) of parkland and forest, ideal for walking, hiking and horse riding.
Enjoy water skiing or sunset cruises on the dam. 🖥 🎫 ⚡ P 🏊

WINTERTON: *The Nest Resort Hotel* Ⓦ www.thenest.co.za   ⓇⓇⓇ | 54
R74. Champagne Castle Rd, 3340. **Road map E3.** 【 *(036) 468-1068.* FAX *(036) 468-1390.*
The resident coach teaches guests the art of bowls at this Drakensberg
hotel, which also holds tournaments. 🖥 🎫 ⚡ 🔌 🎾 P 🏊

DURBAN AND ZULULAND

BABANANGO: *Babanango Valley Lodge*   ⓇⓇⓇⓇ | 6
Off the R68. **Road map F3.** 【 *(035) 835-0062.* FAX *(035) 835-0160.*
Ⓦ www.babanangovalley.co.za Set in a 2,025-ha (5,000-acre) natural heritage site, this
is a good base for exploring Isandhlwana, Rorke's Drift, Zulu country and the
Hluhluwe-Umfolozi Game Reserve. Candlelit dinners and fine views. 🖥 🎫 ⚡ 🔌 P

BALLITO: *The Boathouse* Ⓦ www.theboathouse.co.za   ⓇⓇⓇ | 22
Compensation Beach Rd, 4420. **Road map F3.** 【 *(032) 946-0300.* FAX *(032) 946-0184.*
Situated on the beachfront of one of South Africa's prime holiday destinations
and enjoying sweeping ocean views. Rooms are tastefully decorated and well
equipped. Golf courses and attractions nearby. 🖥 TV 🎫 ≡ ⚡ 🔌 P 🏊

Price categories for a standard double room per night including tax and service charges, but not including breakfast:
Ⓡ under R150
ⓇⓇ R150–R300
ⓇⓇⓇ R300–R500
ⓇⓇⓇⓇ R500–R1000
ⓇⓇⓇⓇⓇ over R1000

SWIMMING POOL
These are usually quite small and outdoors.

RESTAURANT
Restaurant on the premises, usually open to non-residents.

CHILDREN'S FACILITIES
Baby-sitting services, cots for small children and play parks are available. Some hotels also provide half portions and high chairs in their restaurants.

GARDEN
Hotel with a garden or terrace.

	Number of Rooms	Swimming Pool	Restaurant	Children's Facilities	Garden
BOTHA'S HILL: *Falcon Crest* Ⓦ www.falconcrestestate.co.za **ⓇⓇ** 18 Old Main Rd, 3660. **Road map** F3. ☎ *(031) 765-5419.* FAX *(031) 765-1122.* Comfortable cottages nestle in a beautiful garden overlooking the Valley of a Thousand Hills. 🖵 TV ✉ ♿ P ♦	20	■	●	■	●
BOTHA'S HILL: *Rob Roy Hotel* Ⓦ www.robroyhotel.co.za **ⓇⓇⓇ** Rob Roy Crescent, 3660. **Road map** F3. ☎ *(031) 777-1305.* FAX *(031) 777-1364.* Revamped and refurbished in 1997, this hotel has unsurpassed views over the unspoilt Valley of a Thousand Hills, near Pietermaritzburg. 🖵 TV ✉ ♿ P ♦	39	■	●	■	●
DURBAN CENTRAL: *Durban City Lodge* Ⓦ www.citylodge.co.za **ⓇⓇ** Cnr Old Fort & Brickhill rds, 4001. **Road map** F3. ☎ *(031) 332-1447.* FAX *(031) 332-1483.* A large, well-run chain hotel that is centrally located within easy distance of the beaches and the city centre. 🖵 TV ✉ ▤ 🛏 ♿ P 🛎 ♦	161	■			●
DURBAN CENTRAL: *Holiday Inn Garden Court South Beach* **ⓇⓇ** 73 Marine Parade, 4001. **Road map** F3. ☎ *(031) 337-2231.* FAX *(031) 337-4640.* Ⓦ www.southernsun.com Clean, no-frills accommodation right on Durban's beachfront, opposite a shopping complex. 🖵 TV ✉ ▤ 🛏 ♿ P ♦	414	■	●	■	
DURBAN CENTRAL: *Beach Hotel* @ lodges@goodersons.co.za **ⓇⓇⓇ** 107 Marine Parade, 4001. **Road map** F3. ☎ *(031) 337-5511.* FAX *(031) 337-5409.* Cheap, clean and comfortable accommodation on the Golden Mile beachfront, close to the aquarium, paddling pools and amusement park. 🖵 TV ✉ ▤ P	112		●	■	
DURBAN CENTRAL: *Hotel Tropicana* **ⓇⓇⓇ** 85 Marine Parade, 4001. **Road map** F3. ☎ *(031) 368-1511.* FAX *(031) 332-6890.* @ tropicana@goodersons.co.za Affordable accommodation close to Golden Mile beaches, walkways, restaurants, entertainment and shopping. 🖵 TV ✉ ▤ P ♦	168		●	■	
DURBAN CENTRAL: *Protea Hotel Edward* **ⓇⓇⓇⓇ** 149 Marine Parade, 4001. **Road map** F3. ☎ *(031) 337-3681.* FAX *(031) 307-1692.* Ⓦ www.proteahotels.com One of the oldest hotels in Durban, opposite the Golden Mile beaches, with views of the Indian Ocean. 🖵 TV ✉ ▤ 🛏 ♿ ♦	101	■	●	■	
DURBAN CENTRAL: *The Royal Hotel* Ⓦ www.theroyal.co.za **ⓇⓇⓇⓇ** 267 Smith St, 4001. **Road map** F3. ☎ *(031) 333-6000.* FAX *(031) 307-5247.* This 151-year-old hotel near the Victoria Embankment was voted best city hotel in the country for five consecutive years. Impeccable service is its hallmark. 🖵 TV ✉ ▤ 🛏 ♿ 🛎 P	272	■	●	■	
ESHOWE: *Protea Hotel Shakaland* Ⓦ www.proteahotels.com **ⓇⓇⓇⓇ** R68. Box 103, Eshowe, 3815. **Road map** F3. ☎ *(035) 460-0912.* FAX *(035) 460-0824.* A living museum in the Nkwaleni valley, near Eshowe. Accommodation in beehive huts in a replica Zulu village, overlooking the Umhlatuze Lake. Share the secrets of local culture in the Shakaland theme park. 🖵 ✉ P ♦	50	■	●	■	
GINGINDHLOVU: *Mine Own Country House* @ remark@active.co.za **ⓇⓇⓇ** R102. Box 25, 3800. **Road map** F3. ☎ *(035) 337-1262.* FAX *(035) 337-1025.* American colonial-style home on a sugar-cane plantation. Conveniently situated for excursions to Shakaland, game reserves and the battlefields. 🖵 TV ✉ ▤ 🛏	5	■	●		
HLUHLUWE: *Hluhluwe River Lodge* Ⓦ www.hluhluwe.co.za **ⓇⓇⓇⓇⓇ** N2. Box 105, Hluhluwe, 3960. **Road map** F3. ☎ *(035) 562-0246.* FAX *(035) 562-0248.* Superior air-conditioned timber-and-thatch lodges on the western shore of the Greater St Lucia Wetland Park. Game drives, boat cruises and walking trails in the surrounding sand forest. 🖵 ✉ ▤ 🛏 P ♦	12	■	●	■	
HLUHLUWE: *Zulu Nyala Heritage Hotel* **ⓇⓇⓇⓇⓇ** Old Hluhluwe Main Rd, 3960. **Road map** F3. ☎ *(035) 562-0177.* FAX *(035) 562-0582.* Ⓦ www.zulunyala.com This exclusive hotel is set in typical Zululand countryside and offers wildlife viewing, birdwatching and a true taste of the rich culture and traditions of the Zulu people. 🖵 ✉ 🛏 P ♦	63	■	●	■	●

HLUHLUWE: *Zulu Nyala Game Lodge* ⓇⓇⓇⓇ 37
Mzinene Rd, 3960. **Road map** F3. & FAX *(035) 562-0169.*
W www.zulunyala.com Thatched stone cottages on a hilltop with wonderful views of the indigenous bush, as well as wildlife and birds.

HLUHLUWE: *Zululand Tree Lodge* W www.ubizane.co.za ⓇⓇⓇⓇ 24
Ubizane Game Reserve. **Road map** F3. *(035) 562-1020.* FAX *(035) 562-1032.*
Elevated chalets set in a forest of fever trees in private reserve adjoining the Hluhluwe-Umfolozi Park. Game drives and horse trails.

PORT SHEPSTONE: *Kapenta Bay All-suite Resort Hotel* ⓇⓇⓇ 50
Princess Elizabeth Dr, 4240. **Road map** E4. *(039) 682-5528.* FAX *(039) 682-4530.*
W www.kapentabay.co.za This friendly beachfront Mediterranean-style hotel on the South Coast also has a magnificent swimming pool.

SALT ROCK: *Salt Rock Hotel and Beach Resort* ⓇⓇⓇⓇ 69
Basil Hulett Dr, 4391. **Road map** F3. *(032) 525-5025.* FAX *(032) 525-5071.*
W www.saltrockbeach.co.za This established North Coast hotel has waves breaking on the lawn at high tide. Dolphin dives arranged.

SODWANA BAY: *Rocktail Bay Lodge* ⓇⓇⓇⓇⓇ 10
Between Kosi and Sodwana bays. **Road map** F3. *(011) 257-5200.*
FAX *(011) 234-4978.* @ info@wildernis.co.za Wooden chalets built on stilts nestle under gigantic Natal mahogany trees. The lodge forms part of the Maputaland Coastal Forest Reserve, offering 25 km (15 miles) of unspoilt wilderness. All meals are included. Booking is through the Johannesburg office.

SOUTHBROOM: *The Country Lodge* W www.thecountrylodge.co.za ⓇⓇⓇ 24
Old South Coast Rd, 4277. **Road map** E4. *(039) 316-8380.* FAX *(039) 313-0157.*
Set in a forest, this natural heritage site offers tranquillity amid sub-tropical gardens. Golf nearby.

SOUTHBROOM: *Sanlameer Estate Hotel* W www.sanlameer.com ⓇⓇⓇⓇ 40
Lower S Coast Main Rd, 4277. **Road map** E4. *(039) 313-0011.* FAX *(039) 313-0157.*
Accommodation at this popular golfing resort with its own stretch of beach is in the luxury hotel or villas.

UMHLALI: *Shortens Country House* W www.shortenshotel.com ⓇⓇⓇⓇ 15
Compensation Rd, 4390. **Road map** F3. *(032) 947-1140.* FAX *(032) 947-1144.*
Gracious country hotel in a colonial homestead (c.1903) on the lush North Coast, about 30 minutes' drive from Durban.

UMHLANGA ROCKS: *Oyster Box Hotel* W www.oysterbox.co.za ⓇⓇⓇ 95
2 Lighthouse Rd, 4320. **Road map** F3. *(031) 561-2233.* FAX *(031) 561-4072.*
North Coast Mediterranean-style hotel right on the beach near the lighthouse. Children and pets are welcome at this family-oriented hotel.

UMHLANGA ROCKS: *Umhlanga Sands Hotel* ⓇⓇⓇ 237
Lagoon Dr, 4320. **Road map** F3. *(031) 561-2323.* FAX *(031) 561-2333.*
W www.southernsun.com The Southern Sun hotel chain ownes this resort hotel in the popular North Coast holiday town.

GAUTENG AND SUN CITY

BOKSBURG: *Airport Grand* W www.legacyhotels.co.za ⓇⓇⓇ 151
100 North Rd, 1459. **Road map** E2. *(011) 823-1843.* FAX *(011) 823-2194.*
Executive accommodation just five minutes' drive from Johannesburg International Airport.

JOHANNESBURG: *Airport Holiday Inn* W www.southernsun.com ⓇⓇⓇ 366
Johannesburg International Airport. **Road map** E2. *(011) 975-1121.* FAX *(011) 975-5846.*
Conveniently situated for transit passengers, or those with an early morning departure or late-night arrival.

JOHANNESBURG: *5th Avenue Gooseberry* W www.gooseberry1.co.za ⓇⓇⓇ 7
44 5th Ave, Linden, 2195. **Road map** E2. *(011) 888-5587.* FAX *(011) 782-4905.*
In the northern suburbs of Johannesburg, this guesthouse exudes Old English charm. Every room is individually decorated.

JOHANNESBURG: *The Cottages Guesthouse* ⓇⓇⓇ 13
30 Gill St, Observatory, 2198. **Road map** E2. *(011) 487-2829.* FAX *(011) 487-2404.*
@ mckenna@iafrica.com The original thatched stone house was built in the 1920s. Individually decorated cottages adjoin the Mervin King hiking trail and offer a 360-degree panorama of Johannesburg.

Price categories for a standard double room per night including tax and service charges, but not including breakfast: Ⓡ under R150 ⓇⓇ R150–R300 ⓇⓇⓇ R300–R500 ⓇⓇⓇⓇ R500–R1000 ⓇⓇⓇⓇⓇ over R1000	**SWIMMING POOL** These are usually quite small and outdoors. **RESTAURANT** Restaurant on the premises, usually open to non-residents. **CHILDREN'S FACILITIES** Baby-sitting services, cots for small children and play parks are available. Some hotels also provide half portions and high chairs in their restaurants. **GARDEN** Hotel with a garden or terrace.			

	NUMBER OF ROOMS	SWIMMING POOL	RESTAURANT	CHILDREN'S FACILITIES	GARDEN
JOHANNESBURG: *B&B at Wedgewood* ⓇⓇⓇ 75 Second Ave, Melville, 2092. **Road map** E2. 【 *(011) 482-4124*. ꜰᴀx *(011) 726-7557*. ⓌⓌ www.wedgewoodmews.co.za This elegant accommodation lies in the safe 'village' of Melville, with its trendy restaurants, bistros and shops. 🛏 📺 🍽 🌿 🅿 🔲	6				●
JOHANNESBURG: *No 10 2nd Avenue, Houghton Estate* ⓇⓇⓇⓇ 10 2nd Ave, Houghton, 2041. **Road map** E2. 【 *(011) 483-3037*. ꜰᴀx *(011) 483-3051*. ⓌⓌ www.houghtonestate.com Private, informal bed-and-breakfast establishment in a restored manor house in a quiet garden suburb. 🛏 📺 🍽 🅿 ♿ 🔲	12	■	●		
JOHANNESBURG: *Sunnyside Park* ⓌⓌ www.legacyhotels.co.za ⓇⓇⓇⓇ 2 York Rd, Sunnyside, 2193. **Road map** E2. 【 *(011) 643-7226*. ꜰᴀx *(011) 642-0019*. Suburban hotel located in the Victorian manor house that was the residence of Lord Milner during the Anglo-Boer War. 🛏 📺 🍽 🍴 🌿 🅿 🔲	96	■	●	■	●
JOHANNESBURG: *Protea Hotel Balalaika* ⓇⓇⓇⓇⓇ Maud St, Sandown. **Road map** E2. 【 *(011) 322-5000*. ꜰᴀx *(011) 322-5022*. ⓌⓌ www.proteahotels.com A tranquil hotel in extensive grounds, yet not too far from the main Pretoria/Johannesburg highway. 🛏 📺 🍽 🍴 🌿 ♿ 🅿 🔲	325	■	●	■	●
JOHANNESBURG: *The Westcliff* ⓌⓌ www.westcliff.com ⓇⓇⓇⓇⓇ 67 Jan Smuts Dr, Westcliff, 2193. **Road map** E2. 【 *(011) 646-2400*. ꜰᴀx *(021) 646-3500*. This elegant Italianate villa, built by Orient Express Hotels in 1997, has superb views, valet parking and a golf cart to transport guests. The top restaurant serves northern Mediterranean specialities. 🛏 📺 🍽 🍴 🌿 ♿ 🍷 🅿 🔲	121	■	●	■	●
MAGALIESBURG: *Mount Grace Country House Hotel* ⓇⓇⓇⓇ Magaliesburg, 2805. **Road map** D2. 【 *(014) 577-1350*. ꜰᴀx *(014) 577-1202*. ⓌⓌ www.grace.co.za Country retreat set in 4 ha (10 acres) of exquisite gardens. Newly rebuilt after a devastating fire, the stone and thatch bedrooms include luxury suites with private patios. Superb cuisine and excellent wine list. Enjoy walking, trout fishing, birdwatching, swimming and croquet. 🛏 📺 🍽 ♿ 🅿 🔲	65	■	●		●
MAGALIESBURG: *Valley Lodge* @ res@valleylodge.co.za ⓇⓇⓇⓇ Jennings St, 2805. **Road map** D2. 【 *(014) 577-1301*. ꜰᴀx *(014) 577-1306*. Hospitable country retreat set in 40 ha (100 acres) of gardens on the banks of the Magalies River, an hour's drive from Pretoria. 🛏 📺 🍽 🍴 🅿	60	■	●	■	●
MAGALIESBURG: *De Hoek Country House* ⓇⓇⓇⓇⓇ Portion 7, Zeekoehoek, 2805. **Road map** D2. 【 *(014) 577-1198*. ꜰᴀx *(014) 577-4530*. ⓌⓌ www.dehoek.com This gracious sandstone manor house on the Magalies River is surrounded by gardens and riverine bush. The baronial dining hall boasts an 18-seat mahogany table and the cuisine combines Mediterranean, Swiss and French influences. 🛏 📺 🍽 🌿 🅿 🔲	7	■	●		●
MIDRAND: *Constantia Hotel* @ conhot@global.co.za ⓇⓇⓇ 546 16th Ave, Constantia Park, 1685. **Road map** E2. 【 *(011) 315-5035*. ꜰᴀx *(011) 315-1466*. Provençal-type lodge offering pleasant accommodation or travellers or business executives. Conveniently situated with easy access to the motorways. Swimmingpool and tranquil garden provide soothing relief. 🛏 📺 🍽 🌿 🅿 🔲	34	■		■	●
MIDRAND: *Protea Hotel Landmark Lodge Midrand* ⓇⓇⓇ Samrand, Sterling Street, 1690. **Road map** E2. 【 *(011) 805-3885*. ꜰᴀx *(011) 657-0133*. ⓌⓌ www.proteahotels.com With a swimming pool and sun deck in the park-like grounds, a cosy lounge and comfortable rooms, this hotel offers unrivalled convenience and value for money. 🛏 📺 🍽 🍴 🌿 🅿	112	■	●		●

MIDRAND: *Midrand Protea Hotel* w www.proteahotels.com $\circledR\circledR\circledR\circledR$ 14th St, Noordwyk, 1687. **Road map** E2. [(011) 318-1868. FAX (011) 318-2429. An up-market chain hotel in this busy commercial hub between Sandton and Pretoria, yet retaining an air of tranquillity. Tastefully decorated, using local Rustenburg granite and cherry wood furnishings. 🛏 TV 🖉 🗐 ✄ 🕭 👖 P 🔥	177	■	●	■	●
PILANESBERG: *Tshukudu Lodge* w www.legacyhotels.co.za $\circledR\circledR\circledR\circledR\circledR$ Box 6805, Rustenburg, 0300. **Road map** D2. [(014) 552-6255. FAX (014) 552-6266. Built on a rocky outcrop, this upmarket lodge overlooks a beautiful valley and a waterhole where the animals gather to drink. 🛏 🖉	8	■			
PILANESBERG: NATIONAL PARK: *Bakubung Game Lodge* $\circledR\circledR\circledR\circledR\circledR$ Box 294, Sun City, 0136. **Road map** D2. [(014) 552-6000. FAX (014) 552-6300. w www.legacyhotels.co.za Ensuite, air-conditioned chalets on the edge of the 55,000-ha (136,000-acre) Pilanesberg National Park, which is situated in an ancient volcanic crater. View lion, leopard, cheetah and a variety of antelope. There is a regular shuttle bus to nearby Sun City. 🛏 TV 🖉 🗐 🕭 👖 P 🔥	142	■	●	■	●
PRETORIA: *Brooklyn Lodge* w www.blodge.global.co.za $\circledR\circledR\circledR$ Bronkhorst St, New Muckleneuk, 0181. **Road map** E2. [(012) 460-3936. FAX (012) 460-2988. Located in a shopping complex, this hotel is only a block away from the Austin Roberts Bird Sanctuary. 🛏 TV 🖉 🗐 ✄ P 🔥	10				●
PRETORIA: *Meintjieskop Guesthouse* w www.meiguest.co.za $\circledR\circledR\circledR$ 145 Eastwood St, Arcadia, 0083. **Road map** E2. [(012) 342-0738. FAX (012) 430-4037. Executive accommodation in the heart of Pretoria, 400 m (430 yd) from the Union Buildings, and adjoining the presidential estate. 🛏 TV 🖉 🗐 🕭 P 🔥	8	■			
PRETORIA: *Oxnead Guesthouse* @ oxnead-guesthouse@mweb.co.za $\circledR\circledR\circledR$ Marnewick St, Moreleta Park, 0044. **Road map** E2. [(012) 993-4515. FAX (012) 998-9168. Cape Georgian-style manor, offering exclusivity, good cuisine and fine wines. Easy access to a driving range for golfing enthusiasts. 🛏 TV 🖉 P	10	■		■	
PRETORIA: *La Maison Guesthouse* w www.lamaison.co.za $\circledR\circledR\circledR\circledR$ 235 Hilda St, Hatfield, 0083. **Road map** E2. [(012) 430-4341. FAX (012) 342-1531. This quality establishment, 30 minutes from Johannesburg International Airport, has a wonderful garden with prolific birdlife. 🛏 TV 🖉 🗐 P 🔥	6	■	●	■	●
PRETORIA: *Leriba Lodge & Conference Centre* $\circledR\circledR\circledR\circledR$ End St, Centurion, 0149. **Road map** E2. [(012) 660-3300. FAX (012) 660-2433. w www.leriba.co.za An African-style lodge on the banks of the river in the bushveld, yet only 10 minutes' walk from all amenities. 🛏 TV 🖉 🕭 P 🔥	41	■	●		
PRETORIA: *Whistletree Lodge* @ wtree@icon.co.za $\circledR\circledR\circledR\circledR$ 1267 Whistletree Dr, Queenswood. **Road map** E2. [(012) 333-9915. FAX (012) 333-9917. Set on the slopes of a wooded hill, in a lush landscape of trees, lawns and gardens. Old world charm is combined with a unique modern style. 🛏 TV 🖉 ✄ 🕭 P 🔥	10	■			●
PRETORIA: *Illyria House* w www.illyria.co.za $\circledR\circledR\circledR\circledR\circledR$ 327 Bourke St, Muckleneuk, 0002. **Road map** E2. [(012) 344-5193. FAX (012) 344-3978. Magnificent colonial manor boasting fine antiques, exquisite cuisine and unrivalled personal service. 🛏 TV 🖉 ✄ P 🔥	6	■			●
PRETORIA: *Manor House Tswane* $\circledR\circledR\circledR\circledR\circledR$ 358 Aries St, Waterkloof, 0145. **Road map** E2. [(012) 346-1774. FAX (012) 346-1776. @ marvolmh@global.co.za An exclusive retreat, built in the Cape Dutch style, in a quiet location, 10 km (6 miles) from downtown Pretoria. 🛏 TV 🖉 🗐 ✄ 👖 P	13	■	●	■	●
PRETORIA: *Toadbury Hall* @ enquiries@toadbury.co.za $\circledR\circledR\circledR\circledR\circledR$ Swartkop Rd, Lanseria. **Road map** E2. [(011) 659-0335. FAX (011) 659-0058. A small elegant country hotel set in lush gardens. Gracious rooms with top quality finishes and attention to detail. 🛏 TV 🖉 ✄ 🕭 P 🔥	8	■	●		
ROSEBANK: *The Rosebank Hotel* w www.rosebankhotel.co.za $\circledR\circledR\circledR$ Tyrwhitt Ave, 2196. **Road map** E2. [(011) 447-2700. FAX (011) 447-3276. A long-standing favourite among business travellers, as it is ideally situated for both city centre and the northern suburbs. Live jazz on Saturday nights in the Silver Rose restaurant. 🛏 TV 🖉 🗐 ✄ P	318	■	●	■	
ROSEBANK: *Park Hyatt* w www.johannesburg.park.hyatt.com $\circledR\circledR\circledR\circledR\circledR$ 191 Oxford Rd, 2196. **Road map** E2. [(011) 280-1234. FAX (011) 280-1238. Five-star international hotel, close to shops and restaurants. Sip a sundowner in Jabulani's Bar or relax over coffee and cake in the Conservatory. Regent's Club caters exclusively for businessmen. 🛏 TV 🖉 🗐 ✄ 🕭 👖 P 🔥	244	■	●	■	●

	Number of Rooms	Swimming Pool	Restaurant	Children's Facilities	Garden

Price categories for a standard double room per night including tax and service charges, but not including breakfast:
Ⓡ under R150
ⓇⓇ R150–R300
ⓇⓇⓇ R300–R500
ⓇⓇⓇⓇ R500–R1000
ⓇⓇⓇⓇⓇ over R1000

SWIMMING POOL
These are usually quite small and outdoors.
RESTAURANT
Restaurant on the premises, usually open to non-residents.
CHILDREN'S FACILITIES
Baby-sitting services, cots for small children and play parks are available. Some hotels also provide half portions and high chairs in their restaurants.
GARDEN
Hotel with a garden or terrace.

ROSEBANK: *The Grace* 🔳 www.grace.co.za ⓇⓇⓇⓇ 54 Bath Ave, 2196. **Road map** E2. 📞 *(011) 280-7300.* 📠 *(011) 280-7333.* Elegant five-star hotel in leafy suburb, minutes from city centre and upmarket shopping complexes. High levels of personal service and luxury, including fax modem lines in all bedrooms. Member of the Small Luxury Hotels of the World, affiliated to Cape Town's Cape Grace and Magaliesberg's Mount Grace. There are also 12 suites, three penthouse suites. 🛏 📺 🔲 🔳 🔲 🔲 🔲 **P** 🔲	75	▦	●	▦	●
SANDTON: *Holiday Inn Garden Court* 🔳 www.southernsun.com ⓇⓇ 1 Cullinan Cl, Morningside, 2146. **Road map** E2. 📞 *(011) 884-1804.* 📠 *(011) 884-6040.* This inn offers affordable luxury with a marvellous swimming pool area, close to the heart of Sandton. 🛏 📺 🔲 🔳 🔲 🔲 **P** 🔲	150	▦	●	▦	●
SANDTON: *Town Lodge Sandton* 🔳 www.citylodge.co.za ⓇⓇ Grayston Dr & Webber rd, 2146. **Road map** E2. 📞 *(011) 784-8850.* 📠 *(011) 784-8888.* Functionality and efficiency are the hallmarks of this chain. Perfect for the business traveller or for overnight stops. 🛏 📺 🔲 🔳 🔲 🔲 **P**	142	▦		▦	
SANDTON: *City Lodge Morningside* 🔳 www.citylodge.co.za ⓇⓇⓇ Cnr Rivonia & Hill rds, 2146. **Road map** E2. 📞 *(011) 884-9500.* 📠 *(011) 884-9440.* Affordable quality accommodation in the heart of one of Johannesburg's most fashionable suburbs. Close to exclusive shops and restaurants. Children sharing with parents stay free. 🛏 📺 🔲 🔳 🔲 🔲 **P**	161	▦	●	▦	
SANDTON: *Holiday Inn Hotel & Suites* 🔳 www.southernsun.com ⓇⓇⓇ 115 Katherine St, Sandown, 2146. **Road map** E2. 📞 *(011) 884-8544.* 📠 *(011) 884-8545.* French colonial elegance close to Sandton CBD, shops and entertainment. Easy access from freeway. 🛏 📺 🔲 🔳 🔲 🔲 **P** 🔲	122	▦	●	▦	●
SANDTON: *Zulu Nyala Country Manor* 🔳 www.zulunyala.co.za ⓇⓇⓇⓇ 70E Third Rd, Chartwell, 2146. **Road map** E2. 📞 *(011) 708-1969.* 📠 *(011) 708-2220.* A thatched country manor set in 2-ha (6-acre) estate on the outskirts of Sandton, within easy reach of the airport. The Lion Park is also close by. Comfortable, spacious rooms and warm hospitality. 🛏 📺 🔲 🔲 **P** 🔲	16	▦			●
SANDTON: *The Michelangelo* 🔳 www.legacyhotels.co.za ⓇⓇⓇⓇⓇ Sandton Square, 2146. **Road map** E2. 📞 *(011) 282-7000.* 📠 *(011) 282-7170.* Prestigious five-star Renaissance-style hotel set in a piazza featuring a host of upmarket shops and restaurants. Discreet, quality service and the sort of attention to detail one expects from a top-class hotel. Gourmet African cuisine that blends flavours from across the continent. 🛏 📺 🔲 🔳 🔲 🔲 🔲 **P** 🔲	242	▦	●	▦	
SANDTON: *Sandton Sun Inter-Continental* ⓇⓇⓇⓇⓇ Fifth St, Sandton, 2146. **Road map** E2. 📞 *(086) 144-7744.* 📠 *(011) 780-5002.* @ joburg@interconti.com Luxury glass-and-marble five-star hotel adjacent to Sandton City, the largest shopping complex in Africa. Four themed restaurants: African, Mediterranean, Portuguese and high-quality Japanese. 🛏 📺 🔲 🔳 🔲 🔲 🔲 **P** 🔲	564	▦	●		
SUN CITY: *Sun City Hotel, Cascades and Cabanas* ⓇⓇⓇⓇ Box 2, 0316. **Road map** D2. 📞 *(011) 780-7800.* 📠 *(011) 780-7443.* 🔳 www.suninternational.com Accommodation in three different venues at the hub of the complex, close to the entertainment centre and casino. The Cabanas are suitable for families. The luxury five-star Cascades and Main Hotel both offer direct access to the complex's many facilities. Water is a special feature of the Cascades, which is surrounded by pools. 🛏 📺 🔲 🔳 🔲 🔲 🔲 **P** 🔲	340	▦	●	▦	●
SUN CITY: *The Palace of the Lost City* ⓇⓇⓇⓇⓇ Box 308, 0316. **Road map** D2. 📞 *(011) 780-7800.* 📠 *(011) 780-7443.* 🔳 www.suninternational.com Spectacular architecture recreates an ancient African fantasy temple, rising out of a subtropical jungle, complete with animal statuary and exotic works of art. Ultimate luxury and hospitality. 🛏 📺 🔲 🔳 🔲 🔲 🔲 **P** 🔲	338	▦	●	▦	●

SWAZILAND: *Mlilwane Lodge* Ⓦ www.biggame.co.sz   ⓇⓇ 22
Mlilwane Wildlife Sanctuary. **Road map** F2. 【 *(09268) 528-3992.* FAX *(09268) 528-3924.*
Accommodation is in chalets, a choice of 16 traditional beehive huts or
an inexpensive youth hostel, all situated right in the sanctuary. 🛏 🖫

SWAZILAND: *Malolotja Lodge* @ malolotja@sntc.org.sz   ⓇⓇⓇ 37
Malolotja Nature Reserve. **Road map** F2. 【 *(09268) 416-1151.* FAX *(09268) 416-1480.*
Apart from the 15 campsites and five rustic log cabins at the main camp, a
further 17 campsites throughout the scenic reserve cater for self-sufficient
hikers. The shop at the main gate sells basic provisions. 🛏 🖫

SWAZILAND: *Tavern Inn* @ headoffice@ninggroup.com   ⓇⓇⓇ 16
Cnr Allister Miller and Gilfillian sts, Mbabane. **Road map** F2. 【 *(09268) 404-2361.*
FAX *09268) 404-2469.* Centrally situated, this Tudor-style hotel consists of private,
self-catering apartments, and is a perfect base for exploring Mbabane. 🛏 🖫

SWAZILAND: *Ezulwini Sun* Ⓦ www.suninternational.com   ⓇⓇⓇⓇ 120
Between Mbabane & Manzini. **Road map** F2. 【 *(09268) 416-6800.* FAX *(09268) 416-1782.*
This comfortable family hotel in the picturesque Ezulwini valley is
signposted from the Oshoek/Ngwenya border post. 🛏 TV 🖫 📋 ⛤ P

VANDERBIJLPARK: *Riverside Sun* Ⓦ www.southernsun.com   ⓇⓇ 169
Kemmons Wilson Dr, 1900. **Road map** E2. 【 *(016) 932-1111.* FAX *(016) 932-1348.*
Modern resort hotel on the banks of the Vaal River. Enjoy boating and
water-skiing facilities or relax at the pool. 🛏 TV 🖫 📋 ⛤ ⛳ P 🗲

VEREENIGING: *Riviera International Hotel*   ⓇⓇⓇ 104
Maria Milani Dr, 1930. **Road map** E2. 【 & FAX *(016) 420-1300.*
Ⓦ www.rivieraonvaal.co.za Country club with full sporting facilities including an
18-hole golf course. On the banks of the Vaal River. 🛏 TV 🖫 📋 ⛤ P

BLYDE RIVER CANYON AND KRUGER

DULLSTROOM: *Walkersons* Ⓦ www.walkersons.co.za   ⓇⓇⓇⓇ 20
Waboomkop–Lydenburg Rd. **Road map** E2. 【 *(013) 254-0999.* FAX *(013) 254-0262.*
Luxury stone-and-thatch lodge set in 600-ha (1,500-acre) estate in the heart of
flyfishing country. Bedrooms all have lake views and fireplaces. Enjoy fishing
for rainbow trout on private river and lakes. Equipment provided. TV 🖫 🗲

GRASKOP: *The Graskop Hotel* Ⓦ www.graskophotel.co.za   ⓇⓇⓇ 41
3 Main St, 1270. **Road map** F2. 【 & FAX *(013) 767-1244.*
Comfortable hotel with ethnic decor, within easy reach of the superb sights of
the area, including God's Window, Pilgrim's Rest and the Blyde River Canyon.
Crafts studio and gallery on site. 🛏 TV 🖫 ⛤ 🗲

HAENERTSBURG: *Glenshiel Country Lodge*   ⓇⓇⓇⓇ 15
R71 to Magoebaskloof, 0730. **Road map** E1. 【 *(015) 276-4335.* FAX *(015) 276-4338.*
@ info@glenshiel.co.za Owner-managed retreat on a scenic farm, bordering on the
Ebenezer Dam. Suites open onto the gardens and have fireplaces for cold nights.
Rolling hills, tea and tropical fruit plantations, forests and magnificent gardens.
Perfect for walking, trout fishing and bird watching. 🛏 TV 🖫 ⛤ ⛳ P 🗲

HAZYVIEW: *Chestnut Country Lodge*   ⓇⓇⓇⓇ 9
Emmet Rd, Kiepersol, 1241. **Road map** F2. 【 *(013) 737-8195.* FAX *(013) 737-8196.*
@ reservations@chestnutlodge.co.za Renovated farmhouse in a lush garden teeming
with birdlife. Wonderful views, country cooking and good walks. 🛏 🖫 📋 P 🗲

HAZYVIEW: *Sabi River Sun* Ⓦ www.southernsun.com   ⓇⓇⓇⓇ 60
Main Rd, Perry's Farm, 1242. **Road map** F2. 【 *(013) 737-7311.* FAX *(013) 737-7314.*
Situated 20 km (12 miles) from the Kruger National Park, this comfortable
hotel has a golf course, bowling greens, squash and tennis courts and
five swimming pools. 🛏 TV 🖫 📋 ⛤ P

HAZYVIEW: *Highgrove House* @ highgrove@ns.lia.net   ⓇⓇⓇⓇⓇ 8
R40. Box 46, Kiepersol, 1241. **Road map** F2. 【 *(013) 764-1844.* FAX *(013) 764-1855.*
Colonial-style, award-winning lodge offers easy access to the area's many
panoramic drives and wildlife reserves. A pastoral setting, gourmet cuisine
and excellent wine list have earned international acclaim. 🛏 🖫 P

HAZYVIEW: *Umbhaba Lodge* @ reservations@umbhaba.com   ⓇⓇⓇⓇⓇ 23
Box 1677, 1242. **Road map** F2. 【 *(013) 737-7636.* FAX *(013) 737-7629.*
Luxuriously appointed lodge, set in magnificent subtropical gardens, close to
the many scenic wonders of the area. Fishing, horse riding and hiking can be
arranged and children are welcome. 🛏 TV 🖫 🗲 P 🗲

For key to symbols see back flap

Price categories for a standard double room per night including tax and service charges, but not including breakfast:
Ⓡ under R150
ⓇⓇ R150–R300
ⓇⓇⓇ R300–R500
ⓇⓇⓇⓇ R500–R1000
ⓇⓇⓇⓇⓇ over R1000

SWIMMING POOL
These are usually quite small and outdoors.

RESTAURANT
Restaurant on the premises, usually open to non-residents.

CHILDREN'S FACILITIES
Baby-sitting services, cots for small children and play parks are available. Some hotels also provide half portions and high chairs in their restaurants.

GARDEN
Hotel with a garden or terrace.

	NUMBER OF ROOMS	SWIMMING POOL	RESTAURANT	CHILDREN'S FACILITIES	GARDEN
HENDRIKSDAL: *Artist's Cafe and Guesthouse* ⓇⓇⓇ Hendriksdal Siding, Sabie. **Road map** F2. 📞 & ☎ FAX *(013) 764-2309.* @ artscafe@mweb.co.za Restaurant and accommodation in the converted rooms of this former station, built circa 1920. 🔧 🏛 & 🅿	4		●		■
KRUGER NATIONAL PARK: *Public Camps* 🌐 www.sanparks.co.za ⓇⓇⓇ Box 787, Pretoria, 0001. **Road map** F2. 📞 *(012) 428-9111.* FAX *(012) 343-0905.* @ reservations@saparks.co.za Bookings via head offices in Pretoria or Jo'burg. *Balule:* (Central) Six three-bed rondavels; barbeque sites; no electricity. 🅰 *Berg-en-Dal:* (South) Six-bed bungalows; three-bed rondavels; two cottages; laundry facilities and an information centre. 🔧 & 🏛 🅰 *Crocodile Bridge:* (South) Camp with about 20 three-bed bungalows. 🏛 🅰 & *Letaba:* (Central) Large camp with bungalows, rondavels and cottages, as well as an auto repair workshop and an education centre. 🔧 & 🏛 *Lower Sabie:* (South) Bungalows, rondavels and cottages. 🔧 & 🏛 *Mopani:* (North) Three-bed rondavels and six-bed cottages. 🔧 🏛 *Olifants:* (Central) Thatched bungalows and cottages, as well as an information centre, a petrol station, a museum and an amphitheatre. 🔧 🏛 *Orpen:* (Central) Small camp with two- and three-bed bungalows. 🏛 🅰 *Pretoriuskop:* (South) Bungalows, rondavels and cottages. 🔧 & 🏛 *Punda Maria:* (North) Family bungalows, two- and three-bed cottages. 🏛 *Satara:* (Central) Large camp with family bungalows, as well as rondavels and cottages. There's an auto repair workshop and petrol station. 🔧 & 🏛 *Shingwedzi:* (North) Large camp with bungalows and rondavels. 🔧 🏛 *Skukuza:* (South) The largest camp, with bungalows, rondavels and cottages, as well as banking facilities and a doctor's surgery. 🔧 & 🏛 ✉		■ ■ ■ ■ ■ ■ ■	● ● ● ● ● ● ● ● ●		
KRUGER NATIONAL PARK: *Bushveld Camps* ⓇⓇⓇ *Bateleur:* (North) Small camp with 10 self-catering cottages. 🔧 *Mbyamiti:* (South) Fifteen self-catering family cottages. 🔧 *Sirheni:* (North) Fifteen self-catering family cottages. 🔧 *Shimuwini:* (North) Six self-catering cottages. 🔧 *Talamati:* (Central) Fifteen self-catering family cottages. 🔧					
KRUGER NATIONAL PARK: *Private Camps* ⓇⓇⓇⓇⓇ *Boulders:* (North) Four two-bed bungalows and one cottage. 🔧 *Malelane:* (South) Five luxury cottages can accommodate 18 visitors. 🔧 *Nwanetsi:* (Central) This camp caters for 16 persons. 🔧 *Roodewal:* (Central) A 19-person camp with communal kitchen facilities. 🔧					
MAGOEBASKLOOF: *Magoebaskloof Hotel* ⓇⓇⓇ Between Pietersburg & Tzaneen. **Road map** E1. 📞 *(015) 276-4776.* FAX *(015) 276-4780.* @ enquiries@magoebaskloof.co.za Affordable yet comfortable accommodation in a scenic mountain location. Access to several hikes and walks. 🔧 📺 🍽 💈 🅿 🛗	60	■	●	■	
MALELANE: *Buhala Game Lodge* 🌐 www.buhala.co.za ⓇⓇⓇⓇⓇ N4. Box 165, Malelane, 1320. **Road map** F2. 📞 *(013) 792-4372.* FAX *(013) 792-4306.* Colonial-style comfort awaits the visitor in this grass-thatched guest-house overlooking the Crocodile River and fenced into the Kruger National Park. 🔧 🍽 💈 🅿 🛗	7	■			
MALELANE: *Malelane Sun Inter-Continental Lodge* ⓇⓇⓇⓇⓇ Riverside Farm. Box 392, 1320. **Road map** F2. 📞 *(013) 792-3304.* FAX *(013) 792-3303.* 🌐 www.southernsun.com Individual thatched chalets on the Crocodile River, only a few minutes' drive from the Kruger National Park. Ideal resort-type accommodation for visitors unable to obtain a place in the park itself. 🔧 🍽 💈 🍴 & 🅿 🛗	102	■	●	■	●
NELSPRUIT: *Holiday Inn Express* 🌐 www.southernsun.com ⓇⓇ White River Rd, 1200. **Road map** F2. 📞 *(086) 144-7744.* FAX *(013) 757-0008.* Simple no-frills accommodation for travellers who wish to overnight en route to the Kruger National Park. 🔧 🍽 💈 🅿 🛗	89	■	■		●

NYLSTROOM (MODIMOLLE): *Protea Hotel Shangri-La Lodge* ®®® | 34
Eersbewoond Rd, 0570. **Road map** E2. ((014) 717-5381. FAX (014) 717-3188.
W www.proteahotels.com Family-run country retreat 15 km (9 miles) from
Nylstroom. Thatched rondavels surround a sparkling pool. ⬛ TV 🗌 P 🗌

PILGRIM'S REST: *Crystal Springs Mountain Lodge* ®®® | 164
Box 10, Pilgrim's Rest, 1290. **Road map** F2. ((013) 768-5000. FAX (013) 768-5024.
W www.crystalsprings.co.za Individual, self-catering cottages situated within a
game reserve high above Pilgrim's Rest. Tennis and squash courts, mini-golf and
a gym surround an indoor heated pool and Jacuzzi area. ⬛ TV 🗌 🗌 P 🗌

PILGRIM'S REST: *Inn on Robber's Pass* ®®® | 9
Box 76, 1290. **Road map** F2. ((013) 768-1491. FAX (013) 768-1386.
@ innonrp@global.co.za Quaint accommodation in converted stables, 17 km
(10 miles) from Pilgrim's Rest. Tranquil haven for nature lovers. ⬛ 🗌 P 🗌

PILGRIM'S REST: *Mount Sheba Country Lodge* ®®®® | 25
Box 100, Pilgrim's Rest, 1290. **Road map** F2. ((013) 768-1241. FAX (013) 768-1248.
W www.mountsheba.co.za On a plateau 25 km (15.5 miles) from Pilgrim's Rest.
Surrounded by indigenous forest with walking trails and trout dams. Clear
air, mountain mists and spectacular scenery. ⬛ TV 🗌 🗌 P 🗌

PILGRIM'S REST: *Royal Hotel* W www.royal-hotel.co.za ®®® | 50
Main Rd, 1290. **Road map** F2. ((013) 768-1100. FAX (013) 768-1188.
The tin and wood buildings of this national monument date from the 1900s.
Enjoy home-style cooking and explore the historic town. ⬛ 🗌 🗌 🗌 🗌 P 🗌

SABIE SAND RESERVE: *Chitwa Chitwa* ®®®®® | 14
PO Box 781854, Sandton. **Road map** F2. ((013) 735-5357. FAX (013) 735-5595.
Chitwa Chitwa offers a relaxed atmosphere along with a sophisticated style. Superbly
located infront of the dam where guests can view game. ⬛ 🗌 🗌 🗌 🗌 P 🗌

SABIE SAND RESERVE: *Idube Game Reserve* ®®®®® | 10
Box 2617, Northcliff, 2115. **Road map** F2. ((011) 888-3713. FAX (013) 735-5432.
W www.idube.com Thatched chalets on stilts have private open-air showers,
air conditioning and fans. Twice daily game drives to view lion, leopard and
cheetah. Price includes all meals, game drives and bush walks. ⬛ 🗌 🗌 🗌 P

SABIE SAND RESERVE: *Sabi Sabi* W www.sabisabi.com ®®®®® | 57
Box 52665, Saxonwold, 2132. **Road map** F2. ((011) 483-3939. FAX (011) 483-3799.
This multi-award-winning establishment has three unique rest camps,
Bush, River and Selati, each of which offers the ultimate, luxury safari
experience. Experienced guides accompany visitors on day and night
game-viewing drives in open vehicles. Fully inclusive. ⬛ 🗌 🗌 P 🗌

SABIE SAND RESERVE: *Singita Private Game Reserve* ®®®®® | 18
Box 650881, Benmore, 2010. **Road map** F2. ((021) 683-3424. FAX (021) 683-3502.
W www.singita.com Ebony and Boulders lodges offer exceptional standards
and luxury. Gourmet cuisine, extensive wine cellar, day and night drives
and walking safaris. Member of Relais et Châteaux. ⬛ 🗌 🗌 🗌 P

SABIE SAND RESERVE: *Ulusaba Private Game Reserve* ®®®®® | 20
Box 239, Lonehill, 2062. **Road map** F2. ((011) 465-4240. FAX (011) 465-6649.
@ safaris@ulusaba.com Sweeping views from Rock Lodge, forest shade at Safari
Lodge. Ethnic ambience with subtle sophistication is the hallmark of this
upmarket lodge. ⬛ 🗌 🗌 P

SCHOEMANSKLOOF: *Old Joe's Kaia Country Lodge* ®®®® | 14
Schoemanskloof Valley Rd, 1207. **Road map** F2. ((013) 733-3045. FAX (013) 733-3777.
W www.oldjoes.co.za A choice of log cabins and rondavels decorated in African
colonial style. Superb birdwatching – over 170 species have been observed.
Relax in sub-tropical gardens, or at the pool. All-inclusive tariff. ⬛ 🗌 P

TIMBAVATI PRIVATE GAME RESERVE: *King's Camp* ®®®®® | 10
Box 427, Nelspruit, 1200. **Road map** F2. ((015) 793-3633. FAX (015) 793-3634.
W www.kingscamp.com An unbeatable, if pricey, Africa experience is offered by
this exclusive camp. Air-conditioned thatched bungalows; and day and night game
drives in open vehicles to view the "Big Five". Tariff is all-inclusive. ⬛ 🗌 🗌 🗌

TIMBAVATI PRIVATE GAME RESERVE: *Motswari Camp* ®®®®® | 15
Box 67865, Bryanston, 2021. **Road map** F2. ((011) 463-1990. FAX (011) 463-1992.
W www.motswari.co.za Thatch, timber and canvas tree houses on stilts in a
luxury camp. Private verandahs overlook the lake. Game drives in open vehicles,
walks with experienced guides and fine cuisine are highlights. ⬛ 🗌 P 🗌

For key to symbols see back flap

		NUMBER OF ROOMS	SWIMMING POOL	RESTAURANT	CHILDREN'S FACILITIES	GARDEN

Price categories for a standard double room per night including tax and service charges, but not including breakfast:
ℝ under R150
ℝℝ R150–R300
ℝℝℝ R300–R500
ℝℝℝℝ R500–R1000
ℝℝℝℝℝ over R1000

SWIMMING POOL
These are usually quite small and outdoors.
RESTAURANT
Restaurant on the premises, usually open to non-residents.
CHILDREN'S FACILITIES
Baby-sitting services, cots for small children and play parks are available. Some hotels also provide half portions and high chairs in their restaurants.
GARDEN
Hotel with a garden or terrace.

	NUMBER OF ROOMS	SWIMMING POOL	RESTAURANT	CHILDREN'S FACILITIES	GARDEN
TIMBAVATI PRIVATE GAME RESERVE: *Tanda Tula Safari Camp* ℝℝℝℝℝ Box 32, Constantia, 7848. **Road map** F2. (*(015) 793-3191.* FAX *(015) 793-0496.* @ tandatula@worldonline.co.za Luxury tented camp in this exclusive reserve near Kruger Park. Each suite has its own wooden deck overlooking the bush. 🛏 🍴	12	▪			
TZANEEN: *Coach House* w www.coachhouse.co.za ℝℝℝ Old Coach Rd, Agatha, 0850. **Road map** E1. (*(015) 306-8000.* FAX *(015) 306-8008.* Built in 1892 to serve travellers en route to the coast. Spectacular setting on a high plateau. Individual chalets set in beautiful gardens. The 8000-bottle wine cellar on the premises is an attraction in itself. 🛏 📺 🍴 ♿ 🍴 P	47	▪	●		●
WATERVAL ONDER: *Bergwaters Lodge* w www.bergwaters.co.za ℝℝ Box 71, 1195. **Road map** F2. (& FAX *(013) 257-7059.* Stone building dating to the Anglo-Boer War. Affordable accommodation close to the area's many sites. Flyfishing can be arranged. 🛏 📺 🍴 🍴 P	13	▪	●		●
WHITE RIVER: *Kirby Country Lodge* ℝℝℝ Jatinga Rd, 1240. **Road map** F2. (*(013) 751-2645.* FAX *(013) 750-1836.* w www.kirbycountrylodge.co.za Tranquil thatched lodge set in large woodland gardens, home to a variety of birds. Only 25 minutes' drive from Kruger Park. 🛏 🍴 P	10	▪			●
WHITE RIVER: *Hulala Lakeside Lodge* w www.hulala.co.za ℝℝℝ R40. 23 km (14 miles) past White River. **Road map** F2. (*(013) 764-1893.* FAX *(013) 764-1864.* Tranquil lakeside setting amid bushveld scenery. Birdwatching, boating and fishing. Children over 10 welcome. 🛏 🍴 P	21	▪	●	▪	
WHITE RIVER: *Jatinga Country Lodge* w www.jatinga.co.za ℝℝℝ Jatinga Rd, 1240. **Road map** F2. (*(013) 751-5059.* FAX *(013) 751-5119.* The thatched cottages on the banks of the White River are ideal for exploring the nearby game reserves. The restaurant uses fruit and vegetables from the garden to cater for diabetics and vegetarians. 🛏 📺 🍴 P	14	▪	●		●
WHITE RIVER: *Cybele Forest Lodge* w www.cybele.co.za ℝℝℝℝℝ R40. Box 346, White River, 1240. **Road map** F2. (*(013) 764-1823.* FAX *(013) 764-9510.* Exclusive country retreat in the heart of the forest, with antiques, art and exquisite fabrics. Spectacular mountain views, trout rivers and stables, and gourmet cuisine. All-inclusive tariff. 🛏 📺 🍴 ♿ P	12	▪	●		●

SOUTH OF THE ORANGE

	NUMBER OF ROOMS	SWIMMING POOL	RESTAURANT	CHILDREN'S FACILITIES	GARDEN
BEAUFORT WEST: *Hotel Formule 1* ℝℝ 144 Donkin Rd, 6970. **Road map** C4. (*(023) 415-2421.* FAX *(023) 415-2358.* Chain hotel offering no-frills basics for budget travellers. 🛏 📺 🍴 P	52				
BEAUFORT WEST: *Matoppo Inn* w www.matoppoinn.mrinfo.co.za ℝℝℝ 7 Bird St, 6970. **Road map** C4. (*(023) 415-1055.* FAX *(023) 415-1080.* Historic residence (1834) with yellowwood floors, high wooded ceilings and fine antiques, 2 km (1 mile) from the Karoo National Park. 🛏 📺 🍴 ♿ P	9	▪	●		
COLESBERG: *Sunset Chalets* @ sunset99@telkomsa.net ℝℝ 14 Torenberg St, 9795. **Road map** C4. (*(082) 493-8814.* FAX *(051) 753-0589.* Newly built accommodation close to shops, restaurant and golf course. 🛏 P	15			▪	
COLESBERG: *Kuilfontein Stable Cottages* w www.kuilfontein.co.za ℝℝℝ N1. Box 17, 9795. **Road map** C4. (*(051) 753-1364.* FAX *(051) 753 0200.* The stable block of this historic racehorse stud and sheep farm (in the family since 1876) has been converted to Provençal-style accommodation. 🛏 🍴	5	▪	●		
CRADOCK: *Die Tuishuise* w www.tuishuise.co.za ℝℝℝ 36 Market St, 5880. **Road map** D5. (*(048) 881-1322.* FAX *(048) 881-5388.* Cottages built in the 1840s have been carefully restored to depict 19th-century Karoo architecture. Die Tuishuise is near the Mountain Zebra National Park and the Olive Schreiner Museum. 🛏 📺 🍴 P	27		●	▪	

GRAAFF-REINET: *Drostdy Hotel* W www.drostdy.co.za   ⓡⓡⓡ   55
30 Church St, 6280. **Road map** C4. ⓒ (049) 892-2161. ⒻⒶⓍ (049) 892-4582.
Quaint accommodation in an historic gabled building in a former frontier town.
Built in 1806 as the residence of an early magistrate *(landdrost)*, the building
exudes charm. The suites are restored labourers' cottages. 🏠 📺 🅢 🗒 🅿 🛁

GRAAFF-REINET: *Andries Stockenstrom Guest House*   ⓡⓡⓡⓡⓡ   6
100 Cradock St, 6280. **Road map** C4. ⓒ & ⒻⒶⓍ (049) 892-4575.
W www.stockenstrom.co.za Comfortable accommodation in a Georgian house in
the historic town of Graaff-Reinet. Food is a passion here and owner/chef
Beatrice Barnard's dinners are legendary. 🏠 🅢 🗒 🅗 🅿 🛁

NORTH OF THE ORANGE

ALLEMANSKRAAL DAM: *Africa's Aldam Resort*   ⓡⓡⓡ   68
N1. P/Bag X06, Ventersburg, 9450. **Road map** D3. ⓒ (057) 652-2200. ⒻⒶⓍ (057) 652-0014.
One of a chain of self-catering inland resorts around dams, rivers and
hot springs. It caters for families and has various sports facilities. 🅿

AUGRABIES NATIONAL PARK: *Kalahari Adventure Centre*   ⓡ   8
10 km (6 miles) from Augrabies Falls National Park. **Road map** B3. ⓒ (054) 451 0177.
ⒻⒶⓍ (054) 451-0218. @ reservations@parks.sa.co.za Inexpensive hotel for guests wishing
to stay near the Augrabies Falls and the Kakamas wine cellars. 🗒 🅿

BLOEMFONTEIN: *De Oude Kraal* W www.oudekraal.co.za   ⓡⓡⓡ   8
35 km (22 miles) N of city on N1 South, 9325. **Road map** D3. ⓒ (051) 564-0636.
ⒻⒶⓍ (051) 564-0635. Rustic accommodation in a restored farmhouse that formed
part of a farm, which originally belonged to the Griqua tribe. 🏠 📺 🅢 🅿 🛁

BLOEMFONTEIN: *Hobbit House* W www.hobbit.co.za   ⓡⓡⓡ   12
19 President Steyn Ave, 9301. **Road map** D3. ⓒ & ⒻⒶⓍ (051) 447-0663.
This award-winning Victorian-style double-storey guesthouse was named in
honour of JRR Tolkien's book *The Hobbit*. Situated in a quiet residential area
yet close to the city, with a swimming pool and cosy pub. 🏠 📺 🅢 🗒 🗒 🅿

BLOEMFONTEIN: *Bains Game Lodge* @ chaletpark@mweb.co.za   ⓡⓡⓡ   124
Kimberley Rd, Bainsulei, 9305. **Road map** D3. ⓒ & ⒻⒶⓍ (051) 451-1761.
In the heart of the Free State, just outside Bloemfontein, this site has
log cabins, chalets and camping facilities. It offers the perfect blend of
clean, high veld air with city convenience. 🏠 📺 🅢 🗒 🅿 🛁

GARIEP DAM: *Gariep Dam Hotel*   ⓡⓡⓡ   23
N1. PO 20, Gariep Dam, 9922. **Road map** D4. ⓒ (051) 754-0060. ⒻⒶⓍ (051) 754-0268.
The hotel provides a welcome break if travelling from Gauteng to the Cape.
Clean, comfortable accommodation without frills. 🏠 📺 🅢 🗒 🗒 🅗 🅿 🛁

KALAHARI: *Molopo Kalahari Lodge* W www.molopolodge.co.za   ⓡⓡⓡ   35
R31 (near Kgalagadi Transfrontier Park). **Road map** B2. ⓒ & ⒻⒶⓍ (054) 511-0008.
Only 60 km (37 miles) from the red sands of the Kalahari, the hotel offers
guests the opportunity to enjoy the peaceful scenery and the spectacular
moonlit nights of the desert. 🏠 🅢 🅗 🅿

KALAHARI: *Tswalu Kalahari Reserve* W www.tswalu.com   ⓡⓡⓡⓡⓡ   9
N14 (near Kuruman). **Road map** C2. ⓒ (021) 426-4137/9. ⒻⒶⓍ (021) 426-4150.
A 100,000-ha (247,000-acre) private wildlife reserve at the southern
tip of the Kalahari Desert, offering game drives, bushwalks
and horse riding. 🏠 🅢 🗒 🅗 🅿 🛁

KIMBERLEY: *Protea Hotel Diamond Lodge* W www.proteahotels.com   ⓡⓡ   32
124 Du Toitspan Rd, 8300. **Road map** D3. ⓒ (053) 831-1281. ⒻⒶⓍ (053) 831-1284.
This comfortable family hotel offers value-for-money accommodation in
the vicinity of the Big Hole and Mine Museum. 🏠 📺 🅢 🗒 🗒 🅿 🛁

KIMBERLEY: *Edgerton House* @ edgerton@mweb.co.za   ⓡⓡⓡ   12
5 Edgerton Rd, 8300. **Road map** D3. ⓒ (053) 831-1150. ⒻⒶⓍ (053) 831-1871.
Located in the historical part of town, across the road from the McGregor
Museum, this lovingly restored 98-year-old building offers comfortable
accommodation in garden rooms. There is a swimming pool on the premises
and a tea garden. Lunch and dinner by arrangement. 🏠 📺 🅢 🗒 🗒 🅗 🅿 🛁

UPINGTON: *Protea Hotel Upington* W www.proteahotels.com   ⓡⓡⓡ   57
24 Schroder St, 8801. **Road map** B3. ⓒ (054) 337-8500. ⒻⒶⓍ (054) 337-8499.
This modern hotel in central Upington is a good stop en route to the Kgalagadi
Transfrontier and Augrabies Falls national parks. 🏠 📺 🅢 🗒 🗒 🅿 🛁

WHERE TO EAT

SOUTH AFRICA has a wide variety of restaurants and eateries, from franchise steakhouses and sizzling street-corner *boerewors* stands to elegant business venues and seafood, Oriental, French and Mediterranean-style restaurants. Whenever the weather is fine, eating is done outside, and coffee shops do a roaring trade. African eateries for the Western palate are found in the cities, while some township tours *(see p364)* include traditional meals. South Africa's multi-cultural heritage is also evident in the proliferation of Indian restaurants and stalls serving spicy eastern and Kwa-Zulu-Natal-style curries. In the Western Cape, fragrant, sweet Malay curries are popular quick lunches and in the winelands, more formal fare.

Mr. DELIVERY

Home delivery service

Village Walk in Sandton, Gauteng

SOUTH AFRICAN EATING PATTERNS

RESTAURANTS ARE most likely to be open for lunch from Mondays to Fridays and for dinner from Tuesdays to Sundays. It is common to find restaurants closed on Mondays (Italian restaurants often close on Tuesdays). Coffee shops are open during the day, usually from 9am to 5pm, and serve breakfasts, light lunches and teas. For breakfasts, try the traditional cooked dish of eggs, bacon and sausages. Healthy muffins (also available at supermarkets, delis and even petrol-station stores) such as bran, banana and date are popular, too. Salads, open sandwiches and quiches are good choices for lunch, while cakes (carrot, chocolate and cheese) are usual afternoon-tea fare. Dinner is the main meal of the day, served from 6:30pm to 10pm. In the urban areas, bars, popular restaurants and fast-food outlets stay open until midnight or even later.

PLACES TO EAT

YOU CAN ALWAYS EAT WELL in the cities and in the well-visited outlying and country areas and smaller towns.

The annual guide, *Eat Out* magazine, available at newsagents, recommends restaurants nationwide, while the monthly listings magazine *SA City Life* lists places in Durban, Johannesburg and Cape Town.

BOOKING AHEAD

IT IS BEST to phone ahead and reserve a table in order to avoid disappointment.

Established or fashionable venues may be booked up for weeks in advance. If you cannot keep a reservation, call the restaurant and cancel.

PRICES AND TIPPING

EATING OUT in South Africa is usually inexpensive. The average price of a three-course meal for one (excluding wine and a tip) at a good restaurant is about R100–120. But certain items, such as seafood, can increase the total substantially. A freshly-made deli sandwich with delicious fillings will seldom cost more than R20, while a large, hearty breakfast costs around R40.

Tipping should always be based on service. If simply average, leave 10 per cent; if excellent, 15 per cent. Tips are sometimes placed in a communal jar near the cashier.

Seafood *braai* at a *skerm* (sheltered barbecue area) on the West Coast

WHAT TO EAT

TRY TO VISIT one of the
African, Indian (in Kwa-
Zulu-Natal) or Malay (in
Cape Town) restaurants in
the cities. If you're at the
coast, don't miss the
delicious seafood –
calamari, mussels, tuna,
crayfish, yellowtail and
kabeljou (cob). On the
West Coast there are
scenic open-air seafood
braais (barbecues).
The cities and larger
towns offer excellent
international cuisine:
Portuguese, Thai, Indo-
nesian, Italian, Greek,
French and Chinese. There
are also typical South African
restaurants, where traditional
fare and drinks like *witblits*,
strong spirit distilled from
peaches, are served.

**Witblits
(peach brandy)**

South Africa is a meat-loving
nation; beef steaks are good,
and franchise steakhouses
offer great value for money;
the selection of substantial
salads and vegetable dishes
will satisfy vegetarians, too.
Boerewors (spicy-sausage) on
a bread-roll can be bought
from informal street vendors.
At someone's home, you
might sample a South African
meat *braai (see p17)*, or barbecue. Pizza chains are very
popular and offer good value.

WINE CHOICES

SOUTH AFRICAN wines offer
something for everybody,
and most restaurants stock a
mainstream selection of local
labels – usually with a significant price mark-up. Many
serve a great variety: from
easy-drinking wines to vintage
bottlings. Some venues offer a
choice of bottled wines by
the glass, although house
wines are, more usually, from
an inexpensive 5-litre box.
Fine-dining venues provide
an international winelist, and
the better Italian eateries, for
example, offer Italian wines.
Corkage (from R10) is charged
if you bring your own bottle.

DELIVERY SERVICES

IN THE CITIES and larger towns
food-delivery services are
popular. The company known
as "Mr Delivery" is contracted
to a variety of eateries and
restaurants (not only fast-food
outlets) and will deliver hot
food, for a reasonable fee,
during lunch times and
from early to late evening.
The local telephone directory will provide details.

SMOKING

STRICT ANTI-TOBACCO LAWS
are enforced in South
Africa. Smoking in the
main dining area of
restaurants is not
allowed. At present,
most restaurants have
a smoking section, and
patrons should specify their
requirements when booking.

CHILDREN

RESTAURANTS AND EATERIES are
not always child-friendly
in South Africa, especially at
dinner times when, for many
patrons, dining out is the entertainment for the evening
and children are left at home.

Outdoor, informal and day-
time venues (and their menus)
are more likely to suit little
people. High chairs and mini
menus are not common; ex-
pect to pay three-quarters of
the price for a half-size meal.

Franchises like the Spur
Steakhouses are a very good
bet: they all have an appetiz-
ing children's menu; crayons,
colouring-in competitions,
balloons and resident clowns.

The Spur Steakhouse franchise
also caters for younger patrons

DRESS CODE

MANY UPMARKET restaurants
do require patrons to
wear smart, but not formal
attire. While you will not be
able to wear jeans, shorts and
sports shoes at such venues,
you may comfortably do so
just about anywhere else.

WHEELCHAIR ACCESS

A GROWING AWARENESS for the
special needs of the phy-
sically disabled visitor has led
to the construction of ramps
and wider toilet doors at some,
mostly upmarket, venues.
Many restaurants, however,
still cannot accommodate visitors in wheelchairs, and it is
advisable to check in advance.

Eating on the patio at Tradouw Guesthouse in Barrydale

What to Eat in South Africa

RESTAURANTS IN SOUTH AFRICA cover a wide spectrum of national cuisines and tastes, from Italian pizza parlours to Chinese takeaways. Visitors who wish to taste regional specialities will delight in the excellent Cape Malay fare of the Cape, the Indian curries of KwaZulu-Natal and the exotic culinary marvels offered by African restaurants. The Atlantic and Indian oceans provide a smorgasbord of seafood, prepared in restaurants countrywide. For the real thing, however, join a seafood *braai* (barbecue) on a lonely West Coast beach.

Koeksisters, sweet dessert

Rooibos tea and Mrs Ball's chutney
Caffeine-free herbal tea and chutney (a fruity, spicy sauce) are two classic local products.

Snoek paté
Samoosas
Chilli bites
Bobotie
Potato and green beans

Spicy Malay cuisine *excludes pork and alcohol, which are taboo for the Muslim Malays. Samoosas (deep-fried, filled pastries) and chilli bites (deep-fried spicy dough) are often vegetarian; Bobotie is a lamb stew.*

Breyani *consists of baked rice and lentils with lamb or chicken. This tasty Cape Malay dish is spiced with dried coriander.*

Waterblommetjie bredie *is a stew made with the flower stems of a certain type of water lily that is found in the Cape.*

Portuguese food *features in many South African restaurants. Nando's is a particularly popular franchise chain that also makes its own range of spicy sauces.*

The braai, *weekend fare for South Africans, consists of boerewors (farmer's sausage), chops and sosaties (kebabs).*

Smoorsnoek *is a lightly curried stew of onions and snoek, a barracuda-like fish found along the West Coast.*

AFRICAN FOOD

Potjie (cast-iron pot)

An increasing number of superb, upmarket African restaurants are available in South Africa's major cities. Menus do not only offer a choice of traditional dishes from indigenous South African cultures; they may also include the specialities of several other countries, such as Ethiopia, Mali, Senegal, Kenya and Morocco. While these restaurants certainly offer a culinary tour of Africa, they may also be priced accordingly. For an affordable taste of the real South Africa, visitors should embark on one of the "township tours", which are offered by independent tour companies. Most of these include a visit to a *shebeen* (typical "township" bar), where the standard fare can be sampled.

Chilli with lemon juice
Papaya stuffed with rice
Vetkoek (deep-fried dough)
Mince pastries
Sweet potato and cheese
Lamb stew
Curd cheese with herbs
Chicken wings

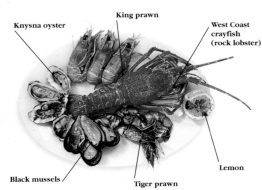

Knysna oyster

King prawn

West Coast crayfish (rock lobster)

Black mussels

Tiger prawn

Lemon

South African seafood *is harvested from the country's long coastline which supports a vast number of fish and other marine life. Most species of fish are exploited commercially. Lobsters, prawns, mussels, oysters and a large variety of edible fish are served in restaurants countrywide.*

DRIED MEATS

In the early years, the hot climate and a lack of adequate cooling facilities led to the creation of some unusual local delicacies that have, since then, become firm favourites with most South Africans. Meat had to be salted, spiced and dried quickly in order to preserve it. Today, *biltong* (the word is derived from "bull tongue") is a sought-after delicacy. Beef biltong is always available, but the connoisseur will settle for nothing less than venison. The *droëwors* (dried sausage) and *bok-koms* (salted fish, a true West Coast speciality) have a similar history.

Biltong

Droëwors

Grated mango

Mixed vegetables

Tomato and onion mix

Cucumber in yoghurt

Crab

Mussels

Indian curry *usually includes either lamb, chicken, beef or vegetables. Crab is one of the more unusual components of this popular dish. A variety of cooling sauces is served to lessen the impact on the tastebuds*

Fruit kebabs *make up an attractive fruit-on-a-stick dessert; this African speciality, uses whatever is in season.*

Malay desserts *are often very rich: Malva (geranium) pudding, melk tert (milk tart) and brandy pudding.*

To make glacé fruit, *slices of orange, whole cherries and pieces of fig and melon are preserved in sugar syrup.*

SOUTH AFRICAN FRUIT

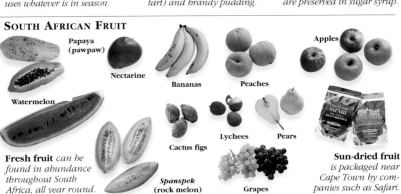

Papaya (pawpaw)

Nectarine

Bananas

Peaches

Apples

Watermelon

Lychees

Pears

Cactus figs

Sun-dried fruit *is packaged near Cape Town by companies such as Safari.*

Fresh fruit *can be found in abundance throughout South Africa, all year round.*

Spanspek (rock melon)

Grapes

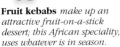

Choosing a Restaurant

THE RESTAURANTS in this guide have been selected for their good value, interesting location and exceptional food. This chart lists additional factors which may assist your choice. Entries are alphabetical within price categories. The thumb tabs on the side of the page use the same colour coding as the corresponding regional chapters in the main section of this guide.

	CREDIT CARDS	CHILDREN'S FACILITIES	OUTSIDE TABLES	BAR	TWO SITTINGS

CAPE TOWN

CITY BOWL: *Noon-Gun Tea Room and Restaurant* ℝ 273 Longmarket St, 8001. **Map** 5 A2. 📞 *(021) 424-0529.* This Cape Malay restaurant at the foot of Signal Hill serves halaal dishes. In strict keeping with the Muslim custom, no alcohol is permitted. 🆅 ⚡		●	■		
CITY BOWL: *Chief Pan Asian Kitchen* ℝℝℝ 12 Mill St, 8001. **Map** 5 B3. 📞 *(021) 465-6058.* Enjoy traditional Cape fare, like Malay curry, *bobotie*, ostrich and *potjiekos*, in this informal, zebra-striped venue. 🆅 ● *Sun.*	AE DC MC V		■	●	
CITY BOWL: *Anatoli* ℝℝℝ 24 Napier St, 8001. **Map** 2 D5. 📞 *(021) 419-2501.* An old Edwardian warehouse (1904) with an indoor garden, tastefully redecorated in Turkish style. This restaurant serves tasty Middle Eastern, as well as vegetarian and halaal dishes. 🆅 ⚡ ● *Mon.*	AE DC MC V			●	
CITY BOWL: *Café Paradiso* ℝℝℝ 110 Kloof St, 8001. **Map** 5 A2. 📞 *(021) 423-8653.* A trendy restaurant-cum-bar, deli and bakery offering Mediterranean-style cuisine, views and friendly service. 🅿 🆅 ⚡ ● *Good Friday, 25 Dec & 1 Jan.*	AE DC MC V		■		
CITY BOWL: *Col'Cacchio Restaurant* ℝℝℝ 42 Hans Strydom Ave, 8001. **Map** 2 E5. 📞 *(021) 419-4848.* This trendy, loft-style pizzeria serves a wide range of pizzas. Open for dinner daily, and lunch from Monday to Friday. 🆅 ⚡ ● *Sat & Sun L.*	AE MC V		■		
CITY BOWL: *Kotobuki Japanese Restaurant* ℝℝℝ 3 Avalon Centre, Mill St, 8001. **Map** 5 B3. 📞 *(021) 462-3675.* An authentic Japanese restaurant offering traditional sushi, sashimi, tempura and tepanyaki dishes, prepared by Japanese chefs. ● *Sat L; Mon.*	AE DC V			●	
CITY BOWL: *De Goewerneur Restaurant* ℝℝℝℝ Castle of Good Hope, Darling St, 8001. **Map** 5 A2. 📞 *(021) 461-4895.* Set in the historic Castle of Good Hope *(see pp68–9)* the restaurant is tastefully furnished and serves excellent Cape Malay cuisine. 🅿 ⚡ 🎵 ● *Sun & eves.*	DC MC V		■	●	■
CITY BOWL: *Madam Zingara* ℝℝℝℝ 192 Loop Street, 8001. **Map** 5 B1. 📞 *(021) 426-2458.* Situated in the centre of Cape Town, this buzzing restaurant serves spicey dishes, including green lipped mussels in a Thai sauce. 🆅 ⚡ ● *L, Sun.*	AE DC MC V			●	
CITY BOWL: *Restaurant Bukhara* ℝℝℝℝ 33 Church St, 8001. **Map** 5 B1. 📞 *(021) 424-0000.* Sophisticated North Indian cuisine prepared in tandoors (clay ovens) in an open-plan kitchen. Try the butter chicken or rogan josh. 🆅 ⚡	AE DC MC V			●	■
CITY BOWL: *Saigon Vietnamese Restaurant* ℝℝℝℝ Cnr Kloof and Camp sts, 8001. **Map** 4 F3. 📞 *(021) 424-7670.* The first authentic Vietnamese restaurant in the country. Dishes include coconut prawns on a skewer; wok beef with watercress. 🆅 ⚡ ● *Sat L.*	AE DC MC V				■
CITY BOWL: *Aubergine Restaurant* ℝℝℝℝ 39 Barnet St, 8001. **Map** 5 B3. 📞 *(021) 465-4909.* **FAX** *(021) 461-3781* One of Cape Town's top ten, this restaurant offers a fusion of east and west, mingling tastes and flavours with inventiveness and flair. 🅿 🆅 🍴 ⚡ 🍷 ● *Sun.*	AE DC V		■	●	
CITY BOWL: *Cape Colony Restaurant* ℝℝℝℝ Mount Nelson Hotel, 76 Orange St, 8001. **Map** 5 A3. 📞 *(021) 483-1000.* This expensive restaurant in Cape Town's *grande dame* of hotels serves a melange of superb international fare and regional specialities. 🅿 🆅 ⚡ 🍷 🎵	AE DC MC V			●	■

Price categories for a three-course meal and one half-bottle of house wine, as well as unavoidable costs such as service and couvert charges:
Ⓡ under R45
ⓇⓇ R45–R70
ⓇⓇⓇ R70–R90
ⓇⓇⓇⓇ R90–R115
ⓇⓇⓇⓇⓇ over R115

CREDIT CARDS
Indicates which credit cards are accepted: AE American Express; DC Diners Club; MC MasterCard; V Visa.

CHILDREN'S FACILITIES
Small portions and high chairs available, and there may also be a special children's menu.

OUTSIDE TABLES
Meals can be served al fresco.

TWO SITTINGS
Bookings are taken for more than one sitting per table at peak times.

	Credit Cards	Children's Facilities	Outside Tables	Bar	Two Sittings
CITY BOWL: *Cara Lazulli* ⓇⓇⓇⓇ 11 Buiten St, 8001. Map 5 A2. (021) 426-2351. FAX (021) 426-4554. Recline in a shadowy corner spread with cushions and enjoy contemporary Moroccan cuisine as well as traditional confectionary. ● Sun; Mon–Sat L.	AE V				
CITY BOWL: *Floris Smit Huijs Restaurant* ⓇⓇⓇⓇ Cnr Church and Loop sts, 8001. Map 5 B1. (021) 423-3415. This gourmet restaurant, located in an eclectically decorated national monument, dating to 1758, is renowned for its venison and seafood dishes. ● Sat & Sun L.	AE DC MC V				
CITY BOWL: *Ginja* ⓇⓇⓇⓇ 121 Castle St, 8001. Map 5 B1. (021) 426-2368. FAX (021) 422-3079. Situated in the trendy Bo-Kaap district of Cape Town, Ginja offers international fusion cuisine in a French brasserie style setting. ● Sun; Mon–Sat L.	AE DC V				■
CITY BOWL: *Leinster Hall Restaurant* ⓇⓇⓇⓇ 7 Weltevreden St, 8001. Map 5 A3. (021) 424-1836. Set in a lovely old house (1850) with seating on the verandah. The superb menu consists of classic dishes, light lunches, seafood, and haute cuisine with Cape Malay touches.	AE DC MC V	■	●		
CITY BOWL: *Mama Africa Restaurant & Bar* ⓇⓇⓇⓇ 178 Long St, 8001. Map 5 A2. (021) 424-8634. An ethnic restaurant serving Cape Malay dishes and exotic game, like crocodile and ostrich. Wattle sapling ceilings add a charming ethnic feel. African bands provide background music. ● Sun; Mon–Sat L.	AE DC MC V			●	■
CITY BOWL: *Maximilians* ⓇⓇⓇⓇ 52 Barnet Street, 8001. Map 5 B3. (021) 434-5420. This restaurant is housed in a 19th Century monumental structure. Serves European food with a South African tang. ● Sat-Mon L; Jul–Aug: Mon.	AE DC MC V	■	●		
CITY BOWL: *Rozenhof* ⓇⓇⓇⓇ 18 Kloof Street Gardens, 8001. Map 4 F3. (021) 424-1968. Now in its 18th year of business, this delightful restaurant serves a wide range of cosmopolitan dishes. Situated near the city centre. ● Sat L; Sun.	AE DC MC V			●	■
V & A WATERFRONT: *Hildebrand Restaurant* ⓇⓇⓇ Pierhead, 8001. Map 2 E3. (021) 425-3385. Recipient of the sought-after "Ristorante Italiano" award, in recognition of its traditional, classic Italian cuisine. Superb food and views.	AE DC MC V	■	●		
V & A WATERFRONT: *The Sports Café* ⓇⓇⓇ Victoria Wharf, 8001. Map 2 E3. (021) 419-5558. A popular bistro with 70 television sets and two big screens covering a variety of world sport. Pub-style meals complement the sports theme.	AE DC MC V	●	■	●	■
V & A WATERFRONT: *Quay Four Restaurant and Tavern* ⓇⓇⓇ Quay Four, 8001. Map 2 E3. (021) 419-2008. Popular waterside duo, comprising a smart seafood restaurant upstairs, while the informal Tavern serves pub fare and live music nightly. ● Sat L.	AE DC MC V	●	■	●	
V & A WATERFRONT: *Atlantic Grill* ⓇⓇⓇⓇ Table Bay Hotel, Quay Six, 8001. Map 2 E3. (021) 406-5000. The sophisticated menu combines the best of global cuisine, enhanced by eastern flavours. Flawless presentation and attention to detail throughout. The wine list includes over 300 top South African wines.	AE DC MC V	●	■		
V & A WATERFRONT: *The Conservatory* ⓇⓇⓇ Table Bay Hotel, Victoria and Alfred Waterfront. Map 2 E3. (021) 406-5000. Intimate waterside restaurant presenting customers with fine cosmopolitan cuisine. Its location embraces views of both the working harbour and Tabletop Mountain. ● L, Sun & Mon.	AE DC MC V			●	

Price categories for a three-course meal and one half-bottle of house wine, as well as unavoidable costs such as service and couvert charges:
Ⓡ under R45
ⓇⓇ R45–R70
ⓇⓇⓇ R70–R90
ⓇⓇⓇⓇ R90–R115
ⓇⓇⓇⓇⓇ over R115

Credit Cards
Indicates which credit cards are accepted: AE American Express; DC Diners Club; MC MasterCard; V Visa.

Children's Facilities
Small portions and high chairs available, and there may also be a special children's menu.

Outside Tables
Meals can be served *al fresco*.

Two Sittings
Bookings are taken for more than one sitting per table at peak times.

Restaurant	Credit Cards	Children's Facilities	Outside Tables	Bar	Two Sittings
V & A Waterfront: *The Green Dolphin Restaurant* ⓇⓇⓇⓇⓇ Victoria and Alfred Mall, Pierhead, 8001. **Map 2 E3.** *(021) 421-7471.* A bistro-style eatery that offers the best of Cape Town jazz every night. Specialities include seafood platters and ostrich meat dishes. P V	AE DC MC V		■	●	■
V & A Waterfront: *One.Waterfront* ⓇⓇⓇⓇⓇ Cape Grace Hotel, West Quay. **Map 2 E3.** *(021) 418-0520.* This luxurious restaurant affords the diner more than magnificent Table Mountain views. Home to London-trained executive chef Bruce Robertson, it also features daring 'fusion fine' cuisine with enormous attention to presentation. The wine list is also highly acclaimed. P V	AE DC MC			●	■
V & A Waterfront: *Quay West* ⓇⓇⓇⓇⓇ Cape Grace Hotel, West Quay, 8001. **Map 2 E4.** *(021) 418-0520.* An elegant, upmarket restaurant with a nautical feel and wonderful views. The menu is complemented by an award-winning wine list. P V	AE DC MC V	●	■	●	
Further Afield: *Ari's Souvlaki* Ⓡ 83a Regent Rd, Sea Point, 8001. **Map 3 C1.** *(021) 439-6683.* A popular Greek taverna that is open for dinner till late at night. V	DC MC V		■		
Further Afield: *Obz Café* ⓇⓇ 115 Lower Main Rd, Observatory, 7925. *(021) 448-5555.* A trendy, deli-style eatery, with a good wine and cocktails list as well. V	AE MC V			●	■
Further Afield: *Tarkaris Indian Restaurant* ⓇⓇ 305 Main Rd, Sea Point, 8001. **Map 1 A5.** *(021) 434-4266.* Renowned for spicy South Indian cuisine, the curries are regarded as among the best in town. Try the mixed seafood curry with 12 spices. V ● *Mon.*	AE DC MC V				■
Further Afield: *Africa Café* ⓇⓇⓇ 108 Short Market Street, 8001. *(021) 422-0221.* Decorated in an ethnic style, this elegant African restaurant serves a selection of dishes from all over Africa. V ● *Sun; 25 Dec & 1 Jan.*	AE DC MC V	●		●	
Further Afield: *Café Bijou* ⓇⓇⓇ 313 Beach Rd, Sea Point, 8001. **Map 1 A4.** *(021) 439-8888.* This acclaimed restaurant offers selected dishes from around the world. There are lovely sea views. P V ● *Sun.*	AE DC MC V	●		●	
Further Afield: *Clifton Beach House Restaurant* ⓇⓇⓇ 4th Beach, 72 The Ridge, Clifton, 8001. **Map 3 A5.** *(021) 438-1955.* Known especially for its French and Italian cuisine, the menu also includes seafood and Thai curries. There are great sea views from the deck. V	AE DC MC V	●	■	●	
Further Afield: *Mr Chan Chinese Restaurant* ⓇⓇⓇ 178a Main Rd, Sea Point, 8001. **Map 1 A5.** *(021) 439-2239.* The authentic culinary delights from Canton, Beijing and Hunan are popular not only with the locals, but also with many Chinese tourists. V	AE DC MC V	●			
Further Afield: *Peddlars on the Bend* ⓇⓇⓇ Spaanschemat River Rd, Constantia, 7800. *(021) 794-7747.* This cosy tavern, housed in a converted farmstall, offers hearty country fare like livers with onion and chicken-and-leek pie. P ● *25 Dec & 1 Jan.*	AE DC MC V		■	●	■
Further Afield: *Blues* ⓇⓇⓇⓇ The Promenade, Camps Bay, 8001. *(021) 438-2040.* This trendy beachfront restaurant offers wonderful sea views, and a blend of Californian and Mediterranean fare from a London-trained chef. P V	AE DC MC V		■	●	■

FURTHER AFIELD: *Café Macchiato* ⓇⓇⓇⓇ AE DC MC V
92 Main Rd, Sea Point, 8001. **Map** 1A5. ▌ *(021) 439-2758.*
An Italian classic, serving a variety of pasta and seafood dishes, the restaurant
has also gained fame for its delicious homemade ice cream. ▌ ▌ *Tue.*

FURTHER AFIELD: *Cape Malay Kitchen* ⓇⓇⓇⓇ AE DC MC V
Cellars-Hohenort Hotel, Constantia, 7800. ▌ *(021) 794-2137.*
An amazing selection of traditional dishes, delicious Cape Malay curries
bredies and *breyanis* is offered by this refined restaurant. ▌ ▌ ▌ ▌ *L.*

FURTHER AFIELD: *Clementine's* ⓇⓇⓇⓇ AE DC MC V
23 Wolfe St, Wynberg, 7800. ▌ *(021) 797-6168.*
The warm atmosphere and muted music make for fine dining in this
restaurant, which uses only local produce to prepare its wide range of
traditional South African and international dishes. ▌ ▌ ▌ ▌ ▌ ▌ *Sun.*

FURTHER AFIELD: *Inside Out* ⓇⓇⓇⓇ AE DC MC V
114 Constantia Rd, Constantia, 7800. **Map** B5. ▌ *(021) 797-8202.*
One of Cape Town's top ten, set in a pretty Victorian-style house. The menu
blends classic and new world cuisine with style and care. ▌ ▌

FURTHER AFIELD: *Two Oceans Restaurant* ⓇⓇⓇⓇ AE DC MC V
Cape of Good Hope Nature Reserve, 7975. ▌ *(021) 780-9200.*
Traditional Cape and seafood dishes are served in this quaint stone building.
As this venue is in a nature reserve, it is closed in the evenings. ▌ ▌

FURTHER AFIELD: *Wharfside Grill* ⓇⓇⓇⓇ AE DC MC V
Mariner's Wharf, Hout Bay, 7800. ▌ *(021) 790-1100.*
Great harbour views are offered by this popular restaurant that prides itself on
its freshly prepared seafood dishes. Cape lobster is the speciality here. ▌ ▌ ▌

FURTHER AFIELD: *Au Jardin* ⓇⓇⓇⓇⓇ AE DC MC V
Vineyard Hotel, Colinton Rd, Newlands, 7700. ▌ *(021) 683-1520.*
Emanating gracious Cape Georgian charm, this award-winning restaurant is
renowned for its classic French cuisine, especially the *bouillabaisse du Cap.*
Superb views through floor-to-ceiling windows. ▌ ▌ ▌ ▌ *Sat & Mon L.*

FURTHER AFIELD: *Buitenverwachting* ⓇⓇⓇⓇ AE DC MC V
Klein Constantia Rd, Constantia, 7800. ▌ *(021) 794-3522.*
Awarded the Blazon of Excellence by Chaine des Rotisseurs, this is one
of the Cape's finest restaurants. International haute cuisine is prepared and
presented with flair. Excellent wine list. ▌ ▌ ▌ ▌ ▌ ▌ *Sun & Mon.*

FURTHER AFIELD: *The Chef* ⓇⓇⓇⓇ
3 Rose Street, Green Point. ▌ *(021) 419-6767.*
Located inbetween the Bo-Kaap and Green Point and decorated in Tuscan
style, this restaurant's menu consists of traditional Italian cuisine. Fully air
conditioned with good views. There is also an extensive wine list on offer
here. ▌ ▌ ▌ ▌ ▌ ▌ ▌ *Sun & Mon.*

FURTHER AFIELD: *Constantia Uitsig Restaurant* ⓇⓇⓇⓇ AE DC MC V
Constantia Uitsig Farm, Constantia, 7800. ▌ *(021) 794-4480.*
A member of the South African Restaurant Guild and one of Cape Town's best
restaurants, this award-winner serves Italian and Mediterranean cuisine and
has an international connoisseurs wine list. ▌ ▌ ▌ ▌ ▌ ▌ *Mon L.*

FURTHER AFIELD: *Blue Danube* ⓇⓇⓇⓇ AE DC MC V
102 New Church Street, Cape Town. ▌ *(021) 423-3624.*
Based in a gracious Victorian house in Tamboerskloof, this restaurant offers
the finest continental cuisine. Utilises fresh local produce whilst retaining a
distinct French and Austrian influence. This highly acclaimed establishment
boasts a Diner's Club wine list award. ▌ ▌ ▌ ▌ ▌ ▌ *Sat-Mon L.*

FURTHER AFIELD: *La Colombe Restaurant* ⓇⓇⓇⓇ AE DC MC V
Constantia Uitsig Farm, Constantia, 7800. ▌ *(021) 794-2390.*
Another one of Cape Town's top ten, this restaurant serves superb French
Provençal dishes in a serene vineyard setting. ▌ ▌ ▌ ▌ *Tue.*

FURTHER AFIELD: *Greenhouse Restaurant* ⓇⓇⓇⓇ AE DC MC V
Cellars-Hohenhort Hotel, Constantia, 7800. ▌ *(021) 794-2137.*
A member of the South African Restaurant Guild and Relais et Châteaux. Run
in association with London's Christophe Novelli. An innovative, sophisticated
menu backed by attentive service, and a lovely garden setting. ▌ ▌ ▌ ▌

<table>
<tr><td colspan="2">

Price categories for a three-course meal and one half-bottle of house wine, as well as unavoidable costs such as service and couvert charges:
® under R45
®® R45–R70
®®® R70–R90
®®®® R90–R115
®®®®® over R115
</td><td colspan="2">

CREDIT CARDS
Indicates which credit cards are accepted: AE American Express; DC Diners Club; MC MasterCard; V Visa.

CHILDREN'S FACILITIES
Small portions and high chairs available, and there may also be a special children's menu.

OUTSIDE TABLES
Meals can be served *al fresco*.

TWO SITTINGS
Bookings are taken for more than one sitting per table at peak times.
</td></tr>
</table>

	CREDIT CARDS	CHILDREN'S FACILITIES	OUTSIDE TABLES	BAR	TWO SITTINGS
CAPE WINELANDS					
FRANSCHHOEK: *La Petite Ferme* ®®®® Franschhoek Pass Rd, 7690. **Road map** B5. **(** *(021) 876-3016.* The speciality of this well-loved country restaurant overlooking the beautiful Franschhoek valley is local rainbow trout, deboned, smoked and served whole. Enjoy it with wine made in the tiny winery next door. **P V 🍷 ●** *eve.*	AE DC MC V	●	▣		
FRANSCHHOEK: *Le Quartier Français* ®®® 16/18 Huguenot Rd, 7690. **Road map** B5. **(** *(021) 876-2151.* Breakfast, tea, lunch, dinner are served in a fusion of Cape Provençal style, in this restaurant in the heart of Franschhoek's main street. **V T**	AE DC MC V	●	▣	●	
FRANSCHHOEK: *Haute Cabrière* ®®®® Cabrière Estate, Franschhoek Pass Rd, 7690. **Road map** B5. **(** *(021) 876-3688.* This top-rated restaurant, located in a wine cellar built into the mountainside, offers gourmet cuisine with French and eastern influences, complemented by the estate's range of still and sparkling wines. **P V T 🍷**	AE DC MC V	●		▣	
FRANSCHHOEK: *Monneaux* ®®®® Franschhoek Country House, Main Road. **Road map** 1 A4. **(** *(021) 876-3386.* Quality fusion cookery is offered at this country restaurant. Whilst the setting of the establishment may be rustic and traditional, the food is decidedly contemporary. Offers good, shady, outdoor dining. **P V 🔁**	AE DC MC V		▣	●	
MONTAGU: *Preston's* ®®® 17 Bath St, 6720. **Road map** B5. **(** *(023) 614-3013.* The menu offers traditional home-cooked South African cuisine such as lamb casserole and *bobotie*, and a selection of wines from the area. **P V 🍷**	DC MC V	●	▣	●	
PAARL: *Rhebokskloof Restaurant* ®®®® Rhebokskloof Wine Estate, 7646. **Road map** B5. **(** *(021) 869-8386* Continental as well as Cape gourmet dishes and an award-winning wine list offered in two separate venues on this beautiful estate. **P V ●** *Tue eve, Wed eve.*	AE DC MC V	●	▣	●	
PAARL: *Bosman's* ®®®®® Grande Roche Hotel, Plantasie St, 7646. **Road map** B5. **(** *(021) 863-2727.* Consistently rated as one of the top restaurants in the country, the outstanding interpretations of Cape cuisine take Bosman's to international levels. Set menus change nightly. Presentation and service are impeccable, and the award-winning wine list is spectacular. Light lunches on the terrace. **P V T 🔁 🍷 ●** *Jun–Aug.*	AE DC MC V		▣	●	
PAARL: *Roggeland Country House* ®®®® Roggeland Rd, Dal Josaphat Valley, 7646. **Road map** B5. **(** *(021) 868-2501.* Local wines and traditional fare with French influences are served in this 250-year-old Cape Dutch homestead where simplicity and freshness are the keynotes. Try the home-smoked, deboned guinea fowl. **🔁**	AE DC MC V		▣		
SOMERSET WEST: *96 Winery Road* ®®® Zandberg Farm, Winery Rd, 7130. **Road map** B5. **(** *(021) 842-2020.* Fresh farm fare and quality cooking, combining Cape, Provençal and Eastern influences, are the style at this award-winning country inn whose pumpkin-coloured walls are hung with the works of local artists. **P V 🔁 ●** *Sun eve.*	AE DC MC V	●	▣		
SOMERSET WEST: *The Restaurant at Erinvale* ®®®® Erinvale Estate Hotel, 1 Erinvale Ave, 7130. **Road map** B5. **(** *(021) 847-1160.* This country restaurant, located in an early-18th-century Cape Dutch building, serves classic Cape cuisine with an emphasis on seafood. **P V**	AE DC MC V		▣	●	
SOMERSET WEST: *Willowbrook Lodge Restaurant* ®®®® 1 Morgenster Ave, 7130. **Road map** B5. **(** *(021) 851-3759.* French cuisine with South African overtones includes rillettes of duck confit, roasted pork on potato and olive puree. Good wine list. **P V 🔁**	AE DC MC V		▣	●	

STELLENBOSCH: *Boschendal* ⓇⓇⓇⓇ
Pniel Rd (R310), Groot Drakenstein, 7680. **Road map** B5. 【 *(021) 870-4274.*
Located in the original cellar of the manor (built in 1812), the Taphuis menu
offers an extensive traditional Cape buffet and Boschendal wines. In summer,
visitors can enjoy Le Pique-Nique in the shade of the pine trees next to the lake.
Teas and lighter fare are available at Le Café, the estate's other restaurant.
🄿 Ⓥ 🕭 🕻 ⬤ *Good Fri, 1 May, 16 Jun.*

	AE	⬤	▪	
	DC			
	MC			
	V			

STELLENBOSCH: *De Volkskombuis* ⓇⓇⓇ
Aan de Wagenweg, 7600. **Road map** B5. 【 *(021) 887-2121.*
Traditional Cape cuisine like succulent Karoo lamb, and an extensive wine
list are the culinary delights offered in this historic cottage, originally
designed by Sir Herbert Baker. 🄿 🕭 🕻 ⬤ *Sun eve.*

	AE	⬤	▪	⬤
	DC			
	MC			
	V			

STELLENBOSCH: *Lord Neethling & The Palm Terrace* ⓇⓇⓇ
Neethlingshof Wine Estate,7600. **Road map** B5. 【 *(021) 883-8966.*
The award-winning Lord Neethling features Thai, Indonesian, Vietnamese
and Cape Malay dishes. The less formal Palm Terrace offers light à la carte
lunches with views over the gardens. 🄿 Ⓥ 🕭

	AE	⬤	▪	
	DC			
	V			

STELLENBOSCH: *Spier* ⓇⓇⓇ
Spier Estate, Lynedoch Rd, 7600. **Road map** B5. 【 *(021) 809-1172.*
A tourist Mecca with own steam train, Cape Dutch buildings and concerts in
landscaped gardens. Three separate eating venues (The Jonkershuis, Taphuis
Grill & Riverside Pub and the Café Spier) offer a variety of choices. 🄿 Ⓥ 🕭

	AE	⬤	▪	⬤	▪
	DC				
	MC				
	V				

STELLENBOSCH: *The Green Door* ⓇⓇⓇⓇⓇ
Delaire Wine Farm, Helshoogte Pass. **Road map** B5. 【 *(021) 885-1149.*
Best known for its innovative, cosmopolitan cuisine and the spectacular views of
vine-clad mountainside and verdant valley. There is a large cosy dining room
with open fires in winter. Ⓥ 🕭 🎵 ⬤ *Sun eve.*

	AE	⬤	▪	
	DC			

TULBAGH: *Paddagang* ⓇⓇⓇ
23 Church St, 6820. **Road map** B5. 【 *(023) 230-0242.*
This cozy restaurant is located in a historical monument (1821). The Cape
farmhouse fare features local delicacies like *waterblommetjie bredie, smoorsnoek* and *malva* pudding. 🄿 Ⓥ 🕭 ⬤ *Eve, Good Fri, 1 May, 25 Dec, 1 Jan.*

	AE	⬤	▪	
	DC			
	MC			
	V			

WORCESTER: *Kleinplasie Restaurant* ⓇⓇⓇ
Kleinplasie Museum Rest, Traubstr. 23. 【 *(023) 347-5118*
This hospitable and classy restaurant, specialising in traditional fare, is located
on the premises of the Living Open Air Museum. Has a large lawn from where
children can see the nearby working farm. 🄿 Ⓥ 🕭 🕻 ⬤ *Good Fri, 1 Jan, Sun eve.*

	AE	⬤		⬤	▪
	DC				
	MC				
	V				

WESTERN COASTAL TERRACE

BLOUBERGSTRAND: *The Blue Peter* ⓇⓇⓇ
2 Popham Rd, 7441. **Road map** B5. 【 *(021) 554-1956.*
A firm favourite with Capetonians, especially with the younger crowd at
weekends. Dine in style upstairs or sip your sundowner on the wide lawn,
enjoying the superb view of Table Mountain across the bay. 🄿 🕭 🎵

	AE	⬤	▪	⬤
	DC			
	MC			
	V			

BLOUBERGSTRAND: *On the Rocks* ⓇⓇⓇ
45 Stadler Rd, 7441. **Road map** B5. 【 *(021) 554-1988.*
Overlooking the beach, with superb views of Table Mountain and Robben Island.
Fresh seafood is the speciality of the kitchen. 🄿 Ⓥ

	AE			⬤
	DC			
	MC			
	V			

LAMBERT'S BAY: *Die Muisbosskerm* ⓇⓇⓇ
Elands Bay Rd, 8130. 【 *(027) 432-1017.*
One of the West Coast's open-air beach restaurants, Lambert's Bay seats
about 150 people. Enjoy traditional seafood, *potjiekos* and dessert in a
three-hour feast. 🄿 🎵

	AE		▪	
	DC			
	MC			
	V			

LANGEBAAN: *Die Strandloper* ⓇⓇⓇ
On the beach, 7357. **Road map** A5. 【 *(022) 772-2490.*
Just an hour from Cape Town, this West Coast seafood eatery on the beach does
not mind if you come to lunch in your bathing suit. Communal feast served
directly from the fire or pot, eaten with fingers. 🄿 🕭 🎵 ⬤ *in bad weather.*

			▪	

LANGEBAAN: *Pearlie's on the Beach* ⓇⓇⓇ
On the beach, 7357. **Road map** A5. 【 *(022) 772-2734.*
This casual beachfront café and restaurant serves generous seafood platters,
steaks, pizza, pasta and a range of fresh salads. 🄿 Ⓥ

	AE	⬤	▪	⬤	▪
	DC				
	MC				
	V				

For key to symbols see back flap

Price categories for a three-course meal and one half-bottle of house wine, as well as unavoidable costs such as service and couvert charges:
Ⓡ under R45
ⓇⓇ R45–R70
ⓇⓇⓇ R70–R90
ⓇⓇⓇⓇ R90–R115
ⓇⓇⓇⓇⓇ over R115

CREDIT CARDS
Indicates which credit cards are accepted: AE American Express; DC Diners Club; MC MasterCard; V Visa.

CHILDREN'S FACILITIES
Small portions and high chairs available, and there may also be a special children's menu.

OUTSIDE TABLES
Meals can be served al fresco.

TWO SITTINGS
Bookings are taken for more than one sitting per table at peak times.

	CREDIT CARDS	CHILDREN'S FACILITIES	OUTSIDE TABLES	BAR	TWO SITTINGS
MALMESBURY: *Die Herehuis* ⓇⓇⓇ 1 Loedolf St, 7300. **Road map** B5. ☏ (02248) 7-1771. The traditional country fare at this quaint inn includes dishes like *bobotie*. The wine list features some of the Swartland's best wines. 🄿 Ⓥ ● *Sun eve.*	AE DC MC V	●	■	●	
MILNERTON: *Maestro's on the Beach* ⓇⓇⓇⓇ Bridge Rd, 7441. **Road map** B5. ☏ (021) 551-4992. Mediterranean-style restaurant overlooking Table Bay and Robben Island. Fresh seafood and a relaxed ambience. 🄿 ⚡	AE DC MC V			●	
YZERFONTEIN: *Strandkombuis* ⓇⓇⓇⓇ 16-Mile Beach, 7351. **Road map** A5. ☏ (0825) 759-683. Booking is essential at this alfresco seafood eatery some 80 km (50 miles) from the city. Relax on the wooden deck, with wonderful views of the stormy Atlantic, enjoying a feast of Cape seafood, hot off the fire. 🄿 ● *Jun–Jul.*	DC MC V	●	■		

SOUTHERN CAPE

	CREDIT CARDS	CHILDREN'S FACILITIES	OUTSIDE TABLES	BAR	TWO SITTINGS
GREYTON: *Greyton Lodge* ⓇⓇⓇ 46 Main Rd, 7233. **Road map** B5. ☏ (028) 254-9876. One of the oldest buildings in the village, this former fishing cottage (now a national monument) still features the original stone floors and serves mainly seafood delicacies and vegetarian dishes. 🄿 Ⓥ ⚡ 🍷	AE DC MC V	●	■		
HERMANUS: *The Burgundy Restaurant* ⓇⓇⓇ Market Square, 7200. **Road map** B5. ☏ (028) 312-2800. The specialities of this historical monument restaurant, just a stone's throw from the whale-watching viewpoints, are seafood and choice cuts of venison. Emphasis on wines from the area. 🄿 Ⓥ ⚡ ● *Sun eve, 25 Dec, 1 Jan.*	AE DC MC V	●	■		
OUDTSHOORN: *Bernhard's Taphuis* ⓇⓇⓇ 10 Baron van Rheede St, 6620. **Road map** C5. ☏ (044) 272-3208. This country restaurant offers typical Karoo-style hospitality and wonderful regional dishes with an international flair, such as carpaccio of ostrich. 🄿 Ⓥ ⚡ ● *Sun.*	MC V		■	●	
OUDTSHOORN: *De Fijne Keuken* ⓇⓇⓇ 114 Baron van Rheede St, 6620. **Road map** C5. ☏ (044) 272-6403. Mouthwatering local specialities like panfried ostrich fillet, as well as a variety of salads and desserts are served on the wooden sun deck and interleading dining rooms. 🄿 Ⓥ ⚡ ● *Sun & Mon.*	AE DC MC V	●	■	●	
SWELLENDAM: *Zanddrift Restaurant* ⓇⓇⓇ 32 Swellengrebel St, 6740. **Road map** B5. ☏ (028) 514-1789. Tastefully refurbished farmhouse dating to 1746. 🄿 Ⓥ ● *every eve.*	DC MC V		■		

GARDEN ROUTE TO GRAHAMSTOWN

	CREDIT CARDS	CHILDREN'S FACILITIES	OUTSIDE TABLES	BAR	TWO SITTINGS
GEORGE: *The Copper Pot* ⓇⓇⓇ 12 Montague St, Blanco, 6529. **Road map** C5. ☏ (044) 870-7378. An elegant restaurant with an award-winning wine list, and a lovingly prepared fusion of French and traditional South African dishes. 🄿 Ⓥ ⚡ 🍷 ● *Sat L, Sun L, Sun eve.*	AE DC MC V		■	●	
GRAHAMSTOWN: *The Cock House* ⓇⓇⓇ 10 Market St, 6139. **Road map** D5. ☏ (046) 636-1287. Located in a charming national monument building (1826), this restaurant's menu always features traditional and vegetarian dishes. 🄿 Ⓥ	AE DC MC V		■	●	■
KNYSNA: *Belvidere House* ⓇⓇⓇ Lower Duthie Dr, Belvidere Est, 6570. **Road map** C5. ☏ (044) 387-1055. This restaurant, part of an upmarket guesthouse, uses fresh produce in season and has a short but excellent wine list. 🄿 Ⓥ ⚡ 🍷 🎵	AE DC MC V		■	●	

KNYSNA: *The Phantom Forest*　　　　　ⓇⓇⓇⓇ　　DC
Phantom Pass Rd, 6001. **Road map** C5. ▯ *(044) 386-0046.* F̲A̲X̲ *(044) 387-1944.*　MC
Leave your car at the entrance to the eco-reserve and climb into a 4WD
for a steep ride up the mountain slope. The cosmopolitan food here is as
adventurous as the setting. Ⓥ 🔆 🍷 ● *Mon–Sun L.*

MOSSEL BAY: *The Gannet*　　　　　ⓇⓇⓇ　　AE ● ■ ■
Market St, 6500. **Road map** C5. ▯ *(044) 691 1885*　DC
Situated within the Bartolomeu Dias Museum Complex, this restaurant　MC
specializes in seafood, and prepares an excellent mussel pot. Also superb
for outdoor dining - the garden overlooks the bay where dolphins and whales　V
can often be spotted. Ⓟ Ⓥ 🔆

MOSSEL BAY: *The Post Tree*　　　　　ⓇⓇⓇⓇ　　AE ■ ●
10 Powrie St, 6500. **Road map** C5. ▯ *(044) 691 1177*　DC
Paraffin lamps and old-fashioned decor recreate a bygone era. This tiny,　MC
intimate restaurant is located in one of Mossel Bay's oldest buildings, dating　V
from the 1850s. Enjoy the day's catch, rich tomato-basil seafood soup, or
stick with choice cuts of beef and ostrich. Ⓟ Ⓥ 🔆 ● *Mon L, Sat L, Sun.*

PLETTENBERG BAY: *The Islander*　　　　　ⓇⓇⓇⓇ　　AE ● ■ ●
N2. Harkerville, 6600. **Road map** C5. ▯ *(044) 532-7776.*　DC
The tropical atmosphere of this restaurant is complemented by its buffet-style　MC
menu reminiscent of Indonesian, Creole and Polynesian seafood dishes.　V
Dine on locally caught fish prepared in a variety of ways, seafood soup, and
fresh crayfish in season. Ⓟ Ⓥ 🔆 ● *part June, check beforehand.*

PLETTENBERG BAY: *The Plettenberg*　　　　　ⓇⓇⓇⓇ　　AE ● ■ ●
40 Church St, 6600. **Road map** C5. ▯ *(044) 533-2030.*　DC
This elegant and expensive dining room offers superb views　MC
over the bay, gourmet food, and an excellent wine list. Menus　V
change seasonally to take advantage of fresh ingredients. Local
dishes served with flair. Ⓟ Ⓥ 🍷 🔆

PORT ELIZABETH: *Royal Delhi*　　　　　ⓇⓇⓇ　　AE ■ ●
10 Burgess St, 6001. **Road map** D5. ▯ *(041) 373-8216.*　DC
This is the best place in town for lovers of hot curries, but the restaurant　MC
also serves a variety of seafood and steak dishes, as well as non-meat　V
dishes suitable for vegetarians. Ⓟ Ⓥ ● *Sun.*

PORT ELIZABETH: *Bay Café & Plate*　　　　　ⓇⓇⓇⓇ　　AE ● ■
7 Lutman Street, Central, 6000. ▯ *(041) 585-1558.*　DC
There is a choice of dining here - the upmarket, café interior of one half　MC
of this eatery, or the plush restaurant setting of the other half. Shrimp,　V
calamari and crab feature regularly whilst daily specials will depend on the
catch. All fare is made up of fresh, local produce. The establishment is located
in the historical part of Port Elizabeth. Ⓟ Ⓥ 🍷 🔆 🍷 🎵 ● *Sun.*

WILD COAST, DRAKENSBERG & MIDLANDS

EAST LONDON: *Le Petit Restaurant*　　　　　ⓇⓇⓇⓇ　　AE ● ●
54 Beach Rd, Nahoon, 5201. **Road map** E5. ▯ *(043) 735-3685.*　DC
A solid favourite amongst locals in the area, this restaurant has the feel of a　MC
warm, inviting, country manor house. The food is likewise excellent - the　V
Ostrich Steak Flambé is a particularly inviting dish, and customers can watch
as it's prepared at their tables. Ⓟ 🔆 ● *Sat L, Sun.*

KEI MOUTH: *Kei Mouth Beach Hotel Restaurant*　　　　ⓇⓇⓇ　　MC ● ■ ●
Kei Mouth, Wild Coast, 5260. **Road map** E5. ▯ *(043) 841-1017.*　V
This wonderful restaurant, set on a hill overlooking the ocean, offers a wide
variety of seafood from grilled crayfish to prawns and calamari. Ⓟ 🎵

HATTINGSPRUIT: *Farmer's Brewery*　　　　　ⓇⓇⓇ　　MC ● ■ ●
R621. The Bier Farm, 3081. **Road map** E3. ▯ *(0342) 18-1735.*　V
Eisbein with sauerkraut, Kassler rib, and beer brewed on the premises are part
of the hearty fare at this Austrian tavern. Ⓟ Ⓥ ● *24–26 Dec, Good Fri, Sun eve.*

HOWICK: *Afton Restaurant*　　　　　ⓇⓇⓇ　　AE ●
Cnr Bell & Somme sts, 3290. **Road map** E3. ▯ *(033) 330-5256.*　DC
Housed in the residence built in 1886 for the first district surgeon, and　MC
reputed to be haunted, this restaurant serves hearty meals like duck, lamb,　V
casseroles and pies. The name of the establishment is derived from lines of the
Robert Burns poem "Flow Gently Sweet Afton", the spirit of which can be
imbibed whilst dining here. Ⓟ Ⓥ 🔆 ● *Mon, Tue.*

Price categories for a three-course meal and one half-bottle of house wine, as well as unavoidable costs such as service and couvert charges:
Ⓡ under R45
ⓇⓇ R45–R70
ⓇⓇⓇ R70–R90
ⓇⓇⓇⓇ R90–R115
ⓇⓇⓇⓇⓇ over R115

CREDIT CARDS
Indicates which credit cards are accepted: AE American Express; DC Diners Club; MC MasterCard; V Visa.

CHILDREN'S FACILITIES
Small portions and high chairs available, and there may also be a special children's menu.

OUTSIDE TABLES
Meals can be served *al fresco.*

TWO SITTINGS
Bookings are taken for more than one sitting per table at peak times.

	CREDIT CARDS	CHILDREN'S FACILITIES	OUTSIDE TABLES	BAR	TWO SITTINGS
HOWICK: *Protea Hotel Old Halliwell* ⓇⓇⓇⓇ Curry's Post Rd, 3290. **Road map** E3. 【 *(033) 330-2602.* Classic country cooking and an excellent choice of wines are served in this historic building dating from around 1830. Menus change frequently to reflect seasonal fare. **P V** 👶	AE DC MC V		■	●	
LESOTHO: *Katse Lodge* ⓇⓇⓇ Katse Dam. **Road map** E3. 【 *(09266) 2291-0202.* The restaurant, which caters mainly for guests residing at the lodge, is open for breakfast, lunch and dinner seven days a week. Delicious carvery as well as à la carte meals are offered. **P V**	MC V			●	
LESOTHO: *Ximenia* ⓇⓇⓇ Maseru Sun Hotel, 12 Orpen Rd, Maseru. **Road map** D3. 【 *(09266) 2231-2434.* The Ximenia Restaurant is open for breakfast, lunch and dinner seven days a week, and serves carvery and salad buffets. **P V** 🔲	AE DC MC V	●	■	●	■
LESOTHO: *Vic Restaurant* ⓇⓇⓇ Victoria Hotel, Kingsway, Maseru. **Road map** D3. 【 *(09266) 2231-2922.* Open for lunch and dinner seven days a week. Fairly standard buffet fare. **P**	DC MC V			●	■
LESOTHO: *Lehaha Grill* ⓇⓇⓇⓇ Lesotho Sun Hotel, Hilton Rd, Maseru. **Road map** D3. 【 *(09266) 2231-3111.* The hotel has several restaurants: Lehaha Grill, which offers a choice of buffet or à la carte, serves a variety of seafood, grills and the best pork spare ribs in Maseru; Nala Coffee Shop and Leifo Lounge serve light meals at breakfast, lunch and dinner, and occasional open-air barbeque evenings. **P V** 🔲	AE DC MC V	●	■	●	■
LIDGETTON: *Caversham Mill* ⓇⓇ Midlands Meander, 3616. **Road map** E3. 【 *(033) 234-4524.* Located in an old mill overlooking a waterfall and stone bridge, this quaint restaurant serves Mediterranean specialities. **P V ●** *Mon–Tue.*	AE DC MC V		■		
MORGAN'S BAY: *Morgan's Bay Hotel* ⓇⓇ Morgan's Bay Hotel, 5292. **Road map** E5. 【 *(043) 841-1062.* This affordable Wild Coast venue, perched 30 m (100 ft) above the Indian Ocean, offers unlimited sea views and five-course set meals. **P** 🔲	AE DC MC V	●			
PIETERMARITZBURG: *Turtle Bay* ⓇⓇ 7 Wembley Terrace, 3201. **Road map** E3. 【 *(033) 394-5390.* The international menu includes venison, seafood and vegetarian dishes. Especially good are steamed langoustines in soy sauce. **P V** 🔲 🎵 **●** *Sun.*	AE DC MC V	●		●	■
PIETERMARITZBURG: *Els Amics* ⓇⓇⓇ 380 Longmarket St, 3201. **Road map** E3. 【 *(033) 345-6524.* This restaurant, whose name means 'The Friends' in Catalan, offers mouth-watering Spanish fare. The paella is legendary. **P V** 🔲 **●** *Sun, Mon.*	AE DC MC V	●			
PIETERMARITZBURG: *Le Gourmet Restaurant* ⓇⓇⓇ 80 Roberts Rd, Clarendon, 3201. **Road map** E3. 【 & FAX *(033) 342-3280.* This restaurant is set in a charming Victorian house, in the leafy suburb of Clarendon. The menu is made up of delectable French cuisine as well as seafood and good vegetarian options. **V** 🔲 👶 **●** *Sat L, Sun.*	MC V	●	■		
PIETERMARITZBURG: *The Blue Room* ⓇⓇⓇ 1 George McFarlane Lane, 3201. **Road map** E3. 【 *(033) 394-3333.* The continental fare at this restaurant includes such delicacies as crispy duck and lamb with a herbed, minted crust. **P** 🪑 **●** *Sun.*	AE DC MC V		■	●	
PORT EDWARD: *Glenmore Sands Restaurant* ⓇⓇ 1 Boulder Rd, Glenmore Beach, 4295. **Road map** E4. 【 *(039) 319-2313.* Located right on the beach, this family restaurant is renowned for its tasty seafood dishes and has wonderful views of the Indian Ocean. **P V**	AE DC MC V	●	■	●	

DURBAN AND ZULULAND

BEREA: *Havana El Cubano Latin Quarter* ®®®
Silvervaux Centre, cnr Silverton & Vaux rds, 4001. **Road map** F3. ((031) 202-9198.
A restaurant with a Caribbean ambience that offers Cajun-style dishes and
Cuban cigars. **P** **V** ● *Sat L, Sun & Mon.*
AE DC MC V

BEREA: *Café 1999* ®®®
Silvervaux Centre, cnr Silverton & Vaux rds, 4001. **Road map** F3. ((031) 202-3406.
This popular Mediterranean-style restaurant uses only the freshest
ingredients for its dishes and caters extensively for vegetarians. Winner of a
Diner's Club cellar selection award. **P** **V** ● *Mon, Tue L.*
AE DC MC V

CENTRAL: *Christina's Restaurant* ®®®
130–4 Florida Rd, 4001. **Road map** F3. ((031) 303-2111.
Superb multi national cuisine and a pleasant setting in this restaurant located
in the Christina Martin School of Food and Wine. **P** **V** **!** ● *Sun, Mon.*
AE DC MC V

CENTRAL: *Rainbow Terrace* ®®®
Hilton Hotel, 12–14 Walnut Rd, 4001. **Road map** F3. ((031) 336-8100.
Located in a popular family hotel, this South African Restaurant Guild member
offers a mouthwatering buffet selection, as well as several traditional and
Indian specialities from their a là carte menu. **P** **V** **T** **⚡** **!** **♫** ● *Sun, Mon.*
AE DC MC V

ELANGENI: *Daruma Restaurant* ®®®®
63 Snell Parade, Holiday Inn. ((031) 337-0423.
This newly renovated seafood restaurant offers a Sushi Bar and Tepenyaki
grill. It has a fixed price menu. **V** **T** **⚡** **!**
AE DC MC V

HILLCREST: *House Sweet* ®®®®
Shop 22, Heritage Market, Old Main Rd. **Road map** F3. ((031) 765-5114.
House Sweet is a decidedly quaint Shanghai restaurant, replete with eye--
catching décor and lanterns. Offers four fixed menus. **P** **V** **⚡** ● *Mon.*
AE DC MC V

HILLCREST: *Aubergine & Lemongrass* ®®®®
20 Hillcrest Centre, Old Main Rd. **Road map** F3. ((031) 765-6050.
A mixure of European, American and Thai cuisine is on offer at this centrally-
located restaurant. Great for breakfast, lunch and dinner. **V** **⚡** **!** ● *Sat L, Sun D.*
MC V

MORNINGSIDE: *Catmandu* ®®®
413 Windermere Rd, 4001. **Road map** F3. ((031) 312-7893.
This small restaurant, decorated with Persian rugs and copper ornaments,
serves Middle Eastern fare, like mezze platters and kebabs. **P** **V** ● *Sat L, Sun.*
AE DC MC V

MORNINGSIDE: *El Bandido Mexican Quarter* ®®®
411 Windermere Rd, 4001. **Road map** F3. ((031) 303-3827.
This restaurant is for *hombres* who like fajitas, enchiladas, steak filled with
jalapeño chillis, and tequila pork roast. **P** **V** ● *Sat L, Sun.*
AE DC MC V

MORNINGSIDE: *Bistro 136* ®®®
136 Florida Rd, 4001. **Road map** F3. ((031) 303-3440.
The Swiss chef of this elite establishment offers a choice of European dishes,
as well as mouthwatering vegetarian creations. **P** **V**
AE DC MC V

MORNINGSIDE: *Baanthai* ®®®®
138 Florida Rd, 4001. **Road map** F3. ((031) 303-4270.
Thai chefs prepare authentic Thai specialities like Banthaai duck, and red
and green curries. **P** **V** ● *Sat L, Sun.*
AE DC MC V

MORNINGSIDE: *Bean Bag Bohemia* ®®®
18 Windermere Rd. **Road map** F3. ((031) 309-6019.
This eccentric, avant-garde venue organizes poetry and theme-party evenings,
has live jazz on Sundays and the menu is superb. **P** **V** **♫**
AE DC MC V

MORNINGSIDE: *Marco's Restaurant* ®®®®
45 Windermere Rd, 4001. **Road map** F3. ((031) 303-3078.
For an unadulterated taste of Italian cuisine, this upmarket family-owned
restaurant offers homemade pastas and is simply unsurpassed. **P** **V** ● *Sun.*
AE DC MC V

MORNINGSIDE: *9th Avenue Bistro & Bar* ®®®®
Shop 2, Avonmore Centre, 9th Avenue. ((031) 312-9134.
This boutique restaurant presents cosmopolitan American specialities. Offers
delights such as San Francisco-style fish stew with saffron, roasted red pepper
rouille and croutons. **P** **V** **⚡** ● *Sat & Mon L, Sun.*
AE DC MC V

Price categories for a three-course meal and one half-bottle of house wine, as well as unavoidable costs such as service and couvert charges:
Ⓡ under R45
ⓇⓇ R45–R70
ⓇⓇⓇ R70–R90
ⓇⓇⓇⓇ R90–R115
ⓇⓇⓇⓇⓇ over R115

CREDIT CARDS
Indicates which credit cards are accepted: AE American Express; DC Diners Club; MC MasterCard; V Visa.

CHILDREN'S FACILITIES
Small portions and high chairs available, and there may also be a special children's menu.

OUTSIDE TABLES
Meals can be served *al fresco*.

TWO SITTINGS
Bookings are taken for more than one sitting per table at peak times.

	CREDIT CARDS	CHILDREN'S FACILITIES	OUTSIDE TABLES	BAR	TWO SITTINGS
THE POINT: *Famous Fish Company* ⓇⓇⓇⓇ King's Battery, 4001. **Road map** F3. 𝄃 *(031) 368-1060.* Spectacular setting in the harbour houses one of South Africa's top seafood restaurants. Specialities of the house include mussels in white wine, grilled calamari, seafood platter and fresh linefish. 🅿	AE DC MC V	●	■	●	
RAMSGATE: *La Petite Normandie* ⓇⓇⓇⓇ 73 Marine Dr, 4285. **Road map** F3. 𝄃 *(039) 317-1818.* Judged one of the top ten in KwaZulu-Natal, this restaurant offers the best in French cuisine. It has a private dining room. 🅿 🆅 ● *Sun & Mon.*	AE DC MC V		■		
SALT ROCK: *Beira Mar Restaurant Portuguese* ⓇⓇⓇⓇⓇ Mall 505, Basil Hulett Dr, 4391. **Road map** F3. 𝄃 *(032) 525-8505.* This restaurant offers delicious Portuguese cuisine with a warm welcome. The crab and prawn curries are a must. 🅿 🆅 *by arrangement* ● *out of season.*	AE DC MC V	●	■	●	■
SOUTHBROOM: *Trattoria La Terrazza* ⓇⓇⓇⓇ Outlook Rd, 4277. **Road map** F3. 𝄃 *(039) 316-6162.* This cozy restaurant, situated under milkwood trees on the Umkobi Lagoon, offers home-made pasta and regional Italian dishes. 🅿 🆅 ● *Mon.*	AE MC V	●	■	●	
UMBILO: *Coimbra Portuguese Restaurant* ⓇⓇⓇ Queensmead Mall, Hillier Rd, 4001. **Road map** F3. 𝄃 *(031) 205-5447.* Reputed to be the best Portuguese restaurant in Durban, the peri-peri chicken is heavenly, but don't overlook the traditional-style seafood. Live Latin American music on Friday and Saturday evenings. 🅿 🎵	AE DC MC V			●	
UMHLALI: *Shortens Country House* ⓇⓇⓇ Compensation Rd, 4390. **Road map** F3. 𝄃 *(032) 947-1140.* Guests at this award-winning farmhouse restaurant, built in 1903, can choose to dine inside or in the garden. A la carte menu includes daily specials. Try char-grilled quail on garlic puree; nougatine parfait with passion fruit. 🅿 🆅 🍴 🍷	DC MC V		■	●	
WESTVILLE: *Ma Cucina* ⓇⓇⓇⓇ 124 Jan Hofmeyr Road. 𝄃 *(031) 266-5737* Ma Cucina is a Mediterranean-style café offering breakfast, lunch and dinner. Try the croissants with egg and mozarella, or the bruschettas. 🆅 🍽 ● *Mon.*	AE DC MC V		■		■

GAUTENG & SUN CITY

	CREDIT CARDS	CHILDREN'S FACILITIES	OUTSIDE TABLES	BAR	TWO SITTINGS
FAIRWAYS: *Medeo Restaurant* ⓇⓇⓇⓇⓇ Palazzo Intercontinental c/o William Nicol Dr. & Monte Casino Blvd. 𝄃 *(011) 510-3000.* A Mediterranean restaurant set in beautiful grounds and boasting fine views. Regularly serves dishes such as seafood broth, ostrich strips or trout. 🅿 🆅 🍷	AE DC MC V	●	■	●	■
JOHANNESBURG: *Sam's Café* ⓇⓇⓇ 11 Seventh St, Melville 2092. **Road map** E2. 𝄃 *(011) 726-8142.* A popular and trendy place, where creative flair is evident in the select choice of Mediterranean and oriental dishes. Starter portions throughout allow for a wider choice, but do leave room for dessert. 🅿 🆅 ● *Sun eve, Sat, Sun L.*	AE DC MC V		■		
JOHANNESBURG: *Singing Fig* ⓇⓇⓇ 44 The Avenue, Norwood, 2192. **Road map** E2. 𝄃 *(011) 728-2434.* This popular eatery is minimalistic in style, reminiscent of a country kitchen, but the fare is far from minimalistic. 🅿 🆅 🍽 🍷 ● *Sun eve, Sat L.*	AE DC MC V		■	●	
JOHANNESBURG: *Chaplin's* ⓇⓇⓇⓇ 85 Fourth Ave, Mellville, 2092. **Road map** E2. 𝄃 *(011) 482-4657.* The menu features unusual combinations, such as deboned duckling in an apple, cherry and cinnamon sauce, and authentic Caesar salad. Vegetarians, diabetics, and those on a fat-free diet are catered for and copies of the menu are available in Braille. Award-winning wine list. 🆅 🍽 ● *Sat L, Sun.*	AE DC MC V		■		

JOHANNESBURG: *Giles Restaurant*   ®®®®   AE
9 Grafton Ave, Craighall Park, 2196. **Road map** E2. 📞 *(011) 442-4056.* **FAX** *(011) 442-4057.*   DC
A lively, unpretentious establishment offering varied and interesting
French-influenced cuisine. A cartoon theme runs across the walls
and tables and there is an inviting shady terrace. 🔳 ⚡ 🍴 ⚫ *Sun.*

JOHANNESBURG: *Gramadoelas*   ®®®®   AE
Market Theatre, Newtown, 2001. **Road map** E2. 📞 *(011) 838-6960.*   DC
Cape Dutch/Malay and African dishes are served, as well as a wide range   MC
of wines and traditional African drinks. The speciality of the house is the   V
Gramadoelas selection platter. 🅿 🔳 ⚡ ⚫ *Sun, Mon L.*

JOHANNESBURG: *The Ritz*   ®®®®   AE
17 Third Ave, Parktown North, 2193. **Road map** E2. 📞 *(011) 880-2470.*   DC
Mediterranean cuisine with eastern influences are on the menu at this popular   MC
restaurant. Teas and light meals are served in the garden. 🅿 🔳 🍴 ⚡ ⚫ *Sun.*   V

JOHANNESBURG: *La Belle Terrasse*   ®®®®®   AE
67 Jan Smuts Ave, Westcliff, 2193. **Road map** E2. 📞 *(011) 646-2400.*   DC
The Westcliff Hotel has a reputation for style and elegance which is upheld   MC
by this top-rated restaurant. Gourmet cuisine in the French tradition is aimed   V
at discerning diners who enjoy only the finest food, accompanied by local
and imported wines that complement and enhance the experience. Superb
service is of a standard that matches the food and the ambience. 🅿 🔳 🎵

JOHANNESBURG: *Lee's Café Zoo Lake*   ®®®®   AE
Zoo Lake Gardens, Parkview, 2193. **Road map** E2. 📞 *(011) 646-8807.*   DC
A popular, elegant venue in a superb setting that serves seasonal dishes,   MC
venison and seafood on a covered terrace. The wine list is superb.   V
🅿 ⚡ 🍴 ⚫ *Mon, Tue–Sun eve.*

JOHANNESBURG: *The Bell Pepper*   ®®®®   AE
176 Queen St, Kensington, 2094. **Road map** E2. 📞 *(011) 615-7531.*   DC
Housed in a former antique store in Kensington's charming Queen Street,
this sleek, modern restaurant serves mainly French cuisine as well as
fusion dishes. Core menus are changed seasonally. 🔳 ⚡ 🍴 ⚫ *Mon & Sun.*

MIDRAND: *Thirty-Three High Street*   ®®®   AE
33 High St, Modderfontein, North Rand, 2065. **Road map** E2. 📞 *(011) 606-3574.*   DC
This tastefully refurnished Victorian manor is set in a tranquil garden with old   MC
oak trees. The menu includes international and South African favourites, such   V
as calamari to start, honey-glazed duck breast to follow. 🅿 🔳 ⚡ 🍴 ⚫ *Mon.*

RANDBURG: *Baytree Restaurant*   ®®®   AE
Cnr North Rd & Hans Strydom Dr, Linden Ext, 2194. **Road map** E2. 📞 *(011) 784-5738.*   DC
This award-winning gourmet restaurant specializes in Provençal dishes and   MC
offers a notable wine list. 🅿 🔳 ⚡ 🍴 ⚫ *Sun, Mon.*   V

RANDBURG: *Casalinga*   ®®®®   AE
Muldersdrift Road, Honeydew, 2040. **Road map** E2. 📞 *(011) 957-2612.*   DC
This classic Italian country restaurant uses organically grown vegetables and   MC
home-made pasta as the basis for superb regional cuisine, which explains why   V
booking is essential, particularly at weekends. 🅿 🔳 ⚫ *Sun eve, Mon, Tue.*

ROSEBANK: *Sophia's*   ®®®   AE
Rosebank Mall, Cradock Ave, Rosebank, 2196. **Road map** E2. 📞 *(011) 880-7356.*   DC
A restaurant with a relaxed Mediterranean flavour and an excellent wine list.   MC
The menu includes Greek and Italian favourites. 🅿 🔳 ⚡ 🍴 ⚫ *Sun eve.*   V

SANDTON: *Raj Indian Restaurant*   ®®®   AE
Cnr Rivonia Rd & 7th Ave, Rivonia, 2128. **Road map** E2. 📞 *(011) 807-0471.*   DC
Indian chefs prepare a wide range of North Indian dishes. The wine list and   MC
service are good and the tandoori excellent. 🅿 ⚡ 🍴   V

SANDTON: *Turtle Creek Winery*   ®®®®   AE
58 Wierda Rd East, Sandton, 2196. **Road map** E2. 📞 *(011) 884-0466.*   DC
Located in an open barn with seating in the garden, this country restaurant has   MC
a Mauritian chef who expertly prepares an international selection of dishes   V
encompassing everything from snack fare to culinary delights. 🅿 🔳 ⚫ *Sun eve.*

SANDTON: *Blues Room*   ®®®®   AE
Village Walk Shopping Centre, Sandown, 2196. **Road map** E2. 📞 *(011) 784-5527.*   DC
A low-lit blues-themed restaurant which offers an international menu and   MC
features local and international blues, rock and jazz. 🅿 🔳 🎵 ⚫ *Sun, Mon*

<table>
<tr><td colspan="2">

Price categories for a three-course meal and one half-bottle of house wine, as well as unavoidable costs such as service and couvert charges:
Ⓡ under R45
ⓇⓇ R45–R70
ⓇⓇⓇ R70–R90
ⓇⓇⓇⓇ R90–R115
ⓇⓇⓇⓇⓇ over R115

</td><td colspan="5">

CREDIT CARDS
Indicates which credit cards are accepted: AE American Express; DC Diners Club; MC MasterCard; V Visa.
CHILDREN'S FACILITIES
Small portions and high chairs available, and there may also be a special children's menu.
OUTSIDE TABLES
Meals can be served *al fresco*.
TWO SITTINGS
Bookings are taken for more than one sitting per table at peak times.

</td></tr>
</table>

	CREDIT CARDS	CHILDREN'S FACILITIES	OUTSIDE TABLES	BAR	TWO SITTINGS
SANDTON: *Le Canard* ⓇⓇⓇⓇ 163 Rivonia Rd, Morningside, 2057. **Road map** E2. ((011) 884-4597. Set in a beautiful Georgian house surrounded by a tranquil garden, this expensive restaurant offers French haute cuisine and is a must for discerning diners. There is an *alfresco* terrace for lighter lunches. 🅿 Ⓥ 🍴 ⚡ ● *Sun.*	AE DC MC V		▪		
SANDTON: *Browns of Rivonia* ⓇⓇⓇ 21 Wessels Rd, Rivonia, 2128. **Road map** E2. ((011) 803-7605. Browns' indoor dining area spills out into a covered patio which looks out into flower filled gardens. 🅿 ⚡ Ⓥ 🍴 🎵 *Thurs and Sat* ● *Sun.*	AE DC MC V		▪		
SANDTON: *Linger Longer* ⓇⓇⓇⓇ 58 Wierda Rd West, Sandton, 2196. **Road map** E2. ((011) 884-0465. This award-winning restaurant, one of the country's top ten, is set in a gracious colonial home. Classic dishes such as poached Scottish salmon and the trio of lamb, beef and venison roasts, or fusion cooking blending east and west, are complemented by a superb selection of wines. 🅿 Ⓥ 🍴 ⚡ 🍷 ● *Sat L, Sun.*	AE DC MC V		▪		
MULDERSDRIFT: *Bellgables Country Restaurant* ⓇⓇⓇⓇ Off DF Malan Dr, 1747. **Road map** E2. ((011) 659-0430. This farmhouse, with its old slave bell, is said to be one of the prettiest in the province. Decorated with original art, it offers beautifully presented, inspired, classic cuisine. Sunday lunch is served al fresco on the pool terrace. 🅿 Ⓥ 🍴 ● *Mon, Tue.*	AE DC MC V		▪	●	
PRETORIA: *Café Riche* ⓇⓇⓇ 2 Church Sq, 0002. **Road map** E2. ((012) 328-3173. Enter this beautiful Art Nouveau-style national monument building, and enjoy the selection of fresh salads and baguettes with a variety of fillings. 🅿 ⚡ 🎵	AE DC MC V		▪	●	
PRETORIA: *Villa Do Mar* ⓇⓇⓇ Waterkloof Heights Centre, Club Ave, 0181. **Road map** E2. ((012) 460-5140. This Portuguese restaurant with a rustic feel offers authentic, spicy specialities and Portuguese wines and port, supplemented by a good local list. Try the Portuguese-style chunky fish soup or calamari. 🅿 Ⓥ ⚡ ● *Sat L, Mon.*	AE DC MC V	●	▪		
PRETORIA: *The Odd Plate* ⓇⓇⓇⓇ 262 Rhino St, Hennops Park, Centurion, 0157. **Road map** E2. ((012) 660-3260. Plates are the only mismatched items to be found in this Prue Leith-run cooking school. Daily lessons dictate the fare, which ranges from classic to contemporary, all served with skill and enthusiasm by Leith's students. 🅿 Ⓥ 🍴 ● *L, Sun, Mon, Tue.*	AE DC MC V		▪		
PRETORIA: *Ritrovo Ristorante* ⓇⓇⓇⓇ Waterkloof Heights Shopping Centre, Club Ave, 0181. **Road map** E2. ((012) 460-4367. This award-winning Italian venue offers South Italian cuisine and wonderful views. The Espresso Café next door serves home-made pasta. 🅿 Ⓥ ⚡ 🍷	AE DC MC V	●	▪	●	
SWAZILAND: *Phoenix Spur* ⓇⓇ Shop 210, Mall, Mbabane. **Road map** E2. ((09268) 404-9103. Family restaurant serving a variety of grills and burgers, with an extensive and varied salad buffet. The Phoenix Spur is part of a national chain offering excellent value. 🅿 Ⓥ ⚡	AE DC MC V	●	▪	●	
SWAZILAND: *Cleopatras on the Nile* ⓇⓇⓇ Gilfillian Road, Mbabane. **Road map** E2. ((09268) 404-4880. Portuguese-style restaurant specializing in seafood and grills. Try king-size prawns or grilled chicken with fiery peri-peri sauce from Mozambique. 🅿	AE DC MC V			●	
SWAZILAND: *Mliwane Lodge* ⓇⓇⓇ 12 km (7 miles) outside Mbabane on the Manzini road. **Road map** E2. ((09268) 416-1591. The buffet-style restaurant at this game lodge, which caters mainly for residents, is open for breakfast, lunch and dinner daily. 🅿	MC V			●	

BLYDE RIVER CANYON & KRUGER

DULLSTROOM: *Die Tonteldoos Bistro*　　　　　　ⓇⓇⓇ
Hugenote St, 1110. **Road map** E2. 【 *(013) 254-0115.*
At 2,100 m (6 800 ft) above sea level, it is often misty and cold here, which
explains why fireplaces are used in summer. Good British home-style cooking.
Sensational grilled trout with lemon herb butter. 🅿 🆅 ⚡ ● *Mon–Thurs eve.*

	AE	●	■		
	DC				
	MC				
	V				

DULLSTROOM: *Harrie's Pancakes*　　　　　　　ⓇⓇⓇ
Main Rd, 1110. **Road map** E2. 【 *(013) 254-0801.*
A great place to try if you enjoy pancakes. Harrie's offers a variety of savoury
and sweet fillings, and four breakfast menus. 🅿 🆅

	AE	●	■		
	DC				
	MC				
	V				

HENDRIKSDAL: *Artists' Café*　　　　　　　　ⓇⓇⓇⓇ
Between Sabie & Nelspruit. **Road map** F2. 【 *(013) 764-2309.*
This trattoria in the tin-roofed house of the former station master offers Tuscan
cuisine, alongside dishes made from local game. Much use made of fresh herbs
and the pasta is homemade. The Café also exhibits local and tribal art. 🅿 🆅

	AE	●	■		
	DC				
	MC				
	V				

NYLSTROOM: *Shangri-La Country Lodge*　　　　ⓇⓇⓇ
Eersbewoond Rd, 0510. **Road map** E2. 【 *(014) 718-1600.*
The lodge offers a choice of options. A variety of African and Cape Malay
dishes are served by candlelight in the Kraal (semi-enclosed, thatched area),
with local drinks like *maroela, mampoer*, sorghum beer. In the Heritage
Room, the à la carte menu blends classic cuisine with African influences. 🅿 🆅

	AE		■	●	■
	DC				
	MC				
	V				

PILGRIM'S REST: *Chandelier*　　　　　　　　ⓇⓇⓇⓇ
Lydenberg Rd, Grootfonteinberg, 1290. **Road map** F2. 【 *(013) 768-1241.*
Locally caught trout and Sheba-style beef are among the specialities prepared
by the cordon bleu chef at this elegant English country-style restaurant on the
road to the historical mining town. 🅿 🆅 🍴 ♟

	AE	●		●	
	DC				
	MC				
	V				

SOUTH OF THE ORANGE

BEAUFORT WEST: *Saddles Steak Ranch*　　　　　　ⓇⓇ
144 Donkin St. **Road map** C4. 【 *(023) 415-2310.*
Traditional, lively steak house, often crowded with locals congregating to
watch sport on large-screen TV. Try the Karoo lamb chops. 🆅 ⚡

	AE	●			
	DC				
	MC				
	V				

GRAAFF-REINET: *The Coral Tree*　　　　　　ⓇⓇⓇⓇ
3 Church Square. 【 *(049) 892-5947.*
This restaurant is minimalistic in style, and is set in a 128 year old building.
Dishes include Karoo Lamb and Venison. 🅿 🆅 ⚡ ● *Sun.*

			■	●	

NORTH OF THE ORANGE

BLOEMFONTEIN: *Beef Baron*　　　　　　　　ⓇⓇⓇ
22 Second Ave, Westdene, 9301. **Road map** D3. 【 *(051) 447-4290.*
As its name implies, this restaurant serves mainly beef cuts, and they are
masters at it. Try the Diplomat Fillet or the Bookmaker's Rump. Non-beef
dishes, such as Portuguese-style prawns, are also available. 🅿 🆅 ● *Sun.*

	AE			●	
	DC				
	MC				
	V				

BLOEMFONTEIN: *The Mexican Restaurant*　　　ⓇⓇⓇⓇⓇ
19a Second Avenue, Westdene. 【 *(051) 430-4526.*
A winner of several prestigious awards, this restaurant offers fine vegetarian and
seafood dishes. Fresh coastal oysters are available, as well as mustard fillets.
🅿 🆅 ⚡ ♟ 🎵 ● *Dec school holidays, Sun (exc first Sun of month), Sat L.*

	AE			●	■
	DC				
	MC				
	V				

KIMBERLEY: *Mario's*　　　　　　　　　　ⓇⓇⓇ
159 Du Toitspan Rd, 8301. **Road map** D3. 【 *(053) 831-1738.*
A charming Mediterranean restaurant with friendly service and a warm, Italian
ambience, this restaurant serves delicacies like chicken breast with almonds
and Emmenthal cheese, and breast of duck in port sauce. 🅿 🆅 ● *Sat L, Sun.*

	AE	●	■	●	
	DC				
	MC				
	V				

KIMBERLEY: *Umberto's*　　　　　　　　　ⓇⓇⓇ
229 Du Toitspan Rd, 8301. **Road map** D3. 【 *(053) 832-5741.*
The pizzas are baked in a wood-burning pizza oven in this lively Italian
restaurant. Next door is South Africa's only drive-in pub, which was frequented
by Cecil John Rhodes. 🅿 ● *Sun, Good Fri, 25 & 26 Dec, 1 Jan.*

	AE	●		●	
	DC				
	MC				
	V				

UPINGTON: *Le Raisin*　　　　　　　　　　ⓇⓇ
67 Market St, 8801. **Road map** B3. 【 *(083) 771-3934.*
An affordable yet elegant small town restaurant that serves a variety of meat
and seafood dishes, as well as vegetarian meals. 🅿 🆅 ⚡

	DC	●			
	MC				
	V				

SHOPPING IN SOUTH AFRICA

SOUTH AFRICA's principal shopping attraction is, undoubtedly, its superb range of handcrafted goods, as well as jewellery made from locally mined gold, inlaid with precious or semi-precious stones. Intricate beadwork, woven rugs and carpets, decorative baskets, stone and wood carvings, wood-and-bone spoons and traditional, flowing African garments with geometric motifs are sold at curio shops and

Natural cluster of amethyst crystals

markets countrywide. Crafters from the rest of Africa, attracted by South Africa's thriving tourism industry, frequent markets in the bigger centres, selling, for example, ceremonial wooden masks and malachite bracelets. All manner of other handworks can be found in craft markets, too, from wind chimes, wooden beach chairs and painted duvet covers to African chilli sauces and leather goods.

Eye-catching works in malachite

SHOPPING HOURS

CITY SHOPPING MALLS have adopted extended hours, staying open until around nine o'clock at night for the convenience of their patrons, while most small-town shops observe the nine-to-five rule. Village shops may even close at noon as siestas are still very much a part of rural South Africa.

Outdoor fleamarkets usually begin trading around 10am and end at sunset.

HOW TO PAY

VISA AND MASTERCARD are readily accepted in malls and city shops. Similarly, VISA, American Express and Thomas

Cook traveller's cheques are accepted against proof of identity. Small shops and informal traders prefer cash. In remote areas and rural villages, it is advisable to carry cash in a concealed wallet or pouch. If you need cash after hours, most banks have automatic teller machines (ATMs) that allow you to make withdrawals with your credit card or international ATM card.

BARGAINING

AFRICAN TRADERS are always prepared to bargain hard, mostly because they would rather make a sale than lose it. Indian salespeople also enjoy haggling over prices and seem to expect a little resistance from their customers.

VAT

MOST GOODS (except basic foodstuffs) are subject to 14 per cent Value Added Tax (VAT), included in the price. Expensive antiques, art and jewellery are best bought from reputable dealers who issue

foreign clients with a VAT refund document, which can be used to claim the VAT amount paid, prior to departure from the international airports.

Vibrant colour at a market stall

A WORD OF WARNING

HAWKERS OF GOLD JEWELLERY and watches, theatrically concealed under a jacket or inside a folded piece of cloth commonly hang around open air markets and parking lots of shopping malls. Although they approach potential buyers with a very convincing act of secrecy and a lowered voice, the goods are usually cheap brass imitations. They may also be real – and perhaps stolen. In either case, decline briskly and walk away.

REFUNDS

IF THE MERCHANDISE you have bought is defective in any way, you are entitled to a refund. If you decide that you don't like an item, you may have to settle for a credit note or an exchange. In general, the larger the store, the more

The Workshop *(see pp218–21)* in Durban during the festive season.

protected you are; if you are unhappy with the service, talk to the customer services department or the manager.

WHERE TO SHOP

MANY INTERESTING STORES have moved away from the malls and main centres. Specialist book, design and wine stores jostle with delis and art studios in the city side streets. There are also always surprises in the small-town bric-a-brac shops. Gold and diamond jewellery, however, is best sought in the malls; the variety is more extensive.

SHIPPING PACKAGES

THE POST OFFICE will send parcels of up to 30 kg (66 lb) to Great Britain, Australia and New Zealand and up to 20 kg (44 lb) to the United States. They may not be larger than 2.5 sq metres (8 sq feet). A fixed handling fee is payable, with additional charges per 100 g. Insurance is an option, with an upper limit of around R2,000. Surface mail will take about 6–8 weeks; airmail one week.

Many upmarket stores will arrange all packaging and shipping. To organize your own exports, contact a shipper such as **Trans Global Freight International.** They will arrange customs and packaging, and will deliver to your home or the office of their local agent. There is no maximum or minimum size or weight, and prices are competitive.

A bottle of wine to suit any taste

Swaziland is a treasure trove of woven baskets and mats

STRICTLY SOUTH AFRICAN

IN JOHANNESBURG and other large cities, you can buy almost anything. Johannesburg, in particular, attracts consumers from all over the subcontinent. It is the queen of the mall culture, and the best place to find indigenous arts and crafts. But much of the wood and stone carving is from West and Central Africa and Zimbabwe.

The crafts in Durban *(see pp 218–21)* and KwaZulu-Natal *(see pp194–95)*, on the other hand, are more likely to be local. Zulu baskets are usually of outstanding quality, as are the woven beer strainers, grass brooms, pots, shields and drums. Sometimes brightly coloured baskets are made from telephone wire.

These wares, as well as many charming and often brightly painted wooden animal and bird figures, can be found on the side of the N2 highway from Durban to the game parks: Hluhluwe-Umfolozi and Mkuzi.

Gazankulu and Venda also have a reputation for crafts. Clay pots with distinctive angular designs in gleaming silver and ochre are popular, as are the woodcarvings, tapestries, fabrics and batiks.

Ndebele bead blankets, belts, aprons and dolls are also worth looking out for *(see p254)*. They can be found at Botshabelo Museum and Nature Reserve near Fort Merensky, 13 km (8 miles) north of Middelburg.

Knysna *(see pp176–7)* is yet another craftwork "capital". A major timber centre, this is the place to buy stinkwood and yellowwood chairs and tables, door knobs and other unusual decor accessories. Colourful, woven mohair blankets, shawls, cushion covers and jackets are also found in this region.

The label "Scarab Paper", represents a truly unique South African craft: handmade papers, notelets and cards in nationwide craft and curio stores – produced from (now fragrance free) elephant dung!

Swazi candles are also sold countrywide: look out for the distinctive "stained-glass" effect of these slow-burning bright candles in animal, bird and more traditional candle shapes.

Throughout the country, gift stores and jewellers offer an unusual array of necklaces, rings, earrings and bracelets using local diamonds and semi-precious stones, often combined with South African gold and platinum.

DIRECTORY

SHIPPING AGENCIES

Trans Global Freight International
☏ *(021) 419-5610.*

Seaclad Maritime (shipping line)
☏ *(021) 419-1438.*

AfroMar (ship brokers)
☏ *(011) 803-0008.*

ENTERTAINMENT IN
SOUTH AFRICA

CAPAB ballet dancers

JOHANNESBURG IS reputed to be the entertainment and night-life hub of South Africa. In this entrepreneurial city people party as hard as they work, and there is always something happening. This does not mean, however, that other South African cities and towns are dull. Even rural places have their music, restaurant and clubbing venues. The demand for cinemas and casinos is high, and exciting new venues are opened regularly. The dramatic arts are innovative and of a very high standard, with theatre companies committed to the development of a local arts culture. The vibrant music scene spans classical, jazz and the African *genre*.

The Oude Libertas amphitheatre, Stellenbosch *(see p35)*

INFORMATION

FOR DETAILS of entertainment in the cities, check the local daily press and the weekly papers such as the *Mail & Guardian*, available nationwide. They review and list theatre productions, current film festivals, art exhibitions, music performances and other interesting events.

Reviews and listings also appear in a number of magazines that are sold in book stores and at newsagents. A good choice is *SA City Life*, which includes restaurant reviews and details of workshops, gay and lesbian and kids' events in Cape Town, Johannesburg and Durban.

BOOKING TICKETS

SEATS FOR MOST EVENTS can be reserved by calling **Computicket**, which has branches in all the major centres and larger towns countrywide. To make telephone bookings for Ster-Kinekor cinemas, call Ticketline, or **Ticketweb**.

Most South African theatres and cinemas do not accept telephone bookings without credit card payment.

CINEMA

MAINSTREAM HOLLYWOOD film productions and foreign-language films with subtitles are the main fare in South African cinemas, because the local film industry is still in the fledgling stage.

The cities host regular film festivals: themes range from French, Italian and Dutch to natural health, the environment and gay and lesbian.

THEATRE, OPERA AND DANCE

COMEDY, SATIRE, cabaret and musicals are particularly popular in South Africa, as are modernized and "localized" adaptations of Shakespeare. Theatres are committed to the development of scriptwriting and directing talent, and talent-scouting festivals are becoming annual events.

Arts Alive, a Johannesburg festival held in September, is a major celebration of the performing arts. The FNB Vita Dance Umbrella, held in Johannesburg in February and March, is an important platform for new choreographers. The Standard Bank National Arts Festival *(see p57)* held in

The State Theatre, Pretoria *(see p254)*

"Cross Roads", Rembrandt van Rijn Art Museum, Stellenbosch

Grahamstown in July is, of course, the best place to go for an overview of the innovative, exciting South African theatre, dance, artistic and musical talent.

In KwaZulu-Natal, the annual Massed Choir Festival, toward the end of the year is a celebration of African voices harmonizing oratorio, opera and traditional music. Watch the press for details.

Opera, too, is well supported. The five-month, annual Spier Festival of Music, Theatre and Opera attracts national and international artists.

Zulu dancer at Heia Safari Ranch

Soweto String Quartet charm audiences with their unique compositions and African-flavoured interpretations of classical pieces.

Local rock bands such as Springbok Nude Girls and Sons of Trout enjoy a loyal following, and appear at clubs countrywide. Check the listings guides and local radio stations for details of gigs and venues. Music from the rest of Africa is filtering down to South Africa, and clubs are rocking to sounds from Ghana, Mali and Benin.

MUSIC

THE FIVE SYMPHONY SEASONS throughout the year are well supported in the cities; concerts are held in venues such as the Durban City Hall (see p219), Cape Town's Baxter Theatre (see p106) and the Johannesburg College of Music in Parktown.

Outdoor, twilight performances, for example at Durban's Botanic Gardens (see p221) and Kirstenbosch Gardens in Cape Town (see p100), are popular. Look out for the musical fireworks shows in the cities every December.

Nowadays, international bands, pop and opera singers regularly include South Africa on their world tours.

Nevertheless, local bands are far from neglected, and they offer a wide range of sounds: rock, jazz, gospel, reggae, rap and Afro-fusion. The members of the popular

ART

JOHANNESBURG, DURBAN, Cape Town, Port Elizabeth and Bloemfontein, as well as some of the larger towns such as Knysna, have excellent art galleries. These showcase local and international works, from the traditional to the somewhat more bizarre, from ceramics and photography to multi-media works and installations. Exhibitions change regularly, and exhibition openings are popular social events, with a high-profile speaker as well as a buffet and drinks.

GAMING

INVESTORS, DEVELOPERS and casino operators have poured billions of rand into this industry. South Africa is said to be the one of the biggest emerging gaming markets in the world.

Spectacular gaming and entertainment centres with names like **Graceland**, **Sun City**, **Carousel** and **Emnotweni** are now dotted all over the country. Their architectural styles are detailed and lavish, blending fun and fantasy with the latest in technology.

Limited payout machines (see pp256–7), one-arm bandits and slot machines are found in theme bars, while gaming tables include blackjack, roulette, poker and punto banco. Larger casinos usually have a *salon privé*.

Merry-go-round at the Carousel

DIRECTORY

BOOKING TICKETS

Computicket
(083) 915-8000.
www.computicket.com

Ticketweb
(083) 915-1234.

CINEMAS

Ster-Kinekor Ticket-Line
Cape Town, Durban, Pretoria and Johannesburg (0861) 300-444.

NuMetro booking line
Cape Town, Durban, Pretoria and Johannesburg (0861) 100-220.

GAMING

Carousel (012) 718-7566.
Sun City (014) 557-1000.
Wild Coast Sun (039) 305-9111.
Graceland (011) 620-1000.
Sundome (011) 794-5800.
Emnotweni (013) 757-0021.

SPECIAL-INTEREST VACATIONS

SOUTH AFRICANS, in general, enjoy the great outdoors. With its moderate climate, long hours of sunshine, endless coastline and varied interior landscape, the country offers a wealth of outdoor pursuits virtually all year round. During summer, visitors to Cape Town may well believe that the entire city is in training for forthcoming running and cycling marathons, as Capetonians take to the streets to get fit. Activities go beyond competitive sports, however.

Bungee jumping

From canoeing on the Orange or Tugela rivers to plant-discovery trips in the coastal forests of KwaZulu-Natal, from mountaineering in the Drakensberg to bungee jumping along the Garden Route, to board-sailing in the Western Cape and visiting historic battlefields and museums, there is something to interest everyone. South Africa's interesting multi-cultural past and present are easily accessible by means of many regional festivals *(see pp34–3)* and special tours on offer.

HIKING, KLOOFING AND ROCK CLIMBING

HIKING IS an extremely popular pastime. Even the smallest farms in the most remote regions have laid-out trails; the paths have distance markers and maps are provided upon booking and payment. Most overnight hikes are situated on private land or state reserves, with accommodation in rustic huts (wood, mattresses and cold-water washing facilities are usually provided). Favourite trails such as the two Garden Route trails *(see pp170–1)* – the four-night Otter Trail and four-night Tsitsikamma Trail – can be booked more than a year in advance. Good bookstores stock a host of trail guides. Most outdoor equipment stores are able to advise on day and longer hikes, and they also sell guide books, maps and trail provisions.

Sport fishing at Cape Vidal, in the Greater St Lucia Wetlands *(see p232)*

Kloofing is a newly popular offshoot of hiking: it involves boulder hopping and wading while following the course of a river. It requires a certain level of daring, with long jumps into mountain pools.

The **Hiking South Africa** has a list of some 250 hiking clubs around the country, which arrange weekend and day hikes for beginners and seasoned walkers. These clubs alternatively sometimes organize longer, more challenging trails.

Rock climbing (traditional, sport and bouldering) has a large following in South Africa. Climbing equipment stores will help visiting climbers with information and route ideas. Some of the best traditional climbing is found in the KwaZulu-Natal Drakensberg *(see pp206–7)*, while Cape Town's Table Mountain *(see pp74–5)* offers interesting challenges for experienced climbers.

FISHING

MORE THAN A MILLION anglers enjoy the local waters, which are subject to strict regulations – enquire at the nearest police station. More than 250 species of fish can be caught through fly, line, game, surf or reef fishing. The merging of the cool Atlantic and the warm Indian oceans off the Southern Cape coast creates a high concentration of game fish, including marlin and tuna. Mpumalanga and KwaZulu-Natal offer excellent trout fishing. Kalk Bay in Cape Town has one of the few line-fishing harbours in the world. **Grassroutes Tours** organizes day fishing trips on one of these vessels. Almost all harbours and marinas offer the opportunity to join commercial or semi-commercial boats on short trips, and a myriad tour groups offer fishing charters and expeditions.

Hiking in KwaZulu-Natal

Mountain biking in Knysna

HUNTING

Hunting is a multi-million rand industry, and in the hunting reserves, such as in the Waterberg region of Northern Province, the land is stocked with game specifically for that purpose. The law stipulates that foreign hunters must be accompanied by a professional South African hunter. Contact the **Professional Hunters Association of South Africa (PHASA)** for details of members who will be able to organize your hunting trip for you.

CYCLING

Even the cities offer spectacular cycling routes: after all, 35,000 cyclists take to the streets for the annual marathon around the Cape Peninsula *(see pp60–1)*, and most drivers are remarkably tolerant of cyclists. Specialist shops sell top-of-the range and second-hand equipment and can advise about rides and routes. Cycling organizations such as the **Pedal Power** associations organize weekend rides (which often include off-road routes on otherwise out-of-bounds farmlands.) They are also able to offer advice about renting bicycles. Adventure holiday agencies organize a variety of cycling tours – both off-road and on smooth tar – along the Garden Route, for example, and in the Karoo. Meals, accommodation and luggage transport are provided and cycles can often be hired.

AIR SPORTS

The AERO CLUB OF SOUTH Africa is the controlling and co-ordinating body for all sport aviation: ballooning, hang-gliding, microlighting and parachuting. Winelands and game-viewing hot-air ballooning trips are romantic treats. Contact **Pilansberg Safaris** for game-viewing trips *(see p257)*. Paragliding and parachuting courses and tandem flights are popular. Bridge jumping and bungee jumping are for the real adrenaline junkie, but you may not simply stop, rig up and launch yourself off a bridge. It is safer to book your jump through one of the many adventure travel agencies, such as **Face Adrenalin** in Cape Town. Extreme jumps can be found on the Garden Route.

White-water rafting on the Orange River *(see pp284–5)*

WATER SPORTS

South Africa has 2,500 km (1,553 miles) of coastline and many rivers and dams. The country has some of the world's greatest surf. Perfect waves abound in Jeffrey's Bay, but the surf is great from Namibia to Mozambique. Windsurfing and sailing are also popular, and many of the resorts rent out equipment.

Scuba diving is taught even in Johannesburg. Instructors should be accredited to the **National Association of Underwater Instructors** (NAUI) or **Professional Association of Diving Instructors** (PADI)

The best diving is along the St Lucia Marine Reserve in KwaZulu-Natal, with its coral reefs. In Cape Town, wreck-diving is popular. Swimming with the dolphins is another option. Johannesburg-based **Dolphin Encounters**, for example, organizes three-day trips to the remote east-coast.

River rafting has a growing number of addicts in the country. Qualified guides take rafters in two- or eight-person inflatable rafts on a variety of waters. From white-water running to quiet paddling, there is a trip for everyone and overnight accommodation and meals are always superb. Popular routes include the Blyde River Canyon and the Breede, Orange and Zambezi rivers. One-day or overnight sea or river kayaking trails are available, too, usually around Cape Town, along the Garden Route and in KwaZulu-Natal.

Hot-air ballooning is a popular pastime

Pony trekking in Lesotho *(see pp204–5)*

HORSE RIDING AND PONY TREKKING

SPORT RIDING is controlled by the South African National Equestrian Federation. Leisure riding is very popular; sunset rides along a beach or wine-tasting trails are memorable options.

Pony-trekking in Lesotho *(see pp204–5)* offers a real African experience. Lodges such as **Malealea** can organize guides to accompany riders through unfenced landscapes to see dinosaur tracks or San Bushman rock art. Accommodation is in Basotho huts, with traditional food and dancing provided by the local people.

WILDERNESS TRAILS, FLORA AND BIRD-WATCHING

MOST PRIVATE RESERVES and some of the provincial reserves and national parks offer guided game- and birdwatching walks, as well as overnight bushveld or wilderness trails. The real attraction of these trails, which do not necessarily bring the visitor any closer to the wildlife than a driving tour would, is the unrivalled experience of strolling through the African bush, surrounded by the sounds and smells of the diverse fauna and flora.

The Kruger National Park *(see pp272–5)* offers at least seven such trails: the Bushman Trail includes rock paintings in the hill shelters. At Kosi Bay, the four-day Amanzimnyama

Trail is one of the few ways to see the country's northernmost section of Indian ocean coastline. Cycad, giant raffia palm groves and leatherback turtles on the beach are the star attractions here.

Due to the popularity of these trails, bookings should be made months in advance. Contact the **Wildlife Society of South Africa** and **Kwa-Zulu-Natal Conservation Services** for details. The Wildlife Society, as well as most of the local birding and botanic societies (all of which belong to the Botanic Institute), regularly offer courses on indigenous birds and plants, and arrange outings. Various topics such as medicinal plants, orchids and spiders are covered. Watch the press for details or contact the organizations directly.

TOWNSHIP, HISTORY AND CULTURAL TOURS

A VISIT TO SOWETO is almost always a highlight of a visit to South Africa. In fact, this city receives at least 1,000 foreign visitors a day, and for many it is a destination that is more desirable than Sun City or the game parks.

Experienced guides accompany the visitors to jazz clubs, clinics, schools, *shebeens* (bars) and cemeteries. Overnight stays and visits to the cultural village of African mystic and writer, Credo Mutwa, can also be arranged.

Crowned Crane

Other fascinating tours in and around Johannesburg include a visit to the Lesedi Cultural Village, to encounter Zulu, Xhosa and Sotho culture, and to a Ndebele village near Bronkhorstspruit, close to Pretoria. The best bet is to contact tour operators such as **Jimmy's Face to Face Tours**.

In Cape Town, tours visit the Malay Quarter *(see p71)*, and include traditional meals and hospitality. Contact agencies such as **African Adventure** and **Legend Tours**. District Six, craft and education centres, mosques and the rather drab suburbs known as the Cape Flats are also included on the itinerary.

For those with an interest in life under the apartheid regime, a trip to the infamous Robben Island *(see pp84–5)* is a must, as are tours of places where protest action occurred. Some of these are led by former *uMkhonto-we-Sizwe* (Spear of the Nation) activists.

In central Zululand, 18th and 19th century battlefields of the Great Trek *(see pp48–9)*, Anglo-Zulu War *(see p51)* and South African War *(see pp210–11)* are firm fixtures on the tourist map. Many of the local museums and lodges organize guided tours: the storytelling skills of many of these guides, such as those of the **Fugitives' Drift Lodge** and the **Isibindi Lodge,** are remarkable.

Durban tours offer insights into the Indian community and the nearby townships, while a trip to Shakaland *(see p229)* will explain traditional Zulu society, crafts and medicine.

A visit to a private home is part of most township tours

DIRECTORY

HIKING TRAILS

Hiking South Africa
358 Christoffel St, Pretoria West, Pretoria 0183.
☎ *(0) 83 535-4538.*
@ *christine.frost@ pfizer.com*

Tony Lourens Hiking, Rock climbing and Mountaineering
☎ *(021) 439 8199.*

Abseil Africa
229 Long St, Cape Town 8000.
☎ *(021) 424-1580.*

FISHING

Grassroutes Tours
908 Bree St, Cape Town 8001.
☎ *(021) 706-1006.*

South African Deep Sea Angling Association
PO Box 4191, Cape Town 8000.
☎ *(021) 976-4454.*

Big Game Fishing Safaris
Simons Town Pier, Cape Town 7700.
☎ *(021) 674-2203.*

Lynski Deep Sea Fishing Charters
26 Manaar Rd, Umhlanga Rocks, Durban 4320.
☎ *082 445 6600.*

HUNTING

Professional Hunters Association of South Africa
PO Box 10264, Centurion, Pretoria 0046.
☎ *(012) 667-1023.*

CYCLING

South African Cycling Federation
104 Raats Dr, Tableview Cape Town 7441.
☎ *(021) 794-7887.*

Pedal Power Association
Cape Town 8000
☎ *(021) 689-8420.*

South African Mountain Bike Association
Cape Town 8000
☎ *(021) 856 1284.*

AIR SPORTS

Aero Club of South Africa
49 New Rd, Midrand 1685.
☎ *(011) 805-0366.*

Face Adrenalin
Mossel Bay.
☎ *(044) 697-7001.*

South African Hang Gliding and Para-gliding Association
49 New Road, Il Piachere, Midrand, 1685.
☎ *(012) 668-1219.*

Pilanesberg Safaris
PO Box 79, Sun City 0316.
☎ *(014) 555-5469.*

WATER SPORTS

Felix Unite River Trips
141 Lansdowne Rd, Claremont, Cape Town 7700.
☎ *(021) 670-1300.*

River Rafters
45 Kendal Rd, Diep River, Cape Town 7800.
☎ *(021) 712-5094.*

Coastal Kayak Trails
179 Beach Rd, Three Anchor Bay 8001.
☎ *(021) 439-1134.*

Gary's Surf School
For surfing, board-sailing tuition and tours.
☎ *(021) 783-2915.*

Real Cape Adventures
PaddleYak, Hout Bay.
☎ *(021) 790-5611.*

(NAUI) National Association of Underwater Instructors
40 Gordonia Centre, Gordon's Bay 7150.
☎ *(021) 856-5184.*
W *www.naui.co.za*

Orca Diving Academy
3 Bowwood Rd, Claremont 7708.
☎ *(021) 671-9673.*

Shark Cage Diving
South Coast Safaris 124 Cliff St, De Kelders, Gansbaai 7220.
☎ *(028) 384-1380.*

HORSE RIDING AND PONY TREKKING

Malealea Lodge and Horse Treks
Malealea, Lesotho.
☎ *(051) 447-3200.*

WILDERNESS, BIRD-WATCHING AND FLORA TRAILS

Cape Nature Conservation
Utilitas Bldg, 1 Dorp St, Cape Town 8000.
☎ *(021) 426-0723.*

Wildlife Society of South Africa
31 The Sanctuary Rd, Kirstenhof 7945.
☎ *(021) 701-1397.*

South African National Parks Board
PO Box 787, Pretoria 0001.
☎ *(012) 428-9111.*
W *www.saparks.co.za*

KwaZulu-Natal Conservation Services
Queen Elizabeth Pk, Pietermaritzburg 3200.
☎ *(033) 845-1000.*
W *www.kznwildlife.com*

National Botanical Institute
Kirstenbosch, Rhodes Dr, Newlands, Cape Town 7700.
☎ *(021) 799-8783.*
W *www.nbi.ac.za*

World of Birds Bird Sanctuary
Valley Rd, Hout Bay, Cape Town.
☎ *(021) 790-2730.*

TOWNSHIP TOURS

African Adventure
14 Mooiverwacht St, Stellenridge.
☎ *(021) 785-3374.*

Legend Tours
26 Hayward Rd, Crawford, Cape Town.
☎ *(021) 697-4056/7.*

Gold Reef Guides
Northern Parkway Avenue, Ormonde.
☎ *(011) 496-1400.*

Grassroute Tours
90B Bree St, Cape Town 8001.
☎ *(021) 706-1006.*

Imbizo Tours
1 President St, Johannesburg 2001.
☎ *(011) 838-2667.*

Jimmy's Face to Face Tours
130 Main St, 2nd Fl, Budget House, Johannesburg 2001.
☎ *(011) 331-6109.*

HISTORY AND BATTLEFIELD TOURS

Fugitives' Drift Lodge
PO Rorke's Drift, 3016.
☎ *(034) 642-1843.*

Isibindi Lodge
PO Box 124, Dundee 3000.
☎ *(034) 642-1620.*

Babanango Valley Lodge
PO Box 10, Babanango 3850.
☎ *(035) 835-0062.*

KZN Battlefields Tour Guides
Talana Museum, Dundee 3000.
☎ *(034) 212-2654.*

National Parks and Wildlife Reserves

TEMPORARY PERMITS, at a reasonable cost, are issued by National Parks Board officials at the main entrance gates of most reserves. Maps and information are also available. Accommodation, however, must be booked in advance through the National Parks Board head office in Pretoria, or its representative offices in Cape Town and at the Tourist Junction in Durban (see p220).

Impala

	Number of Rooms	Swimming Pool	On-Site Restaurant	On-Site Fuel	Malaria Risk
CAPE TOWN					
CAPE TOWN: *Cape Peninsula National Park* W www.saparks.co.za Cape Peninsula. **Road map** B5. ☎ (012) 428-9111, (021) 701-8692. Protecting Table Mountain and the peninsular chain, this park sports some 2,285 plant species. Animals: bontebok, Cape mountain zebra and baboon.		●			
WESTERN COASTAL TERRACE					
LANGEBAAN: *West Coast National Park* W www.saparks.co.za West Coast Rd (R27). **Road map** A5. ☎ (012) 428-9111, (021) 422-2816. Encompassing Langebaan lagoon, four islands and the surrounding land, this park protects the largest wetland on the West Coast. Some 30,000 waders may be seen, as well as superb wildflower displays in spring.		●			
SOUTHERN CAPE					
BREDASDORP: *De Hoop Nature Reserve* 56 km (35 miles) E of Bredasdorp on dirt road. **Road map** B5. ☎ (028) 425-5020. This reserve protects a 40-km (25-mile) stretch of coastal wetland. De Hoop also incorporates a marine reserve that is visited by southern right whales annually. Animals: over 400 bontebok, zebra, endangered Cape vulture.	11	●			
THE GARDEN ROUTE TO GRAHAMSTOWN					
PLETTENBERG BAY: *Tsitsikamma National Park* W www.saparks.co.za N2 from Plettenberg Bay. **Road map** C5. ☎ (012) 428-9111. South Africa's first marine park conserves 90 km (56 miles) of coastline. Animals: monkeys, bushbuck, blue duiker, whales and dolphins.	193	■	●		
PORT ELIZABETH: *Addo Elephant National Park* W www.addoelephantpark.com N2 from city, then R335. **Road map** D5. ☎ (012) 428-9111, (042) 233-0556. Since its proclamation in the 1930s, the park has been enlarged to incorporate the Zuurberg mountains. The main rest camp overlooks a floodlit waterhole. Animals: elephant, Cape buffalo, black rhino, eland, kudu.	100	■	●	■	
WILD COAST, DRAKENSBERG AND MIDLANDS					
CLARENS: *Golden Gate Highlands National Park* W www.saparks.co.za R711 or R712. **Road map** E3. ☎ (012) 428-9111, (058) 255-0012. Sandstone rock formations and unspoilt grassland are some of the attractions in this highland park. Animals: blesbok, mountain reedbuck, black wildebeest, eland, *lammergeier* (bearded vulture), black eagle, bald ibis.	100		●	■	
MOOI RIVER/BERGVILLE: *Natal Drakensberg Park* W www.kznwildlife.com N3 via Mooi River, or Harrismith and Estcourt. **Road map** E3. ☎ (033) 845-1000. This park conserves South Africa's highest peaks. Visitors have a choice of four rest camps; hikers stay in caves once inhabited by San Bushmen. Animals: eland, mountain reedbuck, grey rhebok, oribi, baboon.	87				■
DURBAN AND ZULULAND					
EMPANGENI: *Greater St Lucia Wetland Park* W www.leisure.satel.co.za N2 from Mtubatuba. **Road map** F3. ☎ (035) 550-4059. South Africa's most important wetland reserve incorporates bushveld, sand forest, grassland, wetland, coastal forest, swamp, beach, coral reef and sea. Animals: hippo, crocodile, pelican, Caspian tern, fish eagle.	85	■	●	■	●
EMPANGENI: *Hluhluwe Umfolozi Park* W www.kznwildlife.com N2 to signposted turn-off at Mtubatuba. **Road map** F3. ☎ (033) 845-1000, (035) 562-0255. This park has three rest camps and five bush camps, and is most often associated with rhino conservation. Animals: over 1,200 white rhino, 300 black rhino, lion, cheetah, leopard, elephant, buffalo, giraffe, antelope, wild dog.	96	■	●	■	

	NUMBER OF ROOMS	SWIMMING POOL	ON-SITE RESTAURANT	ON-SITE FUEL	MALARIA RISK

NUMBER OF ROOMS
Total number of *rondavels* (also known locally as chalets, and cottages) in the reserve. There may be more than one rest camp.

SWIMMING POOL
Swimming pool located within the rest camp.

ON-SITE RESTAURANT
Restaurant or communal dining area located within the rest camp.

ON-SITE FUEL
Petrol (gas) stations are a necessity, especially in the larger parks where vast distances can be covered in a single day.

MALARIA RISK
Visitors are advised to take the necessary precautions before travelling into any of the areas where malaria is prevalent.

Entry	NUMBER OF ROOMS	SWIMMING POOL	ON-SITE RESTAURANT	ON-SITE FUEL	MALARIA RISK
MKUZE: *Ndumo/Tembe Elephant Reserve* w www.tembe.co.za N2 past Mkuze, Jozini turn-off. **Road map** F3. (033) 845-1000. This isolated wilderness in northern KwaZulu-Natal was established to conserve the region's last elephants. The park is rich in mammal and birdlife.	7				●
VRYHEID: *Itala* w www.kznwildlife.com R69 from Vryheid to signposted turn at Louwsburg. **Road map** F3. (033) 845-1000. A reserve in the catchment of the Phongolo River. Animals: elephant, buffalo, rhino, leopard, giraffe, eland, red hartebeest, kudu, waterbuck.	68	■	●	■	

GAUTENG AND SUN CITY

Entry	NUMBER OF ROOMS	SWIMMING POOL	ON-SITE RESTAURANT	ON-SITE FUEL	MALARIA RISK
HEIDELBERG: *Suikerbosrand Nature Reserve* Outside Heidelberg. **Road map** E2. (011) 904-3930. A prominent range studded with proteas *(suikerbos)*, some 10 km (6 miles) from Johannesburg. Animals: wildebeest, eland, springbok, blesbok.		■	●		
RUSTENBURG: *Pilanesberg National Park* w www.goldenleopard.co.za 50 km (31 miles) NW of Rustenburg. **Road map** D2. (014) 553-6135. The reserve lies in an ancient volcano. Animals: lion, leopard, cheetah, elephant, buffalo, rhino, hippo, giraffe, zebra, 17 antelope species.	182	■	●	■	
ZEERUST: *Madikwe Game Reserve* 70 km (43 miles) north of Zeerust on R49. **Road map** D2. (011) 315-6194. Situated in the extreme northwest corner of Northwest Province, bordering on Botswana. Animals: lion, cheetah, wild dog, spotted hyena, elephant, rhino, eland, giraffe and red hartebeest, among others.	46	■	●	■	

BLYDE RIVER CANYON AND MPUMALANGA

Entry	NUMBER OF ROOMS	SWIMMING POOL	ON-SITE RESTAURANT	ON-SITE FUEL	MALARIA RISK
GRASKOP: *Blyderivierspoort Nature Reserve* R534 from Graskop. **Road map** F2. (013) 761-6019. A reserve in South Africa's largest, 1,000-m (3,281-ft) deep canyon. Animals: variety of smaller mammals and birdlife, five primates.	157	■	●	■	
NELSPRUIT AND PHALABORWA: *Kruger National Park* w www.saparks.co.za N4, R538, R569, or R536. **Road map** F2. (012) 428-9111. South Africa's conservation flagship measures 352 km (219 miles) from north to south and averages 60 km (37 miles) across. The abundant wildlife can be viewed along 2,400 km (1,491 miles) of all-weather roads. For accommodation *(see pp335–6)*.	4000	■	●	■	●

SOUTH OF THE ORANGE

Entry	NUMBER OF ROOMS	SWIMMING POOL	ON-SITE RESTAURANT	ON-SITE FUEL	MALARIA RISK
BEAUFORT WEST: *Karoo National Park* w www.saparks.co.za N1 to Beaufort West. **Road map** D2. (012) 428-9111, (023) 415-2828. The park was established to protect a part of the semi-arid Karoo that is unique to South Africa. Animals: Cape mountain zebra, springbok, gemsbok, red hartebeest, black wildebeest.	22	■	●		
UPINGTON: *Augrabies Falls National Park* w www.parks-sa.co.za N14, 120 km (74 miles) W of Upington. **Road map** B3. (012) 343-1991, (054) 452-9200. This desert park surrounds the spectacular waterfall formed by the Orange River. Animals: black rhino, eland, springbok, gemsbok, giraffe.	59	■	●	■	

NORTH OF THE ORANGE

Entry	NUMBER OF ROOMS	SWIMMING POOL	ON-SITE RESTAURANT	ON-SITE FUEL	MALARIA RISK
UPINGTON: *Kgalagadi Transfrontier Park* w www.saparks.co.za R360 from Upington. **Road map** B2. (012) 428-9111, (054) 561-2000. In the Northern Cape, a desert wilderness of red sand dunes bisected by two dry rivers forms the second largest park in the country. It adjoins a vast national park in Botswana – the combined International Peace Park covers almost twice the area of the Kruger National Park. Animals: lion, cheetah, eland, springbok, gemsbok, brown- and spotted hyena, bat-eared fox, 260 bird species.	165	■	●	■	

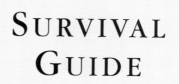

SURVIVAL
GUIDE

PRACTICAL INFORMATION

SOUTH AFRICA HOSTS around 4.5 million foreign visitors a year. Throughout the country, the peak seasons coincide with the South African school holidays – the busiest times are from early December to late February, especially along the south and east coasts. The Easter weekend is also busy at both inland and seaside resorts, as are the four-week winter school holidays over June and July. Although the number of tourists increases every year, the country nevertheless offers a sense of the "undiscovered". Local people still have wide, sandy beaches largely to themselves, and road travel between cities and the sea is easy. In the interior, the natural splendour of game parks and nature reserves draw crowds of visitors.

National Monument logo

WHEN TO GO

MANY PARTS of South Africa are at their best in September and October, when the spring season's growth is fresh and the temperature comfortably warm. Game-watchers may prefer June to August, when many trees are bare and large numbers of animals converge on the diminishing number of drinking places. Winter days are usually sunny and warm, but temperatures drop as the sun sets.

Temperatures from December to February may be close to unbearable in high-lying areas such as the Northern Cape and along the East Coast, but relief is delivered through thunderstorms almost every afternoon. The moderating influence of the sea is welcome at the coast, although some people find the increased humidity difficult to deal with. The southwestern areas have winter rainfall and hot summers. Much of the southern coast receives rain throughout the year. Almost all attractions stay open all through the year.

WHAT TO TAKE

DON'T UNDERESTIMATE South African winters, or the wind-chill factor in summer; bear in mind that central heating is the exception and pack warm clothes. Sunblock, film and specialized provisions can be bought locally, but do carry a supply of medication if you suffer from a chronic condition.

VISA AND PASSPORTS

EUROPEAN UNION nationals need only a valid passport in order to stay in South Africa for six months. Citizens of the United States, Canada, Australia and New Zealand, who have a valid passport, can stay for three months.

Visas to enter Swaziland are issued free of charge at the border. Visa requirements for Lesotho are about to change. The South African consulate or embassy in your country will be able to advise.

All visitors must complete a temporary residence permit at the point of entry into South Africa. It shows length and

Tourist Information kiosk

purpose of the visit and a contact address. Visitors may also be asked to prove that they can support themselves financially while in the country and own a return ticket or have the means to buy one. No inoculations are necessary, however, if you arrive from a country where yellow fever is endemic you will need a vaccination certificate. Malaria is still prevalent in parts of KwaZulu-Natal and Mpumalanga, and caution is advised.

TOURIST INFORMATION

TOURIST OFFICES, identified by the letter "i" on a green background, offer invaluable advice about what to see and where to go. They may also carry the name of an umbrella organisation or a local publicity association. The offices are usually sited on the main road in the smaller towns, sometimes adjoining (or inside) the offices of the local authority or forming part of the local museum or public library. You should be able to obtain advance information in your own country from **South African Tourism**.

Summer game-viewing at Addo Elephant Park, Port Elizabeth *(see p186)*

The *John Benn* takes sightseers around the Knysna Lagoon *(see p176)*

OPENING TIMES AND ADMISSION PRICES

Most businesses (other than retail outlets), museums and galleries open from 8 or 9am until 4 or 5pm. Many, particularly in the smaller towns, close for lunch between 1 and 2pm, except during the peak summer season. Larger museums or galleries usually close for one day each week (usually on a Monday). Entry charges vary. Nature reserves, game parks and botanic gardens all charge entry fees, most of them very reasonable.

ETIQUETTE

Dress code in South African cities is casual, except for a few top restaurants and for events noted as formal. On the beach, however, it is illegal for women to either swim or sunbathe topless. The consumption of alcohol on beaches and in public places is illegal, as is smoking in buses, trains, taxis and most public buildings.

It is very important to observe religious customs when visiting mosques, temples and other places of worship.

DISABLED TRAVELLERS

Facilities for the disabled are not as sophisticated as they are in the United States and Europe, but wheelchair users, for example, will nevertheless have a satisfactory holiday. If you're renting a car, ask about a special parking disk, allowing parking concessions. Local airlines provide assistance for disabled passengers, if given prior notice. South Africa also has a growing number of hotels that cater for the disabled, and the Kruger and Karoo national parks have specially adapted huts. Contact the **Association for Persons with Physical Disabilities** *(see p373)* for further information and contact numbers.

Disabled parking

VAT AND TAXES

See p358 and p381.

Visitors must remove their shoes before entering a Hindu temple

DIRECTORY

EMBASSIES AND CONSULATES

Australian High Commission
Pretoria (012) 342-3740.
Durban (031) 208-4163.

British High Commission
Johannesburg (011) 327-0163.
Pretoria (012) 421-7800.
Cape Town (021) 405-2400.

Canadian High Commission
Johannesburg (011) 442-3130.
Pretoria (012) 422-3000.
Cape Town (021) 423-5240.

Embassy of Ireland
Pretoria (012) 342-5062.

New Zealand High Commission
Pretoria (012) 342-8656.

US Consulate General
Johannesburg (011) 646-6900.
Cape Town (021) 421-4280.
Durban (031) 304-4737.

US Embassy
Pretoria (012) 342-1048.

TOURIST OFFICES

Cape Town Tourism
(021) 405-4500.
w www.cape-town.org

Durban Publicity
(031) 304-4934.
w www.durban.co.za

Eastern Cape Tourism Board
(041) 585-7761.

Free State Tourism
(051) 405-8111.
w www.freestate.co.za

Johannesburg Tourism
(011) 784-9596 / 7 / 8.

Mpumalanga Tourism
(013) 752-7001.

South African Tourism
(021) 421-6274.

Tswane Pretoria Tourism
(012) 337-4337.

Discovery tour at Oudtshoorn's Cango Wildlife Farm *(see p166)*

TRAVELLING WITH CHILDREN

Travelling with children is fairly easy, as the sunny weather allows for a variety of outdoor entertainment. Make sure that they drink plenty of water, though, and that they wear a high-protection sun screen. Consult your doctor about travelling with children in a malaria zone.

Children can be great "ice-breakers" in getting to meet the locals, but do not let them out of your sight.

If you travel during local school holidays, you'll find that even the smaller towns offer children's activities – from aquarium and zoo tours to theatre, baking and craft workshops. The local press, libraries and the monthly entertainment guide, *SACityLife*, are good sources of ideas. Look out for "Touch and Feed" farms, where children can encounter farm animals.

WOMEN TRAVELLERS

South Africa has an extremely high incidence of rape *(see p374)*, although the careful tourist should be reasonably safe. There are **Rape Crisis** centres in major towns and cities. Travelling alone is not recommended. Women are potential victims of mugging, so keep to well-lit public areas during the day and night and don't exhibit any valuables. Always look as if you know where

you are going and don't offer or accept a lift from anyone.

Sexual harassment is not too common, although a great many South African males do hold rather chauvinistic attitudes, so be careful not to come across as too friendly, as your interest may be perceived as sexual. The incidence of HIV/Aids is high, so don't ever have unprotected sex. Condoms are readily available at pharmacies and supermarkets.

GAY AND LESBIAN TRAVEL

Enshrined in the new constitution is a clause protecting the rights of gays and lesbians. But while Cape Town is certainly the "gay capital of Africa", the smaller towns still retain conservative attitudes.

The cities have a host of gay bars and theatre venues. *SACityLife* magazine has a monthly gay and lesbian

event listing. **TOGS**, The Organization for Gay Sport, is among several sports organisations operating in the major cities.

The drag/theme party held in Cape Town each December by Mother City Queer Projects draws almost 10,000 party goers – at least 1,000 of them foreign visitors. In September you can join Johannesburg's annual Gay and Lesbian Pride Parade, billed as the greatest parade in Africa.

Gay and Lesbian Pride Parade

STUDENT TRAVEL

Students with a valid International Student Identity Card (ISIC) benefit from good airline travel discounts, but reduced admission to venues and events has not taken off in South Africa. The STA travel agency, which specialises in student travel, has branches world-wide, and backpacking is gaining in popularity.

Backpackers' accommodation in the centre of Cape Town

TIME

SOUTH AFRICAN Standard Time (there is only one time zone) is two hours ahead of Greenwich Mean Time (GMT) all year round, seven hours ahead of the United States' Eastern Standard Winter Time and seven hours behind Australian Central Time.

PUBLIC TOILETS

THERE ARE public toilets in shopping malls and in many public buildings such as civic centres, libraries or town halls. Most large urban vehicle service stations have toilets, but these are intended for the use of clients. On major tourist routes, most garages that have refreshment centres also usually have well-kept toilets. Public toilets can be found at railway and bus stations, although these are often not very clean. Many have no soap or any means of drying your hands.

An alternative is to use the toilets in a restaurant where you are a customer. Large shopping centres and tourist attractions usually have well-maintained facilities and customised toilets for wheelchair users. Baby-changing facilities are also available.

ELECTRICAL SUPPLY

VIRTUALLY ALL electricity (alternating current) is supplied by the state-owned utility company Eskom. Mains voltage is 220/230 volts (220V) at 50 cycles (50Hz). Most local power plugs are 5A (amperes) with twin pins, or 15A with three rounded pins, with the longest of the three carrying the earth connection (brown wire). Standard South African plugs do not contain safety fuses. An open circuit within an appliance should cause a circuit-breaker to trip at the distribution board, cutting off electricity from that board or

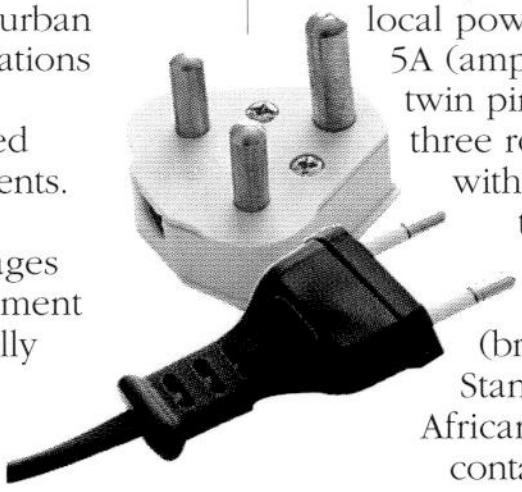

South African two- and three-prong plugs

the electricity to the section in which the fault has occurred. Seek advice about adaptors from a local electrical supplier.

WEIGHTS AND MEASURES

SOUTH AFRICA uses the metric system and SI (Système International) units. Normal body temperature of 98.4° F is equal to 37° C. If the weather chart shows 30° C, you're in for a hot day. A pressure of 30 pounds per square inch is equal to two bars.

CONVERSION CHART

Imperial to Metric
1 inch = 2.54 cm
1 foot = 30 cm
1 mile = 1.6 km
1 ounce = 28 g
1 pound = 454 g
1 pint = 0.6 litres
1 gallon = 4.6 litres

Metric to Imperial
1 mm = 0.04 inches
1 cm = 0.4 inches
1 m = 3 feet 3 inches
1 km = 0.6 miles
1 g = 0.04 ounces
1 kg = 2.2 pounds
1 litre = 1.8 pints

DIRECTORY

DISABLED TRAVELLERS

Titch Travel
26 Station Rd,
Rondebosch,
Cape Town.
(021) 686-5501.
Tours for the physically disabled or visually impaired.
www.titchtours.co.za
titcheve@iafrica.com

Association for Persons with Physical Disabilities

Cape Town
(021) 555-2881.

Durban
(031) 403-7041.

Johannesburg
(011) 726-8040.

Kimberley
(053) 833-3315.

Disabled People of South Africa
(043) 743-1579.

CHILDREN

Childline
0800-05-5555.
National toll-free number.
www.childline.org.za

GAY AND LESBIAN

Gay and Lesbian Coalition
Cape Town
(011) 487-3810.
www.q.co.za

Gayteway to South Africa
Cape Town.
(021) 462-4679.
Gay and lesbian travel.

TOGS (The Organization for Gay Sport)
Cnr Putney and Cheswick sts, Brixton, Johannesburg.
(011) 802-5589.
www.togs.co.za

RAPE CRISIS

Cape Town
(021) 447-9762 or
(021) 361-9085.

Durban
(031) 204-4862.

Johannesburg
(011) 642-4345.

Pretoria
(012) 342-2222.

AIDS COUNSELLING

Cape Town
(021) 797-3327.

Durban
(031) 300-3104.

Johannesburg
(011) 725-6711.

Pretoria
(012) 312-0122.

Port Elizabeth
(041) 506-1415.

STUDENT TRAVEL

STA Travel
62 Strand St,
Cape Town.
(021) 418-6570.

34 Mutual Gardens,
Rosebank, Johannesburg.
(011) 447-5414.

Student Travel Head Office.
(011) 706-0052.
www.statravel.co.za

Personal Security and Health

SA Police logo

SOUTH AFRICA IS EXPERIENCING a period of profound change. For some, the rate of change is overwhelming; for others it is too slow. Democracy has at last been attained, but a great many problems – such as widespread unemployment and poverty – still need to be solved. In some areas, the incidence of serious crime is alarmingly high, but overall, South Africa is a safe place for visitors who take reasonable precautions. The wildlife should always be taken seriously and treated with respect. Bites and stings from venomous creatures are rare, but malaria and bilharzia need to be considered in certain areas.

PERSONAL SAFETY

STAYING SAFE is a question of exercising common sense and extreme caution. While inner-city areas and town-ships are probably the most dangerous, villages may also have crime hot spots.

Do not go out on your own, anywhere, and don't exhibit expensive-looking accessories. Pickpockets may be a problem, and muggers may snatch at a valuable item or handbag and run away.

Don't carry large sums of money, but do keep some change in a side pocket so that you don't have to pro-duce your wallet whenever you need to tip.

Don't put your possessions down when you need your hands (for examining an intended purchase, perhaps). Carry with you only what you are likely to need. A money belt worn under your clothing is useful for keeping documents and banknotes.

Police officer

Don't go near deserted or impoverished areas except as part of a tour group.

Avoid any place where unrestricted consumption of liquor takes place.

Leave valuables and purchases in your hotel's safe-deposit box.

Avoid any of the sub-urban trains at off-peak times, unless you're in a group of at least ten.

Don't go exploring without a guide. Call the **police flying squad** in an emergency, or report the incident to the nearest police station or police officer. You will need to produce identification. To make an insurance claim you will need to obtain a case reference number from the police sta-tion. A free assistance service called Eblockwatch also has a call centre which tourists can ring if they need assistance. You can register at www. eblockwatch.co.za. The centre will then send one of its members to assist you in an emergency.

Tow truck

ON THE ROAD

WHEN TRAVELLING by car, always keep the doors locked and the windows only slightly open. When you do leave the car, lock it, even if you're getting out for just a few moments (*see p384*). Make sure that nothing of value is visible inside – leave the glove compartment open to show that there's nothing in there either. Use undercover or supervised parking wherever possible. Do not stop for hitch-hikers or to offer any help, even to an accident victim. If a hijacker or other criminal points a firearm at you, obey his or her orders.

Pharmacies offer valuable medical advice and services

MEDICAL FACILITIES

STATE AND PROVINCIAL hos-pitals do offer adequate facilities, but they tend to be under-funded and under-staffed. Patients who are mem-bers of medical insurance schemes are usually admitted to a private hospital, such as the **Sandton Medi-Clinic**. If you suffer from any pre-existing medical condition or are on any long-term medi-cation, make sure those who try to help you are aware of it.

FOOD AND WATER

TAP WATER is safe to drink, although chlorinated. There is a wide range of bottled – still and sparkling – waters available. Be careful of river or mountain water in heavily populated areas.

Female police officer   Police officer on horseback

Ambulance

Police vehicle

Fire engine

The preparation of food in most restaurants and hotels meets international standards, but do exercise common sense. In the informal markets, avoid meat or dairy products that may have been lying in the sun, and wash all fruit and vegetables carefully.

Travellers to South Africa do not generally suffer the same stomach upsets as they may in the rest of the continent.

OUTDOOR HAZARDS

I N MANY PARTS of South Africa, forest and bush fires are a major hazard, especially during the dry winter months. Don't ever discard burning matches and cigarette ends.

Always protect yourself from the harsh sun with a hat and sunblock.

Before you climb or hike at high altitude, ask about the

No fires

expected weather conditions. These change very quickly. If you are caught in cloud, keep warm and wait for the weather to lift. Make sure you tell a responsible person your route and the time you expect to return. Ensure that you are familiar with your route.

POISONOUS BITES AND STINGS

F EW TRAVELLERS are likely to find themselves in danger of being bitten or stung by any one of the venomous creatures of South Africa. People on safari or on hiking trails should nevertheless watch where they place their hands and feet.

Few snakes in South Africa are deadly, and most are not poisonous at all. They strike only when attacked or threatened. The most dangerous spider is the seldom-encountered button spider (*Latrodectus species*). Most of the species of scorpion are only slightly venomous. In general, those with thick tails and small pincers tend to be more poisonous. Because of their lower body weight, children are more susceptible to the toxins than adults.

MALARIA AND BILHARZIA

M ALARIA is most likely to be contracted in Mpumalanga, Northern Province and northern KwaZulu-Natal. The risks of contracting malaria can be minimised by starting a course of anti-malaria

tablets a week before travelling to an affected area and continuing with the treatment for a month after your return.

Bilharzia (*schistosomiasis*) results from contact (whether on the skin or by drinking) with affected water. Areas in which the disease is most likely to be contracted are Northern Province, Mpumalanga, North-West Province, KwaZulu-Natal and Eastern Cape. Suspect water should not be used for washing or bathing, and should be boiled if intended for consumption.

DIRECTORY

EMERGENCY NUMBERS

Police Flying Squad
10111 all areas.

Ambulance
10177 all areas.

Private Ambulance
ER24 Service (021) 551-6823

Fire
Jo'burg (011) 624-2800.
Pretoria 10177.
Cape Town (021) 535-1100.
Durban (031) 361-0000.

AA Emergency Road Service
Free call 0800-01-0101.
24-hours, all areas.

MEDICAL FACILITIES

After-Hours Pharmacies
Jo'burg (011) 624-2800.
Pretoria (012) 460-6422.
Cape Town (021) 797-5094.
Durban (031) 368-3666.

Christiaan Barnard Memorial Hospital
181 Longmarket St. Cape Town.
(021) 480-6111.

Poison Information
0800 33 3444 all areas.

Sandton Medi-Clinic
Peter Place, Bryanston, Jo'burg.
(011) 709-2000.

St. Augustine's Hospital
107 Chelmsford Rd, Glenwood,
Durban (031) 268-5000.

The charming police station in Pietermaritzburg

Banking and Local Currency

The Standard Bank

THE SOUTH AFRICAN BANKING system is similar to that in most industrialized Western countries. There are no restrictions on the amount of foreign currency that may be brought into the country. There are, however, limits to the amount of any currency that may be taken out of South Africa. These amounts, like rates of exchange, are subject to fluctuation, so always check with your travel agent. Travellers' cheques may be exchanged at banks, bureaux de change, some hotels and some shops. Banks generally offer the best rate of exchange.

Foreign exchange bureau, V&A Waterfront, Cape Town

BANKING HOURS

IN THE LARGER towns, week day banking hours are from 9am to 3:30pm, and on Saturdays from 9am to 11am. Smaller branches and agencies may have shorter hours and be closed on Saturdays. They are all closed on public holidays. A number of sites, such as the Victoria and Alfred Waterfront in Cape Town and the Johannesburg International Airport, offer a convenient, 24-hour foreign-exchange service. At all the other airports, the reception areas for international arrivals and departures have special banking facilities for international passengers.

AUTOMATIC BANKING

AUTOMATIC TELLER machines (ATMs) are widely distributed in the cities and towns. Cash withdrawals, up to a set limit per day per card, are made with bank-issued debit cards, but transactions may also be done with local or foreign-issued

A convenient Bankteller ATM

credit cards encoded with a PIN number. The cards most widely used in South Africa are VISA and Master-Card. If you find the daily limit inadequate, go to the bank and arrange to draw more. You will need your passport for any transactions at the bank counter. ATMs may run out of notes at week-ends, especially if there is a public holiday on the Monday, so draw money early.

Avoid drawing money while on your own, or at deserted ATM's after-hours, and decline all unsolicited offers of "help". ATM fraud is common: a fraudster may, for example, jam the machine slot so you can't retrieve your card. While you alert the bank officials inside, the fraudster un-jams the slot and withdraws money from your account. Rather wait outside at the ATM while a companion goes for help. All ATM's display a 24-hour emergency telephone number to call in the event of any problems with your card.

CREDIT CARDS

MOST BUSINESSES accept all major credit cards. They will be electronically validated, which usually takes no longer than a few minutes. Informal traders do not normally accept credit cards. It is not possible to purchase petrol or oil with a credit card; most banks issue a separate petrol card. Your car-rental company can help with arrangements. Find out what charges your bank will levy for use of your credit card in South Africa.

CHANGING MONEY

AMONG THE RECENTLY introduced foreign exchange facilities are automatic teller machines in larger cities that handle only the exchange of foreign currency. While these machines are still scarce, they do offer a very convenient means of exchanging notes after hours. It is planned to install more machines.

DIRECTORY

ABSA/Maestro
National free-call, 24-hours.
0800 11 1155.

American Express
☎ *0800 11 0929, 24-hours.*

Diners Club
☎ *(011) 358-8400.*
◷ *8am–4:45pm Mon–Fri.*

First National Bank
National free-call, 24-hours.
0800 11 0132.

MasterCard
National free-call, 24-hours.
0800 99 0418.

Nedbank
National free-call, 24-hours.
0800 11 0929.

Rennies Foreign Exchange Bureaux (Thomas Cook)
National free-call, 24-hours.
0800 99 8175.

Standard Bank/Master-Card
National free-call, 24-hours.
0800 02 0600.

VISA International
National free-call, 24-hours.
0800 99 0475.

TRAVELLERS' CHEQUES

THESE MAY BE cashed at any bank – provided the currency of issue is acceptable. No commission is charged by a branch of the bank that issued the cheque.

CURRENCY

THE SOUTH AFRICAN unit of currency is the rand, indicated by the letter "R" before the amount ("rand" is short for "Witwatersrand", Gauteng's gold-bearing reef).

The rand is divided into 100 cents (c). Older issues of coins and notes are still legal tender. South African currency circulates – usually at face value – in the neighbouring Lesotho, Namibia, Swaziland and Botswana.

Bank Notes
Bank notes, on which the "Big 5" wildlife animals are represented, are issued in R10, R20, R50, R100 and R200 denominations.

R200 note

R100 note

R50 note

R20 note

R10 note

1-cent piece

2-cent piece

Coins (actual size)
Copper-coloured, smooth-edged coins are in denominations of 1cent, 2cents and 5cents. The 10cents, 20cents and 50cents coins are a brassy yellow and have milled edges. The R1, R2 and R5 coins are milled in a bright, silver colour.

5-cent piece

10-cent piece

20-cent piece

50-cent piece

R1

R2

R5

Telecommunications

SOUTH AFRICAN telecommunications systems are among the most advanced in the world. The national telecommunications agency is Telkom SA Limited, and a wide variety of postal options, from insured or signature-on-delivery mail to courier services, are offered by post offices countrywide. Public telephones (payphones) are found in every city and town, and include both coin- and card-operated models. Telephone cards and postage stamps may be bought at many shops and supermarkets. Some shops, especially in the rural areas, have one or more public telephone (rented from Telkom) on their premises.

Telkom logo

Roadside SOS telephone

TELEPHONES

MOST TELEPHONE exchanges in South Africa are automatic, so it is possible to dial direct if the correct dialling code is used. Public, or payphones are found at post offices, train stations and in shopping malls, but don't rely on finding a phone directory there. Post offices, however, usually keep a complete range of South African telephone directories. Businesses and restaurants often have a table-model payphone – aptly known as a Chatterbox. Even if you are not a patron, ask if you may use the phone. The staff are

Telkom payphones

unlikely to refuse your request. Payphones accept a range of South African coins.

Telephone cards are available from most post offices, cafés and newsagents. Note that payphone models accept either coins or cards, but not both.

Reduced rates are in effect after hours, typically from 7pm–7am on weekdays; and on weekends from 1pm Saturday to 7am Monday. Calls made from hotels may carry a substantial levy.

ROADSIDE TELEPHONES

PLACED AT REGULAR intervals along all the major roads, these telephone boxes are connected directly to an emergency monitoring service and should be used only in an emergency or to summon help in case of an accident.

MOBILE PHONES

ALSO KNOWN AS cell phones, mobile telephones are obtainable on contract from a private service provider.

Quite often nowadays, cell phones are offered as part of a car-hire contract.

Cell phone coverage is very good in most of the larger towns, as well as in the cities and along the main highways.

Legislation forbidding the use of hand-held cell phones while driving is expected to be introduced. Cell phone rental facilities can be found at the major airports.

USING A PUBLIC TELEPHONE IN SOUTH AFRICA

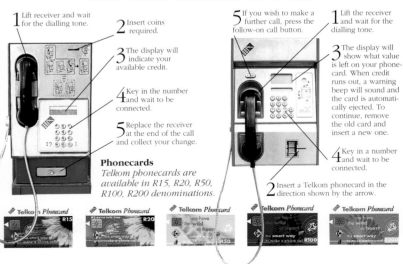

1 Lift receiver and wait for the dialling tone.

2 Insert coins required.

3 The display will indicate your available credit.

4 Key in the number and wait to be connected.

5 Replace the receiver at the end of the call and collect your change.

5 If you wish to make a further call, press the follow-on call button.

1 Lift the receiver and wait for the dialling tone.

3 The display will show what value is left on your phonecard. When credit runs out, a warning beep will sound and the card is automatically ejected. To continue, remove the old card and insert a new one.

4 Key in a number and wait to be connected.

2 Insert a Telkom phonecard in the direction shown by the arrow.

Phonecards
Telkom phonecards are available in R15, R20, R50, R100, R200 denominations.

Telkom Phonecard R15
Telkom Phonecard R20
Telkom Phonecard R50
Telkom Phonecard R100
Telkom Phonecard R200

Standard South African postbox

POSTAL SERVICE

THE POSTAL service is under-going extensive reorgani-zation, because the delivery rate of letters and parcels is erratic. Letters or goods may be sent registered, cash-on-delivery (COD), insured, express delivery service, Fastmail and Speed Services (for guaranteed delivery within 24 hours in South Africa). Private courier services are popular. Postage stamps are sold at newsagents, grocery stores and corner cafés. Post offices are open from 8am–4:30pm on week-days and from 8am–noon on Saturdays. Smaller centres usually close for lunch hour.

Aerogramme

FACSIMILE SERVICES

FACSIMILE (fax), Internet and email (electronic mail) facilities are widely available. Most photocopying outlets, like **Copy Wizards** and the **Internet Café** offer interna-tional and local fax and tele-phone facilities, as well as email connections. You will find them in large shopping centres and business areas.

POSTE RESTANTE

IF YOU REQUIRE a "poste restante" service (there is no charge), address your request, in writing, to the postmaster of the post office in the area where you will be travelling. Supply your sur-name, the date on which you wish the service to begin and an address to which uncol-lected post should be sent. Instruct your correspondents to address all mail to the designated post office, for example, "J Jones, Poste Restante, Cape Town 8000, South Africa." Post will then safely be retained for you at that post office for a month.

NEWSPAPERS AND MAGAZINES

DAILY NEWSPAPERS are found in all major cities; most have both morning and after-noon papers as well as Sat-urday and Sunday editions. A number of national weekly or bi-weekly news tabloids are also published.
English language newspapers are widespread in the cities, but rural towns may receive fewer copies, often up to a day later. A variety of local and international magazines is widely available. Topics include travel, sport, wildlife and outdoor life. South Africa receives editions of some overseas newspapers (mainly British), as well as a number of foreign magazines. All of these are distributed through selected newsagents or placed in upmarket hotels.

A selection of local daily and weekly newspapers

COURIER SERVICES

WORLDWIDE COURIERS like **DHL** and **Speed Servi-ces** have branches in larger South African centres. They all offer a collection service and deliver parcels, priced per kilo, country- and worldwide.

RADIO AND TELEVISION

THE SOUTH AFRICAN Broad-casting Corporation (SABC) is responsible for four tele-vision channels and a number of national and regional radio stations. The principal lan-guage of television is English. British and American pro-gramming dominate, but there are some good local productions. Local radio stations target specific audi-ences and language groups. Cable and satellite television services are provided by the private company MNet.

TRAVEL INFORMATION

SOUTH AFRICA, historically a welcome stopover for seafarers, is well served by air links with most parts of the globe and by road and rail connections to the rest of Africa. The national carrier, South African Airways (SAA), operates 50 passenger aircraft, while some 45 foreign airlines make around 180 landings in South Africa every week. There are many internal flights

Tail of an SAA 747

operated by SAA and other airlines. The rail network covers the country and extends beyond the borders to give access to Southern and Central Africa. The road system is comprehensive. Roads are generally in good condition, though the accident rate is high. Intercity bus services operate between major cities. Public transport within cities and towns is seldom satisfactory.

Brightly coloured carrier of the South African Airways fleet

ARRIVING BY AIR

MOST VISITORS to the country arrive at Johannesburg International Airport. Direct international flights also leave from and arrive in Cape Town and Durban; some flights to other African destinations are routed through Upington in the Northern Cape.

Internal destinations served by SAA, the national carrier, are Johannesburg, Durban, Cape Town, Port Elizabeth, Bloemfontein, East London,

Kimberley, Ulundi, George and Upington. Smaller centres, as well as the airport at Skukuza in the Kruger National Park, are linked by regular feeder services. Air charter services, both fixed wing and rotary, are available at most of the larger airports.

Public transport to and from the major airports includes airline or privately operated shuttle buses to the city centre. Radio taxi services are also available, while most of the hotels, guesthouses and some

backpackers' lodges in the larger cities, will be able to provide transport on request.

Facilities at the international airports include banking, currency exchange, car rental, post offices, information centres, duty-free shops (for outbound passengers only), restaurants and bars.

CUSTOMS

NO DUTY IS PAYABLE on any personal effects, which must be carried in unsealed or unwrapped packages.

Current customs legislation allows visitors to bring duty-free goods to the value of R500 into the country.

Visitors may also bring in a limited amount of perfume, 2 litres (3.5 pints) wine, 1 litre (1.75 pints) of spirits, 250 g tobacco, 400 cigarettes and 50 cigars. Further items to the value of R10,000 per person are charged at a flat rate of 20 per cent of their value. On amounts above R10,000, the rate is 30 per cent of the value, plus VAT. Lesotho, Swaziland and South Africa

AIRPORT	INFORMATION	DISTANCE FROM CITY	TAXI FARE TO CITY	BUS TRANSFER TO CITY
✈ Johannesburg	((086) 727-7888	24 km (15 miles)	R210	20–25 mins
✈ Cape Town	((086) 727-7888	20 km (12 miles)	R180	30–45 mins
✈ Durban	((086) 727-7888	20 km (12 miles)	R180	20–30 mins
✗ Port Elizabeth	((086) 727-7888	3 km (2 miles)	R75	7–10 mins
✗ Bloemfontein	((086) 727-7888	15 km (9 miles)	R140	20–40 mins
✗ East London	((086) 727-7888	15 km (9 miles)	R140	10–15 mins
✗ George	((086) 727-7888	10 km (6 miles)	R120	10 mins
✗ Skukuza *	((013) 735-5644			

* Skukuza, the largest camp in the Kruger National Park has three flights daily arriving from Johannesburg.

Customs area

are members of the Southern African Common Customs Union, so there are no internal customs duties.

INTERNATIONAL FLIGHTS

FARES TO SOUTH AFRICA are generally at their highest from September to February, but how much you pay will depend on the type of ticket you buy. Savings can also be made by booking an APEX (Advance Purchase Excursion) ticket in advance, although these are subject to minimum and maximum time limits, thus restricting the visitor's stay.

Specialist agents offer many good deals. Discount agents may also offer attractive student or youth fares.

Make sure that your booking agent is a licensed member of ABTA (the Association of British Travel Agents) or a similar authority; you will then be assured of compensation should something go wrong with your bookings.

DOMESTIC FLIGHTS

SOUTH AFRICAN AIRWAYS, British Airways/Comair and Nationwide offer regular inter-city services.

The current price structures are competitive, with return-fare and other attractive specials regularly on offer. In general, the earlier one books, the cheaper the fare (seven-day advance specials are common). Booking is essential.

PACKAGE HOLIDAYS

PACKAGE TOURS almost always offer reduced airfare and accommodation costs, making them cheaper than independent travel, unless you are travelling on a tight budget and wish to stay in back-packers' lodges, self-catering accommodation or campsites.

Popular package tours and deals include trips to Durban, Cape Town, Johannesburg, Port Elizabeth, the Garden Route, the Wild Coast, Sun City and the Palace of the Lost City, as well as the Kruger National Park.

FLY-DRIVE DEALS

MANY TRAVEL AGENTS and car-rental firms organize fly-drive packages that enable you to book a flight and have a rental car waiting for you at your destination. This is usually cheaper and involves fewer formalities than renting a car on arrival. Most major car-rental firms such as Avis, Hertz, Budget and Imperial have offices at the airports.

AIRPORT TAX

SOUTH AFRICAN AIRPORT TAX is paid upon purchase of your ticket. The tax to be paid per international departure is R78. Domestic flights are taxed at R22 per departure. The tax on flights to Botswana, Namibia, Lesotho or Swaziland is R44.

DIRECTORY

AIRPORT SHUTTLES

Cape Town Magic Bus
Domestic Arrivals Hall, Cape Town International Airport.
((021) 934-5455.

Durban Magic Bus
Suite 7, Grenada Centre, 16 Chartwell Dr, Umhlanga Rocks.
((031) 561-1096.

East London Shuttle
Domestic Arrivals Hall, East London National Airport.
((082) 569-3599.

Johannesburg Magic Bus
Domestic Arrivals, Terminal 3, Johannesburg International.
((011) 249-8800.

Pretoria Airport Shuttle
Cnr Prinsloo & Vermeulen sts.
((012) 991-0085.

DOMESTIC AIRLINES

British Airways Comair
((021) 936-9000, Cape Town.
(011) 921-0222, Johannesburg.
(031) 450-7000, Durban.
(041) 508-8099, Port Elizabeth.
W www.comair.co.za

Nationwide
((021) 936-2050, Cape Town.
(011) 390-1660, Johannesburg.
(031) 450-2087, Durban.

South African Airways
((021) 936-1111, Cape Town.
(011) 978-1111, Johannesburg.
(031) 250-1111, Durban.
(041) 507-1111, Port Elizabeth.
W www.saa.co.za

CAR-RENTAL SERVICES

See p385 for information on Avis, Hertz, Imperial and Budget car-rental services.

The interior of Johannesburg International Airport

Travelling by Train

Blue Train logo

TRAIN TRAVEL in South Africa is quite comfortable and economical, but seldom very fast. Power is provided by electric and diesel-electric locomotives on a standard gauge of 3 ft 6 in (1.65 m). Enormously popular, particularly with foreign visitors, are the luxurious train safaris offered by the Blue Train. The company offers a choice of four excellent scenic routes, the unhurried journeys lasting anything from 16 hours to two days and nights (on the Pretoria–Victoria Falls route). Another company, Rovos Rail, offers similar excursions to other destinations. Suburban train travel is not a very popular option among foreign tourists as routes are limited, trains run too infrequently and personal safety cannot be guaranteed.

Suburban trains are the main transport for many commuters

SUBURBAN TRAINS

SUBURBAN SERVICES operated by Spoornet are available in most cities. In Cape Town, Metrorail provides this transport service. These trains are used mainly for commuting to and from work and run less frequently during the rest of the day and at weekends.

Timetables and tickets are available at the stations. First-class tickets cost approximately twice that of those in third class and offer better seating and security.

Tickets are clipped by train conductors, but you will need to produce your ticket again in order to get off at the main stations (failure to do so can result in a fine). Weekly and monthly passes are available at reduced rates. Be careful not to lose the tickets, they have no passenger identity mark and can, therefore, be used by anyone else.

No discounts are offered for students or pensioners, while children under seven years of age travel free and those under 13 for half price.

It is recommended that suburban trains be used in daylight hours only, and preferably during peak periods in the morning and afternoon. Do not travel alone on suburban trains at any time.

Metrorail weekly and monthly ticket

Some suburban trains have a restaurant compartment. Try the comfortable **Biggsy's Restaurant Carriage & Wine Bar** along the False Bay coast; the trip from Cape Town to Simon's Town *(see p94)* takes about an hour.

MAINLINE PASSENGER SERVICES

MAINLINE PASSENGER SERVICES, operated by Spoornet, offers fairly comprehensive nationwide rail coverage.

Daily "name" trains run between Cape Town and Johannesburg (Trans-Karoo Express), Johannesburg and Port Elizabeth (Algoa Express), Johannesburg and Durban (Trans-Natal Express) and Johannesburg and East London (Amatola Express).

But the express trains are not particularly fast: an idea of the word "express" may be given by the Trans-Karoo, for example, which takes almost 24 hours to cover approximately 1,500 km (930 miles).

Mainline Passenger Services also services two of the neighbouring states, Zimbabwe and Mozambique.

Timetables (free) and tickets are available at most central stations and Mainline offices countrywide. Third-class tickets cost about half that of first class, and second class tickets somewhere in-between. First-class carriages seat four people, second-class carriages six. Seating in third class is open. Booking is necessary during holiday season.

European-style discount travel passes do not apply in South Africa, although the holders of valid university student cards will receive a

The stately Pretoria Railway Station *(see p255)*

40 per cent discount between February and November. Pensioners qualify for 25 per cent discount during this period. Children under five travel free all year round, children under 11 travel for half price.

SCENIC TRAIN TRAVEL

W HILE CAPE TOWN to Pretoria is the main route of the **Blue Train**, famous for its luxury accommodation, excellent cuisine and impeccable service, the company also offers scenic trips to the Valley of the Olifants (near Kruger National Park), the Garden Route and the Victoria Falls in Zimbabwe.

The only South African line that is routinely worked by steam train is the scenic stretch between George and Knysna on the Garden Route. The **Outeniqua Choo-Tjoe** (see pp174–5) offers a wonderful day's outing, passing sea, lakes, forest and mountains.

An open day at the **South African National Railway and Steam Museum** in Johannesburg is held on the first Sunday of every month. A number of steam train safaris give a taste of what train travel was about in years gone by.

From Cape Town, the **Spier Vintage Train Company** (see p133) runs luxury trips in gleaming vintage carriages through beautiful vineyards, directly to the estate.

The Blue Train on its way through the scenic Hex River Valley

Rovos Rail logo

Union Limited offers popular day trips through the Franschhoek Valley or across the mountains to Ceres and the six-day Golden Thread Tour travels to Oudtshoorn. Other holiday steamers are the **Banana Express** (see p225) from Port Shepstone in KwaZulu-Natal, and the little **Apple Express** that leaves from Port Elizabeth in the Eastern Cape on its 24-inch (61-cm) gauge for a trip through the countryside.

On **Rovos Rail**, sleepers and dining cars are in period style, but the comforts are modern. Rovos Rail takes travellers all over the country including to historical places such as Matjiesfontein and Kimberley.

DIRECTORY

PASSENGER SERVICES

Cape Metrorail
[(080) 065-6463.

Mainline Passenger Services (Shosholozameyl)
[(086) 000-8888.

Spoornet
[(011) 773-7743, (031) 361-3388, (041) 507-2042.
W www.spoornet.co.za

LEISURE TOURS

Apple Express
[(041) 507-2333.

Biggsy's
[(021) 449-3870.

Blue Train
[(011) 774-4555.

Outeniqua Choo-tjoe
[(044) 801-8288.

Rovos Rail
[(012) 323-6052.
W www.rovos.com

SA National Railway and Steam Museum
[(011) 888-1154.

Spier Vintage Train Company
[(021) 419-5222.

Union Limited Steam Railtours
[(021) 449-4391.

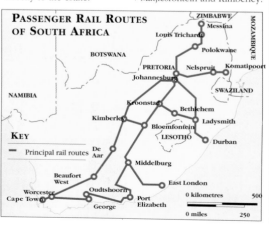

PASSENGER RAIL ROUTES OF SOUTH AFRICA

ZIMBABWE
Messina
Louis Trichardt
Polokwane
MOZAMBIQUE
BOTSWANA
PRETORIA Nelspruit Komatipoort
Johannesburg
NAMIBIA
SWAZILAND
Kroonstad
Kimberley Bethlehem
Bloemfontein Ladysmith
LESOTHO
Durban
KEY
— Principal rail routes
De Aar
Middelburg
Beaufort West
Oudtshoorn East London
Worcester
Cape Town George Port Elizabeth

0 kilometres 500
0 miles 250

Travelling by Road

AA logo

Overall, South Africa's road network is good, although individual roads, even those that are part of the N-prefixed national road system, range from very poor to excellent. In rural areas, only main arteries may be tarred, but dirt roads are usually levelled and in good condition. Long distances and other road users, unfortunately, constitute one of the major hazards. Intercity bus services are fast, affordable and comprehensive, but own transport is necessary to visit remote areas. Most sightseeing can be done along tarred roads. Fuel is inexpensive, and busy routes have many service stations.

Six-lane freeway between Pretoria and Johannesburg

The alcohol limit of 0.08 g, is equivalent to about two tots of spirit, or two glasses of beer or wine. Anyone caught driving above this limit, is liable for a fine of up to R120 000,00 or six years' imprisonment.

Service-cum-refreshment stations are welcome stop-offs on long routes

DRIVER'S LICENCE

Persons over 18, who are in possession of a locally issued driver's licence that is printed in English and includes a recent photograph of the owner, will not require an international licence to drive in South Africa. However, if you need an international licence, you must obtain one before you arrive in South Africa.

Your licence and a red warning triangle (for emergency use) must be carried in the vehicle at all times.

Animal and rock falling warning signs

RULES OF THE ROAD

Traffic drives on the left side of the road. Except where granted right of way by a sign or by an official on duty, yield to traffic approaching from your right. It is common courtesy to pull over onto the hard shoulder to let faster traffic

pass on the right. Seat belts are compulsory in the front (and back if your car has them). Children must be properly restrained. The speed limit in urban areas, whether there are regulatory signs or not, is 60 km per hour (37 mph). On freeways and roads not regulated to a lower speed, the limit is 120 km per hour (75 mph). In the event of a vehicle breakdown, pull over onto the extreme left, activate your hazard lights and place a red warning triangle at a distance of 50 m (164 ft) behind your car.

In the event of an accident, you may move your vehicle if there are no injuries, but have to notify the nearest police station within 24 hours. If there are any injuries, notify the police immediately and do not move vehicles until they have arrived. Swap names, addresses, car and insurance details with the other party.

SAFETY

Police advise travellers not to pick up strangers. Keep car doors locked and windows well wound up. When parking the car, leave nothing of value in plain sight (see p374). At night, be sure to park only in well-lit areas.

Many road users – both pedestrians and motorists – are undisciplined to the point of negligence. In the rural areas, and when passing peri-urban townships, be alert for pedestrians and straying livestock.

Due to the vast distances that separate the country towns and villages, especially in the arid interior, it is advisable to refuel in good time and plan regular rest stops.

Emergency telephones are sited at regular intervals on major roads

Display | Insert coins
Take ticket | Parking bay number

Hi-tech parking meters accept coins and low-denomination notes

PARKING

M OST SOUTH AFRICAN towns nowadays have parking meters, so check for numbered bays painted on the tarmac or at the kerb, and for signposts on a nearby pole. In towns and cities, unofficial "parking attendants" are a nuisance and may guide you to a no-parking zone. Many demand payment when you arrive and may also expect a tip when you leave. Some have been known to damage the cars of unobliging drivers.

Whenever you are able to do so, park in a regulated area where an official is on duty.

FUEL

M OTOR VEHICLES run on 97 Octane petrol, unleaded petrol or diesel fuel, and the

unit of liquid measurement is the litre (0.22 UK gallons or 0.264 US gallons). Service station attendants see to refuelling and other checks like tyre pressure, oil, water, and cleaning the front and rear windows. A tip is always appreciated.

CAR RENTAL

C AR RENTAL IS EXPENSIVE in South Africa and is best arranged through fly-drive packages *(see p381)* or pre-booked with international agents at home. All the international airports have car-rental offices on site. To rent a car you must be over 23 and have held a valid driver's licence for at least five years. Check the small print for insurance cover. There are usually specials on offer.

Some of the most common and trusted car rental firms

BUS SERVICES

G REYHOUND, INTERCAPE and Translux coaches travel to almost every town in the country, and the journeys are safe, comfortable and reasonably inexpensive – they are also faster than travelling by train. Both the Greyhound and Translux coaches offer savings in the form of "frequent traveller" passes.

The City Liner hop-on/hop-off system, aimed at backpackers and budget travellers, runs along the coast between Durban and Cape Town. Trips can be booked at Computicket branches countrywide.

Conventional bus services operate along the main cross-country routes. Minibus taxis transport workers, but the service has a poor safety record and is not recommended.

There is no central system for taxis in South Africa. If you need a taxi, ask your place of accommodation or the nearest tourism office to recommend a reliable service, or use the Yellow Pages.

DIRECTORY

Area codes
Johannesburg (011).
Pretoria (012).
Cape Town (021).
Durban (031).
Port Elizabeth (041).

CAR RENTAL

Avis
📞 *(086) 102-1111.*
🔲 www.avis.co.za

Budget
📞 *(086) 101-6622.*
🔲 www.budget.co.za

Hertz
📞 *(086) 160-0136.*
🔲 www.hertz.co.za

Imperial
📞 *(011) 390-3909.*
📞 *(021) 386-3239.*
📞 *(031) 469-0066.*
📞 *(041) 581-4214.*
🔲 www.imperialcarrental.co.za

BUS SERVICES

City Liner
📞 *(083) 915-8000.*

Computicket
📞 *(083) 915-8000.*
🔲 www.computicket.com

Greyhound
📞 *(011) 249-8700.*
🔲 www.greyhound.co.za

Intercape
📞 *(021) 380-4400.*
🔲 www.intercape.co.za

Translux
📞 *(012) 334-8000.*
🔲 www.translux.co.za

The bus terminus in Adderley Street, Cape Town

General Index

Acknowledgments

DORLING KINDERSLEY would like to thank the following people whose contributions and assistance have made the preparation of this book possible.

MAIN CONTRIBUTORS

Michael Brett has visited many African countries, including Kenya, Malawi, Zimbabwe, Namibia and Mozambique, and has an extensive knowledge of South Africa. His first book, a detailed guide to the Pilanesberg National Park in North West Province, South Africa, was published in 1989. In 1996, he co-authored the *Touring Atlas of South Africa*. He has written *Great Game Parks of Africa: Masai Mara* and *Kenya the Beautiful*. Articles by Michael Brett have been published in several travel magazines, as well as in *Reader's Digest*.

Brian Johnson-Barker was born and educated in Cape Town, South Africa. After graduating from the University of Cape Town and running a clinical pathology laboratory for some 15 years, he turned to writing. His considerable involvement in this field has also extended to television scripts and magazine articles. Among his nearly 50 book titles are *Off the Beaten Track* (1996) and *Illustrated Guide to Game Parks and Nature Reserves of Southern Africa* (1997), both published by Reader's Digest.

Mariëlle Renssen wrote for South African general-interest magazine *Fair Lady* before spending two years in New York with *Young & Modern*, a teenage publication owned by the Bertelsmann publishing group. After returning to South Africa, several of her articles were published in magazines such as *Food and Home SA* and *Woman's Value*. Since 1995 she has been the publishing manager of Struik Publishers' International Division, during which time she also contributed to *Traveller's Guide to Tanzania*.

ADDITIONAL CONTRIBUTORS
Duncan Cruickshank, Claudia Dos Santos, Peter Joyce, Gail Jennings.

ADDITIONAL PHOTOGRAPHY
Charley van Dugteren, Anthony Johnson.

ADDITIONAL ILLUSTRATIONS
Anton Krugel.

ADDITIONAL CARTOGRAPHY
Genené Hart, Eloïse Moss.

RESEARCH ASSISTANCE
Susan Alexander, Sandy Vahl.

PROOF READER
Mariëlle Renssen.

INDEXER
Brenda Brickman.

DESIGN AND EDITORIAL ASSISTANCE
Arwen Burnett, Sean Fraser, Thea Grobbelaar, Freddy Hamilton, Lesley Hay-Whitton, Victoria Heyworth-Dunne, Alfred Lemaitre, Glynne Newlands, Marianne Petrou, Gerhardt van Rooyen, Mitzi Scheepers.

SPECIAL ASSISTANCE
Joan Armstrong, The Howick Publicity Bureau; Coen Bessinger, Die Kaapse Tafel; Tim Bowdell, Port Elizabeth City Council; Dr Joyce Brain, Durban; Katherine Brooks, MuseuMAfrikA (Johannesburg); Michael Coke, Durban; Coleen de Villiers and Gail Linnow, South African Weather Bureau; Dr Trevor Dearlove, South African Parks Board; Louis Eksteen, Voortrekker Museum (Pietermaritzburg); Lindsay Hooper, South African Museum (Cape Town); Brian Jackson, The National Monuments Commission; Linda Labuschagne, Bartolomeu Dias Museum Complex (Mossel Bay); Darden Lotz, Cape Town; Tim Maggs, Cape Town; Hector Mbau, The Africa Café; Annette Miller, Bredasdorp Tourism; Gayla Naicker and Gerhart Richter, Perima's; Professor John Parkington, University of Cape Town; Anton Pauw, Cape Town; David Philips Publisher (Pty) Ltd, Cape Town; Bev Prinsloo, Palace of the Lost City; Professor Bruce Rubidge, University of the Witwatersrand; Jeremy Saville, ZigZag Magazine; Mark Shaw, Barrister's; Dr Dan Sleigh, Cape Town; Anthony Sterne, Simply Salmon; David Swanepoel, Voortrekker Museum; Johan Taljaard, West Coast National Park; Pietermaritzburg Publicity Association; Beyers Truter, Beyerskloof wine farm, Stellenbosch; Dr Lita Webley, Albany Museum, Grahamstown; Lloyd Wingate and Stephanie Pienaar, Kaffrarian Museum (King William's Town); and all provincial tourist authorities and national and provincial park services.

PHOTOGRAPHIC AND ARTWORK REFERENCE
Vida Allen and Bridget Carlstein, McGregor Museum (Kimberley); Marlain Botha, Anglo American Library; The Cape Archives; Captain Emilio de Souza; Petrus Dhlamini, Anglo American Corporation (Johannesburg); Gawie Fagan and Tertius Kruger, Revel Fox Architects (Cape Town); Jeremy Fourie, Cape Land Data; Graham Goddard, Mayibuye Centre, The University of the Western Cape; Margaret Harradene, Public Library (Port Elizabeth); Maryke Jooste, Library of Parliament (Cape Town); Llewellyn Kriel, Chamber of Mines; Professor André Meyer, Pretoria University; Julia Moore, Boschendal Manor House; Marguerite Robinson, Standard Bank National Arts Festival; Christine Roe and Judith Swanepoel, Pilgrim's Rest Museum; Dr F Thackeray, Transvaal Museum (Pretoria); Marena van Hemert, Drostdy Museum (Swellendam); Kees van Ryksdyk, South African Astronomical Observatory; Cobri Vermeulen, The Knysna Forestry Department; Nasmi Wally, The Argus (Cape Town); Pam Warner, Old Slave Lodge (Cape Town).

PHOTOGRAPHY PERMISSIONS
DORLING KINDERSLEY would like to thank the following for their assistance and kind permission to photograph at their establishments:
African Herbalist's Shop, Johannesburg; Alanglade, Pilgrim's Rest; Albany Museum Complex, Grahamstown; Bartolomeu Dias Museum Complex, Mossel Bay; BAT (Bartel Arts Trust) Centre, Durban; Bertram House, Cape Town; BMW Pavilion, Victoria & Alfred Waterfront; Bo-Kaap Museum, Cape Town; Cango Caves, Oudtshoorn; The Castle of Good Hope; Department of Public Works, Cape Town; Drum Magazine/Bailey's Archives; Dutch Reformed Church, Nieu Bethesda; The Edward Hotel, Port Elizabeth; Gold Reef City, Johannesburg; Groot

Constantia; Heia Safari Ranch; Highgate Ostrich Farm, Oudtshoorn; Hindu (Hare Krishna) Temple of Understanding; Huguenot Museum, Franschhoek; Johannesburg International Airport; Kimberley Open-Air Mine Museum; Kirstenbosch National Botanical Garden; Kleinplasie Open-Air Museum; Koopmans-De Wet House, Cape Town; Mala Mala Private Reserve; MuseuMAfricA, Johannesburg; Natural Science Museum, Durban; Old Slave Lodge, Cape Town; Oliewenhuis Art Gallery, Bloemfontein; Oom Samie se Winkel, Stellenbosch; Owl House, Nieu Bethesda; Paarl Museum; Pilgrim's Rest; Rhebokskloof Wine Estate; Robben Island Museum Service; Sandton Village Walk; Shakaland; Shipwreck Museum, Bredasdorp; Simunye; South African Library; South African Museum, Cape Town; Tatham Art Gallery, Pietermaritzburg; Two Oceans Aquarium, Victoria & Alfred Waterfront; Victoria & Alfred Waterfront; The Village Museum, Stellenbosch; Sue Williamson, Cape Town; The Workshop, Durban.

PICTURE CREDITS

t = top; tl = top left; tlc = top left centre; tc = top centre; tr = top right; cla = centre left above; ca = centre above; cra = centre right above; cl = centre left; c = centre; cr = centre right; clb = centre left below; cb = centre below; crb = centre right below; bl = bottom left; b = bottom; bc = bottom centre; bcl = bottom centre left; br = bottom right; d = detail.

Works of art have been reproduced with the permission of the following copyright holders:

Lead Ox, 1995–6, © Cecil Skotnes, Incised, painted wood panel 306br; *Portrait of a Lady*, Frans Hals (1580–1666), Oil on canvas, Old Town House (Cape Town), © Michaelis Collection 66bl; *Rocco Catoggio and Rocco Cartozia de Villiers*, artist unknown, c.1842, Oil on canvas, © Huguenot Museum (Franschhoek) 137bc; *Untitled work*, 1998, Hannelie de Clerq, Tempera, © Stellenbosch Art Gallery 131tr.

Every effort has been made to trace the copyright holders and we apologize in advance for any unintentional omissions. We would be pleased to insert the appropriate acknowledgements in any subsequent edition of this publication.

The publisher would like to thank the following individuals, companies and picture libraries for permission to reproduce their photographs:

ACSA (AIRPORTS COMPANY OF SOUTH AFRICA): 380t, 381b; SHAEN ADEY: 1t, 24cl, 28t, 71bl, 80t, 80b, 102cr, 276tl, 276cla, 276cl, 276b, 277t, 277cr; ANITA AKAL: 37cl; ANGLO AMERICAN CORPORATION OF SOUTH AFRICA LIMITED: 16c, 240clb, 240b, 240–241c, 241tl, 241tr, 241cr, 241r, 305t, 305bl; THE ARGUS: 53bl, 54tl, 55cla; AA (AUTOMOBILE ASSOCIATION OF SOUTH AFRICA): 384tl.

DARYL BALFOUR: 277b; BARNETT COLLECTION: © The Star 50cla; BARRY FAMILY COLLECTION: 269bl; BIBLE SOCIETY OF SOUTH AFRICA: 26tl, 53b; THE BLUE TRAIN: 382tl; BOOMSHAKA/POLYGRAM: 55tl; MICHAEL BRETT: 27t, 238cl, 239bl, 239br, 256b, 257tl, 303c, 361b.

THE CAMPBELL COLLECTION OF THE UNIVERSITY OF NATAL, Durban: 52clb, 137cr; CAPAB (CAPE PERFORMING ARTS BOARD): © Pat Bromilow-Downing 360t; CAPE ARCHIVES: 4t, 26tr, 44b, 45b, 45c, 46t, 46ca, 51cr, 51br; CAPE LEGENDS: 121br; CAPE PHOTO LIBRARY: © Alain Proust 17t; 17c, 31c, 85tl, 120cla, 120ca, 120cra, 121tr, 134cl, 135cra, 135crb; THE CORY LIBRARY OF RHODES UNIVERSITY, Grahamstown: 49cb; RUPHIN COUDYZER: 26b.

DE BEERS: 50b; ROGER DE LA HARPE: 5t, 30cl, 31b, 35tr, 202b, 203b, 204tl, 205t, 205cr, 206c, 208–209, 211b, 224tl, 228t, 229t, 231b, 313t, 362c, 362b, 363b; NIGEL DENNIS: 20cr, 24–25c, 282tl, 283clb, 283crb, 296–297; DEPARTMENT OF TRANSPORT: 371c; DEPARTMENT OF WATER AFFAIRS AND FORESTRY: 177b; DIGITAL PERSPECTIVES: 10bl; GERHARD DREYER: 20br, 100tl, 151cl, 154b.

THE FEATHERBED COMPANY: 176t; FOTO HOLLER, © Schirmer, Hermanus: 122cl, 122–123c, 122bl.

GALLO IMAGES: © Anthony Bannister 20cl, 21cr, 252tr, 282–283c; © David Gikey 36t; © Kevin Carter Collection 31tr; © Rod Haestier 21tr; G'ECHO DESIGN: 36b; GLEANINGS IN AFRICA: (1806) 123b; BENNY GOOL/Trace: 19c, 54–55c; BOB GOSANI: 250cla; GREAT STOCK: © Jürgen Schadeberg 250t, 250cra, 250cr, 250clb, 250b; GREEN DOLPHIN: 105b; GUARDIAN NEWSPAPERS LIMITED: 53t.

ROD HAESTIER: 123cr, 180bl; GEORGE HALLETT: 53br, 55tr; LEX HES: 23cr, 24bc, 25bl, 25bc; HULTON PICTURE COMPANY: 305cra.

i-AFRICA: © Nic Bothma 197t, 197cra; © Sasa Kralj 27b, 42cl; © Eric Muller 17b; INTERNATIONAL EISTEDDFOD: © Bachraty Ctibor 34tl.

J&B PHOTOGRAPHERS: 25cra; JACOBSDAL WINE ESTATE: 120bl.

KING GEORGE VI ART GALLERY, Port Elizabeth: 49crb; KLEIN CONSTANTIA: 97cl; WALTER KNIRR: 35cl, 53cr, 71cl, 71br, 210ca, 222cla, 242b, 248tr, 249br, 254b, 255t, 257tr, 257b, 267b, 340c, 358cl, 360b, 370cr, 382bl.

ANNE LAING: 18b; STEFANIA LAMBERTI: 81cl, 223b; LEVI'S: 55cl; LIBRARY OF PARLIAMENT, Cape Town: © Mendelssohn Collection of watercolour paintings by Francois Vaillant 25tl; LOCAL HISTORY MUSEUM, Durban: 51bl.

MAYIBUYE CENTRE, University of the Western Cape: 52tl, 52–53c, 54clb; MEERENDAL WINE ESTATE: 120bc; MICHAELIS COLLECTION (Old Town House): 66b; MONEX CONSTRUCTION (PTY) LIMITED: 99c; MR DELIVERY: 340t; MUSEUMAFRICA: 9t, 42ca, 44tl, 48ca, 48cl, 49t, 57t, 117t, 191t, 235t, 279t, 309t, 369t.

THE NATIONAL ARCHIVES, Pretoria: 241b; IMPERIAL WAR MUSEUM, London: 50–51; NICO MALAN THEATRE: 104b.

COLIN PATERSON-JONES: 15t, 22cra; ANTON PAUW: 5c, 74b, 153tr; DAVID PHILIPS PUBLISHER (PTY) LTD: 18tl, 18tc, 27cr; PHOTO ACCESS: © Getaway/C Lanz 341b; © Getaway/ D Rogers 252cla; © Getaway/P Wagner 364t; © Clarke Gittens 46b; © Walter Knirr 240tl, 358b; © Photo Royal 204b; © Mark Skinner 62; © David Steele 34c, 204cla, 204clb; © Patrick Wagner 205b; © Alan Wilson 36c, 85ca; HERMAN POTGIETER: 2–3; THE PURPLE TURTLE: 106tl.

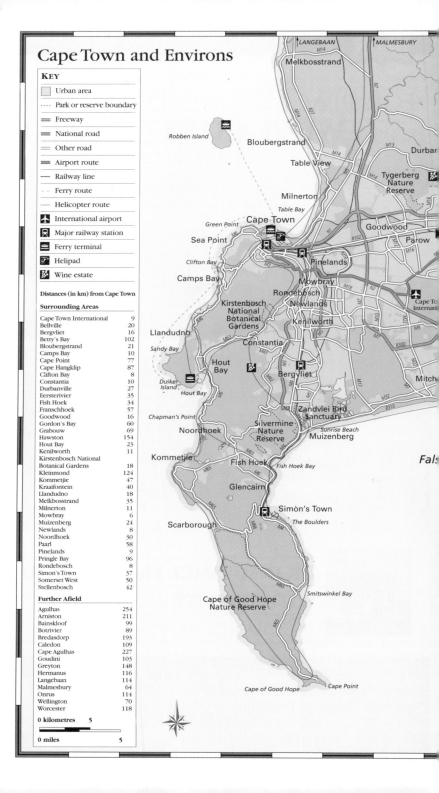

Cape Town and Environs

KEY

- Urban area
- ···· Park or reserve boundary
- Freeway
- National road
- Other road
- Airport route
- Railway line
- Ferry route
- Helicopter route
- International airport
- Major railway station
- Ferry terminal
- Helipad
- Wine estate

Distances (in km) from Cape Town

Surrounding Areas

Cape Town International	9
Bellville	20
Bergvliet	16
Betty's Bay	102
Bloubergstrand	21
Camps Bay	10
Cape Point	77
Cape Hangklip	87
Clifton Bay	8
Constantia	10
Durbanville	27
Eersterivier	35
Fish Hoek	34
Franschhoek	57
Goodwood	16
Gordon's Bay	60
Grabouw	69
Hawston	154
Hout Bay	23
Kenilworth	11
Kirstenbosch National Botanical Gardens	18
Kleinmond	124
Kommetjie	47
Kraaifontein	40
Llandudno	18
Melkbosstrand	35
Milnerton	11
Mowbray	6
Muizenberg	24
Newlands	8
Noordhoek	30
Paarl	58
Pinelands	9
Pringle Bay	96
Rondebosch	8
Simon's Town	37
Somerset West	50
Stellenbosch	42

Further Afield

Agulhas	254
Arniston	211
Bainskloof	99
Botrivier	89
Bredasdorp	193
Caledon	109
Cape Agulhas	227
Goudini	103
Greyton	148
Hermanus	116
Langebaan	114
Malmesbury	64
Onrus	114
Wellington	70
Worcester	118

0 kilometres   5

0 miles   5